Contemporary Linguistic Analysis

An Introduction

FOURTH EDITION

Edited by

William O'Grady
University of Hawaii

and

John Archibald
University of Calgary

Toronto

D0619991

Canadian Cataloguing in Publication Data

Main entry under title:

Contemporary linguistic analysis: an introduction

4th ed.
Includes index.
ISBN 0-201-47812-9

1. Linguistics. I. O'Grady, William D. (William Delaney), 1952– . II. Archibald, John, 1959– .

P126.C66 2000   410   C99-932647-3

©2000 Pearson Education Canada Inc.

ISBN 0-201-47812-9

Printed and bound in Canada.

  3 4 5   04 03 02 01

Vice President, Editorial Director: Michael Young
Art Director: Mary Opper
Developmental Editor: Laura Paterson Forbes
Production Editor: Matthew Christian
Copy Editor: Pamela Erlichman
Production Coordinator: Wendy Moran
Permissions Research: Susan Wallace-Cox
Cover Design: Julia Hall
Cover Image: Digital Vision
Interior Design and Page Layout: Jack Steiner Graphic Design

To the memory of our friend and colleague
Ewa Iwanicka
1950–1986

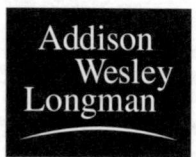

Brief Contents

Convinced at once that, in order to break loose from the beaten paths of opinions and systems, it was necessary to proceed in my study of man and society by scientific methods, and in a rigorous manner, I devoted one year to philology and grammar; linguistics, or the natural history of speech, being, of all the sciences, that which best suited the researches which I was about to commence.

PIERRE-JOSEPH PROUDHON, *WHAT IS PROPERTY?* (1840)

Contents

Preface

The fourth edition of *Contemporary Linguistic Analysis* has been updated and modified to reflect changes in the discipline as well as comments from faculty and students who used the third edition. Particularly extensive revisions have been made to the chapters on phonology, morphology, syntax, and first language acquisition, and we present an entirely new chapter on language in social contexts.

Another major change in this edition of *Contemporary Linguistic Analysis* involves the editorial team. Michael Dobrovolsky, co-editor for the first three editions, has stepped aside in order to pursue other projects, and John Archibald, professor of linguistics at the University of Calgary, has joined the editorial team as new co-editor. We extend our thanks to Michael Dobrovolsky for his many contributions to the first three editions of *Contemporary Linguistic Analysis*.

As has been the case since its inception, *Contemporary Linguistic Analysis* has benefited from the generous comments and advice provided by various colleagues. In addition to the many individuals whose assistance is acknowledged in the first three editions and whose names we list below, we would especially like to acknowledge the help that we received in preparing this edition of our book.

A special debt of gratitude is due to Keira Ballantyne and Hsiu-chuan Liao, who carefully read through drafts of several chapters, noting many problems and inconsistencies. We are also grateful to Ed Burstynsky, Denise Devenuto, Alice Harris, Kevin Gregg, Terry Pratt, and Byron Bender for valuable comments and suggestions.

Since the early 1980s, when this project was first conceived, we have enjoyed extraordinary support from our publisher's executive team, first at Copp Clark and later at Addison Wesley Longman. We would particularly like to acknowledge the efforts of Brian Henderson, Les Petriw, Jeff Miller, and the late Linda Scott and Steve Mills. Preparation of the current edition was facilitated through the efforts of the Pearson Education team, especially Matthew Christian, Laura Paterson Forbes, and Dawn Lee.

The assistance of the many individuals who contributed comments and advice on the first three editions continues to manifest itself in our fourth edition. Heartfelt thanks are due (in no particular order) to: Sheila Embleton, Jack Chambers, Steven Carey, Matthew Dryer, David Ingram, Gary Byma, Gary Libben, Robert Murrary, R. Radhakrishnan, Ronald Southerland, Mary Pepper, Derek Bickerton, Robert Blust, Ricky Jacobs, Donald Frantz, John Haiman, John Hewson, Nicole Domingue, Lydia White, George Patterson, Donna Gerdts, Elan Dresher, Keren Rice, Robert Fisher, Marilyn Philips, Lorna Rowsell, Joyce Hildebrand, Coral Sayce, Lynda Costello, Patrick Burke, Margaret Larock, Yutaka Sato, Peter Seyffert, Mark Aronoff, Howard Aronson, Norio Yamada, Shuji Chiba, Michael Forman, Robert Hsu, Kazue Kanno, Anatole Lyovin, Woody Mott, Peter Avery, John Davison, Patricia Shaw, Allison Teasdale, Charles Ulrich, Howard Aronson, Vit

Bubenik, Andrew Carnie, Vanna Condax, Eung-Do Cook, John DeFrancis, Brian King, Barry Meislin, Yves-Charles Morin, Michael O'Grady, the students in Terry Pratt's linguistics course at the University of Prince Edward Island, Albert Schütz, Stanley Starosta, Lawrence Reid, Theo Venneman, Tim Vance, Douglas Walker, and Nava Zvaig.

Finally, we owe a special debt of gratitude to our superb editor, Pamela Erlichman, for advice and encouragement over the past years. Her dedication and talent have kept this project on course through the past three editions and have contributed in countless substantial ways to its success.

Preface to the first edition

Thanks to the application of rigorous analysis to familiar subject matter, linguistics provides students with an ideal introduction to the kind of thinking we call 'scientific'. Such thinking proceeds from an appreciation of problems arising from bodies of data, to hypotheses that attempt to account for those problems, to the careful testing and extension of these hypotheses. But science is more than a formal activity. One of the great pleasures offered introductory students of linguistics is the discovery of the impressive body of subconscious knowledge that underlies language use. This book attempts to emphasize the extent of this knowledge as well as to introduce the scientific methodology used in linguistic analysis.

Although this is the first linguistics textbook designed primarily for a Canadian readership, we have tried to do much more than simply provide coverage of linguistic phenomena peculiar to Canada. As the title suggests, we have attempted an introduction to linguistic analysis as it is practised at this stage in the development of our discipline. While we do not ignore or reject other fruitful approaches to linguistics, we have taken the generative paradigm as basic for two reasons. First, generative linguistics provides a relatively coherent and integrated approach to basic linguistic phenomena. Phonetics, phonology, morphology, syntax, and semantics are viewed within this framework as perhaps in no other as fully integrated and interrelated. Secondly, the generative approach has been widely influential in its application to a broad range of other linguistic phenomena over the past twenty years.

The extent of our 'contemporariness' has been limited by the inevitable compromise between the need to present basic concepts and the demands of sophisticated and competing recent approaches. In many cases, early versions of our chapters were judged 'too contemporary' by instructors who were not specialists in the subfields in question. This led to substantial revisions and a somewhat more traditional approach to certain issues than was originally intended. Where possible, however, later sections of the chapters are used to present more contemporary material. In this way, we have attempted to provide what is promised by the title— an introductory text that provides a solid grounding in basic linguistic concepts, but one that also prepares the student to go on to current work in the discipline. For this reason, the student is introduced to multilevelled phonology (in preparation for further tiered analyses), allophonic/morphophonemic distinctions (in preparation for lexical phonology), interaction among components of the grammar (in preparation for a more extended modular approach), word formation rules in morphology, and examples of parametric variation in syntax.

To the extent possible, we have attempted to integrate the basic mechanisms outlined in the first five chapters of the book into our discussion of phenomena in later chapters. Thus, our discussion of semantics, historical linguistics, first and second language acquisition, and neurolinguistics draws to some degree on the notions presented in our introduction to generative grammar.

No textbook can be all things to all users. We hope that this book will provide students not only with a springboard to the realm of scientific linguistic analysis, but with a greater appreciation for the wonder of human language, the variety and complexity of its structure, and the subtlety of its use.

We gratefully acknowledge the assistance of Jack Chambers and Sheila Embleton, both of whom read the manuscript in its entirety and provided invaluable comments. Thanks are also due to those who have read and commented upon individual chapters and sections, including Steven Carey, Matthew Dryer, David Ingram, Gary Byma, Gary Libben, Robert Murray, R. Radhakrishnan, Ronald Southerland, Mary Pepper, Derek Bickerton, Robert Blust, Ricky Jacobs, Don Frantz, John Haiman, John Hewson, Nicole Domingue, Lydia White, George Patterson, Donna Gerdts, Elan Dresher, Keren Rice, Robert Fisher, Marilyn Philips, Lorna Rowsell, and Joyce Hildebrand. For assistance in the planning, editing, and production of the manuscript, we are grateful to Coral Sayce, Lynda Costello, Joyce Hildebrand, Brian Henderson, Patrick Burke, Les Petriw, and our project editor at Copp Clark, Margaret Larock.

List of technical abreviations

*	(in syntactic rules) one or more
*	(in front of words or sentences) unacceptable
#	word boundary
1	first person
1	primary stress
2	second person
2	secondary stress
3	third person
A	adjective
Abl	ablative case
Abs	absolutive case
Acc	accusative case
Adv	adverb
AdvP	adverb phrase
Af	affix
ag	agent
AP	adjective phrase
Aux	auxiliary verb
B	bound root
C	complementizer
C	consonant
caus	cause
CG	constricted glottis
cmpl	completed action
C_o	any number of consonants
Co	coda
CP	complementizer phrase
CT	computerized axial tomography
CYC	Cape York Creole
DA	derivational affix
Dat	dative case
Deg	degree word
DR	delayed release
EEG	electroencephalogram
Erg	ergative case
ESL	English as a second language
FN	first name
Fut	future tense
Gen	genitive case
go	goal
H	high tone
IA	inflectional affix
indic	indicative
IP	inflectional phrase (=S)
IPA	International Phonetic Alphabet
L	low tone
L1	first language
L2	second language
LN	last name
Loc	locative case
Loc	location
M	man
M	mid tone
N	noun
N	nucleus
Nom	nominative case
NP	noun phrase
O	(direct) object
O	onset
Obl	oblique
OE	Old English
P	preposition, postposition
Pass	passive
PC	Principal Component
PCA	Principal Components Analysis
PET	Positron Emission Tomography
PIE	Proto-Indo-European
pl	plural
PP	prepositional phrase
PR	phonetic representation
Prs	present tense
Pst	past tense
R	rhyme
R	rounded
RC	relative cause
REA	right ear advantage
recip	recipient
S	sentence
S	subject
σ	syllable
SES	socioeconomic status
SG	spread glottis
sg	singular
SLA	second language acquisition
th	theme
T	title alone
TLN	title + last name
Top	topic
UG	Universal Grammar
UR	underlying representation
UR	unrounded
V	verb
V	vowel
VP	verb phrase
W	woman
Wd	word

William O'Grady

Language: a preview

*The gift of language is the single human trait
that marks us all genetically, setting us
apart from the rest of life.*

LEWIS THOMAS, *THE LIVES OF A CELL*

Language is many things—a system of communication, a tool for thought, a medium for self-expression, a social institution, a source of ethnic pride and political controversy. All normal human beings have at least one language, and it is difficult to imagine much significant social, intellectual, or artistic activity taking place in the absence of language.

The centrality of language to virtually every aspect of human life gives each of us a reason to want to understand more about its nature and use. This book takes a first step in that direction by providing a basic introduction to **linguistics**, the discipline that studies language.

1 Specialization for language

Modern *homo sapiens* (our species) made their appearance 200 000 years ago, by many estimates. Early humans were anatomically just like us—they had large brains and vocal tracts capable of producing speech. Archeological evidence (such as tools, carvings, and cave paintings) suggest that they also had the type of intellect that could support language.

Hundreds of thousands of years of evolution created a special capacity for language in humans not found in any other species. The evidence is literally inside us. For example, our speech organs (the lungs, larynx, tongue, teeth, lips, soft palate, and nasal passages) were—and still are—directly concerned with breathing and eating. However, they have also all become highly specialized for use in language. Their structure and shape is unique to our species, as is the highly developed network of neural pathways that exercises control over them during speech production.

Table 1.1	Dual functions of the speech organs	
Organ	**Survival function**	**Speech function**
Lungs	to exchange CO_2 and oxygen	to supply air for speech
Vocal cords	to create seal over passage to lungs	to produce vibrations for speech sounds
Tongue	to move food to teeth and back into throat	to articulate vowels and consonants
Teeth	to break up food	to provide place of articulation for consonants
Lips	to seal oral cavity	to articulate vowels and consonants
Nose	to assist in breathing	to provide nasal resonance during speech

Breathing during speech is associated with higher lung pressure and a longer exhalation time than ordinary respiration, and abdominal muscles that are not normally employed for respiration are brought into play in order to regulate the air pressure needed for speech.

Human beings are also especially equipped for the perception of speech. Newborns respond differently to human voices than to other types of sounds, and six-month-old infants are able to perceive subtle differences among sounds in languages that they have never heard before (this is discussed in more detail in chapter 10).

Even the ability to deal with non-vocal, cognitive aspects of language—such as word formation, sentence building, the interpretation of meaning—seems to be the product of neurological specialization. Particular parts of the brain tend to be associated with specific types of linguistic phenomena (see chapter 13 for discussion), and species with different types of brains appear to be unable to acquire or use human language (see chapter 16).

2 A creative system

Knowing that human beings are especially suited for language only increases the mystery that surrounds this phenomenon. What, precisely, is language? What does it mean to know a language? To answer these questions, it is first necessary to understand the resources that a language makes available to its **native speakers**, those who have acquired it as children in a natural setting (say, a home rather than a classroom).

The breadth and diversity of human thought and experience place great demands on language. Because communication is not restricted to a fixed set of topics, language must do something more than provide a package of ready-made messages. It must enable us to produce and understand new words and sentences as the need arises. In short, human language must be **creative**—allowing novelty and innovation in response to new thoughts, experiences, and situations.

The creativity of language goes hand in hand with a second defining characteristic—the presence of systematic constraints that establish the boundaries within which innovation can occur. As a preliminary illustration of this, let us consider the process that creates verbs from nouns in English. (For now, you can think of verbs as words that name actions and nouns as words that name things.)

Table 1.2	Nouns used as verbs
Noun use	**Verb use**
pull the boat onto the *beach*	*beach* the boat
keep the airplane on the *ground*	*ground* the airplane
tie a *knot* in the string	*knot* the string
put the wine in *bottles*	*bottle* the wine
catch the fish with a *spear*	*spear* the fish
clean the floor with a *mop*	*mop* the floor

As the following sentences show, there is a great deal of freedom to innovate in the formation of such verbs.

1)
a. I *wristed* the ball over the net.
b. He would try to *stiff-upper-lip* it through.
c. She *Houdini'd* her way out of the locked closet.

However, there are also limits on this freedom. For instance, a new verb is rarely coined if a word with the intended meaning already exists. Although we say *jail the robber* to mean 'put the robber in jail', we do not say *prison the robber* to mean 'put the robber in prison'. This is because the well-established verb *imprison* already has the meaning that the new form would have.

There are also special constraints on the meaning and use of particular subclasses of these verbs. One such constraint involves verbs that are created from time expressions such as *summer, holiday*, and so on.

2)
a. Julia *summered* in Paris.
b. Harry *wintered* in Mexico.
c. Bob *holidayed* in France.
d. Harry and Julia *honeymooned* in Hawaii.

Although the sentences in *2)* are all natural-sounding, not all time expressions can be used in this way. (Throughout this book an asterisk is used to indicate that an utterance is unacceptable.)

3)
a. *Jerome *midnighted* in the streets.
b. *Andrea *nooned* at the restaurant.
c. *Philip *one o'clocked* at the airport.

These examples show that when a verb is created from a time expression, it must be given a very specific interpretation—roughly paraphrasable as 'to be somewhere for the period of time X'. Thus, *to summer in Paris* is 'to be in Paris for the summer', *to holiday in France* is 'to be in France for the holidays', and so on. Since *noon* and *midnight* express *points* in time rather than extended *periods* of time, they cannot be used to create new verbs of this type.[1]

Systematic constraints are essential to the viability of the creative process. If well-established words were constantly being replaced by new creations, a language's vocabulary would be so unstable that communication could be jeopardized. A similar danger would arise if there were no constraints on the meaning of words newly derived from other words. If *They winter in Hawaii* could mean 'They make it snow in Hawaii' or 'They wish it were winter in Hawaii' or any other arbitrary thing, the production and interpretation of new forms would be chaotic and unsystematic, undermining the usefulness of language for communication.

Some other examples

Systematic creativity is the hallmark of all aspects of language. For instance, consider the way in which sounds are combined to form words. Certain patterns of sounds, like the novel forms in *4)*, have the 'look' of English words—we recognize that they could become part of the language and be used as names for new products or processes, for example.

4)
a. prasp
b. flib
c. traf

In contrast, the forms in *5)* contain combinations of sounds that English just does not permit. As a result, they simply do not have the shape of English words.

5)
a. *psapr
b. *bfli
c. *ftra

Still other constraints determine how new words can be created from already existing forms with the help of special endings. Imagine, for example, that the word *soleme* entered the English language (used perhaps for a newly discovered atomic particle). As a speaker of English, you would then automatically know that something with the properties of a soleme could be called *solemic*. You would also know that to make something solemic is to solemicize it, and you would call this process *solemicization*. Further, you would know that the *c* is pronounced as *s* in *solemicize* but as *k* in *solemic*. Without hesitation, you would also recognize that *solemicize* is pronounced with the stress on the second syllable. (You would say soLEmicize, not SOlemicize or solemiCIZE.)

Nowhere is the ability to deal with novel utterances more obvious than in the production and comprehension of sentences. Apart from a few fixed expressions and greetings, much of what you say, hear, and read in the course of a day consists of sentences that are new to you. In conversations, lectures, newscasts, and textbooks, you are regularly exposed to novel combinations of words, unfamiliar ideas, and new information. Consider, for instance, the paragraph that you are currently reading. While each sentence is no doubt perfectly comprehensible to you, it is extremely unlikely that you have ever seen any of them before.

Not all new sentences are acceptable, however. For example, the words in *6)* are all familiar, but they are simply not arranged in the right way to make a sentence of English.

6)
*Frightened dog this the cat that chased mouse a.
(cf. This dog frightened the cat that chased a mouse.)

As with other aspects of language, the ability to form and interpret sentences is subject to systematic limitations. One of the principal goals of contemporary linguistic analysis is to identify and understand these limitations.

3 Grammar and linguistic competence

As we have just seen, speakers of a language are able to produce and understand an unlimited number of utterances, including many that are novel and unfamiliar. At the same time, they are able to recognize that certain utterances are not acceptable and simply do not belong in their language. This ability, which is often called **linguistic competence**, constitutes the central subject matter of linguistics and of this book.

In investigating linguistic competence, linguists focus on the mental system that allows human beings to form and interpret the sounds, words, and sentences of their language. Linguists call this system a **grammar** and often break it down into the following components.

Table 1.3	The components of a grammar
Component	**Domain**
Phonetics	the articulation and perception of speech sounds
Phonology	the patterning of speech sounds
Morphology	word formation
Syntax	sentence formation
Semantics	the interpretation of words and sentences

As you can see, the term *grammar* is used in a special way within linguistics. A linguist's grammar is not a book and it is not concerned with just the form of words and sentences. Rather, it is an intricate system of knowledge that encompasses sound and meaning as well as form and structure.

The study of grammar lies at the core of our attempts to understand what language is and what it means to know a language. Five simple points should help clarify why the investigation of grammatical systems is so important to contemporary linguistic analysis.

3.1 Generality: all languages have a grammar

One of the most fundamental claims of modern linguistic analysis is that all languages have a grammar. It could not be any other way. If a language is spoken, it must have a phonetic and phonological system; since it has words and sentences, it must also have a morphology and a syntax; and since these words and sentences have systematic meanings, there must obviously be semantic principles as well. Of course, these are the very things that make up a grammar.

It is not unusual to hear the remark that some language—Acadian French, Cree, or Swahili—has no grammar. (This is especially common in the case of languages that are not written or are not taught in schools and universities.) Unfamiliar languages sometimes appear to an untrained observer to have no grammar simply because their grammatical systems are different from those of better-known languages. In Walbiri (an indigenous language of Australia), for example, the relative ordering of words is so free that the English sentence *The two dogs now see several kangaroos* could be translated by the equivalent of any of the following sentences.

7)
a. Dogs two now see kangaroos several.
b. See now dogs two kangaroos several.
c. See now kangaroos several dogs two.
d. Kangaroos several now dogs two see.
e. Kangaroos several now see dogs two.

Although Walbiri may not restrict the order of words in the way English does, its grammar imposes other types of requirements. For example, in the sentence types we are considering, Walbiri speakers must place the ending *lu* on the word for 'dogs' to indicate that it names the animals that do the seeing rather than the animals that are seen. In English, by contrast, this information is conveyed by placing *two dogs* in front of the verb and *several kangaroos* after it.

Rather than showing that Walbiri has no grammar, such differences simply demonstrate that it has a grammar that is unlike the grammar of English in certain respects. This point holds across the board: although no two languages have exactly the same grammar, there are no languages without a grammar.

A similar point can be made about different varieties of the same language. To some extent, for instance, each of the many varieties of English spoken in today's world (Newfoundland English, Jamaican English, Boston English) has its own characteristic pronunciation, vocabulary, and sentence patterns. Crucially, though, these differences exist not because the various varieties of English have no grammar, but rather because they have grammars that differ from each other in particular ways.

3.2   Parity: all grammars are equal

Contrary to popular belief, there is no such thing as a 'primitive' language, even in places untouched by modern science and technology. Indeed, some of the most complex linguistic phenomena we know about are found in societies that have neither writing nor electricity.

Moreover, there is no such thing as a 'good grammar' or a 'bad grammar'. In fact, all grammars do essentially the same thing: they tell speakers how to form and interpret the words and sentences of their language. The form and meaning of those words and sentences vary from language to language and even from community to community, of course, but there is no such thing as a language that doesn't work for its speakers.

Linguists sometimes clash over this point with people who are upset about the use of 'non-standard' varieties of English that permit sentences such as *I seen that, They was there, He didn't do nothing, He ain't here,* and so forth. Depending on where you live and who you talk to, speaking in this way can have negative consequences: it may be harder to win a scholarship, to get a job, to be accepted in certain social circles, and so forth. This is an undeniable fact about the social side of language and we'll return to it in chapter 14. From a purely linguistic point of view, however, there is absolutely nothing wrong with grammars that permit such structures. They work for their speakers, and they deserve to be studied in the same objective fashion as the varieties of English spoken by the rich and educated.

The bottom line for linguistics is that the analysis of language must reflect the way it is actually used, not someone's idealized vision of how it should be used. The linguist Steven Pinker offers the following illustration to make the same point.

> *Imagine that you are watching a nature documentary. The video shows the usual gorgeous footage of animals in their natural habitats. But the voiceover reports some troubling facts. Dolphins do not execute their swimming strokes properly. White-crowned sparrows carelessly debase their calls. Chickadees' nests are incorrectly constructed, pandas hold bamboo in the wrong paw, the song of the humpback whale contains several well-known errors, and the monkey's cries have been in a state of chaos and degeneration for hundreds of years. Your reaction would probably be, What on earth could it mean for the song of the humpback whale to contain an "error"? Isn't the song of the humpback whale whatever the humpback whale decides to sing? . . .*

As Pinker goes on to observe, language is like the song of the humpback whale. The way to determine whether a particular sentence is permissible is to find people who speak the language and observe how they use it.

In sum, linguists don't even think of trying to rate languages as good or bad, simple or complex. Rather, they investigate language in much the same way that other scientists study snails or stars—with a view to simply figuring out how it works. This same point is sometimes made by noting that linguistics is **descriptive**, not **prescriptive**. Its goal is to describe and explain the facts of language, not to change them.

3.3 Universality: grammars are alike in basic ways

In considering how grammars can differ from each other, it is easy to lose sight of something even more intriguing and important—the existence of principles and properties shared by all human languages.

For example, all languages use a small set of contrastive sounds that help distinguish words from each other (like the *t* and *d* sounds that allow us to recognize *to* and *do* as different words). Not all languages use the same sounds, but there are real constraints on which ones they can and cannot use. For instance, all languages have more consonant sounds (*p*, *t*, *d*, etc.) than vowel sounds (*a, e, i*); any language that has a *b* sound also has a *p* sound; and all languages have a vowel that sounds like the 'ah' in *father*. (For more on this, see chapter 8.)

There are also universal constraints on how words can be put together to form sentences. For example, no language can use the second of the sentences in *8)* for a situation in which *he* refers to *Ned*.

8)
a. Ned lost his wallet.
b. He lost Ned's wallet.

Moreover, even when languages do differ from each other, there are often constraints on how much variation is possible. For example, some languages (like English) place question words at the beginning of the sentence.

9)
Mary sees a book. **What** do you see?

Other languages, like Mandarin, make no such changes.

10)
Mali kanjian shu.   Ni kanjian **sheme**?
Mary sees   book you see   what
'Mary sees a book. What do you see?'

But no language uniformly places question words at the end of the sentence.

In other cases, variation is constrained by strong tendencies rather than absolute prohibitions. Take three-word sentences such as *Canadians like hockey*, for instance. There are six logically possible orders for such sentences.

11)
  a. Canadians like hockey.
  b. Canadians hockey like.
  c. Like Canadians hockey.
  d. Like hockey Canadians.
  e. Hockey like Canadians.
  f. Hockey Canadians like.

All other things being equal, we would expect to find each order employed in about one-sixth of the world's languages. In fact, though, more than 95 percent of the world's languages adopt one of the first three orders for basic statements (and the vast majority of those use one or the other of the first two orders). Only a handful of languages use any of the last three orders as basic.

These are not isolated examples. As later chapters will show, languages—like the people who use them—are fundamentally alike in important ways.

3.4   Mutability: grammars change over time

The features of language that are not universal and fixed are subject to change over time. Indeed, within these limits, the grammars of all languages are constantly changing. Some of these changes are relatively minor and occur very quickly (for example, the addition of new words such as *morphing, Internet, e-mail,* and *cyberspace* to the vocabulary of English). Other changes have a more dramatic effect on the overall form of the language and typically take place over a long period of time. One such change involves the manner in which we negate sentences in English. Prior to 1200, English formed negative constructions by placing *ne* before the verb and a variant of *not* after it.

12)
  a. Ic *ne* seye *not*. ('I don't say.')
  b. He *ne* speketh *nawt*. ('He does not speak.')

By 1400 or thereabouts, *ne* was used infrequently and *not* (or *nawt*) typically occurred by itself after the verb.

13)
a. I seye *not* the wordes.
b. We saw *nawt* the knyghtes.

It was not until several centuries later that English adopted its current practice of allowing *not* to occur after only certain types of verbs (such as *do, have, will,* and so on).

14)
a. I will *not* say the words. (versus *I will say not the words.)
b. He did *not* see the knights. (versus *He saw not the knights.)

These changes illustrate the extent to which grammars can be modified over time. The structures exemplified in *13)* are archaic by today's standards and those in *12)* sound completely foreign to most speakers of modern English.

Through the centuries, those who believe that certain varieties of language are better than others have frequently expressed concern over what they perceive to be the deterioration of English. In 1710, for example, the writer Jonathan Swift (author of *Gulliver's Travels*) lamented 'the continual Corruption of our English Tongue.' Among the corruptions to which he objected were contractions such as *he's* for *he is*, although he had no objection to *'Tis* for *It is*.

Similar concerns have been expressed about the state of English spoken in Canada. In 1857, members of the Canadian Institute in Toronto heard a speech describing Canadian English as 'a corrupt dialect growing up amongst our population.' The speaker objected to the use of words such as *lot* (for 'a division of land'), *boss* (for 'master'), *store* (for 'shop'), *fix* (for 'mend'), and *guess* (for 'think', as in *I guess I'll go*). Judging by current usage, he objected in vain.

Linguists reject the view that languages attain a state of perfection at some point in their history and that subsequent changes lead to deterioration and corruption. As noted above, there are simply no grounds for claiming that one language or variety of language is somehow superior to another.

3.5 Inaccessibility: grammatical knowledge is subconscious

Knowledge of a grammar differs in important ways from knowledge of arithmetic, traffic rules, and other subjects that are taught at home or in school: it is largely subconscious and not accessible to introspection (that is, you can't figure out how it works just by thinking about it). As an example of this, consider your pronunciation of the past tense ending written as *ed* in the following words.

15)
a. hunted
b. slipped
c. buzzed

You probably didn't notice it before, but the *ed* ending has a different pronunciation in each of these words. Whereas you say *id* in *hunted*, you say *t* in *slipped* and *d* in *buzzed*. Moreover, if you heard the new verb *flib*, you would form the past tense as *flibbed* and pronounce the ending as *d*. If you are a native speaker of English, you acquired the grammatical subsystem regulating this aspect of speech when you were a child and it now exists subconsciously in your mind, allowing you to automatically make the relevant contrasts.

The same is true for virtually everything else about language. Once we go beyond the most obvious things (like whether words like *the* and *a* come before or after a noun), there is not much that the average person can say about how language works. For example, try explaining to someone who is not a native speaker of English why we can say *I went to school* but not **I went to movie*. Or try to figure out for yourself how the word *too* works. Notice that it sounds perfectly natural in sentences like the following.

16)
a. Mary ate a cookie, and then Johnnie ate a cookie too.
b. Mary ate a cookie, and then she ate some cake too.

For some reason, though, it doesn't sound so natural in the following sentence.

17)
*Mary ate a cookie, and then Johnnie ate some cake too.

You may be thinking that that is because Mary and Johnnie didn't eat the same thing. But, if that's so, then why does *too* sound natural in the next sentence, even though Johnnie didn't have a cookie for his snack?

18)
Mary ate a cookie, and then Johnnie had a snack too.

Speakers of a language know what sounds right and what doesn't sound right, but they are not sure how they know.

Because most of what we know about our language is subconscious, the analysis of human linguistic systems requires considerable effort and ingenuity. As is the case in all science, information about facts that can be observed (the pronunciation of words, the interpretation of sentences, and so on) must be used to draw inferences about the sometimes invisible mechanisms (atoms, cells, or grammars, as the case may be) that are ultimately responsible for these phenomena. A good deal of this book is concerned with the findings of this research and with what they tell us about the nature and use of human language and about how it is represented in the mind.

Summing up

Human language is characterized by **creativity**. Speakers of a language have access to a **grammar**, a mental system that allows them to form and interpret both familiar and novel utterances. The grammar governs the articulation, perception, and patterning of speech sounds, the formation of words and sentences, and the interpretation of utterances. All languages have grammars that are equal in their expressive capacity, and all speakers of a language have (subconscious) knowledge of its grammar. The existence of such linguistic systems in humans is the product of unique anatomical and cognitive specialization not found in other species.

Notes

1 Not all nouns naming periods of time can be converted into verbs, however. Thus, for reasons that are not understood, the nouns *autumn* and *week* do not make very good verbs.

  *They autumned/weeked in the Maritimes.

Sources

The discussion of word creation is based on an article by Eve Clark and Herb Clark, "When Nouns Surface As Verbs" in *Language* 55:767–811 (1979). The Walbiri data are based on K. Hale's article "Person Marking in Walbiri" in *A Festschrift for Morris Halle*, edited by S. Anderson and P. Kiparsky (New York: Holt, Rinehart and Winston, 1973). The quote at the end of section 3.2 is from the book by Steven Pinker (p. 370) cited below. The 1857 speech on the status of Canadian English is cited in Mark Orkin's *Speaking Canadian English* (Toronto: General Publishing Company, 1970). The data on the word order preferences is from *Typology and Universals* by William Croft (New York: Cambridge University Press, 1990), p. 46. The books by Bickerton and Pinker, cited below, provide different views of the emergence of language in the human species.

The exercises for this chapter were prepared by Joyce Hildebrand.

Recommended reading

Bickerton, Derek. 1990. *Language and Species*. Chicago: University of Chicago Press.
Crystal, David. 1997. *Cambridge Encyclopedia of the English Language*. New York: Cambridge University Press.
Pinker, Steven. 1994. *The Language Instinct: How the Human Mind Creates Language*. New York: Morrow.

Questions

1. The following sentences contain verbs created from nouns in accordance with the process described in section 1 of the chapter. Describe the meaning of each of these new verbs.
   a) We punk-rocked the night away.
   b) He dog-teamed his way across the Arctic.
   c) We MG'd to Oregon.
   d) They Concorded to London.
   e) He Gretzky'd his way to the net.
   f) We Greyhounded to Toronto.
   g) We'll have to Ajax the sink.
   h) She Windexed the windows.

    i) You should Clairol your hair.

    j) Let's carton the eggs.

2. Using the examples in the preceding exercise as a model, create five new verbs from nouns. Build a sentence around each of these new verbs to show its meaning.

3. Which of the following forms are possible words of English? Solicit the help of an acquaintance and see if you agree on your judgments.

    a) mbood   e) sproke

    b) frall   f) flube

    c) coofp   g) wordm

    d) ktleem   h) bsarn

4. Imagine that you are an advertising executive and that your job involves inventing new names for products. Create four new forms that are possible words of English and four that are not.

5. Part of linguistic competence involves the ability to recognize whether novel utterances are acceptable. Consider the following sentences and determine which are possible sentences in English. For each unacceptable sentence, change the sentence to make it acceptable, and compare the two.

    a) Jason's mother left himself with nothing to eat.

    b) Miriam is eager to talk to.

    c) This is the man who I took a picture of.

    d) Colin made Jane a sandwich.

    e) Is the dog sleeping the bone again?

    f) Wayne prepared Zena a cake.

    g) Max cleaned the garden up.

    h) Max cleaned up the garden.

    i) Max cleaned up it.

    j) I desire you to leave.

    k) That you likes liver surprises me.

6. Consider the following sentences, each of which is acceptable to some speakers of English. Try to identify the prescriptive rules that are violated in each case.

    a) He don't know about the race.

    b) You was out when I called.

    c) There's twenty horses registered in the show.

    d) That window's broke, so be careful.

    e) Jim and me are gonna go campin' this weekend.

    f) Who did you come with?

    g) I seen the parade last week.

    h) He been lost in the woods for ten days.

    i) My car needs cleaned 'cause of all the rain.

    j) Julie ain't got none.

    k) Somebody left their book on the train.

    l) Murray hurt hisself in the game.

What is the reaction of linguists to the claim that sentences of this sort are 'wrong'?

Michael Dobrovolsky

Phonetics: the sounds of language

Heavenly labials in a world of gutturals

WALLACE STEVENS

We do not need to speak in order to use language. Language can be written, broadcast from tapes and CDs, and even produced by computers in limited ways. Nevertheless, speech remains the primary way humans encode and broadcast language. Our species spoke long before we began to write and, as we saw in the first chapter of this book, this long history of spoken language is reflected in our anatomical specialization for it. Humans also appear to have specialized neural mechanisms for the perception of speech sounds. Because language and speech are so closely linked, we begin our study of language by examining the inventory and structure of the sounds of speech. This branch of linguistics is called **phonetics**.

Human languages display a wide variety of sounds, called **phones** (from Greek *phōnē* 'sound, voice') or **speech sounds**. There are a great many speech sounds, but not an infinite number of them—the class of possible speech sounds is finite, and a portion of the total set will be found in the inventory of any human language. Certain sounds that humans are capable of producing with the vocal tract do not occur in speech, such as the sound made by inhaling through one corner of the mouth, or the 'raspberry' produced by sticking out the tongue and blowing hard across it. Nonetheless, a very wide range of sounds is found in human language, including such sounds as the click made by drawing the tongue hard away from the upper molars on one side of the mouth, or the sound made by constricting the upper part of the throat as we breathe out. The class of possible speech sounds is universal and can be learned by any human, child or adult.

There are two ways of approaching phonetics. One approach studies the physiological mechanisms of speech production. This is known as **articulatory phonetics**. The other, known as **acoustic phonetics**, is concerned with measuring and analyzing the physical properties of the sound waves we produce when we speak. Both approaches are indispensable to an understanding of phonetics. This chapter focuses on articulatory phonetics, but also makes some reference to the acoustic properties of sounds and to acoustic analysis.

1 Phonetic transcription

Since the sixteenth century, efforts have been made to devise a universal system for transcribing the sounds of speech. The best-known system, the **International Phonetic Alphabet (IPA)**, has been developing since 1888. This system of transcription attempts to represent each sound of human speech with a single symbol. These symbols are enclosed in brackets [ ] to indicate that the transcription is phonetic and does not represent the spelling system of a particular language. For example, the sound spelled *th* in English *this* is transcribed as [ð] (pronounced *eth*, as in *weather*). The IPA uses this symbol to represent the sound in whichever language it is heard, whether it is English, Spanish, Turkmen (a Turkic language spoken in Central Asia and written with the Cyrillic alphabet), or any other (see table 2.1).

Table 2.1	Use of [ð] in the International Phonetic Alphabet		
Language	**Spelling**	**IPA**	**Meaning**
English	<u>th</u>is	[ðɪs]	'this'
Spanish	bo<u>d</u>a	[bɔða]	'wedding'
Turkmen	a<u>д</u>ak	[aðak]	'foot'

The use of a standardized phonetic alphabet enables linguists to transcribe languages consistently and accurately. In North American (NA) usage, though, some phonetic symbols differ from those employed by IPA transcription. For example, the sound heard at the beginning of the English word *shark* is transcribed as [ʃ] in IPA, but usually as [š] in North America. This book employs IPA transcription, but notes common North American symbols where relevant.

If you wish to start practising the phonetic transcription of English, turn to tables 2.16 and 2.17, pages 33–35, for examples.

1.1 Units of representation

Anyone who hears a language spoken for the first time finds it hard to break up the flow of speech into individual units. Even when hearing our own language spoken, we do not focus attention on individual sounds as much as we do on the meanings of words, phrases, and sentences. Many alphabets, including the IPA, represent speech in the form of **segments**—individual phones like [p], [s], or [m]. Using segments, however, is only one way to represent speech. The **syllable**, presented in chapter 3, is also represented in some writing systems (see chapter 15, sections 1.2, 3.2, and 4.2). In one form of Japanese writing, for example, signs such as か [ka], と [to], and み [mi] represent syllables without recourse to segmental transcription.

Segments are produced by coordinating a number of individual articulatory gestures including jaw movement, lip shape, and tongue placement. Many of these individual activities are represented as smaller subunits called **features** that segments are assumed to be made up of. Even though features are almost never represented in writing systems, they are important elements of linguistic representation. Features reflect individual aspects of articulatory control or acoustic effects produced by articulation. This chapter presents segmental transcription, since it is the most widely used way of representing speech. Features and syllables are introduced in the following chapter.

1.2   Segments

We have defined the **segment** as an individual speech sound (phone). There are several kinds of evidence that suggest that speakers have the linguistic knowledge that makes it possible to break down a stream of speech into sound segments.

Errors in speech production provide one kind of evidence for the existence of segments. Slips of the tongue such as *Kolacodor* for *Kodacolor* and *melcome wat* for *welcome mat* show segments shifting and reversing position within and across words. This suggests that segments are individual units of linguistic structure and can be represented individually in a system of transcription.

The relative invariance of speech sounds in human language also suggests that segmental phonetic transcription is a well-motivated way of transcribing speech. It is impossible to represent all variants of human speech sounds, since no one says the same sound in exactly the same way twice. Nonetheless, the sounds of speech remain invariant enough from language to language for us to transcribe them consistently. A *p* sound is much the same in English, Russian, or Uzbek. The fact that when producing a *p* sound, English speakers press their lips together but Russian speakers draw theirs slightly inward does not make the sounds different enough to warrant separate symbols. But the sounds *p* and *t* are distinct enough from each other in languages the world over to be consistently transcribed with separate symbols.

2   The sound-producing system

Sound is produced when air is set in motion. Think of the speech production mechanism as consisting of an air supply, a sound source that sets the air in motion in ways specifically relevant to speech production, and a set of filters that modifies the sound in various ways. The air supply is provided by the lungs. The sound source is in the larynx, where a set of muscles called the **vocal folds** (or **vocal cords**) are located. The filters are the organs above the larynx: the tube of the throat between the larynx and the oral cavity, which is called the **pharynx**, the oral cavity, and the nasal cavity. These passages are collectively known as the **vocal tract**.

2.1   The lungs

In order to produce the majority of sounds in the world's languages, we take air into the lungs and then expel it during speech. (A small number of phones are made with air as it flows into the vocal tract.) A certain level of air pressure is needed to keep the speech mechanism functioning steadily. The pressure is maintained by the action of various sets of muscles coming into play during the course of an utterance. The muscles are primarily the **intercostals** (the muscles between the ribs) and the **diaphragm** (the large sheet of muscle separating the chest cavity from the abdomen).

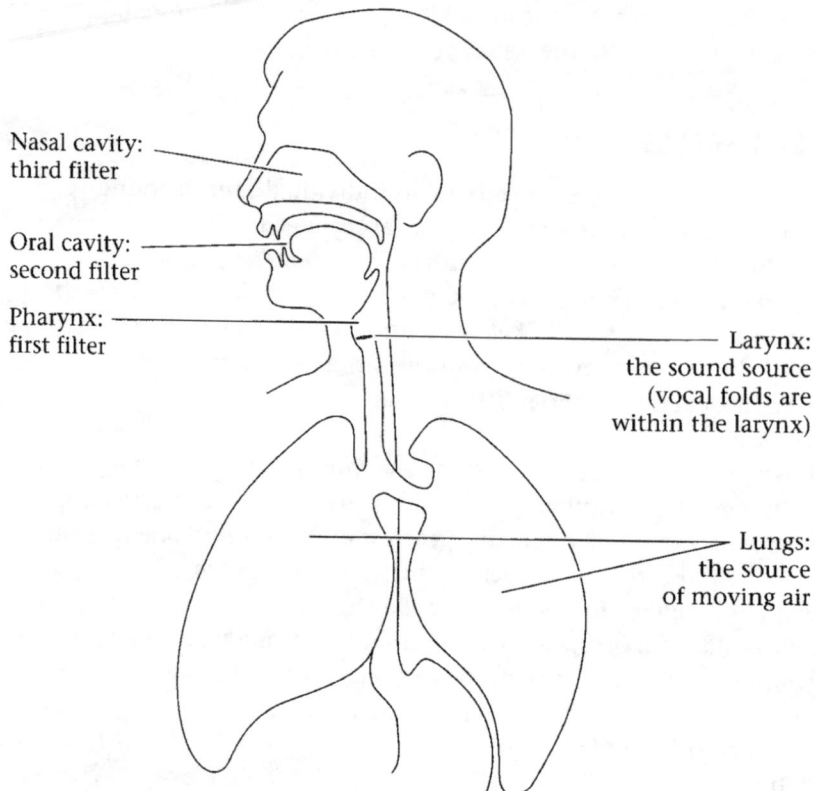

Figure 2.1 The sound-producing system

2.2   The larynx

As air flows out of the lungs up the **trachea** (windpipe), it passes through a box-like structure made of cartilages and muscle; this is the larynx (commonly known as the voice box or

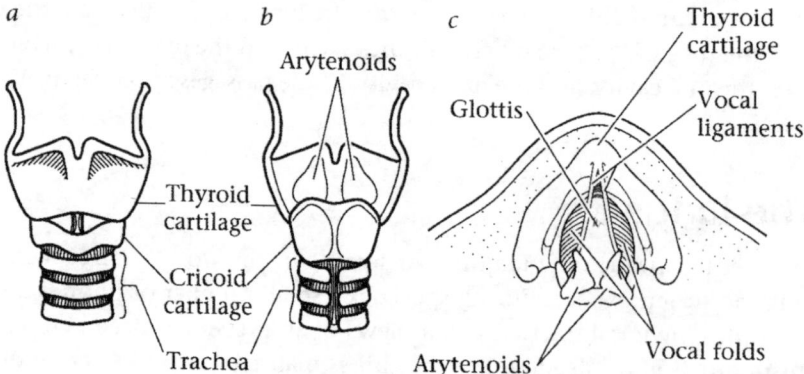

Figure 2.2 The larynx: *a* from the front; *b* from the back; *c* from above, with the vocal folds in
open position. The striated lines in *c* indicate muscles, a number of which have been eliminated from
the drawings in order to show the cartilages more clearly

Adam's apple). The main portion of the larynx is formed by the thyroid cartilage, which spreads outward like the head of a plow. The thyroid cartilage rests on the ring-shaped **cricoid cartilage**. Fine sheets of muscle flare from the inner sides of the thyroid cartilage, forming the paired vocal folds (vocal cords). The inner edges of the vocal folds are attached to the vocal ligaments. The vocal folds can be pulled apart or drawn closer together, especially at their back or posterior ends, where each is attached to one of two small cartilages, the **arytenoids**. The arytenoids are opened, closed, and rotated by several pairs of small muscles (not shown in figure 2.2). As air passes through the space between the vocal folds, which is called the **glottis**, different glottal states are produced, depending on the positioning of the vocal folds.

2.3   Glottal states

The vocal folds may be positioned in a number of ways to produce different glottal states. The first two glottal states presented in figure 2.3 are commonly encountered in most of the world's languages. The third diagram describes the glottal state that underlies a common speech phenomenon, and the fourth illustrates one of a number of glottal states not encountered in English.

Voicelessness

When the vocal folds are pulled apart as illustrated in figure 2.2, air passes directly through the glottis. Any sound made with the vocal folds in this position is said to be **voiceless**. You can confirm a sound's voicelessness by touching your fingers to the larynx as you produce it. You will not feel any vibration from the vocal folds being transmitted to your fingertips. The initial sounds of *fish*, *sing*, and *house* are all voiceless. Voicelessness is a true speech state; the vocal folds are not as far apart as they are in silent breathing.

Voicing

When the vocal folds are brought close together, but not tightly closed, air passing between them causes them to vibrate, producing sounds that are said to be voiced. (See figure 2.3, where the movement of the vocal folds during voicing is indicated by the wavy line.) You can determine whether a sound is voiced in the same way you determined voicelessness. By lightly touching the fingers to the larynx as you produce an extended version of the initial sounds of the words *zip* or *vow*, or any vowel, you can sense the vibration of the vocal folds within the larynx.

Whisper

Another glottal state produces a **whisper**. Whispering is voiceless, but, as shown in figure 2.3, the vocal folds are adjusted so that the anterior (front) portions are pulled close together, while the posterior (back) portions are apart.

Murmur

Yet another glottal state produces a **murmur**, also known as **whispery voice**. Sounds produced with this glottal configuration are voiced, but the vocal folds are relaxed to allow enough air to escape to produce a simultaneous whispery effect.

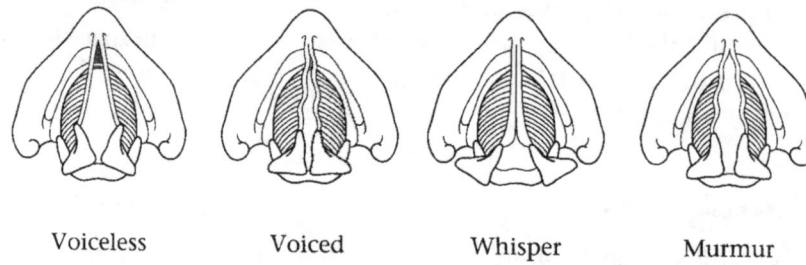

| Voiceless | Voiced | Whisper | Murmur |

Figure 2.3 Four glottal states: the stylized drawing represents the vocal folds and glottis from above; the anterior portion at the larynx is towards the top. The small triangles represent the arytenoid cartilages, which help spread or close the vocal folds

These four glottal states represent only some of the possibilities of sound production at the glottis. The total number of glottal states is still undecided, but is over a dozen. Combined with various articulations made above the larynx, they produce a wide range of phones. Before examining phones in more detail, we will first consider the three major classes of speech sound.

3   Sound classes

The sounds of language can be grouped into **classes** based on the phonetic properties that they share. You have already seen what some of these properties can be. All voiced sounds, for example, form a class, as do all voiceless sounds. The most basic division among sounds is into two major classes, **vowels** and **consonants**. Another class of sounds, the **glides**, shares properties of both vowels and consonants. Each of these classes of sounds has a number of distinguishing features.

3.1   Vowels, consonants, and glides (syllabic and non-syllabic elements)

Vowels, consonants, and glides can be distinguished on the basis of differences in articulation, or by their acoustic properties. We can also distinguish among these elements with respect to whether they function as syllabic or non-syllabic elements.

The articulatory difference

Consonantal sounds, which may be voiced or voiceless, are made with either a complete closure or narrowing of the vocal tract. The airflow is either blocked momentarily or restricted so much that noise is produced as air flows past the constriction. Vowels are produced with little obstruction in the vocal tract and are usually voiced.

The acoustic difference

As a result of the difference in articulation, consonants and vowels differ in the way they sound. Vowels are more sonorous (acoustically powerful) than consonants, and so we perceive them as louder and longer lasting.

Syllabic and non-syllabic sounds

The greater sonority of vowels allows them to form the basis of **syllables**. A syllable can be defined as a peak of sonority surrounded by less sonorous segments. For example, the words *a* and *go* each contain one syllable, the word *laughing* two syllables, and the word *telephone* three syllables. In counting the syllables in these words, we are in effect counting the vowels. A vowel is thus said to form the **nucleus** of a syllable. In section 5.7, it will be shown that certain types of consonants can form syllabic nuclei as well. It is a good idea, therefore, to think of vowels and consonants not simply as types of articulations, but as elements that may or may not be syllabic. In *1)*, the initial sounds of the words in the left column are all consonants; those on the right are all vowels.

1)
take   above
cart   at
feel   eel
jump   it
think   ugly
bell   open

Table 2.2 sums up the differences between consonants and vowels:

Table 2.2 Major differences between syllabic and non-syllabic elements	
Vowels (and other syllabic elements)	Consonants (non-syllabic elements)
• are produced with relatively little obstruction in the vocal tract	• are produced with a complete closure or narrowing of the vocal tract
• are more sonorous	• are less sonorous

Glides

A type of sound that shows properties of both consonants and vowels is called a glide. Glides may be thought of as rapidly articulated vowels—this is the auditory impression they produce. Glides are produced with an articulation like that of a vowel. However, they move quickly to another articulation, as do the inital glides in *yet* or *wet*, or quickly terminate, as do the word-final glides in *boy* and *now*.

Even though they are vowel-like in articulation, glides pattern as consonants. For example, glides can never form the nucleus of a syllable. Since glides show properties of both consonants and vowels, the terms *semivowel* and *semiconsonant* may be used interchangeably with the term *glide*.

4 Consonant articulation

Airflow is modified in the vocal tract by the placement of the tongue and the positioning of the lips. These modifications occur at specific **places** or **points of articulation**. The major places of articulation used in speech production are outlined in this section. Figure 2.4 provides a midsagittal section, or cutaway view, of the vocal tract on which each place of articulation has been indicated.

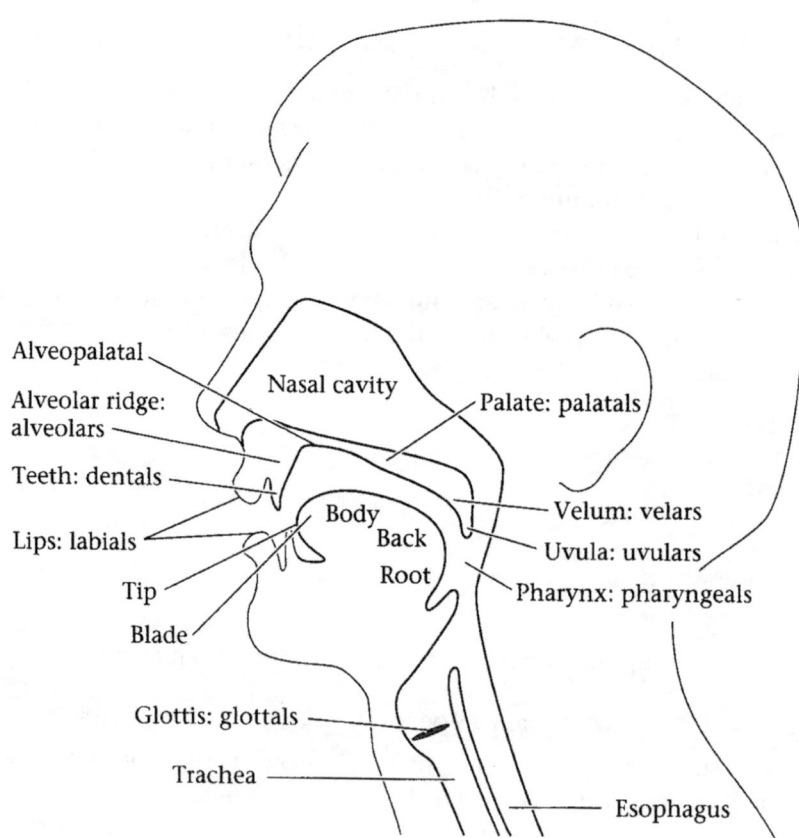

Figure 2.4 The vocal tract

4.1 The tongue

The primary articulating organ is the tongue. It can be raised, lowered, thrust forward or drawn back, and even rolled back. The sides of the tongue can also be raised or lowered.

Phonetic description refers to five areas of the tongue. The **tip** is the narrow area at the front. Just behind the tip lies the **blade**. The main mass of the tongue is called the **body**, and the hindmost part of the tongue that lies in the mouth is called the **back**. The body and back of the tongue can also be referred to jointly as the **dorsum**. The **root** of the tongue is contained in the upper part of the throat (pharynx).

4.2   Places of articulation

Each point at which the airstream can be modified to produce a different sound is called a place of articulation. Places of articulation are found at the lips, within the oral cavity, in the pharynx, and at the glottis.

Labial

Any sound made with closure or near-closure of the lips is said to be **labial**. Sounds involving both lips are termed *bilabial*; sounds involving the lower lip and upper teeth are called **labiodentals**. English includes the bilabials heard word-initially in *peer*, *bin*, and *month*, and the labiodentals heard initially in *fire* and *vow*.

Dental and interdental

Some phones are produced with the tongue placed against or near the teeth. Sounds made in this way are called **dentals**. European French has dental sounds at the beginning of the words *temps*, *dire*, *sept*, and *zizi*.

If the tongue is placed between the teeth, the sound is said to be **interdental**. Interdentals in English include the initial consonants of the words *this* and *thing*. (Some English speakers produce *s* and *z* as dentals; see section 5.3 for more details.)

Alveolar

Within the oral cavity, a small ridge protrudes from just behind the upper front teeth. This is called the **alveolar ridge**. The tongue may touch or be brought near this ridge. Alveolar sounds are heard at the beginning of the following English words: *top*, *deer*, *soap*, *zip*, *lip*, and *neck*. Some languages, such as Spanish, have an *r* that is made by touching the tongue to the alveolar ridge

Alveopalatal and palatal

Just behind the alveolar ridge, the roof of the mouth rises sharply. This area is known as the **alveopalatal** area (**palatoalveolar** in some books).

The highest part of the roof of the mouth is called the **palate**, and sounds produced with the tongue on or near this area are called **palatals**. The word-initial phone in *yes* is a palatal glide. Alveopalatal consonants are heard in the following English words: *show*, *measure*; *chip*, and *judge*.

Velar

The soft area towards the rear of the roof of the mouth is called the **velum**. Sounds made with the tongue touching or near this position are called **velars**. Velars are heard in English at the beginning of the words *call* and *guy*, and at the end of the word *hang*. The glide heard word-initially in *wet* is called a **labiovelar**, since the tongue is raised near the velum and the lips are rounded at the same time.

Uvular

The small fleshy flap of tissue known as the **uvula** hangs down from the velum. Sounds made with the tongue near or touching this area are called **uvulars**. English has no uvulars, but the *r* sound of standard European French is uvular.

Pharyngeal

The area of the throat between the uvula and the larynx is known as the pharynx. Sounds made through the modification of airflow in this region by retracting the tongue or constricting the pharynx are called **pharyngeals**. Pharyngeals can be found in many dialects of Arabic, but not in English.

Glottal

Sounds produced using the vocal folds as primary articulators are called **glottals**. The sound at the beginning of the English words *heave* and *hog* is made at the glottis.

5 Manners of articulation

The lips, tongue, velum, and glottis can be positioned in different ways to produce different sound types. These various configurations are called the **manners of articulation**.

5.1 Oral versus nasal phones

A basic distinction in manner of articulation is between **oral** and **nasal** phones. When the velum is raised, cutting off the airflow through the nasal passages, oral sounds are produced. The velum, however, can be lowered to allow air to pass through the nasal passages, producing a sound that is nasal. Both consonants and vowels can be nasal, in which case they are generally voiced. (Unless otherwise noted, all nasals represented in this chapter are voiced.) The consonants at the end of the English words *sun, sum,* and *sung* are nasal. For many speakers of English, the vowels of words such as *bank* and *wink* are also nasal.

5.2 Stops

Stops are made with a complete and momentary closure of airflow through the vocal tract. In the world's languages, stops are found at bilabial, dental, alveolar, palatal, velar, uvular, and glottal points of articulation.

In English, bilabial, alveolar, and velar oral and nasal stops occur in the words shown in table 2.3. Note that [ŋ] does not occur word-initially in English.

The glottal stop is commonly heard in English in the expression *uh-uh* [ʔʌʔʌ], meaning 'no'. The two vowels in this utterance are each preceded by a momentary closing of the airstream at the glottis. In some British dialects, the glottal stop is commonly heard in place of the [t] in a word like *bottle*. This glottal stop is often spelled with an apostrophe *(bo'l)*.

Table 2.3	English stops and their transcription	
Bilabial		**Transcription**
Voiceless	span	[p]
Voiced	ban	[b]
Nasal	man	[m]
Alveolar		
Voiceless	stun	[t]
Voiced	dot	[d]
Nasal	not	[n]
Velar		
Voiceless	scar	[k]
Voiced	gap	[g]
Nasal	wing	[ŋ]
Glottal		
Voiceless	(see above)	[ʔ]

A grid for stops

Table 2.4 presents a grid on which the stop consonants of English are arranged horizontally according to point of articulation. As you can see, each stop, with one exception, has voiced and voiceless counterparts. The glottal stop is always voiceless. It is produced with the vocal folds drawn firmly together and the arytenoids drawn forward; and since no air can pass through the glottis, the vocal folds cannot be set in motion.

Table 2.4	English stop consonants			
	Bilabial	**Alveolar**	**Velar**	**Glottal**
Voiceless	[p]	[t]	[k]	[ʔ]
Voiced	[b]	[d]	[g]	
Nasal	[m]	[n]	[ŋ]	

5.3 Fricatives

Fricatives are consonants produced with a continuous airflow through the mouth. They belong to a large class of sounds called **continuants** (a class that also includes vowels and glides), all of which share this property. The fricatives form a special class of continuants; during their production, they are accompanied by a continuous audible noise because the air used in their production passes through a very narrow opening either at the glottis or in the vocal tract.

English fricatives

English has voiceless and voiced labiodental fricatives at the beginning of the words *fat* and *vat*, voiceless and voiced interdental fricatives word-initially in the words *thin* and *those*, alveolar fricatives word-initially in *sing* and *zip*, and a voiceless alveopalatal fricative word-initially in *ship*. The voiced alveopalatal fricative is rare in English. It is the first consonant in the word *azure*, and is also heard in the words *pleasure* and *rouge*. The voiceless glottal fricative of English is heard in *hotel* and *hat*.

Special note must be taken of the alveolar fricatives [s] and [z]. There are two ways that English speakers commonly produce these sounds. Some speakers raise the tongue tip to the alveolar ridge (or to just behind the upper front teeth) and allow the air to pass through a grooved channel in the tongue. Other speakers form this same channel using the blade of the tongue; the tip is placed behind the lower front teeth.

Table 2.5	The transcription of English fricatives	
Glottal state	**Point of articulation**	**Transcription**
	Labiodental	
Voiceless	fan	[f]
Voiced	van	[v]
	Interdental	
Voiceless	thin	[θ]
Voiced	then	[ð]
	Alveolar	
Voiceless	sun	[s]
Voiced	zip	[z]
	Alveopalatal	
Voiceless	ship	[ʃ]
Voiced	azure	[ʒ]
	Glottal	
Voiceless	hat	[h]

A grid for fricatives

Table 2.6 presents a grid on which the fricative consonants of English are ranged according to point of articulation. As in table 2.5, dentals are not distinguished from alveolars, since most languages have sounds with either one or the other point of articulation, but not both. Note that IPA [ʃ] and [ʒ] correspond respectively to North American [š] and [ž].

Table 2.6	English fricatives				
	Labiodental	**Interdental**	**Alveolar**	**Alveopalatal**	**Glottal**
Voiceless	[f]	[θ]	[s]	[ʃ]	[h]
Voiced	[v]	[ð]	[z]	[ʒ]	

5.4   Affricates

When a stop articulation is released, the tongue moves rapidly away from the point of articulation. Some non-continuant consonants show a slow release of the closure; these sounds are called **affricates**. English has only two affricates, both of which are alveopalatal. They are heard word-initially in *church* and *jump*, and are transcribed as [tʃ] and [dʒ], respectively.

A grid for affricates

Table 2.7 presents a grid showing the two English affricates. Note that IPA [tʃ] and [dʒ] correspond to North American [č] and [ǰ], respectively.

Table 2.7	English affricates
	Alveopalatal
Voiceless	[tʃ]
Voiced	[dʒ]

Stridents and sibilants

At the beginning of this chapter, it was noted that acoustic as well as articulatory criteria are sometimes used in describing speech sounds. An acoustic criterion comes into play to describe fricatives and affricates. These sounds are subdivided into two types, some of which are distinctly louder than others. The noisier fricatives and affricates are called **stridents** (see table 2.8). Their quieter counterparts, such as [θ] or [ð], which have the same or nearly same place of articulation, are considered non-strident. Stridents are also known as **sibilants**.

Table 2.8	Strident fricatives and affricates in English	
Place of articulation	**Strident**	
	Voiceless	*Voiced*
Alveolar	[s]	[z]
Alveopalatal	[ʃ]	[ʒ]
	[tʃ]	[dʒ]

5.5   Voice lag and aspiration

After the release of certain voiceless stops in English, you can sometimes hear a lag or brief delay before the voicing of a following vowel. Since the lag in the onset of vocalic voicing is accompanied by the release of air, the traditional term for this phenomenon is **aspiration**. It is transcribed with a small raised [ʰ] after the aspirated consonant. Table 2.9 provides some examples of aspirated and unaspirated consonants in English (some vowel symbols are introduced here as well). Notice that the sounds that have both aspirated and unaspirated varieties are all voiceless stops. In other languages, voiceless fricatives and affricates may also be aspirated or unaspirated.

Table 2.9	Aspirated and unaspirated consonants in English		
Aspirated		**Unaspirated**	
[pʰæt]	pat	[spæt]	spat
[tʰʌb]	tub	[stʌb]	stub
[kʰowp]	cope	[skowp]	scope

Figure 2.5 shows how aspiration of a voiceless consonant takes place, using the aspirated consonant [pʰ] as an example. Though the sequence of articulations takes place continuously, the figure illustrates only certain moments.

a)   As articulation of the voiceless consonant is begun, the glottis is open.

b)   The closure for the consonant is released and the vowel articulation begins; however, the glottis is not yet closed enough to permit voicing to begin. Because of this, the vowel is briefly voiceless, giving the impression of an extra release of air that we call **aspiration**.

c)   After a short delay, measurable in milliseconds, voicing of the vowel begins.

d)   The lips remain open and voicing continues during the articulation of the final consonant of the word.

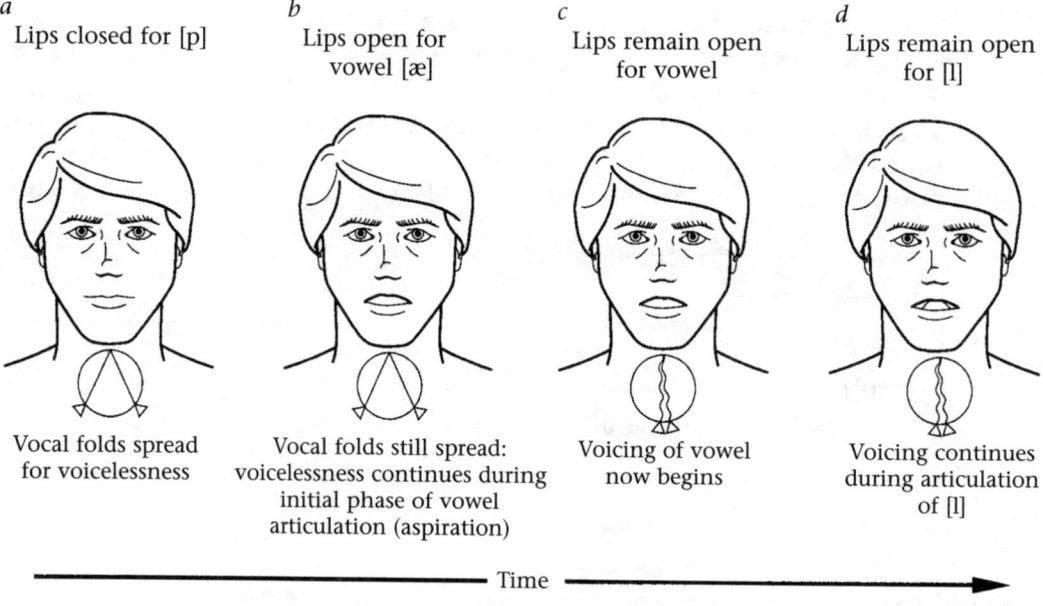

Figure 2.5 Aspirated consonant production (English *pal*)

Figures 2.6 and 2.7 show the relation between articulation and voicing for unaspirated and voiced consonants. The unaspirated consonant, such as the [p] of English *spill*, shows voicing of the vowel starting very soon after release of the consonant articulation. The voiced initial [b] of English *bill* shows voicing starting just before the release of the bilabial articulation. In figure 2.7, note how voicing precedes the release of the labial articulators.

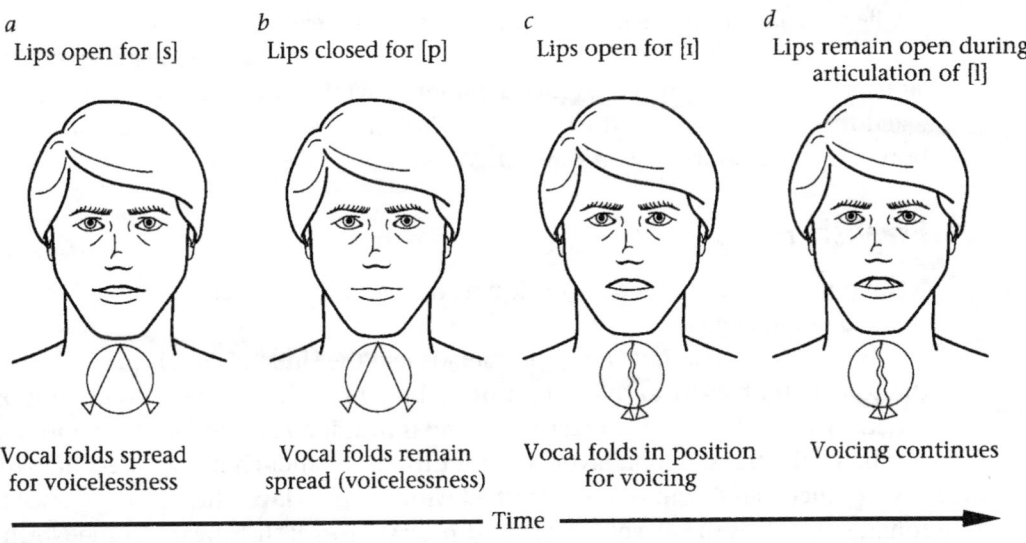

a
Lips open for [s]

b
Lips closed for [p]

c
Lips open for [ɪ]

d
Lips remain open during articulation of [l]

Vocal folds spread for voicelessness

Vocal folds remain spread (voicelessness)

Vocal folds in position for voicing

Voicing continues

Time

Figure 2.6 Unaspirated consonant production (English *spill*)

a
Lips closed for [b]

b
Lips open for [ɪ]

c
Lips remain open during articulation of [l]

Vocal folds in position for voicing, which starts slightly after lip closure

Voicing continues

Voicing continues

Time

Figure 2.7 Voiced consonant release (English *bill*)

5.6 Liquids

Among the sounds commonly found in the world's languages are *l* and *r* and their numerous variants. They form a special class of consonants known as *liquids*.

Laterals

Varieties of *l* are called **laterals**. As laterals are articulated, air escapes through the mouth along the lowered sides of the tongue. When the tongue tip is raised to the dental or alveolar position, the dental or alveolar laterals are produced. Both may be transcribed as [l].

Because laterals are generally voiced, the term *lateral* used alone usually means 'voiced lateral'. Still, there are instances of voiceless laterals in speech. The voiceless dental or alveolar lateral is written with an additional phonetic symbol, called a **diacritic**. In this case, the diacritic is a circle beneath the symbol: [l̥]. Voiceless laterals can be heard in the pronunciation of the English words p̥lease and c̥lear.

English *r*'s

Numerous varieties of *r* are also heard in the world's languages. This section describes the types found in English.

The *r* of English as it is spoken in Canada and the United States is made either by curling the tongue tip back into the mouth or by bunching the tongue upward and back in the mouth. This *r* is known as a **retroflex** *r* and is heard in *ride* and *car*. It is transcribed as [r] in this book. IPA transcription favours [ɹ] for this sound, though it also offers the symbol [r].

Another sound commonly identified with *r* is the **flap**. The flap is produced when the tongue tip strikes the alveolar ridge as it passes across it. It is heard in the North American English pronunciation of *bitter* and *butter*, and in some British pronunciations of *very*. It is commonly transcribed as [ɾ] and is generally voiced. Table 2.10 presents the laterals *r*, *l*, and the flap of Canadian English.

Table 2.10	**English liquids**		
	Alveolar		
Laterals		voiced	[l]
		voiceless	[l̥]
r's	retroflex	voiced	[r]
		voiceless	[r̥]
	flap		[ɾ]

5.7   Syllabic liquids and nasals

Liquids and nasals are more sonorous than other consonants and in this respect are more like vowels than are the other consonants. In fact, they are so sonorous that they may function as syllabic nuclei. When they do so, they are called **syllabic liquids** and **syllabic nasals** (see table 2.11). Syllabic liquids and nasals are found in many of the world's languages,

Table 2.11	**Syllabic liquids and nasals in English**		
	Syllabic	**Non-syllabic**	
bottle	[bɑdl̩]	lift	[lɪft]
funnel	[fʌnl̩]	pill	[pʰɪl]
bird	[bərd], [bɚd], or [br̩d]	rat	[ræt]
her	[hər], [hɚ], or [hr̩]	car	[kʰar]
button	[bʌtn̩]	now	[naw]
'm-m'	[ʔm̩ʔm̩] (meaning 'no')	mat	[mæt]

including English. In transcription, they are usually marked with a short diacritic line underneath. Unfortunately for beginning linguistics students, North American transcription is not always consistent here. The syllabic *r* sound heard in words like *bird* and *her* is often transcribed in North America as a vowel-*r* sequence: [ər]. (The vowel symbol is presented in section 6.2 of this chapter.) The IPA symbol for this sound is [ɚ].

5.8 Glides

Recall that a glide is a very rapidly articulated non-syllabic segment. The two glides of Canadian English are the jod [jɑd] (NA 'y-glide') [j] of *yes* and *boy*, and the w-glide [w] of *wet* and *now*. The [j] in IPA transcription corresponds to the [y] of North American transcription.

The [j] is a palatal glide (often cited as alveopalatal as well) whose articulation is virtually identical to that of the vowel [i] of *see*. You can verify this by pronouncing a [j] in an extended manner; it will sound very close to an [i].

The glide [w] is made with the tongue raised and pulled back near the velum and with the lips protruding, or **rounded**. For this reason, it is sometimes called a labiovelar. The [w] corresponds closely in articulation to the vowel [u] of *who*. This can be verified by extending the pronunciation of a [w]. We will consider [w] a rounded velar glide for purposes of description. Some speakers of English also have a voiceless (labio)velar glide, transcribed [ʍ], in the words *when*, *where*, and *which* (but not in *witch*).

Given that non-syllabic [j] corresponds closely in articulation to syllabic [i], and non-syllabic [w] corresponds closely in articulation to syllabic [u], we could argue that non-syllabic [r] is the glide counterpart of syllabic [r̩] in English. (No such claim has been made for [l]/[l̩]). However, since most linguistics books clearly place [r] among the liquids and not the glides, we will continue to do so here.

Table 2.12	English consonants: places and manners of articulation						
Manner of articulation	**Place of articulation**						
	Labial	Labiodental	Interdental	Alveolar	Alveopalatal	Velar	Glottal
Stop voiceless	p			t		k	ʔ
voiced	b			d		g	
Fricative voiceless		f	θ	s	ʃ		h
voiced		v	ð	z	ʒ		
Affricate voiceless					tʃ		
voiced					dʒ		
Nasal voiced	m			n		ŋ	
Liquid voiced							
lateral voiced				l			
retroflex				r			
Glide voiced	(w)					j	w
(voiceless)							(ʍ)

Table 2.12 provides a summary of the places and manners of articulation of English consonants.

6   Vowels

Vowels are sonorous, syllabic sounds made with the vocal tract more open than it is for consonant and glide articulations. Different vowel sounds (also called vowel *qualities*) are produced by varying the placement of the body of the tongue and shaping the lips. The shape of the vocal tract can be further altered by protruding the lips to produce rounded vowels, or by lowering the velum to produce a nasal vowel. Finally, vowels may be tense or lax, depending on the degree of vocal tract constriction during their articulation.

In the following section on vowels you are introduced to most of the basic vowels of English. Some phonetic detail is omitted that will be introduced in the following chapter.

6.1   Simple vowels and diphthongs

English vowels are divided into two major types, **simple vowels** and **diphthongs**. Simple vowels do not show a noticeable change in quality during their articulation. The vowels of *pit, set, cat, dog, but, put,* and the first vowel of *suppose* are all simple vowels.

Diphthongs are vowels that exhibit a change in quality within a single syllable. English diphthongs show changes in quality that are due to tongue movement away from the initial vowel articulation towards a glide position. This change in vowel quality is clearly perceptible in words such as *say, buy, cow, ice, lout, go,* and *boy*. The change is less easy to hear, and in fact is not made by all English speakers, in the vowels of words like *heed* and *lose*. Table 2.13 presents the simple vowels and diphthongs of English. The diphthongs are transcribed as vowel-glide sequences.

Table 2.13 Some simple vowels and diphthongs of Canadian English			
Simple vowel		**Diphthong**	
p_i_t	[ɪ]	h_ea_t	[i] or [ij]
s_e_t	[ɛ]	s_ay_	[ej]
p_u_t	[ʊ]	l_o_se	[u] or [uw]
_o_r	[o]	gr_ow_	[ow]
c_u_t	[ʌ]	m_y_	[aj]
m_a_t	[æ]	n_ow_	[aw]

In all cases, the diphthongs are somewhat longer than the simple vowels.[1] Notice that the diphthongs [aj] and [aw] are transcribed with a low back unrounded vowel symbol that is different than the one used to transcribe the vowel of, say, *hot*: [ɑ]. This symbol represents a vowel that is both lax and less back than [ɑ]. Try to pronounce the vowel [ɑ] in place of the [a] in these diphthongs; you will hear why a different vowel symbol is needed.

6.2   Basic parameters for describing vowels

Vowel articulations are not as easy to feel at first as consonant articulations, since the vocal tract is not narrowed as much. To become acquainted with vowel articulation, alternately pronounce the vowels of *he* and *paw*. You will feel the tongue move from a **high** front to a **low** back position. Once you feel this tongue movement, alternate between the vowels of *paw* and *pat*. You will feel the tongue moving from the low **back** to low **front** position. Finally, alternate between the vowels of *he* and *who*. You will notice that in addition to a tongue movement between the high front and high back position, you are also rounding your lips for the [u]. Figure 2.8 shows a midsaggital view of the tongue position for the vowels [i], [ɑ], and [u] based on X-ray studies of speech.

Figure 2.8 Tongue position and transcription for three English vowels

Vowels for which the tongue is neither raised nor lowered are called **mid vowels**. The front vowel of English *m<u>a</u>de* or *f<u>a</u>me* is mid, front, and unrounded. The vowel of *c<u>o</u>de* and *s<u>oa</u>k* is mid, back, and rounded. In the case of diphthongs, the articulatory descriptions refer to the tongue position of the vowel nucleus. The vowels presented so far in this section are summed up in table 2.14. Note that in describing the vowels, the articulatory parameters are presented in the order *height, backness, rounding*.

Table 2.14	Basic phonetic parameters for describing Canadian English vowels	
h<u>ea</u>t	[i]	high front unrounded
f<u>a</u>te	[ej]	mid front unrounded
m<u>a</u>d	[æ]	low front unrounded
S<u>ue</u>	[u]	high back rounded
b<u>oa</u>t	[ow]	mid back rounded
s<u>u</u>n	[ʌ]	mid back unrounded
c<u>o</u>t, c<u>au</u>ght	[ɑ]	low back unrounded

In standard Canadian English, there is no difference between the vowels of a pair of words like *cot* [ɑ] and *caught*, whose vowel is also [ɑ]. In some dialects of North American English, as well as in many other dialects of English worldwide, the vowel of *caught* (and certain other words such as *law*) is the mid back rounded lax vowel [ɔ].

Tongue positions for these vowels are illustrated in figure 2.9. The trapezoid corresponds roughly to the space within which the tongue moves, which is wider at the top of the oral cavity and more restricted at the bottom. Non-front vowels are traditionally divided into central and back vowels (see figures 2.9 and 2.10); often the term *back* alone is used for all non-front vowels.

Figure 2.9 Basic tongue positions for English vowels

6.3   Tense and lax vowels

All of the vowels illustrated in figure 2.9 except [æ] and [ʌ] are **tense**; they are produced with a placement of the tongue that results in greater vocal tract constriction than that of non-tense vowels; as well, tense vowels are longer than non-tense vowels. Some vowels of English are made with roughly the same tongue position as the tense vowels, but with a less constricted articulation; they are called **lax** vowels.

Table 2.15 provides examples from English comparing tense and lax vowels. Note that not all the vowels come in tense/lax pairs.

Table 2.15	Tense and lax vowels in Canadian English		
	Tense	**Lax**	
h<u>ea</u>t	[i]	h<u>i</u>t	[ɪ]
m<u>a</u>te	[ej]	m<u>e</u>t	[ɛ]
—	—	m<u>a</u>t	[æ]
sh<u>oo</u>t	[u]	sh<u>ou</u>ld	[ʊ]
c<u>oa</u>t	[ow]	(<u>ou</u>ght	[ɔ] in some dialects)
—	—	c<u>u</u>t	[ʌ]
—	—	Can<u>a</u>da	[ə]
l<u>o</u>ck	[ɑ]	—	—
l<u>ie</u>s	[aj]		
l<u>ou</u>d	[aw]		

The difference in two vowels illustrated in table 2.15 is often not easy to hear at first. Both the vowel [ʌ] in *cut, dud, pluck,* and *Hun,* and the vowel [ə] of *Can<u>a</u>da, <u>a</u>bout, tom<u>a</u>hawk,* and *sof<u>a</u>* are mid, back, unrounded, and lax. The vowel of the second set of examples, called **schwa**, is referred to as a **reduced vowel**. In addition to being lax, it is characterized by very brief duration (briefer than that of any of the other vowels).

There is a simple test that helps determine whether vowels are tense or lax. In English, monosyllabic words spoken in isolation do not end in lax vowels. We find *see* [si], *say* [sej], *Sue*

[su], *so* [sow], and *saw* [sɑ] in English, but not *s[ɪ], *s[ɛ], *s[æ], *s[ʊ], or *s[ʌ]. Schwa, however, frequently appears in unstressed position in polysyllabic words like *sof* [ə] and *Can<u>a</u>d<u>a</u>* [ə]. It should be pointed out—especially for those who think their ears are deceiving them—that many speakers produce the final vowel in the last two examples not as [ə] but as [ʌ].

The representation of vowels and their articulatory positions (figure 2.9) is expanded in figure 2.10 to include both tense and lax vowels.

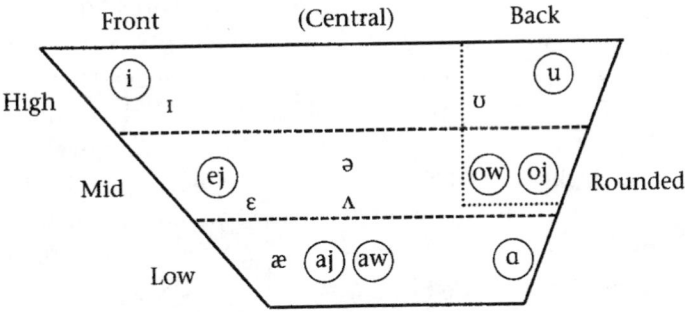

Figure 2.10 Canadian English vowels (tense vowels are circled)

This rather formidable crowd of vowels should not intimidate you. If you are a native speaker of English, you have been using these vowels (and others, some of which you will be introduced to in the next chapter) most of your life. Learning to hear them consciously and transcribe them is not a difficult task. The next section provides more examples of the transcription of English consonants and vowels.

7 Phonetic transcription of Canadian English consonants and vowels

The following tables 2.16 and 2.17 show the phonetic symbols for consonants and vowels commonly used to transcribe Canadian English. To show how each symbol is used, one word is transcribed completely, and then some other words in which the same sound is found are given. You will notice that in the example words, the spelling of the sound may vary. Be careful of this when you transcribe words phonetically—the sound of a word, not its spelling, is what is transcribed!

Table 2.16	Transcribing English consonants		
Symbol	**Word**	**Transcription**	**More examples**
[pʰ]	pit	[pʰɪt]	<u>p</u>ain, u<u>p</u>on, a<u>p</u>art
[p]	spit	[spɪt]	s<u>p</u>ar, cris<u>p</u>y, u<u>pp</u>er, Yu<u>pp</u>ie, cul<u>p</u>rit, bum<u>p</u>er
[tʰ]	tick	[tʰɪk]	<u>t</u>ell, a<u>tt</u>ire, <u>t</u>error, <u>T</u>utu
[t]	stuck	[stʌk]	s<u>t</u>em, hun<u>t</u>er, nas<u>t</u>y, mos<u>tl</u>y
[kʰ]	keep	[kʰip]	<u>c</u>ow, <u>k</u>ernel, re<u>c</u>ur

Table 2.16	**(continued)**	Transcribing English consonants	
Symbol	Word	Transcription	More examples
[k]	skip	[skɪp]	scatter, uncle, blacklist, likely
[tʃ]	chip	[tʃɪp]	lunch, lecher, ditch, belch
[dʒ]	judge	[dʒʌdʒ]	germ, journal, budgie, wedge
[b]	bib	[bɪb]	boat, liberate, rob, blast
[d]	dip	[dɪp]	dust, sled, draft
[ɾ]	butter	[bʌɾər]	madder, matter, hitting, writer, rider
[g]	get	[gɛt]	gape, mugger, twig, gleam
[f]	fit	[fɪt]	flash, coughing, proof, phlegmatic, gopher
[v]	vat	[væt]	vote, oven, prove
[θ]	thick	[θɪk]	thought, ether, teeth, three, bathroom
[ð]	though	[ðow]	then, bother, teethe, bathe
[s]	sip	[sɪp]	psychology, fasten, lunacy, bass, curse, science
[z]	zap	[zæp]	Xerox, scissors, desire, zipper, fuzzy
[ʃ]	ship	[ʃɪp]	shock, nation, mission, glacier, wish
[ʒ]	azure	[æʒər]	measure, rouge, visual, garage (for some speakers), Taj Mahal
[h]	hat	[hæt]	who, ahoy, forehead, behind
[j]	yet	[jɛt]	_use, f_ew, yes
[w]	witch	[wɪtʃ]	wait, weird, queen, now
[ʍ]	which	[ʍɪtʃ]	what, where, when (only for some speakers)
[l]	leaf	[lif]	loose, lock, alive, hail
[l̩]	huddle	[hʌdl̩]	bottle, needle (for many speakers)
[r]	reef	[rif]	rod, arrive, tear
[r̩]	bird	[br̩d] [bɚd], [bərd]	early, hurt, stir, purr, doctor
[m]	moat	[mowt]	mind, humour, shimmer, sum, thumb
[m̩]	'm-m'	[ʔm̩ʔm̩]	bottom, random
[n]	note	[nowt]	now, winner, angel, sign, wind
[n̩]	button	[bʌtn̩]	Jordan, batten
[ŋ]	sing	[sɪŋ]	singer, longer, bank, twinkle

Table 2.17	Transcribing English vowels		
Symbol	Word	Transcription	More examples
[i]	fee	[fi]	she, cream, believe, receive, serene, amoeba, highly
[ɪ]	fit	[fɪt]	hit, income, definition, been (for some speakers)
[ej]	fate	[fejt]	they, clay, grain, gauge, engage, great, sleigh
[ɛ]	let	[lɛt]	led, head, says, said, sever, guest
[æ]	bat	[bæt]	panic, racket, laugh, Vancouver
[u]	boot	[but]	to, two, loose, brew, Louise, Lucy, through
[ʊ]	book	[bʊk]	should, put, hood

Table 2.17	(continued)	Transcribing English vowels	
Symbol	Word	Transcription	More examples
[ow]	note	[nowt]	no, throat, though, slow, toe, oaf, O'Conner
[oj]	boy	[boj]	voice, boil, toy
[ɑ]	saw	[sɑ]	cot, caught, father, bought, across, Toronto
[ʌ]	shut	[ʃʌt]	other, udder, tough, lucky, was, flood
[ə]	roses	[rowzəz]	collide, hinted, telegraph, (to) suspect
[aw]	crowd	[krawd]	(to) house, plow, bough
[aj]	lies	[lajz]	my, tide, thigh, buy

8   Suprasegmentals

All phones have certain inherent **suprasegmental** or **prosodic** properties that form part of their makeup no matter what their place or manner of articulation. These properties are **pitch**, **loudness**, and **length**.

All sounds give us a subjective impression of being relatively higher or lower in pitch. Pitch is the auditory property of a sound that enables us to place it on a scale that ranges from low to high. Pitch is especially noticeable in sonorous sounds like vowels, glides, liquids, and nasals. Even stop and fricative consonants convey different pitches. This is particularly noticeable among the fricatives, as you can hear by extending the pronunciation of [s] and then of [ʃ]; the [s] is clearly higher pitched. All sounds have some degree of intrinsic loudness as well or they could not be heard. Moreover, all sounds occupy a certain stretch of time—they give the subjective impression of length.

8.1   Pitch: tone and intonation

Speakers of any language have the ability to control the level of pitch they speak on. This is accomplished by controlling the tension of the vocal folds and the amount of air that passes through the glottis. The combination of tensed vocal folds and greater air pressure results in higher voice pitch on vowels and sonorant consonants, while less tense vocal folds and lower air pressure result in lower voice pitch. Two kinds of controlled pitch movement found in human language are called **tone** and **intonation**.

Tone

A language is said to have tone or be a **tone language** when differences in word meaning are signalled by differences in pitch. Pitch on forms in tone languages functions very differently from the movement of pitch in a non-tone language. When a speaker of English says *a car?* with a rising pitch, the word *car* does not mean anything different from the same form pronounced on a different pitch level or with a different pitch contour. In contrast, when a speaker of a tone language such as Mandarin pronounces the form *mà* [ma] with a falling pitch, it means 'scold', but when the same form (*ma*) is pronounced with a rising pitch, as [má], the meaning is 'hemp' (see figure 2.13). There is no parallel to anything like this in non-tone languages such as English and French.

Some tone languages show tones at only certain pitch levels. Sarcee, an Athapaskan language spoken in Alberta, has tones heard at high, mid, and low pitch levels. In figure 2.11, the uppercase letters H, M, and L stand for high, mid, and low tones, respectively. A line called an **association line** drawn from the letters to the vowel links the segments with their respective tones. This type of notation is known as autosegmental notation (see chapter 3, section 7.2).

Figure 2.11 Sarcee level tones ([ɬ] is a voiceless lateral fricative)

Level tones that signal meaning differences are called **register tones**: two or three register tones are the norm in most of the world's register tone languages, though four have been reported for Mazatec, a language spoken in Mexico.

A single tone may be associated with more than one syllabic element. In Mende, a language spoken in West Africa, there are certain polysyllabic forms that show the same tone on each syllable (here, the diacritic [ˊ] indicates a high tone and the diacritic [ˋ] indicates a low tone).

Table 2.18	High-tone and low-tone words in Mende
pélé	'banana'
háwámá	'waistline'
kpàkàlì	'tripod chair'

Autosegmental notation and association lines allow us to represent the tone as characteristic of an entire form. The single underlying tone unit is associated with all vowels.

Figure 2.12   Tone as a word feature

In some languages, tones change pitch on single syllabic elements. Moving pitches that signal meaning differences are called **contour tones**. In Mandarin, both register and contour tones are heard. Contour tones are shown by pitch level notation lines that converge above the vowel, as shown in figure 2.13.

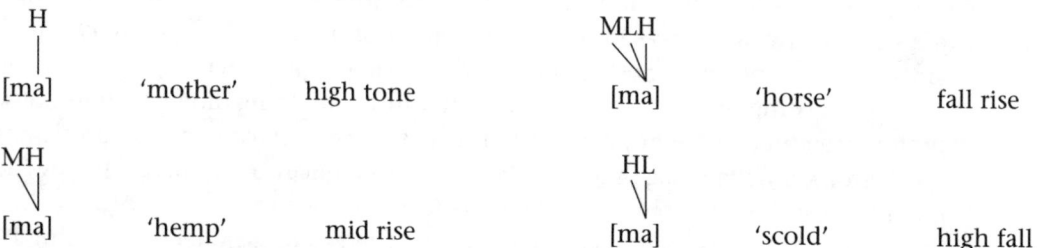

Figure 2.13 Register and contour tones in Mandarin

In figure 2.13, there is one (high) register tone. The other tones are all contour tones.

In other languages, tone can have a grammatical function. In Bini, a language spoken in Nigeria, tone can signal differences in the tense of a verb (such as past versus present), as figure 2.14 shows.

Timeless   ima   'I show'

Continuous   ima   'I am showing'

Past   ima   'I showed'

Figure 2.14   Tense and tone in Bini

Although tones may seem exotic to native speakers of Western European languages, they are very widespread. Tone languages are found throughout North and South America, sub-Saharan Africa, and the Far East.

Intonation

Pitch movement in spoken utterances that is not related to differences in word meaning is called intonation. It makes no difference to the meaning of the word *seven*, for example, whether it is pronounced with a rising pitch or a falling pitch.

Intonation often does serve to convey information of a broadly meaningful nature, however. For example, the falling pitch we hear at the end of a statement in English such as *Fred parked the car* signals that the utterance is complete. For this reason, falling intonation at the end of an utterance is called a **terminal (intonation) contour**. Conversely, a rising or level intonation, called a **non-terminal (intonation) contour**, often signals incompleteness. Non-terminal contours are often heard in the non-final forms found in lists and telephone numbers.

Sally Fred Helen and Joe

two eight four two five one three

Figure 2.15   Rising non-terminal intonations in a list and a telephone number

In questions, final rising intonations also signal a kind of incompleteness in that they indicate that a conversational exchange is not finished.

Did you have a nice time

Figure 2.16   Non-terminal intonation in a question

However, English sentences that contain question words like *who, what, when,* and *how* (for example, *What did you buy?*) ordinarily do not have rising intonation. It is as if the question word itself is enough to indicate that an answer is expected.

Intonation can be represented graphically as in figures 2.15 and 2.16. A more formal way of representing intonation is shown in figure 2.17. Here, as in tonal representation, L and H are relative terms for differences in pitch. The letters HL are placed above the syllabic elements on which the pitch change occurs. The dotted lines indicate that the lowering pitch spreads across the remaining pitch-bearing elements.

L   H L

There's an elephant in here.

Figure 2.17 A terminal contour

Rising intonation on names or requests is commonly heard in addressing people. Its use indicates that the speaker is opening a conversation or that some further action is expected from the addressee.

L H   H   L H

Margo? Is that you?

Figure 2.18 Two non-terminal contours

The complex uses of intonation have just been touched on here. Consider, for example, that rising intonation is often used to express politeness, as in *Please sit down*. Some linguists think that this use is an extension of the 'open-ended mode' of intonation, and that since a rising intonation indicates that further response is expected (but not demanded) of the addressee, a sentence uttered with a rising intonation sounds less like an order and so is more polite.

Intonation and tone

Tone and intonation are not mutually exclusive. Tone languages show intonation of all types. This is possible since the tones are not absolute but relative pitches. A tone is perceived as high if it is high relative to the pitches around it. As long as this relative difference is maintained, the pitch distinctions will also be maintained. Figure 2.19 shows this graphically. It represents the overall pitch of a declarative sentence in Igbo, a West African language with register tones. Note how an Igbo speaker clearly maintains the distinction among the pitch registers even as the overall pitch of the utterance falls. Each high tone is always lower than the preceding high tone, but higher than the low tone that immediately precedes it. This phenomenon is known as **downdrift**.

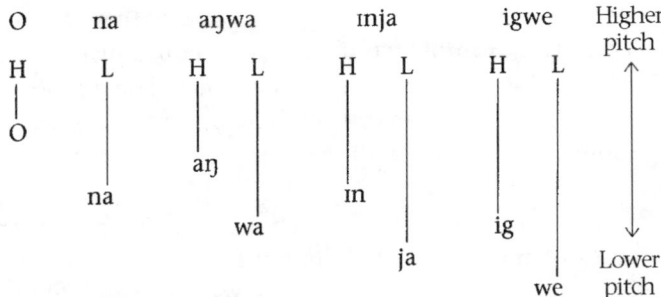

'He is trying to ride a bicycle.'

Figure 2.19 Tone and intonation: downdrift in Igbo

8.2 Length

In many languages there are both vowels and consonants whose articulation takes longer relative to that of other vowels and consonants. This phenomenon, known as length, is widespread in the world's languages. Length is indicated in phonetic transcription by the use of an IPA style colon [ː] (or simply a colon in North American transcription [:]) placed after the segment in question.

Italian, Hungarian, German, Cree, and Finnish are a few of the many languages that have long and short vowels. Yap, a language spoken on the island of Yap in the Western Pacific, shows short and long vowels in pairs of words such as in table 2.19.

Table 2.19	Short and long vowels in Yap		
[θis]	'to topple'	[θiːs]	'(a) post'
[pul]	'to gather'	[puːl]	'moon'
[ʔer]	'near you'	[ʔeːr]	'part of a lagoon'

Italian shows short and long consonants in pairs of words such as those shown in table 2.20. Long and short consonants are also found in many other languages, including Finnish, Turkish, and Hungarian.

Table 2.20	Short and long consonants in Italian			
fato	[fatɔ]	'fate'	fatto	[fatːɔ]	'fact'
fano	[fanɔ]	'grove'	fanno	[fanːɔ]	'they do'
casa	[kasa]	'house'	cassa	[kasːa]	'box'

8.3 Stress

In any utterance, some vowels are perceived as more prominent than others. In a word such as *telegraphic* [tʰɛləgræfɪk], the two vowel nuclei that are more prominent than the others are [ɛ] and [æ]. Syllabic segments perceived as relatively more prominent are stressed. Stress is a cover term for the combined effects of pitch, loudness, and length—the result of which is perceived prominence. In each language, the effect of these prosodic features varies. In general, English stressed vowels are higher in pitch, longer, and louder than unstressed ones. But this is not always the case. The example word *telegraphic* could just as well be pronounced with the stressed syllables lower than the unstressed ones. The important thing is that they be prominent with respect to the syllables around them, and this is usually accomplished by a relatively large shift in one, two, or all three of the parameters of pitch, loudness, and length.

In some languages, the impression of vowel prominence results from an interaction of the prosodic parameters that is different from that found in English. In Modern Greek, for example, syllables tend to be of equal length. Stress, therefore, is manifested by a change only in pitch and loudness and not in syllable length. Tone languages do not change the pitch level or contour of tones to mark stress. In many of these languages, relative prominence is marked by exaggerating the vowel length or pitch contour.

There are various ways to mark stress in phonetic transcription. North American transcription commonly uses an acute accent [´] placed over the vowel nucleus in question to mark the most prominent or **primary** stress, and a grave accent [`] to mark the second most prominent or **secondary** stress or stresses. (This should not be confused with the use of the same diacritics to mark tone in tone languages.) Stress can also be marked by placing numbers above the stressed vowels, usually [1] for a primary stress and [2] for a secondary stress. The word *telegraphic* is transcribed as either of the following:

2)

$$
\overset{2}{[t^h\grave{\varepsilon}l\ni\,gr\acute{æ}f\mathrm{I}k]} \quad \text{or} \quad \overset{1}{[t^h\varepsilon l\ni\,gr\acute{æ}f\mathrm{I}k]}
$$

The examples in table 2.21 show some differences in English stress placement.

Table 2.21	Differing stress placement in English		
(an) éxport	[ɛ́ksport]	(to) expórt	[ɛkspórt]
(a) présent	[prɛ́zənt]	(to) presént	[prəzɛ́nt]
télegràph	[tʰɛ́ləgræ̀f]		
telégraphy	[tʰəlɛ́grəfì]		
tèlegráphic	[tʰɛ̀ləgrǽfɪk]		

In the last four examples, you can also see that the quality of certain vowels varies depending on whether they are stressed or unstressed. This phenomenon is common in English, Russian, Palauan, and many other languages, but is not universal.

9   Processes

Speech production is not a series of isolated events. The process of articulation is a complex one. The articulatory organs are operating independently of each other, and many fine adjustments are carried out very rapidly as we speak. As a consequence, speech production often results in the articulation of one sound affecting that of another sound.

9.1 Co-articulation

Figures 2.5 to 2.7 showed how aspiration results from co-articulation. Figure 2.20 shows some more complex aspects of co-articulation. Here, some of the articulatory organs involved in the production of the word *pan* are represented. Reading from top to bottom, the actions of the lips, tongue, velum, and larynx are shown. The bold black line in each box represents the state of articulation listed to the right of the box.

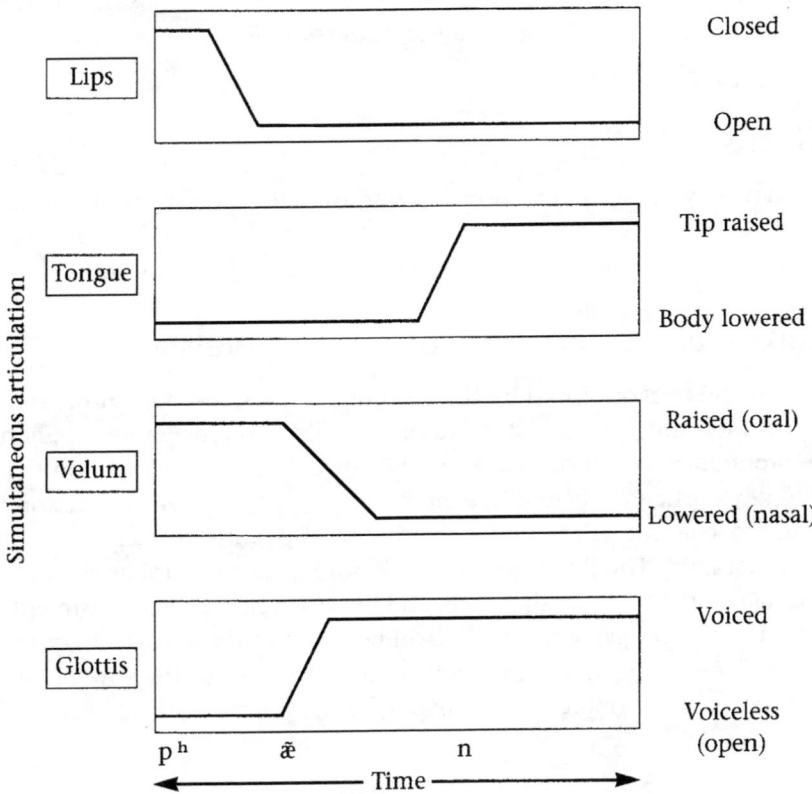

Figure 2.20 Co-articulation among several articulatory parameters of the word *pan*

Lips

The raised line in the upper box indicates that the lips are closed for the articulation of the initial [p] of *pan*. In order to articulate the vowel, the lips are opened—represented by the change in the position of the line—and they stay open during the articulation of the [n].

Tongue

The tongue body is lowered in anticipation of the low front vowel [æ] during articulation of the word-initial consonant. As the vowel articulation ends, the tongue tip is raised to articulate the final [n] of the word.

Velum

You have seen how nasal consonants are produced with the velum lowered to allow air to pass through the nasal cavities. The raising and lowering of the velum is not always precisely co-ordinated with other speech production activity. Speakers often anticipate lowering the velum for nasal consonants and, consequently, produce a nasal vowel before a nasal consonant. Many English speakers do this consistently in fluent speech when they pronounce words like *pan* [pʰæ̃n] or *bank* [bæ̃ŋk] (the tilde [~] over the vowel indicates nasality). This is reflected in figure 2.20. The line representing the velum closure changes to the open (lowered) position during the articulation of the vowel, before the tongue tip raises to articulate the word-final [n].

Glottis

You have already seen in section 5.5 how aspiration results from a delay in voicing after the release of a voiceless stop. Aspiration is shown in figure 2.20 by the black line remaining in the voiceless position even after the lips have opened and the vowel articulation is in place.

Consonant co-articulation with vowels

All speech is characterized by the kind of complex co-articulation among the articulatory organs illustrated in figure 2.20. Another typical co-articulation phenomenon occurs when we pronounce the sound [k] before the vowel [i] in English in words such as *keys* and *keel*. The [k] we articulate before [i] is pronounced with the back of the tongue so far forward it nearly touches the palate (and is transcribed as [k̟]). It is scarcely a velar articulation at all for many speakers. The [k] we pronounce before the vowels [ɑ] and [ow] in words such as *call* and *cold* is articulated further back, and is a true velar. These adjustments are made in anticipation of the tongue position that will be needed for the vowel in question: front for the [i] and back for the [ɑ] and [ow]. The [k] pronounced before the vowel [u] in a word such as *cool* also shows lip rounding in anticipation of the following (back) rounded vowel and is transcribed as [kʷ].

9.2   Processes and efficiency

Articulatory adjustments that occur during the production of connected speech are called **processes**. Their cumulative effect often results in making words easier to articulate, and in this sense they are said to make speech more efficient. For example, when speakers of English nasalize the vowel of *bank* they do not delay lowering the velum until the exact moment the nasal consonant articulation is reached. Most English speakers begin lowering the velum for a nasal consonant almost as soon as they articulate the vowel that precedes it.

In a parallel manner, when speakers pronounce [k̟] as more palatal in a word such as *key*, they are speaking more efficiently from the point of view of articulation since they are making a less drastic adjustment in moving from the articulation of a more palatal [k̟] to that of a high front vowel than they would make in moving from a velar [k] to a high front vowel. Even more drastically, a speaker of English who says [pɹ̥ejd] for *parade* is making a major adjustment that results in a more efficient articulation: the two syllables of a careful pronunciation of *parade* are reduced to one by dropping the unstressed vowel of the first syllable; the tongue position for [r] can be anticipated during pronunciation of the [p]; finally, the voicelessness of the initial stop is carried on through the [ɹ̥].

9.3 Processes and clarity

Some processes appear to make articulation less, not more efficient. For example, English speakers often lengthen consonants and vowels when they are asked to repeat a word that someone has not heard clearly. The following kind of exchange is typical.

> 3)
> "It's Fred."
> "Did you say, 'It's red'?"
> "No, I said, 'Fffreeed!'"

Lengthening segments results in a greater articulatory effort, but the process results in a form being more distinct and therefore easier to perceive.

Another process that results in more easily perceivable speech adds a segment under certain conditions. When speaking slowly and carefully in a noisy environment, for example, English speakers often insert a vowel inside a group of consonants. This breaks up the sequence of consonants into separate syllables. To judge from the use people often make of this process when they wish to be clearly understood, it may well make words easier to perceive.

> 4)
> "Stop screaming!"
> "What?"
> "I said, 'Stop sc[ə]reaming.'"

These examples show that there are two basic reasons for the existence of articulatory processes. Some processes result in a more efficient articulation of a series of sounds in that the precise timing and co-ordination of speech is relaxed to various degrees. Other processes result in a more distinct output, which is easier to perceive than fluent or rapid everyday speech. Although these two types of processes might at first appear to be contradictory, each serves a particular end in speech production.

9.4 Articulatory processes

Only a finite number of processes operate in language, though their end result is a great deal of linguistic variability. In this section, we survey some of the most common of these processes.

Assimilation

A number of different processes, collectively known as **assimilation**, result from the influence of one segment on another. Assimilation always results from a sound becoming more like another nearby sound in terms of one or more of its phonetic characteristics.

Nasalization of a vowel before a nasal consonant is caused by speakers anticipating the lowering of the velum in advance of a nasal segment. The result is that the preceding segment takes on the nasality of the following consonant as in [kʰǽnt] 'can't'. This type of assimilation is known as **regressive assimilation**, since the nasalization is, in effect, moving *backwards* to a preceding segment.

The nasalization of vowels following nasal consonants in Scots Gaelic is an example of **progressive assimilation**, since the nasality moves *forward* from the nasal consonant onto the vowel. It results from not immediately raising the velum after the production of a nasal stop.

Table 2.22	Progressive nasalization of vowels in Scots Gaelic
[mõːr]	'big'
[nĩ]	'cattle'
[mũ]	'about'
[nẽːl]	'cloud'

Voicing assimilation is also widespread. For many speakers of English, voiceless liquids and glides occur after voiceless stops in words such as *please* [pl̥iz], *proud* [pr̥awd], and *pure* [pj̥uwr]. These sounds are said to be devoiced in this environment. **Devoicing** is a kind of assimilation. Here, the vocal folds are not set in motion immediately after the release of the voiceless consonant closure. The opposite of devoicing is **voicing**. In Dutch, voiceless fricatives assimilate to the voicing of the stops that follow them, in anticipation of the voiced consonant. For example, the word *af* [ɑf] 'off, over' is pronounced with a [v] in the words *afbelen* 'to ring off' and *afdeken* 'to cover over'.

Assimilation for place of articulation is also widespread in the world's languages. Nasal consonants are very likely to undergo this type of assimilation, as shown in table 2.23.

Table 2.23	Assimilation for place of articulation in English
possible	impossible
potent	impotent
tolerable	intolerable
tangible	intangible

The negative form of each of these words is made with either *im* or *in*. In both cases, the form shows a nasal consonant that has the same place of articulation as the stop consonant that follows it: labial in the case of *possible* and *potent*, and alveolar in the case of *tolerable* and *tangible*. In informal speech, many English speakers pronounce words like *inconsequential* and *inconsiderate* with an [ŋ] where the spelling shows *n*. Assimilation can also be heard in pronunciations such as *Va*[ŋ]*couver* and *Ba*[ɱ]*ff* (the symbol [ɱ] represents a labiodental nasal). Assimilation may even cross the boundaries between words. In rapid speech, it is not uncommon to hear people pronounce phrases such as *in code* as [ɪŋkʰowd].

The preceding English example shows regressive assimilation to place of articulation. The following example, taken from German, shows progressive assimilation that again affects nasal consonants. In careful speech, certain German verb forms are pronounced with a final [ən], as in *laden* 'to invite', *loben* 'to praise', and *backen* 'to bake'. In informal speech, the final [ən] is reduced to a syllabic nasal, which takes on the point of articulation of the preceding consonant. (Recall that the diacritic line under the phonetically transcribed nasals indicates that they are syllabic.)

Table 2.24	Progressive assimilation in German		
Careful speech		**Informal speech**	
laden	[laːdən]	[laːdn̩]	'to invite'
loben	[loːbən]	[loːbm̩]	'to praise'
backen	[bakən]	[bakŋ̩]	'to bake'

Flapping is a process in which a dental or alveolar stop articulation changes to a flap [ɾ] articulation. In English, this process applies to both [t] and [d] and occurs between vowels, the first of which is generally stressed. Flaps are heard in the casual speech pronunciation of words such as *butter, writer, fatter, wader,* and *waiter,* and even in phrases such as *I bought it* [ajbáɾɪt]. The alveolar flap is always voiced. Flapping is considered a type of assimilation since it changes a non-continuant segment (a stop) to a continuant segment in the environment of other continuants (vowels). In addition, we may note that voicing assimilation also occurs in the change of the voiceless [t] to the voiced [ɾ].

Dissimilation

Dissimilation, the opposite of assimilation, results in two sounds becoming less alike in articulatory or acoustic terms. The resulting sequence of sounds is easier to articulate and distinguish. It is a much rarer process than assimilation. One commonly heard example of dissimilation in English occurs in words ending with three consecutive fricatives, such as *fifths*. Many speakers dissimilate the final [fθs] sequence to [fts], apparently to break up the sequence of three fricatives with a stop.

Deletion

Deletion is a process that removes a segment from certain phonetic contexts. Deletion occurs in everyday rapid speech in many languages. In English, a schwa [ə] is often deleted when the next vowel in the word is stressed.

Table 2.25	Deletion of [ə] in English	
Slow speech	**Rapid speech**	
[pʰəréjd]	[p̥réjd]	parade
[kʰərówd]	[k̥rówd]	corrode
[səpʰówz]	[spówz]	suppose

Deletion also occurs as an alternative to dissimilation in words such as *fifths*. Many speakers delete the [θ] of the final consonant cluster and say [fɪfs]. In very rapid speech, both the second [f] and [θ] are sometimes deleted, resulting in [fɪs].

Epenthesis

Epenthesis is a process that inserts a syllabic or a non-syllabic segment within an existing string of segments. For example, in careful speech, the words *warmth* and *something* are pronounced [wɑrmθ] and [sʌ̃mθɪ̃ŋ] (see table 2.26). It is common in casual speech for speakers to insert a [p] between the *m* and the *th* and pronounce the words [wɑrmpθ] and [sʌ̃mpθɪ̃ŋ]. Consonant epenthesis of this type is another example of a co-articulation phenomenon. In English, the articulatory transition from a sonorant consonant to a non-sonorant appears to be eased by the insertion of a consonant that shares properties of both segments. Notice that the epenthesized consonants are all non-sonorant, have the same place of articulation as the sonorant consonant to their left, and have the same voicing as the non-sonorant consonant to their right.

Table 2.26	Some examples of English consonant epenthesis	
Word	**Non-epenthesized pronunciation**	**Epenthesized pronunciation**
something	[sʌ̃mθɪ̃ŋ]	[sʌ̃mpθɪ̃ŋ]
warmth	[wɑrmθ]	[wɑrmpθ]
length	[lɛ̃ŋθ]	[lɛ̃ŋkθ]
prince	[prɪ̃ns]	[prɪ̃nts]
tenth	[tɛ̃nθ]	[tɛ̃ntθ]

Vowels may also be epenthesized. In Turkish, a word may not begin with two consonants. When words are borrowed into Turkish, an epenthetic vowel is inserted between certain sequences of two initial consonants, creating a new and permissible sequence (see table 2.27). (The reason for the differences among the vowels need not concern us here; note, though, that the vowel is always high; see section 10.1 for further presentation of these and other unfamiliar symbols.)

Table 2.27	Vowel epenthesis in Turkish
Source word	**Turkish form**
train	t̪iren
club	kyl̪vp
sport	sɯpor

Metathesis

Metathesis is a process that reorders a sequence of segments. Metathesis often results in a sequence of phones that is easier to articulate. It is common to hear metathesis in the speech of children, who often cannot pronounce all the consonant sequences that adults can. For example, some English-speaking children pronounce *spaghetti* as *pesghetti* [pəskɛɾi]. In this form, the initial sequence [spə], which is often difficult for children to pronounce, is metathesized to [pəs].

The pronunciations of *prescribe* and *prescription* as *perscribe* and *perscription* are often-cited examples of metathesis in adult speech. In these cases, metathesis appears to facilitate the pronunciation of two successive consonant-*r* sequences in each word.

Vowel reduction

In many languages, the articulation of vowels may move to a more central position when the vowels are unstressed. This process is known as **(vowel) reduction**. Typically, the outcome of vowel reduction is a schwa [ə]; this can be observed in pairs of related words that show different stress placement such as *Canada* [kʰǽnədə] versus *Canadian* [kʰənéjdiən]. Note that the first vowel of the words *Canada/Canadian* is [æ] when stressed but a schwa when unstressed, while the second vowel is [ej] when stressed and a schwa when unstressed. Since we cannot predict what vowel a schwa may 'turn into' when it is stressed, we assume that [æ] and [ej] are basic to the words in question and are reduced in unstressed position.

10   Other vowels and consonants (*Advanced*)

This chapter has considered only the vowels and consonants of English, many of which are found in other languages. There are also many speech sounds found in the world's languages that are not heard in English. Since phonetic descriptions are universally valid, once the basic articulatory parameters have been mastered it is not too difficult to describe and even to pronounce less familiar sounds. This section presents a number of speech sounds found in other languages.

10.1 Vowels

Front vowels, which in English are always unrounded, can also be rounded. A high front tense rounded vowel is heard in French *pur* 'pure', German *Bücher* 'books', and Turkish *düğme* 'button'. It is transcribed as [y] in IPA transcription, but as [ü] in North America—a difference that sometimes leads to confusion. A rounded high front lax vowel, [ʏ] is heard in Canadian French *lune* 'moon' and *duc* 'duke'. A rounded mid front tense vowel, transcribed [ø] (NA [ö]), is found in French *peu* 'few' and German *schœn* 'beautiful'. A rounded mid front lax vowel, transcribed [œ], is heard in French *oeuf* 'egg' and *peur* 'fear', German *örtlich* 'local', and Turkish *göl* 'lake'. Back vowels may be unrounded; a high back unrounded vowel, transcribed as [ɯ], is heard in Russian words like *byl* 'was', and Rumanian *mînă* 'hand'. These vowels, as well as other 'exotic' ones, are found in many other languages as well. Table 2.28 illustrates the vowels presented in this chapter (UR = unrounded; R = rounded). Note carefully that the tense vowels are presented without glides. This is intentional; whereas certain English tense vowels are followed by glides, the tense vowels of the languages cited here (and many others) are not.

Table 2.28	Articulatory grid of vowels presented in this chapter					
	Front		**Central**		**Back**	
	UR	R	UR	R	UR	R
High	i	y			ɯ	u tense
	ɪ	Y				ʊ lax
Mid	e	ø	ə (reduced)			o tense
	ɛ	œ	ʌ			ɔ lax
Low	æ (lax)		a (lax)		ɑ (tense)	

Nasal vowels

Nasal vowels, like nasal consonants, are produced with a lowered velum. Air passes simultaneously through the oral and nasal cavities. Nasal vowels can be heard in English, French, Portuguese, Hindi, and a wide variety of other languages (see table 2.29). They are often transcribed with a tilde [˜] over the vowel symbol.

Table 2.29	Some nasal vowels			
English	win	[wɪ̃n]	'win'	
French	pain	[pɛ̃]	'bread'	
Portuguese	sento	[sẽntu]	'one hundred'	
Polish	ząb	[zɔ̃p]	'tooth'	

10.2 Consonants

The same consonants found in English are widespread in other languages. A few additional consonants are introduced in this section.

Stops

In many European languages, we find not the alveolar stops [t], [d], and [n], but dental stops [t̪], [d̪], and [n̪]. Although this seems like a very slight difference in articulation, it can be readily observed in the speech of French, Spanish, or Italian speakers.

Other stop positions are common in the world's languages. Serbo-Croatian has both a voiceless and a voiced palatal stop in words like ćaśa 'dish', and đak 'pupil'. These are transcribed as [c] and [ɟ], respectively. Inuktitut dialects show a voiceless and voiced uvular stop pair in words like imaq 'sea', and ugsik 'cow'. These are transcribed as [q] and [G], respectively. A nasal stop is also made at the palatal point of articulation, as in Spanish año 'year' (transcribed [ɲ] in IPA and as [ñ] in North America), and at the uvula as well, where it is transcribed as [N].

We now return to the glottal state known as *whispery voice* or *murmur* that was introduced in section 2.3. In Hindi there is a series of stops sometimes incorrectly referred to as 'voiced aspirated stops' that make use of whispery voice (murmur). These stops are traditionally represented with a following h (e.g., bh, dh, sh); the double underdots of IPA standard are used here.

In table 2.30, examples of non-English stop articulations and glottal states are laid out. The distinction between dentals and alveolars is not indicated in the transcription, since most of the world's languages have either dental or alveolar stop articulations, but not both. Sounds found in English are set off in boxes.

Table 2.30	Stops					
	Bilabial	**Dental/ alveolar**	**Palatal**	**Velar**	**Uvular**	**Glottal**
Voiceless	[p]	[t]	[c]	[k]	[q]	[ʔ]
Voiced	[b]	[d]	[ɟ]	[g]	[ɢ]	
Murmured	[b̤]	[d̤]	[ɟ̤]	[g̤]		
Nasal	[m]	[n]	[ɲ]	[ŋ]	[ɴ]	

Fricatives

Fricatives other than those of English are found in the world's languages. A bilabial fricative, produced by drawing the lips almost together and forcing the airstream through the narrow opening, is found in many languages. The voiceless bilabial fricative [ɸ] is heard word-initially in the Japanese word *Fuji* (the mountain). The voiced bilabial fricative [β] is found in Spanish words like *deber* 'to owe'. A voiceless palatal fricative [ç] is found in Standard German as in the word *ich* 'I'. Velar fricatives are not found in English but are widespread in the world's languages. The voiceless velar fricative [x] is common in German and Russian. (The composer Bach's name, pronounced in German, has this sound.) A voiced velar fricative [ɣ] is commonly heard in Spanish words like *agua* 'water'.

Table 2.31 presents a grid on which some common fricative consonants are ranged according to point and manner of articulation. As in table 2.30, dentals are not distinguished from alveolars, as most languages have sounds with either one or the other point of articulation, but not both. Sounds found in English are set off in boxes.

Table 2.31	Fricatives							
	Bilabial	**Labio-dental**	**Inter-dental**	**Alveolar**	**Alveo-palatal**	**Palatal**	**Velar**	**Glottal**
Voiceless	[ɸ]	[f]	[θ]	[s]	[ʃ]	[ç]	[x]	[h]
Voiced	[β]	[v]	[ð]	[z]	[ʒ]	[ʝ]	[ɣ]	

Affricates

Affricates are found at most points of articulation. In German, a voiceless labiodental affricate, transcribed as [pf] is heard at the beginning of the word *Pferd* horse. Many dialects of Canadian French have voiceless and voiced dental (or alveolar) affricates, [ts] and [dz], in words like *tu* 'you' and *dire* 'to say'.

Table 2.32 presents a grid including the two English affricates and some others commonly found in other languages. The English sounds are again set off in a box.

Table 2.32	Affricates			
	Labiodental	**Alveolar**	**Alveopalatal**	**Velar**
Voiceless	[pᶠ]	[tˢ]	[tʃ]	[kx]
Voiced	[bᵛ]	[dᶻ]	[dʒ]	[gɣ]

Liquids

As with the stops, laterals may be dental as well as alveolar. Laterals can also be made with the tongue body raised to the palate. Such a sound is called a palatal lateral, and is transcribed with the symbol [ʎ]. It is heard in some pronunciations of the Spanish words *caballo* 'horse' and *calle* 'street', and in the Serbo-Croatian words *dalje* 'farther' and *ljudi* 'people'. The palatal lateral may also be voiceless, in which case it is transcribed as [ʎ̥].

Lateral fricatives are produced when a lateral is made with a narrow enough closure to be classified as a fricative. This sound is transcribed as [ɮ] when voiced and [ɬ] when voiceless. Lateral fricatives can be heard in many American Indian languages, in Welsh, and in the languages spoken in the Caucasus. Table 2.33 shows some examples of voiceless alveolar lateral fricatives from Welsh.

Table 2.33	Voiceless lateral fricatives in Welsh	
llan	[ɬan]	'clan'
ambell	[ambɛɬ]	'some'

Other *r*-like sounds are widely heard in the world's languages. A common one is the **trill**, which is made by passing air over the raised tongue tip and allowing it to vibrate. Trills are commonly transcribed as (IPA) [r], but North American [r̃]. They can be heard in the Spanish words *perro* 'dog' and *río* 'river', and the Italian words *carro* 'wagon' and *birra* 'beer'. A similar trilling effect can be made with the uvula, and is called a uvular trill. Its IPA symbol is [ʀ].

A uvular *r* made without trilling is more commonly heard, however. This is the voiced *r* of Standard European French, and is also widespread in German. IPA transcription classifies this sound along with the fricatives. It is transcribed as [χ] when voiceless and as [ʁ] when voiced.

Table 2.34 presents the liquids. As before, sounds found in English are set off in boxes.

Table 2.34	Liquids		
	Dental/alveolar	**Palatal**	**Uvular**
Laterals			
Voiced	[l]	[ʎ]	
Voiceless	[l̥]	[ʎ̥]	

Table 2.34	Liquids (continued)			
		Dental/alveolar	Palatal	Uvular
Lateral fricatives				
	Voiced	[ɮ]		
	Voiceless	[ɬ]		
r's				
	Retroflex	[ɽ]		
	Flap	[ɾ]		
	Trill	[r̃]		[ʀ]

Flaps and trills can be voiceless as well. Voicelessness for these sounds is usually indicated by a small open circle beneath the symbol, as in [r̥] or [ʀ̥].

Glides

Other glides are found in the world's languages. A commonly heard one is made with the tongue position of [j] but with the lips rounded. It is transcribed as [ɥ] and can be heard in French words such as [ɥit] *huit* 'eight', [ɥil] *huile* 'oil', and [ɥitχ] *huitre* 'oyster'.

Summing up

The study of the sounds of human language is called *phonetics*. These sounds are widely transcribed by means of the **International Phonetic Alphabet**.

The sounds of language are commonly described in **articulatory** and **acoustic** terms, and fall into two major types: syllabic sounds (**vowels, syllabic liquids,** and **syllabic nasals**) and non-syllabic sounds (**consonants** and **glides**). Sounds may be **voiced** or **voiceless**, and **oral** or **nasal**. Consonants are produced at various places of articulation: labial, dental, alveolar, alveopalatal, palatal, velar, uvular, glottal, and pharyngeal. At the places of articulation, the airstream is modified by different **manners of articulation** and the resulting sounds are **stops, fricatives,** or **affricates**. Vowels are produced with less drastic closure and are described with reference to tongue position (**high, low, back,** and **front**), tension (**tense** or **lax**), and lip rounding (**rounded** or **unrounded**). Language also exhibits **suprasegmental** phenomena such as **tone, intonation,** and **stress**.

Notes

1 There is still a great deal of discussion among linguists on the subject of diphthongs. English vowels that show a change in quality are considered diphthongs as long as the change in quality *follows* the vowel nucleus. Words such as *yes* and *wet* are considered to begin with a glide that is not an integral part of the vocalic nucleus. However, in transcribing other languages (Finnish, for example), sounds like [jɛ] and [wo] are considered to

be diphthongs. For now, treat the diphthongs presented in table 2.15 as unit vowels, and the initial two sounds of words like *yes* and *wet* as distinct segments. This approach will be revised somewhat in chapter 3.

Sources

Information on the International Phonetic Alphabet can be obtained from the International Phonetic Association, University College, Gower Street, London, WC1E 6BT, England (Web site: http://www.arts.gla.ac.uk/IPA/ipa.html). Sarcee data are taken from E.-D. Cook, "Vowels and Tones in Sarcee" in *Language* 47:164–79; Gaelic data are courtesy of James Galbraith. Bini data are adapted from Ladefoged (cited below). For a discussion of glottal states, see Jimmy G. Harris, "The State of the Glottis for Voiceless Plosives" in *Proceedings of the 14th International Congress of Phonetic Sciences,* Vol. 3, pp. 2041–2044. More detailed reading on the phonetics of English and other languages is reported below.

Recommended reading

Catford, J.C. 1977. *Fundamental Problems in Phonetics*. Bloomington, IN: Indiana University Press.

Cruttenden, Alan. 1986. *Intonation*. Cambridge, UK: Cambridge University Press.

Fromkin, V.A., ed. 1978. *Tone: A Linguistic Survey*. New York: Academic Press.

Ladefoged, P. 1982. *A Course in Phonetics*. 2nd ed. Toronto: Harcourt Brace Jovanovich.

Ladefoged, P., and I. Maddieson. 1995. *The Sounds of the World's Languages*. Cambridge, MA: Blackwell.

Pullum, G.K., and W.A. Ladusaw. 1986. *Phonetic Symbol Guide*. Chicago: University of Chicago Press.

Rogers, H. 1991. *Theoretical and Practical Phonetics*. Toronto: Copp Clark Pitman.

Shearer, William M. 1968. *Illustrated Speech Anatomy*. Springfield, IL: Charles C. Thomas.

Walker, Douglas C. 1984. *The Pronunciation of Canadian French*. Ottawa: University of Ottawa Press.

Questions

1. In order to become more aware of the differences between spelling and pronunciation, answer the following questions about English spelling.
   a) Find four words that show four alternative spellings of the sound [f].
   b) Find six words that have the letter 'a' pronounced differently.
   c) Find four words in which different groups of letters represent only one sound.
   d) Find two words in which two different sounds are pronounced but not spelled out.

2. How many segments are there in the following words?
   a) at   e) psychology
   b) math   f) knowledge
   c) cure   g) mailbox
   d) hopping   h) awesome

3. Is the first sound in each of the following words voiced or voiceless?

   a) though   e) zoom   i) huge   m) when (*may vary*)
   b) thought   f) silk   j) choose   n) ghetto
   c) form   g) pan   k) judge   o) pneumatic
   d) view   h) boat   l) buns   p) winced

4. Using the words presented in question 3, state whether the last sound of each word is voiced or voiceless.

5. For each of the following pairs of sounds, state whether they have the same or a different place of articulation. Then identify the place of articulation for each sound.

   a) [s] : [l]   e) [m] : [n]   i) [b] : [f]
   b) [k] : [ŋ]   f) [dʒ] : [ʃ]   j) [tʃ] : [dʒ]
   c) [p] : [g]   g) [f] : [h]   k) [s] : [v]
   d) [l] : [r]   h) [w] : [j]   l) [θ] : [t]

6. For each of the following pairs of sounds, state whether they have the same or different manners of articulation. Then identify the manner of articulation for each sound.

   a) [s] : [θ]   e) [l] : [t]   i) [r] : [w]
   b) [k] : [g]   f) [ð] : [v]   j) [tʃ] : [dʒ]
   c) [w] : [j]   g) [tʃ] : [s]   k) [h] : [ʔ]
   d) [f] : [ʃ]   h) [m] : [ŋ]   l) [z] : [dʒ]

7. After each of the following articulatory descriptions, write the sound described in phonetic brackets.

   a) voiceless velar stop   e) voiced velar nasal
   b) voiced labiodental fricative   f) voiceless interdental fricative
   c) voiced alveopalatal affricate   g) high back rounded lax vowel
   d) voiced palatal glide   h) low front unrounded vowel

8. Which of the following pairs of words show the same vowel quality? Mark each pair as *same* or *different*. Then transcribe the vowels of each word.

   a) back   sat   h) hide   height
   b) cot   caught   i) least   heed
   c) bid   key   j) drug   cook
   d) luck   flick   k) sink   fit
   e) ooze   deuce   l) oak   own
   f) cot   court   m) pour   port
   g) fell   fail   n) mouse   cow

9. Using descriptive terms like sibilant, fricative, and so on, provide a single phonetic characteristic that all the segments in each group share. Try to avoid over-obvious answers such as 'consonant' or 'vowel'.
   Example: [b d g œ m j] are all voiced.

   a) [p t k g ʔ]   e) [ʌ ə ʊ a]   i) [l r m n ŋ j w]
   b) [i e ɛ æ]   f) [h ʔ]   j) [t d l r n s z]
   c) [tʃ ʒ ʃ dʒ]   g) [u o]
   d) [p b m f v]   h) [s z t ʃ dʒ ʃ ʒ]

10. Transcribe the following sets of words. You may use these words to practise transcribing aspiration.

a) tog	i) peel	q) spell
b) kid	j) stun	r) cord
c) attain	k) Oscar	s) accord
d) despise	l) cooler	t) astound
e) elbow	m) sigh	u) pure
f) haul	n) hulk	v) wheeze
g) juice	o) explode	w) remove
h) thimble	p) tube	x) clinical

11. Using H, L, and association lines, transcribe the intonation of the following English phrases. Compare your results with the transcriptions of several classmates. Are they the same? If they aren't, discuss what aspects of intonation (such as emotion or speech context) might account for the differences in transcription.
    a) 'Hi, Alice.'
    b) 'Three people got off the bus at the last stop.'
    c) 'My uncle likes to mountain climb.'

12. Mark primary and secondary (where present) stresses on the following words. It is not necessary to transcribe them.

a) sunny	f) arrive	k) secret
b) banana	g) defy	l) exceed
c) blackboard	h) summary	m) summery
d) Canada	i) Canadian	n) Canadianize
e) (to) reject	j) (a) reject	o) difficult

13. Find a fluent speaker of a language other than English and transcribe phonetically ten words of that language. If you encounter any sounds for which symbols are not found in this chapter, attempt to describe them in phonetic terms and then invent diacritics to help you transcribe them.

14. Using figure 2.20 as your model, provide co-articulation diagrams for the following words. Be sure that your diagrams capture the movement of the lips, tongue, velum, and glottis as in the model.
    a) had   c) please
    b) snap   d) dome

15. Compare the careful speech and rapid speech pronunciations of the following English words and phrases. Then, name the process or processes that make the rapid speech pronunciation different from the careful speech. (Stress is omitted here.)

	Careful speech	Rapid speech
a) in my room	[ɪn maj rum]	[ɪm maj rum]
b) I see them	[aj si ðɛm]	[aj siəm]
c) I see him	[aj si hɪm]	[aj siəm]
d) within	[wɪθɪn]	[wɪðɪn]
e) balloons	[bəlunz]	[blunz]

f) popsicle   [pʰɑpsɪkʊl]   [pʰɑpskəl]
g) sit down   [sɪt dawn]   [sɪɾawn]
h) my advice   [maj ədvʌjs]   [maj əvʌjs]
i) Scotch tape   [skɑtʃ tʰejp]   [kʰɑtʃ stejp]
j) protection   [p̥rowtʰɛkʃən]   [pərtʰɛkʃən]
k) hand me that   [hænd mi ðæt]   [hæmiðæt]
l) Pam will miss you   [pæm wɪl mɪs juw]   [pæm|mɪʃjə]

CHAPTER
Three

Michael Dobrovolsky
Ewa Czaykowska-Higgins

Phonology: the function and patterning of sounds

A person's tongue is a twisty thing, there are
plenty of words there of every kind, and the
range of words is wide, and their variation.

HOMER, *THE ILIAD*, 20

We saw in chapter 2 that human beings can produce and perceive a large number of speech sounds. No human language exploits all of these phonetic possibilities. Instead, every language makes its own particular selection from the range of all possible speech sounds, and organizes them into a more or less regular system. The component of grammar that determines the selection of speech sounds and that governs both the sound patterns and the systematic phonetic variation found in language is known as **phonology**.

Speakers have (at least) some subconscious knowledge of the phonetic patterns that make up phonological systems. For example, as we saw in chapter 1, speakers of English recognize without being taught that certain combinations of consonants are acceptable in English, even if those combinations occur in forms that are not real words, while other combinations are not acceptable; thus, *slish* and *screnk* are acceptable to English speakers, while *srish* and *screpk* are not. In fact, speakers can do more than recognize that certain forms are unnatural in their system; they can even correct unnatural forms to make them conform to the patterns that are acceptable in their own language. Without knowing exactly why, most English speakers would pronounce a form like *srish* as [sərɪʃ] breaking up the unacceptable consonant combination with a vowel, rather than, say, deleting one of the consonants to form [sɪʃ] or [rɪʃ]. The task of phonologists, then, is (1) to discover and describe the systematic phonetic patterns found in individual languages and (2) to discover the general principles that underlie the patterning of sounds across all human languages. In doing this, phonologists hope to uncover the largely subconscious knowledge that speakers have of sound patterns.

The existence of phonological patterns in language is a result of the organization of certain basic elements or units that combine to make up these patterns. In our discussion of phonology we will examine three of the major phonological units: the **feature**, the **segment**, and the **syllable**.

We are already acquainted with the idea that the flow of speech can be divided into segments and that segments are characterized by specific phonetic properties. In this chapter we will investigate the types of patterned phonetic variation that segments exhibit in individual languages and cross-linguistically. We will also learn that segments are composed of features. Features correspond to articulatory or acoustic categories such as [voice] or [strident]. They are the smallest building blocks of phonological structure, and, as we will see, the types of phonological patterns found in language are directly related to the properties of the features that make up segments. Finally, we will learn about the ways in which segments combine to form syllables. Syllables consist of a syllabic element—usually a vowel—and any preceding or following segments that are associated with it. As the representation of the word *segment* in figure 3.1 illustrates, features, segments, and syllables are organized into hierarchical levels, where each level is composed of units from the level beneath it. In figure 3.1, *segment* is a word-level unit represented by the abbreviation *Wd*. This word in turn consists of two syllables, each of which is represented by the Greek letter σ (sigma). Each syllable itself consists of several segments. Finally, each segment is composed of features. (For purposes of illustration, only a few features are provided for each segment and the internal hierarchical structure of syllables and segments is not represented; these are treated below, in sections 4, 5.2, and 5.3, respectively.)

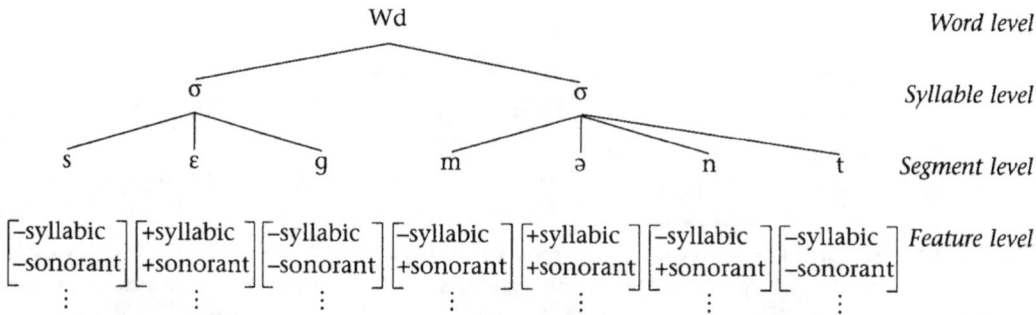

Figure 3.1 Partial phonological representation of *segment*

As units of phonological structure, syllables, segments, and features play major roles in the processes we investigated in the previous chapter, and, in combination with certain general principles of phonology, produce the sound patterns of language. In the next sections we examine these sound patterns and the phonological knowledge that enables speakers to distinguish among forms and to deal with the systematic phonetic variation found in the pronunciation of speech sounds.

1 Segments in contrast

All speakers know which segments of their language **contrast** and which do not. Segments are said to contrast (or to be *distinctive* or be in *opposition*) in a particular language when their presence alone may distinguish forms with different meanings from each other. Thus, for instance, in the English words *sip* and *zip*, the phonetically distinct segments [s] and [z] are in contrast; similarly, in *hit*, *hate*, and *hot*, the vowels are in contrast.

In this section we will consider how to determine which segments contrast in a language. In section 2 we will consider the systematic patterns associated with phonetically similar segments when they do not contrast.

1.1   Minimal pairs

Since knowledge of segmental contrasts is fundamental to knowing any language, the first step in an analysis of the phonology of a language is to establish which sounds in that language are in contrast with each other. In order to establish contrasts, it is necessary to examine the distribution of sounds in words and to compare word meanings. The most straightforward way to accomplish this examination is by way of the **minimal pair** test.

A minimal pair consists of two forms with distinct meanings that differ by only one segment found in the same position in each form. The examples [sɪp] *sip* and [zɪp] *zip* given previously form a minimal pair and show that the sounds [s] and [z] contrast in English.

A number of minimal pairs that demonstrate consonant contrasts for English are given in table 3.1; it is important to remember that it is on the basis of *sound* and not spelling that minimal pairs are established. In displaying contrasts, contrasting words are often placed along the horizontal axis with respect to their place of articulation, reading from left to right (labial, alveolar, and so on), and vertically with respect to manner of articulation, in order to show which places and manners of articulation are exploited by the language in question.[1]

Table 3.1	Contrasts among consonants in English				
Stops and affricates (non-continuants)					
Labial		*Alveolar*	*Alveopalatal*	*Velar*	*Glottal*
tap [p]		pat [t]	match [tʃ]	pick [k]	
tab [b]		pad [d]	Madge [dʒ]	pig [g]	
Continuants					
	Interdental				
leaf [f]	thigh [θ]	sip [s]	mesher [ʃ]		hip [h]
leave [v]	thy [ð]	zip [z]	measure [ʒ]		
Nasals					
sum [m]		sun [n]		sung [ŋ]	
Liquids and glides					
wet ([w])			yet [j]	wet [w]	
		leer [l]			
		rear [r]			

The phonetic context in which a sound occurs is called its **environment**. Pairs that have segments in nearly identical environments, such as *assure* [əʃʊ́r] /*azure* [ǽʒər], which contrast [ʃ] and [ʒ], or *author* [ɑ́θər]/*either* [íðər], which contrast [θ] and [ð], are called **near-minimal pairs**. They can be used to establish contrasts if no minimal pairs for a particular set of segments can be found.

Once you have established the existence of a minimal or a near-minimal pair for a set of two segments, you may assume that those two segments contrast or are distinctive. Segments that contrast with each other in a particular language are said to belong to separate **phonemes** (contrastive phonological units) of that language. Thus all the consonants in table 3.1 belong to separate phonemes in English, since all of them are contrastive in the language.

When looking for the contrastive sounds of a language, it is in fact rare to find minimal pairs for all such sounds, since the historical evolution of every language has led to some sounds being used more frequently than others, or to being eliminated from some environments. For example, you will find no minimal pairs involving [h] and [ŋ] in word-initial or word-final position in English, because there are no words that begin with [ŋ] or end in [h]. It is also difficult to find minimal pairs in English that have the phone [ʒ], which occurs for the most part in words borrowed from French such as *azure* and *mirage*.

Vowel contrasts in English

Vowel contrasts in English can be established with a few sets of examples. We assume in table 3.2 that English vowel-glide sequences like [ej] and [ow] are single vowels. From this perspective, we can say that the vowels [ej] and [ɛ] and [aw] and [aj], etc., contrast.

Table 3.2	Vowel contrasts in Canadian English	
beet	[bit]	[i]
bit	[bɪt]	[ɪ]
bait	[bejt]	[ej]
bet	[bɛt]	[ɛ]
bat	[bæt]	[æ]
cooed	[kʰud]	[u]
could	[kʰʊd]	[ʊ]
code	[kʰowd]	[ow]
cod	[kʰɑd]	[ɑ]²
cud	[kʰʌd]	[ʌ]
lewd	[lud]	[u]
loud	[lawd]	[aw]
lied	[lajd]	[aj]
Lloyd	[lojd]	[oj]

1.2   Language-specific contrasts

Whether or not segments contrast with each other is determined on a language-particular basis. In other words, just because two sounds are phonetically distinct, does not mean that they necessarily behave as phonologically distinct or contrastive. Therefore, sounds that are contrastive in one language will not necessarily be contrastive in another. For example, the difference between the two vowels [ɛ] and [æ] is crucial to English, as we can see from minimal pairs like *Ben* [bɛn] and *ban* [bæn] (see table 3.3). But in Turkish, this difference in pronunciation is not distinctive. A Turkish speaker may pronounce the word for 'I' as [bɛn] or [bæn], and it will make no difference to the meaning.

Conversely, sounds that do not contrast in English, such as long and short vowels, may be distinctive in another language. There are no minimal pairs of the type [hæt]:[hæːt] or [lus]:[luːs] in English. But in Japanese and Finnish, short and long vowels contrast, as the examples in table 3.4 show.

Table 3.3	Language-specific vowel contrasts: English versus Turkish		
English		**Turkish**	
[bɛn]	'Ben'	[bɛn]	'I'
[bæn]	'ban'	[bæn]	'I'

Table 3.4	Short/long vowel contrasts in Japanese and Finnish		
Japanese			
[tori]	'bird'	[toriː]	'shrine gate'
[kibo]	'scale'	[kiboː]	'hope'
Finnish			
[tuli]	'fire	[tuːli]	'wind'
[hætæ]	'distress'	[hæːtæː]	'to evict'

Establishing the contrasting segments in a language is a first step in phonological analysis. However, in any language there are also many sounds that never contrast. The following section deals with this aspect of phonology.

2 Phonetically conditioned variation: phonemes and allophones

Everyday speech contains a great deal of phonetic variation that speakers pay little or no attention to. Some of this variation arises from non-linguistic factors such as fatigue, excitement, orthodontic work, gum chewing, and the like. This kind of variation is not part of the domain of phonology. But much phonetic variation is systematic. It occurs most often among phonetically similar segments and is conditioned by the phonetic context or environment in which the segments are found. This variation occurs because segments are affected and altered by the phonetic characteristics of neighbouring elements or by the larger phonological context in which they occur. We rarely notice this kind of variation unless we are trained to do so, because every speaker has the ability to factor it out in order to focus attention on only those contrasts of the language that affect meaning. In this section we will consider the patterns of variation exhibited by non-contrastive sounds, how to analyze these patterns, and the conclusions that can be drawn from them.

2.1   Complementary distribution

When first learning phonetic transcription, English speakers are often surprised that all the *l*s they pronounce are not identical. In table 3.5, the *l*s in column A are voiced, while those in column B are voiceless (indicated here by a subscript ̥). Many speakers of English are unaware that they routinely produce this difference in articulation, which can be heard clearly when the words in column B are pronounced slowly.

Table 3.5	Voiced and voiceless *l* in English		
A		**B**	
blue	[blu]	plow	[pl̥aw]
gleam	[glim]	clap	[kl̥æp]
slip	[slɪp]	clear	[kl̥ir]
flog	[flɑg]	play	[pl̥ej]
leaf	[lif]		

In fact, as it turns out, the two *l*s never contrast in English: there are no minimal pairs like [plej] and [pl̥ej] in which the phonetic difference between [l] and [l̥] functions to signal a difference in meaning.

Moreover, when one examines the distribution of the two *l*s, it becomes apparent that voiced and voiceless *l*s vary systematically: all of the voiceless [l̥]s occur after the class of voiceless stops in English, while the voiced [l]s never occur after voiceless stops. The voicelessness of the *l*s in column B is thus a consequence of their phonetic environment; it is also a predictable property of the phonology of English, in the sense that in English only voiceless [l̥]s occur after voiceless stops.

Since no voiced [l] ever occurs in the same phonetic environment as a voiceless one (and vice versa), we say that the two variants of *l* are in **complementary distribution**.

In the data in table 3.5, voiced [l] occurs in a greater number of different phonetic environments (after voiced stops, voiceless fricatives, and in word-initial position) than does voiceless [l̥], and in addition those different environments for voiced [l] cannot be easily described as they do not naturally fall together as a class. Therefore, when two (or more) segments are in complementary distribution, the term *elsewhere* is used, as in table 3.6, to indicate the kind of wider distribution exhibited by [l] in table 3.5. Specifically, we find [l̥] after voiceless stops, and [l] elsewhere.

Table 3.6	Complementary distribution of [l] and [l̥] in English	
	[l]	[l̥]
After voiceless stops	no	yes
Elsewhere	yes	no

In spite of these differences in their phonetic environments, native speakers of English consider the two *l*s to be instances of the same segment, since they are not contrastive, but are nevertheless similar phonetically (they are both types of *l*s), and since the differences between them are systematic and predictable. We can sum up the relationship that the two *l*s bear to each other by stating that, for speakers of English, the two *l*s are *phonetically* distinct but in the sound system of English, given their phonetic similarity, predictable distribution, and non-contrastiveness, they are *phonologically* the same.

2.2　Phonemes and allophones

When two (or more) segments are phonetically distinct, but phonologically the same, they are referred to as **allophones** (predictable variants) of one **phoneme** (contrastive phonological unit). The ability to group phonetically distinct sounds into the phonological units known as phonemes is shared by all speakers of all languages. Phonologists represent this phonological knowledge formally by distinguishing two levels of representation: the **phonetic representation** that consists of predictable variants or allophones, and the **phonemic** (or phonological) **representation** that consists of the phonemes to which the allophones belong. A representation of the relationship between phonemes and their allophones is given in figure 3.2.

Phonemic representation (phoneme →)　　　　　　　　　　/l/

Phonetic representation (allophones →)　　　[l̥]　　　　　　　　　　　[l]

　　　　　　　　　　　　　　　　After voiceless stops　　　　　Elsewhere

Figure 3.2　The phoneme /l/ and its allophones [l̥] and [l] in English

In figure 3.2 the symbols for allophones are enclosed in square brackets, while the symbol for the phoneme is placed between slashes. This is standard notation in phonology. Notice that the phoneme /l/ in figure 3.2 is the same as its voiced allophone [l]. In most cases the elsewhere variant or allophone of a phoneme can be chosen to represent the phoneme itself.

As we have seen, segments which can be considered to be allophones of one phoneme are phonetically similar and occur in phonetically predictable environments. In fact, it is frequently the case that allophones of one phoneme are in complementary distribution with each other. Consequently, we can use the fact that allophones occur in complementary distribution as a way of testing whether or not two (or more) segments should be considered to be allophones of one phoneme.

Allophonic variation is found throughout language. In fact, every speech sound we utter is an allophone of some phoneme and can be grouped together with other phonetically similar sounds into a class that is represented by a phoneme on a phonological level of representation. An important part of phonological analysis thus deals with discovering inventories of the phonemes of languages and accounting for allophonic variation.

Some problematic distributions

At this point, some other considerations in determining phonemes and allophones must be taken into account. So far, we have seen that a minimal pair test is a quick and direct way of establishing that two sounds belong to separate phonemes in a language. If the sounds contrast, they are members of different phonemes. We have also seen that if certain sounds are non-contrastive and in complementary distribution, they may be considered allophones of one phoneme. In some cases, however, we must go beyond these procedures to discover the phonemic inventory of a language.

As noted in section 1.1, certain patterns of distribution prevent some sounds in a language from ever contrasting with each other. In cases like these, we can establish the phonemic status of a sound by default. If the sound cannot be grouped together with any other phonetically similar sounds as an allophone of a phoneme, we may assume that it has phonemic status. The following data from English help to illustrate this point.

1)
*[ŋowp]   (does not exist)   [howp]   'hope'
*[ŋejt]   (does not exist)   [hejt]   'hate'

We can see here that [h] and [ŋ] do not contrast in initial position in English. The following examples show that they do not contrast in final position either.

2)
[laŋ]   'long'   *[lah]   (does not exist)
[sɪŋ]   'sing'   *[sɪh]   (does not exist)
[kl̥æŋ]   'clang'   *[kl̥æh]   (does not exist)

These lists could be extended for pages, but a minimal pair involving [h] and [ŋ] could never be found in English. Additionally, as *1)* and *2)* have shown, [h] and [ŋ] are in complementary distribution. Do these facts taken together not lead us to conclude that [h] and [ŋ] are allophones of one phoneme? No. Since [h] and [ŋ] are so distinct phonetically, we assume that each one is a member of a separate phoneme and that the pattern of distribution is of secondary importance in this instance.

Minimal pairs or near-minimal pairs help us establish which sounds contrast in a language; phonetic similarity and complementary distribution help us decide which sounds are allophones of a particular phoneme. But not all examples of variation among sounds can be dealt with through these approaches.

In some cases, phonetically similar sounds are neither in complementary distribution nor are they found to contrast. It is still possible, nevertheless, to determine which phonemes these sounds belong to. A case in point is the variation in English voiceless stops when they are found in word-final position, as in the word *stop*. Sometimes an English speaker releases the articulation of these sounds rather forcefully. Let us represent this with a diacritic sign [!]. At other times, the same speaker may keep the articulators closed for a moment after the articulation; the diacritic [˺] can represent this. Some speakers may even co-articulate a glottal closure (represented here with the raised symbol for a glottal stop following the consonant in question) and produce the word as [stɑpˀ]. Thus, we can find at least three pronunciations of *stop* : [stɑp!], [stɑp˺], and [stɑpˀ]. Since there is no difference in the meaning of these forms and since the final consonants are phonetically similar, we say that these sounds are in **free variation**, and that they are all allophones of the phoneme /p/. The same pattern holds for the other voiceless stops of English.

2.3 Classes and generalization in phonology

Phonological analysis permits us to account for the great amount of phonetic variation in everyday speech. This variation, which is usually systematic, is found throughout language. Evidence of its systematic nature comes from the fact that allophones in languages do not pattern piecemeal, but rather according to their membership in phonetic classes. This point can be illustrated by comparing the patterns of distribution of *r*s and glides in English to the patterning of *l*s that was illustrated earlier in table 3.5.

Table 3.7	Voiced and voiceless allophones of English /r/		
A		**B**	
brew	[bru]	prow	[pr̥aw]
green	[grin]	trip	[tr̥ɪp]
drip	[drɪp]	creep	[kr̥ip]
frog	[frɑg]	pray	[pr̥ej]
shrimp	[ʃrɪmp]		

The data in table 3.7 shows that in English, voiceless [r̥] occurs after voiceless stops, while voiced [r] occurs elsewhere. Based on this information we can conclude that there is an /r/ phoneme in English with (at least) two allophones—one voiced, the other voiceless, and that the allophones of English /r/ thus pattern like those of /l/. But if we were to stop there, we would overlook an important point. The phonemes /r/ and /l/ belong to the same class of sounds: both are *liquids*. By taking this information into account, we can state a general fact about English.

3)
In English, liquids have voiceless allophones after voiceless stops and voiced allophones elsewhere.

Now examine the data in table 3.8.

Table 3.8	Voiced and voiceless allophones of English glides		
A		**B**	
beauty	[bjuɾi]	putrid	[pjutr̥ɪd]
Duane	[dwejn]	twin	[tw̥ɪn]
Gwen	[gwɛn]	quick	[kw̥ɪk]
view	[vju]	cute	[kj̥ut]
swim	[swɪm]		
thwack	[θwæk]		

These forms demonstrate that the contrasting glides /j/ and /w/ pattern like the liquids. We can now extend our general statement even further.

4)
In English, liquids and glides have voiceless allophones after voiceless stops, and voiced allophones elsewhere.

When we consider the fact that liquids and glides all belong to the same phonetic class, namely the class of non-nasal sonorant consonants, we can understand why the allophones of liquids and glides pattern similarly. One of the major goals of phonological description is the discovery of such broad patterns of variation, and the formulation of the most general statements possible to capture these broad patterns.

2.4   Canadian Raising

Another example of allophonic variation is taken from English. In most Canadian and some American dialects, pronunciations like those illustrated in table 3.9 are common.

Table 3.9	Low and central vowel allophones in Canadian English		
[ajz]	eyes	[ʌjs]	ice
[lajz]	lies	[lʌjs]	lice
[tr̥ajd]	tried	[tr̥ʌjt]	trite
[tr̥ajb]	tribe	[tr̥ʌjp]	tripe
[hawz]	(to) house (verb)	[hʌws]	house (noun)
[lawd]	loud	[lʌwt]	lout
[kaw]	cow	[skʌwt]	scout
[flaj]	fly	[flʌjt]	flight

In table 3.9, the vowels [aj] and [ʌj] are in complementary distribution. The [aj] occurs before the class of voiced consonants or in word-final position, and the [ʌj] occurs before the class of voiceless consonants. The two are allophones of a single phoneme /aj/. The same relationship holds between the vowels [aw] and [ʌw], which are allophones of /aw/.

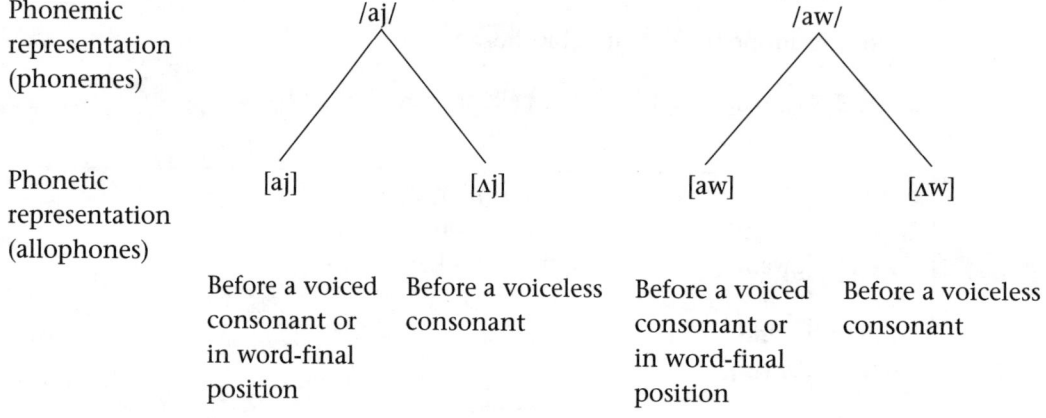

Figure 3.3 Allophones of /aj/ and /aw/ in Canadian English

Again, we see this phonological fact reflected in everyday language use. Most speakers of Canadian English find it difficult to distinguish between these allophones, even when the difference is pointed out to them. This is because the difference is not contrastive. On the other hand, many people who speak varieties of English that do not have the [ʌj] or [ʌw] allophones are very much aware of their presence in Canadian English. To them, a Canadian speaker sounds markedly different, even though they may be confused about the nature of the difference.

> *I don't agree he was an American. ... Where all other English-speaking people pronounce OU as a diphthong, the Canadian ... makes a separate sound for each letter. The word about, for instance, he pronounces as ab-oh-oot.*
>
> Philip MacDonald, *The List of Adrian Messenger*

This phenomenon is sometimes referred to as Canadian Raising, since the allophones [ʌj] and [ʌw] have higher vowel components than the elsewhere variants [aj] and [aw].

2.5   English mid vowels and glides

The vowels that exhibit the Canadian Raising alternation are all and only the central (unreduced) vowels of Canadian English; the two mid allophones [ʌj] and [ʌw] both occur before voiceless consonants, while the two low allophones [aj] and [aw] both occur elsewhere. Just as in the case of the liquid and glide patterns seen in section 2.3, the allophones that participate in the Canadian Raising pattern are distributed according to their membership in phonetic classes. A final example of predictable variation that refers to classes of segments but that differs crucially from examples seen so far is again taken from English.

Table 3.2 showed contrasts among English vowels. In most dialects of English, the mid, tense vowels [ej] and [ow] are always diphthongized and thus end in the glide [j] or [w]. Significantly, the non-back (i.e., front) vowel [e] is always followed by the palatal glide [j], which is a non-back unrounded segment, while the back rounded vowel [o] is always followed by the labiovelar glide [w], which is a back rounded segment. These facts are summed up in table 3.10.

Table 3.10 Tense vowel-glide combinations in English							
Vowel	**Glide**			**Vowel**	**Glide**		
(both non-back and unrounded)				**(both back and rounded)**			
e	j	[fejt]	fate	o	w	[bowt]	boat
		[kejn]	cane			[kown]	cone

In other words, the occurrence of the glides following the mid tense vowels is predictable. The following generalization states the distribution of the two glides.

5)
The mid tense vowels of English are predictably followed by a glide that has the same backness and roundness as the vowel.

The data in table 3.10 show parallels with the allophonic distribution we have considered so far in the sense that certain elements in it are predictable under certain systematically stateable phonetic conditions. However, there is a difference between allophonic distribution and the kind of distribution exhibited by the glides. Specifically, in table 3.10, instead of a number of variants of one phoneme, we have two segments, [ej] and [ow], whose pronunciation is always the same: the mid tense vowels of English are always followed by glides of the same backness and roundness. When certain sounds are found predictably in a given environment, they are not included in phonemic representations. Thus, although the phonetic representations of English mid vowels include the glides, the corresponding phonemic representations do not.

Phonemic representation	/e/	/o/
	|	|
Phonetic representation	[ej]	[ow]

Figure 3.4 Two representations of mid vowels in English

2.6   Language-specific patterns

The phenomenon of allophonic variation is universal. However, just as the phonemic contrasts found in each language are specific to that language, the actual patterning of phonemes and allophones is also language-specific. Thus, whatever distribution we discover for one language may not hold true for another.

Language-specific variation in allophonic nasalization

Some languages have nasal as well as oral vowels and glides. It is usual in such languages for nasal vowel (and nasal glide) allophones to occur near nasal consonants, but, as tables 3.11 and 3.12 illustrate, the details of the patterning may vary from language to language.

In Scots Gaelic, for instance, whenever a nasal consonant occurs in a word, the vowel adjacent to it appears as nasalized. Glides do not get nasalized.

Table 3.11 Nasal and oral vowels in Scots Gaelic	
[mõːr]	'big'
[nĩ]	'cattle'
[nẽːl]	'cloud'
[mũ]	'about'
[rũːn]	'secret'
[ʃalak]	'hunting'

The generalization governing the distribution of nasal vowels in Scots Gaelic is stated as follows.

6)
Vowels are nasal in Scots Gaelic when preceded or followed by a nasal consonant.

Malay, a language spoken in Malaysia and Singapore, has both nasalized vowels and glides. In Malay, all vowels and glides following a nasal are predictably nasalized until an obstruent, liquid, or glottal ([h], [ʔ]) is reached.

Table 3.12 Nasalization in Malay

[mẽw̃ãh]	'luxurious'
[mãjãn]	'stalk'
[mãrah]	'scold'
[nãɛ̃ʔ]	'ascend'
[məlaraŋ]	'forbid'
[mãkan	'eat'
[rumãh]	'house'
[kəreta]	'car'

For Malay, then, the generalization governing nasalization is different from the Scots Gaelic case both in the direction and the targets of nasalization.

7)
In Malay, all vowels and glides following a nasal consonant and not separated from it by a non-nasal consonant are nasalized.

Language-specific variation in allophonic distribution

In section 1.2 we saw that a phonemic contrast in one language may not prove to be a phonemic contrast in another. This means that the relationship of phonemes to allophones may vary. A comparison of the contrasts among stops in English and Khmer (Cambodian) in table 3.13 illustrates this point. In both languages, aspirated and unaspirated phones can be heard.

Table 3.13 Stop phones in English and Khmer

English		Khmer	
[p]	[pʰ]	[p]	[pʰ]
[t]	[tʰ]	[t]	[tʰ]
[k]	[kʰ]	[k]	[kʰ]

In English, aspirated and unaspirated stops are allophones of their respective phonemes (the distribution is explained in section 4.5 of this chapter); there are no contrasting forms like [pɪk] and [pʰɪk]. In Khmer, though, unaspirated and aspirated voiceless stops contrast (see table 3.14).

Table 3.14 Khmer contrastive voiceless stops

[pɔːŋ]	'to wish'	[pʰɔːŋ]	'also'
[tɔp]	'to support'	[tʰɔp]	'be suffocated'
[kat]	'to cut	[kʰat]	'to polish'

The phonological contrasts of the two languages are different, even though the phones are not (see figure 3.5). These distributions are the same for the other voiceless stops in both languages.

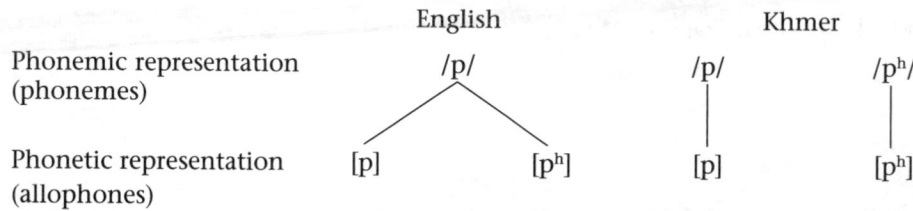

Figure 3.5 English and Khmer voiceless bilabial stop phonemes and allophones

3 Phonetic and phonemic transcription

We have seen so far that each language has a set of contrastive phonemes (which can be established largely by means of the minimal pair test) and that phonemes themselves can have predictable variants or allophones (which are usually in complementary distribution with each other). We have also shown that there are two distinct levels of representation: the phonemic (or phonological) and the phonetic. We can now illustrate more clearly the types of transcription used at each level of representation.

The phonetic level of representation includes both predictable and unpredictable phonetic information. In contrast, the phonemic level includes all and only those aspects of a representation that are unpredictable; all predictable information is excluded. The examples in table 3.15 show this difference for the classes of sounds in English that we have examined so far.

Table 3.15 Phonetic and phonemic transcription of English

Phonetic transcription	Phonemic transcription	Word	Predictable property(s) not represented in phonemic transcription
[pl̥aw]	/plaw/	plow	voicelessness of liquid
[kr̥ip]	/krip/	creep	voicelessness of liquid
[kw̥ɪk]	/kwɪk/	quick	voicelessness of liquid
[lejt]	/let/	late	glide after mid tense vowel
[lɛt]	/lɛt/	let	–
[tʰajd]	/tajd/	tied	aspiration
[tʰʌjt]	/tajt/	tight	aspiration; Canadian Raising

In the phonemic transcriptions in table 3.15 the words are transcribed using only phonemes; in the phonetic transcriptions, however, the allophones of each phoneme are transcribed (in the environments in which they predictably occur). There is thus more phonetic information in the phonetic transcriptions than in the phonemic ones. If one compares the two transcriptions of *tight*, for instance, one sees that the phonetic transcription indicates the aspiration of the initial *t*, and the raised pronunciation of the vowel. In the corresponding phonemic transcription, the aspiration is left out, because its occurrence is predictable, and the [ʌj] allophone of /aj/ is replaced by its phoneme.

The contrast between phonetic and phonemic representation is even more striking for the Malay forms given earlier, as shown in table 3.16.

Table 3.16   Phonetic and phonemic transcription of Malay nasal vowels

Phonetic transcription	Phonemic transcription	Word	Predictable property(s) not represented in phonemic transcription
[mẽw̃ãh]	/mewah/	'luxurious'	nasalization
[mãj̃ãn]	/majan/	'stalk'	nasalization
[nãɛ̃ʔ]	/naɛʔ/	'ascend'	nasalization

Here, nasalization on all vowel and glide segments is predictable and is therefore omitted from the phonemic representation.

3.1   Phonetic and phonemic inventories

All languages have both a phonetic level of representation and a phonemic one. The phonetic level represents the allophones of a language. The phonemic level represents the language's phonemes. What this means is that each language has two inventories of sounds: one for the allophones of the language, which is used to transcribe phonetically; the other inventory is of the phonemes of the language and this inventory is used to transcribe phonemically. Since every language has more allophones of phonemes than it has phonemes, phonetic inventories of sounds are always larger than phonemic ones. Table 3.17 illustrates a partial phonetic inventory and the phonemic inventory for the vowels of English. Only those allophones that we have discussed so far in this chapter are listed (the phonetic inventory is thus obviously incomplete).

Table 3.17   Phonetic and phonemic inventories of the vowels of English

Phonetic inventory				Phonemic inventory		
i			u	i		u
ɪ			ʊ	ɪ		ʊ
ej			ow	e		o
ɛ	ʌ	ʌj	oj	ɛ	ʌ	oj
		ʌw			ə	
	ə			æ	aj	ɑ
æ		aj	ɑ		aw	
		aw				

Table 3.18, on the next page, illustrates a phonetic inventory (again based on allophones discussed so far) and the phonemic inventory of English consonants.

Since there are two levels of representation—the phonetic and the phonemic—one obvious question to ask is how they are related to each other. In sections 6 and 7 we consider in detail the nature of the relationship between phonetic and phonemic levels and inventories and show how to formalize this relationship.

Table 3.18 Phonetic and phonemic inventories of the consonants of English

Phonetic inventory	Phonemic inventory
p t k	p t k
pʰ tʰ kʰ	b d g
b d g	tʃ
tʃ	dʒ
dʒ	f θ s ʃ h
f θ s ʃ h	v ð z ʒ
v ð z ʒ	m n ŋ
m n ŋ	l j w
(w) l j w	r
(w̥) l̥ j̊ w̥	
r	
r̥	

4   Above the segment: syllables

So far we have been discussing the distributional properties of segments, and have established the existence of the segmental units of phonological analysis known as phonemes and their allophones. We have also seen that allophonic variation may be conditioned by neighbouring segments. We turn now to a different unit of phonological representation, namely the **syllable**. We will see that syllables are composed of segments, and thus impose an organization on segments; in this sense syllables are **suprasegmental** (above the segment) units. We will also see that the shapes of syllables are governed by universal and language-specific constraints. Finally, we will examine examples of allophonic variation which is conditioned by syllable structure, rather than by neighbouring segments.

4.1   Defining the syllable

As we saw in chapter 2, vowels, glides, liquids, and nasals are sonorant (singable) sounds, while **obstruents** are not; of the sonorant sounds, vowels are most sonorous, and glides, liquids, and nasals are correspondingly less sonorous. A syllable consists of a sonorous element, and its associated non-syllabic (less sonorous) segments. Since vowels are the most sonorous sounds, syllables usually have a vowel nucleus at their core; less sonorous sounds may appear on either side of a nucleus. Thus the word *telegraph* has three syllables because it has three vowels that serve as syllable nuclei.

Native speakers of a language demonstrate their awareness of the sonority values of segments and of the syllable as a unit of phonological structure whenever they count syllables in a word. No English speaker would hesitate to say that the words *telegraph* and *accident* have three syllables, and most speakers would feel confident that the words could be broken up into the syllables [tɛ.lɛ.græf] and [æk.sə.dənt] (the '.' marks syllable divisions informally).

Speakers also know that syllables have internal subsyllabic structure as well. This internal organization of the syllable unit is shown in figure 3.6 with the monosyllabic English word *sprint*. As you can see, syllables consist of an **onset** and a **rhyme**; the rhyme, in turn, consists of the **nucleus** or syllable core, and a **coda**.

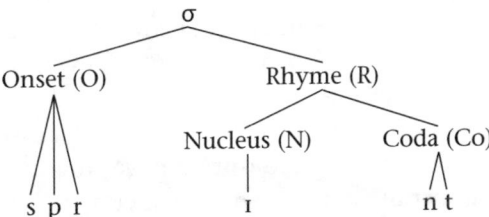

Figure 3.6 Internal structure of a syllable

We will see later on in this chapter that some allophonic variation makes reference to internal subsyllabic structure such as the coda.

There are other kinds of evidence that subsyllabic structure is part of speakers' knowledge. In English rhyming verses, for instance, it is always the rhymes of syllables that match each other (in other words that rhyme), while onsets may vary: thus *sprite* and *fright* rhyme by virtue of having identical rhyme (nucleus and coda) constituents, but the onsets of each are different. In addition, one version of the English language game known as Pig Latin is played by displacing the onset of the first syllable of a word to the end of the word and then tacking on the rhyme *ay* [ej]: thus *strong* becomes *ong-str-ay*, and *swivel* become *ivel-sw-ay*.

Furthermore, when speakers are asked to syllabify words, they are able to do so in ways that are neither random nor variable. The word *extreme* /ɛkstrim/ would never be syllabified as /ɛ.kstrim/ in English, for example. Instead, syllables comply with certain constraints that prohibit them from beginning with a sequence like *kstr* and thus result in the actual syllabification /ɛk.strim/. The examples here are all from English, but similar kinds of evidence for the existence of subsyllabic constituents can be found in many other languages as well.

Table 3.19   Some examples of English syllables

/ə.plɑd/	applaud
/di.klajn/	decline
/ɛk.splen/	explain
/ɪm.prə.vajz/	improvise

All languages have syllables. The shapes of these syllables are governed by various kinds of constraints, but certain universal tendencies are observable: (1) syllable nuclei usually consist of one vowel (V); (2) syllables usually begin with onsets; (3) syllables often end with codas; (4) onsets and codas usually consist of one consonant (C). Putting these tendencies together, we find that the most common types of syllables found in languages throughout the world take the shapes CV and CVC. These are general tendencies, not absolute laws, and languages may, and often do, violate them. But even when a language violates the universal tendencies, the types of syllables that do occur are governed by other constraints on the shapes of the subsyllabic units, O, N, and Co. To illustrate this, we turn to the constraints that govern the phonological shape of consonant sequences in onsets in English.

4.2   Onset constraints and phonotactics

Native speakers of any language intuitively know that certain words that come from other languages sound unusual and they often adjust the segment sequences of these words to conform with the pronunciation requirements of their own language. These intuitions are based on a tacit knowledge of the permissible syllable structures of the speaker's own language. For example, English-speaking students learning Russian have difficulty pronouncing a word like *vprog* /fprɔk/ 'value, good', since the sequence /fpr/ is never found in English onsets. Since speakers typically adjust an impermissible sequence by altering it to a permissible one, many English speakers would pronounce the Russian word [fprɔk] as [fəprɔk], or even delete the initial /f/ and say [prɔk] in order to adjust the impermissible sequence /fpr/ to a permissible English onset. **Phonotactics**, the set of constraints on how sequences of segments pattern, forms part of a speaker's knowledge of the phonology of his or her language.

Some English onsets

English is a language that allows onsets to contain more than one consonant; in this sense, English permits syllables that are more complex than those found in many languages. Nevertheless there are very strict phonotactic constraints on the shapes of English onsets. Table 3.20 contains examples of the possible syllable-initial consonant sequences of English that contain a voiceless stop consonant. These sequences are all illustrated in word-initial position to make them easier to pick out. (Stress marking and phonetic details such as liquid-glide devoicing that are not relevant to the present discussion are omitted here.)

Table 3.20 Initial consonant clusters in English containing a voiceless stop					
Labial + sonorant		**Coronal + sonorant**		**Velar + sonorant**	
[pl]	please	[tl]	—	[kl]	clean
[pr]	proud	[tr]	trade	[kr]	cream
[pw]	—	[tw]	twin	[kw]	queen
[pj]	pure	[tj]	tune (British)	[kj]	cute
[spl]	splat	[stl]	—	[skl]	sclerosis
[spr]	spring	[str]	strip	[skr]	scrap
[spw]	—	[stw]	—	[skw]	squeak
[spj]	spew	[stj]	stew (British)	[skj]	skewer

The examples in table 3.20 show that the first segment of a word-initial three-consonant cluster in English is always *s*; the second consonant in the series is always a voiceless stop, and the third is either a liquid or a glide. These sound patterns can be formally represented as follows:

$$\sigma \left[s \left\{ \begin{matrix} p \\ t \\ k \end{matrix} \right\} \left\{ \begin{matrix} (l) \\ r \\ (w) \\ j \end{matrix} \right. \right.$$

In this formalization, σ indicates the boundary of a syllable and the curly braces designate 'either/or'. The sounds in parentheses are not found in all combinations. An important observation about the types of onsets that are allowed in English is that the consonant combinations are not random: in fact (1) the consonant combinations are dependent primarily on the manners of articulation of the consonants and (2) sonorant consonants (here liquids and glides) are closer to the nucleus than are stops and fricatives. Both these phonotactic constraints reflect universal restrictions on consonant combinations, and are found in other languages that allow complex onsets.

4.3   Accidental and systematic gaps

Although there are twenty-four possible two- and three-consonant syllable-initial sequences in English containing a voiceless stop, not all of these combinations are exploited in the vocabulary of the language.

Some gaps in the inventory of possible English words include *snool, splick, sklop, flis, trok,* and *krif,* although none of these forms violates any constraints on onset combinations found in English. Gaps in a language's vocabulary that correspond to non-occurring but possible forms are called **accidental gaps**. Occasionally, an accidental gap will be filled by the invention of a new word. The word *Kodak* is one such invented word; its shape conforms to the phonotactic constraints of English, but it only became part of English vocabulary in this century. Borrowed words such as *perestroika* (from Russian), *taco* (from Spanish), and *Zen* (from Japanese) are readily accepted by English speakers when, as is the case in these three examples, their syllable structures conform to the phonotactic patterns of the language.

Table 3.20 has shown which syllable-initial consonant clusters involving voiceless stops are permissible in English. Gaps in the occurring syllable structures of a language that result not by accident, but from the exclusion of certain sequences are called **systematic gaps**. Certain onset sequences like /bz/, /pt/, and /fp/ are systematic gaps in the pattern of English. They are outright unacceptable to English speakers, and never occur in spoken English. Instead, such sequences will be adjusted phonologically when they are pronounced in spontaneous speech. This can be seen in the case of borrowings from other languages into English. Many Greek words beginning with *ps-* and *pt-* have been absorbed into English, as the spellings of *psychology, psoriasis,* and *pterodactyl* attest. In all of them the impermissible syllable-initial clusters *ps-* and *pt-* have been reduced to *s-* or *t-* in onsets of spoken English. However, when these same forms occur word-internally, where their syllabification is different, the 'lost' segments may resurface. For example, the *pter* of *pterodactyl* means 'wing'; both consonants are heard in the word *helicopter,* where English syllabification has resulted in a structure *he.li.cop.ter* in which the members of the cluster *pt* belong to different syllables.

There are other words that violate phonotactic constraints but that nonetheless do commonly appear in spoken English, such as *pueblo* [pw̥eblow], and *Tlingit* [tl̥ɪŋɪt]. The fact that such words and pronunciations do occur in spoken English even though they violate phonotactic constraints is due to the fact that some phonotactic constraints are stronger than others and thus less likely to be violated. Thus, the sequences *ps-, *pt-* and *bz-* are excluded from the initial position of English syllables because English has a very strong and thus absolute constraint against allowing stop-stop or stop-fricative clusters in onsets. In contrast, the restriction against sequences like *pw-* and *tl* in English onsets is due to a weaker and thus violable constraint on stop-sonorant onset sequences with the same place of articulation: for example, a labiovelar glide is not usually permitted to occur after a labial consonant, and an alveolar stop such as /t/ is not usually permitted to precede an alveolar /l/ in English words.

Language-specific phonotactics

It is important to emphasize again that certain aspects of the particular constraints discussed in the previous section are universal and thus form part of human linguistic knowledge, whereas others are language-specific. An onset like *pl* is found in many languages besides English (for example, in Russian, Thai, and French), while an onset sequence like *lp* is never found. We may therefore say that no restrictions against an onset like *pl* appear to exist as part of human universal linguistic knowledge, while the non-existence of onsets like **lp* suggest that something in their phonetic makeup disqualifies them from occurring in language. Language-specific constraints, on the other hand, hold true for individual languages such as English, and they may or may not be found in other languages. Each language has its own set of restrictions on the phonological shapes of its syllable constituents. Speakers of Russian, for example, are quite accustomed to pronouncing onset sequences such as *ps-, fsl-,* and *mgl-,* which are not found in English (see table 3.21).

Table 3.21	Some onset sequences in Russian
[psa]	'dog's'
[fslux]	'aloud'
[mgla]	'fog'

Phonotactic constraints of the kind that we have seen for English represent one kind of phonological knowledge. You might, however, wonder what prevents English words like *extreme, applaud, decline, explain,* and *improvise* from being syllabified as the incorrect **/ɛks.trim/, */ʌp.lɑd/, */dik.lajn/, */ɛks.plen/,* and **/ɪmp.rəv.ajz/,* instead of the correct /ɛk.strim/, /ʌ.plɑd/, /di.klajn/, /ɛk.splen/, and /ɪm.prə.vajz/. In the incorrect syllabifications, the syllable divisions do not violate any phonotactic constraints, so the question is why the syllabifications are nevertheless incorrect. The answer to this question is that such syllabifications are prevented by a universal constraint on general syllable shapes, rather than by a phonotactic constraint on segment sequences. As mentioned in section 4.1, there is a universal syllable-shape constraint which encourages languages to make syllables with onsets; as a result, onsets in languages tend to be as large as possible. The next section illustrates the way this universal constraint works by providing a procedure for establishing the association of consonants and vowels within syllables.

4.4   Setting up syllables

Each language defines its own syllable structure through the interaction of universal and language-specific constraints. The process for setting up syllables in a given language involves three steps: Nucleus-formation, Onset-formation, and Coda-formation; a fourth step, Word-level construction, ensures that syllables are incorporated into word-level units. The first step reflects the universal tendency for syllables to have a sonorant core; the second step reflects the tendency for syllables to have onsets, and the third step reflects the tendency for syllables to have codas. Ordering Onset-formation before Coda-formation reflects a crosslinguistic tendency of *Onsets before codas:* (in a sequence of VCV, the consonant C will always be syllabified as an onset rather than a coda), and ensures that onsets gather up as many consonants as possible before any codas are formed.

- **Step a** *Nucleus-formation:* Since the syllable nucleus is the only obligatory constituent of a syllable, it is constructed first. Each vowel segment in a word makes up a syllabic **nucleus**. To represent this, link a vowel to an N above it by drawing an association line. Above each nucleus symbol, place an R (for **rhyme**—in section 4.1 we saw that the rhyme consists of the nucleus plus the coda), which is filled out in step c below. Above each R, place a σ symbol; link all with association lines.

Figure 3.7

- **Step b** *Onset-formation:* The longest sequence of consonants to the left of each nucleus that does not violate the phonotactic constraints of the language in question is the **onset** of the syllable. Link these consonants to an O and join it to the same syllable as the vowel to the right. Note that there is no onset in the first syllable of *extreme*.

Figure 3.8

- **Step c** *Coda-formation:* Any remaining unassociated consonants to the right of each nucleus form the **coda**, and are linked to a Co above them. This Co is associated with the syllable nucleus to its left in the rhyme. A syllable with a coda is called a **closed syllable** (a syllable without a coda is called **open**).

Figure 3.9

- **Step d** *Word-level construction:* Syllables that make up a single form (usually a word) branch out from the representation *Wd* (this step is frequently omitted from phonological representations to save space; the complete representation is understood even when *Wd* is not written out).

Figure 3.10

The steps in the procedure just outlined reflect universal constraints on syllable shapes. These interact with universal and language-specific phonotactic constraints. Given the procedure and the phonotactic constraints, we can now explain why words such as *applaud* and *explain* are syllabified as /ʌ.plɑd/ and /ɛk.splen/. In accordance with step b, Onset-formation, all the consonants in the clusters between the two vowel nuclei in each word (*pl* and *kspl*, respectively) could be syllabified as onsets of the second syllable. Thus *pl* is a possible candidate for an onset. According to the phonotactic constraints that are active in English, it is also a permissible onset, so both consonants are syllabified as part of the second syllable onset. In contrast, *kspl* is not a permissible onset in English; *spl* is a permissible onset, however, so the last three consonants of *kspl* are syllabified as part of the second syllable onset, and the first consonant *k* is left to be syllabified as a coda to the preceding syllable.

Figure 3.11   Syllabification: onsets before codas and phonotactic constraints

Some further syllabification

This procedure is used to syllabify forms in any language. An example from Turkish demonstrates in more detail how this universal syllabification procedure works. Turkish has different syllable structure constraints than English. As in English, onsets are optional in Turkish, but when present, may consist of no more than one segment—clearly not a constraint found in English. A nucleus may consist of a long vowel (which is equivalent to two short vowels in length) or a short vowel. Codas can be no more than two segments long, and are largely limited to the following combinations: fricative-stop (for example, *-ft$_\sigma$*), or sonorant-obstruent (for example, *-rp$_\sigma$*).

The following words can be syllabified in the steps given above (steps c and d have been collapsed here). Note how the procedure leads to different syllabifications of the word *alt* 'bottom' in steps b and c of the examples.

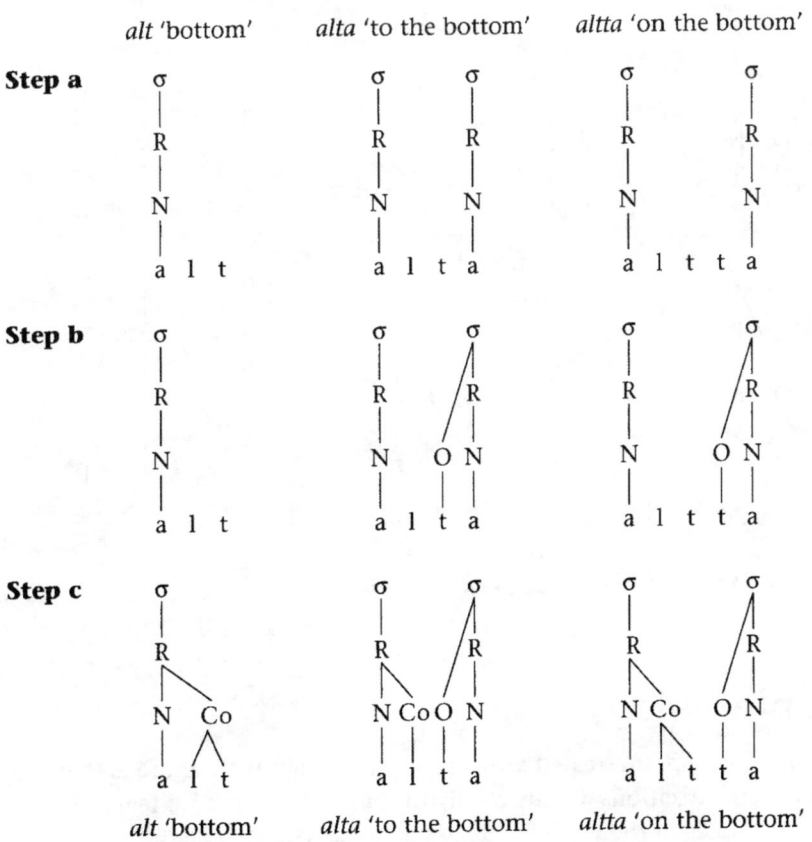

Figure 3.12 Examples of syllabification in Turkish

In these examples, the *t* of *alt* 'bottom' is assigned to the coda of the first syllable, since there is no syllable with an available onset position following it. However, the same phoneme *t* in *alta* 'to the bottom' is assigned to the onset of the second syllable, since onsets are filled first and *t* is available to fill the position. In *altta* 'on the bottom', the two *t*s fill the available coda and onset positions of their respective syllables.

As a final example of the procedure, the following figure demonstrates the syllabification of the English words *slim*, *decline*, and *scrimp*.

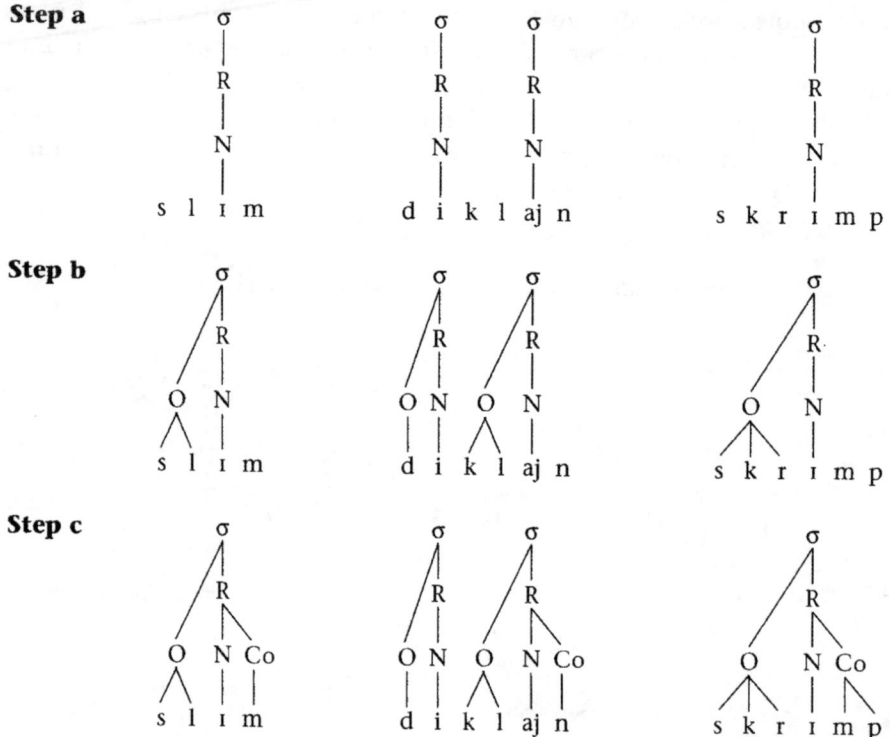

Figure 3.13 Examples of syllabification in English

With this method in mind, we can now consider the relevance of syllables to phonological description.

4.5 Syllabic phonology

One reason that syllables are treated as units of phonological structure is that they are relevant to stating generalizations about the distribution of allophonic features. The next sections provide examples of the role of syllables and subsyllabic constituents in phonological patterns. The fact that syllables and their internal constituents have such a role is thus evidence that they are part of the knowledge that speakers have of the phonology of their language.

Aspiration in English

As table 3.22 shows, the voiceless stops of English each have an aspirated and an unaspirated allophone.[3]

Table 3.22	English aspiration				
A		**B**		**C**	
[pʰǽn]	pan	[spǽn]	span	[slǽp]	slap
[pʰéjn]	pain	[spéjn]	Spain	[slát]	slot
[pʰówk]	poke	[spówk]	spoke	[blák]	block
[tʰówn]	tone	[stówn]	stone		
[kʰín]	kin	[skín]	skin		
[pʰərspájr]	perspire	[splǽt]	splat		
[tʰəméjɾow]	tomato	[ʌpsét]	upset		
[kʰənú]	canoe				
[əpʰán]	upon				
[ətʰǽk]	attack				
[tʰəkʰílə]	tequila				

The distribution of aspiration can be stated generally by referring to syllable structure, and, in the case of the distribution of unaspirated stops, by referring to the subsyllabic units, onset and coda.

Table 3.23	Distribution of aspirated stops in English
Aspirated stops	**Unaspirated stops**
• syllable-initially	Elsewhere • in a syllable onset preceded by *s* (whether another C follows or not) • in a coda

The phonemic representations of the three English stops are unaspirated, since aspiration is predictable. The environments where aspiration occurs can be stated very generally by referring to syllable structure.

8)
English voiceless stops are aspirated syllable-initially.

This statement accounts for all the data in column A of table 3.22, where voiceless stops appear syllable-initially. No aspiration is found in the forms in columns B and C since the voiceless stops appear either as the second member of the syllable onset (in *span, Spain, spoke, stone,* and *skin*), or in a coda, as in *upset*.[4]

Phonetic length in English vowels

English offers a second example of the phonological relevance of syllables. Phonetic length is predictable in English vowels, as the next examples show.

Table 3.24	Phonetic length in English: long vowels before voiced coda consonants		
A		**B**	
bad	[bæ:d]	bat	[bæt]
Abe	[e:jb]	ape	[ejp]
phase	[fe:jz]	face	[fejs]
leave	[li:v]	leaf	[lif]
tag	[tʰæ:g]	tack	[tʰæk]
brogue	[bro:wg]	broke	[browk]
		tame	[tʰẽjm]
		meal	[mil]
		soar	[sor]
		show	[ʃow]

English vowels are shorter before voiceless consonants, before sonorant consonants, and in word-final position; they are longer before voiced non-sonorant consonants as long as these non-sonorant consonants are in coda-position in the same syllable. As the next examples show, if vowels are followed by non-sonorant consonants that are onsets of the following syllable, the vowels are short. Thus in table 3.25, the first-syllable vowels all precede voiced, non-sonorant consonants, but they are short since the voiced consonant is in the following syllable.

Table 3.25	Short vowels before voiced onset consonants in English	
obey	[ow.bej]	/obe/
redo	[ri.du]	/ridu/
regard	[ri.gard]	/rigard/
ogre	[ow.gər]	/ogər/

In order for an English vowel to be long, it must be followed by a voiced obstruent in the same syllable. The following generalization can now be made.

9)
English vowels are long when followed by a voiced obstruent in the coda-position of the same syllable.

As the analyses of the distribution of aspiration and vowel length in English have shown, the use of syllabic representations in phonology permits us to make more general statements about certain allophonic patterns in language than if we use only statements that do not make reference to syllable structure.

Syllables and stress in English

English provides a final example of the relevance of syllabic units to phonological analysis. Recall (from chapter 2, section 8.3) that stress is defined as the perceived prominence of one or more syllabic elements over others in a word. In some languages—English among them—the structure of individual syllables plays a role in determining which vowel is stressed. Consider the data in table 3.26.

Table 3.26	English noun stress	
A	**B**	**C**
agénda	aróma	cínema
consénsus	Manitóba	cábinet
appéndix	horízon	vénison
synópsis	Elíza	América
veránda	Minnesóta	jávelin

The words in columns A and B are all stressed on the next-to-last (penultimate) syllable, while the words in column C are all stressed on the third syllable from the end of the word (the antepenultimate syllable), as the form *America* makes clear. Although the stressing of the words at first may seem arbitrary, reference to syllable structure makes clear that there is some system underlying the assignment of stress here.

Syllabifying the words in each column reveals what stress assignment is based on. Figure 3.14 provides the syllabification of one word from each column. Words are provided in phonetic transcription.

Column A
Penultimate stress

Column B
Penultimate stress

Column C
Antepenultimate stress

Figure 3.14 Syllable-based stress in English

All the words in column A share a correlation between their syllabification and their stress: the stressed penultimate syllable has a coda (recall that a syllable with a coda is said to be closed). All the words in column B also share a syllabic characteristic: their nucleus contains a tense vowel. Although the syllable is not closed, the nucleus vowel with two elements in it (the vowel-glide sequence) is now represented as branching. Tense vowels, in other words, have the same effect on stress assignment in English as closed syllables. Both closed syllables and syllables with two elements in the nucleus are referred to as heavy syllables. Compare these words with the representative item from column C. We see that the penultimate syllable is not heavy: it is neither closed nor does it contain a branching nucleus. With these facts before us, we can state our generalization. We will be careful to limit it to English *nouns*, that is, words that label or describe some thing or state (see chapter 5, section 1).

10)
English nouns are stressed on the penultimate syllable when it is heavy; otherwise, they are stressed on the antepenultimate syllable.

We have limited our generalization to English nouns because the full stress pattern of English is rather elaborate. Nevertheless, there is no doubt that syllabification plays a central role in the determining of stress placement in English.

5 Features

In the previous section, we saw the role that syllable structure plays in verse, language games, and especially in allophonic variation. We also saw that universal and language-specific constraints govern the ways in which segment units combine to form the suprasegmental units of structure known as syllables. In this section we will discover that segments themselves are composed of even smaller, subsegmental, phonological units known as **features**. In fact, features are like atoms: they are the smallest units of phonology and as such are the basic building blocks of human speech sounds.

5.1 Why we use features

There are a number of reasons why linguists consider features to be the most basic units of the phonology.

Features as independent and coordinated phonetic elements

We have already seen in chapter 1 that speech is produced by a number of independent but coordinated articulatory activities such as voicing, tongue position, lip rounding, and so on. For example, when we produce the voiceless bilabial stop [p], the vocal cords in the larynx are open and not vibrating (hence the sound is voiceless), and the lips are actively pressed together to form a complete constriction (hence the sound is a labial stop). Each sound is thus the result of the coordinated articulatory activity of the larynx, and the various articulators, such as the tongue body, the tongue blade, the lips, and the velum, found in the oral and nasal cavities of the vocal tract. We assume that segments are themselves composed of smaller units known as features as a way of modelling this phonetic reality.

Features reflect the articulatory basis of speech in the sense that each feature encodes one of the independently controllable aspects of speech production. For example, in the case of [p], the feature [-voice] reflects laryngeal activity; the feature [oLABIAL] reflects the activity of the lips; and the feature [-continuant] reflects the stop manner of articulation (note that features are written in square brackets; the use of '+' and '-' signs and capital versus lower case letters is explained below); an 'o' before a feature indicates that the articulation is active.

As a further example, consider the sound [ɑ]. This sound is produced with a low, back and tense tongue body (dorsal) position, with no rounding of the lips (therefore no labial activity) and little constriction. It is a vowel, and therefore is voiced and sonorant as well. All these phonetic properties are represented in terms of separate features in the feature representation in figure 3.15. In this representation the features of the segment are listed in an array called a **matrix**. This is a common way of presenting sets of features.

Figure 3.15 Feature representation for the English vowel /ɑ/

Features and natural classes

A second reason for viewing segments as composed of features is that doing so gives us an economical way of characterizing segments as members of natural classes. **Natural classes** are classes of sounds that share a feature or features and that pattern together in sound systems.

To see what is meant by this, consider the set of English sounds /p/, /t/, /k/, /f/, /s/, /ʃ/, and /b/, /d/, /g/, /v/, /z/, /ʒ/ given in figure 3.16. All these sounds belong to the class of obstruents (/tʃ/, /dʒ/, /θ/ and /ð/ are also obstruents, but we will ignore them for now). In order to capture this fact, we can say that they are all [-sonorant] (the '-' means 'not' in this context; definitions of the features are given in section 5.2). In addition, a subset of the members of this [-sonorant] class, namely /p/, /t/, /k/, /f/, /s/, /ʃ/, all of which differ in place and (in part) in manner of articulation, can be readily distinguished from the subset, /b/, /d/, /g/, /v/, /z/, /ʒ/, by the single feature [voice] alone. Finally a third feature, [continuant] (which refers to whether or not a sound is produced with continuous, free airflow) can distinguish all the (non-continuous) stops in the obstruent class, /p/, /t/, /k/, /b/, /d/, /g/ from all the (continuous) fricatives, /f/, /s/, /ʃ/, /v/, /z/, /ʒ/.

	[-sonorant]	
[-voice]		[+voice]
p	b	
t	d	[-continuant]
k	g	
f	v	
s	z	[+continuant]
ʃ	ʒ	

Figure 3.16 Natural classes: obstruents in English

Using these three features we are able to capture nine different natural classes of sounds; these are given in table 3.27.

Table 3.27   Nine natural classes: obstruents in English

$\begin{bmatrix}\text{-sonorant}\end{bmatrix}$	$\begin{bmatrix}\text{-sonorant}\\\text{-continuant}\end{bmatrix}$	$\begin{bmatrix}\text{-sonorant}\\\text{+continuant}\end{bmatrix}$	$\begin{bmatrix}\text{-sonorant}\\\text{-voice}\end{bmatrix}$	$\begin{bmatrix}\text{-sonorant}\\\text{+voice}\end{bmatrix}$	$\begin{bmatrix}\text{-sonorant}\\\text{-continuant}\\\text{-voice}\end{bmatrix}$	$\begin{bmatrix}\text{-sonorant}\\\text{-continuant}\\\text{+voice}\end{bmatrix}$	$\begin{bmatrix}\text{-sonorant}\\\text{+continuant}\\\text{-voice}\end{bmatrix}$	$\begin{bmatrix}\text{-sonorant}\\\text{+continuant}\\\text{+voice}\end{bmatrix}$
p t k b d g f s ʃ v z ʒ	p t k b d g	f s ʃ v z ʒ	p t k f s ʃ	b d g v z ʒ	p t k	b d g	f s ʃ	v z ʒ

Any natural class requires fewer features to define it than to define any one of its members. Thus in table 3.27, the largest class, that of the obstruents, is defined by only one feature, while the four classes containing three segments each are defined by three features each.

Every set of sounds that is characterized by one or more features and that therefore constitutes a natural class has the potential to pattern together in some way in the phonology of a language. For instance, we saw above that aspiration in English affects /p/, /t/, and /k/, the [-sonorant, -continuant, -voice] sounds of the language. All and only these sounds are affected by the aspiration process. An interesting point about features is that their use allows us to exclude sounds from (as well as to include them in) natural classes. Thus, because /b/ is [+voice], it does not belong to the same class in English as /p/, /t/, and /k/. As a result /b/ is not affected by aspiration.

Table 3.28 provides an additional illustration of the use of features to distinguish natural classes, in this case, the class of front and back vowels in English. Again we see that fewer features are needed to define the larger class of English front vowels than to capture the vowel /æ/ alone.

Table 3.28   Two natural classes: front and back vowels in English

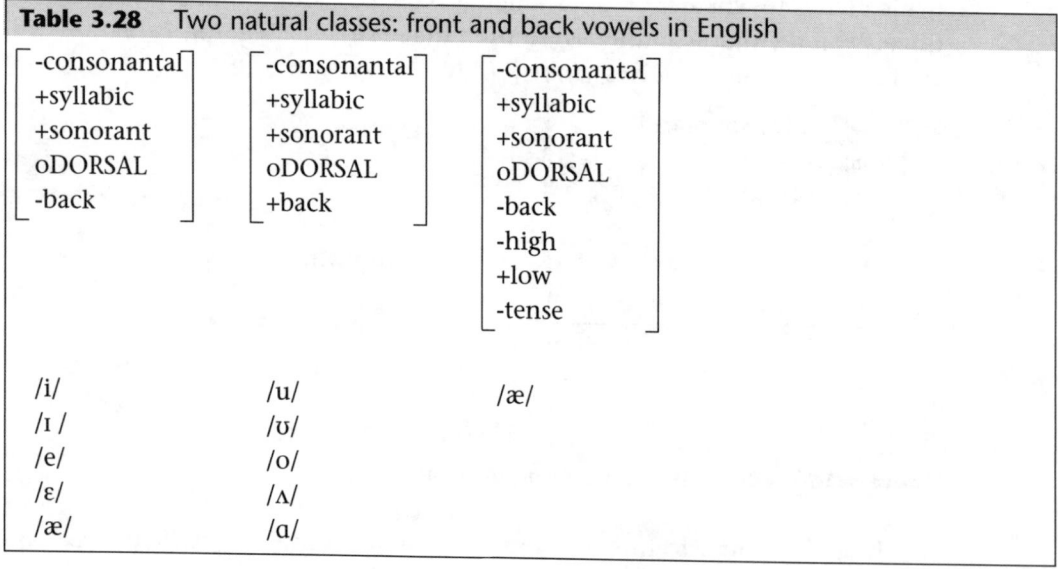

$\begin{bmatrix}\text{-consonantal}\\\text{+syllabic}\\\text{+sonorant}\\\text{oDORSAL}\\\text{-back}\end{bmatrix}$	$\begin{bmatrix}\text{-consonantal}\\\text{+syllabic}\\\text{+sonorant}\\\text{oDORSAL}\\\text{+back}\end{bmatrix}$	$\begin{bmatrix}\text{-consonantal}\\\text{+syllabic}\\\text{+sonorant}\\\text{oDORSAL}\\\text{-back}\\\text{-high}\\\text{+low}\\\text{-tense}\end{bmatrix}$
/i/ /ɪ/ /e/ /ɛ/ /æ/	/u/ /ʊ/ /o/ /ʌ/ /ɑ/	/æ/

In preceding sections we listed those segments of English that contrast, and that are therefore the phonemes of English. Because features define natural classes, it is not just individual phonemes such as /p/, /b/, /k/, and /g/ that contrast in English; in fact, the entire class of voiced stops contrasts with the class of voiceless stops. All the contrasts found in the English sound system (and in the sound system of any language) can be defined in terms of the features that make up those phonemes. Thus, the distinctions between /p/ and /b/, /t/ and /d/, and /k/ and /g/ all reside in the feature [voice]. In addition, words like *pit* and *bit*, which constitute a minimal pair, contrast in the segments /p/ and /b/, and /p/ and /b/ themselves contrast in the feature [voice]. What these examples show us then, is that features as well as segments can be contrastive. When a feature is the source of phonemic contrasts in a language, we say that it is a **distinctive feature** in the language. Thus, [voice] is a distinctive feature in English.

Other features provide for other contrasts. For example, we can capture the contrast between /t/ and /s/ in English with the feature [continuant]. Both /t/ and /s/ are voiceless and have an alveolar point of articulation. By viewing the relevant distinctive feature as [continuant], we can use the same feature to distinguish between /p/ and /f/, /b/ and /v/, and /d/ and /z/.

Table 3.29	Stop-fricative contrasts as a feature
[-continuant]	[+continuant]
p	f
b	v
t	s
d	z

By systematically examining the phonemic contrasts of a language, we can extract the distinctive features and use these irreducible linguistic elements to describe the phonemic inventory.

Features, processes, and allophonic variation

A third reason for using features is that reference to features enables us to understand the nature of allophonic variation more exactly. Viewed from the perspective of features, allophonic variation is seen to be not simply the substitution of one allophone for another, but rather the environmentally conditioned change or specification of a feature or features. The liquid-glide devoicing that occurs in English words like *tree* and *twinkle*, for example, is a change in the value of the feature [voice] from [+voice] to [-voice] after voiceless (i.e., [-voice]) stop consonants. Similarly, the vowel and glide nasalization that occurs in Malay forms like /mewah/ [mẽw̃ãh] 'luxurious' is a change in the value of the feature [nasal] from [-nasal] to [+nasal] following a nasal (i.e., [+nasal]) consonant (see 7)).

We saw above that features reflect the fact that speech is produced by a number of independent but coordinated articulatory activities. Certain features, however, reflect classes of sounds that are not always reflected in the traditional descriptive terminology of phonetics that was introduced in chapter 1, but that are nevertheless relevant to phonological patterning. For example, the feature [CORONAL] (the use of capitals as opposed to lower case letters here reflects a difference in feature type which will be clarified below) refers to the class of sounds made with the tongue tip or blade raised: this class includes sounds made with inter-dental, alveolar, and alveopalatal places of articulation. It turns out that just this feature is required to state a constraint on the selection of consonant sequences in coda position in English: according to this constraint, when a vowel is tense and followed by two consonants (*pint*), or when a vowel is lax and followed by three consonants (*next* [nɛkst]), the final consonant in the coda must always be [CORONAL] (t, d, s, z, θ, ð, ʃ, ʒ, tʃ, or dʒ). Although the feature [CORONAL] does not reflect a traditional phonetic term, it plays a very important role in the phonologies of many languages. This fact shows us that features reflect articulatory reality in a way that is more than just presenting traditional phonetic descriptions in a different guise.

5.2   Feature representations

We have seen that segments are composed of subsegmental units or features and that features reflect phonetic reality. Since features are considered to be the basic building blocks of speech sounds, and thus of phonology, linguists have attempted to state all possible phonological facts about language with the fewest number of features possible. Only a limited number of features—currently around twenty-four—have been proposed. Features thus constitute an important part of a theory of what is possible (and what is not possible) in the phonological behaviour of human beings. In this section we present and define all the features that are needed to characterize the sounds of English, as well as of many other languages.

Defining the features of English

Most features have labels that reflect traditional articulatory terms such as [voice], [consonantal], and [nasal]. These features require little further description. A few features have less familiar labels, such as [CORONAL] and [anterior]. From this point on, features will be used to describe classes of sounds. At the same time, we will continue throughout the book to use terms such as *consonant, glide,* and *obstruent* (a fricative, affricate, or non-nasal stop) in phonetic description. The traditional terminology will be maintained because it is still widely used in phonetic description.

Features are organized into groups that reflect natural classes. The following headings indicate what these classes are and how the features represent them. Most of the features given below are written in lower case and can have one of two values, '+' or '-', each of which defines a particular class of sounds. For example, [+voice] sounds involve vibration or voicing in the larynx, while [-voice] sounds involve an open glottis and therefore no vibration or voicing. Three of the features ([LABIAL], [CORONAL], and [DORSAL]), are written in upper case and do not have '+' and '-' values. Why this is so will be made clear below.

- **Major class features** *features that represent the classes consonant, obstruent, and sonorant (nasal, liquid, glide, vowel)*

   [±consonantal] Sounds that are [+consonantal] are produced with a major obstruction in the vocal tract. All non-sonorant consonants, as well as liquids and nasals are [+consonantal]. Glides and vowels are [-consonantal].

[±syllabic] Sounds that can act as syllable peaks are [+syllabic]; this includes vowels, and syllabic liquids or syllabic nasals. All other sounds are [-syllabic].

[±sonorant] All and only those sounds that are 'singable' are [+sonorant]; this includes vowels, glides, liquids, and nasals (even if the [+sonorant] sounds are voiceless). All non-singable sounds (obstruents) are [-sonorant].

Table 3.30 illustrates how the major class features are used to divide sounds into classes. Note that nasals and liquids have the same values for the three major class features; to distinguish these two classes from each other additional (manner) features are therefore needed.

Table 3.30	Use of major class features				
	Obstruents	**Nasals**	**Liquids**	**Glides**	**Vowels**
[±consonantal]	+	+	+	-	-
[±syllabic]	-	-	-	-	+
[±sonorant]	-	+	+	+	+
Examples:	p d v tʃ	m n	l r	j w	i a

The manner features given next represent manners of articulation. Their use is particularly important in distinguishing the following classes: stops/affricates as opposed to fricatives ([±continuant]); affricates as opposed to stops ([±DR]); nasals from non-nasals ([±nasal]); and laterals from non-laterals ([±lateral]).

- **Manner features** *features that represent manner of articulation*

  [±continuant] Sounds produced with free or nearly free airflow through the centre of the oral cavity are [+continuant]; these include vowels, glides, the non-lateral liquid *r*, and fricatives. All other sounds are [-continuant]; these include nasal and oral stops, and the lateral liquid *l*.

  [±delayed release] ([±DR]) In the stop portion [t] of an affricate sound such as [tʃ], the tongue is slower in leaving the roof of the mouth than when a stop like [t] is produced on its own. Hence affricates are said to be produced with 'delayed release'. All and only affricates such as [tʃ] and [dʒ] are [+delayed release]. All other sounds are [-delayed release].

  [±nasal] Sounds produced with a lowered velum are [+nasal]; this includes nasal stops and all nasalized sounds. Sounds that are oral, and thus produced with a raised velum are [-nasal].

  [±lateral] All and only varieties of *l* are [+lateral]. All other sounds are [-lateral].

Voicing, aspiration, and glottal constriction are all the result of laryngeal activity. To represent different laryngeal states, we use the features [±voice], [±spread glottis], and [±constricted glottis].

- **Laryngeal features** *features that represent laryngeal activity*

  [±voice] All voiced sounds are [+voice]; all voiceless sounds are [-voice].

  [±spread glottis] ([±SG]) All aspirated consonants are [+SG]; all others are [-SG].

[±constricted glottis] ([±CG]) All sounds made with a closed glottis are [+CG]; all others are [-CG]. In English only the glottal stop [ʔ] is [+CG].

The last set of features is used to represent the supralaryngeal (above the larynx) articulatory activity which determines place of articulation. There are two types of articulatory features. The first type includes the features [LABIAL], [CORONAL], and [DORSAL] which are used specifically to represent and to distinguish the *articulators* that are active in executing (producing) particular places of articulation. For instance, the sound [k] is produced when the dorsum or body of the tongue touches the velum (soft palate) to form a constriction. [k] thus has a *velar* place of articulation; this place of articulation is executed (produced) by moving the dorsal (tongue body) articulator. The second type of articulatory feature includes all the other place of articulation features (e.g., [high], [back], etc.) listed below. These features are used to distinguish different settings for each of the active articulators and are in this sense specific to individual articulators. For instance, when [k] is pronounced, the tongue body is always positioned high and back in the oral cavity, and therefore the [k] is [+high] and [+back] as well as being [DORSAL].

- **Place of articulation features** *features that represent supralaryngeal activity*

   [LABIAL] This feature represents the labial articulator: any sound that is produced with involvement of one or both of the lips is [LABIAL].

   [±round] A sound produced with the labial articulator may be produced by protruding the lips; such sounds are [+round]; labial sounds made with no lip protrusion are [-round]. [+round] labial sounds are rounded vowels and the rounded labiovelar glide [w]. [-round] labial sounds are sounds like [p, b, f, v].

   [CORONAL] This feature represents the coronal articulator: any sound that is produced with involvement of the tongue tip or blade raised is [CORONAL].

   [±anterior] All coronal sounds articulated in front of the alveopalatal region (interdentals and alveolars) are [+anterior]; coronal sounds articulated at or behind the alveopalatal region (alveopalatals) are [-anterior].

   [±strident] All 'noisy' coronal fricatives and affricates ([s z ʃ ʒ tʃ dʒ]) are [+strident]; all other coronal fricatives and affricates ([θ, ð]) are [-strident].

   [DORSAL] This feature represents the dorsal articulator: any sound that is produced with involvement of the body of the tongue is [DORSAL].

   [±high] Dorsal consonants (velars or palatals) or vowels produced with the tongue body raised from a central position in the oral cavity are [+high]. Sounds produced with a neutral or lowered tongue body are [-high].

   [±low] Vowels produced with the tongue body lowered from a central position in the oral cavity are [+low]. All other vowels are [-low].

   [±back] Dorsal consonants or vowels produced with the tongue body behind the palatal region (hard palate) in the oral cavity are [+back]. Sounds produced with the tongue body at the palatal region are [-back].

   [±tense] Vowels that are tense are [+tense]; vowels that are lax are [-tense].

   [±reduced] The vowel schwa ([ə]) is a lax and exceptionally brief vowel and is therefore [+reduced]; all other vowels are [-reduced].

To set the articulator features apart from other features, they are written with capitals. They do not have '+' and '-' values associated with them because if they are not being used to execute an articulation, they are simply inactive and are therefore absent from a representation. In other words, if a sound is a velar [k], it is produced with the tongue body, not with the lips or the tongue blade or tip. Consequently, the lips and the tongue blade or tip are not actively involved in the production of the sound and therefore the feature specification for [k] does not include the articulator features [LABIAL] and [CORONAL].

Features like [±round], [±anterior], or [±high], which are executed by particular articulators, are used only to distinguish sounds produced by those articulators. Thus, for instance, only sounds like [k] that are produced with the tongue body and that are thus [DORSAL], may be [±high], [±low], or [±back]. No sounds made with other articulators are represented with values for these features.

To see exactly how the articulation features are used to represent the various places of articulation of the consonants found in English, let us look at table 3.31. In the feature representations, 'o' indicates that the relevant articulator is active in the production of a sound. Where no 'o' is present it means that the articulator is inactive.

Table 3.31   Use of place of articulation features in representing some English consonants

	Labials		Dentals	Alveolars	Alveopalatals[5]	Palatals	Velars
	p	w	θ	s	ʃ	j	k
LABIAL	o	o					
[±round]	-	+					
CORONAL			o	o	o		
[±anterior]			+	+	-		
[±strident]			-	+	+		
DORSAL	o					o	o
[±high]	+					+	+
[±back]	+					-	+
[±low]	-					-	-

The feature representations in table 3.31 can be understood as follows:

- [p] is produced with the lips in an unrounded state. It is therefore a [LABIAL], [-round] sound. The tongue blade and the tongue body are not used in the production of [p] and therefore it has no feature specifications for the coronal and dorsal articulators nor for [CORONAL] or [DORSAL] features.

- [θ s ʃ] are all [CORONAL] sounds because they are produced with the tongue blade. [θ s] are produced with the tongue blade before or at the alveolar ridge and are therefore [+anterior], while [ʃ] is produced with the tongue blade behind the alveolar ridge and is therefore [-anterior]. [θ] is produced with a quiet airflow and so is [-strident], while [s ʃ] are produced with noisy airflow and so are [+strident]. Since neither the lips nor the tongue body are used to produce these sounds they have no specifications for the labial and dorsal articulators nor for [LABIAL] or [DORSAL] features.

- [j k] are both produced with the tongue body and are therefore [DORSAL] sounds. Both have a raised tongue body so are [+high], but [j] is pronounced with the tongue body at the hard palate, so is [-back], while [k] is pronounced with the tongue body behind the hard palate, so is [+back]. Since sounds cannot have both a raised and a lowered tongue body simultaneously, and since [j] and [k] are both [+high], they are also both [-low]. Finally, since neither the lips nor the tongue blade are used to produce these sounds, they have no specifications for the labial and coronal articulators nor for [LABIAL] or [CORONAL] features.

- [w] is a labiovelar sound and is thus coarticulated: it is produced with both a tongue body that is raised and behind the hard palate, *and* with lip rounding. This means that both the dorsum and the lips are used to produce [w], so it is executed with two articulators acting simultaneously. It is therefore both [LABIAL] and [DORSAL]; as a [LABIAL] sound it is [+round], and as a [DORSAL] sound is it [+high, +back, -low]. Since the tongue blade is not used to produce this sound, it has no specifications for the [CORONAL] articulator or for coronal features.

Table 3.32 exemplifies how the place of articulation features are used to represent vowels in English. All the vowels in the table are produced with an active tongue body and therefore are [DORSAL]; this is true of all vowels, in English and in all other languages. Vowels that involve lip rounding are also produced with the [LABIAL] articulator. [CORONAL] is never used in the feature representations of vowels. All vowels except schwa are unreduced and therefore specified as [-reduced].

Table 3.32	Use of place of articulation features in representing some English vowels			
	u	ɛ	ə	ɑ
LABIAL	o			
[±round]	+			
DORSAL	o	o	o	o
[±high]	+	-	-	-
[±low]	-	-	-	+
[±back]	+	-	+	+
[±tense]	+	-	-	+
[±reduced]	-	-	+	-

- [u] is a high, back, tense vowel, and is therefore specified as [+high], [+back], and [+tense]. Since it is round, it is [LABIAL, +round] in addition to being [DORSAL]. Since it is [+high], it is also [-low] (as in the case of consonants, the tongue body cannot be both raised and lowered at the same time, so all [+high] vowels are also [-low]).

- [ɛ] is a mid, front (non-back), lax, unrounded vowel. Since it is unrounded, it does not use the labial articulator. As a mid vowel, it has neither a raised nor a lowered tongue body, so it is [DORSAL] and specified as both [-high] and [-low]. As a front vowel, it is [-back] and as a lax vowel, it is [-tense].

- [ə] is a mid, central, unrounded, lax, and reduced vowel. As mid, it is [DORSAL, -high] and [-low]. As a central and therefore non-front vowel, it is [+back] (all central vowels are always [+back] in feature representations). Being unrounded, it does not involve the labial articulator. Because it is a lax reduced vowel, it is [-tense] and [+reduced].

- [ɑ] is a low, back, unrounded, tense vowel. Since it is produced with a lowered tongue body it is [DORSAL, +low]; because a lowered tongue body cannot be simultaneously raised, it is also [-high]. Since it is back, it is [+back]. Being tense, it is [+tense], and being unrounded, it has no labial specifications.

Feature notation does not provide a convenient way to distinguish diphthongs such as [aj], [aw], and [oj] from the other vowels. These diphthongs may be treated as vowel-glide sequences when using features.

Determining feature representations

We have now defined the phonological features used to represent sounds and have illustrated the feature specifications of some of the consonants and vowels of English. Unlike in the case of constructing syllables, there is no straightforward algorithm for setting up feature representations. It is possible, however, to simplify the task of determining feature representations for individual sounds by going through the process in a step-wise fashion, asking oneself certain key questions in a particular order.

I. What is the manner of articulation of the sound?
    To determine the answer to this question, use the *major class features* and the *manner features*.
    1. Start by asking yourself if the sound is [+sonorant] or [-sonorant].
    2. Is it [-consonantal] or [+consonantal]?
    3. Is it [+continuant] or [-continuant]?
    4. Is it [+syllabic] or [-syllabic]?
    5. Is it [-nasal] or [+nasal]?
    6. If [+sonorant, +consonantal, -nasal], is it [-lateral] or [+lateral]?
    7. If [-sonorant, +consonantal, -continuant], is it [+DR] or [-DR]?

    Once the major class divisions have been determined, the next step is to go on to the laryngeal features.

II. What is the laryngeal setting of the sound?
     To determine the answer to this question, use the *laryngeal features*.
     1. Is it [+voice] or [-voice]?
     2. Is it [+CG] or [-CG]?   This question is only relevant to [ʔ].
     3. Is it [+SG] or [-SG]?   This question is only relevant to [h] and aspirated sounds.

     Finally, place of articulation must be determined.

III. What is the place of articulation of the sound?
      To determine the answer to this question, use the *place of articulation features*.
      1. Which articulator is active in producing the sound?
      2. If [LABIAL], is the sound [+round] or [-round]?

3. If [CORONAL], is the sound [+anterior] or [-anterior]
                                        [+strident] or [-strident]?
4. If [DORSAL], is the sound   [+high] or [-high]
                                        [+low] or [-low]
                                        [+back] or [-back]
                                        [+tense] or [-tense]   } These questions are
                                          [+reduced] or [-reduced]? } only for vowels.

To illustrate how these questions lead one to the right feature representations, consider the sounds [t], [m], and [i].

- [t] is an oral stop (obstruent), is voiceless, and has an alveolar place of articulation.

Manner of articulation: As an obstruent it is [-sonorant] and, since all [-sonorant] sounds are also always consonants, it is [+consonantal, -syllabic]. As an oral stop, it is [-nasal], [-continuant] and [-DR].

Laryngeal setting: As a voiceless sound, it is [-voice] and since it is not glottal stop or [h] it is [-CG, -SG].

Place of articulation: As an alveolar, it is produced with the tongue blade at the alveolar ridge with no obvious noise, so it is [CORONAL, +anterior, -strident].

- [m] is a nasal stop, is voiced, and has a labial place of articulation.

Manner of articulation: As a nasal it is a sonorant consonant, and therefore, it is [+sonorant] and [+consonantal], and [-syllabic] (unless it is a syllabic nasal). Nasals are always stops, therefore it is [-continuant]. It is also crucially [+nasal].

Laryngeal setting: Like all sonorant sounds, in the normal case it is [+voice] and [-CG, -SG].

Place of articulation: As a labial, it is produced with the lips but with no lip-rounding and is therefore [LABIAL, -round].

- [i] is an oral vowel which is high, front, unrounded, and tense.

Manner of articulation: It is nonconsonantal, sonorant, syllabic, and a continuous sound, and therefore is [+sonorant, -consonantal, +syllabic, +continuant]. It is also [-nasal].

Laryngeal setting: Like all sonorant sounds, in the normal case it is [+voice] and [-CG, -SG].

Place of articulation: As an unrounded vowel, it is produced only with the tongue body and is therefore [DORSAL, +high, -low, -back, +tense, -reduced].

To illustrate what complete feature representations look like, figure 3.17 gives feature matrices for [t m i]. In the matrices features are listed following the same basic order as the one we have just followed to arrive at the feature representations: the major class features are followed by the manner features; the manner features are followed by laryngeal features; and, finally, laryngeal features are followed by place of articulation features with the articulator feature given first.[6]

t   m   i

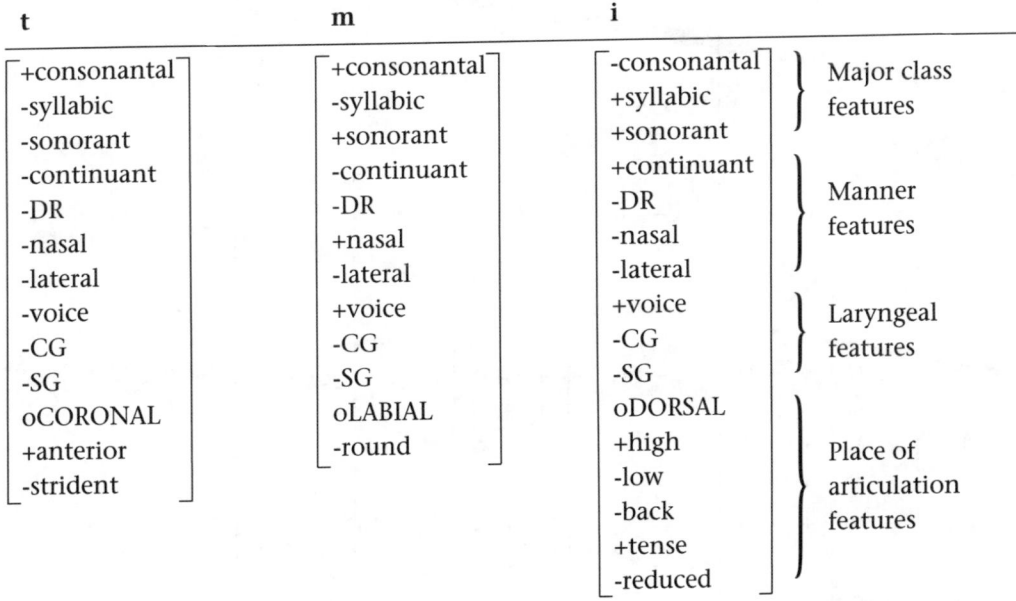

Figure 3.17 Feature matrices for three English sounds

Tables 3.33 and 3.34 provide the feature representations for all the vowels and consonants of English. Go through them keeping in mind the basic questions that need to be answered when determining the feature representation of any sound.

Table 3.33	Feature matrix for English vowels	i	ɪ	e	ɛ	æ	ʌ	ə	ɑ	u	ʊ	o
Major class features	[consonantal]	-	-	-	-	-	-	-	-	-	-	-
	[sonorant]	+	+	+	+	+	+	+	+	+	+	+
	[syllabic]	+	+	+	+	+	+	+	+	+	+	+
Manner feature	[continuant]	+	+	+	+	+	+	+	+	+	+	+
Laryngeal feature	[voice]	+	+	+	+	+	+	+	+	+	+	+
Place of articulation features	LABIAL									o	o	o
	[round]									+	+	+
	DORSAL	o	o	o	o	o	o	o	o	o	o	o
	[high]	+	+	-	-	-	-	-	-	+	+	-
	[low]	-	-	-	-	+	-	-	+	-	-	-
	[back]	-	-	-	-	-	+	+	+	+	+	+
	[tense]	+	-	+	-	-	-	-	+	+	-	+
	[reduced]	-	-	-	-	-	-	+	-	-	-	-

Table 3.34 Feature matrix for English consonants

		p	pʰ	b	t	tʰ	d	k	kʰ	g	f	v	s	z	θ	ð	ʃ	ʒ	tʃ	dʒ	m	n	ŋ	l	r	j	w	ʍ	h	ʔ
Major class features	[consonantal]	+	+	+	+	+	+	+	+	+	+	+	+	+	+	+	+	+	+	+	+	+	+	+	+	−	−	−	−	−
	[sonorant]	−	−	−	−	−	−	−	−	−	−	−	−	−	−	−	−	−	−	−	+	+	+	+	+	+	+	+	−	−
	[syllabic]	−	−	−	−	−	−	−	−	−	−	−	−	−	−	−	−	−	−	−	−	−	−	−	−	−	−	−	−	−
Manner features	[nasal]	−	−	−	−	−	−	−	−	−	−	−	−	−	−	−	−	−	−	−	+	+	+	−	−	−	−	−	−	−
	[continuant]	−	−	−	−	−	−	−	−	−	+	+	+	+	+	+	+	+	−	−	−	−	−	−	+	+	+	+	+	−
	[lateral]	−	−	−	−	−	−	−	−	−	−	−	−	−	−	−	−	−	−	−	−	−	−	+	−	−	−	−	−	−
	[delayed release]	−	−	−	−	−	−	−	−	−	−	−	−	−	−	−	−	−	+	+	−	−	−	−	−	−	−	−	−	−
Laryngeal features	[voice]	−	−	+	−	−	+	−	−	+	−	+	−	+	−	+	−	+	−	+	+	+	+	+	+	+	+	−	−	−
	[CG]	−	−	−	−	−	−	−	−	−	−	−	−	−	−	−	−	−	−	−	−	−	−	−	−	−	−	−	−	+
	[SG]	−	+	−	−	+	−	−	+	−	−	−	−	−	−	−	−	−	−	−	−	−	−	−	−	−	−	−	+	−
Place of articulation features	LABIAL	o	o	o							o	o									o						o	o		
	[round]	−	−	−							−	−									−						+	+		
	CORONAL				o	o	o						o	o	o	o	o	o	o	o		o		o	o	o				
	[anterior]				+	+	+						+	+	+	+	−	−	−	−		+		+	−	−				
	[strident]				−	−	−						+	+	−	−	+	+	+	+		−		−	−	−				
	DORSAL							o	o	o													o			o	o	o		
	[high]							+	+	+													+			+	+	+		
	[back]							+	+	+													+			−	+	+		

Note: [low], [tense], and [reduced] are not used for English consonants.

5.3   The feature hierarchy (*Advanced*)

In the preceding subsection the features of any one segment are listed in a matrix, which has no internal structure of any kind. Listing features in a matrix has long been the most common way to represent the featural composition of segments. It is also possible, however, to group features together into a **feature hierarchy**. Hierarchical feature representations are useful for several reasons: first, they are an even better mirror of vocal tract activity than feature matrices are; and, second, they represent more directly than matrices do how features are related to one other.

Figure 3.18 illustrates the kind of hierarchical representation that features can be grouped into:

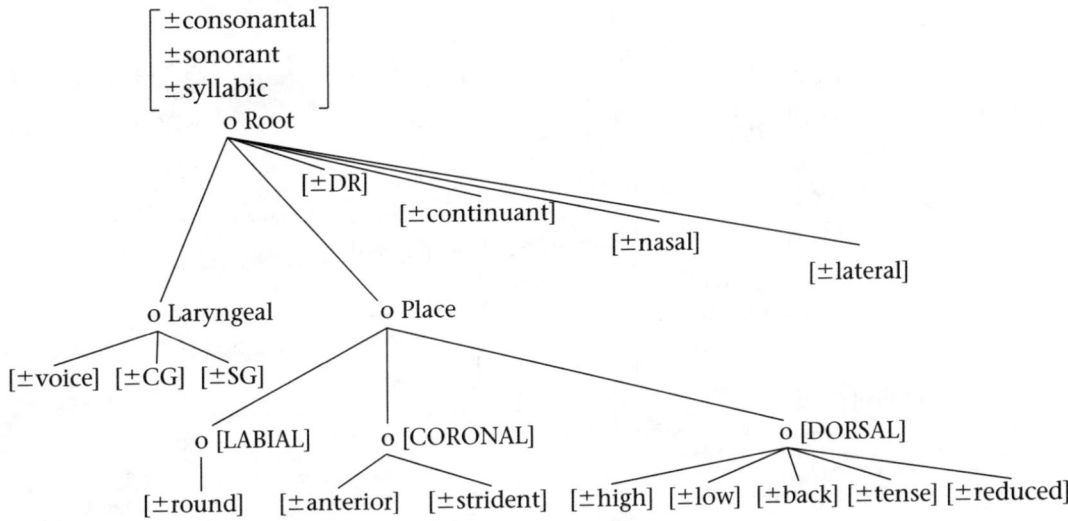

Figure 3.18   The feature hierarchy

In addition to the features themselves (for definitions see section 5.2), three **class nodes** are included in the feature tree: these are the **root node**, the **laryngeal node**, and the **place node**. Each feature grouping in the hierarchy is represented by one of these nodes (the node symbol is a small circle: o). Beneath each node are found the feature or features that make up that grouping. For instance, beneath each of the articulators [LABIAL], [CORONAL], and [DORSAL] are grouped all and only those features that further specify the positioning of the articulators ([±round] for [LABIAL], [±anterior], [±strident] for [CORONAL], etc.). Thus, the nodes and features are ranked on levels or **tiers** that reflect their relation to each other.

Nodes serve three functions in the hierarchy. First, they represent the articulatory organization of the feature hierarchy: the laryngeal node represents laryngeal activity; the place node represents supralaryngeal articulations; the root node groups the major class features together, thus defining whether a segment is a vowel, consonant, or glide; and each articulator node groups together all and only those features which the articulator is able to produce. Second, the nodes function to group together and label natural classes of features. And, third, nodes, like features themselves, may be referred to directly when attempting to describe sound patterns and processes. This property of the hierarchy is illustrated in some detail in section 7.

The manner features are not grouped together under one node, but instead are all linked individually to the root node; this is because segments of each type of place of articulation ([LABIAL], [CORONAL], and [DORSAL]) can have different values for any one of the manner features individually. For instance, a [CORONAL, +anterior] segment can be [±continuant], [±nasal], or [±lateral]. Thus, manner features always seem to pattern individually rather than as a group.

Figure 3.19 illustrates how the feature hierarchy is used to represent the feature specifications of individual segments. No representation of an actual segment makes use of all the features in the hierarchy simultaneously.

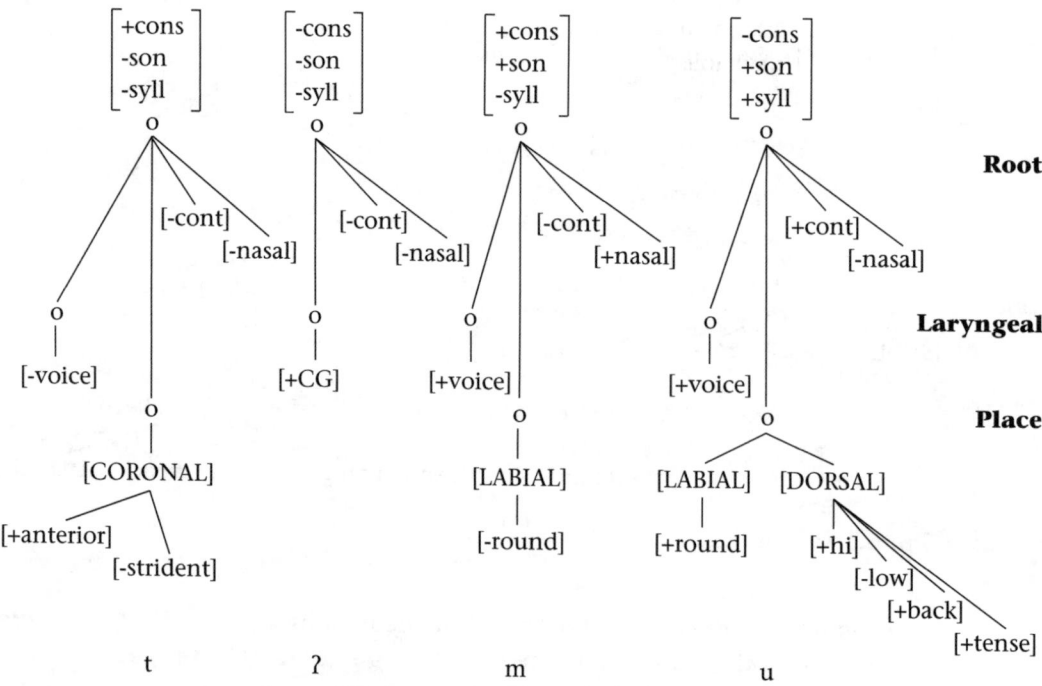

Figure 3.19 The feature hierarchical representations of some English sounds

Notice that in the representation for /ʔ/ there is no place node. Only glottal sounds, which are produced with no supralaryngeal articulation, are represented without this node. Features like [±lateral], [±DR], [±reduced] have been left out of the structures to simplify them somewhat.

While this kind of feature representation may at first look more complex and clumsy than a strictly segmental representation, it is in fact very useful. It allows us to capture contrasts at the level of the feature, instead of listing individual sets of contrastive phonemes. Much allophonic variation can be represented as the addition, loss, or change of a few features. The influence of the conditioning environment is also made more obvious with this type of representation, as shown in section 7 of this chapter.

6 Derivations and rules

To this point we have established the existence of related levels of phonological structure. In this model, phonological units from a lower level of structure are organized and grouped into higher-level structural units. Thus, *features* are grouped into *segments*, which in turn are organized into *syllables*. We have established that segments can be contrastive and hence belong to separate *phonemes*, or non-contrastive and hence function as predictable *allophonic variants* of phonemes. We have also seen that general statements referring to natural classes and to syllable structure can account for the patterning of non-contrastive elements. Finally, we have seen that there are two levels of representation associated with the difference between contrastive and non-contrastive segments: the *phonemic* level represents unpredictable, phonemic properties and units of a language, while the *phonetic* level represents predictable, allophonic properties and units. In this section and in section 7, we will explore the relationship between the phonemic and phonetic levels of representation and illustrate how this relationship is formalized.

Phonologists assume that phonemic representations are equivalent to the mental representations that speakers have of the words in their language, while phonetic representations are equivalent to the actual phonetic outputs that are produced in the course of speech. In this sense, phonemic representations are understood to be the basic representations of units such as the word. The unpredictable phonological information represented in a phonemic representation thus underlies all actual phonetic forms; for this reason, phonemic representations are also called **underlying representations** (or forms) while phonetic representations are also called surface representations (or forms).

Phonemic representations become phonetic representations as a result of being acted upon by *phonological processes* such as the devoicing of liquids and glides following voiceless stops in English, the aspiration of voiceless stops at the beginnings of syllables in English, the lengthening of English vowels preceding voiced coda obstruents, and so on. Thus we say that phonetic or surface forms are **derived** from phonemic or underlying forms by means of the action of phonological processes. These phonological processes are formalized in two ways: as **phonological rules** (formalized statements of phonological processes) or as **phonological representations** (graphic presentations of phonological processes). In this section, we focus on understanding how rules act in derivations and how they should be formalized. Section 7 focuses on phonological representations.

6.1 Derivations

Underlying representations are composed of phonemes (it is important to keep in mind that all phonemes are themselves composed of distinctive features). Phonetic forms are derived by allowing phonological processes—formalized as rules—to operate on underlying representations in those contexts where the processes are relevant.

The derivation of three phonetic representations (PRs) from underlying representations (URs) is presented in figure 3.20. Here, the underlying representation is on the top line (the cross hatch # symbolizes a word boundary); reading downward, each rule applies in sequence, and the underlying representation is adjusted as required. Where a rule fails to apply, the form remains unchanged; this information is conveyed by dashes. The resulting output then serves as the input to the following rule. Finally, when all rules relevant to the derivation in question have applied, a phonetic representation is provided. The two rules presented in the following example are aspiration and vowel lengthening (see section 4.5).

UR	#slæp#	'slap'	#tæp#	'tap'	#pæd#	'pad'
Aspiration	—		#tʰæp#		#pʰæd#	
V-length	—		—		#pʰæːd#	
PR	[slæp]		[tʰæp]		[pʰæːd]	

Figure 3.20 The phonological derivation of three English words

In this example, two rules have applied (since the words being derived are all monosyllabic, the syllable boundaries are equivalent to word boundaries and so are not indicated here). The first accounts for aspiration. Since the initial consonant of the URs #tæp# and #pæd# are voiceless stops found in onset position, they fulfill the conditions under which English stops become aspirated. We therefore indicate that aspiration occurs by providing an intermediate form on a new line.

We have also seen that in English, vowels are predictably long when they occur before a voiced stop in the same syllable. In figure 3.20, the /æ/'s of *slap* and *tap* occur before voiceless stops and so are not lengthened. The vowel of *pad*, however, occurs in just the environment associated with long vowels and so is predictably lengthened.

The use of such derivations underscores the fact that allophonic variation is the result of processes that apply in the course of language use. Underlying representations capture the knowledge that speakers have about the nature of their phonological system, rules reflect the application of allophonic processes, and the phonetic representation reflects the speech output. The relationship between phonemic or underlying representations and phonetic or surface representations is the result of the action of phonological processes.

6.2   Rule application

We have seen that more than one rule may be employed in a derivation. Consequently, we must now ask how several rules are applied to a given underlying form when these rules interact.

Unordered rule application and feeding

In figure 3.20 we saw the application of the rules of English aspiration and vowel lengthening, which apply to voiceless stops and vowels, respectively. Note that the environments in which each of these rules apply (onset and pre-coda position, respectively) are entirely different. Therefore, these rules do not interact or affect each other in any way; the order in which they are applied makes no difference to the outcome of the derivation. Figure 3.21 shows the same rules applied in reverse order; there is no difference in the outcome.

We therefore say that the rules of aspiration and vowel lengthening are *unordered* with respect to each other.

UR	#slæp#	'slap'	#tæp#	'tap'	#pæd#	'pad'
V-length	—		—		#pæ:d#	
Aspiration	—		#tʰæp#		#pʰæ:d#	
PR	[slæp]		[tʰæp]		[pʰæ:d]	

Figure 3.21 Unordered rule application

A second type of rule ordering is called feeding. Rules are said to be in a feeding order when the application of one rule creates an environment that makes possible the application of another rule that could otherwise not apply. The rules of English schwa-deletion and liquid-glide devoicing (given in example 4)) are in a feeding relation in the casual speech pronunciation of a word like *parade*. In this word, the schwa between *p* and *r* gets deleted because it is unstressed. After the schwa has been lost, through schwa deletion, a liquid or glide that follows the schwa in the underlying representations gets positioned directly after a voiceless stop, and, therefore, becomes subject to liquid-glide devoicing. This is shown in the next example. The arrows, which are normally not written in derivations, here indicate feeding relationships. Notice that before schwa deletion, a rule has to apply to assign stress to the final vowel.

UR	#pəred#	'parade'
Stress	#pəréd#	
Schwa deletion	#préd#	
Liquid-glide devoicing	#pr̥éd#	
Diphthongization	#pr̥éjd#	
Vowel lengthening	#pr̥é:jd#	
PR	[pr̥é:jd]	

Figure 3.22 Feeding order in a derivation

Notice now that no incorrect forms would result if, say, the schwa-deletion rule attempted to apply before the stress rule. Because its environment is not present, the schwa-deletion rule would simply fail to apply. However, once the stress rule was applied, the schwa-deletion rule could then follow in its turn, ultimately leading to a correct phonetic representation. What these facts suggest is that rules in a feeding relation may apply in *free order*, each attempting to apply wherever the required conditions are met. The result will be the desired phonetic output.

6.3 The form and notation of rules

General statements about allophonic distribution are formalized as rules. These rules are written so as to reflect the dynamic nature of processes (chapter 2, section 9.4).

Rules

Rules take the following form.

11)

A → B / X ___ Y

In this notation, *A* stands for an element in the underlying representation, *B* for the change it undergoes, and *X* and *Y* for the conditioning environment. Either *X* or *Y* may be absent (null) if the conditioning environment is found only on one side of the allophone. The ___ (focus bar) indicates the position of the segment undergoing the rule. The slash separates the statement of the change from the statement of the conditioning environment. This rule is read as *A becomes B between X and Y*.

As an example of rule writing, we return to the distribution of liquid-glide devoicing in English (section 2.4): in English, liquids and glides have voiceless allophones after syllable-initial voiceless stops and voiced allophones elsewhere. The rule statement treats the voiced allophones of liquids and glides as basic (underlying) and changes the feature [+voice] to [-voice] in the appropriate environment. This rule is read as follows:

12)

Liquids and glides become voiceless after syllable-initial voiceless stops.

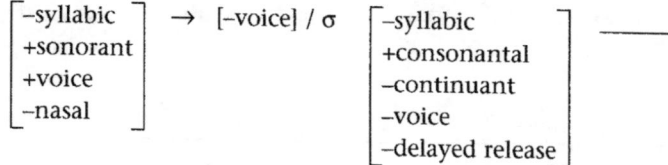

Figure 3.23 Liquid-glide devoicing in English expressed as a rule

Rule and feature notation formally represents the origin of allophones in phonetic processes that arise in the course of speech. For example, the devoicing of liquids and glides in English is a typical process of assimilation. The rule notation in figure 3.23 shows explicitly how this change of [+voice] to [-voice] occurs in a specific class of sounds following the class of sounds that is [-voice]. Features in figure 3.23 and others below are listed in matrices (between square brackets), rather than as trees to simplify the forms of the rules.

Deletion as a rule

We have already seen that English speakers (optionally) drop a schwa [ə] in an open syllable when it is followed by a stressed syllable, as in *police* [plis] and *parade* [prejd]. The rule can be formalized as in figure 3.24. Here, Cø is an abbreviation for any number of successive consonants from zero on up and the σ represents a syllable boundary.

$$[ə] → ø / Cø ___ σ Cø \qquad V$$
$$[+\text{stress}]$$

Figure 3.24 Schwa deletion in English

The English schwa-deletion rule interacts with the constraint on possible consonant sequences. It automatically fails to apply when an impermissible sequence would result. Since σ[pt^h and σ[dl are impermissible onsets in English, there are no forms like *[pt^héjɾow] *potato* or *[dlít] *delete* (except in very, very fast speech).

Epenthesis and alpha rules

Recall that epenthesis involves the insertion of a segment (chapter 2, section 9.4) into a sequence of other segments. In section 2.5 we saw that the glides following English tense non-low vowels are predictable by a general rule: the tense mid [-back] vowel /e/ is followed by the [-back] glide /j/; the tense mid [+back] vowel /o/ is followed by the [+back] glide/w/.

In order to represent this epenthesis, we can make use of a type of notation called *alpha notation*. Here, the Greek letter α is a variable (like *x* in algebra) that can stand for either feature value. For example, a feature statement like [α round] can be read as either [+round] or [-round], but the alpha variable or variables used in a rule must match. Whenever the alpha is used in a rule, it must have the same value wherever it occurs. Since alpha notation is used to capture two rules, alphas are read twice, once as '+' and once as '-'. When the first alpha is read as '+', all other alphas in the same rule are to be read as '+'; when it is read as '-', all other alphas in the same rule are read as '-'.

With alpha notation, we can capture the variability of the glide insertion in English as follows.

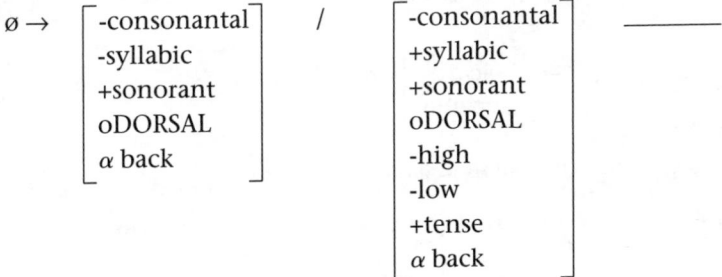

Figure 3.25 Alpha notation in English glide epenthesis

Remember: in reading an alpha, you are reading a rule twice, once with the plus value for the alpha feature, and once with the minus value. The rule in figure 3.25 states that a [+back] glide is inserted after a [+back] mid tense vowel and that a [-back] glide is inserted after a [-back] mid tense vowel. Since there are only two glides in the phonological inventory of English, [+back] /w/ and [-back] /j/, the correct glide will be inserted by the rule.

Rules that refer to syllable structure

The rule of vowel lengthening in English makes reference to syllable structure. The boundary of the syllable may be represented by a syllable marker σ. Recall the rule of vowel lengthening in English.

13)
English vowels are long when followed by a voiced obstruent consonant in the same syllable.

The corresponding rule (in figure 3.26) states that an underlying short vowel is lengthened in the appropriate context.
Notice here that the onset of the syllable is irrelevant to the statement of the rule and so is not included in the formalization.

$$\begin{bmatrix} +\text{syllabic} \\ -\text{consonantal} \\ +\text{sonorant} \\ -\text{long} \end{bmatrix} \rightarrow \begin{bmatrix} +\text{long} \end{bmatrix} \ / \ \underline{\hspace{1cm}} \begin{bmatrix} -\text{syllabic} \\ +\text{consonantal} \\ -\text{sonorant} \\ +\text{voice} \\ -\text{nasal} \end{bmatrix} \sigma$$

Figure 3.26 Vowel lengthening in English

Notice here that the onset of the syllable is irrelevant to the statement of the rule and so is not included in the formalization.

Vowel epenthesis

Vowel epenthesis is frequently triggered when an impermissible phonotactic structure is encountered in a borrowed word, as in the English pronunciation of the name *Dmitri*. It is also the case that in some dialects of English, a coda consisting of *l* and another consonant is not permitted. In these dialects, *milk* is pronounced [mɪlək] and *film* [fɪləm]. This change can be represented in rule format as in figure 3.27.

$$\emptyset \rightarrow [\text{ə}] \ / \ [+\text{lateral}] \ \underline{\hspace{1cm}} \begin{bmatrix} -\text{syllabic} \\ +\text{consonantal} \end{bmatrix} \sigma$$

Figure 3.27 Schwa epenthesis in English as a rule

A more complete representation of this process requires showing the change of syllable structure, as in figure 3.28.

Figure 3.28 Syllabic representation of schwa epenthesis in English

7   Representations (*Advanced*)

In recent years, the formalization of rules has become more graphic. This change has taken place because certain types of processes, especially processes of assimilation (where one segment becomes similar in one or more features to a neighbouring segment), have been viewed as the spreading of features from one segment (represented as a feature hierarchy) to another one. It has also been claimed that a simple set of principles governs the way in which features spread.

These graphic presentations of feature changes are referred to as **representations**. The features themselves are referred to as **autosegments**—the label suggests that each feature has a certain autonomy in its operation.

7.1 Assimilation and the feature hierarchy

Assimilation processes are particularly amenable to autosegmental representation using the feature hierarchy. This is the case because the overlapping production typical of co-articulation (see chapter 2, section 9.1) is neatly represented by the spread of individual features from one 'segment' to another.

Assimilation of [+nasal]

In English, a vowel nasalizes when it is immediately followed by a nasal consonant in the same syllable. One or more consonants may follow the nasal consonant. (For some speakers, the vowels must also be stressed.) The words *banks*, *shunted*, and *nimble*, for example, are pronounced [bæ̃ŋks], [ʃʌ̃ntəd], and [nĩmbəl]. This regressive nasalization in English can be represented as in figure 3.29 (the symbol σ following the feature matrices indicates the boundary of the syllable—that is, that the nasal consonant is in the coda; the change undergone by the word *bank* is provided below the representation).

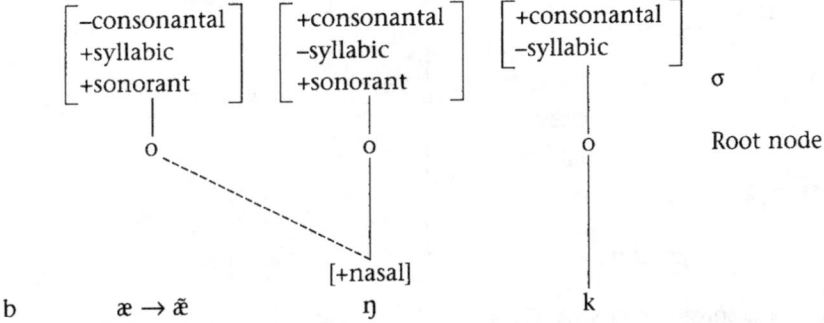

Figure 3.29 Vowel nasalization in English (regressive assimilation)

Note that the English non-nasal vowel is represented as having no feature [nasal]. This fact will be very important in our discussion of representations below. With autosegmental representations, there is no need to list individual segments or even to write a rule. The next section outlines the principles that govern the spreading of features.

7.2 Autosegmental principles

It is claimed that only three principles account for the many processes that can be represented with **autosegmental notation**.

- **Association: feature-to-segment** Each autosegment (feature) is associated with at least one segment by an association line.

- **Association: segment-to-feature** Each segment is associated with at least one autosegment (feature) by an association line.

- **Crossing** Association lines do not cross.

Feature spreading

We are now in a position to understand how English nasalization can be viewed as a form of feature spreading. Since English vowels never contrast for the feature [nasal], they can be unspecified for nasality (in other words, the feature [±nasal] can be left out of their representations). Our principles note that each feature must be associated with at least one segment, and vice-versa. But nasality is not part of the specification of English vowels. A language-specific rule of English allows leftward spreading. The feature [nasal] on /n/ therefore will 'automatically' spread leftward whenever it finds a vowel that is not specified for nasality. This spreading is not accomplished by a rule, but by a general principle.

Compare nasal spreading in English with nasal spreading in Scots Gaelic (see figure 3.30). Remember that nasal assimilation in Scots Gaelic can occur progressively (see section 2.6). To capture this fact autosegmentally, we do not have to write a new rule; we merely state that spreading in Scots Gaelic can operate rightward. The general principles take care of the rest.

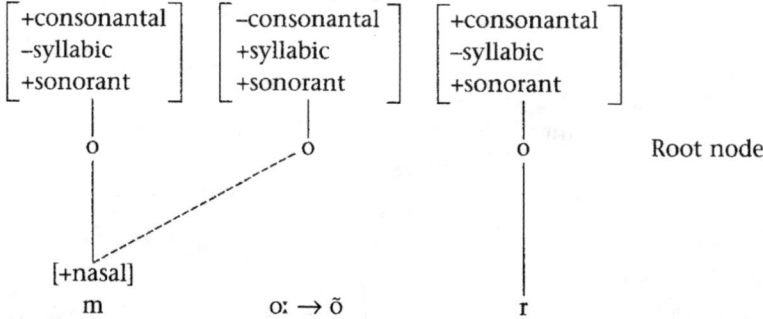

Figure 3.30 Nasal spreading in Scots Gaelic

The spreading of autosegments need not apply only to the feature [nasal]. In theory, just about any feature should follow the same principles. The next section shows how spreading can apply to voicing features.

Laryngeal assimilation: English liquid-glide devoicing revisited

We have already seen (figure 3.23) how English liquid-glide devoicing is stated in rule format. This particular variation is in fact assimilatory, in the sense that the liquids and glides take on the voiceless quality of a preceding voiceless stop. For this reason, devoicing lends itself well to statement as a representation (see figure 3.31).

The root node and manner features represent the leftmost class as stops and the class to its right as liquids or glides. The place node is not represented since the place of articulation of both the stops and the liquids and glides is irrelevant to the process in question here as it is not affected by the rule. The dotted line represents the spreading of the laryngeal node feature [-voice] from the voiceless stop to the liquid or glide.

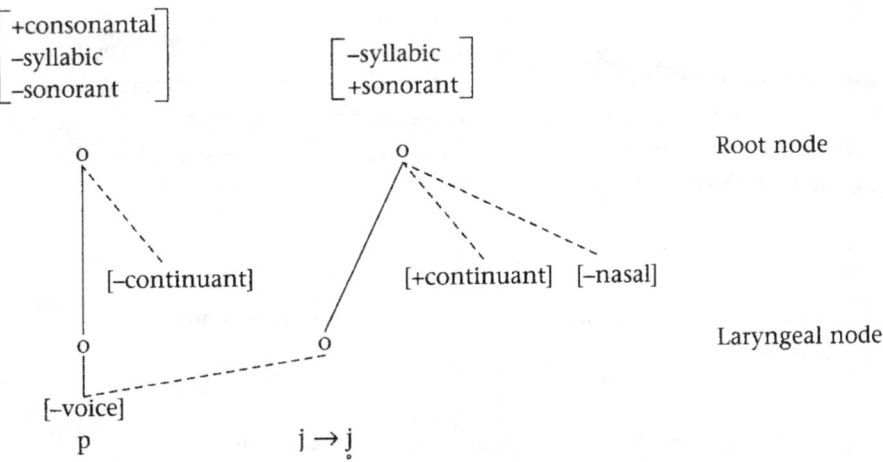

Figure 3.31 Liquid-glide devoicing in English as a representation

7.3 Tonal assimilation as a representation

In chapter 2, we saw how tone is represented on separate levels or tiers of phonological description. Association lines link the tone to the appropriate vowel. A representation of the word *tunko* 'sheep' from Duwai, a language spoken in West Africa, is shown in figure 3.32, where L indicates low tone, and H high tone.

```
L    H
|    |
t u n k o
```

Figure 3.32 Representing tone

This type of representation has the advantage of being able to show explicitly certain facts about tone languages. Tones, like other phonological phenomena, are subject to contextually conditioned variation. A good example of this comes from Duwai (see figure 3.33). In Duwai, many words show the tonal pattern LH (low-high).

```
L H              L H
| |              | |
kəvus  'warthog'   məri  'beard'

L  H             L  H
|  Λ             |  |
uːdau  'mush'    tunko  'sheep'
```

Figure 3.33 Low-high tonal patterns in Duwai

When a word with a LH tonal pattern is followed by a word with a L tone, such as the form *bàì* '(is) not', the H tone of the first word becomes L: *kəvús* 'warthog' becomes *kəvùs bàì* 'it's not a warthog'; *mərí* 'beard' becomes *mərì bàì* 'it's not a beard', and so on.

This tonal change is a kind of assimilation, and parallels common processes of assimilation of segmental features. This assimilation is viewed as a spreading of the L tone backwards from the word *bài* to the final vowel of the preceding word, and is represented by drawing a dotted association line as in figure 3.34 (which represents the change in tone) and breaking the original association line from the vowel to the former tone value (the short double lines indicate the loss of association).

Figure 3.34   Tone assimilation in Duwai

Thus, both features and tonal material are handled by the same type of representation and the same principles.

7.4   Processes, rules, and representations: a last word

The combined use of features and processes in phonological description reflects the dynamic nature of linguistic behaviour. First, the use of features reflects a basic level of phonological activity—contrasts take place on the feature level, not on the level where segments are represented. Secondly, the use of process notation and formalization with rules and representations reflects the realities of linguistic production, in which sounds are affected by the context in which they are pronounced as we speak.

Overall, the patterning of phonological units is seen to be based on the interaction of a universal set of features, universal and language specific phonotactic constraints and syllabification procedures, and the use of rules and representations. This current theory of phonology is based on principles that are applicable to the study of any human language.

Summing up

Phonology deals with the sequential and phonetically conditioned patterning of sounds in language. To account for this patterning, three units of phonological representation have been established: the **feature**, the **phoneme**, and the **syllable**. Phonemes are contrastive segmental units composed of distinctive features. Phonetically conditioned variants of phonemes are called **allophones**.

Phonology makes use of **underlying forms**, **derivations**, **phonological rules**, and **representations** in its formal notation. Some rules apply in **free** order. **Autosegments**—features that are autonomous to varying degrees—spread or delete on the basis of a few principles.

Notes

1   Of course, words can differ in meaning without contrasting phonetically. In every language, there are words (called *homophones*) that are identical in pronunciation but that differ in meaning, such as English *well* 'spring' and *well* 'all right'. The following French words provide a more dramatic example of homophones.

vert   [vɛːʀ]   'green'
vers   [vɛːʀ]   'towards'
vers   [vɛːʀ]   'verse'
verre   [vɛːʀ]   'glass'
ver   [vɛːʀ]   'worm'

2   In some dialects of English there is also a contrast between [a] and the mid back rounded lax vowel [ɔ] in words like *cot* [kʰat] and *caught* [kʰɔt]. In Canadian English, these words and other analogous ones are both pronounced [kʰɑt].

3   Perhaps you have noticed that voiceless sonorant allophones occur in the same context as aspiration: in syllable onsets. Both types of voicelessness are indeed a manifestation of voice lag. It would not be inappropriate to represent aspiration as [p̥ɪn] 'pin' or liquid-glide devoicing as [pl̥ʰʌk]. This book, however, will stick to the traditional distinct representations.

4   Some English words, such as *upper, happy,* and *walking,* do not show aspiration where it is expected, given that the syllabification procedure results in the following: /ʌ.pər/, /hæ.pi/, and /wɑ.kɪŋ/. This fact is accounted for by assuming that the voiceless stops in these forms are simultaneously in both syllables, a phenomenon that is known as **ambisyllabicity**:

We will not address the details and motivations of ambisyllabicity here.

5   Alveopalatals may pattern together with high front vowels and glides for purposes of some rules. In such cases, we can assume they are specified with the features [DORSAL, +high, -back] as well as [CORONAL, -anterior, +strident].

6   In the feature matrices in figure 3.17 a complete set of features is given for every phoneme. However, it is not always necessary to give a complete set of features for a sound, and so in some cases in this chapter we leave predictable features out. The reason for this is that in some situations certain features are inherently predictable and so can be left out of feature representations. For example, as we saw above, segments that are [+high] are always [-low] because the two tongue positions represented by these features are mutually exclusive. Conversely, segments that are [+low] are always [-high]. When giving feature representations for [+high] segments, therefore, it is not absolutely necessary to include the feature [-low], since this feature is predictable; similarly for [+low] segments it is not necessary to include the feature [-high] in the representation, since [-high] is predictable. The

phoneme /l/ is another example: this segment is the only [+lateral] sound in the language; to represent it therefore it is sufficient to represent it simply as [+lateral]. All its other features are predictable. Other examples of features that are predictable include [+voice] on sonorant consonants and vowels and [-nasal] on vowels. Since sonorant consonant and vowel phonemes are always [+voice] (unless they become devoiced by a phonological process such as liquid-glide devoicing), [+voice] can be left out of the feature representations for these phonemes. Similarly, since vowel phonemes in English are never contrastively nasal, they are always [-nasal]; therefore, [-nasal] does not have to be part of the representation of vowel phonemes.

Sources

A classic and still valuable presentation of phonemic analysis is found in H.A. Gleason, Jr.'s *An Introduction to Descriptive Linguistics* (Toronto: Holt, Rinehart and Winston, 1961). Tone data on Mende are from W.R. Leben's "The Representation of Tone" and on Duwai from R.G. Schuh's, "Tone Rules" both in *Tone: A Linguistic Survey*, edited by V.A. Fromkin (New York: Academic Press, 1978). Syllabification, tone, and autosegmental analysis are drawn from numerous sources, all summarized recently in Goldsmith (cited below). The Malay data are adapted from M. Kenstowicz and C. Kisseberth, *Generative Phonology* (New York: Academic Press, 1979) with additional examples provided by S.L. Lee (personal communication).

Data sources for problems are as follows: for Inuktitut, B. Harnum (personal communication); for Mokilese, S. Harrison's *Mokilese Reference Grammar* (Honolulu: University of Hawaii Press, 1976); for Tamil, R. Radhakrishnan (personal communication); for Gascon, R.C. Kelly's *A Descriptive Analysis of Gascon* (Amsterdam: Mouton, 1978); for Plains Cree, Y. Carifelle and M. Pepper (personal communication); for Canadian French, D.C. Walker's *The Pronunciation of Canadian French* (Ottawa: University of Ottawa Press, 1984) and A. Teasdale (personal communication); for English fast speech, G. Zhang, *Phonological Representation and Analyses of Fast Speech Phenomena in English*, M.A. thesis, Memorial University of Newfoundland, 1994; for Mende, L. Hyman and D. Pulleyblank, "The Basics of Autosegmental Phonology Applied to Tone"; for Moru, A.N. Tucker, *The Eastern Sudanic Languages* (London: Dawsons, 1976/1940), pp. 112, 271.

Recommended reading

Anderson, Stephen R. 1985. *Phonology in the Twentieth Century.* Chicago: University of Chicago Press.

Carr, Philip. 1993. *Phonology.* London: Macmillan.

Clements, George N., and Samuel Jay Keyser. 1983. *CV Phonology.* Cambridge, MA: MIT Press.

Goldsmith, John. 1990. *Autosegmental and Metrical Phonology.* Cambridge, MA: Blackwell.

Goldsmith, John, ed. 1995. *The Handbook of Phonological Theory.* Cambridge, MA: Blackwell.

Hyman, Larry M. 1975. *Phonology: Theory and Analysis.* New York: Holt, Rinehart and Winston.

Keating, Patricia. 1988. "The Phonology-Phonetics Interface." In *Linguistics: The Cambridge Survey.* Vol. 1. Edited by F. Newmeyer, 281–302. London: Cambridge University Press.

Kenstowicz, Michael. 1994. *Phonology in Generative Grammar.* Cambridge, MA: Blackwell.

Stampe, David. 1980. *A Dissertation on Natural Phonology.* New York: Garland.

Appendix: hints for solving phonology problems

The task of solving a phonology problem is made easier if certain facts presented in this chapter and summarized here are kept in mind. The data that we consider below are taken from Tagalog, a language spoken in the Philippines.

1. In the following data, consider the phones [h] and [ʔ] and determine whether they contrast, or whether they are allophones of one phoneme.

   a) kahon   'box'   d) ʔari   'property'
   b) hariʔ   'king'   e) kaʔon   'to fetch'
   c) ʔumagos 'to flow'   f) humagos   'to paint'

   In order to determine whether the phones contrast, we begin by looking for minimal pairs. These establish which segments are contrastive. For example, in the data in a) through f), minimal pairs occur in items a–e and c–f; the pair b–d is a near minimal pair. The existence of minimal and near minimal pairs of words indicates that [h] and [ʔ] contrast. Therefore we can conclude that /h/ and /ʔ/ are separate phonemes.

2. Now consider the following data, and determine whether the two sounds [d] and [r] contrast or whether they are allophones of one phoneme.

   a) datiŋ   'to arrive'   f) daraʔiŋ   'will complain'
   b) dami   'amount'   g) marumi   'dirty'
   c) dumi   'dirt'   h) marami   'many'
   d) daratiŋ   'will arrive'   i) daʔiŋ   'to complain'
   e) mandurukot 'pickpocket'   j) mandukot   'to go pickpocketing'

   Since there are no minimal pairs in the data which contrast [d] and [r], we proceed to check whether the two sounds are in complementary distribution. Normally, when two sounds are in complementary distribution and therefore allophones of one phoneme, they must be phonetically similar. In Tagalog, [d] and [r] are both voiced alveolar segments; thus they are sufficiently similar phonetically to be viewed as potential allophones of one phoneme.

   To check whether two (or more) sounds are in complementary distribution, the best thing to do is to list the environments in which the sounds occur:

[d] occurs:	[r] occurs:
–word-initially (e.g., *dami*)	–between two vowels (e.g., *marami*)
–following a nasal (e.g., *mandukot*)	

   [d] never occurs between two vowels, and [r] never occurs word-initially or following a nasal. The two sounds never occur in identical environments, therefore they are in complementary distribution and their distributions are predictable.

3. If two potential allophones of one phoneme are in complementary distribution, we can be reasonably sure that they are allophones of one phoneme. We can therefore make a general statement about their distribution, in terms of some natural phonological class. For example:

Tagalog [d] and [r] are in complementary distribution and are allophones of one phoneme. The allophone [r] occurs between vowels; [d] occurs elsewhere—here, word-initially, as in items a), b), c), f), and so on, and after nasal consonants, as in items e) and j).

4. Once we have determined that two sounds are allophones of one phoneme, we need to determine what the phoneme that they are both derived from is. Usually this can be done by selecting one of the allophones as basic. In most cases, the allophone chosen as the phoneme is the one with the widest distribution (the elsewhere variant). In the Tagalog case, the elsewhere variant is [d], so we posit the phoneme /d/, which has two allophones, [d] and [r]. It may be helpful to set up a traditional phoneme-allophone diagram to illustrate this (see figure 3.2).

       [r]   [d]
Between vowels Elsewhere

5. Now that we know that [d] and [r] are allophones of the phoneme /d/, we need to determine the phonological rule or the representation that accounts for the predictable features of the other allophones. Our rule or representation is probably correct if it describes a common linguistic process (such as assimilation) in terms of natural classes of sounds interacting with neighbouring segments and/or syllable structure.

For example, for the above: d → r / V___V

Here the process that leads to the allophony is a form of assimilation, in that an underlying voiced stop consonant becomes a continuant when found between two continuants (vowels).

6. We can assume that segments are phonemic if there are no minimal pairs for them but they cannot be shown to be allophones of one phoneme. In such a case, we can conclude that the data simply did not provide minimal pairs.

Questions

Assume phonetic transcription of the data in all exercises.
1. *Inuktitut* (Eastern) (Native Canadian)

a) iglumut	'to a house'	h) pinna	'that one up there'
b) ukiaq	'late fall'	i) ani	'female's brother'
c) aiviq	'walrus'	j) iglu	'(snow)house'
d) aniguvit	'if you leave'	k) panna	'that place up there'
e) aglu	'seal's breathing hole'	l) aivuq	'she goes home'
f) iglumit	'from a house'	m) ini	'place, spot'
g) anigavit	'because you leave'	n) ukiuq	'winter'

i) List all the minimal pairs in this data. Based on the minimal pairs you have found, list all the contrastive pairs of vowels.

ii) Using the vowel charts in figures 2.9 and 2.10 as your models, make a chart of Inuktitut vowel phonemes.

iii) Now consider the data again; here it is transcribed in more phonetic detail. In it, there are phonetically similar segments that are in complementary distribution. Look for them and then answer the question that follows the data.

aa)	iglumut	'to a house'	hh)	pinna	'that one up there'
bb)	ukiaq	'late fall'	ii)	anɪ	'female's brother'
cc)	aivɪq	'walrus'	jj)	iglʊ	'(snow)house'
dd)	aniguvit	'if you leave'	kk)	panna	'that place up there'
ee)	aglʊ	'seal's breathing hole'	ll)	aivʊq	'she goes home'
ff)	iglumit	'from a house'	mm)	inɪ	'place, spot'
gg)	anigavit	'because you leave'	nn)	ukiʊq	'winter'

iv) List the phonetically similar segments that are in complementary distribution. State their distribution in words.

2. *Hindi* (Hindi is a language of the Indo-European family spoken in India)
Consider the segments [b] and [b̤] in the data below and answer the questions that follow. The segment transcribed [b̤] is a murmured voiced stop; it was presented in chapter 2, section 10.2.

a)	[bara]	'large'	f)	[b̤ɛd]	'disagreement'
b)	[b̤ari]	'heavy'	g)	[bais]	'twenty-two'
c)	[bina]	'without'	h)	[b̤əs]	'buffalo'
d)	[b̤ir]	'crowd'	i)	[bap]	'father'
e)	[bori]	'sackcloth'	j)	[b̤ag]	'part'

i) Are the segments [b] and [b̤] allophones of the same phoneme or do they belong to separate phonemes? If you believe they belong to separate phonemes, give evidence from the data to support your analysis. If you believe they are allophones of the same phoneme, list the conditioning environments.

3. *Mokilese* (Mokilese is an Austronesian language of the South Pacific)
Examine the following data from Mokilese carefully, taking note of where voiceless vowels occur.

a)	pi̥san	'full of leaves'	g)	uduk	'flesh'
b)	tu̥pu̥kta	'bought'	h)	kaskas	'to throw'
c)	pu̥ko	'basket'	i)	poki	'to strike something'
d)	ki̥sa	'we two'	j)	pil	'water'
e)	su̥pwo	'firewood'	k)	apid	'outrigger support'
f)	kamwɔki̥ti	'to move'	l)	ludʒuk	'to tackle'

i) The vowel phonemes of Mokilese are /i e ɛ u o ɔ a/. In Mokilese, [i̥] is an allophone of /i/, and [u̥] is an allophone of /u/. No other vowels have voiceless allophones. State in words the conditioning factors that account for this. Be as general as possible in referring to classes of sounds.

ii) If you have completed the section on rule formalization, write a rule (using features) that accounts for the derived allophones.

4. *Gascon* (Gascon is spoken in southwest France)

The phones [b], [β], [d], [ð], [g], and [ɣ] are all found in Gascon, as the following examples show. The phone [β] is a voiced bilabial fricative; [ɣ] is a voiced velar fricative (see chapter 2, section 10.2).

a)	brẽn	'endanger'	n)	gat	'cat'
b)	bako	'cow'	o)	lũŋg	'long'
c)	ũmbro	'shadow'	p)	saliβo	'saliva'
d)	krãmbo	'room'	q)	noβi	'husband'
e)	dilys	'Monday'	r)	aβe	'to have'
f)	dũŋko	'until'	s)	ʃiβaw	'horse'
g)	duso	'sweet'	t)	byðɛt	'gut'
h)	taldepãn	'leftover bread'	u)	eʃaðo	'hoe'
i)	pũnde	'to lay eggs'	v)	biɣar	'mosquito'
j)	dudze	'twelve'	w)	riɣut	'he laughed'
k)	guteʒa	'flow'	x)	agro	'sour'
l)	ẽŋgwãn	'this year'	y)	ʒuɣɛt	'he played'
m)	puðe	'to be able'			

i) Which pairs among the phones [b], [β], [d], [ð], [g], and [ɣ] are the most phonetically similar? Support your claim with phonetic descriptions of the similar pairs.

ii) List the environments in which the phones [b], [β], [d], [ð], [g], and [ɣ] are found. You may ignore word-final position in your consideration.

iii) Is there any evidence for grouping these pairs of sounds into phonemes? State the evidence for each pair.

iv) Make a general statement about the patterning of the phonemes you have established.

v) Following your analysis, write the following forms in phonemic transcription.

a) [puɣo]   b) [deðat]   c) [ʃiβaw]   d) [krãmbo]

5. *Plains Cree* (Plains Cree is a Native Canadian language of the Algonquian family)

The following data from Plains Cree shows a number of different voiced and voiceless consonantal segments.

a)	niska	'goose'	l)	nisto	'three'
b)	kodak	'another'	m)	tʃiːgahigan	'axe'
c)	asabaːp	'thread'	n)	aːdim	'dog'
d)	waskoːw	'cloud'	o)	miːbit	'tooth'
e)	paskwaːw	'prairie'	p)	pimeː	'lard'
f)	niːgi	'my house'	q)	mide	'heart'
g)	koːgos	'pig'	r)	oːgik	'these'
h)	tahki	'often'	s)	tʃiihtʃij	'finger'
i)	namwaːtʃ	'not at all'	t)	waːbos	'rabbit'
j)	ospwaːgan	'pipe'	u)	naːbeːw	'man'
k)	midʒihtʃij	'hand'	v)	miːdʒiwin	'food'

i) Do [p] and [b] belong to separate phonemes, or are they allophones of one phoneme? If you think they belong to separate phonemes, list data to support your case. If you think they are allophones, first state the conditioning factors in words, and then, using features, write a rule that accounts for their distribution.

ii) Do the same for [t] and [d], [k] and [g], and [tʃ] and [dʒ].

iii) Can you make a general statement about the relationship among all the consonantal pairs whose distribution you have examined?

iv) Using figure 3.17 as your model, provide complete derivations of the forms for k) *hand*, m) *axe*, and o) *tooth*.

6. There are a number of natural classes in the vowel and consonant data below. Circle three natural classes in each set of data. Indicate which feature or features define the class, as in the example.

Example: [+voice] —— b d tʃ k h ——[–continuant]

a) i   u

   e   o

        a

b) p   tʃ   k

              dʒ

    f   θ   ʃ   x

    m   ŋ

7. Name the single feature that distinguishes the following pairs of sounds.

a) [θ] : [ð]   e) [b] : [m]   i) [ʌ] : [ə]
b) [p] : [f]   f) [s] : [ʃ]   j) [s] : [θ]
c) [u] : [ʊ]   g) [i] : [ɪ]   k) [e] : [ɛ]
d) [i] : [e]   h) [k] : [x]   l) [u] : [o]

8. Complete the feature matrix for each of the sounds indicated. The V abbreviates the features [+syllabic, –consonantal], and the C abbreviates the features [–syllabic, +consonantal].

a) [e]   V
   ⎡ +sonorant ⎤
   ⎢ oDORSAL   ⎥
   ⎢ –high   ⎥
   ⎣ –low   ⎦

b) [ʃ]   C
   ⎡ –sonorant ⎤
   ⎢ –voice   ⎥
   ⎣ –nasal   ⎦

c) [m]   C
   ⎡ +sonorant ⎤
   ⎣ oLABIAL   ⎦

d) [s]   C
   ⎡ –sonorant ⎤
   ⎢ +strident ⎥
   ⎣ oCORONAL ⎦

e) [g]   C
   ⎡ +sonorant ⎤
   ⎢ oDORSAL   ⎥
   ⎣ +high   ⎦

f) [j]
   ⎡ –syllabic   ⎤
   ⎣ –consonantal ⎦

Using the appropriate features, represent each segment on a feature hierarchy tree.

9. *English/Korean*

As we have seen, phonological adaptation of loan words may reflect facts about syllable structure. Recently, the Korean automobile name *Hyundai* has been adapted into English in various ways, one of which follows. Give the Korean form and the English adaptation provided, state two reasons based on syllable structure conditions that explain why the English form is pronounced the way it is.

Korean form		English form
/hjʌndæ/	→	/hʌnde/ [hʌndej]

10. *English*

Many speakers of English have two variants of [l]. One, called *clear l*, is transcribed as [l] in the following data. The other, called *dark l*, is transcribed with [ɫ]. Examine the data, and answer the questions that follow.

a) [lʌjf]	'life'		g) [pʰɪɫ]	'pill'
b) [lip]	'leap'		h) [fiɫ]	'feel'
c) [luːz]	'lose'		i) [hɛɫp]	'help'
d) [ilowp]	'elope'		j) [bʌɫk]	'bulk'
e) [dilʌjt]	'delight'		k) [sowɫd]	'sold'
f) [slip]	'sleep'		l) [fʊɫ]	'full'

Do [l] and [ɫ] belong to separate phonemes or are they allophones of the same phoneme? If you think they belong to separate phonemes, answer question *i*). If you think they are allophones of the same phoneme, answer question *ii*).

i) List the evidence that makes your case for considering [l] and [ɫ] as separate phonemes.

ii) State the distribution of [l] and [ɫ] in words.

iii) Which variant makes the best underlying form? Why?

iv) Can you make reference to syllable structure in your distribution statement? If you can, do so in rule form.

11. *Canadian French*

For the purposes of this problem, you may assume that syllables in Canadian French have the following structure:

- Maximum number of consonants in an onset: 2. Where there are two onset consonants, the first must be an obstruent, the second a sonorant or a fricative.
- Each vowel forms a syllable nucleus.
- Maximum number of consonants in a coda: 2.

With these stipulations in mind, syllabify the following forms:

a) bukan 'smoke'   b) erite 'to inherit'   c) pudrœri 'snowstorm'
d) liɔ̃ 'lion'

In the following data from Canadian French, each pair of phones is in complementary distribution.

[i] and [ɪ]   are allophones of one phoneme
[y] and [ɣ]   are allophones of a second phoneme
[o] and [ɔ]   are allophones of a third phoneme
[u] and [ʊ]   are allophones of a fourth phoneme

It is possible to make a general statement about the distribution of the vowel allophones that accounts for all four phonemes.

Examine the data and answer the questions that follow.

a)	pilɣl	'pill'	s)	lɣn	'moon'
b)	griʃe	'to crunch'	t)	pɪp	'pipe'
c)	grɪʃ	'it crunches'	u)	grimas	'grimace'
d)	pətsi	'little (masc.)'	v)	fini	'finished'
e)	pətsɪt	'little (fem.)'	w)	fɪj	'girl'
f)	vitamɪn	'vitamin'	x)	dzɣr	'hard'
g)	salɣ	'hi'	y)	tryke	'to fake'
h)	ʒɣp	'skirt'	z)	fʊl	'(a) crowd'
i)	fyme	'smoke'	aa)	plɣs	'more'
j)	lynɛt	'glasses'	bb)	fɔl	'crazy (fem.)'
k)	frole	'to skim'	cc)	ru	'wheel'
l)	pɔrt	'door'	dd)	rʊt	'road'
m)	bote	'beauty'	ee)	suvã	'often'
n)	bɔt	'boot'	ff)	trupo	'herd'
o)	fo	'false'	gg)	sʊp	'flexible'
p)	tɔrdzy	'twisted'	hh)	tʊʃ	'touch'
q)	zero	'zero'	ii)	fu	'crazy (masc.)'
r)	pɔm	'apple'	jj)	trɣk	'(a) trick'

i) Provide a statement of the distribution of [i] and [ɪ], [y] and [ɣ], [o] and [ɔ], [u] and [ʊ] in words. Make your statement as general as possible, but be precise!

ii) If you have completed the section on rule formalization, write a single rule that derives the allophones of each phoneme from the underlying form. Use features! Be sure to give your rule a mnemonic name; use this name in the answer to question *iii).*

iii) Provide derivations for the following underlying forms.

UR	#	#	'vitamin'	#	#	'glasses'
PR	[vitamɪn]			[lynɛt]		

12. *English*

The following data contains both careful speech and fast speech forms. Note the differences and answer the questions that follow. Some phonetic detail irrelevant to the question has been omitted from the transcription. Remember that an asterisk before a form indicates that it is not acceptable to (most) native speakers.

Careful speech	Fast speech	Spelled form
a) [ǽspərən]	k) [ǽsprən]	aspirin
b) [pɔ́rsələn]	l) [pɔ́rslən]	porcelain
c) [nǽʃənəlàjz]	m) [nǽʃnəlàjz]	nationalize
d) [rízənəbl̩]	n) [ríznəbl̩]	reasonable
e) [ɪmǽdʒənətɪv]	o) [ɪmǽdʒnətɪv]	imaginative
f) [sɛ̀pərəbílɪri]	p) [sɛ̀prəbílɪri]	separability
g) [mɛ́θəd]	q) [mɛ́θəd] *[mɛ́θd]	method
h) [féjməs]	r) [féjməs] *[féjms]	famous
i) [mɛ́məràjz]	s) [mɛ́məràjz] *[mɛ́mràjz]	memorize
j) [kʰənsìdəréjʃən]	t) [kʰənsìdəréjʃən] *[kʰənsìdréjʃən]	consideration

i)   The schwa deletion between the careful speech forms and the rapid speech forms in items a–f is systematic. State in words the phonetic conditions that account for the deletion.

ii)   The same pattern that occurs between the careful speech forms and the rapid speech forms in items a–f does not occur in items g–j. State in words the phonetic difference between these sets of forms that accounts for the lack of schwa deletion.

iii)   Now that you have taken items g–j into account, will you have to change your original statement of the phonetic conditions governing schwa deletion in the fast speech forms? If so, do this in words.

iv)   If you have completed the section on rule formalization, convert your statement in *iii)* into formal notation.

13.   The English data below provide examples of stress placement on certain verbs.

A	*B*	*C*
contáin	adápt	astónish
collíde	collápse	consíder
eráse	eléct	imágine
caróuse	obsérve	detérmine
corróde	tormént	prómise

i)   Describe in words the stress placement on these verbs. Be sure to make reference to syllable structure in your statement.

ii)   Provide syllabified representations of the words *collide, elect,* and *consider* in order to illustrate your conclusions about stress placement on these forms.

14.   State each of the following rules in English, making reference to natural classes and common linguistic processes.

Example: $\begin{bmatrix} \text{-syllabic} \\ \text{+consonantal} \\ \text{-sonorant} \end{bmatrix} \rightarrow \emptyset / \_\_\_\_ \#$ *(an obstruent is deleted word-finally)*

a) Ø →
$$\begin{bmatrix}+\text{syllabic}\\-\text{consonantal}\\+\text{sonorant}\\o\text{DORSAL}\\-\text{high}\\-\text{low}\\-\text{back}\\+\text{tense}\end{bmatrix}$$ / # ____ $$\begin{bmatrix}-\text{syllabic}\\+\text{consonantal}\\-\text{sonorant}\end{bmatrix}\begin{bmatrix}-\text{syllabic}\\+\text{consonantal}\\-\text{sonorant}\end{bmatrix}$$

b) $$\begin{bmatrix}-\text{syllabic}\\+\text{consonantal}\\-\text{sonorant}\\-\text{nasal}\\-\text{continuant}\\-\text{delayed release}\\+\text{voice}\\o\text{CORONAL}\\+\text{anterior}\end{bmatrix}$$ → [+nasal] /____ $$\begin{bmatrix}-\text{syllabic}\\+\text{consonantal}\\+\text{sonorant}\\+\text{nasal}\end{bmatrix}$$

c) $$\begin{bmatrix}+\text{syllabic}\\-\text{consonantal}\\+\text{sonorant}\end{bmatrix}$$ → [+round] / $$\begin{bmatrix}-\text{syllabic}\\+\text{consonantal}\\o\text{LABIAL}\end{bmatrix}$$ ———— $$\begin{bmatrix}-\text{syllabic}\\+\text{consonantal}\\o\text{LABIAL}\end{bmatrix}$$

15. Change the following statements into rule notation. Be sure to name the process in question for each case.
    a) Voiceless stops become corresponding fricatives between vowels.
    b) A schwa is inserted between a voiced stop and a word-final voiced fricative.
    c) Low unrounded vowels become rounded before *m*.

16. *Tamil* (Tamil is a Dravidian language spoken in South India and Sri Lanka)
    In the following Tamil data, some words begin with glides while others do not. The symbol [d] represents a voiced retroflex stop and the diacritic [̪] indicates dentals.

Initial j-glide		Initial w-glide		No initial glide	
a) jeli	'rat'	f) woɖi	'break'	k) arivu	'knowledge'
b) jiː	'fly'	g) woːlaj	'palm leaf'	l) ai̪n̪tu	'five'
c) jilaj	'leaf'	h) wuːsi	'needle'	m) aːsaj	'desire'
d) jeŋgeː	'where'	i) wujir	'life'	n) aːru	'river'
e) jiɖuppu	'waist'	j) woːram	'edge'	o) aːɖi	'origin'

    i) The occurrence of these glides is predictable. Using your knowledge of natural classes, make a general statement about the distribution of the glides.
    ii) Assuming the glides are not present in the underlying representations, name the process that accounts for their presence in the phonetic forms.
    iii) Using features, write a rule using alpha notation that formalizes this process. Show the derivation of the forms for *fly* and *break*.

17. *Mende* (Mende is spoken in Liberia and Sierra Leone)

In Mende, the forms that mean 'on' (*ma*) and 'in' (*hu*) are suffixes (they are attached to a preceding word; see chapter 4, section 1.3). Notice in the data below that suffixes all bear tone, but that the tone varies on different words. In the examples, ´ indicates a high tone, ` a low tone, and ^ a falling (high-to-low) tone.

a)	kɔ́	'war'	kɔ́má	'on war'	kɔ́hú	'in war'
b)	pélέ	'house'	pélέmá	'on (the) house'	pélέhú	'in (the) house'
c)	bὲlὲ	'trousers'	bὲlὲmà	'on trousers'	bὲlὲhù	'in trousers'
d)	ngílà	'dog'	ngílàmà	'on (the) dog'	ngílàhù	'in (the) dog'

i) Can you account for the differences in tone on the suffixes for 'on' and 'in' in Mende? Provide a solution using autosegmental notation. [Hint: assume that the suffixes have no tone to begin with, but that the words to which they are attached do have tone.]

ii) Assuming that you have answered question a) successfully, account for the tones of the suffixes meaning 'on' and 'in' in the remaining examples.

e)	mbû	'owl'	mbúmà	'on (the) owl'	mbúhù	'in (the) owl'
f)	njáhâ	'woman'	njàhámà	'on (the) woman'	njàháhù	'in (the) woman'

18. *Moru* (Miza dialect; Moru is a Sudanic language)

In Moru, contour tones are not found on short vowels in underlying representations. However, phonetic forms of combined lexical items do show contour tones. Can you represent this using autosegmental notation? [Hint: a segmental process is involved as well as a typical suprasegmental process and the two processes must be ordered.] In the data provided, ´ indicates a high tone; ` a low tone; ^ a falling (high-to-low) tone; and ˇ a rising (low-to-high) tone. Vowels with no tone mark need not be considered.

a) màá → [mǎ] 'we'
   we

b) ká ùmu → [kûmu] 'he runs'
   he runs

c) ká ɔ̀nga → [kɔ̂nga] 'he jumps'
   he jumps

d) njá àdì ùzi ja → [njâdùzi ja] 'who are you calling?'
   you call who?

CHAPTER *Four*

William O'Grady
Videa de Guzman

Morphology: the analysis of word structure

Carve every word before you let it fall.

OLIVER WENDELL HOLMES, SR.

Nothing is more important to language than words. Unlike phonemes and syllables, which are simply elements of sound, words carry meaning in addition to their phonological form. And unlike sentences, which are made up as needed and then discarded, words are permanently stored in a speaker's mental dictionary or **lexicon**. They are arguably the fundamental building blocks of language.

The average high school student knows about 60 000 basic words—items such as *read, language, on, cold,* and *if,* whose form and meaning cannot be predicted from anything else. Countless other words can be constructed and comprehended by the application of general rules to these and other elements. For example, any speaker of English who knows the verb *fax* recognizes *faxed* as its past tense form, and can construct and interpret words such as *faxable* (for things that can be faxed) and *fax machine* (for the device that sends and receives faxes). Linguists use the term **morphology** to refer to the part of the grammar that is concerned with word formation and word structure.

1 Words and word structure

As literate speakers of English, we rarely have difficulty segmenting a stream of speech sounds into words or deciding where to leave spaces when writing a sentence. What, though, is a word?

Linguists define the **word** as the smallest **free form** found in language. A free form is simply an element that does not have to occur in a fixed position with respect to neighbouring elements; in many cases, it can even appear in isolation. Consider the words making up the following sentence.

1)
The birds left.

The plural marker *-s* is not a free form (and therefore not a word) since it never occurs in isolation and cannot be separated from the noun to which it belongs. (Elements that must be attached to another category are written here with a hyphen.)

2)
*The bird left -s.

In contrast, *birds* is a word since it can occur in isolation, as in the following example.

3)
Speaker A: What are those things in the tree?
Speaker B: Birds.

Moreover, even when *birds* occurs as part of a larger sentence, it is not attached to anything else. This is why it can appear in different positions within a sentence, as illustrated in *4)*.

4)
a. birds occurring in front of a verb:
Birds avoid cats.

b. birds occurring after a verb:
Cats chase birds.

Some words—like *the* in sentence *1)*—normally do not occur in isolation. However, they are still free forms since their positioning with respect to neighbouring words is not entirely fixed. As shown by the following example, *the* can be separated from an accompanying noun by an intervening word.

5)
the birds
the young birds
the very young birds

1.1   Morphemes

Like syllables and sentences, words have an internal structure consisting of smaller units organized with respect to each other in a particular way. The most important component of word structure is the **morpheme**, the smallest unit of language that carries information about meaning or function. The word *builder*, for example, consists of two morphemes: *build* (with the meaning of 'construct') and *-er* (which indicates that the entire word functions as a noun with the meaning 'one who builds'). Similarly, the word *houses* is made up of the morphemes *house* (with the meaning of 'dwelling') and *-s* (with the meaning 'more than one').

Some words consist of a single morpheme. For example, the word *train* cannot be divided into smaller parts (say, *tr* and *ain* or *t* and *rain*) that carry information about its meaning or function. Such words are said to be **simple** and are distinguished from **complex** words, which contain two or more morphemes (see table 4.1).

| Table 4.1 | Words consisting of one or more morphemes | | |
One	Two	Three	More than three
and			
boy	boy-s		
hunt	hunt-er	hunt-er-s	
act	act-ive	act-iv-ate	re-act-iv-ate

Free and bound morphemes

A morpheme that can be a word by itself is called **free** whereas a morpheme that must be attached to another element is said to be **bound**. The morpheme *boy*, for example, is free since it can be used as a word on its own; plural *-s*, on the other hand, is bound.

Concepts that are expressed by free morphemes in English do not necessarily have the same status in other languages. For example, in Hare (an Athapaskan language spoken in Canada's Northwest Territories), morphemes that indicate body parts must always be attached to a morpheme designating a possessor (see table 4.2). (The diacritic ´ marks a high tone.)

Table 4.2	Some body part names in Hare		
Without a possessor		**With a possessor**	
*fí	'head'	sefí	'my head'
*bé	'belly'	nebé	'your belly'
*dzé	'heart'	ʔedzé	'someone's heart/a heart'

In English, of course, these body part names are free morphemes and do not have to be attached to another element.

Conversely, there are also some bound forms in English whose counterparts in other languages are free. For example, the notion 'past' or 'completed' is expressed by the bound morpheme *-ed* in English, but by the free morpheme *lɛɛw* in Thai. As the following sentence shows, this morpheme can even be separated from the verb by an intervening word. (Tone is not marked here.)

6)
Boon thaan khaaw lɛɛw.
Boon eat   rice   past
'Boon ate rice.'

Allomorphs

Morphemes do not always have an invariant form. The morpheme used to express indefiniteness in English, for instance, has two forms—*a* before a word that begins with a consonant and *an* before a word that begins with a vowel.

7)
an orange   a building
an accent   a car
an eel   a girl

The variant forms of a morpheme are called its **allomorphs**.

Another example of allomorphic variation is found in the pronunciation of the plural morpheme *-s* in the following words.

8)
cats
dogs
judges

Whereas the plural is /s/ in the first case, it is /z/ in the second, and /əz/ in the third. Here again, selection of the proper allomorph is dependent on phonological facts. We will examine this phenomenon in more detail later in this chapter.

Other examples of patterns in which a morpheme's form changes when it combines with another element are easy to find in English. The final segment in *assert*, for instance, is /t/ when this morpheme stands alone as a separate word but /ʃ/ when it combines with the morpheme *-ion* in the word *assertion*. Similar alternations are found in words such as *permit/permiss-ive*, *include/inclus-ive*, *electric/electric-ity*, *impress/impress-ion*, and so on.

It is important not to confuse spelling changes with allomorphic variation. For example, the final *e* in the spelling of *create* and *ride* is dropped in *creat-ive* and *rid-ing*. However, since there is no change in pronunciation, this is not allomorphic variation.

1.2   Analyzing word structure

In order to represent the internal structure of words, it is necessary not only to identify each of the component morphemes but also to classify them in terms of their contribution to the meaning and function of the larger word.

Roots and affixes

Complex words typically consist of a **root** morpheme and one or more **affixes**. The root constitutes the core of the word and carries the major component of its meaning. Roots typically belong to a **lexical category**, such as noun (N), verb (V), adjective (A), or preposition (P). These categories will be discussed in more detail in chapter 5, section 1.1. For now it suffices to note that nouns typically refer to concrete and abstract 'things' (*tree, intelligence*), verbs tend to denote actions (*treat, teach*), adjectives usually name properties (*kind, red*), and prepositions encode spatial relations (*in, near*).

Unlike roots, affixes do not belong to a lexical category and are always bound morphemes. For example, the affix *-er* is a bound morpheme that combines with a verb such as *teach*, giving a noun with the meaning 'one who teaches'. The internal structure of this word can be represented in diagram form as in figure 4.1. (The symbol 'Af' stands for affix.)

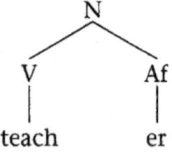

Figure 4.1 The internal structure of the word *teacher*

Figure 4.2 on page 125 provides some additional examples of word structure.

The structural diagrams in figures 4.1 and 4.2 are often called **trees**. The information they depict can also be represented by using labeled bracketing—[_A_ [_Af_ un] [_A_ kind]] for *unkind* and [_N_ [_N_ book] [_Af_ s]] for *books*. (This is somewhat harder to read, though, and we will generally use tree structures in this chapter.) Where the details of a word's structure are irrelevant to the point being considered, it is traditional to use a much simpler system of representation that indicates only the location of the morpheme boundaries: *un-kind*, *book-s*, and so on.

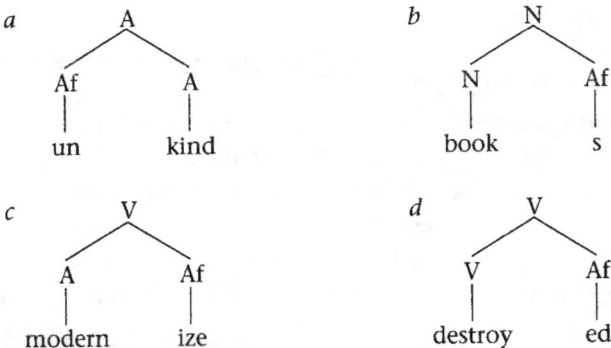

Figure 4.2 Some other words with an internal structure consisting of a root and an affix

Bases

A **base** is the form to which an affix is added. In many cases, the base is also the root. In *books,* for example, the element to which the affix *-s* is added corresponds to the word's root. In other cases, however, the base can be larger than a root. This happens in words such as *blackened,* in which the past tense affix *-ed* is added to the verbal base *blacken*—a unit consisting of the root morpheme *black* and the suffix *-en* (see figure 4.3).

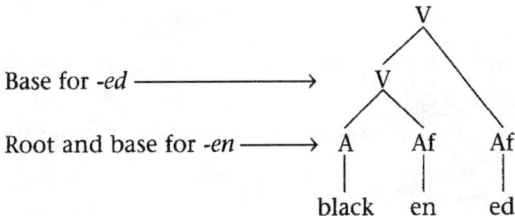

Figure 4.3 A word illustrating the difference between a root and a base

In this case, *black* is not only the root for the entire word but also the base for *-en.* The unit *blacken,* on the other hand, is simply the base for *-ed.*

Problematic cases (*Advanced*)

The majority of complex words in English are built from roots that are free morphemes. In the words *re-do* and *treat-ment,* for example, the root (*do* and *treat,* respectively) is a V that can appear elsewhere in the language without an affix. Because most complex words are formed from a root that can itself be a word, English morphology is said to be **word-based**.

Not all languages work this way, however. In Japanese and Spanish, for instance, verbal roots must always appear with an affix; they never stand alone as separate words.

English too has some bound roots. For example, the word *unkempt* seems to consist of the prefix *un-* (with the meaning 'not') and the root *kempt* (meaning 'groomed'), even though *kempt* cannot be used by itself. Other common words of this type include *in-ept,* *venge-ance,* and *salv-ation,* to name but a few.[1]

There is a good historical explanation for why English has words of this type. For example, there was once a word *kempt* in English (with the meaning 'combed'), and it was to this base that the affix *un-* was originally attached. However, *kempt* later disappeared from the language, leaving behind the word *unkempt* in which an affix appears with a bound root.

Still other words with bound roots were borrowed into English as whole words. *Inept*, for instance, comes from Latin *ineptus* 'unsuited'. Its relationship to the word *apt* may have been evident at one time, but it now seems to consist of a prefix and a bound root.

Another class of words that are notoriously problematic for morphological analysis includes items such as *receive, deceive, conceive,* and *perceive* or *permit, submit,* and *commit*. These items were borrowed into English from Latin (usually via French) as whole words and their component syllables have no identifiable meaning of their own. (The *re* of *receive*, for instance, does not have the sense of 'again' that it does in *redo*.) For this reason we will assume that words of this type consist of a single morpheme.[2]

1.3   Some common morphological phenomena

Words can be extended and modified in a variety of ways—sometimes by adding an additional morpheme and sometimes by making an internal change. As the next step in our survey of word structure, we will examine some of the more common of these morphological processes.

Compounding

One of the most common and important word-building processes in language involves **compounding**, the combination of two or more existing words to create a new word. The effects of compounding can be seen in countless English words, including the examples in table 4.3.

Table 4.3 Some examples of English compounds			
Noun + noun	**Adjective + noun**	**Verb + noun**	**Preposition + noun**
street light	bluebird	swear word	overlord
campsite	happy hour	washcloth	outhouse
bookcase	high chair	scrub lady	in-group

Compounding plays a central role in word formation in many languages, as we will see in more detail in section 3.

Affixation

Another extremely common morphological process in language is **affixation**, the addition of an affix. Normally, linguists distinguish among three types of affixes. An affix that is attached to the front of its base is called a **prefix** whereas an affix that is attached to the end of its base is termed a **suffix**. Both types of affix occur in English, as table 4.4 shows.

Table 4.4	Some English prefixes and suffixes
Prefixes	**Suffixes**
de-activate	vivid-*ly*
re-play	govern-*ment*
il-legal	hunt-*er*
in-accurate	kind-*ness*

We will consider the nature and properties of English affixes in more detail in sections 2.1 and 5.

Far less common than prefixes and suffixes are **infixes**, a type of affix that occurs within a base. The data in table 4.5 from the Philippine language Tagalog contains examples of the infix -*in*-, which is inserted after the first consonant of the base to mark a completed event.

Table 4.5	Some Tagalog infixes		
Base		**Infixed Form**	
bili	'buy'	b-*in*-ili	'bought'
basa	'read'	b-*in*-asa	'read' (Past)
sulat	'write'	s-*in*-ulat	'wrote'

Beginning students sometimes think that a morpheme such as -*ish* in *boy-ish-ness* is an infix since it occurs between two other morphemes (*boy* and -*ness*), but this is not so. To be an infix, an affix must occur inside its base (as when -*in*- in Tagalog occurs inside *sulat* 'write'). Nothing of this sort happens in the case of -*ish*, since its base is *boy* not the impossible **boyness*.

A very special type of infixing system is found in Arabic, in which a typical root consists simply of three consonants. Affixes consisting of two vowels are then inserted into this root in a manner that intersperses the vowels among the consonants. (In the examples that follow, the segments of the root are written in boldface.)

9)

katab	**kutib**	**aktub**	**uktab**
'write'	'have been written'	'be writing'	'being written'

One way to represent the structure of such words is shown in figure 4.4, with the root and affix assigned to different **tiers**, or levels of structure, that are intercalated in the actual pronunciation of the word.

Figure 4.4 Two tiers are used to represent the structure of infixed words in Arabic

Cliticization

Some morphemes behave like words in terms of their meaning and function, but are unable to stand alone as independent forms for phonological reasons. Called **clitics**, these elements must be attached to another word (known as a **host**). A good example of this can be found in English, where certain verb forms have reduced variants (*'m* for *am*, *'s* for *is*, and *'re* for *are*) that cannot stand alone since they no longer constitute a syllable. Cliticization occurs, attaching these elements to the preceding word.

> 10)
> *a.* I*'m* leaving now.
> *b.* Mary*'s* going to succeed.   *enclitics*
> *c.* They*'re* here now.

Cliticization is also common in French, which has a set of unstressed clitic pronouns that must be attached to the verb. (Although not evident in the written language, the clitic and the verb are pronounced as if they formed a single word.)

> 11)
> Suzanne *les* voit.
> Suzanne them-sees   *proclitics*
> 'Suzanne sees them.'

Clitics that attach to the end of their host (as in the English examples) are called **enclitics**; those that attach to the beginning of their host (as in the French example) are known as **proclitics**.

The effects of cliticization can bear a superficial resemblance to affixation since in both cases an element that cannot stand alone is attached to a base. The key difference is that—unlike affixes—clitics are members of a lexical category such as verb, noun (or pronoun), or preposition.

Internal change

Internal change is a process that substitutes one non-morphemic segment for another to mark a grammatical contrast, as illustrated in the pairs of words in table 4.6.

internal change

Table 4.6	Internal change in English
sing (present)	sang (past)
sink (present)	sank (past)
drive (present)	drove (past)
foot (singular)	feet (plural)
goose (singular)	geese (plural)

Verbs such as *sing, sink,* and *drive* form their past tense by changing the vowel (e.g., from *i* to *a* in the first two examples). The term **ablaut** is often used for vowel alternations that mark grammatical contrasts in this way.

Some internal changes reflect phonologically conditioned alternations from an earlier stage in the language's history. The irregular plurals *geese* and *feet* came about in this way: the original vowel in the words *goose* and *foot* was fronted under the influence of the front vowel in the old plural suffix /i/, which was subsequently dropped. This type of change in English and other Germanic languages is known as **umlaut.**

12)

Old singular form of *goose*:	/gos/
Old plural form:	/gos-i/
Umlaut:	/gœs-i/
Loss of the plural suffix:	/gœs/
Other changes (see ch. 7)	/ges/ and then /gis/ 'geese'

Internal change differs from infixing in important ways. As shown by the Tagalog examples in table 4.5, the base into which a real infix is inserted typically exists as a separate form elsewhere in the language (compare *sulat* 'write' with *s-in-ulat* 'wrote'). Matters are quite different in the case of alternations such as *foot/feet* or *sing/sang* in English, since we have no form *ft* meaning 'lower extremity of the leg' or *sng* meaning 'produce words in a musical tone'. Moreover, in contrast to the situation in either Tagalog or Arabic, the segments affected by internal change are not themselves morphemes: the *a* of *ran* and the *o* of *drove* do not in general carry the meaning 'past' in English any more than the *ee* of *geese* normally carries the meaning 'plural'.

The existence of internal change and of infixing illustrates an important point about word structure: morphology is not always **concatenative**. That is, not all word structure is built by assembling morphemes in an additive, linear fashion. The morphological processes considered in the remainder of this section provide additional illustrations of this point.

Suppletion

Suppletion is a morphological process that replaces a morpheme by an entirely different morpheme in order to indicate a grammatical contrast (see table 4.7). Examples of this phenomenon in English include the use of *went* as the past tense form of the verb *go* and *was* and *were* as the past tense forms of *be*.

Table 4.7	Suppletion in some European languages	
Language	**Basic form**	**Suppletive form**
French	*avoir* 'to have'	*eu* 'had'
Spanish	*ir* 'to go'	*fue* '(s/he) went'
German	*ist* 'is'	*sind* 'are'
Russian	*xoroʃo* 'good'	*lutʃʃe* 'better' ('more good')

In some cases, it is hard to distinguish between suppletion and internal change. For example, is the past tense of *think* (*thought*) and *seek* (*sought*) an instance of suppletion or internal change? Because the initial phoneme of these verbs remains unchanged and because the phenomenon shows up in several words (see also *catch/caught* and *wreak/wrought*), this type of alternation is often treated as an extreme form of internal change. (However, the term **partial suppletion** is used by some linguists for these cases.)

Reduplication

A common morphological process in some languages involves **reduplication**, which marks a grammatical or semantic contrast by repeating all or part of the base to which it applies. Repetition of the entire base yields **full reduplication**, as in the data in table 4.8 from Turkish and Indonesian, respectively.

Table 4.8	Some examples of full reduplication		
Base		**Reduplicated form**	
Turkish			
tʃabuk	'quickly'	tʃabuk tʃabuk	'very quickly'
javaʃ	'slowly'	javaʃ javaʃ	'very slowly'
iji	'well'	iji iji	'very well'
gyzel	'beautifully'	gyzel gyzel	'very beautifully'
Indonesian			
oraŋ	'man'	oraŋ oraŋ	'all sorts of men'
anak	'child'	anak anak	'all sorts of children'
maŋga	'mango'	maŋga maŋga	'all sorts of mangoes'

In contrast, **partial reduplication** copies only part of the base. In the data from Tagalog in table 4.9, for instance, reduplication affects only the first consonant-vowel sequence.

Table 4.9	Reduplication in Tagalog		
Base		**Reduplicated form**	
takbuh	'run'	tatakbuh	'will run'
lakad	'walk'	lalakad	'will walk'
pili?	'choose'	pipili?	'will choose'

English makes limited use of reduplication in diminutive expressions such as *teeny-weeny* and *itsy-bitsy.*

Stress and tone placement

Sometimes, a base can undergo a change in the placement of stress or tone to reflect a change in its category. In English, for example, there are pairs of words such as those in table 4.10 on page 131, in which the verb has stress on the final syllable while the corresponding noun is stressed on the first syllable. (Stress is represented here by ´.)

In the language Mono-Bili (spoken in the African country of Zaire; see table 4.11), tone is used to make the distinction between past and future tense. (A high tone is marked by ´ and a low tone by `.)

Table 4.10	Stress placement in English
Verb	**Noun**
implánt	ímplant
impórt	ímport
presént	présent
subjéct	súbject
contést	cóntest

Table 4.11	Past versus future in Mono-Bili		
Past		**Future**	
dá	'spanked'	dà	'will spank'
zî	'ate'	zì	'will eat'
wó	'killed'	wò	'will kill'

As you can see, high tone is associated with the past tense and low tone with the future.

Of the morphological operations we have been considering, two deserve special attention because of the crucial role they play in the formation of new words in English and many other languages—derivation (a special type of affixation) and compounding. The next sections of this chapter focus on these processes.

2 Derivation

Derivation is an affixational process that forms a word with a meaning and/or category distinct from that of its base. Table 4.12 contains words formed by adding the suffix *-er* to a verb to form a noun with the meaning 'one who does X'. (Do not confuse this suffix with the *-er* that applies to a noun in cases such as *Quebecer* and *islander* or the *-er* that combines with an adjective in cases such as *taller* and *smarter*.)

Table 4.12	The *-er* affix
Verb base	**Resulting noun**
sell	sell-er
write	writ-er
teach	teach-er
sing	sing-er
discover	discover-er

Once formed, derived words become independent lexical items that receive their own entry in a speaker's mental dictionary. As time goes by, they often take on special senses that are not predictable from the component morphemes. The word *writer*, for example, is often used not just for someone who can write but rather for someone who writes for a living (e.g., *He's a writer*); *comparable* (with stress on the first syllable) means 'similar' rather than 'able to be compared'; *profession* usually denotes a career rather than the act of professing; and so on.

2.1   English derivational affixes

Table 4.13 lists some English derivational affixes, along with information about the category of their usual base (ignoring bound roots) and of the resulting new word. The first entry states that the affix *-able* applies to a verb base and converts it into an adjective. Thus, if we add the affix *-able* to the verb *fix*, we get an adjective (with the meaning 'able to be fixed').

Table 4.13	Some English derivational affixes	
Affix	**Change**	**Examples**
Suffixes		
-able	V → A	fix-able, do-able, understand-able
-al	V → N	refus-al, dispos-al, recit-al
-ant	V → N	claim-ant, defend-ant
-(at)ion	V → N	realiz-ation, assert-ion, protect-ion
-er	V → N	teach-er, work-er
-ing$_1$	V → N	the shoot-ing, the danc-ing
-ing$_2$	V → A	the sleep-ing giant, a blaz-ing fire
-ive	V → A	assert-ive, impress-ive, restrict-ive
-ment	V → N	adjourn-ment, treat-ment, amaze-ment
-ful	N → A	faith-ful, hope-ful, dread-ful
-(i)al	N → A	president-ial, nation-al
-(i)an	N → A	Arab-ian, Einstein-ian, Albert-an
-ic	N → A	cub-ic, optimist-ic, moron-ic
-ize$_1$	N → V	hospital-ize, crystal-ize
-less	N → A	penni-less, brain-less
-ous	N → A	poison-ous, lecher-ous
-ate	A → V	activ-ate, captiv-ate
-en	A → V	dead-en, black-en, hard-en
-ity	A → N	stupid-ity, prior-ity
-ize$_2$	A → V	modern-ize, national-ize
-ly	A → Adv	quiet-ly, slow-ly, careful-ly
-ness	A → N	happi-ness, sad-ness
Prefixes		
anti-	N → N	anti-abortion, anti-pollution
de-	V → V	de-activate, de-mystify
dis-	V → V	dis-continue, dis-obey
ex-	N → N	ex-president, ex-wife, ex-friend
in-	A → A	in-competent, in-complete
mis-	V → V	mis-identify, mis-place
re-	V → V	re-think, re-do, re-state
un$_1$-	A → A	un-happy, un-fair, un-intelligent
un$_2$-	V → V	un-tie, un-lock, un-do

It is sometimes difficult to determine the category of the base to which an affix is added. In the case of *worker*, for instance, the base (*work*) is sometimes used as a verb (as in *they work hard*) and sometimes as a noun (as in *the work is time-consuming*). How can we know which of these forms serves as the base for -*er*? The key is to find words such as *teacher* and *writer*, in which the category of the base can be unequivocally determined. Because *teach* and *write* can only be verbs, we can infer that the base with which -*er* combines in the word *worker* is also a verb.

Words formed by derivation exhibit the type of internal structure illustrated in figure 4.5.

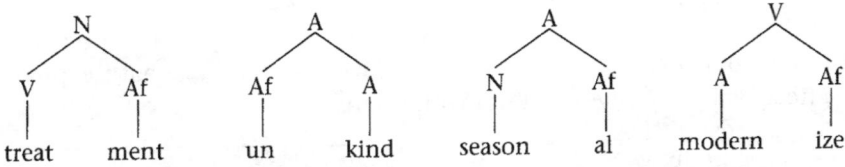

Figure 4.5 Some words formed by derivation

In each of these structures, an affix combines with a base of a particular type to give a new word, in accordance with the properties listed in table 4.13. In the case of *treatment*, for instance, the affix -*ment* combines with the V *treat* to give the N *treatment*.

Complex derivations

Since derivation can apply more than once, it is possible to create multiple levels of word structure, as in figure 4.6.

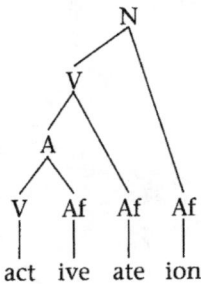

Figure 4.6 A word with a multilayered internal structure

The word *activation* contains several layers of structure, each of which reflects the attachment of an affix to a base of the appropriate type. In the first layer, the affix -*ive* combines with the verbal base *act* to give an adjective. (As noted in table 4.13, -*ive* is the type of affix that converts a verb into an adjective.) In the next layer, the affix -*ate* combines with this adjective and converts it into a verb (*activate*). At this point, the affix -*ion* is added, converting the verb into a noun and giving the word *activation*.

In some cases, the internal structure of a complex word is not so obvious. The word *unhappiness*, for instance, could apparently be analyzed in either of the ways indicated in figure 4.7.

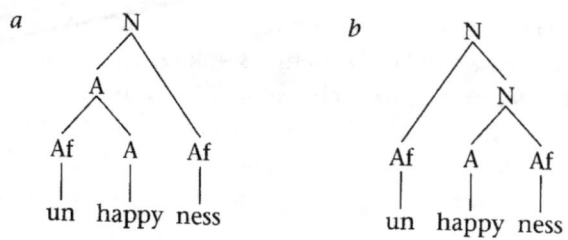

Figure 4.7 Two possible structures for the word *unhappiness*

However, by considering the properties of the affixes *un-* and *-ness*, it is possible to find an argument that favours figure 4.7a over 4.7b. The key observation is that the prefix *un-* combines quite freely with adjectives, but not with nouns.

Table 4.14	The prefix *un-*
***un* + A**	***un* + N**
unable	*unknowledge
unkind	*unhealth
unhurt	*uninjury

This suggests that *un-* must combine with the adjective *happy* before it is converted into a noun by the suffix *-ness*, exactly as depicted in figure 4.7a.

By contrast, in a word such as *unhealthy*, the prefix *un-* can be attached only AFTER the suffix *-y* has been added to the root. That is because *-y* turns nouns into adjectives, creating the type of category with which *un-* can combine.

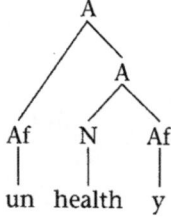

Figure 4.8 The internal structure of the word *unhealthy*

Constraints on derivation

Derivation is often subject to special constraints and restrictions. For instance, the suffix *-ant* (see table 4.13) can combine with bases of Latin origin such as *assist* and *combat*, but not those of native English origin such as *help* and *fight*. Thus, we find words such as *assistant* and *combatant*, but not **helpant* and **fightant*.

Sometimes, a derivational affix is able to attach only to bases with particular phonological properties. A good example of this involves the suffix *-en*, which can combine with some adjectives to create verbs with a causative meaning (*whiten* means roughly 'cause to become white').

Table 4.15	Restrictions on the use of *-en*
Acceptable	**Unacceptable**
whiten	*abstracten
soften	*bluen
madden	*angryen
quicken	*slowen
liven	*greenen

The contrasts illustrated in table 4.15 reflect the fact that *-en* can only combine with a mono-syllabic base that ends in an obstruent. Thus, it can be added to *white*, which is both mono-syllabic and ends in an obstruent. But it cannot be added to *abstract*, which has two syllables, or to *blue*, which does not end in an obstruent.

2.2 Two classes of derivational affixes (*Advanced*)

It is common to distinguish between two types of derivational affixes in English. **Class 1** affixes often trigger changes in the consonant or vowel segments of the base and may affect stress placement. In addition, they often combine with bound roots, as in the final two of the following examples (see table 4.16).

Table 4.16	Typical effects of Class 1 affixes	
Affix	**Sample word**	**Change triggered by affix**
-ity	san-ity	vowel in the base changes from /e/ to /æ/ (cf. *sane*)
	public-ity	final consonant of the base changes from /k/ to /s/, stress shifts to second syllable (cf. *públic* vs. *publícity*)
-y	democrac-y	final consonant of the base changes from /t/ to /s/ stress shifts to second syllable (cf. *démocrat* vs. *demócracy*)
-ive	product-ive	stress shifts to second syllable (cf. *próduct* vs. *prodúctive*)
-(i)al	part-ial	final consonant of the base changes from /t/ to /ʃ/ (cf. *part*)
-ize	public-ize	final consonant of the base changes from /k/ to /s/ (cf. *public*)
-ion	nat-ion	final consonant of the base changes from /t/ to /ʃ/ (cf. *native*)

In contrast, **Class 2** affixes tend to be phonologically neutral, having no effect on the seg-mental makeup of the base or on stress placement (see table 4.17).

Table 4.17 Some typical Class 2 affixes		
Affix	**Sample word**	**Change triggered by affix**
-ness	prompt-ness	None
-less	hair-less	None
-ful	hope-ful	None
-ly	quiet-ly	None
-er	defend-er	None
-ish	self-ish	None

When both types of affix appear in the same word, the Class 1 affix must normally occur closer to the root than does the Class 2 affix. As the following examples help illustrate, forms in which a Class 2 affix appears closer to the root are typically not possible words.

13)

relat-ion-al	divis-ive-ness	*fear-less-ity	fear-less-ness
ROOT 1 1	ROOT 1 2	ROOT 2 1	ROOT 2 2

3 Compounding

Another common technique for word building in English involves compounding, the combination of two already existent words. With very few exceptions, the resulting **compound** word is a noun, a verb, or an adjective (see figure 4.9). (Possible examples of compound prepositions include the words *into* and *onto*.)

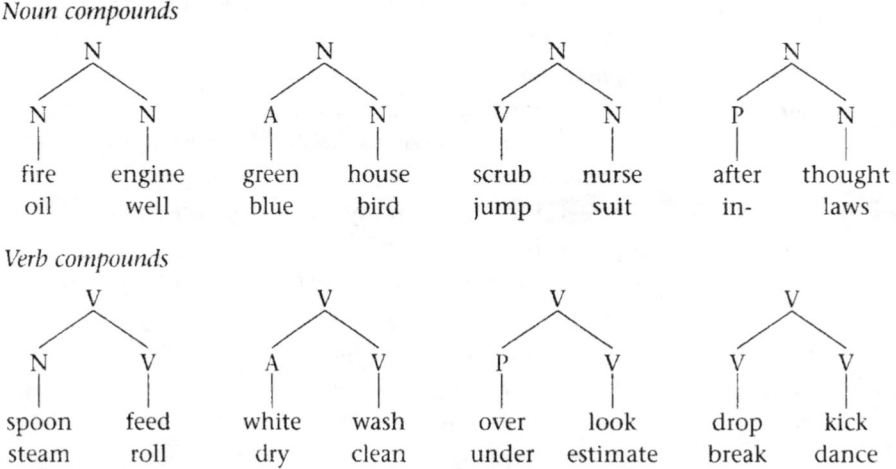

Figure 4.9 Some English compounds

Adjective compounds

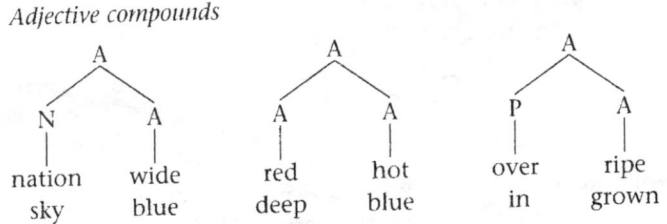

Figure 4.9 (continued) Some English compounds

In these and most other compounds of this type, the rightmost morpheme determines the category of the entire word. Thus, *greenhouse* is a noun because its rightmost component is a noun, *spoonfeed* is a verb because *feed* also belongs to this category, and *nationwide* is an adjective just as *wide* is. The morpheme that determines the category of the entire word is called the **head**.

Once formed, compounds can be combined with other words to create still larger compounds, as the examples in figure 4.10 help show.

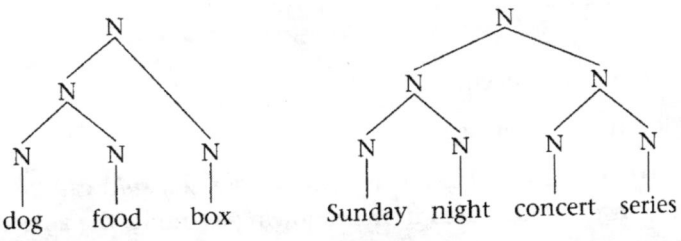

Figure 4.10 Compounds formed from smaller compounds

In addition, compounding can interact with derivation, yielding forms such as *abortion debate*, in which the first word in the compound is the result of derivation (see figure 4.11).

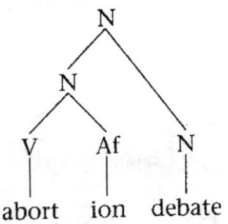

Figure 4.11 The interaction of derivation with compounding

3.1 Properties of compounds

English orthography is not consistent in representing compounds, which are sometimes written as single words, sometimes with an intervening hyphen, and sometimes as separate words. In terms of pronunciation, however, there is an important generalization to be made (see table 4.18). In particular, adjective-noun compounds are characterized by a more prominent stress on their first component. In non-compounds consisting of an adjective and a noun, in contrast, the second element is generally stressed.

Table 4.18 Compounds versus non-compounds			
Compound word		**Non-compound expressions**	
greénhouse	'a glass-enclosed garden'	green hoúse	'a house painted green'
bláckboard	'a chalkboard'	black boárd	'a board that is black'
wét suit	'a diver's costume'	wet suít	'a suit that is wet'

A second distinguishing feature of compounds in English is that tense and plural markers can typically not be attached to the first element, although they can be added to the compound as a whole. (There are some exceptions, however, such as *passers-by* and *park<u>s</u> supervisor.*)

14)
*The player [drop<u>ped</u> kick] the ball through the goal posts.

The player [drop kick]<u>ed</u> the ball through the goal posts.

15)
*The [fox<u>es</u> hunter] didn't have a licence.

The [fox hunter]<u>s</u> didn't have a licence.

Compounds whose first element is an adjective (*greenhouse, wet suit*) can be identified with the help of a different test. As illustrated in the following example, the adjectival component of a compound cannot be preceded by a word such as *very*.

16)
Compound with *very*:
*We live next to a very [greenhouse].

In contrast, an adjective that is not part of a compound can typically be accompanied by this type of word.

17)
Very with an adjective that is not part of a compound:
We live next to a very green house.

3.2   Endocentric and exocentric compounds

Compounds are used to express a wide range of meaning relationships in English. Table 4.19 contains examples of just some of the semantic patterns found in noun–noun compounds.

In most cases, a compound denotes a subtype of the concept denoted by its head (the rightmost component). Thus *dog food* is a type of food, a *cave man* is a type of man, *sky-blue* is a type of blue, and so on. Such compounds, including all the examples in table 4.19, are called **endocentric**. In a smaller number of cases, however, the meaning of the compound does not follow from the meanings of its parts in this way. Thus, a *redhead* is not a type of head; rather, it is a person with red hair. Similarly, a *redneck* is a person and not a type of neck. Such compounds are said to be **exocentric**.

Table 4.19	Some noun–noun compounds
Example	**Meaning**
steamboat	'a boat powered by steam'
airplane	'a conveyance that travels through the air'
air hose	'a hose that carries air'
air field	'a field where airplanes land'
fire truck	'a vehicle used to put out fires'
fire drill	'a practice in the event of a fire'
bath tub	'a place in which to bathe'
bath towel	'a towel used after bathing'

A very striking difference between English endocentric and exocentric compounds sometimes shows up in cases where the head is a word like *tooth* or *foot*, which has an irregular plural form. Consider in this regard the following examples.

Table 4.20	Pluralization in English compounds
In endocentric compounds	**In exocentric compounds**
wisdom t<u>ee</u>th	saber t<u>oo</u>ths (extinct species of carnivore)
club f<u>ee</u>t	bigf<u>oo</u>ts (mythical creatures; 'Sasquatch')
police<u>me</u>n	Walk<u>ma</u>ns ('a type of portable radio')
oak lea<u>ve</u>s	Maple Lea<u>f</u>s (Toronto's NHL hockey team)

Notice that whereas the endocentric compounds employ the usual irregular plural (*teeth*, *feet*, etc.), the exocentric compounds permit the plural suffix *-s* for words such as *tooth*, *foot*, and *man*.

3.3 Compounds in other languages

Although the rules for forming compounds differ from language to language, the practice of combining lexical categories to build a word is very widespread. As the examples in table 4.21 help illustrate, compound nouns are especially common. With the exception of Tagalog, in which compounds are left-headed, the languages exemplified in table 4.21 all have compounds in which the rightmost element is the head.

A special type of compounding process involves **incorporation**, the combination of a word (usually a noun) with a verb to form a compound verb. Although incorporation is not a productive word formation process in English, it is common in other languages. The following examples are from Chukchee, spoken in northeastern Siberia, and the Micronesian language Ponapean. (As these examples help illustrate, incorporation often involves phonological adjustments to the noun and/or the verb.)

Table 4.21   Noun compounds in various languages

Korean

kot elum	isul pi	nwun mwul
straight ice	dew rain	eye water
'icicle'	'drizzle'	'tears'

Tagalog

tubig ulan	tanod bayan	anak araw
water rain	guard town	child sun
'rainwater'	'policeman'	'albino'

German

Gast-hof	Wort-bedeutungs-lehre	Fern-seher
guest inn	word meaning theory	far seer
'hotel'	'semantics'	'television'

Finnish

lammas-nahka-turkki	elin-keino-tulo-vero-laki
sheep skin coat	life's means income tax law
'sheepskin coat'	'income tax law'

Tzotzil

piʃ-xól	méʔ- k'ínobal	ʔóra-tʃón
wrap-head	mother-mist	rightaway-snake
'hat'	'rainbow'	'deadly viper'

18)

   a. Chukchee

Without incorporation	*With incorporation*
tə-pelarkən qoraŋə.	tə-qora-pelarkən
I leave reindeer	I-reindeer-leave
'I'm leaving the reindeer.'	'I'm in the process of reindeer-leaving.'

   b. Ponapean

Without incorporation	*With incorporation*
I pahn pereki lohs	I pahn perek-los
I will unroll mats	I will unroll-mats
'I will unroll the mats.'	'I will engage in mat unrolling.'

4   Other types of word formation

Derivation and compounding are the two most common types of word formation in English, but they are not the only ones. As the examples presented in this section will show, there are various other ways to create new words.

4.1   Conversion

Conversion is a process that assigns an already existing word to a new syntactic category. Even though it does not add an affix, conversion is often considered to be a type of derivation because of the change in category and meaning that it brings about. For this reason, it is sometimes called **zero derivation**.

Table 4.22 contains examples of the three most common types of conversion in English. (As noted in section 1.3 above, nouns derived from verbs sometimes undergo stress shift, which moves the stress to the initial syllable. The effects of this phenomenon can be seen in the first three examples in the middle column of table 4.22.)

Table 4.22 Some examples of conversion		
V derived from N	**N derived from V**	**V derived from A**
ink (a contract)	(a building) pérmit	dirty (a shirt)
butter (the bread)	(an exciting) cóntest	empty (the box)
ship (the package)	(a new) súrvey	better (the old score)
nail (the door shut)	(a brief) report	right (a wrong)
button (the shirt)	(an important) call	total (a car)

Less common types of conversion can yield a noun from an adjective (*the poor, gays*) and even a verb from a preposition (*down a beer, up the price*).

Conversion is usually restricted to words containing a single morpheme, although there are a few exceptions such as *propos-ition* (noun and verb), *refer-ee* (noun and verb), and *dirt-y* (adjective and verb). In some cases, conversion can even apply to a compound, as when the noun *showboat* is used as a verb in the sense of 'show off' (*he likes to showboat*).

4.2   Clipping

Clipping is a process that shortens a polysyllabic word by deleting one or more syllables. Some of the most common products of clipping are names—*Liz, Ron, Rob, Sue*, and so on. Clipping is especially popular in the speech of students, where it has yielded forms like *prof* for *professor*, *phys-ed* for *physical education*, *poli-sci* for *political science*, and *burger* for *hamburger*. However, many clipped forms have also been accepted in general usage: *doc, ad, auto, lab, sub, deli, porn, demo*, and *condo*.

In some cases, speakers may not even realize that a particular word is the product of clipping: the word *zoo*, for instance, was formed in this manner from *zoological garden*. A more recent example of this sort that has become part of general English vocabulary is *fax*, from *facsimile* (meaning 'exact copy or reproduction').

4.3   Blends

Blends are words that are created from non-morphemic parts of two already existing items, usually the first part of one and the final part of the other. Familiar examples include *brunch* from *breakfast* and *lunch*, *smog* from *smoke* and *fog*, *spam* from *spiced* and *ham*, *telethon* from *telephone* and *marathon*, *aerobicise* from *aerobics* and *exercise*, *chunnel* (for the new underwater link between Britain and the continent) from *channel* and *tunnel*, and *infomercial* from *information* and *commercial*.

In some languages, blending can bring together parts of three words. The following examples are from Malay.

19)

pembangunan lima tahun > pelita 'five-year plan'
development   five   year

universeti utara malaysia > unitama 'University of North Malaysia'
university north Malaysia

Some blends have become so integrated into the standard vocabulary of English that speakers are unaware of their status. For example, relatively few people know that blending has produced *chortle* (coined by author Lewis Carroll) from *chuckle* and *snort*, *motel* from *motor* and *hotel*, *bit* (in computer jargon) from *binary* and *digit*, and *modem* from *modulator* and *demodulator*.

Sometimes, a word is formed by a process that is on the borderline between compounding and blending in that it combines all of one word with part of another. Examples of this in English include *perma-press* (for *permanent-press*), *workaholic*, *medicare*, *guesstimate*, and *threepeat* (used by sports fans to refer to the winning of a championship in three successive years).

4.4   Backformation

Backformation is a process that creates a new word by removing a real or supposed affix from another word in the language. *Resurrect* was originally formed in this way from *resurrection*. Other backformations in English include *enthuse* from *enthusiasm*, *donate* from *donation*, *orient* or *orientate* from *orientation*, and *self-destruct* from *self-destruction*.

Sometimes, backformation involves an incorrect assumption about a word's form: for example, the word *pea* was derived from the singular noun *pease*, whose final /z/ was incorrectly interpreted as the plural suffix.

Words that end in *-or* or *-er* have proven very susceptible to backformation in English. Because hundreds of such words are the result of affixation (*runner, walker, singer*, etc.), any word with this shape is likely to be perceived as a verb + *er* combination. The words *editor, peddler*, and *swindler* were (mis)analyzed in just this way, resulting in the creation of the verbs *edit, peddle*, and *swindle* (see table 4.23). A more recent backformation of this type is the verb *lase*, produced by backformation from *laser*, which itself had an unusual origin (see section 4.5).

Backformation continues to produce new words in modern English. For instance, the form *attrit*, from *attrition*, was used by military officials during the 1991 Gulf War (as in *The enemy is 50 percent attritted*). Among the backformations noticed by the authors of this chapter are *liposuct* (from *liposuction*, seen in a magazine article), *orate* (from *oration*, used in a newspaper editorial), and *tuit* (from *intuition*, heard on CBC Radio).

Table 4.23   Some examples of backformation

Original word	Misanalysis	Verb formed by backformation
editor	edit + or	edit
peddler	peddle + er	peddle
swindler	swindle + er	swindle

4.5   Acronyms

Acronyms are formed by taking the initial letters of (some or all) the words in a phrase or title and pronouncing them as a word. This type of word formation is especially common in names of organizations and in military and scientific terminology. Common examples include UNICEF for United Nations International Children's Emergency Fund, CIDA for Canadian International Development Agency, NATO for North Atlantic Treaty Organization, and AIDS for acquired immune deficiency syndrome.

In some cases, speakers may not know that a word in their vocabulary originated as an acronym. Three commonly used words of this type are *radar* (from radio detecting and ranging), *scuba* (self-contained underwater breathing apparatus), and *laser* (light amplification by stimulated emission of radiation).

4.6   Onomatopoeia

All languages have some words that have been created to sound like the thing that they name. Examples of such **onomatopoeic** words in English include *buzz, hiss, sizzle,* and *cuckoo.* Since onomatopoeic words are not exact phonetic copies of noises, their form can differ from language to language (see table 4.24).

Table 4.24   Onomatopoeia across languages

English	Japanese	Tagalog
cock-a-doodle-doo	kokekokko	kuk-kukaok
meow	nyaa	ngiyaw
chirp	pii-pii	tiririt
bow-wow	wan-wan	aw-aw

English does not always have an equivalent for the onomatopoeic words found in other languages. The Athapaskan language Slavey, for instance, has the onomatopoeic word *sah sah sah* for 'the sound of a bear walking unseen not far from camp', *ðik* for 'the sound of a knife hitting a tree', and *ɬóòtʃ* for 'the sound of an egg splattering'.

4.7   Other sources

Sometimes, a word may be created from scratch. Called **word manufacture** or **coinage**, this phenomenon is especially common in the case of product names, including *Kodak, Dacron, Orlon,* and *Teflon.* (Notice how the *-on* of the final three words makes them more scientific-sounding, perhaps because an affix of this form occurs in words of Greek origin such as *phenomenon* and *automaton.*)

New words can also sometimes be created from names. Familiar words of this type include *watt, curie, fahrenheit,* and *boycott,* all of which originated from the names of the inventors or discoverers of the things to which they refer.

In still other cases, brand names can become so widely known that they are accepted as generic terms for the product with which they are associated. The words *kleenex* for 'facial tissue' and *xerox* for 'photocopy' are two obvious examples of this.

5   Inflection

Virtually all languages have contrasts such as **singular** versus **plural** and past versus non-past. Such contrasts are often marked with the help of **inflection**, the modification of a word's form (through affixation, internal change, reduplication, or suppletion) to indicate the grammatical subclass to which it belongs. (The base to which an inflectional affix is added is sometimes called a **stem**.)

5.1   Inflection in English

Affixation is the dominant inflectional process in language, and many languages (e.g., Japanese, Swahili, Inuktitut, and Finnish) have dozens of inflectional affixes. With only eight inflectional affixes (all suffixes), English is not a highly inflected language. Table 4.25 gives a complete list of English inflectional affixes.[3]

Table 4.25 English inflectional affixes	
Nouns	
Plural *-s*	the book<u>s</u>
Possessive *-'s*	John<u>'s</u> book
Verbs	
3rd person sg non-past *-s*	He read<u>s</u> well.
Progressive *-ing*	He is work<u>ing</u>.
Past tense *-ed*	He work<u>ed</u>.
Past participle *-en/-ed*	He has eat<u>en</u>/stud<u>ied</u>.
Adjectives	
Comparative *-er*	the small<u>er</u> one
Superlative *-est*	the small<u>est</u> one

Although most inflection in English involves regular affixation, some words mark inflectional contrasts in less regular ways. This is most obvious in the case of verbs, a number of which indicate past tense by internal changes of various sorts and even by suppletion: *come-came, see-saw, fall-fell, eat-ate, drink-drank, lose-lost, think-thought, is-was, go-went*, and so on.

Regular and irregular inflection appear to operate in fundamentally different ways: whereas regular inflected forms are constructed as needed in accordance with a general morphological rule (such as 'Add -*ed* to mark the past tense'), irregular forms must be stored permanently in the language user's memory. Evidence for this difference comes from studies of how long it takes speakers to utter the past tense form of a verb when presented with the base. For irregular forms, there is a correlation between response time and frequency of the verb: thus it takes less time to recall the past form of frequent verbs such as *see* and *find* than it does for infrequent verbs such as *stride* and *bid*—presumably because it takes longer to locate infrequently used forms in one's memory. For regular verbs, in contrast, response time is independent of frequency: because the past tense is formed by a regular rule, there is no need to 'look up' the word in the mental dictionary and all verbs—frequent ones like *walk* and infrequent ones like *discern*—can be handled with equal speed.

5.2   Inflection versus derivation

Because inflection and derivation are both marked by affixation, the distinction between the two can be a subtle one and it is sometimes unclear which function a particular affix has. Three criteria are commonly used to help distinguish between inflectional and derivational affixes.

Category change

First, inflection does not change either the grammatical category or the type of meaning found in the word to which it applies (see figure 4.12).

Figure 4.12   The output of inflection: there is no change in either the category of the base or the type of meaning it denotes.

The form produced by adding the plural suffix -*s* in figure 4.12a is still a noun and has the same type of meaning as the base. Even though *books* differs from *book* in referring to several things rather than just one, the type of thing(s) to which it refers remains the same. Similarly, a past tense suffix such as the one in figure 4.12b indicates that the action took place in the past, but the word remains a verb and it continues to denote the same action.

In contrast, derivational suffixes characteristically change the category and/or the type of meaning of the form to which they apply and are therefore said to create a new word. Consider the examples of derivation in figure 4.13.

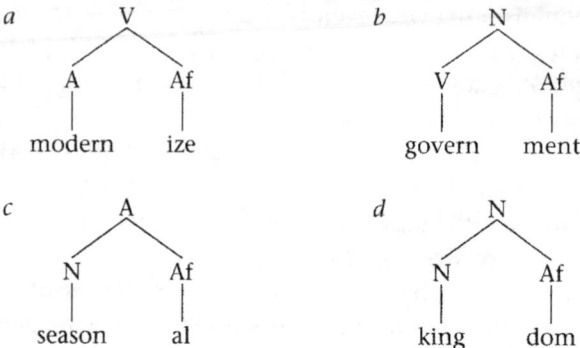

Figure 4.13 The output of derivation: there is a change in the category of the base and/or the type of meaning it denotes.

As figure 4.13a shows, *-ize* makes a verb out of an adjective, changing the type of meaning it expresses from a property (*modern*) to an action (*modernize*). Parallel changes in category and type of meaning are brought about by *-ment* (V to N) and *-al* (N to A). Matters are a little different in the case of *-dom*, which does not bring about a category change in the word *kingdom* (since both the base and the resulting word are nouns). However, *-dom* does modify the type of meaning from 'person' (for *king*) to 'place' (for *kingdom*).

Order

A second property of inflectional affixes has to do with the order in which they are combined with a base relative to derivational affixes. As figure 4.14 illustrates, a derivational affix must combine with the base before an inflectional affix does (IA = inflectional affix; DA = derivational affix).

Figure 4.14 The relative positioning of derivational and inflectional affixes: the derivational affix must be closer to the root.

The positioning of inflectional affixes outside derivational affixes in these examples reflects the fact that inflection takes place after derivation.

Productivity

A third criterion for distinguishing between inflectional and derivational affixes has to do with **productivity**, the relative freedom with which they can combine with bases of the appropriate category. Inflectional affixes typically have relatively few exceptions. The suffix

-s, for example, can combine with virtually any noun that allows a plural form (aside from a few exceptions such as *oxen* and *feet*). In contrast, derivational affixes characteristically apply to restricted classes of bases. Thus, *-ize* can combine with only certain adjectives to form a verb.

20)

modern-ize	*new-ize
legal-ize	*lawful-ize
final-ize	*permanent-ize

In the case of verbs, matters are somewhat more complicated, since many English verbs have irregular past tense forms (*saw, left, went*, and so on). Nonetheless, the distribution of the inflectional affix *-ed* is still considerably freer than that of a derivational affix such as *-ment*. In table 4.26, for example, all the verbs can take the regular past tense ending, but only those in the first three rows are able to take the *-ment* suffix.

Table 4.26 Compatibility of verb bases with inflectional *-ed* and derivational *-ment*

Verb	With *-ed*	With *-ment*
confine	confined	confinement
align	aligned	alignment
treat	treated	treatment
arrest	arrested	*arrestment
straighten	straightened	*straightenment
cure	cured	*curement

6 Further examples of inflection (*Advanced*)

As we have already seen, language uses inflection to mark grammatical information of various sorts. Some of this information, such as the contrast between past and non-past or singular and plural, is familiar to English speakers. However, as we will see in this section, inflection can also be used to mark less familiar sorts of contrasts.

6.1 Number

Number is the morphological category that expresses contrasts involving countable quantities. The simplest number contrast consists of a two-way distinction between singular (one) and plural (more than one). This is the contrast found in English, where a noun usually takes the suffix *-s* if it refers to two or more entities.

Although most languages express number, not all do. In Nancowry (spoken in India's Nicobar Islands), for example, number is not marked on nouns at all. A sentence such as *21* is therefore ambiguous since *nɔ́t* 'pig' can refer to one or more pigs.

21)
sák   nɔ́t ʔin tsiʔə́j.
spear pig the we
'We speared the pig(s).'

In Inuktitut (spoken in northern Canada), on the other hand, there is a three-way number contrast involving singular, dual (two and only two), and plural (more than two).

22)
iglu   'a house'
iglu-k   'two houses'
iglu-t   'three or more houses'

6.2   Noun class

Some languages divide nouns into classes based on shared phonological and/or semantic properties. A familiar example of noun classification for many Canadian students is the so-called gender system of French, which divides nouns into two classes—masculine and feminine. (Despite the noun class names, the gender system of French is not based on a male–female contrast, since it applies even to nouns with inanimate referents: *monde* 'world' and *livre* 'book' are 'masculine' while *chaise* 'chair' and *lune* 'moon' are 'feminine'.) Other languages have far more elaborate noun classes—Latin recognized six classes, for instance, and the Bantu language SiSwati distinguishes among more than a dozen.

Noun class can be marked in a variety of ways. In some languages, the determiner (the equivalent of words such as *the* and *a*) is inflected to indicate the class of the noun. For example, singular nouns in French take the definite determiner *le* if masculine but *la* if feminine. In other languages, inflectional affixes are used to indicate the gender class of the noun. For instance, Russian employs one set of suffixes for nouns in the feminine, animate class and another set for nouns in the masculine, animate class. The examples in table 4.27 show the gender inflection for nouns that function as subject of a sentence.

Table 4.27	Gender distinctions in Russian		
Class	**Suffix**	**Example**	
Masculine	-Ø	dom	'house'
Feminine	-a	ulic-a	'street'
Neuter	-o	tʃuvstv-o	'sensation'

SiSwati makes use of prefixes to distinguish among its noun classes. (Tone is not represented in the examples in table 4.28.)

Table 4.28	Some noun classes in SiSwati		
Prefix	**Description of class**	**Example**	
um(u)-	persons	um-fana	'boy'
li-	body parts, fruit	li-dvolo	'knee'
s(i)-	instruments	si-tja	'plate'
in-	animals	in-ja	'dog'
bu-	abstract properties	bu-bi	'evil'
pha-	locations	pha-ndle	'outside'

6.3 Case

Still another type of inflectional contrast associated with nouns in many languages involves **case**—a category that encodes information about an element's grammatical role (subject, direct object, and so on). As an illustration of this, consider the set of related nominal forms (called a **nominal paradigm** or **declension**) for the Turkish word *ev* 'house' in table 4.29. The contrasts represented in the Turkish case system are intermediate in complexity compared to Finnish, which has fifteen distinct case categories, and to Rumanian, which has only two.

Table 4.29	Turkish case	
Case	**Form**	**Type of element that it marks**
Nominative	ev-Ø	the subject
Accusative	ev-i	the direct object
Dative	ev-e	the recipient
Genitive	ev-in	the possessor
Locative	ev-de	a place or location
Ablative	ev-den	direction away from somewhere

The following sentences illustrate the use of these case suffixes.

23)
a. Adam-Ø   ev-i   Ahmed-e   göster-di.
   Man-Nom house-Ac Ahmed-Dat show-past.
   'The man showed the house to Ahmed.'

b. Ev-in   rengi-Ø   māvidir.
   house-Gen colour-Nom blue
   'The house's colour is blue.'

c. Adam-Ø   ev-de   kaldɨ.
   man-Nom house-Loc stayed
   'The man stayed in the house.'

d. Adam-Ø   ev-den   tʃɨktɨ.
   man-Nom house-Abl went
   'The man went from the house.'

In the final sentence, for example, *Adam* 'man' bears the zero ending of the nominative to indicate that it is the subject of the sentence, while *ev* 'house' bears the ablative suffix indicating the place from which the man went.

Case is most often manifested as affixation on nouns and pronouns, as in Turkish. In some languages, though, it is expressed through changes in the form of the determiner.

24)
German
Der   Mann sieht *den*   Hund.
The (Nom) man sees   the (Ac) dog
'The man sees the dog.'

Because case provides a reliable way to distinguish between subjects and direct objects, there is no need to rely on word order for this purpose. For this reason, languages with case often have relatively free word order.

25)

Japanese

a. subject-direct object-verb order:
   Yumiko-ga   sono kodomo-o sikat-ta.
   Yumiko-Nom that child-Ac   scold-Pst
   'Yumiko scolded the child.'

b. direct object-subject-verb order:
   Sono kodomo-o Yumiko-ga   sikat-ta.
   that child-Ac Yumiko-Nom scold-Pst
   'Yumiko scolded the child.'

Ergative case marking

Some languages use case marking to encode grammatical contrasts quite unlike those found in familiar European languages. In the Australian language Yidin^y, for instance, the case system groups together the subject of an intransitive verb and the direct object of a transitive verb (both of which receive a zero ending) while using a special marker (-*ngu*) for the subject of a transitive verb. (A verb is transitive if it takes a direct object; otherwise, it is intransitive. We will talk more about this in chapter 5.)

26)

a. Yidin^y sentence with a transitive verb:
   Wagudya-ngu dyugi-Ø gundal.
   man-Erg   tree-Abs is cutting.
   'The man is cutting the tree.'

b. Yidin^y sentence with an intransitive verb:
   Wagudya-Ø gundal
   man-Abs   is cutting
   'The man is cutting.'

In this type of system, the case associated with the subject of the transitive verb, *wagudya* 'man' in *26a)*, is called the **ergative**. The case associated with the direct object (*dyugi* 'tree' in the first sentence) and with the subject of an intransitive verb (*wagudya* in the second sentence) is called the **absolutive**.

Ergative case marking is found in a varied set of languages, including Basque (in Spain), Tagalog (in the Philippines), Tabassaran (in the Caucasus), Inuktitut (in northern Canada and Greenland), and Halkomelem (on the west coast of Canada). Ergative case marking is far less common than the nominative-accusative pattern, which groups together the subjects of transitive and intransitive verbs, distinguishing them from direct objects. Nominative-accusative case marking is found in Turkish, German, Russian, Japanese, Korean, and many other languages.

English nouns and pronouns

At one time, English nouns and determiners (words such as *the*) were inflected for case (see discussion in chapter 7). In modern English, however, the only remnant of this case system is the genitive suffix *-'s*, used to mark possessors (*the man's book*). Neither nouns nor determiners are inflected to mark grammatical relations such as subject and direct object.

27)
a. the man in subject position:
   The man left. The man read the book.

b. the man in direct object position:
   A noise frightened the man.

However, English pronouns do exhibit case contrasts, distinguishing a nominative (*I, they, he*), an accusative (*me, them, him*), and a genitive (*my, their, his*).

28)
Nominative: *He* left. *He* read the book.
Accusative: A noise frightened *him*.
Genitive: Sam took *his* car.

These contrasts follow the nominative-accusative pattern: the same form of the pronoun is used for the subject of an intransitive verb (*leave*) and the subject of a transitive verb (*read*) and this form differs from the one used for direct objects.

We will have more to say about case in section 5.2 of chapter 5.

6.4   Person and number agreement

A widely attested type of verbal inflection in human language involves **person**—a category that typically distinguishes among the first person (the speaker), the second person (the addressee), and the third person (anyone else). In many languages, the verb is marked for both the person and number (singular or plural) of the subject. When one category is inflected for properties (such as person and number) of another, the first category is said to **agree** with the second.

A quite rich system of agreement is found in Italian, which exhibits the following contrasts in the present tense (see table 4.30). (The set of inflected forms associated with a verb is called a **verbal paradigm** or a **conjugation**.)

Table 4.30	The Italian present tense paradigm			
	Singular		**Plural**	
1st person	parl-<u>o</u>	'I speak'	parl-<u>iamo</u>	'we speak'
2nd person	parl-<u>i</u>	'you speak'	parl-<u>ate</u>	'you speak'
3rd person	parl-<u>a</u>	'she, he speaks'	parl-<u>ano</u>	'they speak'

Because inflectional affixes in languages like Italian provide so much information about the person and number of the subject phrase, this element need not be overtly present. Thus, *parla italiano* 'speaks Italian' can make up a complete sentence with the meaning 'He/she speaks Italian'.

Modern English has a much more impoverished system of person and number agreement in the verb, and an inflectional affix is used only for the third person singular in the non-past tense (see table 4.31).

Table 4.31 The English verbal paradigm (non-past forms)		
	Singular	**Plural**
1st person	I speak	we speak
2nd person	you speak	you speak
3rd person	she, he, or it speaks	they speak

Except for commands, formal English differs from Italian and many other languages with rich verbal inflection in requiring an overtly expressed subject in a complete sentence.

29)
*Speaks English.

6.5   Tense

Tense is the category that encodes the time of an event with reference to the moment of speaking. There are many different types of tense systems in the languages of the world. For example, English makes a two-way contrast between past (for before the moment of speaking) and the non-past, which can be used for both present and future events (see figure 4.15).

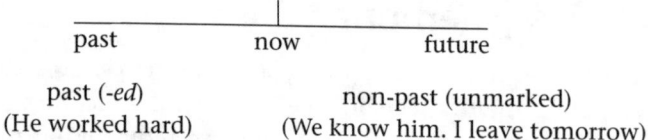

| past | now | future |

past (-*ed*)   non-past (unmarked)
(He worked hard)   (We know him. I leave tomorrow)

Figure 4.15   Tense in English

In the Australian language Dyirbal, in contrast, there is a two-way distinction between future and non-future. As the following examples show, the latter form can be used for both present and past events.

30)
a. Future: *b.* Non-future:
    bani-ɲ   bani-ɲu
    'will come'   'came, is coming'

In Spanish and Lithuanian, on the other hand, inflectional endings are used to express a three-way contrast involving past, present, and future.

31)
    Spanish   *Lithuanian*
a. Juan habl-ó bien.   Dirb-au.
    'John spoke well.'   'I worked.'

b. Juan habl-a bien.   Dirb-u.
    'John speaks well.'   'I work.'

c. Juan habl-ar-á bien.   Dirb-siu.
    'John will speak well.'   'I will work.'

A still richer system of contrasts is found in the Bantu language ChiBemba, which uses its inflectional system to distinguish degrees of pastness and futurity. (In table 4.32, the diacritics mark tone; affixes expressing tense contrasts are underlined.)

Table 4.32 Tense in ChiBemba	
Past	**Future**
Remote past (before yesterday) ba-<u>àlí</u>-bomb-ele 'They worked.'	Remote future (after tomorrow) ba-<u>ká</u>-bomba 'They'll work.'
Removed past (yesterday) ba-<u>àlíí</u>-bomba 'They worked.'	Removed future (tomorrow) ba-<u>kà</u>-bomba 'They'll work.'
Near past (earlier today) ba-<u>àcí</u>-bomba 'They worked.'	Near future (later today) ba-<u>léé</u>-bomba 'They'll work.'
Immediate past (just happened) ba-<u>á</u>-bomba 'They worked.'	Immediate future (very soon) ba-<u>áláá</u>-bomba 'They'll work.'

7   Morphophonemics

As we saw in chapter 3, a word's pronunciation is often sensitive to the particular phonetic context in which phonemes occur. For instance, an /æ/ that occurs before a nasal consonant will be nasalized (e.g., [kæ̃nt] 'can't' vs. [kæt] 'cat'), an /æ/ that occurs before a voiced consonant will be longer than one that occurs before a voiceless consonant (e.g., [hæːd] 'had' vs. [hæt] 'hat'), and so on. Pronunciation can also be sensitive to morphological factors, including a word's internal structure. The study of this phenomenon is known as **morphophonemics** (or **morphophonology**).

Morphophonemic phenomena are extremely common in language. A quite straightforward example from English involves the way that we pronounce the plural suffix -*s*. As first noted in chapter 1, the morpheme can be pronounced as [s], [z], or [əz].

32)
lip[s]
pill[z]
judg[ə z]

We know that this is a morphophonemic alternation because it occurs only in certain morphologically defined contexts. It is perfectly possible to pronounce an [s] sound after an

[l] in English—as in a word like *else*, for instance—but for some reason the plural *-s* has to be pronounced as [z] when it occurs after an [l], as in *pill*-[z]. The fact that this phenomenon is found only in particular morphological contexts underlines its morphophonemic character.

7.1 Deriving allomorphs

When linguists find that the same morpheme has more than one form (or allomorph), they often seek to set up a single underlying representation for the morpheme and to formulate rules that will derive the appropriate pronunciation for any particular context. To see how this works, let us consider in more detail the precise environments in which the different allomorphs of the English plural morpheme occur (see table 4.33).

Table 4.33	English plural allomorphs	
[-s]		Environment
tops	[tɑps]	• base ends in a voiceless consonant that is not strident
mitts	[mɪts]	
backs	[bæks]	
puffs	[pʌfs]	
baths	[bæθs]	
[-z]		Environment
cobs	[kɑbz]	• base ends in a vowel or a voiced consonant that is not
lids	[lɪdz]	strident
lads	[lædz]	
doves	[dʌvz]	
lathes	[lejðz]	
pins	[pɪnz]	
bums	[bʌmz]	
wings	[wɪŋz]	
teas	[tiz]	
days	[dejz]	
[-əz]		Environment
hisses	[hɪsəz]	• base ends in a consonant that is strident (s, z, ʃ, ʒ, tʃ, dʒ)
buzzes	[bʌzəz]	
crutches	[krʌtʃəz]	
judges	[dʒʌdʒəz]	
wishes	[wɪʃəz]	

As you can see, the choice of plural allomorph is determined by the final segment of the base. Bases that end in a non-strident voiceless consonant take the [-s] allomorph. Bases that end in a vowel or a non-strident voiced consonant take the [-z] allomorph. And bases that end in a strident (sibilant) consonant occur with the [-əz] allomorph.

In selecting the underlying representation of a morpheme, it is common to choose the allomorph with the widest distribution. This happens to be [-z] in the case of the English plural morpheme, since it occurs after most voiced consonants and after all vowels (which are also voiced). This is no accident, of course, since [-z] too is voiced.

The words *lips, pills,* and *glasses* therefore have the underlying representations depicted in 33).

33)

lɪp-z 'lips'   pɪl-z 'pills'   glæs-z 'glasses'

Two rules are now required to derive the correct final form of these words. The first rule, which we will call Coda Epenthesis, inserts a schwa whenever the [-z] appears after a base that ends in a strident consonant.

34)

$$\emptyset \rightarrow \begin{bmatrix} \text{+syllabic} \\ \text{+reduced} \end{bmatrix} \quad / \quad \text{[+strident]} \_\_\_\_\_ \text{-z}$$

This rule has a solid perceptual and articulatory motivation since it helps ensure that the resulting word will obey the general phonotactic constraint prohibiting a sequence of strident consonants in the same coda in English. Notice that English permits double strident sequences across word boundaries (as in *crash site* [kræʃ sajt] and *buzz saw* [bʌz sɑ] and across syllable boundaries (as in *posture* [pɑstʃər]), but never within a coda. Our rule of Coda Epenthesis helps rule out illegal codas by applying whenever the plural morpheme [-z], a type of strident, is attached to a base that ends in a strident consonant.

The second rule needed to ensure that the plural morpheme has the right form devoices [-z] when it occurs after a voiceless consonant in the same coda.

35)

Devoicing

-z → [-voice] / [-voice] _____]$_\sigma$

Like Coda Epenthesis, Devoicing helps ensure that English plurals comply with the usual phonotactic constraints of the language: no English words contain a coda in which a voiceless consonant is followed by a voiced one.

Figure 4.16 illustrates the derivations of all three plural allomorphs.

	lips	*pills*	*glasses*
Underlying representation:	lɪp-z	pɪl-z	glæs-z
Coda Epenthesis:	lɪp-z	pɪl-z	glæs-əz
Devoicing:	lɪp-s	pɪl-z	glæs-əz

Figure 4.16 Underlying representations and derivations for the three plural allomorphs in English

Notice that the ordering of the rules is crucial here. If Devoicing applied first, the plural ending of forms such as *glasses* would incorrectly end up as */glæs-s/, since Coda Epenthesis would not apply (see figure 4.17).

Underlying representation:	glæs-z
Devoicing:	glæs-s
Coda Epenthesis:	does not apply

Figure 4.17 Derivation for *glasses* in which Devoicing incorrectly applies before Coda Epenthesis

7.2 Conditioning by morphological class

A second type of morphophonemic phenomenon is manifested in just a subclass of morphemes rather than in the entire class. This too can be illustrated with the help of English
plurals.

As the examples in table 4.34 show, English includes a limited class of words in which an
/f/ in the base alternates with /v/ in the plural.

Table 4.34 Alternating base-final /f/ and /v/ in English			
The *f-v* alternation (irregular forms)		**No alternation (regular forms)**	
wife	wives	whiff	whiffs
thief	thieves	chief	chiefs
leaf	leaves	fife	fifes
knife	knives	laugh	laughs

The alternating class is unproductive, and new words with final [f] entering English do not
exhibit the *f-v* alternation. That is why a hypothetical new word such as *nif* would have [nɪfs]
rather than *[nɪvz] as its plural form.

We can formulate the process that is responsible for the *f-v* alternation as follows.

36)
f → v / ___]Plural

Notice that this rule is morphophonemic in two ways. First, it applies only when the plural
morpheme is present: there is no *f-v* alternation with the possessive morpheme -'s, which is
why we say *my wife*'[s] *car*, not **my wive*'[z] *car*. Second, only certain root morphemes (e.g.,
thief, but not *chief*) can undergo the rule.

This second characteristic illustrates a frequent feature of morphophonemic rules: they
often have exceptions. In this, they contrast with allophonic rules, which apply very generally. Thus, all vowels occurring before a nasal in the same syllable are nasalized; all vowels
occurring before a voiced consonant in the same syllable are lengthened; and so on. But only
some base-final /f/s are converted to /v/ in the plural.

Figure 4.18 illustrates how the plural forms of *thief* and *chief* are derived from the appropriate underlying representations.

	thieves	*chiefs*
Underlying representation:	θif-z	tʃif-z
The */f/-to-/v/* rule:	θiv-z	tʃif-z
Devoicing:	θiv-z	tʃif-s
Other rules:	θiːv-z	tʃif-s

Figure 4.18 Underlying representations and derivations for *thieves* and *chiefs*

Once again, rule ordering is important here. Unless the */f/-to-/v/* rule applies before
Devoicing, the final form of *thieves* will be *[θiv-s], with the [-s] allomorph of the plural (see
figure 4.19).

Underlying representation:	θif-z
Devoicing:	θif-s
The /f/-to-/v/ rule:	*θiv-s
Other rules:	*θiːv-s

Figure 4.19 Derivation for *thieves* in which Devoicing incorrectly applies before the /f/-to-/v/ rule

Abstract underlying representations

As the preceding examples help show, the underlying representations needed to account for morphophonemic phenomena may be quite unlike a word's phonetic form. For example, the word *thieves* is pronounced [θiːvz], but its underlying representation is /θif-z/. Representations that differ from phonetic forms in this way are said to be **abstract**.

In some cases, a morpheme's underlying representation can be very abstract indeed. For example, in order to account for the alternation in the pronunciation of the morpheme *electric* in words like *electrical* and *electricity*, linguists often posit the underlying representations in 37).

37)
ilɛktrɪk-æl   ilɛktrɪk-ɪti

A morphophonemic rule then converts the /k/ of the base to [s] in front of the affix *-ity*. This rule is clearly morphophonemic in character since it applies only before the [ɪ] of *-ity* rather than before any [ɪ]. (Notice that we don't pronounce *kill* as *sill*!)

The variant of the base that ends in *k* is chosen as underlying for two reasons. First, the base *electri*[k] has a wider distribution than the allomorph *electri*[s], since it occurs in words such as *electrical* as well as in the unsuffixed form. Second, a rule that fronts a /k/ to [s] before the high front vowel of the suffix is phonetically more natural than a rule that changes an /s/ to [k] in final position or before the suffix *-al*.

A more complicated example involves the three-way alternation involving *permit, permissive,* and *permission* (see figure 4.20). The underlying representation for the root morpheme is /pərmɪt/, with a *t-to-s* rule accounting for the [s] in the second form and a *t-to-ʃ* rule giving the [ʃ] in the third word.

	permit	*permissive*	*permission*
UR	pərmɪt	pərmɪt - ɪv	pərmɪt - ən
t-to-s		pərmɪsɪv	
t-to-ʃ			pərmɪʃən

Figure 4.20 Derivations for *permit, permissive,* and *permission*

Although very abstract, this sort of analysis has proven to be very popular over the years, primarily because it allows us to posit a single underlying representation for each morpheme and to find general rules that predict its actual pronunciation in particular contexts.

Summing up

This chapter has focused on the structure and formation of **words** in human language. Many words consist of smaller formative elements, called **morphemes**. These elements can be classified in a variety of ways (**free** versus **bound**, **root** versus **affix**, **prefix** versus **suffix**) and can be combined and modified under various conditions to build words. Operations that can combine and modify morphemes include **compounding, affixation, cliticization, internal change, suppletion,** and **reduplication**.

The two basic types of word formation in English are **derivation** and **compounding**. Less common types of word formation include **conversion, blending, clipping,** and **backformation**. Once formed, words may be **inflected** to mark grammatical contrasts in **number, gender, case, person,** and **tense**.

Notes

[1] Such words can be assigned structures such as the following, in which the symbol B stands for 'bound root'.

Figure a The internal structure of words built around a bound root

[2] An interesting fact about these forms is that although *ceive* and *mit* have no identifiable meaning, they undergo certain alternations that suggest that they have a special status in the language. For instance, the *ceive* in words like *receive* and *deceive* becomes *cept* in *receptive* and *deceptive* while the *mit* in words like *submit* and *permit* becomes *miss* in *submissive* and *permissive*. For further discussion of this point, see *Word Formation in Generative Grammar* by Mark Aronoff (Cambridge, MA: MIT Press, 1976).

[3] There are three *-ing* affixes in English, one inflectional and two derivational. Inflectional *-ing* combines with a verb to give another verb, as in *He is breathing*. One derivational *-ing* combines with a verb to give a noun (*the breathing of the runners*) and the other converts a verb into an adjective (*the sleeping giant*)—see table 4.13. There are also two types of *-en/-ed* suffix, one inflectional as noted in table 4.28 and the other derivational. The latter converts verbs into adjectives so that they can appear in structures such as the following:

[a] The *stolen* money

[b] The *escaped* convict

Sources

The estimate that the average high school student knows 60 000 'basic' words come from *The Language Instinct* by S. Pinker (New York: Morrow & Co.), p. 150. The introduction to words and morphemes draws on the classic treatments found in L. Bloomfield's *Language* (New York: Holt, Rinehart and Winston, 1933), Gleason's *An Introduction to Descriptive Linguistics* (cited below), and C.F. Hockett's *A Course in Modern Linguistics* (New York: Macmillan, 1958). The discussion of word formation seeks to portray those aspects of recent and current work that represent widely accepted views and are appropriate for presentation in an introductory textbook. Much of this work is summarized in the books by Jensen, Katamba, and Spencer (cited below) and the many references cited therein. For a detailed discussion on non-concatenative morphology, see *A-Morphous Morphology* by S. Anderson (New York: Cambridge University Press, 1992).

The Arabic examples in section 1.3 are from p. 17 of the book by Spencer cited below. The tier-based analysis of Arabic word structure is based on work by John McCarthy, including his article "A Prosodic Theory of Nonconcatenative Morphology," *Linguistic Inquiry* 12:373–418 (1981). The facts concerning the requirement that -*ant* combine with a base of Latin origin (section 2.2) are noted on p. 71 of the book by Katamba cited below.

The example of Chukchee compound in section 3.3 is from p. 15 of the book by Spencer, cited below. The Ponapean example is from p. 212 of *A Ponapean Reference Grammar* by Kenneth Rehg (Honolulu: University of Hawaii Press, 1981).

The examples of conversion given in section 4.1 come largely from the discussion in the books by Jensen (pp. 92–93) and Bauer (pp. 229–31) cited below. The examples of Malay blends come from "Malay Blends—CV or Syllable Templates" by M. Dobrovolsky, unpublished ms., University of Calgary. The data on Slavey onomatopoeia is from "Slavey Expressive Terms" by M. Pepper, *Kansas Working Papers in Linguistics* 10:85–100 (1985).

The definition of *stem* introduced in section 5 is from the article by S. Anderson cited below (p. 163). The discussion of the difference between regular and irregular inflection draws on information from "Rules of Language" by S. Pinker (*Science* 253, August 1991, pp. 530–35). The Nancowry example in the section on number was provided by R. Radhakrishnan. The data in the section on tense come principally from "Tense, Aspect and Mood" by S. Chung and A. Timberlake in *Language Typology and Syntactic Description*, Vol. 3, edited by T. Shopen (London: Cambridge University Press, 1985), pp. 202–58.

The examples used in the section on morphophonemics were taken from the discussion of this subject written by Michael Dobrovolsky for the third edition of this book. Exercises 1 to 19 were prepared by Joyce Hildebrand and exercise 20 by Michael Dobrovolsky. The data in problem 7 is from *Writing Transformational Grammars* by A. Koutsoudas (New York: McGraw-Hill, 1966).

Recommended reading

Anderson, Stephen. 1988. "Morphological Theory." In *Linguistics: The Cambridge Survey*. Vol. 1. Edited by F. Newmeyer, 146–91. New York: Cambridge University Press.

Bauer, L. 1983. *English Word-Formation*. New York: Cambridge University Press.

Gleason, H. 1955/1961. *An Introduction to Descriptive Linguistics*. New York: Holt, Rinehart and Winston.

Jensen, John. 1990. *Morphology: Word Structure in Generative Grammar*. Amsterdam: John Benjamins.

Katamba, Francis. 1993. *Morphology*. London: Macmillan.

Spencer, Andrew. 1991. *Morphological Theory*. Cambridge, MA: Blackwell.

Appendix: how to identify morphemes in unfamiliar languages

An important part of morphological analysis involves identifying morphemes in unfamiliar languages and determining the nature of the information that they carry. (A number of the problems in the set of exercises that follow this chapter will give you an opportunity to practise this type of analysis.) The key procedure to follow in working on this sort of problem can be stated simply as follows:

- Identify recurring strings of sounds and match them with recurring meanings.

Consider in this regard the small sample of data in table 4.35 from Turkish, consisting of four words along with their English translations. (A more realistic data sample would not only be much larger, but would also include sentences in which it might well be unclear where the word boundaries should be placed.)

Table 4.35 Some Turkish words

/mumlar/	'candles'
/toplar/	'guns'
/adamlar/	'men'
/kitaplar/	'books'

As you can probably see, the syllable /lar/ occurs in all four items in our sample. From the translations of these items, you can see that a particular feature of meaning—namely, plurality—is present in all four cases as well. Using the procedure just stated, we therefore hypothesize that /lar/ is the morpheme marking plurality in Turkish. Once this has been determined, we can then infer that /mum/ in /mumlar/ is also a morpheme (with the meaning 'candle'), that /top/ in /toplar/ is a morpheme (with the meaning 'gun'), and so on. A larger sampling of Turkish data would confirm the correctness of these inferences.

In doing morphological analysis in unfamiliar languages, there are a number of pitfalls to avoid. For the type of data normally investigated at the introductory level, the following guidelines are especially important.

- Do not assume that the morpheme order in the language you are analyzing is the same as in English. In Korean, for example, morphemes indicating location (the rough equivalent of 'at', 'in', and so forth) follow rather than precede the noun (*hakkyo-eyse* 'at school' is literally 'school at').

- Do not assume that every semantic contrast expressed in English will also be manifested in the language you are analyzing. In Turkish, for instance, there is no equivalent for English *the* and *a*. In Mandarin Chinese, the same pronoun form can be used to refer to a male or a female (there is no *he-she* distinction).

- Do not assume that every contrast expressed in the language you are analyzing is manifested in English. For example, some languages distinguish more than two number categories (Inuktitut distinguishes singular, dual, and plural; see section 6.1) and some languages make multiple tense contrasts (ChiBemba, discussed in section 6.5, has an eight-way distinction).

- Remember that a morpheme can have more than one form (allomorph). For example, further study of Turkish would reveal that the plural suffix in this language can also be realized as /ler/, depending on the vowel in the base to which the suffix is attached.

Questions

1. Consider the following words and answer the questions below.

a) fly	f) reuse	k) spiteful	p) preplan
b) desks	g) triumphed	l) suite	q) optionality
c) untie	h) delight	m) fastest	r) prettier
d) tree	i) justly	n) deform	s) mistreat
e) dislike	j) payment	o) disobey	t) premature

   i) For each word, determine whether it is simple or complex.

   ii) Circle all of the bound morphemes. Underline all of the roots.

2. All of the following Persian words consist of more than one morpheme. (*Note: xar* means 'buy' and *-id* designates the past tense.)

a)	xaridam	'I bought'
b)	xaridi	'you (sg) bought'
c)	xarid	'(he) bought'
d)	naxaridam	'I did not buy'
e)	namixaridand	'they were not buying'
f)	naxaridim	'we did not buy'
g)	mixarid	'(he) was buying'
h)	mixaridid	'you (pl) were buying'

   i) Try to match each of the following notions with a morpheme in the Persian data.

a) I	e) they
b) you (sg)	f) not
c) we	g) was/were + -ing (continuous)
d) you (pl)	

   ii) How would you say the following in Persian?
   a) They were buying.
   b) You (sg) did not buy.
   c) You (sg) were buying.

3. Consider the following data from Turkish.

a)	lokanta	'a restaurant'	lokantada	'in/at a restaurant'
b)	kapı	'a door'	kapıda	'in/at a door'
c)	randevu	'an appointment'	randevuda	'in/at an appointment'
d)	baʃ	'a head'	baʃta	'in/at a head'
e)	kitap	'a book'	kitapta	'in/at a book'
f)	koltuk	'an armchair'	koltukta	'in/at an armchair'
g)	taraf	'a side'	tarafta	'in/at a side'

   i) Does the Turkish morpheme meaning 'in/at' have more than one allomorph?

   ii) If so, what are the allomorphs? Describe their distribution as generally as possible.

4. Consider the following words.

a) desks	e) triumphed	i) preplan (V)	m) optionality
b) untie	f) ageless	j) fastest	n) prettier
c) invalid (A)	g) justice	k) reuse	o) mistreat
d) dislike (V)	h) payment	l) disobey	p) preview (V)

   i) Draw a tree structure for each word.

   ii) For the word *optionality*, what is the base for the affix *-ion*? What is the base for the suffix *-ity*? Are either of these bases also the root for the entire word? If so, which one?

5. Each of the following columns illustrates a different morphological process.

Column 1	Column 2	Column 3
a) mouse/mice	f) go/went	k) récord/recórd
b) dive/dove	g) is/was	l) ímport/impórt
c) take/took	h) good/better	m) cónvict/convíct
d) man/men	i) she/her	n) ímprint/imprínt
e) eat/ate	j) am/are	o) óutrage/outráge

   i) What morphological process is at work in column 1? column 2? column 3?

   ii) Describe in your own words the difference between the process exemplified in column 1 versus that in column 2.

   iii) Think of at least one more English example to add to each column.

6. The following words can be either nouns or verbs.

a) record	f) outline	k) report
b) journey	g) convict	l) assault
c) exchange	h) imprint	m) answer
d) remark	i) reply	n) import
e) surprise	j) retreat	o) cripple

   i) For each word, determine whether stress placement can be used to make the distinction between noun and verb.

   ii) Think of two more English examples illustrating the process of stress shift to mark a category distinction.

7. The following Samoan data illustrates one of the morphological processes discussed in this chapter.

a) mate	'he dies'	mamate	'they die'
b) nofo	'he stays'	nonofo	'they stay'
c) galue	'he works'	galulue	'they work'
d) tanu	'he buries'	tatanu	'they bury'
e) alofa	'he loves'	alolofa	'they love'
f) taoto	'he lies'	taooto	'they lie'
g) atamaʔi	'he is intelligent'	atamamaʔi	'they are intelligent'

   i) What morphological process is illustrated by these data?

ii) Describe the process in your own words.

iii) If 'he is strong' in Samoan is *malosi*, how would you say 'they are strong' in Samoan?

8. The following data from Agta (spoken in the Philippines) illustrates a specific type of affix.

   a) dakal 'big'   dumakal 'grow big, grow up'
   b) darág 'red'   dumarág 'redden'
   c) furáw 'white'   fumuráw 'become white'

   i) What is the affix in Agta meaning 'become X'?

   ii) What type of affix is it?

   iii) Describe its placement.

9. The following words from Chamorro, spoken in Guam and the Mariana Islands, illustrate some of the morphological processes described in this chapter.

I. Root		Derived word	
a) adda	'mimic'	aadda	'mimicker'
b) kanno	'eat'	kakanno	'eater'
c) tuge	'write'	tutuge	'writer'

II. Root		Derived word	
d) atan	'look at'	atanon	'nice to look at'
e) sangan	'tell'	sanganon	'tellable'
f) guaiya	'love'	guaiyayon	'lovable'
g) tulaika	'exchange'	tulaikayon	'exchangeable'
h) chalek	'laugh'	chalekon	'laughable'
i) ngangas	'chew'	ngangason	'chewable'

III. Root		Derived word	
j) nalang	'hungry'	nalalang	'very hungry'
k) dankolo	'big'	dankololo	'very big'
l) metgot	'strong'	metgogot	'very strong'
m) bunita	'pretty'	bunitata	'very pretty'

   i) What morphological process is involved in I? in II? in III?

   ii) Do any changes in lexical category take place in I? in II? in III?

   iii) Formulate a general statement as to how the derived words in I are formed. Do the same for III.

   iv) Does the affix in II have more than one allomorph? If so, what are the allomorphs? What is their distribution?

10. In this chapter, an argument was presented in favour of the following structure for the word *unhappiness*.

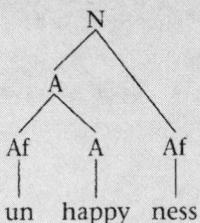

Using the same type of argument, justify tree structures for the words *inexpensive, redisposal,* and *disinvestment.*

(*Hint:* This will involve determining the type of syntactic category with which the affixes in these words can combine; see table 4.13.)

11. In English, the suffix *-er* can be added to a place name. Examine the words in the two columns below.

Column 1	Column 2
Winnipegger	*Denverer
Yellowknifer	*Victoriaer
New Yorker	*Vancouverer
Newfoundlander	*Torontoer
Londoner	*Ganderer

   i)   In general terms, what does the suffix *-er* mean in these words?
   ii) How is this *-er* different in meaning from the *-er* found in the words *skater* and *walker*?
   iii) State the constraint on the distribution of *-er* illustrated in this data.
   iv) Does this constraint also apply to the type of *-er* used in the word *skater*? (*Hint:* What would you call 'one who discovers' or 'one who ploughs'?)

12. The following words have all been formed by compounding. Draw a tree structure for each word. If you are in doubt as to the lexical category of the compound, remember that the category of the head determines the category of the word.

   a) football   i) tree trunk   q) hockey match
   b) billboard   j) lead free   r) coffee table
   c) sunbath   k) shortstop   s) flower-power
   d) in-crowd   l) girlfriend   t) blueprint
   e) fast food   m) city centre   u) Greenpeace
   f) software   n) failsafe   v) space ship
   g) freeze-dry   o) potato peel   w) brain dead
   h) overbook   p) bittersweet   x) kill-joy

13. In this chapter, several ways of identifying compounds were discussed. Using the tests given in the lefthand column, verify the compound status of the forms in the righthand column.

Test	Compound
past tense	blow-dry
compatible with *very*	loudmouth
plural	headlamp
stress	poorhouse

14. Examine the following compounds and answer the questions below.

Column 1	Column 2
a) loudmouth	h) cutthroat
b) skinhead	i) pickpocket
c) kill-joy	j) spoilsport
d) bath towel	k) crybaby

e) death blow
f) bird-brain
g) Walkman

l) brain dead
m) blow-dry
n) armchair

i)   For each of the compounds in column 1, determine whether they are endocentric or exocentric.
ii) How do you form the plural of *Walkman* and *loudmouth*? (*Hint:* see table 4.20. Also, pay special attention to the pronunciation of *mouth.* Is it any different here than when it is an independent word?)

15. Indicate the morphological process responsible for the creation of the items in column 2.

Column 1

Column 2

a) automation → automate
b) humid → humidifier
c) information, entertainment → infotainment
d) love, seat → loveseat
e) prógress → progréss
f) typographical error → typo
g) aerobics, marathon → aerobathon
h) act → deactivate
i) curve, ball → curve ball
j) perambulator → pram
k) (the) comb → comb (your hair)
l) beef, buffalo → beefalo
m) random access memory → RAM
n) megabyte → meg
o) teleprinter, exchange → telex
p) influenza → flu
q) They have finished → They've finished

16. Here are five instances where a new word is needed. Create a word for each of these definitions using the word formation process suggested. Fill in the blanks with your new words.
a) Use an acronym . . . . for your uncle's second oldest brother.
   "We visited my _____ at Christmas."
b) Use onomatopoeia . . . . for the sound of a coffee percolator at work.
   "I can't concentrate because my perc is _____ing."
c) Use conversion . . . . for wrapping something breakable in bubbles.
   "You'd better _____ that ornament or else it might break."
d) Use a compound . . . . for the annoying string of cheese stretching from a slice of hot pizza to one's mouth.
   "As the _____ hung precariously from my lips, our eyes met!"
e) Use backformation . . . . for the action of backformation.
   "We had to _____ words in Linguistics today."

17. Create new words for each of the following situations.
a) Use a product name . . . . for the act of scrubbing with Ajax.

"I _____ed the tub after giving Fido a bath."

b) Use a proper name . . . . for the act of breaking dishes, which Jonathan does regularly.
"He's going to _____ all of my best dishes."

c) Use clipping . . . . for a course in ovinology (the study of sheep).
"Have you done your _____ assignment yet?"

d) Use derivation . . . . for being able to be contacted.
"The counsellor is not very _____."

e) Use a blend . . . . for a hot drink made with chocolate and ginseng.
"I'll have a _____ and two peanut butter cookies, please."

18. Determine whether the words in each of the following groups are related to one another by processes of inflection or derivation.
    a) go, goes, going, gone
    b) discover, discovery, discoverer, discoverable, discoverability
    c) lovely, lovelier, loveliest
    d) inventor, inventor's, inventors, inventors'
    e) democracy, democrat, democratic, democratize

19. The following sentences contain both derivational and inflectional affixes. Underline all of the derivational affixes and circle the inflectional affixes.
    a) The farmer's cows escaped.   e) The strongest rower continued.
    b) It was raining.   f) The pitbull has bitten the cyclist.
    c) Those socks are inexpensive.   g) She quickly closed the book.
    d) Jim needs the newer copy.   h) The alphabetization went well.

20. The following data provides the possible forms of the regular past tense morpheme of English.
    i) List the alternate forms of the past tense morpheme.

a) walked	/wɑkt/	l) heaved	/hivd/
b) cracked	/krækt/	m) wheezed	/wizd/
c) flipped	/flɪpt/	n) fined	/fajnd/
d) hissed	/hɪst/	o) flitted	/flɪtəd/
e) huffed	/hʌft/	p) butted	/bʌtəd/
f) hushed	/hʌʃt/	q) padded	/pædəd/
g) munched	/mʌntʃt/	r) loaded	/lowdəd/
h) drubbed	/drʌbd/	s) collided	/kəlajdəd/
i) dragged	/drægd/	t) allowed	/ʌlawd/
j) jogged	/dʒɑgd/	u) sowed	/sowd/
k) fudged	/fʌdʒd/		

    ii) Which alternate makes the best underlying form? Why?
    iii) State in words the conditioning factors that account for the presence of the alternate forms of the past tense morpheme.

Five

William O'Grady

Syntax: the analysis of sentence structure

. . . the game is to say something new with old words

RALPH WALDO EMERSON, *JOURNALS* (1849)

Not much can be said with a single word. If language is to express complex thoughts and ideas, there has to be a way to combine words to form sentences. In this chapter, we will consider how this is done by focusing on the component of the grammar that linguists call **syntax**.

As noted in chapter 1, speakers of a language are able to combine words in novel ways, forming sentences that they have neither heard nor seen before. However, not just any combination of words will give a well-formed sentence. English speakers recognize that the pattern in *1)* is not permissible even though the same words can be combined in a different way to form the acceptable sentence in *2)*.

1)
*House painted student a the.

2)
A student painted the house.

We say that an utterance is **grammatical** if native speakers judge it to be a possible sentence of their language.

The study of syntax lies very close to the heart of contemporary linguistic analysis and work in this area is notorious both for its diversity and for its complexity. New ideas are constantly being put forward and there is considerable controversy over how the properties of sentence structure should be described and explained.

This chapter will introduce a simple version of **transformational** (or **generative**) **grammar.** Although many linguists disagree with various features of this approach, it is very widely used in linguistics and other disciplines concerned with language (especially cognitive science). For this reason, it is the usual point of departure for introductions to the study of sentence structure. Section 6 provides a brief discussion of some alternatives to transformational analysis.

An intriguing aspect of work within transformational syntax is the emphasis on **Universal Grammar** (UG), the system of categories, operations, and principles that are shared by all languages. The key idea is that despite the many superficial differences among languages, there are certain commonalties with respect to the manner in which sentences are

167

formed. As things now stand, it is widely believed that the syntactic component of any grammar must include at least two subcomponents. The first of these is a **lexicon**, or mental dictionary, that provides a list of the language's words along with information about their pronunciation, their form, and their meaning.

The second subcomponent consists of what can be called a *computational system*—by which we simply mean a system that can carry out operations on words to combine them and arrange them in particular ways. As we will see a little later in this chapter, the two key structure-building operations made available by Universal Grammar are **Merge** (which combines elements to create phrases and sentences) and **Move** (which transports an element to a new position within a particular sentence).

We will begin our discussion of these matters in section 1 by introducing some of the most common categories of words found in language and by investigating how they can be combined into larger structural units. Subsequent sections describe other aspects of sentence structure, using examples and phenomena drawn from English and other languages.

1 Categories and structure

A fundamental fact about words in all human languages is that they can be grouped together into a relatively small number of classes, called **syntactic categories**. This classification reflects a variety of factors, including the type of meaning that words express, the type of affixes that they take, and the type of structures in which they can occur.

1.1 Categories of words

Table 5.1 provides examples of the word-level categories that are most central to the study of syntax.

Table 5.1 Syntactic categories	
Lexical categories	**Examples**
Noun (N)	Harry, boy, wheat, policy, moisture, bravery
Verb (V)	arrive, discuss, melt, hear, remain, dislike
Adjective (A)	good, tall, old, intelligent, beautiful, fond
Preposition (P)	to, in, on, near, at, by
Adverb (Adv)	silently, slowly, quietly, quickly, now
Non-lexical categories	**Examples**
Determiner (Det)	the, a, this, these
Degree word (Deg)	too, so, very, more, quite
Qualifier (Qual)	always, perhaps, often, never, almost
Auxiliary (Aux)	will, can, may, must, should, could
Conjunction (Con)	and, or, but

The four most studied syntactic categories are **noun (N), verb (V), adjective (A)**, and **preposition (P).** These elements, which are often called lexical categories, play a very important role in sentence formation, as we will soon see. A fifth and less studied **lexical category** consists of **adverbs (Adv)**, most of which are derived from adjectives.

Languages may also contain **non-lexical** or **functional** categories, including **determiner (Det), auxiliary verb (Aux), conjunction (Con),** and **degree word (Deg).** Such elements generally have meanings that are harder to define and paraphrase than those of lexical categories. For example, the meaning of a determiner such as *the* or an auxiliary such as *would* is more difficult to describe than the meaning of a noun such as *hill* or *vehicle*.

A potential source of confusion in the area of word classification stems from the fact that some items can belong to more than one category.

3)
comb used as a noun:
The woman found a comb.

comb used as a verb:
The boy should comb his hair.

4)
near used as a preposition:
The child stood near the fence.

near used as a verb:
The runners neared the finish line.

near used as an adjective:
The end is nearer than you might think.

How then can we determine a word's category?

Meaning

One criterion involves meaning. For instance, nouns typically name entities, including individuals (*Harry, Sue*) and objects (*book, desk*). Verbs, on the other hand, characteristically designate actions (*run, jump*), sensations (*feel, hurt*), and states (*be, remain*). Consistent with these tendencies, *comb* in 3) refers to an object when used as a noun but to an action when used as a verb.

The meanings associated with nouns and verbs can be elaborated in various ways. The typical function of an adjective, for instance, is to designate a property or attribute of the entities denoted by nouns. Thus, when we say *that tall building*, we are attributing the property 'tall' to the building designated by the noun.

In a parallel way, adverbs typically denote properties and attributes of the actions, sensations, and states designated by verbs. In the following sentences, for example, the adverb *quickly* indicates the manner of Janet's leaving and the adverb *early* specifies its time.

5)
Janet left quickly.
Janet left early.

A word's category membership does not always bear such a straightforward relationship to its meaning, however. For example, there are nouns such as *difficulty, truth,* and *likelihood,* which do not name entities in the strict sense. Moreover, even though words that name actions tend to be verbs, nouns may also denote actions (*push* is a noun in *give someone a push*).

Matters are further complicated by the fact that in some cases, words with very similar meanings belong to different categories. For instance, the words *like* and *fond* are very similar in meaning (as in *Mice like/are fond of cheese*), yet *like* is a verb and *fond* an adjective.

Inflection

Most linguists believe that meaning is only one of several criteria that enter into determining a word's category. As shown in table 5.2, inflection can also be very useful for distinguishing among different categories of words. (For a discussion of inflection, see chapter 4, section 5.)

Table 5.2	Lexical categories and their inflectional affixes	
Category	**Inflectional affix**	**Examples**
N	plural -*s* possessive -*'s*	books, chairs, doctors John's, (the) man's
V	past tense -*ed* progressive -*ing*	hunted, watched, judged hunting, watching, judging
A	comparative -*er* superlative -*est*	taller, faster, smarter tallest, fastest, smartest

However, even inflection does not always provide the information needed to determine a word's category. In English, for example, not all adjectives can take the comparative and superlative affixes (**intelligenter, *beautifulest*) and some nouns cannot be pluralized (*moisture, bravery, knowledge*).

Distribution

A third and often more reliable criterion for determining a word's category involves the type of elements (especially functional categories) with which it can co-occur (its **distribution**). For example, nouns can typically appear with a determiner, verbs with an auxiliary, and adjectives with a degree word in the sort of patterns illustrated in table 5.3.

Table 5.3	Distributional properties of Ns, Vs, and As	
Category	**Distributional property**	**Examples**
Noun	occurrence with a determiner	a car, the wheat
Verb	occurrence with an auxiliary	has gone, will stay
Adjective	occurrence with a degree word	very rich, too big

Of course, a verb cannot occur with a determiner or degree word in these sorts of patterns and a noun cannot occur with an auxiliary.

6)

a verb with a determiner:
*the destroy

a verb with a degree word:
*very arrive

an auxiliary with a noun:
*will destruction

Distributional tests for category membership are simple and highly reliable. They can be used with confidence when it is necessary to categorize unfamiliar words.

1.2   Phrase structure

Sentences are not formed by simply stringing words together like beads on a necklace. Rather, they have a hierarchical design in which words are grouped together into successively larger structural units. For this reason, the structure of a sentence is often visualized as an 'inverted tree', whose branches reflect the sentence's internal architecture (see figure 5.1).

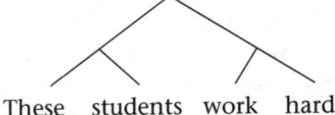

These   students   work   hard

Figure 5.1 A tree structure illustrating the design of the sentence *These students work hard*

This section will focus on the structure of **phrases**, which are the units that stand between words and sentences in syntactic structure.

Heads

Phrases are built around a nucleus called the **head**—a noun in the case of noun phrases (NPs), a verb in the case of verb phrases (VPs), and so on (see figure 5.2). ('Qual' stands for 'qualifier', a type of adverb.)

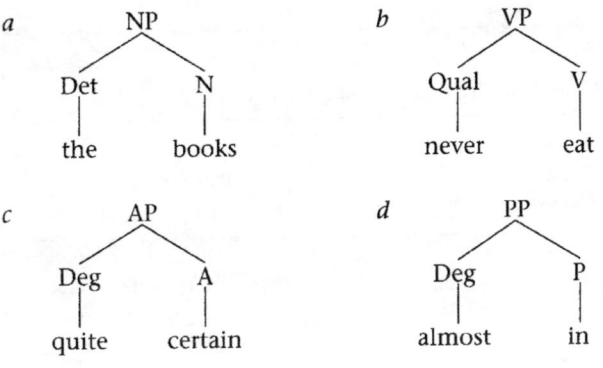

Figure 5.2 Some simple phrases

Although phrases usually consist of two or more words, a head may form a phrase all by itself.

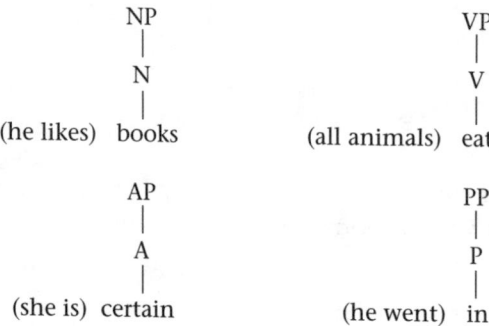

Figure 5.3 Phrases consisting of just a head

Specifiers

Let's go back now to the two-word phrases in figure 5.2. We have already identified the head in these phrases, but we have said nothing about the status of the other word.

Determiners (*the* and *a*), qualifiers (*never* and *often*), and degree words (*quite* or *almost*) function as **specifiers**. Semantically, specifiers help to make more precise the meaning of the head. Hence, the determiner (Det) *the* in *a* indicates that the speaker has in mind specific books, the qualifier (Qual) *never* in *b* indicates a non-occurring event, and the degree words (Deg) *quite* and *almost* in *c* and *d* indicate the extent to which a particular property or relation is manifested.

Syntactically, specifiers typically mark a phrase boundary. In English, specifiers occur at the left boundary (the beginning) of their respective phrases, as illustrated in figure 5.2. However, as we will see in section 4, some languages (Thai, for example) place specifiers in other positions.

The syntactic category of the specifier differs depending on the category of the head. As the examples in figure 5.2 and table 5.4 help show, determiners serve as the specifiers of Ns while qualifiers typically function as the specifiers of Vs and degree words as the specifiers of As and (some) Ps.

Table 5.4	Some specifiers	
Category	**Typical function**	**Examples**
Determiner (Det)	specifier of N	the, a, this, those, no
Qualifier (Qual)	specifier of V	never, perhaps, often, always
Degree word (Deg)	specifier of A or P	very, quite, more, almost

Question 3 at the end of the chapter provides practice in identifying specifiers and heads.

Complements

Consider now some examples of slightly more complex phrases.

7)
a. [NP the <u>books</u> about the war]
b. [VP never <u>eat</u> a hamburger]
c. [AP quite <u>certain</u> about Mary]
d. [PP almost <u>in</u> the house]

In addition to a specifier and the underlined head, the phrases in 7) also contain a **complement.** These elements, which are themselves phrases, provide information about entities and locations whose existence is implied by the meaning of the head. For example, the meaning of *eat* implies an object that is eaten, the meaning of *in* implies a location, and so on.

8)
A vegetarian would never eat [a hamburger].
                    ↑   ↑
                 head   complement naming the thing eaten

9)
in   [the house]
↑   ↑
head   complement naming a location

Complements are attached to the right of the head in English (but to the left in many other languages—see section 4). Figure 5.4 illustrates the structure of a phrase consisting of a specifier, a head, and a complement. (The NP serving as complement of a V is often called a **direct object**; a verb taking a direct object is referred to as **transitive**.)

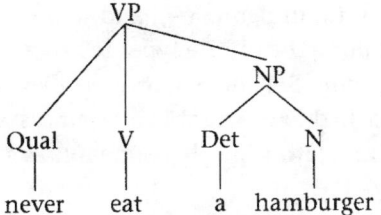

Figure 5.4 A VP consisting of a specifier, a head, and a complement

As noted above, complements are themselves phrases. Thus, the complement of the V *eat* is an NP that itself consists of a determiner (*a*) and a head (*hamburger*). This phrase then combines with the verb and its specifier to form a still larger structural unit.

NPs, APs, and PPs have a parallel internal structure, as the examples in figure 5.5 illustrate. (In order to save space, we do not depict the internal structure of the complement phrases in these examples.) Question 4 at the end of the chapter provides practice in identifying complements.

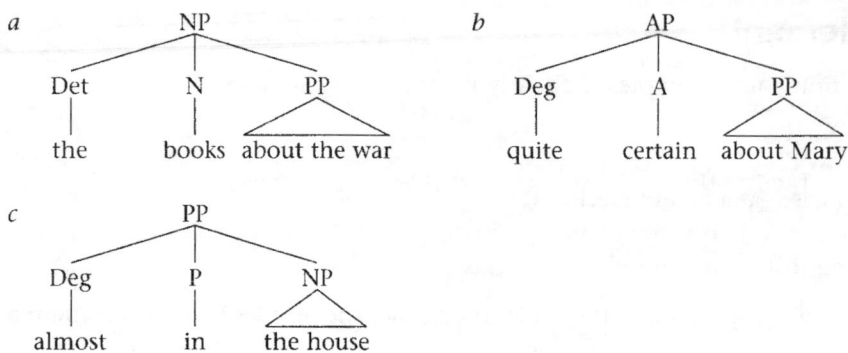

Figure 5.5 Other phrases consisting of a specifier, a head, and a complement

The blueprint

How does the grammar ensure that specifiers, heads, and complements occupy the appropriate positions in a language's sentences? In early work in transformational syntax, a special mechanism known as a **phrase structure rule** was used to describe the composition of phrases. (The arrow in the following sample rules can be read as 'consists of' or 'branches into'. Parentheses are used to indicate that a particular element is optional.)

10)
NP → (Det) N (PP)
VP → (Qual) V (NP)
AP → (Deg) A (PP)
PP → (Deg) P (NP)

The first of these rules states that an NP can consist of a determiner, an N head, and a PP complement (as in figure 5.5a); the second rule captures the fact that a VP can be composed of an optional qualifier, a V, and an NP complement (as in figure 5.4); and so on.

There are very obvious structural similarities among the phrase types referred to by these rules. As you can see by reconsidering the trees in figures 5.4 and 5.5, the specifier is attached to the left of the head while the complement is attached to the right in all four cases. In more recent work, these similarities have been summarized with the help of the following general rule, in which X stands for N, V, A, or P.

11)
The XP Rule
XP → (Specifier) X (Complement)

Put even more explicitly, we can say that the internal structure or 'architecture' of a phrase must comply with the following blueprint, or **phrase structure schema** (see figure 5.6).

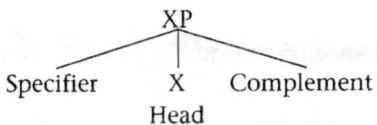

Figure 5.6 The phrase structure schema

We can now formulate the following operation for sentence building.

12)
Merge
Combine words in a manner compatible with the phrase structure schema.

The Merge operation is able to take a determiner such as *the* and combine it with a noun such as *house* to form the NP *the house*. It is then able to take a head such as the preposition *in* and combine it with the NP *the house* to form the PP *in the house* (see figure 5.7).

Step 1: Merge applies to the   Step 2: Merge applies to the preposition
determiner and the noun.   and the NP formed in Step 1.

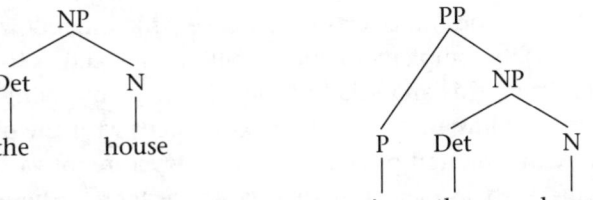

Figure 5.7 The Merge operation in action

Continued application of the Merge operation to additional words can lead the formation of phrases and sentences of unlimited complexity.

1.3   Sentences

The largest unit of syntactic analysis is the sentence (S). Traditionally, sentences are taken to consist of an NP (often called the **subject**) and a VP (sometimes called the *predicate*) to yield structures such as the one in figure 5.8.

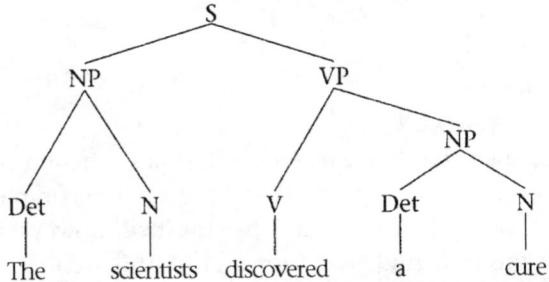

Figure 5.8 The structure of S (traditional view)

This traditional analysis assumes that S is special in not having an internal structure like other phrases (with a head, a complement, and a specifier). However, many linguists now believe that S has the structure depicted in figure 5.9 (Pst = past).

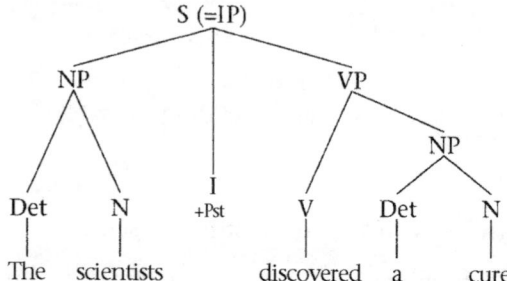

Figure 5.9 The structure of S (popular contemporary view)

The key idea is that sentences have as their head an abstract category dubbed 'I' or 'Infl' (for 'inflection'), which indicates the sentence's tense.[1] Because I, like all heads, is obligatory, this automatically accounts for the fact that all sentences of English have tense (e.g., they are either past or non-past). Other important aspects of sentence structure follows from the fact that the I category takes a VP as its complement and an NP (the subject) as its specifier.

Although somewhat abstract, this analysis has the advantage of giving sentences the same internal structure as other phrases, making them consistent with the phrase structure schema. It also provides us with a natural place in syntactic structure for words such as *can,* *may,* and *will,* which are inherently associated with a particular tense. (These particular elements are invariably non-past, as shown by the unacceptability of patterns such as **He will/can/may work yesterday.*) Although traditionally analyzed as 'auxiliary verbs', these words are commonly treated as instances of the I category in contemporary linguistic analysis and are placed in the I position, as depicted in figure 5.10.

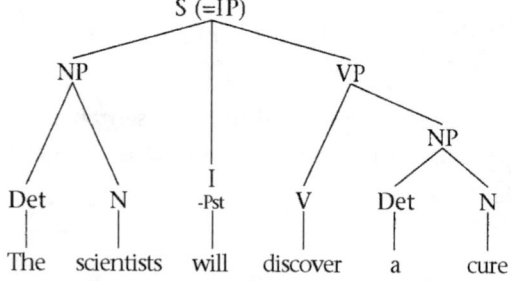

Figure 5.10 An S with an auxiliary in the I position

This neatly accounts not only for the fact that these elements have an inherent tense, but also for their occurrence between the subject (the specifier) and the VP (the complement)—the position reserved for the head of the sentence. (It must be admitted, however, that the use of the term *inflection* by syntacticians to include free forms is unfortunate.)

For the reasons just outlined, we will adopt the view that sentences have I as their head and that this element may be realized as either a tense label (past or non-past) or an auxiliary.[2] Nonetheless, for the sake of exposition, we will also follow the common practice of using the label S rather than IP to designate sentences.

The appendix at the end of the chapter outlines a procedure that should help you assign sentences an appropriate structure. Question 5 provides an opportunity to practice this procedure.

1.4 Tests for phrase structure

How can linguists be sure that they have grouped words together into phrases in the right way? The existence of the syntactic units, or **constituents**, found in tree structures can be independently verified with the help of special tests. We will briefly consider three such tests here.

The substitution test

Evidence that phrases are syntactic units comes from the fact that they can often be replaced by an element such as *they, it,* or *do so.* This is illustrated in *13),* where *they* replaces the NP *the children* and *do so* replaces the VP *stop at the corner.* (This is called a **substitution test**.)

> **13)**
> [$_{NP}$The children] will [$_{VP}$ stop at the corner] if *they* see us *do so.*
> (they = the children; do so = stop at the corner)

The substitution test also confirms that a PP such as *at the corner* is a unit since it can be replaced by a single word in a sentence such as *14).*

> **14)**
> The children stopped [$_{PP}$ at the corner] and we stopped *there* too.
> (there = at the corner)

Elements that do not form a constituent cannot be replaced in this way. Thus, there is no word in English that we can use to replace *children stopped,* for example, or *at the.*

The movement test

A second indication that *at the corner* forms a constituent is that it can be moved as a single unit to a different position within the sentence. (This is called a **movement test**.) In *15),* for instance, *at the corner* can be moved from a position after the verb to the beginning of the sentence.

> **15)**
> They stopped [$_{PP}$ at the corner] → [$_{PP}$ At the corner], they stopped.

Of course, *at the,* which is not a syntactic unit, cannot be fronted in this manner (**At the, they stopped corner*).

The coordination test

Finally, we can conclude that a group of words forms a constituent if it can be joined to another group of words by a conjunction such as *and, or,* or *but.* (This is known as the

coordination test since patterns built around a conjunction are called **coordinate structures.**) The sentence in *16)* illustrates how coordination can be used to help establish that *stopped at the corner* is a constituent.

16)
The children [$_{VP}$ stopped at the corner] but [$_{VP}$ didn't look both ways].

1.5   X' categories (*Advanced*)

Up until now, we have been assuming that the architecture of phrase structure complies with the blueprint in figure 5.11, identical to figure 5.6 above.

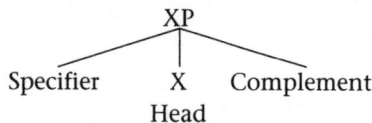

Figure 5.11 The phrase structure schema

In fact, however, this may be a simplification since many syntacticians believe that there is an intermediate level of structure within phrases, as depicted in figure 5.12. The intermediate level of structure is represented by the symbol X, (pronounced 'X-bar').

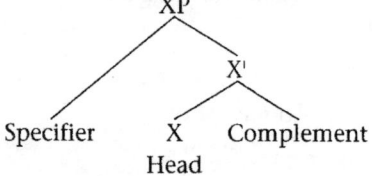

Figure 5.12 The phrase structure template (revised)

According to this viewpoint, the Merge operation combines the head and its complement to form an X'-level constituent, which can then be combined with a specifier to create an XP. Figure 5.13 provides an example of an entire sentence analyzed in this way.

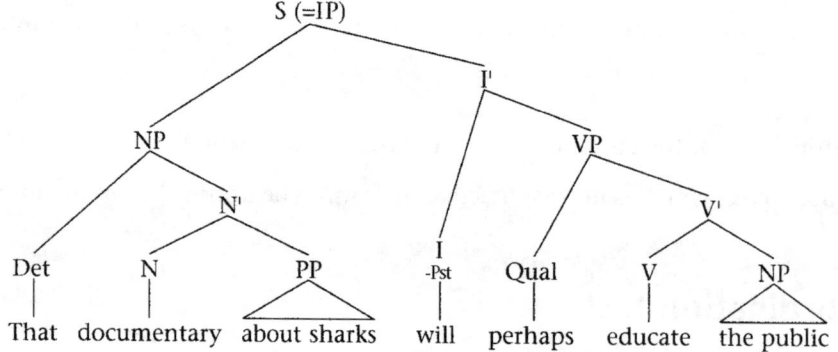

Figure 5.13 Phrase structure containing the intermediate X' level

The existence of X' categories can be verified with the help of the same sort of constituency tests discussed in section 1.4. Consider, for example, the V' *educate the public* in figure 5.13. As the following sentence shows, this constituent can be replaced by *do so*, in accordance with the substitution test.

17)
That documentary about sharks will perhaps [$_V$' educate the public], but media reports never *do so*. (*do so = educate the public*)

Now consider the N' *documentary about sharks* in figure 5.13. As the next sentence shows, this unit can be replaced by the element *one* (the substitution test again).

18)
That [$_N$' documentary about sharks] is more informative than the previous *one*. (*one = documentary about sharks*)

The fact that *one* can replace *documentary about sharks* in this manner confirms that it is a syntactic unit, consistent with the structure in figure 5.13.

Finally, the coordination test can be used to provide evidence for the existence of the I' constituent in figure 5.13.

19)
That documentary about sharks [$_I$' will perhaps educate the public] and [$_I$' may even save the species from extinction].

In order to accommodate these new three-level structures, it is necessary to replace our original XP rule by the pair of rules in *20)*). As before, X can stand for any one of a number of categories, including N, V, A, P or I.

20)
a. XP → (Specifier) X'
b. X' → X (Complement)

The first of these rules stipulates that XP categories of any type consist of an optional specifier and an X'. The second rule then states that an X' consists of a head, X, and its complements (if any). Taken together, these two rules form the three-level structures illustrated in figure 5.13, as desired.

Because three-level structures take up a considerable amount of space and can be tedious to draw, we will not make further use of them here. In order to do more advanced syntactic analysis, though, you need to be familiar with the X' level.

2 Complement options

How can we be sure that individual words will occur with a complement of the right type in the syntactic structures that we have been building? Information about the complements permitted by a particular head is included in its entry in a speaker's lexicon. For instance, the lexicon for English includes an entry for *devour* that indicates its syntactic category (V), its phonological representation, its meaning, and the fact that it takes an NP complement.

21)

devour: category: V
  phonological representation: /dəvawər/
  meaning: EAT HUNGRILY, . . .
  complement: NP

The term **subcategorization** is used to refer to information about a word's complement options.

Subcategorization information helps ensure that lexical items appear in the appropriate types of tree structures. For example, because *devour* belongs to the subcategory of verbs that require an NP complement, it is permitted in the tree structure depicted in figure 5.14a (where there is an NP complement) but not in the tree structure in figure 5.14b.

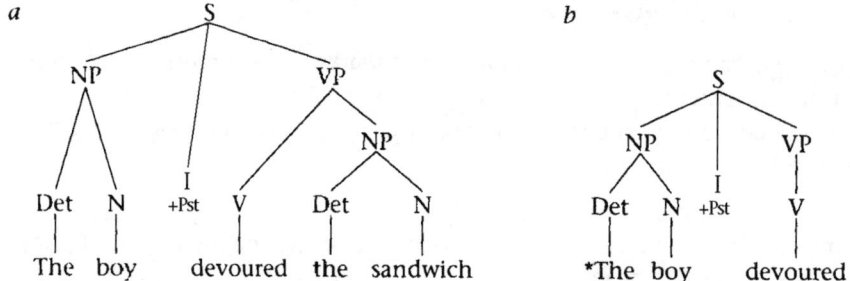

Figure 5.14 Subcategorization determines the type of syntactic structure in which *devour* can occur

Thanks to subcategorization information, heads occur only in tree structures where they have compatible complement phrases.

2.1   Complement options for verbs

Table 5.5 illustrates some of the more common complement options for verbs in English. The subscripted prepositions indicate subtypes of PP complements, where this is relevant. *Loc* stands for any preposition expressing a location (such as *near, on, under*).

Table 5.5	Some examples of verb complements	
Complement option	**Sample heads**	**Example**
Ø	vanish, arrive, die	The rabbit vanished __.
NP	devour, cut, prove	The professor proved [$_{NP}$ *the theorem*].
AP	be, become	The man became [$_{AP}$ *very angry*].
PP$_{to}$	dash, talk, refer	The dog dashed [$_{PP}$ *to the door*].
NP NP	spare, hand, give	We handed [$_{NP}$ *the man*] [$_{NP}$ *a map*].
NP PP$_{to}$	hand, give, send	He gave [$_{NP}$ *a diploma*] [$_{PP}$ *to the student*].
NP PP$_{for}$	buy, cook, reserve	We bought [$_{NP}$ *a hat*] [$_{PP}$ *for Andy*].
NP PP$_{loc}$	put, place, stand	He put [$_{NP}$ *the muffler*] [$_{PP}$ *on the car*].
PP$_{to}$ PP$_{about}$	talk, speak	I talked [$_{PP}$ *to a doctor*] [$_{PP}$ *about Sue*].
NP PP$_{for}$ PP$_{with}$	open, fix	We opened [$_{NP}$ *the door*] [$_{PP}$ *for Andy*] [$_{PP}$ *with a crowbar*].

The verbs in the first line of table 5.5 (*vanish, arrive,* and *die*) can occur without any complement, those in the second line occur with an NP complement, and so on.

A word can belong to more than one subcategory. The verb *eat*, for example, can occur either with or without an NP complement and therefore belongs to both of the first two subcategories in our table.

22)
After getting home, they ate (the sandwiches).

However, not all verbs exhibit this flexibility. Although *devour* is similar in meaning to *eat*, it requires an explicitly stated complement NP and therefore belongs only to the second subcategory in our table.

23)
devour with a complement:
After getting home, they devoured the sandwiches.

devour without a complement:
*After getting home, they devoured.

As the examples in table 5.5 also show, some heads can take more than one complement. The verb *put* is a case in point, since it requires both an NP complement and a PP complement.

24)
put with an NP complement and a PP complement:
The librarian put [NP the book] [PP on the shelf].

25)
put without an NP complement:
*The librarian put [PP on the shelf].

26)
put without a PP complement:
*The librarian put [NP the book].

The VP *put the book on the shelf* has the structure in figure 5.15, in which the VP consists of the head *put* and its two complements—the NP *the book* and the PP *on the shelf.*

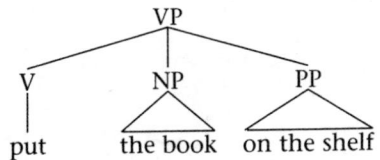

Figure 5.15 A verb with two complements

We can therefore revise our XP rule as follows, using an asterisk after the complement to indicate that one or more of these elements is permitted.

27)
The XP Rule (revised)
XP → (Specifier) X (Complement*)

2.2   Complement options for other categories

Various complement options are also available for Ns, As, and Ps. Tables 5.6, 5.7, and 5.8 provide examples of just some of the possibilities.

Table 5.6	Some examples of noun complements	
Complement option	**Sample heads**	**Example**
Ø	car, boy, electricity	the car __
PP_{of}	memory, failure, death	the memory [$_{PP}$ *of a friend*]
PP_{of} PP_{to}	presentation, description, donation	the presentation [$_{PP}$ *of a medal*] [$_{PP}$ *to the winner*]
PP_{with} PP_{about}	argument, discussion, conversation	an argument [$_{PP}$ *with Stella*] [$_{PP}$ *about politics*]

Table 5.7	Some examples of adjective complements	
Complement option	**Sample heads**	**Example**
Ø	tall, green, smart	very tall __
PP_{about}	curious, glad, angry	curious [$_{PP}$ *about China*]
PP_{to}	apparent, obvious	obvious [$_{PP}$ *to the student*]
PP_{of}	fond, full, tired	fond [$_{PP}$ *of chocolate*]

Table 5.8	Some examples of preposition complements	
Complement option	**Sample heads**	**Example**
Ø	near, away, down	(he got) down __
NP	in, on, by, near	in [$_{NP}$ *the house*]
PP	down, up, out	down [$_{PP}$ *into the cellar*]

Here again, subcategorization ensures that particular heads can appear in tree structures only if there is an appropriate type of complement. Thus, the adjective *curious* (table 5.7) can occur with an '*about* PP', but the adjective *fond* cannot.

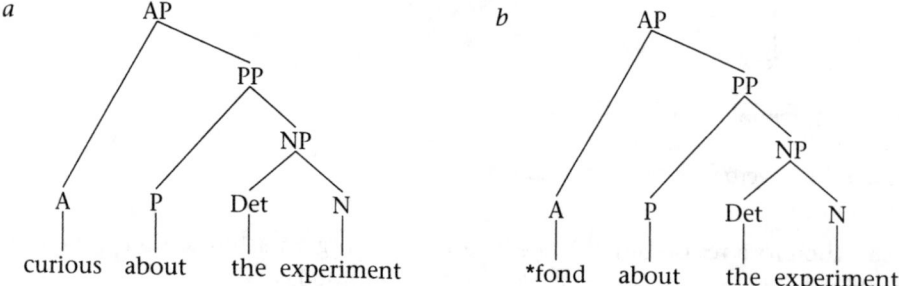

Figure 5.16 Subcategorization permits *curious*, but not *fond*, to take an '*about-PP*' as complement

As you can see, a good deal of what we know about our language consists of information about words and the type of complement with which they can appear. Much of this information must be learned, memorized, and stored in the lexicon since it cannot be predicted from a word's meaning. For example, there seems to be nothing about the meaning of *devour* to predict why it—but not *eat*—must occur with an NP complement. And there is apparently nothing about the meaning of *tired* and *bored* that predicts that the first one takes an *of*-PP (*tired of cafeteria food*) as its complement whereas the second one takes a *with*-PP (*bored with cafeteria food*).

2.3   Complement clauses

All human languages allow sentence-like constructions to function as complements. A simple example of this from English is given in *28)*.

28)

— complement clause —

[The psychic knows [that/whether/if the candidate will succeed]].

— matrix clause —

The smaller bracketed phrase in *28)* is called a **complement clause** while the larger phrase in which it occurs is called the **matrix clause**.

Words such as *that*, *if*, and *whether* are known as **complementizers** (Cs). They take an S complement, forming the CP (complementizer phrase) structure depicted in figure 5.17.

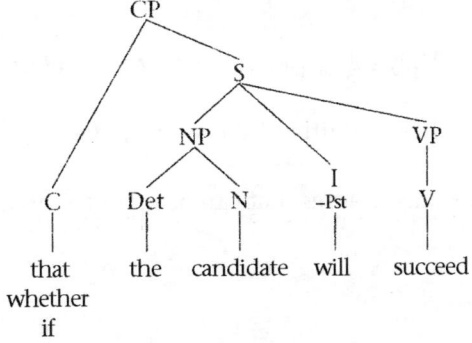

Figure 5.17 The structure of a CP

As we will see in section 3.2, there is even a type of element that can occur in the specifier position under CP.

When a CP occurs in a sentence such as *28)*, in which it serves as complement of the verb *know*, the entire sentence has the structure in figure 5.18.

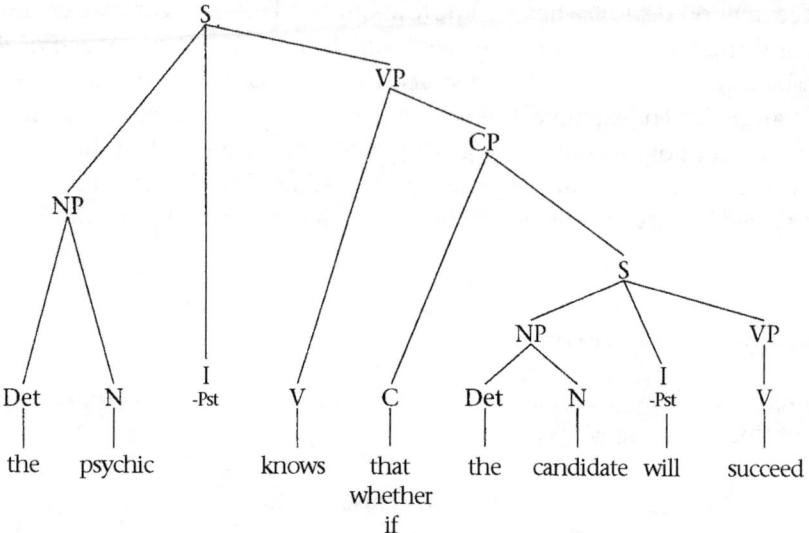

Figure 5.18 The structure of a sentence with an embedded CP

Table 5.9 provides examples of some of the verbs that are commonly found with this type of complement.

Table 5.9	Some verbs permitting CP complements	
Complement(s)	**Sample heads**	**Example**
CP	believe, know think, remember	They believe [_CP_ *that Eric left*].
NP CP	persuade, tell convince, promise	They told [_NP_ *Mary*] [_CP_ *that Eric had left*].
PP_to_ CP	concede, admit	They admitted [_PP_ *to Mary*] [_CP_ *that Eric had left*].

There is no limit on the number of embedded clauses that can occur in a sentence, as figure 5.19 helps show.

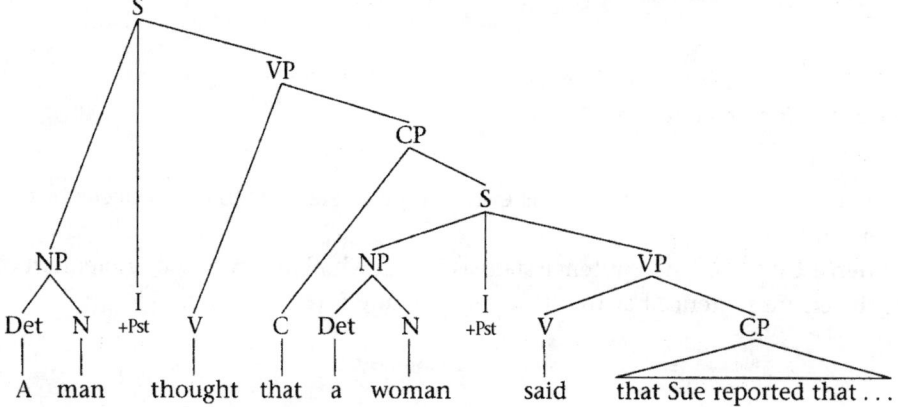

Figure 5.19 The structure of a sentence with more than one embedded CP

This structure is made possible by the fact that any CP can contain a verb that itself takes a complement CP. The topmost clause in our example contains the verb *think*, whose complement clause contains the verb *say*, whose complement clause contains *report*, and so on.

Other categories with CP complements

So far, the embedded CPs in our examples have all occurred as complements of a verb. However, as the examples in figure 5.20 show, a CP may also serve as a complement to an N, an A, or a P.

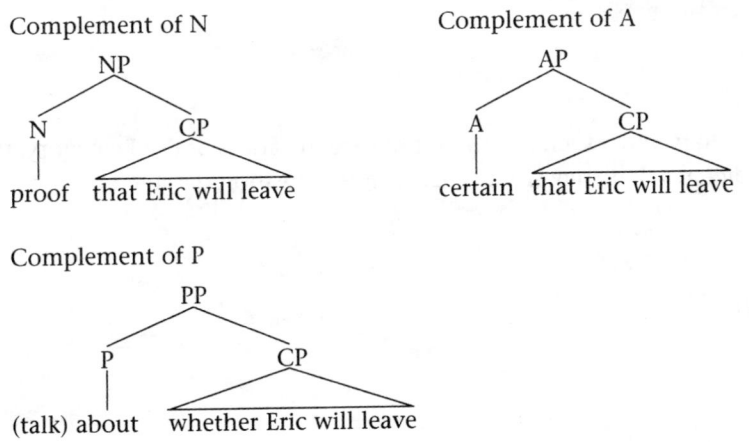

Figure 5.20 An N, an A, and a P with a CP complement

Table 5.10 gives examples of some other adjectives, nouns, and prepositions that can take CP complements.

Table 5.10	Some As, Ns, and Ps permitting CP complements
Items	**Example with CP complement**
Adjectives afraid, certain, aware, confident	They are afraid [$_{CP}$ *that Eric left*].
Nouns claim, belief, fact, knowledge, proof	They lack proof [$_{CP}$ *that Eric left*].
Prepositions over, about	They argued over [$_{CP}$ *whether Eric had left*].

3 Transformations

As we have seen, it is possible to build a very large number of different sentences by allowing the Merge operation to combine words and phrases in accordance with the phrase structure schema and the subcategorization properties of individual words. Nonetheless, there are still a number of sentence types that we cannot build. This section considers two such patterns and discusses the sentence-building operation needed to accommodate them.

3.1   *Yes-no* questions

To begin, let us consider the question sentences exemplified in *29)*. (Such structures are called *yes-no* questions because the expected response is usually 'yes' or 'no'.)

> 29)
> *a. Will* the boy leave?
> *b. Can* the cat climb this tree?

A curious feature of these sentences is that the auxiliary verb occurs to the left of the subject rather than in its more usual position to the right of the subject, as illustrated in *30)*.

> 30)
> *a.* The boy *will* leave.
> *b.* The cat *can* climb this tree.

Given that auxiliary verbs such as *will* and *can* are instances of the I category, the phrase structure schema dictates that they should occur in the position depicted in figure 5.21.

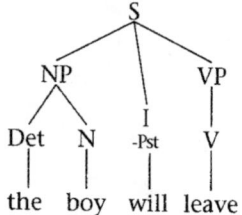

Figure 5.21 *Will* occurring in the head position between the subject (its specifier) and the VP (its complement)

How, then, does the word order found in *29)* come about?

The formation of question structures requires the use of a structure-building operation that we can call '**Move**'. Traditionally known as a **transformation** because it transforms an existing structure, Move applies to structures such as the one in figure 5.21 and moves the auxiliary verb in the I position to a new position to the left of the subject.

> 31)
> Will the boy ⌐ leave?
>   ↑_____⌐

The transformational analysis has at least two advantages. First, it allows us to avoid the conclusion that there are two types of auxiliary verbs in English: one that occurs in the usual I position between the subject and the VP and one that occurs to the left of the subject. Under the transformational analysis, all auxiliaries occur in the I position, consistent with the analysis proposed in section 1.2. Sentences that have an auxiliary verb to the left of the subject simply undergo an 'extra' process—the Move operation that transports the I category to the left of the subject in order to signal a question.

Second, the transformational analysis automatically captures the fact—known to all speakers of English—that the sentence *Will the boy leave?* is the question structure corresponding to *The boy will leave*. According to the analysis presented here, both sentences initially have the same basic structure. They differ only in that the Move operation has applied to the I category in the question structure.

A landing site for I

In what position does the auxiliary verb 'land' when it is moved to the left of the subject? If we assume that sentences such as *31)* are simple Ss, no position is available to the left of the subject. However, the problem can be solved if we assume that all Ss occur within larger CPs, as depicted in figure 5.22.

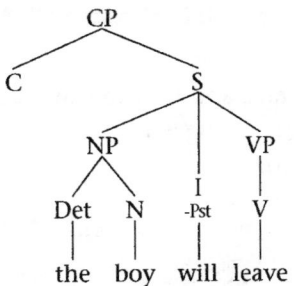

Figure 5.22 An S inside a CP 'shell'

By adopting this structure, we take the position that *all* Ss occur within a CP, whether they are embedded or not. It may help to think of the CP category as a 'shell' that forms an outer layer of structure around an S. When embedded within a larger sentence, the CP can contain an overt complementizer such as *that* or *whether*. Elsewhere, the C position simply contains information about whether the sentence is a statement or a question. For the sake of illustration, let us use the symbol '+Q' to indicate a question; sentences with no such symbol in their C position will be interpreted as statements.

In some languages, the Q feature is 'spelled out' as a separate morpheme (see section 4.2 following). In languages like English, where there is no such morpheme, the feature must attract another element to its position. The auxiliary verb in the I position is that element. This is illustrated in figure 5.23, where the Q feature in the C position attracts the auxiliary verb in the I position, causing it to move to the beginning of the sentence.

a *Structure formed by Merge*   *b* *After Move*

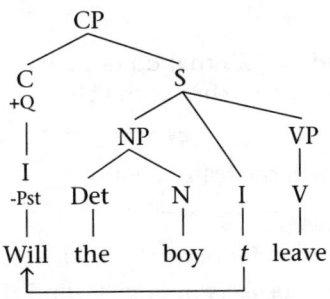

Figure 5.23 Movement of an auxiliary from the I position to C

A transformation (i.e., a Move operation) can do no more than change an element's position. It does not change the categories of any words and it cannot eliminate any part of the structure created by the Merge operation. Thus, *will* retains its I label even though it is moved into the C position, and the position that it formerly occupied remains in the tree structure. Called a **trace** and marked by the symbol *t*, it records the fact that the moved element comes from the head position within S.

The Move operation used for *yes-no* questions is often informally called **Inversion** and formulated as follows.

32)
Inversion:
Move I to C.

Is there any way to be sure that this idea is on the right track and that the auxiliary verb in the I position really does move to the C position? Some interesting evidence comes from the analysis of the embedded CPs in sentences such as the following.

33)
a. The coach wonders [_{CP} <u>if</u> the girl should stay].
b. A fan asked [_{CP} <u>whether</u> the team will win].

The underlined elements in these CPs are complementizers and therefore occur in the C position. Assuming that there can be no more than one overt element in each position in a tree structure, there should be no room for the moved auxiliary under the C label in the embedded CPs in *33)*. We therefore predict that Inversion should not be able to apply in these cases. The ungrammaticality of the sentences in *34)* shows that this is correct.

34)
Inversion in embedded CPs that include complementizers:
a. *The coach wonders [_{CP} if-should the girl *t* stay].

b. *A fan asked [_{CP} whether-will the team *t* win].

Interestingly, the acceptability of Inversion in embedded CPs improves quite dramatically when there is no complementizer and the C position is therefore open to receive the moved auxiliary. (These sentences sound most natural when the embedded clause is interpreted as a sort of quotation.)

35)
Inversion in embedded CPs that do not have complementizers:
a. The coach wondered [_{CP} should the girl *t* stay].

b. A fan asked [_{CP} will the team *t* win].

Although some speakers prefer not to apply Inversion in embedded clauses at all (especially in formal speech), most speakers of English find the sentences in *35)* to be much more natural than those in *34)*. This is just what we would expect if Inversion moves the auxiliary to an empty C position, as required by our analysis.

To summarize before continuing, we have introduced two changes into the system of syntactic analysis used until now. First, we assume that all Ss occur inside CPs. Second, we assume that the Inversion transformation moves the auxiliary from the I position within S to an empty C position to the left of the subject NP. This not only gives the correct word order for question structures, it helps explain why the inversion pattern sounds so unnatural when the C position is already filled by another element, as in *34)*.

Do Insertion

As we have just seen, formation of *yes-no* questions in English involves moving the I category, and the auxiliary verb that it contains, to the C position. How, then, do we form the questions corresponding to sentences such as those in *36)*, which contain no auxiliary?

36)
a. The students liked the movie.
b. Those birds sing.

Since the I category in these sentences contains only an abstract tense marker (see figure 5.24a), applying the Inversion transformation would have no visible effect and there would be no indication that the sentence was being used as a question. English circumvents this problem by adding the special auxiliary verb *do*.

37)
a. Did the students like the movie?
b. Do those birds sing?

As these examples show, *do* is inserted into sentences that do not already have an auxiliary verb, thereby making Inversion possible. We can capture this fact by formulating an **insertion rule**, an operation that adds an element to a tree structure.

38)
Do Insertion
Insert interrogative *do* into an empty I position.

The sentence in *37b)* can now be analyzed in the manner shown in figure 5.24.

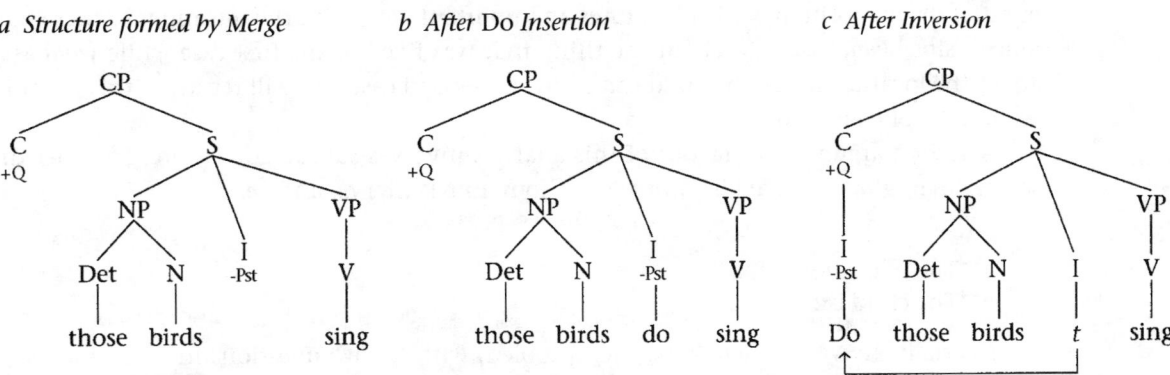

a Structure formed by Merge   *b After Do Insertion*   *c After Inversion*

Figure 5.24 A sentence formed with the help of *Do* Insertion

As these tree structures show, the sentence *Do those birds sing*? is built in three steps. In the initial step, the Merge operation interacts with the phrase structure schema to give the structure in figure 5.24a, which contains no auxiliary verb in the I position. The *Do* Insertion rule then adds the special interrogative auxiliary *do*, at which point it can be moved to the C position.

3.2   *Wh* Movement

Consider now the set of question constructions exemplified in *39)*. These sentences are called **wh questions** because of the presence of a question word beginning with *wh*.

> 39)
> *a.* Which car should the man fix?
> *b.* What can the child sit on?

There is reason to believe that the *wh* elements at the beginning of these sentences have been moved there from the positions indicated in figure 5.25. (Notice that we take *which* to be a determiner and *what* to be a noun in these sentences.)

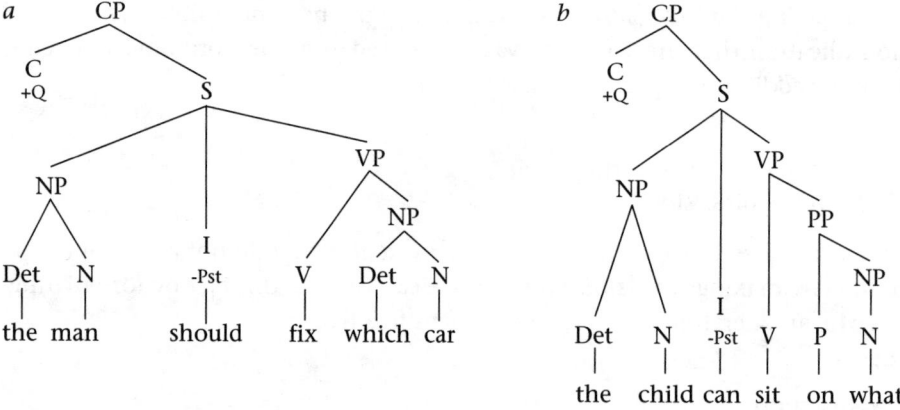

Figure 5.25 Structures depicting the original positions of the *wh* expressions in *39)*

Notice that *which car* occurs as complement of the verb *fix* while *what* appears as complement of the preposition *on*. This captures an important fact about the meanings of these sentences, since *which car* asks about the thing that was fixed in the first case while *what* asks about the location where the child can sit in the second case. We will return to this point in section 3.3 of chapter 6.

A second argument in favour of this analysis involves subcategorization. Consider the sentences in *40)*, which are incomplete without an NP after *fix* and *on*.

> 40)
> *a.* *The man should fix.
> *b.* *The child can sit on.

Crucially, however, there is no such problem with the *wh* questions in *39)*, which suggests that the *wh* phrases must be fulfilling the complement function in these sentences. The structures in figure 5.25 capture this fact by treating the *wh* phrase as complement of the verb in the first pattern and complement of the preposition in the second.

How then do the *wh* phrases end up at the beginning of the sentence? The answer is that they are attracted there by the Q feature, which results in the application of a second Move operation. (Recall that we have already posited one Move operation, which we have been calling Inversion.)

41)

Application of the same two transformations to the structure in figure 5.24b yields the *wh* question in *42)*.

42)

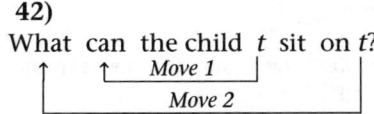

A landing site for *wh* words

As the examples in *41)* and *42)* help illustrate, the Move operation carries the *wh* phrase to the beginning of the sentence, to the left even of the fronted auxiliary. But where precisely does the *wh* phrase land?

Given that the moved auxiliary is located in the C position (see figure 5.23 or 5.24 above, for example), it seems reasonable to conclude that the fronted *wh* phrase ends up in the specifier position of CP. Not only is this the only position in syntactic structure to the left of the C, it is available to receive the moved *wh* phrase: because there is no class of words that serves as specifier of C, this position is empty prior to the application of the Move operation.

We can make this idea precise by formulating the Move operation that applies to *wh* phrases as follows.

43)

Wh Movement:
Move a *wh* phrase to the specifier position under CP.

The sentence *Which car should the man fix?* can now be analyzed in steps, the first of which involves formation of the structure in figure 5.26 by the Merge operation. Consistent with our earlier assumption, the S here occurs within a CP shell.

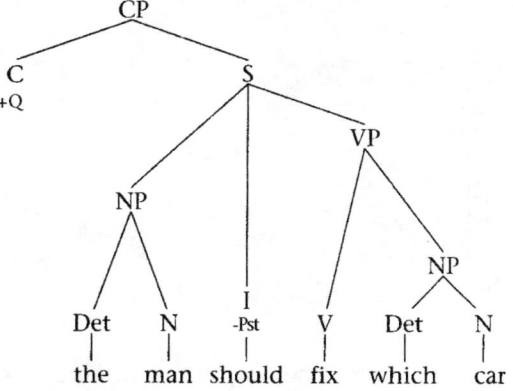

Figure 5.26 Deep structure for *Which car should the man fix?*

Wh Movement and Inversion then apply to this structure, yielding the structure in figure 5.27.

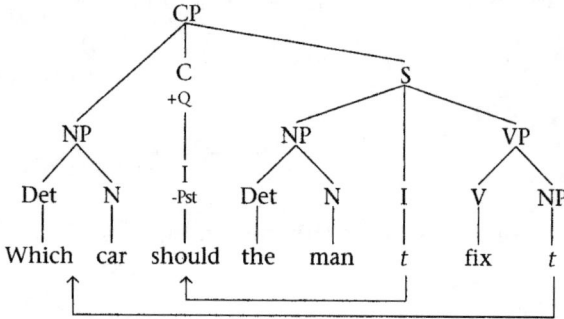

Figure 5.27 Structure for *Which car should the man fix?* The I category moves to the C position and the *wh* phrase moves to the specifier position under CP

Like other transformations, *Wh* Movement cannot eliminate any part of the previously formed structure. The position initially occupied by the *wh* phrase is therefore not lost. Rather, it remains as a trace (an empty category), indicating that the moved element corresponds to the complement of the verb *fix*.

In the examples considered so far, the *wh* word originates as complement of a verb or preposition. In sentences such as the following, however, the *wh* word asks about the subject (the person who does the criticizing).

44)
Who criticized Maxwell?

In such patterns the *wh* word originates in the subject position and subsequently moves to the specifier position within CP even though the actual order of the words in the sentence does not change as a result of this movement. (For reasons that are not fully understood, there is no *Do* Insertion or Inversion in this type of question structure, except for purposes of emphasis, as in *Who DID criticize Maxwell?*)

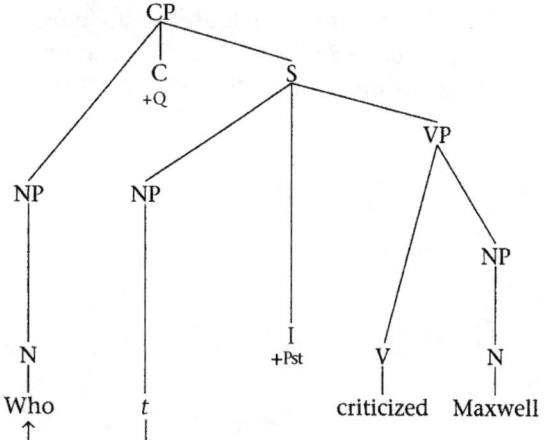

Figure 5.28 Movement of a subject *wh* word Since there is nothing for the *wh* word to move over in such cases, there is no visible change in word order

3.3 Deep structure and surface structure

The preceding examples show that at least some sentences must be analyzed with the help of two distinct types of mechanisms. The first of these is the Merge operation, which creates tree structures by combining categories in a manner consistent with their subcategorization properties and the phrase structure schema. The second is the Move operation, which can modify these tree structures by moving an element from one position to another. The process whereby a syntactic structure is formed by these operations is called a **derivation**.

In traditional work in transformational syntax, all instances of the Merge operation take place before any instances of the Move operation. As a result, the derivation for a sentence typically yields two distinct levels of syntactic structure. The first, called **deep structure** (or **D-structure**), is formed by the Merge in accordance with the head's subcategorization properties and the phrase structure schema. As we shall see in the chapter on semantics, deep structure plays a special role in the interpretation of sentences.

The second level of syntactic structure corresponds to the final syntactic form of the sentence. Called **surface structure** (or **S-structure**), it results from applying whatever transformations are appropriate for the sentence in question.

The deep structure for the question *Which apple will the boy pick?* is given in figure 5.29.

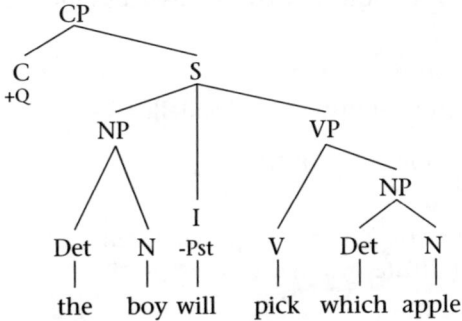

Figure 5.29 The deep structure for the question *Which apple will the boy pick?*

The surface structure for the question pattern is then formed by applying Inversion and *Wh* Movement, yielding figure 5.30.

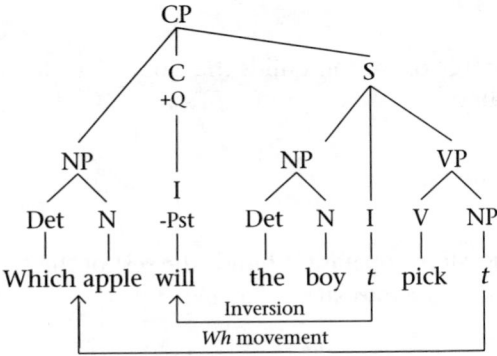

Figure 5.30 Surface structure for *Which apple will the boy pick?*

The organization of the syntactic component of the grammar according to the view put forward in traditional work on transformational syntax can be depicted as follows.

Figure 5.31 The path followed by a derivation

A recent development (*Advanced*)

Within the last few years, matters have changed considerably and it is now believed that the Merge and Move operations interact with each other freely. One consequence of this simpler picture is that derivations no longer include a level of deep structure per se. This is easiest to see if we consider the formation of a two-clause sentence such as the following.

45)
[$_{CP}$ The country wonders [$_{CP}$ what the prime minister will decide]].

In traditional work, this sentence had the following derivation.

46)
The result of all applications of the Merge operation (Deep Structure):
[$_{CP}$ The country wonders [$_{CP}$ the prime minister will decide what]].

47)
The result of applying the Move operation (Surface Structure):
[$_{CP}$ The country wonders [$_{CP}$ what the prime minister will decide *t*]].

However, according to the more recent conception, Merge operations first build just the lower clause. The Move operation then moves the *wh* word to the Spec of CP position in that clause and the Merge operations resume, building the rest of the sentence.

48)
A first series of applications of the Merge operation builds the embedded clause:
[$_{CP}$ the prime minister will decide what].

The Move operation applies:
[$_{CP}$ what the prime minister will decide *t*].

A second series of applications of the Merge operation builds the rest of the sentence:
[$_{CP}$ The country wonders [$_{CP}$ what the prime minister will decide *t*]].

Although the newer derivation produces no deep structure per se for the entire sentence, it does not constitute a complete break with the past either. There are still operations (Merge) that build structure in accordance with the phrase structure schema and other operations (Move) that can change it in the course of the derivation.

3.4 Constraints on transformations (*Advanced*)

A good deal of research in the field of syntax in recent years has been devoted to determining constraints on the Move operation. One such constraint has been dubbed '**Shortest Move**'.

49)
Shortest Move
Moves should be as short as possible.

The effects of Shortest Move can be seen by considering the following structure, which contains two *wh* words.

50)
[$_{CP}$ [$_{IP}$ Marvin should give *what* to *whom*]]

There is only room for one *wh* word in the specifier position under CP, but which one is attracted to that position? As the contrast between the following two sentences shows, it is the nearer *wh* word that moves.

51)
a. The nearer *wh* word moves to the Specifier of CP position:
[$_{CP}$ What should [$_{IP}$ Marvin *t* give *t* to who(m)]]
   ↑   ↑ Inversion |
   |_____*Wh* Movement_____|

b. The more distant *wh* words moves the Specifier of CP position:
*[$_{CP}$ Who should [$_{IP}$ Marvin *t* give what to *t*]]
  ↑   ↑ Inversion |
  |_____*Wh* Movement_____|

This is exactly the result that we would expect, given Shortest Move.

The effects of Shortest Move can also be seen by considering the application of Inversion to a structure such as the following.

52)
[$_{CP}$ [$_{IP}$ The visitors should have stayed longer]]

This structure contains two auxiliary verbs—*should* and *have* (see note 2). Crucially, it is the nearer one that is attracted to the C position, as the contrast between the following two sentences shows.

53)
a. The nearer auxiliary verb moves to the C position:
[$_{CP}$ Should [$_{IP}$ the visitor *t* have stayed longer]]

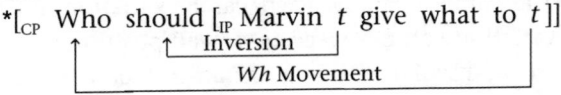

b. The more distant auxiliary moves to the C position:
*[_{CP} Have [_{IP} the visitor should *t* stayed longer]]

b. The more distant auxiliary moves to the C position:
*[_{CP} Have [_{IP} the visitor should *t* stayed longer]]

Shortest Move is sometimes referred to as an **economy constraint**, since it has the effect of making moves as short as possible, which in turn reduces the 'computational cost' of the derivation. A good deal of current research focuses on the notion of derivational economy and its role in explaining syntactic phenomena.

4 Universal grammar and parametric variation

Thus far, our discussion has focused on English. Before looking at any further phenomena in this language, it is important to extend the scope of our analysis to other languages.

As noted at the beginning of this chapter, recent work on Universal Grammar suggests that all languages are fundamentally alike with respect to the basics of syntax. For instance, all languages use the Merge operation to combine words on the basis of their syntactic category and subcategorization properties, creating phrases that comply with the phrase structure schema. Moreover, Move operations are available in all languages and appear to be universally subject to economy constraints such as Shortest Move.

The fact that certain syntactic properties are universal does not mean that languages must be alike in all respects though. Universal Grammar leaves room for variation, allowing individual languages to differ with respect to certain **parameters**. (You can think of a parameter as the set of options that UG permits for a particular phenomenon.) We will consider a few examples of this now, beginning with variation in phrase structure. Some additional instances of cross-linguistic differences in syntax are considered in section 2.3 of chapter 8.

4.1 Variation in phrase structure

Even where languages have the same categories, there can be variation in terms of how they are assembled. Part of this variation can be traced to a head position parameter that offers three options—head-initial, head-medial, and head-final. In Japanese, for example, heads

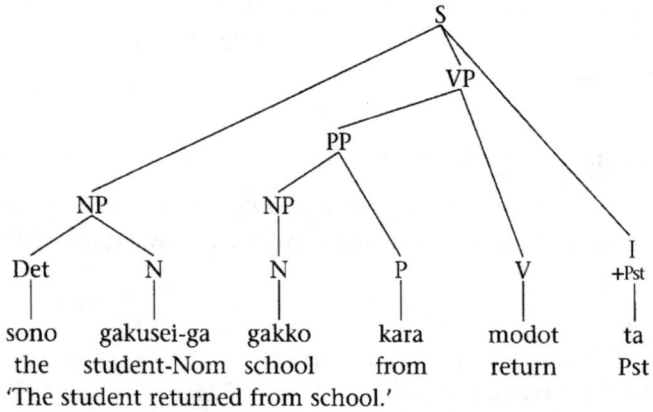

Figure 5.32 Japanese phrase structure: the head is always final

consistently occur in the final position within their phrase. Thus, the noun comes at the end of the NP, the verb at the end of the VP, and so on (see figure 5.32). Because Ps occur at the end of the PP, they are called **postpositions** rather than prepositions. (Nom = nominative, the subject marker; we ignore CP here to save space.)

These word-order differences reflect the positioning of heads with respect to the other elements in their phrases, not the presence of an entirely new type of syntactic system. We can account for these facts by formulating the following phrase structure rule for Japanese.

54)
XP → (Specifier) (Complement*) X

As this rule indicates, the head uniformly follows its specifier and complement(s) in Japanese. In English, on the other hand, the head follows its specifier but precedes any complements.

55)
XP → (Specifier) X (Complement*)

Matters are not always so simple, however. In Thai, for instance, heads precede both complements and specifiers (the head-initial option) within phrases other than S (see figure 5.33). Thus, Ns appear at the beginning of NPs, Ps at the beginning of PPs, Vs at the beginning of VPs, and so on. (Tones have been omitted here.)

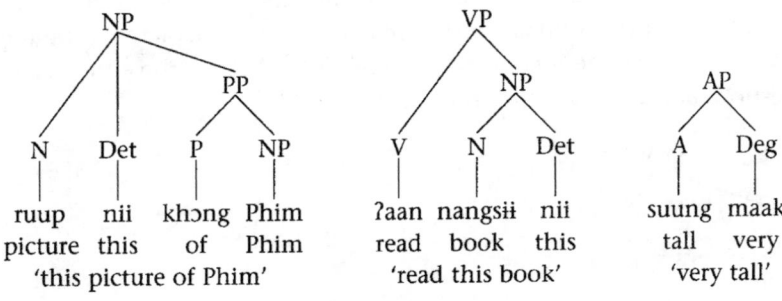

Figure 5.33 Thai phrase structure: the head is initial in phrases other than S

Within S, however, the specifier (the subject NP) comes first, just as it does in English (see figure 5.34).

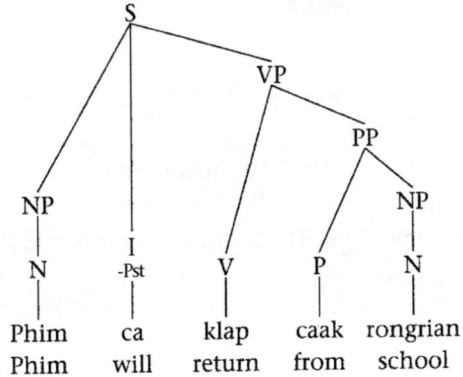

Figure 5.34 Thai sentence structure: the specifier (subject) precedes the head

4.2   Variation in the use of transformations

Languages often differ from each other in the kinds of rules they use to form a particular sentence type. To illustrate this point we will consider four phenomena involving the Move operation.

Yes-no questions

In Tamil (a language of India), *yes-no* questions are signaled by the presence of the morpheme *-ā* at the end of the sentence, rather than by an Inversion transformation. (The diacritic ̣ indicates a dental point of articulation; the diacritic ̄ marks a long vowel; ḷ is a retroflex liquid.)

56)
   a. Muṭṭu paḷam pariṭṭān.
      Muttu fruit   picked
      'Muttu picked the fruit.'

   b. Muṭṭu paḷam pariṭṭān-ā.
      Muttu fruit   picked -Ques
      'Did Muttu pick the fruit?'

The morpheme *-ā* 'spells out' the Q feature in the complementizer position, which occurs at the end of the sentence since Tamil is a head-final language. As depicted in figure 5.35, corresponding to sentence *56b*), the V comes at the end of the VP, I at the end of S, and C (containing the question morpheme) at the end of CP.

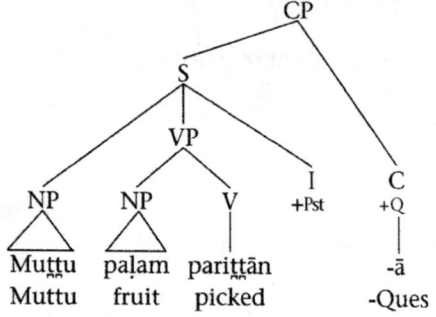

Figure 5.35   A question structure in Tamil

Wh questions

Just as some languages form *yes-no* questions without the help of the Inversion transformation, so some languages form *wh* questions without using *Wh* Movement. Languages of this type include Japanese, Korean, Tamil, Chinese, and Thai. The following example is from Thai.

57)
Khun ʔaan ʔaray?
you read what
'What did you read?'

It seems that the Q feature in languages such as Thai is not 'strong' enough to attract *wh* words, with the result that *wh* questions are formed without the help of a Move operation.

Verb Raising

Consider now the contrast between the following two English sentences.

58)
a. Paul always works.
b. *Paul works always.

This ungrammaticality of the second sentence is expected since the preverbal qualifier *always* functions as specifier of the verb and therefore should occur to its left, as in *58a)*. Surprisingly, however, qualifiers must follow the verb in French.

59)
a. *Paul toujours travaille. (= English *58a*)
   Paul always works

b. Paul travaille toujours. (= English *58b*)
   Paul works always

Why should this be? One possibility is that the tense feature in the I category somehow attracts the verb to that position in French, just as the Q feature can attract verbs to the C position in some languages. As a result, French has the Verb Raising transformation outlined in *60)*.

60)
Verb Raising
Move V to I.

This Move operation brings about the change depicted in figure 5.36.

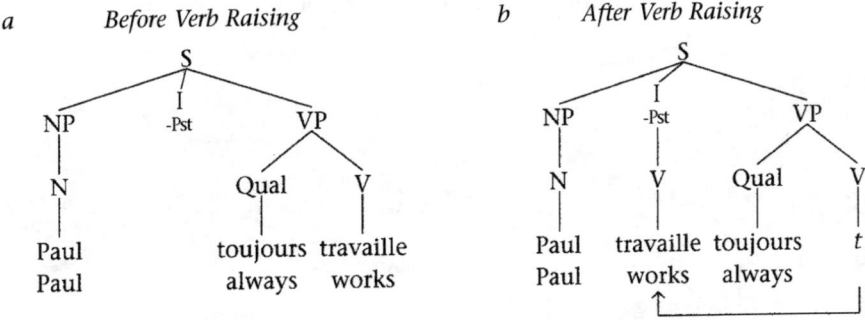

Figure 5.36 Verb Raising in French: the verb moves from within the VP to the I position

A fascinating piece of independent evidence for the existence of Verb Raising in French comes from the operation of the Inversion transformation in that language. As we have already seen (section 3.1), this transformation moves the I category to the C position. Now, in English only auxiliary verbs occur in the I position, which explains why only they can undergo Inversion.

61)

a. Inversion of an auxiliary verb in English:
  Will you *t* stay for supper?
  ⤴_____|

b. Inversion of a non-auxiliary verb in English:
  *Stay you *t* for supper?
  ⤴_____|

In French, however, regular verbs can also occur in the I position, thanks to the Verb Raising transformation. This predicts that Inversion should be able to apply to these Vs in French as well as to auxiliaries. This is correct. Like English, French can form a question by moving an auxiliary leftward, as *62)* illustrates.

62)
Inversion of an auxiliary:
As-tu *t* essayé?
⤴____|

Have you tried?

However, unlike English, French also allows inversion of non-auxiliary Vs.

63)
Inversion of a non-auxiliary verb:
Vois-tu *t* le livre?
 ⤴____|

see you the book
'Do you see the book?'

Figure 5.37 depicts the interaction between Verb Raising and Inversion needed to form this sentence. (We treat the pronoun *tu* 'you' as a type of NP.)

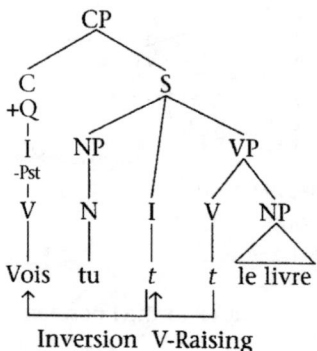

Figure 5.37 The interaction of Verb Raising and Inversion in French

Although Verb Raising is generally not found in English, there is reason to believe that it applies to the 'copula' verb *be* as a special case. As shown in the following example, *be* sounds more natural when it occurs to the left of a qualifier such as *always*.

64)

a. *be* to the left of the specifier:
   Jonathan *is* always on time.

b. *be* to the right of the specifier:
   ?*Jonathan always *is* on time.

This suggests that *be* can be moved leftward to the I position by the Verb Raising transformation.

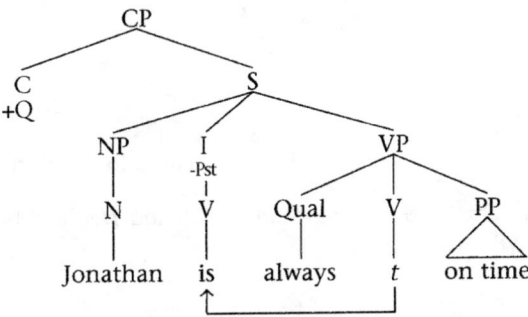

Figure 5.38 Raising of copula *be* in English

As expected, *be* is also able to undergo subsequent movement to the C position (Inversion) in *yes-no* questions, yielding sentences such as *65).*

65)

Is Jonathan *t* always *t* on time?

Verb-initial languages

Languages in which the verb is the first element in the sentence provide a special challenge for syntactic analysis. The following example is from Welsh.

66)
Lladdodd y ddraig y   dyn
killed   the dragon the man
'The dragon killed the man.'

At first glance, it seems impossible to build a legal structure for these sentences, since the subject occurs in the middle of the sentence rather than on the left or right margin.

In order to get around this problem, it has been necessary to consider a radical idea—namely, that the subject originates in the specifier position of VP in all languages. (If this is right, qualifiers have to be reanalyzed as something else—perhaps modifiers; see section 5.1.) This idea is usually implemented in conjunction with the more detailed version of the phrase structure schema discussed in section 1.5 and we will follow this practice here (see figure 5.39). To save space, we ignore the internal structure of NPs.

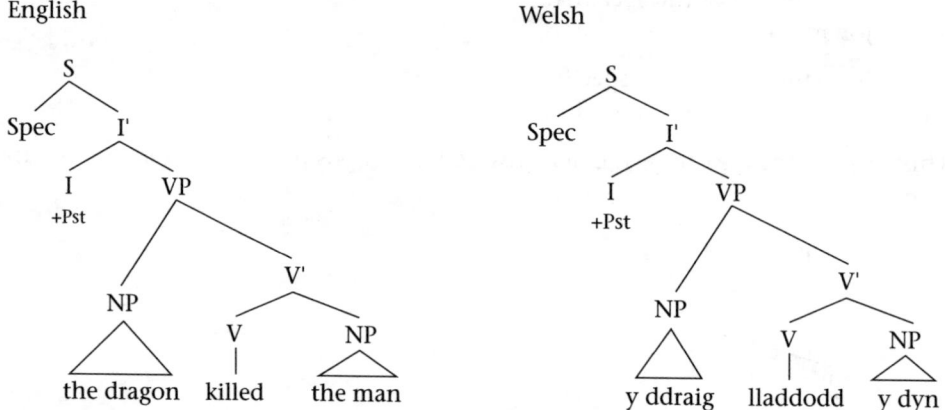

Figure 5.39 The deep structure of a typical transitive sentence in English and Welsh. In both languages, the subject occurs as specifier of VP

In a verb-medial language such as English, the subject raises from the specifier position within VP to the specifier position of S in surface structure. In a verb-initial language such as Welsh, by contrast, the subject remains in the specifier position within VP, but the verb raises to the I position (just as it does in French). As illustrated in figure 5.40, this gives the correct final order for both types of language.

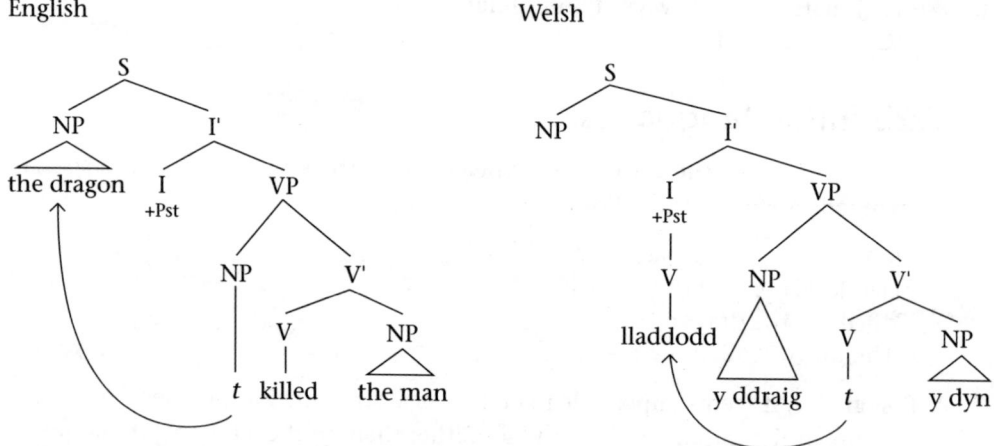

Figure 5.40 The surface structure of a typical transitive sentence in English and Welsh. The subject NP raises in English whereas the verb raises in Welsh

This analysis has two immediate advantages. First, it allow us to extend the X' template to verb-initial languages, which is clearly desirable since this template is supposed to be part of Universal Grammar. Second, it allows us to account for the differences between verb-medial and verb-initial languages in terms of the application of Move operations that are independently attested in human language. We have already seen that the verb-raising operation is needed to account for word order in French and we will see in section 6 that evidence for an NP-raising operation can be found in English and many other languages.

5   Some extensions (*Advanced*)

Now that we have considered some of the basic mechanisms of sentence formation found in human language, it is possible to broaden our treatment of English syntax by briefly examining additional phenomena. We focus in this section on two such phenomena—modifier constructions and case.

5.1   Modifiers

Thus far, our treatment of phrase structure has ignored **modifiers**, a class of elements that encode optionally expressible properties of heads. Although all lexical categories can have modifiers, we will focus here on the types of categories that can modify Ns and Vs.

Adjective phrases (APs) make up the single most commonly used class of modifiers in English. As the following examples show, the principal function of APs is to serve as modifiers of Ns.

67)
APs serving as modifiers of N:
A *very tall* man walked into the room.
She made *exceptional* progress.

The most common modifiers of Vs are adverb phrases (AdvPs) and PPs that describe manner or time.

68)
AdvPs serving as modifiers of V:
describing manner: Ellen left *quickly.*
                       Ellen *quickly* left.
describing time: We arrived *very early.*

PPs serving as modifiers of V:
describing manner: Ellen proceeded *with care.*
describing time: He stayed *for three days.*

As the examples in table 5.11 show, English modifiers vary in terms of their position with respect to the head. APs precede the N while PPs follow the verb, and many AdvPs can occur either before or after the verb that they modify.

Table 5.11	Some modifiers in English	
Modifier	Position	Examples
AP	precedes the head	[very tall] buildings
PP	follows the head	work [with care]
AdvP	precedes or follows the head	walk [carefully] or [carefully] walk

A rule for modifiers

How do modifiers fit into phrase structure? For the purposes of this introduction to syntax, we will attach modifiers at the XP level of phrase structure, in accordance with the following expanded XP rule.

69)
The Expanded XP Rule
XP → (Spec) (Mod) X (Complement*) (Mod)

This rule allows a modifier to occur either before the head (as in figure 5.41a) or after it (see figure 5.41b).

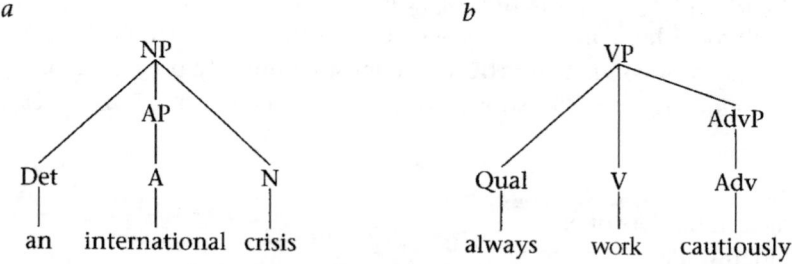

Figure 5.41 Phrases containing modifiers

Where there is a complement, a modifier that occurs after the head will normally occur to the right of the complement as well. This is illustrated in figure 5.42.

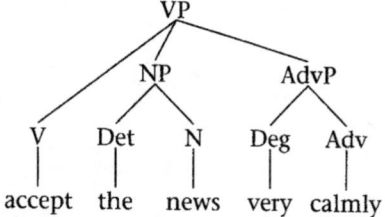

Figure 5.42 A phrase in which both the complement and the modifier occur after the head. In such cases, the modifier occurs after the complement

5.2 Case: the interaction between syntax and morphology

Many linguistic phenomena reflect the interaction of the morphological and syntactic components of the grammar. An important example of this interaction involves case, which indicates an NP's grammatical role in the sentence (see chapter 4, section 6.3).

The sole case marker used with nouns in Modern English is *-'s*, which marks an NP that occupies the specifier position within a larger NP, as depicted in figure 5.43. (We extend our system of phrase structure by allowing an NP to serve as specifier of an N.)

Figure 5.43 The genitive case marks an NP that functions as specifier of an N

However, a richer system of contrasts is found in English pronouns, whose forms reflect a three-way case distinction (see table 5.12).

Table 5.12	Case contrasts for the third person singular masculine pronoun in English		
Case	**Form**	**Function**	**Example**
Nominative	he	subject	*He* left.
Genitive	his	specifier of N	*his* book
Accusative	him	complement of V or P	Mary saw *him.* Mary sat near *him.*

Contemporary transformational syntax accounts for these contrasts by treating the various cases as features that are associated with particular syntactic positions. We capture this idea by having heads of particular types assign case features to NPs in their specifier or complement positions.

70)
The Case Rules for English NPs
a. I assigns a nominative case feature to the subject NP.
b. V and P assign an accusative case feature to their complement NP.
c. N assigns a genitive case feature to an NP in its specifier position.

To see how this works, consider the sentence *She saw him*, with the structure depicted in figure 5.44. (Case features are written as subscripts.)

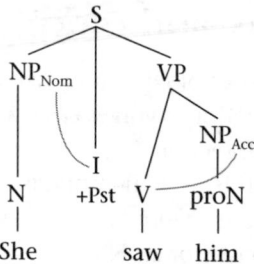

Figure 5.44 An example of case assignment in English

This sentence is well formed, since the pronoun in the subject position has the nominative form required by *70a)* and the pronoun in the complement position has the accusative form required by *70b)*. Had we used the accusative form in the subject position and the nominative in the direct object position (**Her saw he*), the sentence would have been ungrammatical because of the mismatch between the pronoun's form and the case feature that is assigned to the position it occupies.

The Case Filter

You may have noticed that the case rules are formulated in such a way that any NP occurring in the right position—not just a pronoun—will receive case. This means that in a sentence such as *Roberta saw Jean*, *Roberta* will be assigned nominative case and *Jean* will receive accusative case even though there is no inflection to show this. Case that need not have visible effects is known as **abstract case**.

Contemporary versions of transformational syntax require all NPs to have a case feature, even if it is not expressed inflectionally. This requirement is known as the **Case Filter.**

71)
The Case Filter
Every NP in a grammatical sentence must be assigned a case feature.

A major advantage of the Case Filter is that it helps explain why NPs can occur in some positions, but not others. As you may have already noticed, the case rules do not assign a case feature to every imaginable position in syntactic structure. For instance, while the complements of V and P have accusative case (rule *70b)*, the complement of an A or N does not— since no case is assigned to that position. This in turn helps explain why NPs can occur as complements of V and P, but not A or N.

72)

V with NP complement:	P with NP complement:
criticize [NP the girl]	near [NP the girl]
N with NP complement:	A with NP complement:
*criticism [NP the girl]	*critical [NP the girl]

Phrases such as *criticize the girl* and *near the girl*, shown in figure 5.45, satisfy the Case Filter since the NP *the girl* can receive an accusative case feature in that position, in accordance with *70b)*.

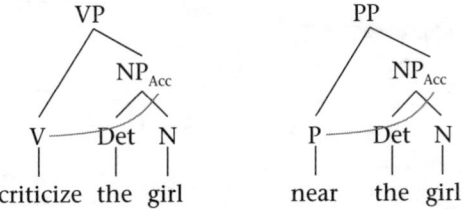

Figure 5.45 Case assignment to the complement of V and P

In contrast, the ill-formed phrases *criticism the girl* and *critical the girl* in *72)* above violate the Case Filter since the NP *the girl* is not in a position to which a case feature is assigned.

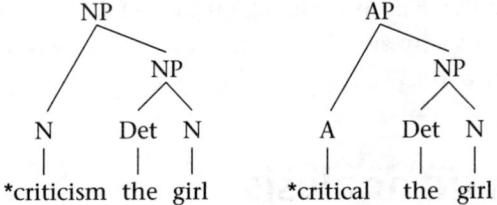

Figure 5.46 The absence of case on the complement of N and A

In order for these phrases to be grammatical, the complement must be realized as a PP (see figure 5.47).

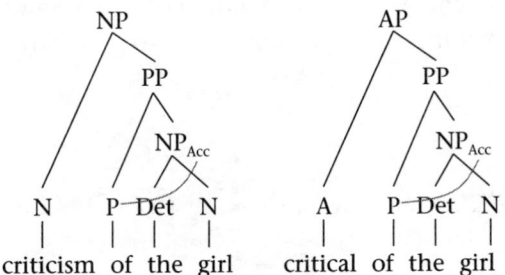

Figure 5.47 Case assignment when the complement of N and A is realized as a PP

As you can see, this structural pattern avoids the problem found in figure 5.46 since the preposition *of* can assign case to the NP, according to the rules in *70)*.

Sometimes, an NP's case is determined by its position prior to movement. A good example of this involves *wh* questions, in which the *wh* word appears in a position (the specifier of CP) to which no case feature is assigned. Under such circumstances, the NP must receive its case feature in the position that it occupies prior to *Wh* Movement. Direct evidence for this comes from conservative varieties of English, in which *who* is associated with the subject position and the special accusative form *whom* with the direct object position.

73)

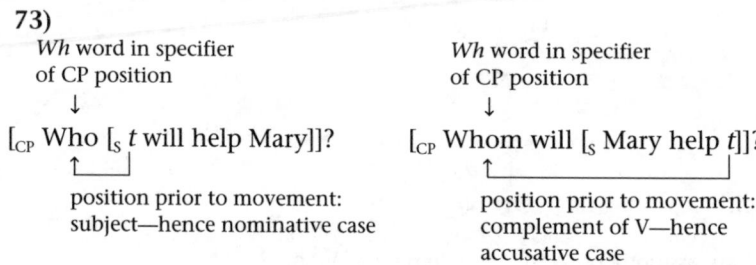

Wh word in specifier
of CP position
↓
[cp Who [s *t* will help Mary]]?

position prior to movement:
subject—hence nominative case

Wh word in specifier
of CP position
↓
[cp Whom will [s Mary help *t*]]?

position prior to movement:
complement of V—hence
accusative case

In summary, then, although case is a morphological category, it encodes syntactic information. This is captured by means of the rules outlined in *70)*, which associate each of the various case forms of English with a different position in syntactic structure (subject, specifier of N, complement of V, and so on). Taking this idea and extending it one step further, the Case Filter then ensures that NP must occupy a position to which a case feature is assigned at some point in the derivation. This explains why an NP may serve as complement of a V or P (figure 5.45), but not of an N or A (figure 5.46).

6 Other types of syntactic analysis

Thus far in this chapter, we have focused our attention on the theory of sentence formation known as transformational syntax. As mentioned at the outset, however, this is not the only type of syntactic analysis used in contemporary linguistics. In this section, we will briefly consider two other approaches to syntax, one focusing on grammatical relations such as subject and direct object, and the other focusing on the way in which syntactic structure is used to communicate information.

In order to illustrate how these approaches work, it is helpful to consider how they—and transformational syntax—deal with the contrast between the two types of sentences illustrated in *74)* and *75)*.

74)
a. The thief took the painting.
b. The painting was taken by the thief.

75)
a. The dog chased the truck.
b. The truck was chased by the dog.

In order to describe the differences and similarities between these two sentences, it is necessary to distinguish between the **agent** (the doer of the action designated by the verb) and the **theme** (the entity directly affected by that action). (These notions are discussed in more detail in chapter 6.)

76)
a. active sentence:
    The thieves took the painting.
      agent   *theme*

b. passive sentence:
   The painting was taken (by the thieves).
       theme   *agent*

The *a* sentence is called **active** because the agent is encoded as subject of the sentence while the *b* sentence is called **passive** in recognition of the fact that the theme is encoded as subject.

The analysis of the relationship between active and passive sentences is an important part of all syntactic theories and therefore provides an ideal 'testing ground' for comparing competing approaches to syntax.

6.1 The transformational analysis

The key generalizations that the transformational analysis of passive sentences tries to capture are as follows:

77)
 a. The agent, which functions as subject in active sentences, is 'downgraded' to a less prominent position in passive sentences.
 b. The vacancy in the subject position is filled in passive sentences by the theme NP, which normally functions as direct object in active sentences.

In a transformational analysis, the first of these generalizations is captured with the help of the deep structure illustrated in figure 5.48. (As indicated in note 2, auxiliary *be* can be treated as a V that takes a VP complement.)

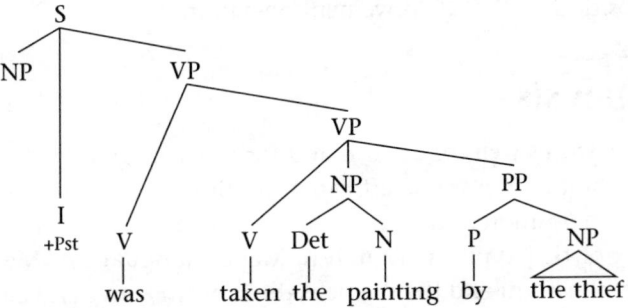

Figure 5.48 Deep structure for *The painting was taken by the thief*

The second generalization is captured by moving the theme NP from the direct object position to the subject position in surface structure. The Move operation needed to bring about this result can be stated as follows.

78)
NP Movement
Move NP into the subject position.

This transformation applies to the deep structure in figure 5.48 to give the surface structure depicted in figure 5.49.

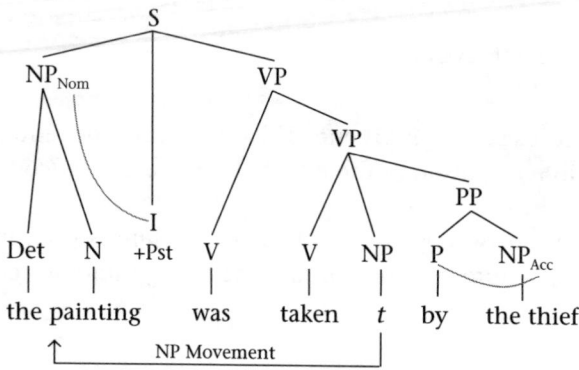

Figure 5.49 Surface structure resulting from NP movement

What ensures that **NP movement** takes place and that the subject position is not simply left empty in the surface structure of a passive sentence? The answer may well lie in the Case Filter discussed in section 5.2.

The key idea is simply that a passive verb is unable to assign a case feature to its complement. Since only transitive verbs are able to assign case, this is just another way of saying that passive verbs are **intransitive**. In fact, it is often suggested that the *-en* or *-ed* suffix found on the passive forms of the verb has a detransitivizing function.

Given that a passive verb cannot assign a case feature to its complement, the direct object must find its case elsewhere if it is to satisfy the Case Filter. As illustrated in figure 5.49, it is 'attracted' to the empty subject position due to the availability of nominative case there and is transported to that position by the NP Movement operation.

6.2   The relational analysis

The transformational analysis works well for English and for other languages in which passivization is marked by a combination of verbal affixation (indicating a loss of the ability to assign case) and a change in the position of the theme (indicating movement). However, not all languages have passives of this type. In Tzotzil (a Mayan language of Mexico), for instance, the relative order of the agent and the theme is the same in active and passive constructions.

79)
a. active sentence:
 Lá snákan ti vīnike ti xpétule.
       theme *agent*
 seated   the man the Peter
 'Peter seated the man.'

b. passive sentence:
 Inákanat ti vīnike yuʔun ti xpétule.
      theme   *agent*
 was seated the man by the Peter
 'The man was seated by Peter.'

Here the passive is signaled by a change in the form of the verb and the appearance of the preposition *yu?un* 'by' before the agent, but there is no change in the relative order of the agent and theme.

Mandarin Chinese employs yet another option.

80)

    a. active sentence:
        Zhu laoshi   piyue-le wode kaoshi.
         agent   *theme*
        Zhu professor marked   my test
        'Professor Zhu marked my test.'

    b. passive sentence:
        Wode kaoshi bei Zhu laoshi   piyue-le.
         theme   *agent*
        my   test by Zhu professor marked.
        'My test was marked by Professor Zhu.'

Here, the passive is marked by a change in word order and by the appearance of the preposition *bei* 'by' before the agent, but the verb has exactly the same form in both patterns.

This has led some linguists to believe syntactic phenomena are best described in terms of grammatical relations such as subject and direct object rather than case or movement. According to proponents of **relational** analysis, the key facts about the contrast between active and passive sentences should be stated as follows in table 5.13. (An NP that occurs with a preposition is said to be **oblique.**)

Table 5.13 Properties of passive structures	
Active pattern	**Passive pattern**
subject →	oblique
direct object →	subject

This works straightforwardly for English, as the following example helps illustrate.

81)

    a. active sentence: The thieves took the painting.
                        subject   *direct object*
                        subject   *oblique*
    b. passive sentence: The painting was taken (by the thieves).

Notice that the direct object in the active *81a)* (*the painting*) is the subject in the passive *81b)* while the subject in *81a)* (*the thieves*) occurs as part of a PP in *81b)*—just as the relational generalization say they should.

Since the criteria used to identify subjects and direct objects differ from language to language, relational changes can be associated with a variety of structural effects. In English, where the direct object appears after the verb and the subject before it, a change in an NP's grammatical relation will also involve a change in its linear position. In other languages, word order may not be so important and the relational changes may be indicated in other ways—by verbal affixation, by case, or by the use of a preposition (as in Tzotzil). By analyzing passivization in terms of processes that affect subjects and direct objects, it is possible to go beyond these differences and to capture the universal properties of this important phenomenon.

Notions like subject and direct object have an important role to play in syntactic analysis and they are often used to describe phenomena in a way that can be understood by linguists of all theoretical orientations. We will see additional examples of this in chapter 8.

6.3   The functional analysis

Some syntactic analysis focuses on the relationship between a sentence's form and the way in which it is used to communicate information. This type of analysis is often called **functional** since it seeks to understand syntactic phenomena in terms of their communicative function. The contrast between active and passive sentences is especially instructive in this regard. Although both sentence types have the same basic meaning, they differ from each other in terms of how they present the situation that they describe. Put another way, they differ from each other in how they 'package' the information to be communicated. Two differences can be noted here.

First, passive sentences tend to de-emphasize the role of the agent in the situation being described. In fact, the vast majority of passive sentences do not mention the agent at all. In English, for instance, we can say simply *The painting was taken* or *The dishes were broken*, without attributing responsibility for these events to any particular person.

Second, passive sentences foreground the theme by making it the subject of the sentence. As a result, the situation is presented from the perspective of that person or thing. (As we will see in chapter 6, the subject usually introduces the entity that the rest of the sentence is about.) Consider in this regard the following passage.

82)
Gretzky raced down the ice, stole the puck, and passed it out in front of the net. An instant later, *he was hit by the defenceman* (compare: An instant later, *the defenceman hit him.*)

The italicized passive sentence sounds more natural than the corresponding active sentence since it brings to the foreground the pronoun *he*, which refers to the person (Gretzky) from whose perspective the entire series of events is being described.

In contrast, the passive is not nearly so natural in the following context.

83)
Gretzky raced down the ice, circled the net, and stopped. *The puck was then stolen by Gretzky* from the defenceman. (compare: *He then stole the puck* from the defenceman.)

Here the passive sentence seems somewhat less natural, since it suddenly foregrounds the puck even though the rest of the passage is about Gretzky. This abrupt shift in the flow of information could be avoided by using the active sentence, with a pronoun referring to Gretzky in the subject position.

As this example illustrates, the functional analysis of the passive pattern focuses on the way in which it packages information compared to active sentences, placing the emphasis on how it is used rather than just on its structure. The key claim is that the function of the passive construction is to de-emphasize the agent (often deleting it entirely) and to draw attention to the theme NP. By analyzing syntactic structures functionally, it is often possible to gain insights into why human language has the particular syntactic patterns that it does and how these patterns contribute to the larger task of communication.

Summing up

Universal Grammar provides all languages with the same general type of syntactic mechanisms. As we have seen, this includes a **Merge** operation that combines words in accordance with their **syntactic category** and their **subcategorization** properties, creating a representation called **deep structure**. Deep structure must comply with the **phrase structure schema**, which stipulates the place of **heads**, **specifiers**, **complements**, and **modifiers** in phrase structure.

Move operations (**transformations**) can modify deep structure by moving words and phrases in ways to produce a **surface structure**. But not just any movement is permitted, since transformations are constrained by economy principles such as **Shortest Move**.

Although the form of sentences can vary considerably from language to language, such differences can for the most part be attributed to a small set of **parameters**, each of which makes available a variety of alternatives from which individual languages may choose.

Notes

[1]　It is commonly assumed that the I node also contains information about subject-verb agreement, which—like tense—is often realized as verbal inflection (see chapter 4, section 6.4). Thus, the tree in figure 5.9 would actually look like this, with the features under the Agr(eement) label matching those on the subject.

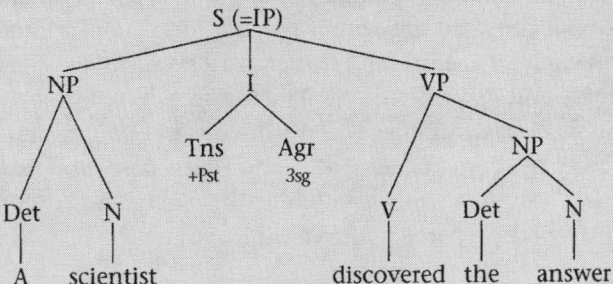

Figure a　The I category contains information about both tense and agreement.

Mechanisms not considered here ensure that the tense and agreement features under I are realized appropriately on the verb. In order to keep this introduction to syntax at a relatively simple level, we will not discuss agreement further in this chapter.

[2]　In this analysis, only the so-called 'modal' auxiliaries mentioned here count as instances of the I category. *Have* and *be* (traditionally called 'aspectual' auxiliaries) are treated as special verbs that take a VP as their complement. For example:

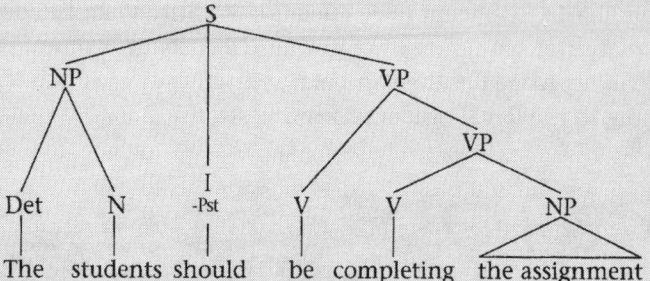

Figure b The modal auxiliary *should* occurs under the I category while the aspectual auxiliary *be* is treated as a V that takes a VP complement.

Here, *should* (an instance of I) takes as its complement the VP headed by *be*, which in turn takes the VP *completing the assignment* as its complement.

Sources

Transformational syntax is the most popular of the half-dozen major contemporary syntactic theories. Traditionally, it is the theory taught in introductory linguistics courses, both because it is so widely used and because many of the other approaches that exist today have developed in response to it. The particular system outlined here involves a variety of simplifications to make it appropriate for presentation in an introductory course.

The system of subcategorization employed here is loosely based on the one outlined in *Generalized Phrase Structure Grammar* by G. Gazdar, E. Klein, G. Pullum, and I. Sag (Cambridge, MA: Harvard University Press, 1979), which describes a non-transformational approach to syntax.

The discussion of the relational analysis of passive sentences is intended to be neutral between Lexical Functional Grammar as outlined in *The Mental Representation of Grammatical Relations*, edited by Joan Bresnan (Cambridge, MA: MIT Press, 1978) and Relational Grammar as described in "Toward a Universal Characterization of Passivization" by D. Perlmutter and P. Postal in *Studies in Relational Grammar I*, edited by D. Perlmutter (Chicago: University of Chicago Press, 1983); the Chinese and Tzotzil examples cited in section 6.2 were taken from this paper. The functional analysis of passives draws on the discussion in *Functional Syntax* by Susumu Kuno (Chicago: University of Chicago Press, 1981) and *Functional Syntax and Universal Grammar* by W. Foley and R. Van Valin (New York: Cambridge University Press, 1980).

The exercises for this chapter were prepared by Joyce Hildebrand.

Recommended reading

Haegeman, Liliane. 1994. *Introduction to Government and Binding Theory.* 2nd ed. Cambridge, MA: Blackwell.

Palmer, F.R. 1994. *Grammatical Roles and Relations.* New York: Cambridge University Press.

Payne, Thomas. 1997. *Describing Morphosyntax: A Guide for Field Linguists.* New York: Cambridge University Press.

Radford, Andrew. 1997. *Syntax: A Minimalist Introduction.* New York: Cambridge University Press.

Shopen, Timothy, ed. 1985. *Language Typology and Syntactic Description*. Vols. 1 – 3. New York: Cambridge University Press.

Appendix: how to build tree structures

Although it is relatively easy to check a tree structure to see if it complies with the phrase structure schema, it is somewhat harder to build a tree structure from scratch when trying to analyze a new phrase or sentence. In such cases, you will probably find it easiest to proceed in steps, working from the bottom up and from right to left. As an illustration, let us first consider the phrase *near the door*.

The first step involves assigning each word to the appropriate category, as depicted in figure 5.50.

```
P    Det    N
|     |     |
near the  door
```

Figure 5.50 The first step: determining the word-level categories

Then, working from right to left, the appropriate XPs are built above each head (see figure 5.51). Thus, we first build an NP above the N *door*. There is clearly no complement here, but there is a specifier (the determiner *the*), which combines with the N in accordance with the phrase structure schema.

Figure 5.51 Building the NP

Next, we carry out the same procedure for the P *near*. The NP to its right of the P clearly functions as its complement, since it names the location entailed by the meaning of *near*. We therefore combine the P and the NP, forming the structure depicted in figure 5.52.

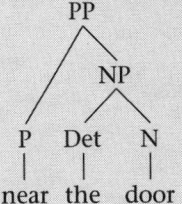

Figure 5.52 The complete PP

A sentential example

Consider now how we proceed in the case of a complete sentence such as *The dog might bite that man*. Assignment of each word to the appropriate category gives the structure depicted in figure 5.53.

Figure 5.53 The categories for each word in the sentence

Working from right to left, it is easy to see that the noun *man* heads an NP that contains a specifier but no complement (see figure 5.54).

Figure 5.54 The structure of the rightmost NP

Next, we focus on the V *bite*, building the required VP and attaching the complement NP *that man* (see figure 5.55).

Figure 5.55 Adding the VP level above the V head

As an instance of the I category, the auxiliary *might* is the head of S, with the VP to the right serving as its complement and the NP to the left functioning as its specifier. This yields the complete sentence illustrated in figure 5.56.

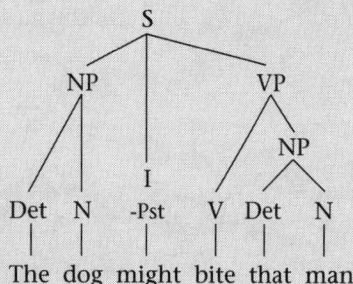

Figure 5.56 The complete sentence

The entire sentence is then embedded in a CP 'shell', giving the tree in figure 5.57.

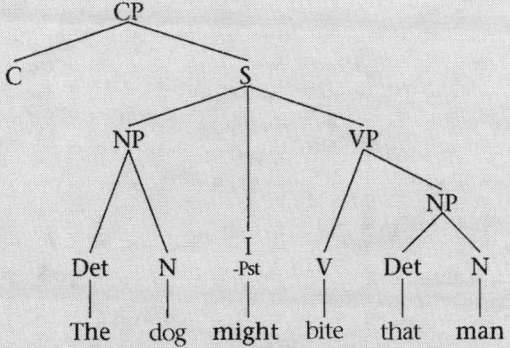

Figure 5.57 The sentence embedded in a CP shell

Transformations

As explained in section 3, the syntactic analysis of some sentences involves the Move operation in addition to Merge. Recognizing that one of the transformations used in this chapter has applied is relatively simple: if a sentence contains an auxiliary verb to the left of the subject, then Inversion has applied; if it begins with a *wh* word, then *Wh* Movement has applied. In the sentence *What should the farmers plant?*, then, both of these transformations have applied.

In order to determine the deep structure, we must 'return' the auxiliary verb to its position under I and we must determine the position from which the *wh* word has been moved. Since the *wh* word in the sentence *What should the farmers plant?* asks about the complement of the verb (the thing that is planted), we place *what* in the complement position within VP in deep structure. This gives the deep structure depicted in figure 5.58.

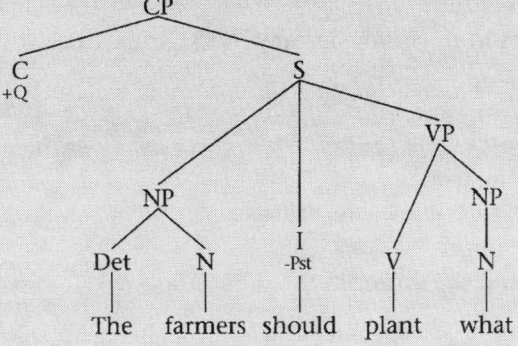

Figure 5.58 The deep structure for the sentence *What should the farmers plant?*

Attracted by the +Q feature, the auxiliary *should* then moves to the C position (Inversion) and *what* to the specifier position under CP (*Wh* Movement), yielding the complete surface structure depicted in figure 5.59.

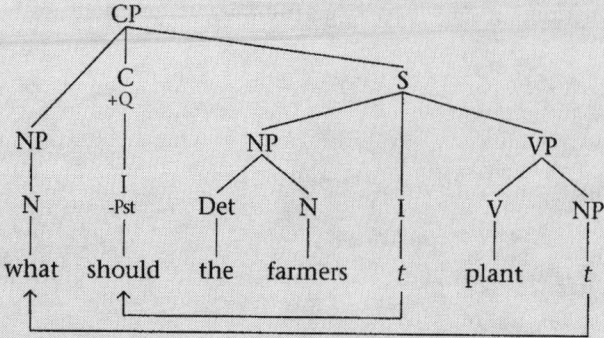

Figure 5.59 The surface structure

Questions

1. Place an asterisk next to any of the sentences that are ungrammatical for you. Can you figure out what makes any of these sentences ungrammatical?
    a) The instructor told the students to study.
    b) The instructor suggested the students to study.
    c) The customer asked for a cold beer.
    d) The customer requested for a cold beer.
    e) He gave the Red Cross some money.
    f) He donated the Red Cross some money.
    g) The pilot landed the jet.
    h) The jet landed.
    i) A journalist wrote the article.
    j) The article wrote.
    k) Jerome is bored of his job.
    l) Jerome is tired of his job.

2. Indicate the category of each word in the following sentences. (It may help to refer back to section 1.1.)
    a) That glass suddenly broke.
    b) A jogger ran toward the end of the lane.
    c) These dead trees are blocking the road.
    d) The detective hurriedly looked through the records.
    e) The peaches never appear quite ripe.
    f) Jeremy will play the trumpet and the drums in the orchestra.

3. Each of the following phrases consists of a specifier and a head. Use the Merge operation to create the appropriate tree structure for each example.
    a) the zoo   f) this house
    b) always try   g) very competent
    c) so witty   h) quite cheap
    d) perhaps pass   i) never surrender
    e) less bleak   j) those books

4. The following phrases include a head, a complement, and (in some cases) a specifier. Use the Merge operation to create the appropriate tree structure for each example. For now, there is no need to depict the internal structure of complements. (See the tree diagrams in figures 5.4 and 5.5 in the chapter.)

   a) into the house
   b) fixed the telephone
   c) full of mistakes
   d) more towards the window
   e) a film about pollution
   f) always study this material
   g) perhaps earn the money
   h) that argument with Owen
   i) the success of the program

5. After carefully reading the first two sections of the appendix, use the Merge operation to create phrase structure trees for each of the following sentences.

   a) Those guests should leave.
   b) Maria never ate a brownie.
   c) That shelf will fall.
   d) The glass broke.
   e) The student lost the debate.
   f) The manager may offer a raise.
   g) The judge often jails shoplifters.
   h) The teacher often organized a discussion.
   i) A psychic will speak to this group.
   j) Marianne could become quite fond of Larry.

6. Apply the substitution test to determine which of the bracketed sequences in the following sentences form constituents.

   a) [The tragedy] upset the entire family.
   b) They hid [in the cave].
   c) The [computer was very] expensive.
   d) [The town square and the civic building] will be rebuilt.
   e) Jane has [left town].
   f) The goslings [swam across] the lake.

7. Apply the movement test to determine which of the bracketed sequences in the following sentences form constituents.

   a) We ate our lunch [near the river bank].
   b) Steve looked [up the number] in the book.
   c) The [island has been] flooded.
   d) I love [peanut butter and bacon sandwiches].
   e) The environmental [movement is gaining momentum].

8. Lexical categories are divided into subcategories on the basis of their complements. For each of the following words, two potential complement options are given. For each of the words:

   i) Determine which one of the two options better matches its subcategorization requirements.
   ii) Justify your choice by creating a sentence using that complement option.

Verb	Options	Verb	Options
a) expire	Ø *or* NP NP	e) clean	NP PP$_{for}$ *or* NP NP
b) destroy	NP *or* Ø	f) mumble	NP *or* NP NP
c) observe	NP *or* PP$_{to}$ PP$_{about}$	g) throw	Ø *or* NP PP$_{loc}$
d) discuss	NP *or* Ø	h) paint	NP PP$_{to}$ *or* NP PP$_{for}$

Noun	Options
a) debate	PP$_{of}$ PP$_{to}$ *or* PP$_{with}$ PP$_{about}$
b) hammer	Ø *or* PP$_{with}$ PP$_{about}$
c) success	PP$_{of}$ PP$_{to}$ *or* PP$_{of}$
d) transfer	PP$_{with}$ PP$_{about}$ *or* PP$_{of}$ PP$_{to}$
e) sickness	Ø *or* PP$_{with}$ PP$_{about}$

Adjective	Options
a) strong	Ø *or* PP$_{about}$
b) sick	NP *or* PP$_{of}$
c) bored	PP$_{with}$ *or* PP$_{of}$
d) knowledgeable	PP$_{to}$ *or* PP$_{about}$
e) small	PP$_{of}$ *or* Ø

9. *i)* The following sentences all contain embedded clauses that function as complements of a verb. Draw a tree structure for each sentence.
   a) The reporter said that an accident injured a woman.
   b) The fishermen think that the company polluted the bay.
   c) Bill reported that a student asked whether the eclipse would occur.

   ii) The following sentences all contain embedded clauses that function as complements of an adjective, a preposition or a noun. Draw a tree structure for each sentence.
   d) The police appeared happy that the criminal would surrender.
   e) That officer was sure that Gerry often speeds down the highway.
   f) Ray wondered about whether the exam would cover that section.
   g) Scientists will never accept the claim that the earth is flat.

10. The derivations of the following sentences involve the Inversion transformation. Give the deep structure and the surface structure for each sentence.
    a) Will the boss hire Hillary?
    b) Can the dog fetch the frisbee?
    c) Should the student report the incident?
    d) Must the musician play that music?
    e) Might that player leave the team?

11. The following sentences involve the rules of *Wh* Movement and Inversion. Give the deep structure and the surface structure for each of these sentences.
    a) Who should the director call?
    b) Who should call the director?
    c) What can Joanne eat?
    d) Who will the visitors stay with?
    e) What might Terry bake for the party?
    f) What could Anne bring to the gathering?

12. The following data is from Igbo, a language spoken in Nigeria.
    a) Nwáànyĩáhũ   b) ṹlṹ   à
       woman that   house this
       'that woman'   'this house'
    i) Draw the phrase structure trees for the two Igbo phrases.

13. The following data is from Malagasy, spoken on the island of Madagascar.
    a) Entin' kafe izy.   b) Mankany amin' ny restauranta izy.
       brings coffee he   goes   to   the restaurant he
       'He brings coffee.'   'He goes to the restaurant.'

    i) Draw the tree structure for each of the Malagasy sentences.
    ii) Do complements precede or follow their heads in Malagasy?

14. Consider the following Selayarese data.
    a) La?allei doe? injo iBaso.
       took   money the Baso
       'Baso took the money.'

    b) nra?bai   sapon injo.
       collapsed house the
       'The house collapsed.'

    c) Lataroi doe? injo ri lamari   injo iBaso.
       put   money the in cupboard the   Baso
       'Baso put the money in the cupboard.'

    i) Draw a tree structure for each of these sentences.
    ii) What is the phrase structure template for Selayarese?

15. The following data is from Korean. You may ignore the nominative (subject) and
    accusative (direct object) markers for the purposes of this question.
    a) Terry-ka   ku yeca-lul coahanta.
       Terry-Nom that girl-Ac   likes
       'Terry likes that girl.'

    b) I   noin-i   hakkyo ey kassta.
       this man-Nom school to went
       'This man went to school.'

    c) Sue-ka   chinkwu eykey chayk-ul ilkessta.
       Sue-Nom friend   to   book-Ac read
       'Sue read the book to a friend.'

    i) Draw the tree structure for each of the Korean sentences.
    ii) What is the phrase structure template for Korean?

16. The following data illustrates the formation of *yes-no* questions in German.
    a) Das Kind wird die Schwester lehren.
       the child will the sister   teach
       'The child will teach the sister.'

b) Wird das Kind die Schwester lehren?
    will   the child the sister   teach
    'Will the child teach the sister?'

c) Der Mann liebt die Frau.
    'The man loves the woman.'

d) Liebt der Mann die Frau?
    loves the man   the woman
    'Does the man love the woman?'

Assuming that German makes use of the same Inversion transformation as English (i.e., 'Move I to the C position'), does the above data tell us whether German employs the Verb Raising transformation? Be sure to include the tree structures for b) and d) in your answer.

17. The following sentences contain modifiers of various types. For each sentence, first identify the modifier(s), then draw the tree structures.
    a) A large iguana suddenly appeared.
    b) The principal made an important announcement after the class.
    c) An unusual event occurred before the game.
    d) The very hazardous waste seeped into the ground quickly.
    e) A huge moon hung in the black sky.
    f) Timothy drew an enormous map during the afternoon.

18. The following Russian sentences contain several different forms for the pronoun 'I'—*ja*, *m^{j}en^{j}a*, *mnoj*, and *mn^{j}e*.

    NOMINATIVE
    a) ja pon^{j}imaju urok
        I understand lesson
        'I understand the lesson.'

    b) ja viʒu joʒika
        I see   hedgehog
        'I see the hedgehog.'

    ACCUSATIVE
    c) on uv^{j}id^{j}el m^{j}en^{j}a
        he saw   me
        'He saw me.'

    d) on^{j}i vstr^{j}et^{j}il^{j}i m^{j}en^{j}a
        they met   me
        'They met me.'

    INSTRUMENTAL
    e) vi poʃl^{j}i sa   mnoj
        you went with me
        'You went with me.'

    f) onʲi pogovorʲilʲi sa   mnoj
       they spoke   with me
       'They were talking with me.'

       DATIVE
    g) onʲi polʃi k mnʲe
       they arrived to me
       'They came to my place.'

    h) on podoʃol k mnʲe
       he approached to me
       'He approached me.'

    i) Draw the tree structure for each of these sentences, and make a statement about the context in which each case form occurs.
    ii) Does the complement of a preposition receive the same case as the complement of a verb?
    iii) Is the case assigned to the complement of a preposition the same for the two prepositions found in the data?

19. In each of the following sentences, indicate above each NP whether it is subject, direct object, or oblique, and indicate below each NP whether it is agent or theme.
    a) Marie purchased a present.
    b) The class was conducted by an expert.
    c) Those books were read by young children.
    d) An expert conducted the class.
    e) A present was purchased by Marie.

Six

William O'Grady

Semantics: the analysis of meaning

. . . in every object there is inexhaustible meaning.

THOMAS CARLYLE

Up to now, this book has focused on the form of utterances—their sound pattern, morphological structure, and syntactic organization. But there is more to language than just form. In order for language to fulfill its communicative function, utterances must also convey a message; they must have content. Speaking very generally, we can refer to an utterance's content as its **meaning**.

This chapter is concerned with **semantics**, the study of meaning in human language. Because some work in this complicated area of linguistic analysis presupposes considerable knowledge of other disciplines (particularly logic, mathematics, and philosophy), not all aspects of contemporary semantics are suitable for presentation in an introductory linguistics textbook. We will restrict our attention here to four major topics in semantics: (1) the nature of meaning, (2) some of the properties of the conceptual system underlying meaning, (3) the contribution of syntactic structure to the interpretation of sentences, and (4) the role of non-grammatical factors in the understanding of utterances.

1 The nature of meaning

Long before linguistics existed as a discipline, thinkers were speculating about the nature of meaning. For thousands of years, this question has been considered central to philosophy. More recently, it has come to be important in other disciplines as well, including psychology and sociology in addition to linguistics. Contributions to semantics have come from a diverse group of scholars, ranging from Plato and Aristotle in ancient Greece to Bertrand Russell in the twentieth century. Our goal in this section will be to consider in a very general way what this research has revealed about meaning in human language. We will begin by considering some of the basic analytic notions used in evaluating the meanings of words and sentences.

1.1   Semantic relations among words

Words and phrases can enter into a variety of semantic relations with each other. Because these relations help identify those aspects of meaning relevant to linguistic analysis, they constitute a good starting point for this chapter.

Synonymy

Synonyms are words or expressions that have the same meaning in some or all contexts. The following pairs of words in table 6.1 provide plausible examples of synonymy in English.

Table 6.1	Some synonyms in English
vacation	holidays
youth	adolescent
automobile	car
remember	recall
purchase	buy
big	large

Because it would be inefficient for a language to have two words or phrases with absolutely identical meanings, perfect synonymy is rare, if not impossible. Words such as *vacation* and *holidays* may be interchangeable in particular contexts *(I spent my vacation/holidays in the Maritimes)*, but their meanings are not always identical. For example, Christmas and Canada Day are holidays, but they are not necessarily part of one's vacation. Similarly, although *youth* and *adolescent* both refer to people of about the same age, only the latter word can be used to imply immaturity—as in *What adolescent behavior!*

Antonymy

Antonyms are words or phrases that are opposites with respect to some component of their meaning. The pairs of words in table 6.2 provide examples of antonymy.

Table 6.2	Some antonyms in English
dark	light
boy	girl
hot	cold
up	down
in	out
come	go

In each of these pairs, the two words contrast with respect to at least one aspect of their meaning. For instance, the meanings of *boy* and *girl* are opposites with respect to gender, although they are alike in other respects (both are human). Similarly, *come* and *go* are opposites with respect to direction, although both involve the concept of movement.

Polysemy and homophony

Polysemy occurs where a word has two or more related meanings. Table 6.3 contains some examples of polysemous words in English.

Table 6.3	Some polysemy in English	
Word	Meaning a	Meaning b
bright	'shining'	'intelligent'
to glare	'to shine intensely'	'to stare angrily'
a deposit	'minerals in the earth'	'money in the bank'

If you consult a reasonably comprehensive dictionary for any language, you will find numerous examples of polysemy. For example, my dictionary lists several related meanings for the word *mark*.

1)
Polysemy in the meaning of *mark*
- a visible trace or impression on something (*The tires left a mark on the road.*)
- a written or printed symbol (*You need a punctuation mark here.*)
- a grade, as in school (*He got a good mark on the math test.*)
- a target (*She hit the mark every time.*)
- an indication of some quality or property (*The mark of a good diplomat is the ability to negotiate.*)

Homophony exists where a single form has two or more entirely distinct meanings (see table 6.4). In such cases, it is assumed that there are separate words with the same pronunciation rather than a single word with different meanings.

Table 6.4	Some homophones in English	
Word	Meaning a	Meaning b
light	'not heavy'	'illumination'
bank	'a financial institution'	'a small cliff at the edge of a river'
club	'a social organization'	'a blunt weapon'
pen	'a writing instrument'	'a small cage'

Homophones need not have identical spellings—*write* and *right* are homophones, as are *piece* and *peace*.

Polysemy and homophony create **lexical ambiguity** in that a single form has two or more meanings. Thus, a sentence such as *2)* could mean either that Liz purchased an instrument to write with or that she bought a small cage.

2)
Liz bought a pen.

Of course, in actual speech the surrounding words and sentences usually make the intended meaning clear. The potential lexical ambiguity in sentences such as the following therefore normally goes unnoticed.

3)

He got a loan from the *bank*.

4)

Because Liz needed a place to keep her guinea pig, she went downtown and bought a *pen* for $20.

1.2 Semantic relations involving sentences

Like words, sentences have meanings that can be analyzed in terms of their relation to other meanings. Three such relations—paraphrase, entailment, and contradiction—are particularly important.

Paraphrase

Two sentences that can have the same meaning are said to be **paraphrases** of each other. The following pairs of sentences provide examples of paraphrase.

5)
a. The police chased the burglar.
b. The burglar was chased by the police.

6)
a. I gave the summons to Erin.
b. I gave Erin the summons.

7)
a. It is unfortunate that the team lost.
b. Unfortunately, the team lost.

8)
a. Paul bought a car from Sue.
b. Sue sold a car to Paul.

9)
a. The game will begin at 3:00 P.M.
b. At 3:00 P.M., the game will begin.

The *a)* and *b)* sentences in each of the above pairs are obviously very similar in meaning. Indeed, it would be impossible for one sentence to be true without the other also being true. Thus, if it is true that the police chased the burglar, it must also be true that the burglar was chased by the police. (Sentences whose meanings are related to each other in this way are said to have the same **truth conditions**.)

For some linguists, this is enough to justify saying that the two sentences have the same meaning. However, you may notice that there are subtle differences in emphasis between the *a)* and *b)* sentences in 5) to 9). For instance, it is natural to interpret *5a)* as a statement about what the police did and *5b)* as a statement about what happened to the burglar. Similarly, *9b)* seems to place more emphasis on the starting time of the game than *9a)* does. As is the case with synonymy, many linguists feel that languages do not permit two or more structures to have absolutely identical meanings and that paraphrases are therefore never perfect.

Entailment

When the truth of one sentence guarantees the truth of another sentence, we say that there is a relation of **entailment**. This relation is mutual in the case of examples *5)* to *9)* since the truth of either sentence in the pair guarantees the truth of the other. In examples such as the following, however, entailment is asymmetrical.

10)
a. The park wardens killed the bear.
b. The bear is dead.

11)
a. Prince is a dog.
b. Prince is an animal.

If it is true that the park wardens killed the bear, then it must also be true that the bear is dead. However, the reverse does not follow since the bear could be dead without the park wardens having killed it. Similarly, if it is true that Prince is a dog, then it is also true that Prince is an animal. Once again though, the reverse does not hold: even if we know that Prince is an animal, we cannot conclude that he is a dog rather than a horse or a cat.

Contradiction

Sometimes, it turns out that if one sentence is true, then another sentence must be false. This is the case with the examples in *12)*.

12)
a. Charles is a bachelor.
b. Charles is married.

If it is true that Charles is a bachelor, then it cannot be true that he is married. When two sentences cannot both be true, we say that there is a **contradiction.**

1.3   What is meaning?

Although it is relatively easy to determine whether two words or sentences have identical or different meanings, it is much more difficult to determine precisely what meaning is in the first place. In fact, despite many centuries of study, we still know very little about the nature of meaning or how it is represented in the human mind. Nonetheless, it is worthwhile to review briefly some of the better known proposals and the problems that they encounter.

Connotation

One notion that is closely linked with the concept of meaning is **connotation**, the set of associations that a word's use can evoke. For most Canadians, for example, the word *winter* evokes thoughts of snow, bitter cold, short evenings, frozen fingertips, and the like. These associations make up the word's connotation, but they cannot be its meaning (or at least not its entire meaning). The word *winter* does not become meaningless just because it is a mild year or because one moves to Florida in November. We must therefore look beyond connotation for our understanding of what meaning is.

Denotation

One well-known approach to semantics attempts to equate the meaning of a word or phrase with the entities to which it refers—its **denotation** or **referents**. The denotation of the word *winter*, for example, corresponds to the season between autumn and spring (regardless of whether it is cold and unpleasant). Similarly, the denotation of the word *dog* corresponds to the set of canines, and so on.

Although a word's denotation is clearly connected to its meaning in some way, they cannot be one and the same thing. This is because there are words such as *unicorn* and phrases such as *the present king of France*, which have no referents in the real world even though they are far from meaningless.

A problem of a different sort arises with expressions such as *the Prime Minister of Canada* and *the leader of the Liberal Party*, both of which refer (in 1999, at least) to Jean Chrétien. Although these two expressions may have the same referent, it seems wrong to say that they mean the same thing. Thus, we would not say that the phrase *Prime Minister of Canada* is defined as 'the leader of the Liberal Party' or that the definition of the phrase *leader of the Liberal Party* is 'Prime Minister of Canada'.

Extension and intension

The impossibility of equating an element's meaning with its referents has led to a distinction between **extension** and **intension**. Whereas an expression's extension corresponds to the set of entities that it picks out in the world (its referents), its intension corresponds to its inherent sense, the concepts that it evokes. Thus, the extension of *woman* is a set of real world entities (women) while its intension involves notions like 'female' and 'human'. Similarly, the phrase *Prime Minister of Canada* has as its extension an individual (Jean Chrétien), but its intension involves the concept 'leader of the governing party' (see table 6.5).

Table 6.5 Extension versus intension		
Phrase	Extension	Intension
Prime Minister of Canada	Jean Chrétien	leader of the governing party
Stanley Cup champions (1999)	Dallas Stars	winners of the NHL championship
Capital of Manitoba	Winnipeg	city containing the provincial legislature

The distinction between intension and extension does not allow us to resolve the question of what meaning is. It simply permits us to pose it in a new way: what are intensions?

One suggestion is that intensions correspond to mental images. This is an obvious improvement over the referential theory since it is possible to have a mental image of a unicorn or even of the king of France, although there are no such entities in the real world. However, problems arise with the meanings of words such as *dog*, which can be used to refer to animals of many different sizes, shapes, and colours. If the meaning of this word corresponds to a mental image, that image would have to be general enough to include Chihuahuas and St. Bernards, yet still exclude foxes and wolves. If you try to draw a picture that satisfies these requirements, you will see just how hard it is to construct an image for word meanings of this sort.

Componential analysis

Still another approach to meaning tries to represent a word's intension by breaking it down into smaller semantic components. Sometimes known as **componential analysis** or **semantic decomposition**, this approach has often been used to analyze the meaning of certain types of nouns in terms of semantic features. The analysis in figure 6.1 for the words *man*, *woman*, *boy*, and *girl* illustrates how this works. (Nothing depends on the choice of feature names here; the analysis would work just as well with the feature ±FEMALE as ±MALE.)

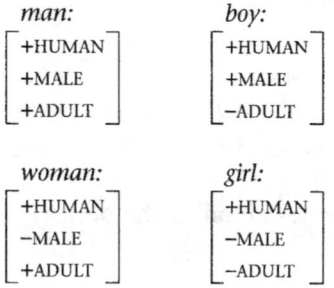

man:
$$\begin{bmatrix} +\text{HUMAN} \\ +\text{MALE} \\ +\text{ADULT} \end{bmatrix}$$

boy:
$$\begin{bmatrix} +\text{HUMAN} \\ +\text{MALE} \\ -\text{ADULT} \end{bmatrix}$$

woman:
$$\begin{bmatrix} +\text{HUMAN} \\ -\text{MALE} \\ +\text{ADULT} \end{bmatrix}$$

girl:
$$\begin{bmatrix} +\text{HUMAN} \\ -\text{MALE} \\ -\text{ADULT} \end{bmatrix}$$

Figure 6.1 Semantic feature composition for *man, woman, boy, girl*

An obvious advantage of this approach is that it allows us to group entities into natural classes (much as we do in phonology). Hence, *man* and *boy* could be grouped together as [+HUMAN, +MALE] while *man* and *woman* could be put in a class defined by the features [+HUMAN, +ADULT].

This in turn can be useful for stating generalizations of various sorts. For instance, there are certain verbs, such as *marry*, *argue*, and the like, that we expect to find only with subjects that are [+human]. Moreover, within the English pronoun system, *he* is used to refer to [+human] entities that are [+male] while *she* is used for [+human] entities that are [-male].

There are limits on the insights into word meaning offered by componential analysis. What value, for example, is there in characterizing the meaning of *dog* as [+ANIMAL, +CANINE] as long as there is no further analysis of these features? Similarly, do we say that the meaning of *blue* consists of the feature [+COLOUR] and something else? If so, what is that other thing? Isn't it blueness? If so, then we have not really broken the meaning of *blue* into smaller components, and we are back where we started.

To date, componential analysis has given its most impressive results in the study of verb meaning. A typical component of verb meaning is the concept GO, which is associated with change of various sorts. (The components of verb meaning tend not to be binary features.)

> 13)
> manifestations of the concept GO:
> *a.* positional change:
> Harvey went from Toronto to Winnipeg.
> *b.* possessional change:
> The inheritance went to Marla.
> *c.* identificational change:
> Max went from being a rational gentleman to being a stark raving maniac.

Despite their somewhat different senses, all three uses of the verb *go* have something in common that can be traced to the GO component of their meaning—they typically occur with a phrase that denotes the entity undergoing change (e.g., the subject in these examples) and with a phrase expressing the endpoint of that change (the *to* complements).

The GO concept is manifested in the meaning of verbs other than just *go*. For instance, positional GO is present in the meaning of *fly* ('go through the air'), *walk* ('go on foot'), *crawl* ('go on hands and knees'), and so forth. Possessional GO is manifested in the meaning of *give*, *buy*, and *inherit*, all of which involve a change of possession, while identificational GO shows up in *become* and *turn into*. Consistent with this fact, each of these verbs is typically used with a phrase denoting the entity undergoing the change (marked below by a single underline) and a phrase denoting the endpoint of that change (marked by a double underline).

14)
   a. positional GO:
      <u>The bird</u> flew to <u>its nest</u>.
   b. possessional GO:
      The coach gave <u>a new ball</u> to <u>the children</u>.
   c. identificational GO:
      <u>The caterpillar</u> turned into <u>a butterfly</u>.

Sometimes, quite surprising features of verb meaning can be relevant to the choice of accompanying phrases. Consider, for instance, the contrast between the verbs in list *a*, which can occur with two NP complements, and the verbs in list *b*, which cannot.

15)
   a. throw [$_{NP}$ the boy] [$_{NP}$ a ball]   *b.* *push [$_{NP}$ the boy] [$_{NP}$ the package]
      toss   *pull
      kick   *lift
      fling   *haul

Can you see the semantic difference? The verbs in list *a* all denote ballistic motion that results from the instantaneous application of force to an object at its point of origin. (When we throw something, for example, we thrust it forward and then release it.) In contrast, the verbs in list *b* all denote motion that is accompanied by the continuous application of force to the object as it moves from one point to another. (Pulling, for instance, typically involves the extended use of force as the object moves rather than a single quick motion.)

Now think about the contrast between the following two sets of verbs.

16)
   a. fax [$_{NP}$ Helen] [$_{NP}$ the news]   *b.* *murmur [$_{NP}$ Helen] [$_{NP}$ the news]
      radio   *mumble
      wire   *mutter
      phone   *shriek

Once again, componential analysis reveals a subtle semantic contrast. The first group of verbs (*phone*, *radio*, etc.) have meanings that include the means by which a message was communicated (by phone, by radio, and so on). In contrast, the verbs in the second group all have meanings that describe the type of voice that was used to communicate the message (murmuring, mumbling, shrieking, etc.). For reasons that are not yet fully understood, meaning differences like these help determine the type of complements that particular verbs can select.

2   The conceptual system

Underlying the use of words and sentences to express meaning in human language is a conceptual system capable of organizing and classifying every imaginable aspect of our experience, from inner feelings and perceptions, to cultural and social phenomena, to the physical world that surrounds us. This section focuses on what the study of this conceptual system reveals about how meaning is expressed through language. We will begin by considering some examples that illustrate the way in which these concepts are structured, extended, and interrelated.

2.1   Fuzzy concepts

We tend to think that the concepts expressed by the words and phrases of our language have precise definitions with clear-cut boundaries. Some concepts may indeed be like this. For example, the concept expressed by the phrase *Member of Parliament* seems to have a clear-cut definition: one is a Member of Parliament if and only if one is duly elected to a particular legislative body; no other person can be truthfully called a Member of Parliament.

But are all concepts so straightforward? Consider the concept associated with the word *rich*. How much does a person have to be worth to be called rich? Five hundred thousand dollars? Eight hundred thousand? A million? Is there any figure that we can give that would be so precise that a person who is short by just five cents would not be called rich? It seems not. While one could miss out on being a Member of Parliament by five votes, it does not seem possible to miss out on being rich by just five cents. Moreover, whereas some people clearly qualify as rich and others uncontroversially do not, an indefinitely large number of people fall into the unclear area at the borderline of the concept and it is just not possible to say definitively whether or not they count as rich. This is because the notion of 'richness' does not have clear-cut boundaries; it is what we call a **fuzzy concept**.

This type of fuzziness pervades the human conceptual system. With only a little effort, you should be able to think of many everyday concepts whose boundaries are fuzzy—*tall, old, playboy, strong, grey-haired, genius, clean,* and *bargain* are just a few examples.

Graded membership

A second important fact about concepts is that their members can be graded in terms of their typicality. Consider first a fuzzy concept such as 'hockey star'. Even within the set of people who we can agree are hockey stars, some provide better examples of this concept than others. At the time of writing, for instance, Wayne Gretzky is a better example of a hockey star than is Mark Messier. Although hockey fans agree that both players are stars, Wayne Gretzky has scored more goals, won more awards, set more records, endorsed more products on TV, received more media attention, and so on. This makes him a better example of a star than Mark Messier.

Even concepts whose boundaries can be scientifically defined exhibit this type of graded membership. A good example of this involves the concept 'bird'. Even assuming that English speakers all think of birds as 'warm-blooded, egg-laying, feathered vertebrates with forelimbs modified to form wings' (the dictionary definition), they still feel that some of these creatures are more birdlike than others. For instance, robins and magpies are intuitively better examples of birds than are hummingbirds, ostriches, or penguins.

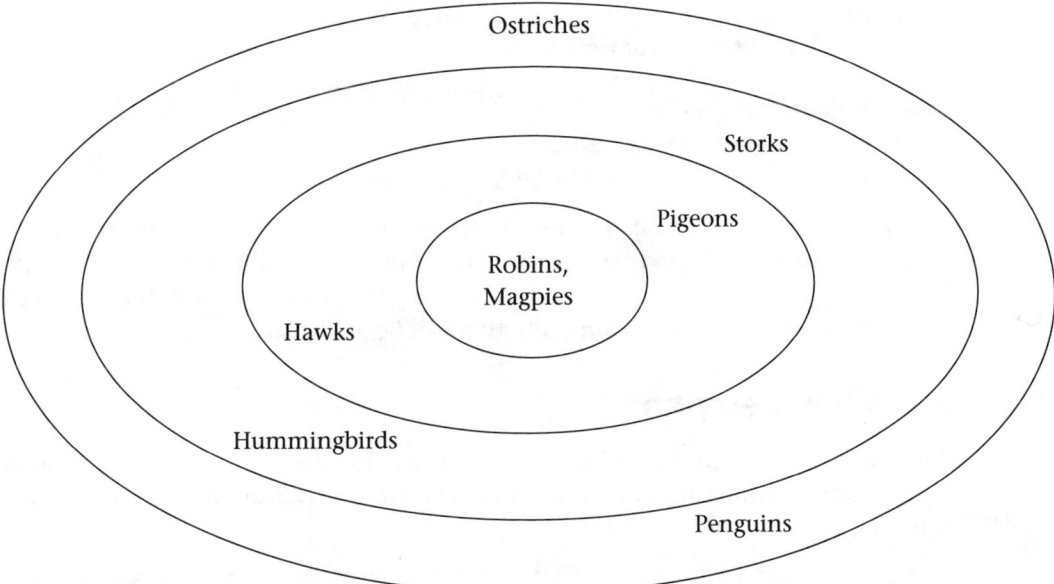

Figure 6.2 Internal structure of the concept 'bird'

Examples like these suggest that concepts have an internal structure, with the best or **prototypical** exemplars (Wayne Gretzky in the case of 'hockey stars', robins in the case of 'birds') close to the core and less typical members arranged in successively more peripheral regions.

The existence of fuzzy concepts and of graded membership provides important insights into the nature of the human conceptual system. In particular, it seems that many (perhaps even most) concepts expressed in language are not rigid all-or-nothing notions with precise and clear-cut boundaries. Rather, they are characterized by an internal structure that recognizes degrees of typicality as well as by fuzzy boundaries that sometimes overlap with those of other concepts.

2.2   Metaphor

The concepts expressed by language make up a giant network, with many interconnections and associations. A good example of these interconnections involves **metaphor**, the understanding of one concept in terms of another.

Many people think of metaphor as a literary device reserved for the use of authors and poets. In fact, however, it has a prominent place in the conceptual system shared by all human beings. This can be seen in the way that we use language to talk about even commonplace notions such as time.

The dominant metaphor for talking about time involves treating it as if it were a concrete commodity that can be saved, wasted, and invested just like other valuable things.

17)
   a. You're *wasting* my time.
   b. This gadget will *save* you hours.
   c. How do you *spend* your time these days?
   d. I have *invested* a lot of time in that project.
   e. You need to *budget* your time.
   f. Is that *worth* your while?
   g. He's living on *borrowed* time.
   h. You don't use your time *profitably*.

What is the basis for this metaphor? There is apparently no objective, inherent similarity between time and commodities such as gold or money. What brings these concepts together is the *perception*, based in part on culture and in part on feelings that all human beings share, that time is like a valuable commodity that can be gained and lost.

A spatial metaphor

Another very prevalent metaphor in our language involves the use of words that are primarily associated with spatial orientation to talk about physical and psychological states (see table 6.6).

Table 6.6	Metaphorical use of spatial terms
Emotions: happy is up, sad is down	
I'm feeling *up*.	I'm feeling *down*.
That *boosted* my spirits.	He *fell* into a depression.
My spirits *rose*.	Her spirits *sank*.
You're in *high* spirits.	He's feeling *low*.
the *height* of ecstasy	the *depths* of depression
That gave me a *lift*.	
Physical health: health and life are up; sickness and death are down	
He's at the *peak* of health.	He's *sinking* fast.
Lazarus *rose* from the dead.	He *fell* ill.
He's in *top* shape.	He came *down* with the flu.
	Her health is *declining*.
	She's feeling *under* the weather.

The basis for these metaphors appears to lie in our physical experience. Unhappiness and ill health tend to be associated with lethargy and inactivity, which often involve being on one's back (physically down). In contrast, happiness and good health are often correlated with energy and movement, which involve being on one's feet (physically up).

These few examples illustrate the more general point that the concepts expressed through language are interrelated in special and intriguing ways. By investigating phenomena such as the use of metaphor to represent abstract concepts in terms of more basic physical and cultural experience, we can gain valuable insights into how language is used to communicate meaning.

2.3 The lexicalization of concepts

Do all human beings share the same conceptual system? Do all languages express concepts in the same way? These are questions that have fascinated and puzzled researchers for many decades. At the present time, there is no reason to believe that human beings in different linguistic communities have different conceptual systems. But there is ample evidence that languages can differ from each other in terms of how they express particular concepts.

Lexicalization

A notorious example of how languages can supposedly differ from each other in the expression of concepts involves the number of words for snow in Inuktitut. Sometimes estimated to be in the hundreds, the number is actually much, much smaller. In fact, one dictionary gives only the four items in table 6.7 (although other dictionaries give a few more, at least for some varieties of Inuktitut).

Table 6.7	Words for 'snow' in Inuktitut
aput	'snow on the ground'
qana	'falling snow'
piqsirpoq	'drifting snow'
qimuqsuq	'snow drift'

As you can see, there is nothing particularly startling about this list of words. In fact, even in English there is more than just one word to describe snow in its various forms—*snow*, *slush*, *blizzard* and *sleet* come to mind, for example.

These examples illustrate the phenomenon of **lexicalization**, the process whereby concepts are encoded in the words of a language. Thus, Inuktitut lexicalizes the concepts 'falling' and 'snow' in a single word (*qana*) while English uses two separate words. While some lexicalization differences may correlate with cultural factors (the relative importance of types of snow in traditional Inuit culture), this is not always so. For example, English has an unusually rich set of vocabulary items pertaining to the perception of light (see table 6.8).

Table 6.8	Some verbs pertaining to light in English	
glimmer	glisten
gleam	glow
glitter	flicker
shimmer	shine
flare	glare
flash	sparkle

Although English speakers know and use the words in this list, it is hard to see how the variety found in this particular area of vocabulary can be correlated with any significant feature of culture or cognition.

As we have tried to emphasize throughout this book, linguistic analysis focuses on the *system* of knowledge that makes it possible to speak and understand a language. The fact that a particular language has more words pertaining to snow or light does not in and of itself provide any insight into the nature of the human linguistic system, and therefore does not merit special attention. However, as we shall see in the next subsection, certain lexicalization differences do shed light on how language expresses meaning.

Motion verbs

All languages have words that can describe motion through space (in English, *come*, *go*, and *move*, among many others). However, there are systematic differences in terms of how languages express motion and the concepts related to it. In English, for example, there are many verbs that simultaneously express both the concept of motion and the manner in which the motion occurs (see table 6.9).

Table 6.9   Some verbs expressing motion and manner in English
The rock *rolled* down the hill.
The puck *slid* across the ice.
She *limped* through the house.
The smoke *swirled* through the opening.

Notice how each of these verbs expresses both the fact that something moved and the manner in which it moved (by rolling, sliding, limping, and so on). We describe this fact by saying that English lexicalization includes a **conflation pattern** that combines manner and motion into a single verb meaning.

Interestingly, Romance languages (descendants of Latin) cannot express motion events in this way. Thus, while Spanish has a verb *rodar* with the meaning 'to roll', it does not use this verb to express both manner and motion as English does.

> 18)
> *La botella rodó en la cueva.
> 'The bottle rolled into the cave.'

Instead, the motion and its manner have to be expressed separately.

> 19)
> La botella entró en la cueva, rodando.
> 'The bottle entered the cave, rolling.'

Although Spanish does not have the motion + manner conflation pattern, it does have verbs whose meaning brings together the concepts of motion and path (see table 6.10). As the English translations show, Spanish verbs of motion express both the concept of movement and the direction of its path—down, up, back, across, out, and so forth. (English too has verbs that can express both motion and path—*descend, ascend, return*, and so on—but these words are not part of its native vocabulary. Rather they were borrowed into English from latinate sources, usually through French.)

Table 6.10   Some verbs expressing motion and path in Spanish

El globo   *bajó*   por la chimenea.
'The balloon moved-down through the chimney'

El globo   *subió*   por la chimenea.
'The balloon moved-up through the chimney'

La botella   *volvió*   a la orilla.
'The bottle moved-back to the bank.'

La botella   *cruzó*   el canal.
'The bottle moved-across the canal.'

La botella   *salió*   de la cueva.
'The bottle moved-out from the cave.'

Yet another conflation pattern is found in the Amerindian language Atsugewi, in which verbs can express both motion and the type of thing that moves (see table 6.11).

Table 6.11   Some verb roots expressing motion and the thing moving in Atsugewi

lup	for movement of a small, shiny spherical object (a hailstone)
t	for movement of a smallish, flat object that can be attached to another (a stamp, a clothing patch, a shingle)
caq	for movement of a slimy, lumpish object (a toad, a cow dropping)
swal	for movement of a limp linear object, suspended by one end (a shirt on a clothes line, a hanging dead rabbit)
qput	for movement of loose, dry dirt
staq	for movement of runny, unpleasant material (manure, guts, chewed gum, rotten tomatoes)

We learn two things from these facts. First, the concept of motion is associated with a number of other concepts, including 'path', 'manner of movement', and 'moving thing'. Second, the way in which these concepts are combined for the purposes of lexicalization can differ systematically from language to language. Languages such as English have verbs that conflate motion and manner while other languages have verbs that conflate motion and path (Spanish) or motion and the type of thing that moves (Atsugewi).

The general picture that is emerging from this type of work is consistent with the key idea underlying componential analysis (section 1.3). In particular, it seems that at least within certain semantic domains, there may be a small universal set of concepts (motion, manner, path, thing that moves, and so on) and a small set of options for how these concepts can be combined for purposes of lexicalization (see figure 6.3).

Unlike the lexicalization differences involving snow and light discussed earlier, these differences appear to be highly systematic and to reveal some general tendencies about the organization of the human conceptual system and the way in which meaning is expressed in language.

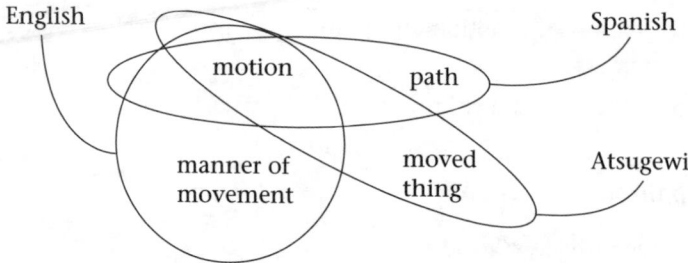

Figure 6.3 Systematic differences in conflation patterns

2.4   Grammaticization

Of the indefinitely large set of concepts expressible in human language, a relatively small subset enjoys a special status. These are the concepts that are expressed as affixes and non-lexical (functional) categories in one language or another. Some of the concepts that are treated this way in English are listed in table 6.12.

Table 6.12	Some concepts associated with affixes and non-lexical categories in English
Concept	**Affix**
Past	*-ed*
More than one	*-s*
Again	*re-*
Negation	*in-, un-*
Concept	**Non-lexical category**
Obligation	*must*
Possibility	*may*
Definite, specific	*the*
Indefinite, non-specific	*a*
Disjunction	*or*
Negation	*not*
Conjunction	*and*

Concepts that are expressed as affixes or non-lexical categories are said to have been **grammaticized**.

Some concepts, such as negation, tense, and number, are highly grammaticizable and are expressed as affixes or special non-lexical categories in most, if not all, of the world's languages. But grammaticization is not restricted to just these familiar concepts, as the example from the Siouan language Hidatsa in table 6.13 illustrates.

Evidentiality in Hidatsa

In Hidatsa, each statement is accompanied by a morpheme to indicate the evidence for its truth. (Morphological contrasts of this sort express **evidentiality**.)

Table 6.13   Evidentiality morphemes in Hidatsa
ski THE SPEAKER IS CERTAIN OF THE STATEMENT'S TRUTH Waceo iikipi kure heo -<u>ski</u> 'The man (definitely) carried the pipe.'
c THE SPEAKER BELIEVES THE STATEMENT TO BE TRUE Waceo iikipi kure heo -<u>c</u>. 'The man (supposedly) carried the pipe.'
wareac THE SPEAKER REGARDS THE STATEMENT TO BE COMMON KNOWLEDGE Waceo iikipi kure heo -<u>wareac</u>. 'The man carried the pipe (they say).'
rahe THE STATEMENT IS BASED ON AN UNVERIFIED REPORT FROM SOMEONE ELSE Waceo wiira rackci heo -<u>rahe</u>. 'The man roasted the goose (it is rumoured).'
toak THE TRUTH OF THE STATEMENT IS UNKNOWN TO BOTH SPEAKER AND LISTENER Waceo cihpa rakci heo -<u>toak</u>. 'The man roasted the prairie dog (perhaps).'

Choice of the appropriate sentence-ender is extremely important in Hidatsa. Speakers who utter a false sentence marked by the morpheme *-ski* are considered to be liars. Had they used the morpheme *-c*, on the other hand, it would be assumed that they simply made a mistake.

While English has ways of indicating these contrasts (by using expressions such as *perhaps*, *I heard that*, and *I guess*), it does not have a grammatical system of morphemes that obligatorily encodes this information in every sentence. By investigating the grammaticization options found in different languages, it may eventually be possible to identify the factors that determine which concepts are singled out for association with affixes and non-lexical categories.

3 Syntax and sentence interpretation

The two preceding sections have focused on the meaning conveyed by the individual words and phrases that make up a sentence. In this section, we turn to the problem of sentence interpretation, with an emphasis on how the positioning of words and phrases in syntactic structure helps determine the meaning of the entire sentence, consistent with the following principle.

20)
The Principle of Compositionality
The meaning of a sentence is determined by the meaning of its component parts and the manner in which they are arranged in syntactic structure.

Syntactic structure is relevant to meaning in a variety of ways. For purposes of illustration, we will consider four aspects of its contribution to the interpretation of sentences—constructional meaning, the representation of structural ambiguity, the assignment of thematic roles, and the interpretation of pronouns.

3.1   Constructional meaning

There is reason to believe that structural patterns are themselves capable of carrying meaning above and beyond the meaning of their component parts. One example of this **constructional meaning** can be seen in 'the caused-motion construction' exemplified in *21)*.

> 21)
> *a.* Seymour pushed the truck off the table.
> *b.* Mabel moved the car into the garage.
> *c.* Perry pulled the dog into the swimming pool.

As these examples help illustrate, the caused-motion construction consists of a structural pattern (NP V NP PP) that is used to express the meaning 'X causes Y to go somewhere'. Thus, the first sentence describes a situation in which Seymour causes the truck to go off the table by pushing it; the second sentence is used for situations in which Mabel causes the car to go into the garage; and so on.

> 22)
> *The caused-motion construction*
> FORM: NP V NP   PP
> MEANING: 'X causes Y to go somewhere'

Striking evidence for the existence of a constructional meaning comes from sentences such as the following.

> 23)
> *a.* Boris sneezed the handkerchief right across the room.
> *b.* The judges laughed the poor guy out the room.
> *c.* Morley squeezed the shirt into the suitcase.

There is clearly nothing in the meaning of verbs such as *sneeze, laugh* and *squeeze* that implies caused motion. Yet, when they occur in the NP V NP PP pattern, the resulting sentence has a meaning in which X causes Y to go somewhere. Thus, sentence *23a)* means that Boris caused the handkerchief to fly across the room by sneezing; *b)* means that the judges forced someone out of the room by laughing at him; and so on.

How can this be? It seems that part of the meaning of these sentences comes from the construction itself: in *23a)*, for instance, the verb *sneeze* provides the meaning 'involuntarily expel air from the mouth and nose', while the structural pattern tells us that this action caused the handkerchief to be propelled across the room. Without both types of information, the sentence could not mean what it does.

Another example of constructional meaning can be found in patterns such as the following.

> 24)
> *a.* Jerry sent Lou a present.
> *b.* The company gave its employees a bonus.

c. The secretary handed Mary a message.
d. Marvin threw Harry the ball.

These sentences are instances of the so-called 'ditransitive construction' that is typically associated with the meaning 'X causes Y to have Z'. Thus *24a)*, for instance, describes a situation in which Jerry causes Lou to have a present by sending it to him.

25)
The Ditransitive Construction
FORM: NP V NP   NP
MEANING: 'X causes Y to have Z'

An indication that the structure itself contributes part of the meaning associated with ditransitive constructions comes from sentences such as *Jerry baked Lou a cake*. This sentence describes a situation in which Lou ends up with a cake, even though there is clearly nothing in the meaning of *bake* that implies that one person causes another person to have something. This part of the sentence's meaning comes from the structure itself—another example of constructional meaning.

3.2 Structural ambiguity

Some sentences are **structurally ambiguous** in that their component words can be combined in more than one way. A simple example of this is found in the phrase *wealthy men and women*, where 'wealthy' can be seen as a property of both the men and the women or of just the men alone. These two interpretations or **readings** are depicted in figure 6.4 (Con = conjunction).

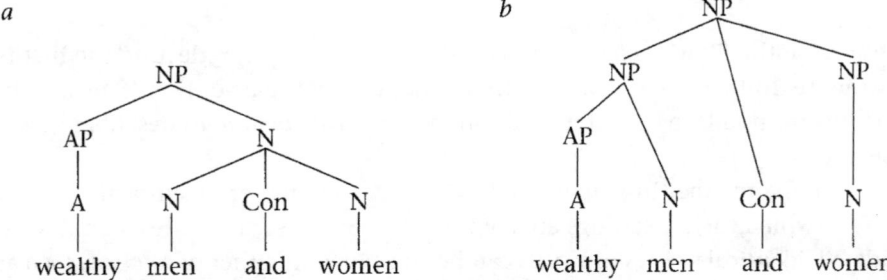

Figure 6.4 An ambiguous phrase. The structure on the left indicates that both the men and the women are wealthy; the structure on the right indicates that only the men are wealthy.

Figure 6.4a corresponds to the reading in which *wealthy* modifies both *men* and *women*. This is shown by having the adjective combine with a category that includes both nouns. In figure 6.4b, on the other hand, the adjective combines only with the N *men*. This structure corresponds to the reading in which 'wealthy' applies only to the men.

Another case of structural ambiguity is found in sentences such as the following.

26)
Nicole saw the people with binoculars.

In one interpretation of *26)*, the people had binoculars when Nicole noticed them (the phrase *with binoculars* modifies the noun *people*) while in the other interpretation Nicole saw the people by using the binoculars (the PP modifies the verb). These two readings are represented in figure 6.5.

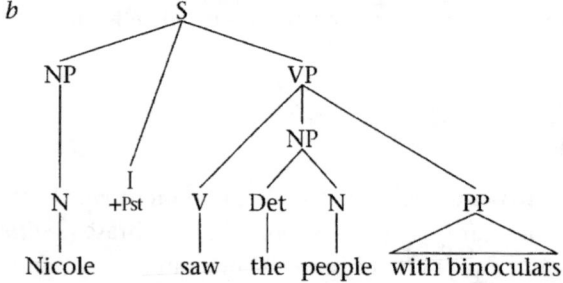

Figure 6.5 An ambiguous sentence. In the first structure, the people have the binoculars; in the second structure, Nicole uses the binoculars to see the people.

In figure 6.5a, the PP *with binoculars* occurs with the N *people*, reflecting the first reading for this sentence. In figure 6.5b, on the other hand, the PP is part of the VP headed by the verb *saw*. This corresponds to the interpretation in which *with binoculars* describes how Nicole saw the people.

In sum, the manner in which words are grouped together in syntactic structure reflects the way in which their meanings are combined. Sometimes, as in the examples we have just considered, identical strings of words can be combined in either of two ways, creating structural ambiguity that can be neatly captured with the help of tree structures.

3.3   Thematic roles

Another aspect of semantic interpretation involves determining the role that the referents of NPs play in the situations described by sentences. Consider in this regard the sentence in *27)*.

27)
The courier carried the document from Halifax to Vancouver.

It would be impossible to understand this sentence if we could not identify the courier as the person who is responsible for carrying something, the document as the thing that is carried, Halifax as the point of origin, and Vancouver as the destination. Linguists often use

thematic roles to categorize the relation between a sentence's parts and the event that it describes. In most linguistic analyses, at least the following thematic roles are recognized (see table 6.14).

Table 6.14	Thematic roles
Agent	the entity that performs an action
Theme	the entity undergoing an action or a movement
Source	the starting point for a movement
Goal	the end point for a movement
Location	the place where an action occurs

Examples of these thematic roles can be seen in sentences such as the following.

28)
  a. The courier carried the document from Halifax to Vancouver.
    agent   *theme*   *source*   *goal*

  b. The athletes practiced in the SkyDome.
    agent   *location*

The notion of movement used in the definition of theme, source, and goal is intended to involve not only actual physical motion, but also changes in possession, as in *29)*, and identity, as in *30)*.

29)
Terry gave the skis to Mary.
agent   *theme*   *goal*

30)
The magician changed the ball into a rabbit.
    agent   *theme*   *goal*

As you may recall, we observed a similar set of contrasts in the manifestation of the GO concept discussed in section 1.3. This is no coincidence. Thematic roles can be traced to particular aspects of word meaning, and the presence of GO in a verb's meaning is specifically linked to the presence of a theme role and a goal role.

Thematic role assignment

How does the grammar ensure that the appropriate thematic role is associated with each NP in a sentence? As we have just seen, thematic roles originate in word meaning. Thus, if the sentence *Marvin purchased a pen at the bookstore* contains an agent and a theme, it is because the verb *purchase* has the type of meaning that implies an entity that does the purchasing (an agent) and an entity that gets purchased (a theme). Similarly, *the bookstore* is taken to denote the location of the action because of the meaning of the preposition *at*. Information about the thematic roles assigned by a particular lexical item is recorded in a **thematic grid**, as depicted in table 6.15.

Table 6.15	Some words and the thematic roles implied by their meanings
purchase	<agent, theme>
walk	<agent>
to	<goal>
from	<source>
at	<location>

The thematic roles implied by the meanings of lexical items are assigned to NPs based on their position in syntactic structure, with each NP receiving a single role. As a first example of this, let us consider the complement of a preposition. In such cases, the process of thematic role assignment can be summarized as follows:

31)
A P assigns a thematic role to its complement NP.

The operation of this convention is illustrated in figure 6.6.

Figure 6.6 Thematic role assignment by prepositions

Matters are slightly more complicated in the case of Vs. Here we must distinguish between the theme role, which is assigned to the V's complement, and the agent role, which is assigned to its subject.

32)
A V assigns a theme role (if it has one) to its complement NP.
A V assigns an agent role (if it has one) to its subject NP.

This is exemplified in the structures in figure 6.7.

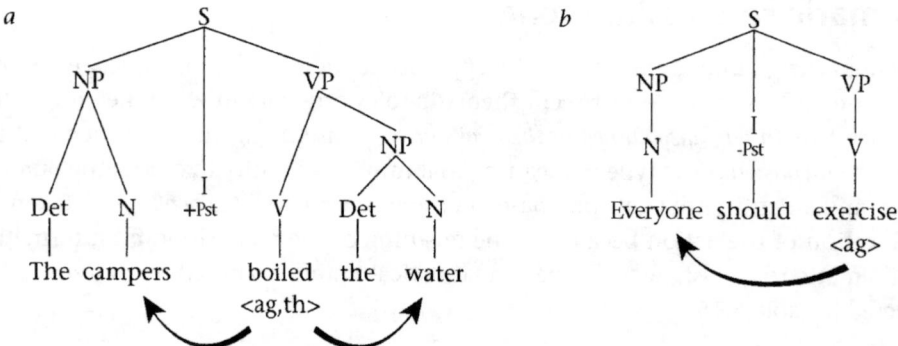

Figure 6.7 Thematic role assignment by verbs

In accordance with *32)*, the theme role is assigned to the V's NP complement while the agent role is assigned to the subject.

The structure in figure 6.8 illustrates the assignment of thematic roles in a sentence that contains a P in addition to a V.

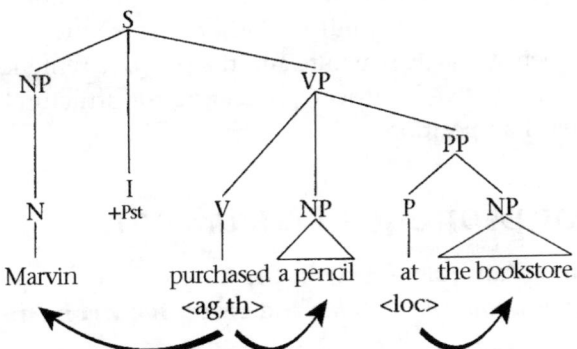

Figure 6.8 Thematic role assignment in complex sentence

Here, the P *at* assigns its location role to its complement NP (*the bookstore*) while the verb *purchase* assigns its theme role to the complement *a pencil* and its agent role to the subject *Marvin*.

Deep structure and thematic roles

In the examples considered to this point, it is unclear whether an NP receives its thematic role on the basis of its position in deep structure or surface structure. This is because our example sentences are all formed without the help of the Move operation, so that each NP occupies the same position in both deep structure and surface structure. But now consider a sentence such as *33)*, which is formed with the help of *Wh* Movement.

33)
Which book should the students read?

This sentence has the deep structure depicted in figure 6.9.

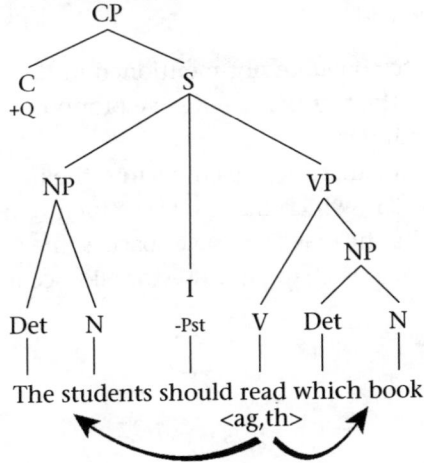

Figure 6.9 Thematic role assignment in a *wh* question

Since the theme role is assigned to the complement of V, it follows that the NP *which book* in the above example receives this role by virtue of its position in deep structure, not surface structure (where it occurs in the specifier of CP position).

In sum, an NP's initial position in syntactic structure (the result of the Merge operation) determines its thematic role. The Move operation may subsequently transport the NP to another position (as is the case with *wh* words), but the original thematic role remains unchanged. The relationship between syntactic structure and the part of a sentence's meaning represented by thematic roles is thus very intricate, reflecting the structural relations manifested in deep structure rather than position in surface structure.

3.4   The interpretation of pronouns (*Advanced*)

Syntactic structure also has an important role to play in the interpretation of **pronouns**, including **pronominals** such as *he, him, she,* and *her* and **reflexive pronouns** such as *himself* and *herself* (see table 6.16).

Table 6.16	Subject and object pronouns in English			
	Pronominals		**Reflexives**	
	Sg	*Pl*	*Sg*	*Pl*
1st person	I, me	we, us	myself	ourselves
2nd person	you	you	yourself	yourselves
3rd person	he, him		himself	
	she, her	they	herself	themselves
	it		itself	

A defining property of pronouns is that their interpretation can be determined by another element, called the **antecedent**. As the following sentences help show, pronominals and reflexive pronouns differ in terms of where their antecedents can occur.

34)
a. [s Claire knew that [s Alexis trusted *her*]].
b. [s Claire knew that [s Alexis trusted *herself*]].

Notice that *her* can refer either to Claire or to someone not mentioned in the sentence, but that *herself* refers only to Alexis. This reflects the fact that a reflexive pronoun typically must have an antecedent in the smallest S containing it.

A somewhat more abstract feature of syntactic structure enters into the interpretation of the reflexive pronouns in sentences such as *35)*, which has the tree structure in figure 6.10. (Pronouns are treated as N-type categories that head NPs; to save space, some word-level category labels are omitted. As noted in the previous chapter, possessor NPs occur in the specifier position within larger NPs.)

35)
That boy's teacher admires himself.

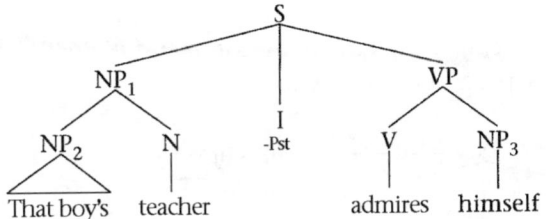

Figure 6.10 Structure containing a reflexive pronoun

Although there are two NPs in the same S as *himself* (namely, *that boy* and *that boy's teacher*), only one (*that boy's teacher*) can serve as antecedent for the reflexive pronoun. Thus, the person who is admired in *35)* must have been the boy's teacher, not the boy.

Principles A and B

The principle needed to ensure this interpretation makes use of the notion **c-command**, which is defined as follows.

36)
NP$_a$ c-commands NP$_b$ if the first category above NP$_a$ contains NP$_b$.

Although c-command might appear to be a rather technical notion, the underlying idea is very simple. Figure 6.11 illustrates the type of configuration in which c-command occurs.

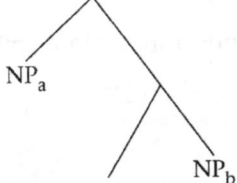

Figure 6.11 The c-command configuration

When trying to determine c-command relations, you can either use the definition in *36)* or apply the template in figure 6.11 to the tree structure being analyzed.

We can now formulate the constraint on the interpretation of reflexives, called **Principle A**, as follows.

37)
Principle A
A reflexive pronoun must have an antecedent that c-commands it in the same minimal S.

When using Principle A, the key step involves determining whether a potential antecedent c-commands the reflexive pronoun. Compare in this regard the status of the NPs *that boy* and *that boy's teacher* in figure 6.12.

Since the first category above *that boy's teacher* (namely, S) contains the reflexive, this NP c-commands *himself* according to our definition and can therefore serve as its antecedent. As we have already seen, the sentence has this interpretation.

In contrast, the first category above NP$_2$ (*that boy*) is NP$_1$, as illustrated in figure 6.12. Since NP$_1$ does not contain the reflexive, *that boy* does not c-command *himself* according to our definition and therefore cannot serve as its antecedent.

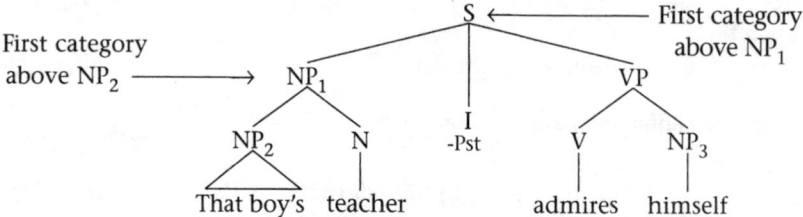

Figure 6.12 Structure illustrating c-command relations. NP$_1$ c-commands NP$_3$ but NP$_2$ does not.

Now let us consider the interpretation of pronominals. As the following example shows, the interpretation of the pronominal *him* contrasts sharply with that of the reflexive *himself* in the structure that we have been considering. Thus, *him* can refer to the boy, but not to the boy's teacher—the opposite of what we observed for *himself*.

38)
That boy's teacher admires him.

How are we to account for these facts? The relevant constraint, called **Principle B**, is stated in *39)*.

39)
Principle B
A pronominal must not have an antecedent that c-commands it in the same minimal S.

To see how this principle works, consider the structure in figure 6.13.

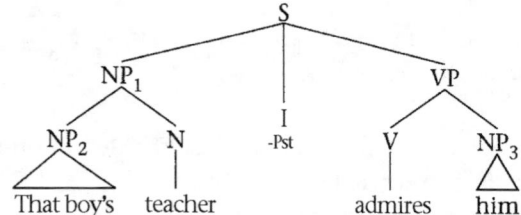

Figure 6.13 Structure containing a pronominal

In this structure, NP$_1$ (*that boy's teacher*) c-commands *him* since the first category above it (namely, S) also contains *him*. Principle B therefore prevents NP$_1$ from serving as antecedent for *him*. In contrast, NP$_2$ (*the boy*) does not c-command *him* since the first category above it (namely, NP$_1$) does not contain the pronoun. Thus, nothing prevents the interpretation in which *him* and *that boy* refer to the same person.

There is much more that can and should be said about the interpretation of pronouns. However, the examples we have just considered suffice to illustrate the crucial point in all of this, which is that syntactic structure plays an important role in the interpretation of both pronominals and reflexive pronouns.

4 Other factors in sentence interpretation

Syntactic structure provides only a part of the information needed to interpret a sentence. Other necessary information comes from **pragmatics**, which includes the speaker's and addressee's background attitudes and beliefs, their understanding of the context in which a sentence is uttered, and their knowledge of how language can be used to inform, to persuade, to mislead, and so forth. This section focuses on the role of pragmatics in sentence interpretation.

4.1 The role of beliefs and attitudes

As we saw in the preceding section, the grammar includes a structural principle (Principle B) that regulates the interpretation of pronominals such as *he* and *they*. However, as the following sentences show, non-linguistic knowledge and beliefs can also play an important role in selecting the antecedent for a pronominal.

40)
a. The judge denied the prisoner's request because he was cautious.
b. The judge denied the prisoner's request because he was dangerous.

These two sentences have identical syntactic structures, differing only in the choice of the adjective in the second clause (*cautious* in the first sentence versus *dangerous* in the second). Yet, most people feel that *he* refers to the judge in *40a)* but to the prisoner in *40b)*. Why should this be?

The crucial factor involves our beliefs about people in our society and their likely characteristics and behaviour. All other things being equal, we are more likely to believe that a judge is cautious and a prisoner dangerous than vice versa. This in turn leads us to interpret the pronoun as referring to the judge in the first sentence in *40)* but to the prisoner in the second.

Presupposition

There are many other ways in which a speaker's beliefs can be reflected in language use. Compare in this regard the following two sentences.

41)
a. Have you stopped exercising regularly?
b. Have you tried exercising regularly?

Use of the verb *stop* implies a belief on the part of the speaker that the listener has been exercising regularly. No such assumption is associated with the verb *try*.

The assumption or belief implied by the use of a particular word or structure is called a **presupposition**. The following two sentences provide another example of this.

42)
a. Nick admitted that the team had lost.
b. Nick said that the team had lost.

Choice of the verb *admit* in *42a)* indicates that the speaker is presupposing the truth of the claim that the team lost. No such presupposition is associated with choice of the verb *say* in *42b)*, where the speaker is simply reporting Nick's statement without taking a position on its accuracy.

Still another type of presupposition is illustrated in *43)*.

43)
a. D'Arcy McGee was assassinated in 1868.
b. D'Arcy McGee was murdered in 1868.

Notice that use of the verb *assassinate* in *43a)* involves the assumption that D'Arcy McGee was a prominent person, but that no such presupposition is associated with the verb *murder*.

4.2   Setting

As noted at the beginning of this section, the pragmatic factors relevant to sentence interpretation can include knowledge of the context in which a sentence is uttered, including its physical environment or setting.

All languages have forms whose use and interpretation depend on the location of the speaker and/or hearer within a particular setting. Called spatial **deictics**, these forms are exemplified in English by words such as *this* and *here* (proximity to the speaker) versus *that* and *there* (proximity to the hearer and/or distance from the speaker). Thus, if Steve and Brian are sitting across from each other at a table, each would refer to a plate directly in front of him as *this plate* and to a plate in front of the other or a plate distant from both as *that plate*. Without an understanding of how the setting in which a sentence is uttered can influence the choice of words such as *this* and *that*, it would be impossible for speakers of English to use or interpret these forms correctly.

As the preceding examples show, English makes a two-way distinction in its expression of deictic contrasts. However, many languages have a three-way system that may be sensitive to distance from the speaker, the addressee, or both (depending on the language) (see table 6.17).

Table 6.17 Languages with a three-way deictic distinction			
Language	**'this'**	**'that'**	**'that over there'**
Spanish	este	ese	aquel
Japanese	kono	sono	ano
Korean	i	ku	ce
Palauan	tia	tilęcha	se
Turkish	bu	ʃu	o

An even more complex system is found in the Amerindian language Tlingit, which makes a four-way distinction: *yáa* 'this one right here', *héi* 'this one nearby', *wée* 'that one over there', and *yóo* 'that one far off'.

Determiners are not the only type of element whose use and interpretation require reference to features of the setting. In English, for example, deictic contrasts are also crucial to the understanding of such commonly used verbs as *come* and *go*. Notice in this regard the striking difference in perspective found in the following two sentences.

44)
a. The bear is coming into the tent!
b. The bear is going into the tent!

Whereas *come* with a third person subject implies movement towards the speaker (hence we can infer that the person who utters *44a)* is probably in the tent), *go* with the same type of subject suggests movement away from the speaker.

4.3   Discourse

An additional source of contextual information relevant to sentence interpretation can be found in **discourse**, the connected series of utterances produced during a conversation, a lecture, a story, or other speech act. The importance of discourse stems from the fact that individual sentences commonly include elements whose interpretation can only be determined with the help of information in preceding utterances. For instance, each of the italicized words in the following passage relies for its interpretation on information encoded in a preceding sentence. We interpret *there* with reference to *in the park*, *she* with reference to *a little girl*, and *it* with reference to *a rabbit*.

45)
A little girl went for a walk in the park. While *there*, *she* saw a rabbit. Since *it* was injured, *she* took *it* home.

One of the most important contrasts in the study of discourse involves the distinction between new and old information. **Old** (or **given**) **information** consists of the knowledge that the speaker assumes is available to the addressee at the time of the utterance, either because it is shared by both or because it has already been introduced into the discourse. In contrast, **new information** involves knowledge that is introduced into the discourse for the first time. Consider the contrast between the following two sentences.

46)
a. The man is at the front door.
b. A man is at the front door.

Choice of *the* as the determiner for *man* in *46a)* suggests that the referent of the phrase is someone who has already been mentioned in the discourse and is therefore known to the addressee (old information). In contrast, choice of the determiner *a* in *46b)* implies that the referent is being introduced into the discourse for the first time (new information).

Notice that both sentences in *46)* use *the* as the determiner for *front door* and that the indefinite determiner *a* would not be natural in this context. This is because the setting for the conversation is likely to include only one front door. Since this information is likely to be known to both the speaker and the addressee (i.e., it is old information), *the* is the right determiner to use in this context.

Topics

Another important notion for the study of discourse is that of **topic**, which corresponds to what a sentence or a portion of the discourse is about. Consider the following passage.

47)

Once upon a time there was a merchant with two sons. The older son wanted to be a scholar. He spent his time reading and studying. As for the younger son, he preferred to travel and see the world.

The first sentence in this passage introduces a merchant and his two sons as new information. A topic (the older son) is selected in the second sentence and maintained in the third, in which *he* refers back to the older son. The final sentence then switches to a new topic (the younger son), providing some information about him. This switch is facilitated by the expression *as for*, which can be used in English to mark new topics.

There is a strong tendency in language to encode the topic as subject of a sentence. This is why (as mentioned in section 1.2) it is natural to interpret the active sentence in *48a)* as being about the police and the passive sentence in *b)* as being about the burglar (see also section 6 of chapter 5).

48)

a. The police chased the burglar.
b. The burglar was chased by the police.

In some languages, a special affix is used to identify the topic. The following sentences from Japanese illustrate this phenomenon (Nom = nominative, the subject marker; Top = topic marker; Ques = question marker).

49)

Speaker A:	Dare-ga kimasita-ka?
	Who-Nom came-Ques?
Speaker B	John-ga kimasita.
	John-Nom came.
Speaker A:	John-wa dare-to kimasita-ka?
	John-Top who-with came-Ques?
	'Who did John come with?'

The topic marker in Japanese (the suffix *-wa*) is distinguished from the subject marker (*-ga*) by its use to mark old or background information. This is why speaker B responds to A's first question by using the subject marker on the NP *John*. Because this NP provides new information (in answer to A's question), the topic marker would be inappropriate. However, once it has been established that John is the person who came, the corresponding NP can then bear the topic marker. This is precisely what happens in Speaker A's final utterance, in which the NP *John* (now associated with previously established information) is marked by the topic suffix *-wa*.

4.4   Conversational maxims

In addition to background beliefs, the setting, and the discourse, there is at least one other major type of information that enters into the interpretation of utterances. This information has to do with the 'rules for conversation'—our understanding of how language is used in particular situations to convey a message. For example, if I ask you, *'Would you like to go to a movie tonight?'* and you respond by saying *'I have to study for an exam'*, I know that you are declining my invitation even though there is nothing in the literal meaning of the sentence that says so. Moreover, I recognize that this is a perfectly appropriate way to respond. (Notice that the same could not be said of a response like *'I have to scratch my arm'* or *'It's a bit warm in here'*.)

As speakers of a language, we are able to draw inferences about what is meant but not actually said. Information that is conveyed in this way is called **conversational implicature**. The ease with which we recognize and interpret implicature stems from our knowledge of how people in our linguistic community use language to communicate with each other.

The general overarching guideline for conversational interactions is often called the **Cooperative Principle**.

50)
The Cooperative Principle
Make your contribution appropriate to the conversation.

More specific maxims or guidelines ensure that conversational interactions actually satisfy the Cooperative Principle as shown in table 6.18.

Table 6.18   Some conversational maxims
The Maxim of Relation Be relevant. **The Maxim of Quality** Try to make your contribution one that is true. (Do not say things that are false or for which you lack adequate evidence.) **The Maxim of Quantity** Do not make your contribution more or less informative than required. **The Maxim of Manner** Avoid ambiguity and obscurity; be brief and orderly.

These maxims are responsible for regulating normal conversation but, as we will see, each can be suspended under certain circumstances to create particular effects.

Relation

The Maxim of Relation gives listeners a 'bottom line' for inferring the intent of other speakers. For example, it is because of this maxim that we are able to interpret the utterance *'I have to study for an exam'* (in response to the question *'Would you like to go to a movie?'*) as a 'no'.

Failure to respect the Maxim of Relation creates a peculiar effect. For example, if someone asks you *'Have you finished that term paper yet?'*, and you respond *'It's been raining a lot lately, hasn't it?'*, you violate the Maxim of Relation by not responding in a relevant way. But by giving this response, you signal that you want to change the topic of conversation.

Quality

The Maxim of Quality requires that the statements used in conversations have some factual basis. If, for example, I ask *'What's the weather like?'* and someone responds *'It's snowing'*, I will normally assume that this statement provides reliable information about the current weather.

In order to achieve irony or sarcasm, however, it is sometimes possible to abandon the Maxim of Quality and say something that one knows to be false. Thus, if two people live in the middle of a sweltering desert and one person insists on asking every morning *'What's the weather like?'*, it might be appropriate for the other person to respond sarcastically *'Oh, today it's snowing, as usual'*, perhaps with a particular facial expression or intonation to indicate that the statement was not intended as a true report of the facts.

Considerations of politeness can also justify suspension of the Maxim of Quality. For instance, in order to avoid hurt feelings, you might congratulate a fellow student on a presentation, even though you thought that it was the worst thing you ever heard.

Quantity

The Maxim of Quantity introduces some very subtle guidelines into a conversation. Imagine, for example, that someone asks me where a famous Canadian author lives. The nature of my response will depend in large part on how much information I believe to be appropriate for that point in the conversation. If I know that the other person is simply curious about which part of the country the author lives in, it might suffice to respond *'in Manitoba'*. On the other hand, if I know that the person wants to visit the author, then much more specific information (perhaps even an address) is appropriate.

The Maxim of Quantity can be suspended in order to mislead a conversational partner. For example, if someone asks me where Mary is and I know that Mary does not want any visitors, I might respond by saying *'I think she went downtown or something'* even though I know precisely where she is. In responding in this way, I am not being untruthful since I have said nothing false, but by giving less information than is appropriate I am violating the Maxim of Quantity and hence being misleading.

Manner

The Maxim of Manner imposes several constraints on language use, two of which will be exemplified here. First, imagine that I refer to a particular person as *the man who Mary lives with*. A listener would be justified in concluding that the man in question is not Mary's husband. This is because, by the Maxim of Manner, a briefer and less obscure description, *Mary's husband*, would have been used if it could have correctly described Mary's companion.

Second, imagine that an employer asks me about a former student of mine who has applied for a job and I say, with some sarcasm, *'You will be fortunate indeed if you can get him to work for you'*. By using a sentence that can be interpreted in two very different ways (*'You will be glad to have him on your staff'* versus *'It is not easy to get him to do any work'*), I violate the Maxim of Manner by using an ambiguous structure. Since the maxims are violated only for specific purposes, the employer would be justified in doubting the sincerity of my recommendation.

Summing up

The study of **semantics** is concerned with a broad range of phenomena including the nature of **meaning**, the role of syntactic structure in the interpretation of sentences, and the effect of **pragmatics** on the understanding of utterances. Although much remains to be done in each of these areas, work in recent years has at least begun to identify the type of relations, mechanisms, and principles involved in the understanding of language. These include the notions of **extension** and **intension** in the case of word meaning, **thematic roles** in the case of NPs, and **c-command** in the case of pronouns. Other factors known to be involved in an utterance's interpretation include **constructional meaning**, the speaker's and hearer's background beliefs (as manifested, for example, in **presuppositions**), the context provided by the setting and the **discourse**, and the **maxims** associated with the **Cooperative Principle**.

Sources

Surveys of the nature of word meaning and semantic relations can be found in many introductory books on semantics, including those recommended below. A prominent advocate of componential analysis is Ray Jackendoff, whose book *Semantic Structures* (Cambridge, MA: MIT Press, 1991) reviews earlier ideas in addition to offering new proposals. The discussion of a semantic constraint on double object patterns draws on the proposal put forward by Steven Pinker in *Learnability and Cognition* (Cambridge, MA: MIT Press, 1989). The discussion of fuzzy categories and graded membership in section 2 draws from Part 1 of *Women, Fire, and Dangerous Things* by G. Lakoff (Chicago: University of Chicago Press, 1987) and the references cited there. The discussion of metaphor takes as its starting point the book *Metaphors We Live By*, cited below. The four Inuktitut words for snow in table 6.7 are from *The Handbook of American Indian Languages* by F. Boas (Washington: Smithsonian Institution, 1911); for a longer list of words for snow, see *Dictionnaire français-eskimau du parler de l'Ungava* (Québec: Presses de l'Université Laval, 1970); see also "The Great Eskimo Vocabulary Hoax" by G. Pullum in *Natural Language and Linguistic Theory* 7:275–81 (1989). The discussion of verbs of motion is based on the paper "Lexicalization Patterns: Semantic Structure in Lexical Form" by L. Talmy in *Language Typology and Syntactic Description*, Vol. 3, edited by T. Shopen (New York: Cambridge University Press, 1985), pp. 57–149. Data on Hidatsa assertion morphemes in the same section is from *Hidatsa Syntax* by G.H. Matthews (The Hague: Mouton, 1965).

The treatment of structural ambiguity, thematic role assignment, and pronoun interpretation in this chapter presents slightly simplified versions of views widely held within generative grammar in the early 1990s. For a summary of the last two issues, see *Introduction to Government and Binding Theory*, 2nd ed., by L. Haegeman (Cambridge, MA: Blackwell, 1994). The discussion of constructional meaning is based on *Constructions: A Construction Grammar Approach to Argument Structure* by A. Goldberg (Chicago: University of Chicago Press, 1995).

The data used in the discussion of deixis and in question 15 comes from "Deixis" by S. Anderson and E. Keenan in *Language Typology and Syntactic Description*, Vol. 3, edited by T. Shopen (New York: Cambridge University Press, 1985), pp. 259–308. The discussion of topicalization draws on the "Major Functions of the Noun Phrase" by A. Andrews in *Language*

Typology and Syntactic Description, Vol. 1, edited by T. Shopen (New York: Cambridge University Press, 1985), pp. 62–154. The discussion of the Cooperative Principle and the maxims of conversation is based primarily on "Logic and Conversation" by Paul Grice in *Syntax and Semantics*, Vol. 3, edited by P. Cole and J. Morgan (New York: Academic Press, 1975), pp. 41–58 and the paper by L. Horn cited below.

The exercises for this chapter were prepared by Joyce Hildebrand.

Recommended reading

Chierchia, Gennaro, and Sally McConnell-Ginet. 1990. *Meaning and Grammar*. Cambridge, MA: MIT Press.

Horn, Laurence. 1988. "Pragmatic Theory." In *Linguistics: The Cambridge Survey*. Vol. 1. Edited by F. Newmeyer, 113–45. New York: Cambridge University Press.

Ladusaw, William. 1988. "Semantic Theory." In *Linguistics: The Cambridge Survey*. Vol. 1. Edited by F. Newmeyer, 89–112. New York: Cambridge University Press.

Lappin, Shalom (ed.). 1997. *The Handbook of Contemporary Semantic Theory*. Boston: Blackwell.

Lakoff, George, and Mark Johnson. 1982. *Metaphors We Live By*. Chicago: University of Chicago Press.

McCawley, James. 1993. *Everything That Linguists Have Always Wanted to Know About Logic*. 2nd ed. Chicago: University of Chicago Press.

Prince, Ellen. 1988. "Discourse Analysis: A Part of the Study of Linguistic Competence." In *Linguistics: The Cambridge Survey*. Vol. 2. Edited by F. Newmeyer, 164–82. New York: Cambridge University Press.

Saeed, John. 1996. *Semantics*. Boston: Blackwell.

Schiffrin, Deborah. 1993. *Approaches to Discourse: Language as Social Interaction*. Boston: Blackwell.

Questions

1. Two relations involving word meanings are antonymy and synonymy. Which relation is illustrated in each of the pairs of words below?

   a) flourish-thrive

   b) intelligent-stupid

   c) casual-informal

   d) young-old

   e) uncle-aunt

   f) intelligent-smart

   g) flog-whip

   h) drunk-sober

2. It was noted in this chapter that a single form can have two or more meanings. Depending on whether these meanings are related to each other, this phenomenon involves polysemy or homophony. Which of these two relations is exemplified by the forms below?

   a) *grass:* herbage used for grazing animals; marijuana

   b) *leech:* a bloodsucking worm; a hanger-on who seeks advantage

   c) *range:* a cooking stove; a series of mountains

   d) *key:* an instrument used to apply to a lock; an answer sheet for a test or assignment

   e) *steal/steel*: rob; a type of metal

   f) *race:* the act of running competitively; people belonging to the same genetic grouping

   g) *flower/flour:* a type of plant; finely ground wheat

3. Three semantic relations among sentences were covered in this chapter: paraphrase, entailment, and contradiction. Which of these relations is exemplified in each of the following pairs of sentences?

   a) I saw Timothy at the anniversary party.
      It was Timothy that I saw at the anniversary party.
   b) Jules is Mary's husband.
      Mary is married.
   c) My pet cobra likes the taste of chocolate fudge.
      My pet cobra finds chocolate fudge tasty.
   d) Vera is an only child.
      Olga is Vera's sister.
   e) It is fifty kilometres to the nearest service station.
      The nearest service station is fifty kilometres away.
   f) My cousin Bryan teaches at the community college for a living.
      My cousin Bryan is a teacher.

4. In discussing the nature of meaning, we noted that it is necessary to distinguish between intension and extension. Describe the intensions and the extensions of each of these phrases.

   a) the President of the United States
   b) the Queen of England
   c) the capital of Canada
   d) women who have walked on the moon
   e) my linguistics professor

5. In our discussion of semantic decomposition, we noted that at least some words have meanings that can be represented in terms of smaller semantic features. Four such words are *dog, puppy, cat,* and *kitten.*

   i) Attempt to provide the semantic features associated with each of these words.
   ii) How are the pairs *dog-puppy* and *cat-kitten* different from *man-boy* and *woman-girl*?
   iii) Try to provide semantic features for the words *circle, triangle,* and *quadrangle.* What problems do you encounter?

6. Each of the following words is associated with a concept.

   a) island   e) food
   b) soft   f) husband
   c) white   g) baseball bat
   d) wristwatch h) mountain

   i) Determine which of these examples are fuzzy concepts.
   ii) Choose one of the fuzzy concepts above. Name one prototypical member of that concept and one member that is closer to the concept boundary.
   iii) Draw a diagram for the concept 'dwelling' similar to that of figure 6.2 in this chapter. Do the same for the concept 'vehicle'.

7. Examine the following sets of sentences, each of which includes words or phrases used metaphorically.
   a) She gave him an icy stare.
      He gave her the cold shoulder.
      He exudes a lot of warmth towards people.
      They got into a heated argument.
   b) He drops a lot of hints.
      The committee picked up on the issue.
      She dumps all her problems on her friends.
      Although he disagreed, he let it go.
   c) the eye of a needle
      the foot of the bed
      the hands of the clock
      the arm of a chair
      the table legs
   d) This lecture is easy to digest.
      He just eats up the lecturer's words.
      Chew on this thought for a while.
      Listen to this juicy piece of gossip.

   For each set of sentences:
   i) Identify the words or phrases that are used metaphorically in each sentence.
   ii) Determine the basis for each of these metaphor sets.
      Use the pattern: 'The metaphors in (x) describe _____ in terms of _____.'
      Example: The metaphors in (a) describe human relationships in terms of temperature.

8. The section on lexicalization of concepts discussed how some languages simultaneously express motion and path, motion and movement, and/or motion and thing moving in motion verbs. Can you change the sentence *He moved the goods by truck to the warehouse* so that both movement and vehicle used to move are lexicalized in one verb? What other verbs express a similar combination of concepts?

9. Consider the following Fijian pronouns.

au	1st person singular 'me'
iko	2nd person singular 'you'
koya	3rd person singular 'him/her/it'
kedaru	1st person dual 'you and me'
keirau	1st person dual 'one other (not you) and me'
kemudrau	2nd person dual 'you two'
rau	3rd person dual 'them two'
kedatou	1st person trial 'two others (including you) and me'
keitou	1st person trial 'two others (excluding you) and me'
kemudou	2nd person trial 'you three'
iratou	3rd person trial 'them three'
keda	1st person plural 'us (more than three, including you)'
keimami	1st person plural 'us (more than three, excluding you)'
kemuni:	2nd person plural 'you (more than three)'
ira	3rd person plural 'them (more than three)'

i) Some concepts are grammaticized in the Fijian pronoun system which are not grammaticized in the English pronoun system. Can you identify them?

ii) Which concept is grammaticized in the English pronoun system but not in the Fijian system?

10. Each NP in the following sentences has a thematic role that represents the part that its referent plays in the situation described by the sentence.

a) The man chased the intruder.

b) The cat jumped from the chair onto the table.

c) Aaron wrote a letter to Marilyn.

d) The premier entertained the guests in the lounge.

e) Henry mailed the manuscript from Halifax.

Using the terms described in this chapter, label the thematic role of each NP in these sentences and identify the assigner for each thematic role.

Example: <u>Bill</u> wrote <u>a novel</u> in <u>the park</u>.

11. Each of the following sentences has undergone a movement transformation.

a) What should Larry give to the bride?

b) Who will Liane kiss?

c) Which house will the group leave from?

d) What might Marvin forget on the bus?

e) The necklace was stolen by the burglar.

f) The ball was thrown to Evan by Louise.

Write out the deep structure string for each of these sentences and mark all thematic roles and thematic role assigners.

Example: a) <u>Larry</u> should give <u>what</u> to <u>the bride</u>

12. One of the relations involved in the interpretation of pronouns is that of c-command. Examine the following tree structure for the sentence *Jack's brother gave himself a haircut*.

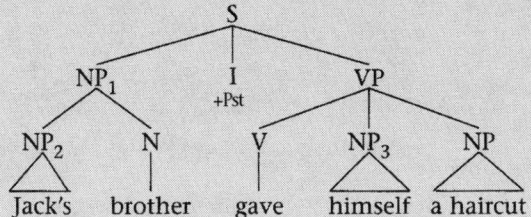

i) Who does *himself* refer to in this sentence?

ii) Does NP$_2$ c-command NP$_3$?

iii) How does your answer to *ii)* relate to your answer to *i)*?

iv) Does the antecedent change if you change *himself* to *him*? Why?

13. In the following sentence, the pronoun *she* could, according to Principle B, refer to either *the architect* or *the secretary*.

    The architect gave the secretary a raise after she typed the report.

    i) Which interpretation for *she* comes to mind first?
    ii) Why?
    iii) What happens to the pronoun's interpretation if you change the word *secretary* to *janitor*?

14. In the following pairs of sentences, one of the two sentences contains a presupposition relating to the truth of the complement clause.
    a) John regrets that Maria went to the graduation ceremony.
       John believes that Maria went to the graduation ceremony.
    b) The captain thought that the ship was in danger.
       The captain realized that the ship was in danger.
    c) It is significant that the criminal was sentenced.
       It is likely that the criminal was sentenced.

    For each pair:
    i) Identify the sentence that contains this presupposition.
    ii) Locate the word that is responsible for the presupposition.

15. In Malagasy, the use of the deictics *ety* 'here' and *aty* 'there' depend on whether the object in question is visible to the speaker.
    a) Ety ny tranony. 'Here is his house (visible to the speaker)'
    b) Aty ny tranony. 'There is his house (not visible to the speaker)'
       How does this differ from the English use of here/there?

16. The syntactic construction *It was _____ that _____* is called a 'cleft construction' and is used in certain discourse contexts. Consider the following conversations involving cleft constructions.
    a) *A*: Did Sally claim that she saw a flying saucer last night?
        B: No, it was <u>a meteorite</u> that <u>Sally claimed she saw last night</u>.
    b) *A*: Did Sally claim that she saw a flying saucer last night?
        B: No, it was <u>Sally</u> that <u>claimed she saw a meteorite last night</u>.
    c) *A*: Did Sally claim that she saw a flying saucer last night?
        B: No, it was <u>last week</u> that <u>Sally claimed she saw a flying saucer</u>.

    i) Is B's response equally acceptable in all three interactions?
    ii) Choose one of the discourses in which B's response is appropriate. How do the underlined parts correspond to new and old information?
    iii) For the discourse in which B's response is unacceptable, can you now explain why it is unacceptable?
    iv) In addition to the cleft construction, identify the way in which new information is marked phonetically in B's responses.

17. Each of the following examples contains a conversational implicature.
    a) *A*: Have you washed the floor and done the dishes?
        B: I've washed the floor.

b) *A*: Did you get hold of Carl yet?
 B: I tried to call him yesterday.

c) *A*: What did you think of the movie?
 B: Well, the supporting actor was great.

d) As the police walked up to John's car, he put on his seat belt.

e) *A*: Do you have any pets?
 B: Yes, I have two cats.

What is the implicature for each example?

Seven

Robert W. Murray

Historical linguistics: the study of language change

Many men sayn that in sweveninges
Ther nys but fables and lesynges;
But men may some swevenes sene
Whiche hardely that false ne bene,
But afterwarde ben apparaunt.

CHAUCER, *THE ROMANCE OF THE ROSE* (C. 1370)

anguage change is both obvious and rather mysterious. The English of the late fourteenth century, for example, is so different from Modern English that without special
training it is difficult to understand the opening lines to *The Romance of the Rose* cited above.
Not only would these sentences have a foreign sound, but words and structures such as
sweveninges, *lesynges*, and *false ne bene* are unfamiliar.[1] The existence of such differences
between early and later variants of the same language raises questions as to how and why
languages change over time.

   Historical linguistics is concerned with both the description and explanation of language change. In this chapter we examine the nature and causes of language change and survey in some detail phonological, morphological, syntactic, lexical, and semantic change. We
also explore techniques used to reconstruct linguistic pre-history and briefly discuss interrelated research into language acquisition and linguistic universals.

1   The nature of language change

All languages undergo change over time. English has undergone continuous and dramatic
change throughout its three major periods: Old English (roughly from 450 to 1100), Middle
English (from 1100 to 1500) and Modern English (from 1500 to the present). While Chaucer's
Middle English is at least partially comprehensible today, Old English looks like a completely
foreign language. The following is an extract from an eighth-century Old English document,
a translation of Bede's Latin history of England. (The letter /þ/, called 'thorn', represented the
phoneme /θ/ in Old English; here and elsewhere in this chapter ‾ marks a long vowel in the
orthography.)

1)

and Seaxan þā sige geslōgan.
and Saxons the victory won
'And the Saxons won the victory.'

þā sendan hī hām ǣrenddracan.
then sent they home a messenger
'Then they sent home a messenger.'

These Old English sentences differ from their Modern English counterparts in many respects. In terms of pronunciation, for instance, the Old English word *hām* [haːm] 'home' in the second sentence became [hɔːm] in Middle English, and then [howm] in Modern English. In its morphology, Old English differed significantly from Modern English. The suffix *-an* on the Old English word for 'sent' indicates both past tense and plurality of the subject (*hī* 'they'). Differences in word order are also readily apparent with the verb following both the subject and the direct object in the first sentence and preceding both the subject and the direct object in the second. Neither of these word orders would be acceptable in the Modern English forms of these sentences.

In addition, some Old English words have disappeared from use, as the unfamiliar *ǣrenddracan* 'messenger' and *sige* 'victory' indicate. Still other words have been maintained, but with a change in meaning. For example, the Old English word *geslōgan* (which we translated as 'won') is the past tense of the verb *slēan*, the Old English predecessor of our word *slay*. Although the Modern English meaning of this word in normal usage is restricted to the act of killing, the Old English verb could also mean 'to strike, beat, coin (money), and forge (weapons)'. As these examples imply, all components of the grammar from meaning (semantics) to individual sounds (phonology) are subject to change.

1.1 Systematicity of language change

A striking fact about language change in general is its regularity and systematicity. For example, the development of a fixed subject-verb-direct object (SVO) word order in English did not affect just a few verbs; all verbs in Modern English appear before rather than after the direct object. Similarly, the changes affecting the vowel in the word *hām* did not occur in that word only; they represent the regular development of the Old English vowel *ā* ([aː]) (see table 7.1).

Table 7.1	Changes affecting Old English [aː]		
Old English	**Middle English**	**Modern English**	
[baːt]	[bɔːt]	[bowt]	'boat'
[aːθ]	[ɔːθ]	[owθ]	'oath'
[staːn]	[stɔːn]	[stown]	'stone'

1.2 Causes of language change

The inevitability of language change is guaranteed by the way in which language is passed on from one generation to the next. Children do not begin with an intact grammar of the language being acquired but rather must construct a grammar on the basis of the available data (see chapter 10). In such a situation it is hardly surprising that differences will arise, even if only subtle ones, from one generation to the next. Moreover, since all children use the same physiological and cognitive endowment in learning language, it is to be expected that the same patterns of change will be consistently and repeatedly manifested in all languages. Following is a brief overview of the principal causes of language change.

Articulatory simplification

As might be expected, most sound changes have a physiological basis. Since such sound changes typically result in **articulatory simplification**, they have traditionally been related to the idea of 'ease of articulation'. Although this notion is difficult to define precisely, we can readily identify cases of articulatory simplification in our everyday speech such as the deletion of a consonant in a complex cluster or, in some dialects, the insertion of a vowel to break up a complex cluster (see table 7.2).

Table 7.2	Simplification of complex clusters	
Deletion of a consonant		
[fɪfθs] →	[fɪfs]	'fifths'
Insertion of a vowel		
[æθlit] →	[æθəlit]	'athlete'

Spelling pronunciation

Not all changes in pronunciation have a physiological motivation. A minor, but nevertheless important, source of change in English and other languages is **spelling pronunciation**. Since the written form of a word can differ significantly from the way it is pronounced, a new pronunciation can arise that seems to reflect more closely the spelling of the word. A case in point is the word *often*. Although this word was pronounced with a [t] in earlier English, the voiceless stop was subsequently lost resulting in the pronunciation [ɑfən] (compare *soften*). However, since the letter *t* was retained in the spelling, [t] has been reintroduced into many speakers' pronunciation of this word.

Another case in point is the pronunciation of [s] in words such as *assume* and *consume*. Although in earlier English such words were pronounced with [s], sound change resulted in a pronunciation with [ʃ] (as in *assure*). Similar to the case of *often* above, a pronunciation with [s] has been reintroduced into many dialects on the basis of the spelling (which remained unchanged even after the sound change took place). Since spelling tends to remain stable even though sound changes have occurred (English spelling began stabilizing more than three hundred years ago), spelling pronunciation can reintroduce a pronunciation that was earlier altered through sound change.

Analogy and reanalysis

Cognitive factors also play a role in change in all components of the grammar. Two sources of change having a cognitive basis are **analogy** and **reanalysis**. Analogy reflects the preference of speakers for regular patterns over irregular ones. It typically involves the extension or generalization of a regularity on the basis of the inference that if elements are alike in some respects, they should be alike in others as well. Both phonological and semantic characteristics can serve as a basis for analogy. For example, on the basis of its phonological similarity with verbs such as *sting/stung* and *swing/swung*, in some dialects *bring* has developed a form *brung*, as in *I('ve) brung it into the house*. The effects of analogy can also be observed in the speech of children, who often produce past tense forms such as *goed* and *knowed* analogous to *flowed* (see chapter 13). As we will see shortly, analogy plays a very important role in morphological change as well.

Reanalysis is particularly common in morphological change. Morphological reanalysis typically involves an attempt to attribute a compound or root + affix structure to a word that formerly was not broken down into component morphemes. A classic example in English is the word *hamburger* which originally referred to a type of meat patty deriving its name from the city of Hamburg in Germany. This word has been reanalyzed as consisting of two components, *ham* + *burger*. The latter morpheme has since appeared in many new forms including *fishburger*, *chickenburger*, and even as a free morpheme *burger*. Note that the resulting reanalysis need not be correct. (There is usually no ham in a burger!)

Language contact

Another cause of language change is **language contact**. Language contact refers to the situation where speakers of a language frequently interact with the speakers of another language or dialect. As a consequence, extensive **borrowing** can occur, particularly where there are significant numbers of bilinguals or multilinguals. Although borrowing can affect all components of the grammar, the lexicon is typically most affected. English, for example, has borrowed many Amerindian words including *Canada*, *moccasin*, *totem*, *tomahawk*, *chinook*, *moose*, and *skunk*.

Among the effects that borrowing can have on the sound system are the introduction of new phonemes or allophones and changes in their distribution. For example, some English speakers pronounce the name of the classical composer, *Bach*, with the final velar fricative [x] found in the German pronunciation. If there is a significant number of borrowings from another language, the borrowed foreign segment can eventually become a new phoneme. In the early Middle English period, the London dialect had [f] but not [v] in word-initial position. The [v] was later introduced as a result of contact with other English dialects and with French, in which it did occur word-initially. This contact was a factor in the development of a contrast between /f/ and /v/ word-initially, as found in Modern English pairs such as *file* and *vile*.

Language (as well as dialect) contact also results in another minor but nevertheless important source of language change, **hypercorrection**. Hypercorrection occurs when a speaker who is attempting to speak another dialect or language overgeneralizes particular rules. For example, most Canadians speak a dialect in which no distinction is made between intervocalic [t] and [d] so that words such as *latter* and *ladder* are both pronounced with an intervocalic flap [ɾ] (see chapter 2). If a speaker from such a dialect attempts to emulate the pronunciation of a speaker from another dialect who does distinguish the two stops intervocalically, hypercorrection could result in the use of intervocalic [t] in words where [d] should be used; for example, the pronunciation *pro*[t]*igy* for *prodigy*.

Another example of hypercorrection is the use of *I* in constructions such as *He saw John and I*. This usage is an overgeneralization of the rule that only *I* should be used in subject position, never *me*. According to this rule, *John and I are going* is correct but *John and me/me and John are going* is incorrect. For some speakers, hypercorrection has resulted in the inference that all coordinate phrases containing *me* (such as *John and me*) are incorrect even when they serve as direct object (complement) of the verb. Note that even a person who says *He gave it to John and I* would not say *He saw I*.

2   Sound change

Although all components of the grammar are susceptible to change over time, some types of change yield more obvious results than others. Variation and change are particularly noticeable in the phonology of a language. Several common types of sound change can be distinguished.

Most sound changes begin as subtle alterations in the sound pattern of a language in particular phonetic environments. The linguistic processes underlying such **phonetically conditioned** change are identical to the ones found in the phonology of currently spoken languages (see chapter 2, section 2). The application of such processes usually brings about an articulatory simplification, and over time significant changes in the phonology of a language can result.

Although all aspects of a language's phonology (e.g., tone, stress, and syllable structure) are subject to change over time, we will restrict our attention here to change involving segments. Since most sound changes involve sequences of segments, the main focus will be on **sequential change**. However, we will also discuss one common type of **segmental** change, involving the simplification of an affricate. In addition, in order to demonstrate that more than just articulatory factors play a role in sound change, we will discuss a case of sound change based on auditory factors. All important sound changes discussed in this section and referred to in this chapter are found in the catalogue of sound changes in table 7.3.

Table 7.3 Catalogue of sound changes	
Sequential change	Consonants
	Degemination
Assimilation	Voicing
Place and/or manner of articulation	Frication
Palatalization/affrication	Rhotacism
Nasalization	Deletion
Umlaut	Consonant strengthening
Dissimilation	Glide strengthening
Epenthesis (segment addition)	
Metathesis (segment movement)	**Segmental change**
Weakening and deletion	
Vowels	Deaffrication
Vowel reduction	**Auditorily based change**
Syncope	
Apocope	Substitution

2.1 Sequential change

Assimilation

The most common type of sequential change is **assimilation**, which has the effect of increasing the efficiency of articulation through a simplification of articulatory movements. We will focus here on the four main types indicated in the catalogue.

Partial assimilation involving **place or manner of articulation** is a very common change which, over time, can result in total assimilation. In the Spanish and Latin examples in table 7.4, the nasal assimilated in place of articulation to the following consonant.

Table 7.4	Assimilation (place of articulation) in Spanish and Latin[2]			
Old Spanish	semda	Modern Spanish	senda	'path'
Early Latin	inpossibilis	Later Latin	impossibilis	'impossible'

The first of the Old English examples in table 7.5 shows voicing assimilation and the second shows the assimilation of nasality.

Table 7.5	Assimilation in manner of articulation in Old English
Early Old English	**Later Old English**	
slæpde	slæpte	'slept'
stefn	stemn	'stem (of a tree)'

In the Italian examples in table 7.6, a stop assimilates totally to a following stop.

Table 7.6	Total assimilation in Italian
Latin	**Italian**	
octo (c = [k])	otto	'eight'
septem	sette	'seven'
damnum	danno	'damage'

Another type of assimilation is **palatalization**—the effect that front vowels and the palatal glide [j] typically have on velar, alveolar, and dental stops, making their place of articulation more palatal. If you compare your pronunciation of *keep* as opposed to *cot*, you will notice that the pronunciation of [k] in the former is much more palatal than in the latter due to the influence of [i]. Palatalization is often the first step in **affrication**, a change in which palatalized stops become affricates, either [ts] or [tʃ] if the original stop was voiceless or [dz] or [dʒ] if the original stop was voiced (see table 7.7).

Nasalization refers to the nasalizing effect that a nasal consonant can have on an adjacent vowel. This change occurred in both French and Portuguese, with the subsequent loss of the nasal consonant. (The pronunciation of the vowels in the examples in table 7.8 underwent additional changes in height and backness in French.)

Table 7.7   Palatalization/affrication induced by front vowels and [j]

Examples from the Romance languages				
Latin	<u>c</u>entum [k]	Old French	<u>c</u>ent	[ts]	'one hundred'
Latin	<u>c</u>entum [k]	Italian	<u>c</u>iento	[tʃ]	'one hundred'
Latin	me<u>d</u>ius [d]	Italian	me<u>zz</u>o	[dz]	'half'
Latin	<u>g</u>entem [g]	Old French	<u>g</u>ent	[dʒ]	'people'

Table 7.8   Nasalization in Portuguese and French

Latin	Portuguese	French	
bon-	bon [bõ]	bon [bɔ̃]	'good'
un-	um [ũ]	un [œ̃]	'one'

Although assimilation is probably most common in the case of adjacent segments, it can also apply at a distance. A case in point is **umlaut**, the effect a vowel or sometimes a glide in one syllable can have on the vowel of another syllable, usually a preceding one. Umlaut (resulting in front rounded vowels [y] and [ø]) played an important role in Old English and is the source of irregular plurals such as *goose/geese* and *mouse/mice* in Modern English. For example, the plural of the pre-Old English words *gōs* 'goose' and *mūs* 'mouse' was formed by adding a suffix -[i]. As a result, umlaut of the vowel in the preceding syllable occurred in the plural forms (see pre-Old English stages 1 and 2) but not in the singular forms. By early Old English, the suffix -[i] had been lost in a separate change leaving the umlauted vowel as the marker of the plural form. (Subsequent changes included the derounding of the umlauted vowels [ȳ] and [ǿ] yielding [ī] and [ē] respectively by Middle English, and the Great Vowel Shift as described in section 2.4 ; see table 7.9).

Table 7.9   Umlaut in English

Pre-Old English 1		Pre-OE 2		Early OE		Subsequent changes	
[gōs]	>	[gōs]	>	[gōs]	>	[gus]	'goose'
[gōsi]	>	[gǿsi]	>	[gǿs]	>	[gis]	'geese'
[mūs]	>	[mūs]	>	[mūs]	>	[maws]	'mouse'
[mūsi]	>	[mȳsi]	>	[mȳs]	>	[majs]	'mice'

Dissimilation

Dissimilation, the process whereby one segment is made less like another segment in its environment, is much less frequent than assimilation. This type of change typically occurs when it would be difficult to articulate or perceive two similar sounds in close proximity. The word *anma* 'soul' in Late Latin, for example, was modified to *alma* in Spanish, thereby avoiding two consecutive nasal consonants. Like assimilation, dissimilation can also operate at a distance to affect non-adjacent segments. For instance, the Latin word *arbor* 'tree' became *arbol* in Spanish and *alboro* in Italian, thereby avoiding two instances of *r* in adjacent syllables. (By contrast, dissimilation did not occur in French where *arbre* has retained both instances of *r*.)

Epenthesis

Another common sound change, **epenthesis**, involves the insertion of a consonant or vowel into a particular environment (see table 7.10). In some cases, epenthesis results from the anticipation of an upcoming sound.

Table 7.10 Epenthesis in Old English

Earlier form	Change			Later form	
ganra	VnrV	>	VndrV	gandra	'gander'
simle	VmlV	>	VmblV	simble	'always'
æmtig	VmtV	>	VmptV	æmptig	'empty'

In these examples, the epenthetic [b], [d], or [p] has the place of articulation of the preceding nasal but agrees with the following segment in terms of voice and nasality. The epenthetic segment therefore serves as a bridge for the transition between the segments on either side.

Table 7.11 The nature of epenthesis

[m]	[b]	[l]	[m]	[p]	[t]
labial	labial	non-labial	labial	labial	non-labial
nasal	non-nasal	non-nasal	nasal	non-nasal	non-nasal
voiced	voiced	voiced	voiced	voiceless	voiceless

In other cases, vowel epenthesis serves to break up a sequence of sounds that would otherwise be difficult to pronounce or even inconsistent with the phonotactic patterns of the language. As mentioned above, some English speakers avoid [θl] clusters by inserting an epenthetic [ə] in their pronunciation of words such as *athlete* as *ath*[ə]*lete*. In the history of Spanish, word-initial [sk] clusters were avoided by inserting a vowel (see table 7.12).

Table 7.12 Examples of epenthesis

Latin	schola [sk]	Spanish	escuela [esk]	'school'
Latin	scrībere [sk]	Spanish	escribir [esk]	'write'

Metathesis

Metathesis involves a change in the relative positioning of segments. This change, like assimilation and dissimilation, can affect adjacent segments or segments at a distance (see table 7.13).

Table 7.13 Metathesis of adjacent segments in Old English		
Earlier form	**Later form**	
wæps	wæ<u>sp</u>	'wasp'
þridda	þ<u>ir</u>dda	'third'

Metathesis at a distance is found in the change from Latin *mīrāculum* 'miracle' to Spanish *milagro*, in which [r] and [l] have changed places although they were not adjacent (see figure 7.1).

mīrāculum

milagro

Figure 7.1 Metathesis of non-adjacent segments in Spanish

Weakening and deletion

Both vowels and consonants are also susceptible to outright **deletion** as well as to various **weakening** processes. We will first treat the effects of these processes on vowels and then turn to their effects on consonants.

Vowel deletion may involve a word-final vowel (**apocope**) or a word-internal vowel (**syncope**) (see table 7.14). A vowel in an unstressed syllable is particularly susceptible to deletion, especially when a nearby neighbouring syllable is stressed.

Table 7.14 Vowel deletion in French		
Apocope		
Latin	*French*	
cū́r<u>a</u>	cure [kyʁ]	'cure'
ōrnā́r<u>e</u>	orner	'decorate'
Syncope		
Latin	*French*	
pér<u>de</u>re	perdre	'lose'
vī́v<u>e</u>re	vivre	'live'

The effects of syncope are also apparent in the loss of the medial vowel in Modern English words such as *veg<u>e</u>table*, *int<u>e</u>rest* and *fam<u>i</u>ly*, which are frequently pronounced as véʤtəbl̩, and [fǽmli].

Vowel deletion is commonly preceded by **vowel reduction**, in which a full vowel is reduced to a schwa-like (i.e., short, lax [ə]) vowel. Vowel reduction typically affects short vowels in unstressed syllables and may affect all or only a subset of the full vowels (see figure 7.2).

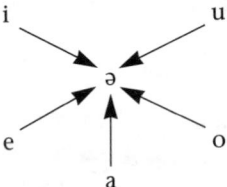

Figure 7.2 Vowel reduction

Vowel reduction with subsequent deletion (syncope and apocope) occurred in Middle English and Early Modern English as shown in table 7.15.

Table 7.15 Vowel reduction and deletion in English		
Syncope		
Old English	*Middle English* (vowel reduction)	*Early Modern English* (vowel deletion)
stānas [a]	stones [ə]	stones ∅
stānes [e]	stones [ə]	stone's ∅
Apocope		
Old English	*Middle English* (vowel reduction)	*Early Modern English* (apocope)
nama [a]	name [ə]	name ∅
talu [u]	tale [ə]	tale ∅

Consonant deletion is also a very common sound change. For example, the word-initial cluster [kn] was found in Old and Middle English, as the spelling of such words as *knight*, *knit*, *knot*, and *knee* implies, but the [k] was subsequently lost giving us our modern pronunciation. The loss of word-final consonants has played a major role in the evolution of Modern French. The final letters in the written forms of the words in table 7.16 reflect consonants which were actually pronounced at an earlier stage of the language.

Table 7.16 Consonant loss in French		
French spelling (masculine form)	**Current pronunciation**	
gros	[gro]	'large'
chaud	[ʃo]	'warm'
vert	[vɛr]	'green'

Just as vowel reduction can be identified as a weakening process since it represents an intermediate step on the pathway from a full vowel to deletion of the vowel, so too can pathways of **consonant weakening** be identified. The scale of **consonantal strength** in figure 7.3 can be helpful in identifying cases of weakening.

Consonantal strength
stronger ↑ voiceless stops
            voiceless fricatives, voiced stops
            voiced fricatives
            nasals
            liquids
weaker   ↓ glides

(*Note:* Geminate consonants are stronger than their non-geminate counterparts.)

Figure 7.3 Scale of consonantal strength

Accordingly, geminates weaken to non-geminates (**degemination**), stops weaken to fricatives (**frication**), and voiceless stops or voiceless fricatives weaken to voiced stops or voiced fricatives respectively (**voicing**).[3] Weakening can ultimately result in the deletion of the consonant. Figure 7.4 is a typical pathway of weakening.

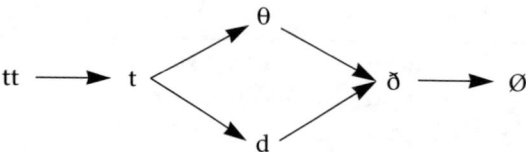

Figure 7.4 Typical pathway of consonant weakening

Consonants are particularly subject to weakening in an intervocalic environment. Parts of the pathway of consonantal weakening are exemplified with developments from the Romance languages shown in table 7.17.

Table 7.17	Consonantal weakening in Romance				
Degemination (tt > t):	Latin	mittere	Spanish	meter	'to put'
Voicing (t > d):	Latin	mātūrus	Old Spanish	maduro	'ripe'
Frication (d > ð):	Old Spanish	maduro	Spanish	maduro [ð]	'ripe'
Deletion (ð > Ø):	Old French	[maðyr]	French	mûr	'ripe'

Rhotacism is a relatively common type of weakening that typically involves the change of [z] to [r]. Often rhotacism is preceded by a stage involving the voicing of [s] to [z]. Within the Germanic family of languages for instance, [s] first became [z] in a particular intervocalic environment. This [z] remained in Gothic but became [r] in other Germanic languages such as in English, German, and Swedish. The effects of the latter part of this change can be seen in the standard spellings of the words in table 7.18.

Table 7.18	Rhotacism in English, German, and Swedish		
Gothic	**English**	**German**	**Swedish**
maiza	more	mehr	mera
diuzam	deer	Tier	djur
huzd	hoard	Hort	——

In Modern English, rhotacism is the source of the alternation between [z] and [r] in *was* and *were*. The [r] resulted from earlier [z] which was originally intervocalic.

Consonantal strengthening

Just as consonants weaken, they can also strengthen. **Glide strengthening** (the strengthening of a glide to an affricate) is particularly common, especially in word-initial position. In the Italian examples in table 7.19, the glide [j] has been strengthened to [dʒ].

Table 7.19	Glide strengthening in Italian					
Latin	iūdicium	[j]	Italian	giudizio	[dʒ]	'justice'
Latin	iuvenis	[j]	Italian	giovane	[dʒ]	'young'

2.2   Segmental change

Segments such as affricates are considered phonologically complex because they represent the fusing of a stop plus a fricative into a single segment, [dʒ] or [ts]. Such complex segments are commonly subject to simplification. A very common type of segmental simplification is **deaffrication** which has the effect of turning affricates into fricatives by eliminating the stop portion of the affricate (see table 7.20).

Table 7.20	Deaffrication in French				
Old French c̲ent	[ts]	French c̲ent	[s]	'one hundred'
Old French g̲ent	[dʒ]	French g̲ent	[ʒ]	'people, tribe'

Since deaffrication of [tʃ] (as well as of [dʒ]) has not occurred in English, early borrowings from French maintain the affricate, while later borrowings have a fricative (see table 7.21).

Table 7.21   Borrowing from French
Early borrowing (before deaffrication occurred in French)

Old French [tʃ]	*English* [tʃ]
c̲haiere	c̲hair
c̲haine	c̲hain

(*Note*: Compare Modern French [ʃ] in *c̲haire* 'throne, seat' and *c̲haîne* 'chain'.)

Later borrowings (after deaffrication occurred in French)

Modern French [ʃ]	*English* [ʃ]
c̲handelier	c̲handelier
c̲hauffeur	c̲hauffeur

2.3   Auditorily based change

Although articulatory factors (particularly relating to 'ease of articulation') are of central importance in sound change as indicated in the discussion above, auditory factors also play a role. **Substitution** is a type of auditorily based change involving the replacement of one segment with another similar-sounding segment. A common type of substitution involves [f] replacing either [x] or [θ]. Earlier in the history of English, [f] replaced [x] in some words in standard varieties of English while [f] replaced [θ] in Cockney, a non-standard dialect spoken in London (see table 7.22).

Table 7.22	Auditorily based substitution			
[x] > [f]	Middle English	laugh [x]	English	laugh [f]
[θ] > [f]	English	thin [θ]	Cockney	[fɪn]

So far we have treated sound changes without consideration of their effect on the sound pattern of the particular language as a whole. All of the foregoing sound changes can lead both to new types of allophonic variation and to the addition or loss of phonemic contrasts. Examples of such cases are presented in the next section.

2.4   Phonetic versus phonological change

The sound changes outlined in the previous sections can affect the overall sound pattern (phonology) of a language in different ways. Commonly, the first stage of a sound change results in the creation of a new allophone of an already existing phoneme. The term **phonetic sound change** can be used to refer to this stage.

A good example of phonetic sound change involves the laxing of short high vowels that has developed in Canadian French (see table 7.23). This change can be seen in closed word-final syllables, among other environments.

Table 7.23	Vowel laxing in Canadian French	
European French	**Canadian French**	
Closed syllable		
[vit]	[vɪt]	'quick'
[libʁ]	[lɪb]	'free'
[ekut]	[ekʊt]	'listen'
[pus]	[pʊs]	'thumb'
Open Syllable		
[vi]	[vi]	'life'
[li]	[li]	'bed'
[vu]	[vu]	'you'
[lu]	[lu]	'wolf'

Whereas Canadian French has the lax vowels [ɪ] and [ʊ] in closed final syllables, European French has kept the tense vowels [i] and [u]. Both dialects of French retain [i] and [u] in open syllables. This suggests that Canadian French has developed the rule in figure 7.5.

$$V \rightarrow [\text{-tense}] / \_\_\_ C (C) \#$$
$$\begin{bmatrix} +\text{high} \\ -\text{long} \end{bmatrix}$$

Figure 7.5 Vowel laxing rule in Canadian French

While this rule did introduce an allophone not present in European French, it did not create any new phonemes since there was no contrast between lax vowels and their tense counterparts in Canadian French.[4]

Splits

Sometimes sound change can lead to changes in a language's phonological system by adding, eliminating, or rearranging phonemes. Such **phonological change** can involve **splits**, **mergers**, or **shifts**.

In a phonological split, allophones of the same phoneme come to contrast with each other due to the loss of the conditioning environment, with the result that one or more new phonemes are created. The English phoneme /ŋ/ was the result of a phonological split (see table 7.24). Originally, [ŋ] was simply the allophone of /n/ that appeared before a velar consonant. During Middle English, consonant deletion resulted in the loss of [g] in word-final position after a nasal consonant, leaving [ŋ] as the final sound in words such as *sing*.

Table 7.24	Phonological split resulting in /ŋ/
Original phonemic form	/sɪng/
Original phonetic form	[sɪŋg]
Deletion of [g]	[sɪŋg] > [sɪŋ]
New phonemic form	/sɪŋ/

The loss of the final [g] in words created minimal pairs such as *sin* (/sɪn/) and *sing* (/sɪŋ/), in which there is a contrast between /n/ and /ŋ/. This example represents a typical phonological split. When the conditioning environment of an allophonic variant of a phoneme is lost through sound change, the allophone is no longer predictable and thus itself becomes phonemic. The original phoneme (in figure 7.6 /n/) splits into two phonemes (/n/ and /ŋ/).

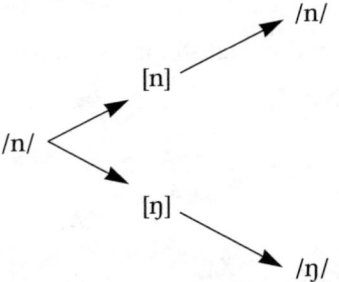

Figure 7.6 A phonological split

Mergers

In a phonological merger, two or more phonemes collapse into a single one, thereby reducing the number of phonemes in the language. The case of auditorily based substitution discussed above has this effect in Cockney English, where all instances of the interdental fricative /θ/ have become /f/ (see figure 7.7). Consequently, the phonemes /θ/ and /f/ have merged into one (/f/) and words such as *thin* and *fin* have the same phonological form (/fɪn/). Similarly, /v/ and /ð/ have merged (e.g., /smuv/ for *smooth*).

Figure 7.7 A phonological merger

Shifts

A phonological shift is a change in which a series of phonemes is systematically modified so that their organization with respect to each other is altered. A well-known example of such a change is called the Great English Vowel Shift. Beginning in the Middle English period and continuing into the eighteenth century, the language underwent a series of modifications to the long vowels (see table 7.25).

Table 7.25	The Great English Vowel Shift		
Middle English	**Great Vowel Shift**	**Modern English**	
[tiːd]	[iː] > [aj]	/tajd/	'tide'
[luːd]	[uː] > [aw]	/lawd/	'loud'
[geːs]	[eː] > [iː]	/gis/	'geese'
[sɛ]	[ɛː] > [iː]	/si/	'sea'
[goːs]	[oː] > [uː]	/gus/	'goose'
[brɔːkən]	[ɔː] > [oː]	/brokən/	'broken'
[naːmə]	[aː] > [eː]	/nem/	'name'

Figure 7.8 illustrates the changes that gradually affected the English long vowels.

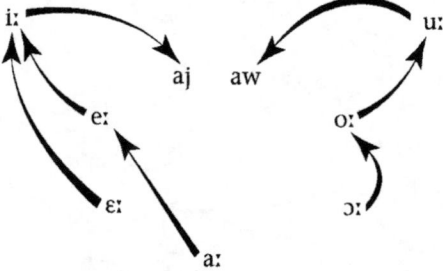

Figure 7.8 Changes brought about by the Great English Vowel Shift

2.5 Explaining phonological shift

The causes and even the details of the Great English Vowel Shift still remain unclear. In fact, the causes of phonological shift in general are not well understood. A possible motivation in some cases appears to involve the phonemic system itself where the notion of phonological space plays a role. As in the case of 'ease of articulation', phonological space is difficult to define precisely. For our purposes and focusing on vowels only, we can consider the vowel quadrangle (a schematicization of the oral cavity) as the phonological space that vowels must occupy. Although the vowel systems of languages can be arranged in various ways (see chapter 8), there is a tendency for languages to maximize the use of space in the quadrangle. Accordingly, if a language has only three vowels, they will likely be [i], [a], and [o] or [u], not (for example) [i], [e], [ɛ]. Similarly, if a language has five vowels, they will be distributed throughout the phonological space typically as [i], [e], [a], [o], [u] rather than [u], [ʊ], [a], [o], [ɔ] for example (see figure 7.9).

a Typical distribution of vowels in phonological space

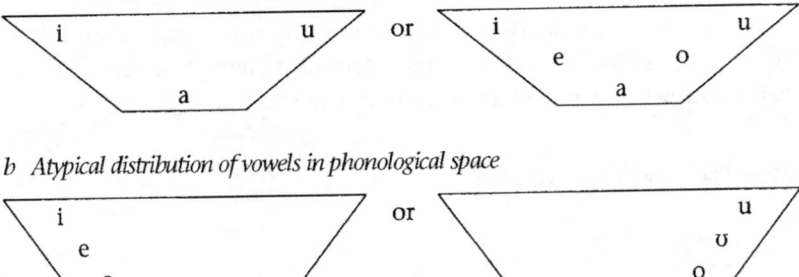

b Atypical distribution of vowels in phonological space

Figure 7.9 Vowel distribution

Languages with seven (or more) vowels (e.g., English at the starting point of the Great English Vowel Shift in figure 7.8) often undergo **diphthongization**. This can be seen as a reaction to the overcrowding of the phonological space since the effect of the diphthongization of a pair of vowels is to reduce a seven-vowel system to a five-vowel system. (Think of the two diphthongs as not infringing on the space of the simple vowels.)

Overcrowding appears to have resulted in diphthongization in many languages, including Old High German and Spanish (see table 7.26).

The diphthongization in these two languages differs from that of the Great English Vowel Shift in two ways. The mid vowels and not the high vowels are affected and different sets of diphthongs result. Nevertheless, in terms of phonological space all these cases of diphthongization achieve the same result: namely, a reduction of the overcrowded seven-vowel system. Although the Great English Vowel Shift was complicated by other developments, diphthongization resulting from overcrowding appears to have been a contributing factor.

Table 7.26   Diphthongization in Old High German and Spanish

Old High German diphthongization	Spanish diphthongization

i: u: i   u
  ia: ua: e   je   we   o
e: ↗   ↖ o: ε ↗   ↖ ɔ
ɛ: a
    a:

Old High German			Latin	Spanish	
Earlier	*Later*				
hēr	hiar	'here'	petra	piedra	'stone'
flōt	fluat	'flood'	mortem	muerte	'death'

2.6   Sound change and rule ordering

In describing language change, it is often crucial to identify the relative chronology, or times at which different changes have occurred. Three important changes in the history of English can be given as the following (somewhat simplified) rules in figure 7.10.

1) Voicing

    C   →   [+voice] / [+voice] ___ [+voice]

2) Syncope

      V   →   Ø / ___ C #
  [-stress]

3) Assimilation

    C   →   [+voice] / C + ___
            [+voice]

Figure 7.10 Three rules in the history of English

These changes have played an important role in the evolution of English plural forms such as *hooves* (versus *hoof*) and *wolves* (versus *wolf*). Of the possible orderings of these three rules, only one will derive the contemporary pronunciation from the earlier (Old English) phonemic form. Two of the possible orderings are given in table 7.27.

Table 7.27   Rule ordering in the history of English

Hypothesis A		Hypothesis B	
Original phonemic form	/wulfas/	Original phonemic form	/wulfas/
Voicing	wulvas	Voicing	wulvas
Syncope	wulvs	Assimilation	(cannot apply)
Assimilation	wulvz	Syncope	wulvs (incorrect)

If we assume hypothesis A with the ordering voicing, syncope, and assimilation, we can account for the [vz] in the modern pronunciation of a word such as *wolves*. By contrast, the ordering proposed in hypothesis B would not account for the present pronunciation.

3 Morphological change

In this section we discuss morphological changes resulting from analogy and reanalysis as well as changes involving the addition or loss of affixes.

3.1 Addition of affixes

Borrowing has been a very important source of new affixes in English. During the Middle English period, many French words containing the suffix *-ment* (e.g., *accomplishment, commencement*) made their way into the language. Eventually, *-ment* established itself as a productive suffix in English and was used with bases that were not of French origin (e.g., *acknowledgement, merriment*). The ending *-able*, which converts a verb into an adjective (e.g., *readable, lovable*, etc.), followed a similar pattern. Although words with this ending (e.g., *favourable, conceivable*) were initially borrowed into English as whole units, eventually the suffix became productive and was used with new bases.

Not all new affixes are the result of borrowing. Lexical forms can become grammatical forms over time through a process called **grammaticalization.** Grammaticalized forms often undergo dramatic phonological reduction, as well as semantic change in which they can lose much of their original content. For example, the Latin word *habeō* '(I) have, hold, grasp' is the source of the Italian future suffix *-ò* (see table 7.30). In the case where two words are frequently adjacent, over time they can become fused together to form a single unit consisting of a base and an affix. **Fusion** refers to this specific type of grammaticalization where words develop into affixes (either prefixes or suffixes) (see table 7.28).

Table 7.28 Fusion		
word word	>	base + affix (suffixation)
word word	>	affix + base (prefixation)

A number of Modern English suffixes are derived from earlier words by means of fusion (see table 7.29).

Table 7.29 English suffixes resulting from fusion		
Suffix	**Old English word**	
-hood (childhood)	hād	'state, condition, rank'
-dom (freedom)	dōm	'condition, power'
-ly (fatherly)	(ge-)līc	'similar, equal, like'

Another case of fusion is the development of the future tense affixes in Italian which are derived from various forms of the Latin word *habere* 'to have' (see table 7.30).

Table 7.30 Fusion resulting in a future tense affix in Italian		
Latin	**Italian**	
amāre + habeō	amerò	'I will love'
amāre + habēmus	ameremo	'we will love'

3.2   Loss of affixes

Just as affixes can be added to the grammar, they can also be lost. Sometimes affixes simply fall into disuse for no apparent reason. For example, a number of Old English derivational affixes, including -*bǣre* and -*bora*, are no longer used (see table 7.31).

Table 7.31	Affixes no longer found in English		
N + bǣre	→	A	(e.g., *lustbǣre* 'pleasant, agreeable' from *lust* 'pleasure')
N + bora	→	N	(e.g., *mundbora* 'protector' from *mund* 'protection')

It is also very common for affixes to be lost through sound change. For example, Old English had a complex system of affixes marking case and gender. Nouns were divided into three gender classes—masculine, neuter, and feminine. Assignment to a class was not based on sex (natural gender) but on grammatical gender; for example, the word for *stone* (Old English *stān*) and even a word for *woman* (*wīfmann*) were masculine, the word for *sun* (*sunne*) was feminine, and another word for *woman* (*wīf*) was neuter. Each gender class was associated with a different set of case endings (see table 7.32).

The following Old English sentence contains all four case categories.

2)
Se cniht   geaf gief-e þæs hierd-es   sun-e.
the youth-Nom gave gift-Acc the shepherd-Gen son-Dat
'The youth gave a gift to the shepherd's son.'

Table 7.32	Old English case affixes		
	Masculine	**Neuter**	**Feminine**
Singular			
	hund 'dog'	dēor 'animal'	gief 'gift'
Nominative	hund	dēor	gief-u
Accusative	hund	dēor	gief-e
Genitive	hund-es	dēor-es	gief-e
Dative	hund-e	dēor-e	gief-e
Plural			
Nominative	hund-as	dēor	gief-a
Accusative	hund-as	dēor	gief-a
Genitive	hund-a	dēor-a	gief-a
Dative	hund-um	dēor-um	gief-um

By the fifteenth century, English case endings had changed radically. Consonant deletion resulted in the loss of the earlier [m] of the dative plural suffix and through vowel reduction all the unstressed vowels of the case endings were reduced to the short, lax vowel [ə] (which was later lost through vowel deletion). Consequently, many of the earlier case and gender distinctions were obliterated. (The examples in table 7.33 also include changes to the base-internal vowels as the result of various processes, including the Great English Vowel Shift.)

Table 7.33	The loss of case affixes through sound change (in English *hound*)		
	Old English	**Middle English (e = [ə])**	**Modern English**
Singular			
Nominative	hund	hund	hound
Accusative	hund	hund	hound
Genitive	hund-es	hund-(e)s	hound's
Dative	hund-e	hund-(e)	hound
Plural			
Nominative	hund-as	hund-(e)s	hounds
Accusative	hund-as	hund-(e)s	hounds
Genitive	hund-a	hund-(e)	hounds'
Dative	hund-um	hund-(e)	hounds

Whereas Old English had five distinct affixes for cases, Middle English had only two suffixes, -*e* and -*es*, which, with the loss of schwa, were ultimately reduced to a single suffix -*s*, still used in Modern English for the plural and the possessive. This represents a typical example of how sound change can result in modification to the morphological component of the grammar.

3.3 From synthetic to analytic to synthetic

Since languages vary greatly in the complexity of their morphology, linguists often make a distinction between analytic and synthetic languages (see chapter 8). Whereas analytic languages have very few inflectional affixes (for example, Modern English), synthetic languages have many (for example, Latin, Old English).

Even in the absence of borrowing, sound change and fusion ensure that there is an endless transition in the morphology of a language over time. As we have seen, due to the loss of case endings through sound change, English has developed from a synthetic language with many inflectional affixes to an analytic one with very few, as the above discussion of nouns such as *hound* indicates.

By contrast, fusion ensures the rise of new synthetic forms. Fusion can be observed in some Modern English dialects in forms such as *coulda* (e.g., *I coulda won*) which represents the fusion of *could* and *have*. For many speakers, the -*a* is treated as a suffix that is no longer related to *have*, as evident in spellings such as *could of* which result from confusion over how to represent the pronunciation of *coulda* in written English. Through fusion, a language with an analytic morphology can become more synthetic over time.

3.4 Analogy

The drastic effects that sound change can have on the morphology of a language are often alleviated through analogy. For example, the plural of Old English *hand* 'hand' was *handa*. Vowel reduction and apocope applying to *handa* would have yielded a Modern English plural form identical to the singular form, namely *hand* (see table 7.34).

Table 7.34	Sound changes applied to Old English *handa* 'hands'
handa	
handə	vowel reduction
hand	apocope

Obviously, then the Modern English plural *hands* cannot be the consequence of sound change. Rather, it is the result of earlier analogy with words such as Middle English *hund* 'hound' (see table 7.33), which did form the plural with the suffix *-s*. This suffix, whose earlier form *-as* was predominant even in Old English, was extended by analogy to all English nouns with a few exceptions (*oxen, men, geese,* etc.). Other plural forms besides *hands* that were created on the basis of analogy include *eyes* (*eyen* in Middle English) and *shoes* (formerly *shooen*).

Continuing analogy along these lines is responsible for the development of the plural form *youse* (from *you*) in some English dialects. Each generation of English-speaking children temporarily extends the analogy still further by producing forms such as *sheeps, gooses,* and *mouses.* To date, however, these particular innovations have not been accepted by adult speakers of Standard English and are eventually abandoned by young language learners.

3.5   Reanalysis

As mentioned in section 1.2, reanalysis can result in a new morphological structure for a word. It can affect both borrowed words and, particularly in cases where the morphological structure of the word is no longer transparent, native words. Reanalysis can result in new productive patterns (as in the case of *(-)burger*) or it can remain quite isolated, affecting perhaps only one word. Since the type of reanalysis exemplified by *hamburger* is not based on a correct analysis of a word (at least from a historical perspective) and does not usually involve a conscious or detailed study of the word on the part of the speaker, it is often called **folk etymology**.

In the case of *hamburger*, the only evidence of folk etymology is the productive use of *(-)burger* as an independent word and in compounds like *fishburger*. However, in other cases, folk etymology commonly involves changes in pronunciation that reflect the new morphological analysis. For example, our word *earwig* derives from Old English *ēarwicga* [ǣərwidʒa], a compound consisting of 'ear' and 'insect'. Taking into consideration sound change alone, the expected Modern English pronunciation of this word would be *earwidge* [ɪrwɪdʒ]. However, the second part of the compound was lost as an independent word by Middle English, so speakers could no longer associate it with the meaning of 'insect'. Subsequently, reanalysis related the second part of the compound to the verb 'wiggle' resulting in Middle English *arwygyll* (literally 'ear + wiggle'). The end result is Modern English *-wig* and not *-widge*. More examples of folk etymology are found in table 7.35.

Although reanalysis of individual words is common, affixes can also be affected, sometimes with new productive morphological rules developing as a result. This is the case of the Modern English adverbial suffix *-ly* (developing from Old English *-lic(e)*). In Old English, adjectives could be derived from nouns by adding the suffix *-lic*. Adverbs, in turn, could be derived by adding the suffix *-e* to adjectives (including those derived with *-lic*) (see table 7.36).

Table 7.35   Folk etymology in English (native words and borrowings)

Modern word	Source
belfry	Middle English *berfrey* 'bell tower' (unrelated to *bell*)
bridegroom	Middle English *bridegome* (unrelated to *groom*)
	(compare Old English *brӯd* 'bride' and *guma* 'man')
muskrat	Algonquian *musquash* (unrelated to either *musk* or *rat*)
woodchuck	Algonquian *otchek* (unrelated to either *wood* or *chuck*)

Table 7.36   The derivation of Old English adjectives and adverbs

Formation of an adjective from a noun

[dæg]$_N$ + lic   →   [dæglic]$_A$ 'daily' (e.g., as in 'daily schedule')

Formation of an adverb from an adjective

[dēop]$_A$ + e   →   [dēope]$_{Adv}$ 'deeply'

Formation of an adverb from a derived adjective with -*lic*

[dæg+lic]$_A$ + e   →   [dæglice]$_{Adv}$ 'daily' (e.g., as in 'she ran daily')

At some point, the entire complex suffix *-lic+e* was reanalyzed as an adverbial suffix (rather than as an adjectival suffix *-lic* plus an adverbial suffix *-e*). It was then used by analogy to derive adverbs from adjectives in forms where it was not used before, resulting in Modern English *deeply* and other such words.

4   Syntactic change

Like other components of the grammar, syntax is also subject to change over time. Syntactic changes can involve modifications to phrase structure rules or transformations, as the following examples illustrate.

4.1   Word order

All languages make a distinction between the subject and direct object. This contrast is typically represented through case marking or word order. Since Old English had an extensive system of case marking, it is not surprising that its word order was somewhat more variable than that of Modern English. In unembedded clauses, Old English placed the verb in second position (much like Modern German). Thus we find subject-verb-object order in simple transitive sentences such as the following.

3)
S   V   O
Hē   geseah   þone mann.
'He   saw   the man.'

When the clause began with an element such as *þa* 'then' or *ne* 'not', the verb preceded the subject as in the following example.

4)

```
        V      S        O
þa   sende  sē cyning  þone disc
then  sent   the king   the dish
'Then the king sent the dish.'
```

Although this word order is still found in Modern English, its use is very limited and subject to special restrictions, unlike the situation in Old English.

5)

```
        V   S             O
Rarely has he ever deceived me.
```

When the direct object was a pronoun, the subject-object-verb order was typical.

6)

```
S    O    V
Hēo  hine  lǣrde.
She  him   advised
'She advised him.'
```

The subject-object-verb order also prevailed in embedded clauses, even when the direct object was not a pronoun.

7)

```
        S      O        V
þa   hē þone cyning sōhte,   hē bēotode.
when  he  the king      visited,   he boasted
'When he visited the king, he boasted.'
```

Since case markings were lost during the Middle English period through sound change, fixed subject-verb-object order became the means of marking grammatical relations. As table 7.37 shows, a major change in word order took place between 1300 and 1400, with the verb-object order becoming dominant.

Table 7.37 Word order patterns in Middle English						
Year	1000	1200	1300	1400	1500	
Direct object before the verb (%)	53	53	40	14	2	
Direct object after the verb (%)	47	47	60	86	98	

From SOV to SVO

Just as languages can be classified in terms of their morphology, languages can also be grouped on the basis of the relative order of subject (S), object (O), and verb (V) in basic sentences. Almost all languages of the world fall into one of three types: SOV, SVO, or VSO, with the majority of languages being one of the first two types. Just as languages change through time from one morphological type to another, they can also change from one syntactic type to another. A case in point is found in the history of English, which shows the development from SOV to SVO syntax.

Evidence indicates that the earliest form of Germanic from which English descended was an SOV language. One of the earliest recorded Germanic sentences, for example, has this word order. The sentence in *8)* was inscribed on a golden horn (now called the Golden Horn of Gallehus) about sixteen hundred years ago.

8)
Horn of Gallehus
```
S                       O     V
ek HlewagastiR HoltijaR horna tawido
I  Hlewagastir of Holt  horn  made
```
'I, Hlewagastir of Holt, made the horn.'

Another type of evidence for an earlier SOV order is found in morphological fusion (see section 3.1). Since fusion depends on frequently occurring syntactic patterns, it can sometimes serve as an indicator of earlier syntax. The OV compound, very common in Old English (as well as in Modern English), likely reflects an earlier stage of OV word order (see table 7.38).

Table 7.38 **Old English compounds with OV structure**		
manslæht	'man' + 'strike'	'manslaughter, murder'
æppelbǣre	'apple' + 'bear'	'apple-bearing'

If the earliest Germanic was SOV and Modern English is firmly SVO, then Old English represents a transitional syntactic type. In developing from SOV syntax to SVO syntax, languages seem to follow similar pathways. For example, Modern German, which developed from the same Germanic SOV source as English, shares two of Old English's distinguishing characteristics. First, the verb is typically placed in the second position of the sentence in main clauses, preceded by the subject or some other element (such as an adverb). Secondly, the SOV order is employed for embedded clauses.

9)
Modern German word order
a. Verb in second position in unembedded clauses
(Compare the Old English sentences in *4)*.)

```
            V    S  O
Gestern   hatte ich keine Zeit.
yesterday had   I   no   time
```
'I had no time yesterday'

b. SOV in embedded clauses
(Compare the Old English sentences in *7)*.)

```
        S    O       V
Als   er den Mann sah ...
when  he the man   saw
```
'When he saw the man ...'

The change from SOV to SVO is not restricted to English and other Germanic languages. The same change is evident, for example, in completely unrelated languages such as those of the Bantu family of Africa. Since linguists are still not sure why languages change from one syntactic type to another, the causes of such change will undoubtedly remain an important area of investigation, especially since the relative order of verb and object (OV versus VO) has been closely linked with other word order patterns (see chapter 8).

4.2   Inversion in the history of English

In Old and Middle English the inversion transformation (see chapter 5) involved in the formation of *yes-no* questions could apply to all verbs, not just auxiliaries, yielding forms that would be unacceptable in Modern English.

> **10)**
> Speak they the truth?

During the sixteenth and seventeenth centuries, the Inversion rule was changed to apply solely to auxiliary verbs.

> **11)**
> *Inversion   (old form)*
> The V moves to the left of the subject
> They speak → Speak they?
> They can speak → Can they speak?
>
> *Inversion   (new form)*
> The Aux moves to the left of subject
> They speak → *Speak they?
> They can speak → Can they speak?

With this change, structures such as *Speak they the truth?* were no longer possible. The corresponding question came to be formed with the auxiliary *do* as in *Do they speak the truth?*[5]

5   Lexical and semantic change

Another obvious type of language change involves modifications to the lexicon. Since we have already dealt with some changes relating to derivational and inflectional morphology in section 3, the main focus here will be on lexical change involving entire words. Simply stated, there are two possible types of lexical change, addition and loss. The addition or loss of words often reflects cultural changes that introduce novel objects and notions, and that eliminate outmoded ones.

5.1   Addition of lexical items

Addition is frequently the result of technological innovations or contact with other cultures. Such developments result in **lexical gaps** that can be filled by adding new words to the lexicon. New words are added either through the word formation processes available to the language or through borrowing.

Word formation

The most important word formation processes are compounding and derivation, although other types including conversion, blends, backformation, clipping, and acronyms (see chapter 4) can play a significant role.

Compounding and derivation have always been available to English speakers for the creation of new words. In fact, much of the compounding and derivation in Old English seems very familiar (see table 7.39).

Table 7.39 Compounding and derivation in Old English			
Noun compounds			
N + N	sunbēam	'sunbeam'	
A + N	middelniht	'midnight'	
Adjective compounds			
N + A	blōdrēad	'blood-red'	
A + A	dēadboren	'stillborn'	
Derived nouns			
[bæc]$_v$ ere	→	bæcere	'baker'
[frēond]$_N$ + scipe	→	frēondscipe	'friendship'
Derived adjectives			
[wundor]$_N$ + full	→	wundorfull	'wonderful'
[cild]$_N$ + isc	→	cildisc	'childish'

Just as speakers of Modern English can use compounding and derivational rules to create new words (e.g., the N + N compound *airhead*) so could Old English speakers create new words such as the poetic N + N compound *hwælweg*, literally 'whale' + 'path' to mean 'sea'.

Note however that even though many Old English compounding and derivational patterns have been maintained in Modern English, words that were acceptable in Old English are not necessarily still in use in Modern English, even though many of them are quite understandable (see table 7.40).

However, not all word formation processes available to Modern English speakers were found in Old English. For example, conversion (as in Modern English [summer]$_N$ → [summer]$_v$) was not possible in Old English. In fact, conversion is typically not available to (synthetic) inflectional languages such as Old English since change in a word category in such languages is usually indicated morphologically and conversion, by definition, does not involve the use of affixes.

Table 7.40 Old English compound and derived forms that are no longer used		
Noun compounds		
N + N	bōccræft ('book' + 'craft')	'literature' (compare *witchcraft*)
A + N	dimhūs ('dim' + 'house')	'prison'
Adjective compounds		
N + A	ælfscīene ('elf' + 'beautiful')	'beautiful as a fairy'
A + A	eallgōd ('all' + 'good')	'perfectly good'
Derived nouns		
[sēam]$_v$ + ere → sēamere		'tailor' (compare *seamster, seamstress*)
[man]$_n$ + scipe → manscipe		'humanity' (compare 'friendship')
Derived adjectives		
[word]$_n$ + full → wordfull		'wordy' (compare *wonderful*)
[heofon]$_n$ + isc → heofonisc		'heavenly' (compare *childish*)

Borrowing

As discussed in section 1.2, language contact over time can result in an important source of new words, borrowing. Depending on the cultural relationship holding between languages, three types of influence of one language on the other are traditionally identified: **substratum**, **adstratum**, and **superstratum** influence.

Substratum influence is the effect of a politically or culturally non-dominant language on a dominant language in the area. Both Canadian and American English and Canadian French, for instance, have borrowed vocabulary items from Amerindian languages (see examples in section 1.2). From a much earlier period in the history of English, the influence of a Celtic substratum is also evident, particularly in place names such as *Thames*, *London*, and *Dover*. Substratum influence does not usually have a major impact on the lexicon of the borrowing language. Borrowed words are usually restricted to place names and unfamiliar items or concepts. This situation reflects the fact that it is usually the speakers of the substratum language who inhabited the area first.

Superstratum influence is the effect of a politically or culturally dominant language on another language or languages in the area. For example, the Athapaskan language Gwich'in (Loucheux) (spoken in Canada's Northwest Territories), has borrowed a number of governmental terms and expressions from English, including *bureaucratic, constituents, program, business, development,* and *political*.

In the case of English, Norman-French had a superstratum influence. The major impact of French on the vocabulary of English is related to a historical event—the conquest of England by French-speaking Normans in 1066. As the conquerors and their descendants gradually learned English over the next decades, they retained French terms for political, judicial, and cultural notions (see table 7.41). These words were in turn borrowed by native English speakers who, in trying to gain a place in the upper middle class, were eager to imitate the speech of their social superiors. Not surprisingly, borrowing was especially heavy in the vocabulary areas pertaining to officialdom: government, the judiciary, and religion. Other areas of heavy borrowing include science, culture, and warfare.

Table 7.41	Some French loan words in English
Government	tax, revenue, government, royal, state, parliament, authority, prince, duke, slave, peasant
Religion	prayer, sermon, religion, chaplain, friar
Judiciary	judge, defendant, jury, evidence, jail, verdict, crime
Science	medicine, physician
Culture	art, sculpture, fashion, satin, fur, ruby
Warfare	army, navy, battle, soldier, enemy, captain

In some cases, French loan words were used in conjunction with native English words to convey distinctions of various sorts. For a minor crime, for example, the English word *theft* was employed, but for a more serious breach of the law the French word *larceny* was used. The English also kept their own words for domesticated animals, but adopted the French words for the meat from those creatures (see table 7.42).

Table 7.42 French loan words used in conjunction with native English words

English origin	French origin
cow	beef
calf	veal
sheep	mutton
pig	pork

Adstratum influence refers to the situation where two languages are in contact and neither one is clearly politically or culturally dominant. In a city such as Montreal with its large number of bilingual speakers, English and French inevitably influence each other (see table 7.43).

Table 7.43 French influence on Montreal English

Montreal English	
subvention	'subsidy'
metro	'subway'
autoroute	'highway'

Earlier in the history of English, when the Scandinavians settled part of England beginning in 800 AD, there was substantial contact between the speakers of English and Scandinavian resulting in an adstratum relationship. As evident in the examples in tables 7.43 and 7.44, adstratum contact usually results in the borrowing of common, everyday words. In fact, without consulting a dictionary, most English speakers could not distinguish between borrowings from Scandinavian and native English words.

Table 7.44 Some loan words from Scandinavian

anger, cake, call, egg, fellow, gear, get, hit, husband, low, lump, raise, root, score, seat, skill, skin, take, their, they, thrust, ugly, window, wing

Borrowed words from many other languages attest to various types of cultural contact and serve often to fill the lexical gaps such contact inevitably brings (see table 7.45).

Table 7.45	Some lexical borrowings into English
Italian	motto, artichoke, balcony, casino, mafia, malaria
Spanish	comrade, tornado, cannibal, mosquito, banana, guitar, vigilante, marijuana
German	poodle, kindergarten, seminar, noodle, pretzel
Dutch	sloop, cole slaw, smuggle, gin, cookie, boom
Slavic languages	czar, tundra, polka, intelligentsia, robot
Amerindian languages	toboggan, opposum, wigwam, chipmunk, Ottawa, Toronto
Hindi	thug, punch (drink), shampoo, chintz

Although borrowing has been a very rich source of new words in English, it is noteworthy that loan words are least common among the most frequently used vocabulary items. This reflects a general tendency for highly frequent words to be relatively resistant to loss or substitution (see table 7.46).

Table 7.46	Origin of the 5000 most frequent words in English			
Degree of frequency	**Source language (%)**			
	English	*French*	*Latin*	*Other*
First 1000	83	11	2	4
Second 1000	34	46	11	9
Third 1000	29	46	14	11
Fourth 1000	27	45	17	11
Fifth 1000	27	47	17	9

5.2   Loss of lexical items

Just as words can be added to the lexicon, they can also be lost. Changes in society play an important role in the loss of words since words are often lost because the object or notion they refer to has become obsolete (see table 7.47).

Table 7.47	Some Old English words lost through cultural change
dolgbōt	'compensation for wounding'
þeox	'hunting spear'
eafor	'tenant obligation to the king to convey goods'
flȳtme	'a blood letting instrument'

5.3   Semantic change

Although changes in word meaning take place continually in all languages, words rarely jump from one meaning to an unrelated one. Typically, the changes are step by step and involve one of the following phenomena.

Semantic broadening is the process in which the meaning of a word becomes more general or more inclusive than its historically earlier form (see table 7.48).

Table 7.48	Semantic broadening	
Word	Old meaning	New meaning
bird	'small fowl'	'any winged creature'
barn	'place to store barley'	'farm building for storage and shelter'
aunt	'father's sister'	'father or mother's sister'

Semantic narrowing is the process in which the meaning of a word becomes less general or less inclusive than its historically earlier meaning (see table 7.49).

Table 7.49	Semantic narrowing	
Word	Old meaning	New meaning
hound	'any dog'	'a hunting breed'
meat	'any type of food'	'flesh of an animal'
fowl	'any bird'	'a domesticated bird'
disease	'any unfavourable state'	'an illness'

In **amelioration** the meaning of a word becomes more positive or favourable. The opposite change, **pejoration**, also occurs (see tables 7.50 and 7.51).

Table 7.50	Amelioration	
Word	Old meaning	New meaning
pretty	'tricky, sly, cunning'	'attractive'
knight	'boy'	'a special title or position'

Table 7.51	Pejoration	
Word	Old meaning	New meaning
silly	'happy, prosperous'	'foolish'
wench	'girl'	'wanton woman, prostitute'

Given the propensity of human beings to exaggerate, it is not surprising that the **weakening** of meaning frequently occurs. For example, our word *soon* used to mean 'immediately' but now simply means 'in the near future'. Other examples are included in table 7.52.

Table 7.52	Weakening	
Word	Old meaning	New meaning
wreak	'avenge, punish'	'to cause, inflict'
quell	'kill, murder'	'to put down, pacify'

Semantic shift is a process in which a word loses its former meaning and takes on a new, but often related, meaning (see table 7.53).

Table 7.53	Semantic shift	
Word	**Old meaning**	**New meaning**
immoral	'not customary'	'unethical'
bead	'prayer'	'prayer bead, bead'

Sometimes a series of semantic shifts occurs over an extended period of time, resulting in a meaning that is completely unrelated to the original sense of a word. The word *hearse*, for example, originally referred to a triangular harrow. Later, it denoted a triangular frame for church candles and later still was used to refer to the device that held candles over a coffin. In a subsequent shift it came to refer to the framework on which curtains were hung over a coffin or tomb. Still later, *hearse* was used to refer to the coffin itself before finally taking on its current sense of the vehicle used to transport a coffin.

One of the most striking types of semantic change is triggered by **metaphor**, a figure of speech based on a perceived similarity between distinct objects or actions. (See chapter 6 for a discussion of metaphor.) Metaphorical change usually involves a word with a concrete meaning taking on a more abstract sense, although the word's original meaning is not lost. The meanings of many English words have been extended through metaphor (see table 7.54).

Table 7.54	Some examples of metaphor in English
Word	**Metaphorical meaning**
grasp	'understand'
yarn	'story'
high	'on drugs'

6 The spread of change

Up to this point, we have been concerned with the causes and description of linguistic change. Still to be dealt with is the question of how linguistic innovations spread. This section focuses on two types of spread, one involving the way in which an innovation is extended through the vocabulary of a language and the other the way in which it spreads through the population.

6.1 Diffusion through the language

Some linguistic change first manifests itself in a few words and then gradually spreads through the vocabulary of the language. This type of change is called **lexical diffusion**. A well-attested example in English involves an ongoing change in the stress pattern of words such as *convert*, which can be used as either a noun or a verb. Although the stress originally fell on the second syllable regardless of lexical category, in the latter half of the sixteenth century three such words, *rebel*, *outlaw*, and *record*, came to be pronounced with the stress on the first syllable when used as nouns. As the figure 7.11 illustrates, this stress shift was extended to an increasing number of words over the next decades.

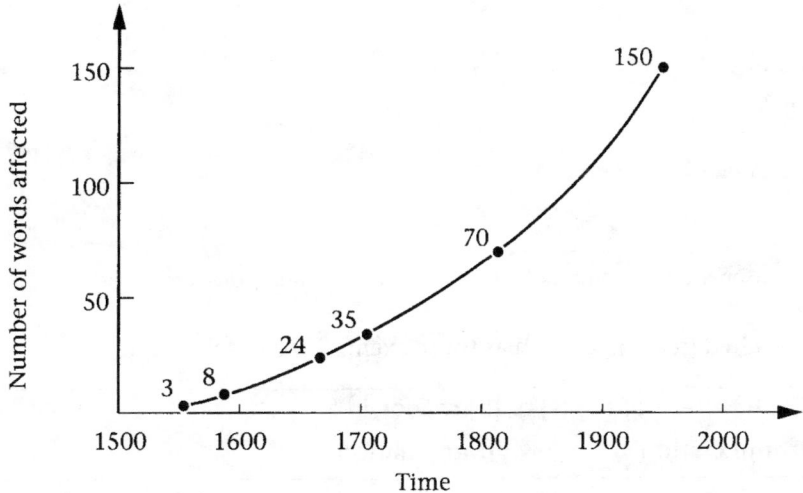

Figure 7.11 Diffusion of stress shift in English

This change has still not diffused through the entire vocabulary of English. There are about a thousand nouns of the relevant sort that still place the stress on the second syllable (e.g., *report*, *mistake*, and *support*). Table 7.55 illustrates the spread of this change to date.

Table 7.55 Stress shift in English (nouns)			
Before the 16th century	**During the 16th century**	**During the 18th century**	**Today**
rebél	rébel	rébel	rébel
affíx	affíx	áffix	áffix
recéss	recéss	recéss	récess
mistáke	mistáke	mistáke	mistáke

This ongoing change can be observed in progress today. The noun *address*, for example, is pronounced by many people with stress on the first syllable as [ǽdrɛs], although the older pronunciation [ədrés] is still heard. Some speakers alternate between the two pronunciations. This change may continue to work its way through the language until all nouns in the class we have been considering are stressed on the first syllable.

The changes discussed in the section on analogy also spread word by word. For example, the transition of strong (irregular) verbs (the *sing/sang/sung* type) to the weak verb class (regular verbs with past tense -*ed*) is an ongoing change. Both strong and weak past tense forms of original strong verbs such as *dive* and *shine* are heard in current English: *dove/dived* and *shone/shined*.

However, not all linguistic change involves gradual diffusion through the vocabulary of a language. Sound changes typically affect all instances of the segment(s) involved. For example, in some dialects of Spanish (such as Cuban) the consonantal weakening of [s] to [h] in syllable-final position affects all instances of *s* in those positions. The relevant rule can be stated as in figure 7.12.

s → h / V ___

Figure 7.12 Consonant weakening of [s] to [h] in certain Spanish dialects

This rule has resulted in changes such as those exemplified in table 7.56.

Table 7.56	The effects of the [s] to [h] change in Spanish dialects	
Standard pronunciation	**New pronunciation**	
[felismente]	[felihmente]	'happily'
[estilo]	[ehtilo]	'type'
[espaɲa]	[ehpaɲa]	'Spain'

This change is entirely regular, affecting all instances of syllable final [s] in the speech of individuals who adopt it.

Accordingly, two types of language change can be identified. One, exemplified by the stress shifts in bisyllabic English nouns of the type we have discussed, affects individual words one at a time and gradually spreads through the vocabulary of the language. The other, exemplified by the consonant weakening of syllable final [s] to [h] in some dialects of Spanish, involves an across-the-board change that applies without exception to all words.

6.2   Spread through the population

For a language change to take place, the particular innovation must be accepted by the linguistic community as a whole. For example, although children acquiring English typically form the past tense of *go* as *goed* instead of *went*, *goed* has never received widespread acceptance. Doubtless the verb form in *he throve on fame* would be equally unacceptable to most speakers today. In earlier English, however, *throve* was the past tense form of *thrive* (compare *drive/drove*). At some point in the past then, the novel form *thrived* did receive general acceptance.

Just as change sometimes begins with a small number of words, often effects of a change only appear first in the speech of a small number of people. Social pressures often play an important role in whether a particular innovation will spread through the entire linguistic community. Since speakers can consciously or subconsciously alter the way they speak to approximate what they perceive to be a more prestigious or socially acceptable variety of speech, once a change has taken hold in the speech of a high prestige group it may gradually spread to other speakers and ultimately affect the entire linguistic community.

There have been numerous examples of this in the history of English, notably the loss of postvocalic [r] along the east coast of the United States. This change, which led to an 'r-less' pronunciation of words such as *far* as [faː], originated in parts of England in the seventeenth and eighteenth centuries. At that time, postvocalic [r] was still pronounced throughout English-speaking settlements in North America. Two factors accounted for its loss in parts of this continent. First, the children of the New England gentry picked up the new pronunciation in British schools and subsequently brought it back to the colony. Second, the speech of newly arrived immigrants, including colonial administrators and church officials who enjoyed high social status in the colony, typically lacked the postvocalic [r]. As a result, the innovation was widely imitated and ultimately spread along much of the east coast and into the south.

Social pressures were also involved in limiting the spread of this innovation. It did not penetrate Pennsylvania or the other Midland states since the most prestigious group of settlers there were Quakers from northern England, an area which retained the postvocalic [r]. Similarly, in Canada, the influence of Scottish and Irish settlers, whose dialects did not undergo the change in question, helped ensure the survival of postvocalic [r] in all but a few areas where contact with New England was strongest, most notably Lunenburg County in Nova Scotia and Grand Manan Island in New Brunswick. More recently the 'r-less' pronunciation has become stigmatized, even in areas where it was previously firmly entrenched, and we now see a trend to restoration of [r] in environments where it had been deleted.

7   Language reconstruction

When we compare the vocabulary items of various languages, we cannot help but notice the strong resemblance certain words bear to each other. By systematically comparing languages, we can establish whether two or more languages descended from a common parent and are therefore **genetically related** (see chapter 8). The **comparative method** refers to the procedure of reconstructing earlier forms on the basis of a comparison of later forms. By means of such comparative reconstruction we can reconstruct properties of the parent language with a great degree of certainty.

7.1   Comparative reconstruction

The most reliable sign of family relationships is the existence of **systematic phonetic correspondences** in the vocabulary items of different languages. Many such correspondences can be found in the sample of vocabulary items in table 7.57 from English, Dutch, German, Danish, and Swedish, all of which are members of the Germanic family of languages.

Table 7.57	Some Germanic cognates			
English	**Dutch**	**German**	**Danish**	**Swedish**
man	man	Mann	mand	man
hand	hand	Hand	hånd	hand
foot	voet	Fuß (β=[s])	fod	fot
bring	brengen	bringen	bringe	bringa
summer	zomer	Sommer	sommer	sommar

Since the relationship between the phonological form and meaning of a word is mostly arbitrary, the existence of systematic phonetic correspondences in the forms of two or more languages must point toward a common source. Conversely, where languages are not related, their vocabulary items fail to show systematic similarities. This can be seen by comparing words from Turkish, which is not related to the Germanic languages, with their counterparts in the languages cited in table 7.58.

Table 7.58	Some words in Turkish, a non-Germanic language (phonemic transcription)
adam	'man'
el	'hand'
ajak	'foot'
getir	'bring'
jaz	'summer'

Words that have descended from a common source (as shown by systematic phonetic correspondences and, usually, semantic similarities) are called **cognates**. Cognates are not always as obvious as the Germanic examples in table 7.57. Where languages from the same family are only distantly related, the systematic correspondences may be considerably less striking. This is exemplified in the data in table 7.59 from English, Russian, and Hindi, all of which are distantly related to each other. Forms from the unrelated Turkish are included to emphasize the similarities among the first three languages.

Table 7.59	Some distantly related cognates compared to non-related Turkish		
English	**Russian**	**Hindi**	**Turkish (phonemic transcription)**
two	dva	dō	iki
three	tri	tīn	ytʃ
brother	brat	bhāī	kardeʃ
nose	nos	na~kh	burun

Once the existence of a relationship between two or more languages has been established, an attempt can be made to reconstruct the common source. This reconstructed language, or **proto-language**, is made up of **proto-forms**, which are written with a preceding * (e.g., *hand*) to indicate their hypothetical character as reconstructions of earlier forms that have not been recorded or are not directly observable.

7.2   Techniques of reconstruction

Reconstruction can be undertaken with some confidence because (as discussed in the previous sections) the processes underlying language change are systematic. Once the processes are uncovered by linguists, they can be reversed, allowing us to infer earlier forms of the language. Although it is possible to reconstruct all components of a proto-language (its phonology, morphology, syntax, lexicon, and semantics), we will focus in the following on phonological reconstruction, the area in which linguists have made the most progress.

Reconstruction strategies

Reconstruction of a proto-form makes use of two general strategies. The most important one is the **phonetic plausibility strategy**, which requires that any changes posited to account for differences between the proto-forms and later forms must be phonetically plausible. Secondarily, the **majority rules strategy** stipulates that if no phonetically plausible change can account for the observed differences, then the segment found in the majority of cognates should be assumed. It is important to note that the first strategy always takes precedence over the second; the second strategy is a last resort.

Consider the cognates in table 7.60 (somewhat simplified) from members of the Romance family.

Table 7.60	Romance cognates			
French	**Italian**	**Rumanian**	**Spanish**	
si	si	ʃi	si	'yes'

The data exemplify a correspondence between [s] and [ʃ] before the vowel [i]. To account for this, we could assume either that Rumanian underwent a change that converted [s] to [ʃ] before [i] or that the other three languages underwent a change converting [ʃ] to [s] before [i] as shown in figure 7.13.

Hypothesis A
Proto-form   *si
Sound change (Rumanian only)   *s > ʃ / ___ i

Hypothesis B
Proto-form   *ʃi
Sound change (French, Italian, and Spanish)   *ʃ > s / ___ i

Figure 7.13 Romance cognates

Both reconstruction strategies favour hypothesis A. Most importantly, the phonetic change needed to account for the Rumanian pronunciation involves palatalization before [i]. Since palatalization in this context is a very common phenomenon in human language, it is reasonable to assume that it occurred in Rumanian. It would be much more difficult to argue that the proto-language contained [ʃ] before [i] and that three languages underwent the change posited by Hypothesis B since depalatalization before [i] would be an unusual phonetic process. (The reconstructed *s posited in hypothesis A is also compatible with the majority rules strategy since three of the four languages in the data have [s] before [i].)

Reconstruction and the catalogue of sound changes

Although there are factors that can confound our attempt to determine the relative plausibility of various sound changes, the changes listed in the catalogue in table 7.3 can generally be considered highly plausible. Table 7.61 lists some plausible versus less plausible or even implausible changes based on that catalogue.

Table 7.61	Different rules in terms of their plausibility based on the catalogue
Rule	**Name of sound change in catalogue**
High probability	
t > tʃ / __ i	palatalization
n > m / __ b	assimilation (place of articulation)
t > d / V __ V	voicing
k > Ø / V __ st	consonant deletion
Low probability	
tʃ > t / __ i	(does not correspond to any listed change)
m > n / __ b	(does not correspond to any listed change)
d > t / V __ V	(does not correspond to any listed change)
Ø > k / V __ st	(does not correspond to any listed change)

Reconstructing Proto-Romance

Consider now the slightly more complex example in table 7.62 involving data from several languages of the Romance family.

Table 7.62	Some Romance cognates				
Spanish	**Sardinian**	**French**	**Portuguese**	**Rumanian**	**Original meaning**
riba [β]	ripa	rive [ʁiv]	riba	rîpă	'embankment'
amiga [ɣ]	amica	amie [ami]	amiga	–	'female friend'
copa	cuppa	coupe [kup]	copa	cupă	'cup, goblet'
gota	gutta	goutte [gut]	gota	gută	'drop'

(*Note*: Orthographic *c* represents [k] in all the above examples. Rumanian ă and î represent the central vowels [ə] and [ɨ], respectively. [β] is a voiced bilabial fricative and [ɣ] a voiced velar fricative. Some details of vowel quality have been ignored.)

Our goal here is to reconstruct the proto-forms for these words in Proto-Romance, the parent language of the Modern Romance languages, which stands very close to Latin.

Let us first consider the reconstruction of the Proto-Romance form for 'embankment'. Since the first two segments are the same in all the cognate languages, we can reconstruct

Proto-Romance *r and *i on the basis of the majority rules strategy. In the case of the second consonant, however, there are differences between the cognates (see table 7.63).

Table 7.63	Systematic correspondences in the cognates for 'embankment'			
Spanish	**Sardinian**	**French**	**Portuguese**	**Rumanian**
-β-	-p-	-v	-b-	-p-

It is most important that we first think in terms of phonetic plausibility. In the absence of evidence to the contrary, we will assume that one of the segments found in the cognates ([p], [b], [v], or [β]) should be reconstructed for Proto-Romance. Logically possible changes ranked with respect to their phonetic plausibility are found in table 7.64.

Table 7.64	Changes based on phonetic plausibility	
Change in V__V	**Name of change based on catalogue**	**Phonetic plausibility**
p > b	voicing	high
p > v	voicing (p > b) and frication (b > v)	high
p > β	voicing (p > b) and frication (b > β)	high
b > p	–	low
β > p	– low	
v > p	–	low

In terms of plausibility, the only possible reconstruction for Proto-Romance is *p. Proto-Romance *p undergoes no change in Sardinian and Rumanian, but in Portuguese it underwent intervocalic voicing and in Spanish it underwent both voicing and frication (that is, weakening) (see table 7.65). (We assume that voicing preceded frication since Portuguese shows voicing but no frication.) If we assume that the final vowel of the proto-form was still present in French when the consonant changes took place, we can conclude that voicing and frication occurred in this language as well. (In its written form, *rive* retains a sign of the earlier reduced vowel [ə].) These changes are phonetically plausible and thus expected.

Table 7.65	Summary of the changes affecting Proto-Romance *p
*p > p /V__V	no change in Sardinian or Rumanian
*p > b /V__V	voicing in Portuguese
*p > b > β /V__V	voicing and frication in Spanish
*p > b > v /V__V	voicing and frication in French

Turning now to the final vowel, we note that three languages have full vowels, Rumanian has [ə], and French has no vowel (see table 7.66). Since vowel reduction and apocope are identified as phonetically plausible changes in the catalogue, it is appropriate to posit a full vowel for the proto-language. Furthermore, since the three languages with a full vowel all have [a] we can posit this vowel on the basis of the majority rules strategy. Accordingly, the reconstructed proto-form is *ripa*.

Table 7.66	Summary of the changes affecting Proto-Romance *a	
Language	**Change (word final)**	**Name of change(s)**
Rumanian	*a > ə	vowel reduction
French	*a > ə > Ø	vowel reduction and deletion

We can now outline the evolution of this word in French, which has the most compli-cated development of the six languages (see table 7.67).

Table 7.67	Evolution of French *rive* from *ripa	
Change	***ripa**	**Name of change**
p > b / V__V	riba	voicing
b > v / V __ V	riva	frication
a > ə / __ #	rivə	vowel reduction
ə > Ø / __ #	riv	apocope

In the case of the cognates for 'female friend' (the second row of table 7.62), the first three segments are the same in all the languages in the data. According to the majority rules strategy we can reconstruct the first three segments as *ami-. In the reconstruction of the sec-ond consonant, however, we must appeal to our strategy of phonetic plausibility (see table 7.68).

Table 7.68	Systematic correspondences in the second consonant of the cognates for 'female friend'			
Spanish	**Sardinian**	**French**	**Portuguese**	**Rumanian**
-ɣ-	-k-	-Ø	-g-	–

Once again, since intervocalic voicing, frication, and deletion are phonetically plausible changes, it is most appropriate to posit *k for the proto-form (see table 7.69).

Table 7.69	Summary of the changes affecting Proto-Romance *k	
Language	**Change (in V_V)**	**Name of change(s)**
Portuguese	*k > g	voicing
Spanish	*k > g > ɣ	voicing and frication
French	*k > g > ɣ > Ø	voicing, frication, and deletion

In the case of the final vowel, we have the same situation we had in the previous form. The full vowel is found in Spanish, Sardinian, and Portuguese but there is no vowel in French. We can therefore assume the full vowel *a for the proto-form, with subsequent vowel reduction and apocope in French. Consequently, we arrive at the proto-form *amika.

Finally, applying the same procedure to the cognates in the final two rows of table 7.62 yields the proto-forms **kuppa* 'cup' and **gutta* 'drop'. All the languages in the data retain the initial consonant of both proto-forms. The vowel **u* is reconstructed on the basis of the majority rules strategy, since we have no phonetic grounds for choosing either [u] or [o] as the older vowel. The systematic correspondences involving the intervocalic consonants are given in table 7.70.

Table 7.70	Systematic correspondences of the medial consonants of **kuppa* and **gutta*			
Spanish	**Sardinian**	**French**	**Portuguese**	**Rumanian**
-p-	-pp-	-p	-p-	-p-
-t-	-tt-	-t	-t-	-t-

Regardless of whether we are dealing with original **pp* or **tt*, the same pattern is evident in the case of both geminate types. There is a geminate stop consonant in Sardinian and a single consonant in Spanish, French, Portuguese, and Rumanian. Since degemination is an expected sound change (see the catalogue in table 7.3), we assume that the proto-forms contained geminate consonants which underwent degemination except in Sardinian. This is an example of a case where the phonetic plausibility strategy overrules the majority rules strategy (since four of the five languages have [p]/[t] whereas only one language has [pp]/[tt]). As far as the final vowels are concerned, the same pattern found in the previous examples is once again evident. Proto-Romance **a* was retained in Spanish, Sardinian, and Portuguese, reduced to [ə] in Rumanian, and deleted in French (see table 7.66).

Of the languages exemplified here, Sardinian is considered the most conservative since it has retained more of the earlier consonants and vowels. (In fact, the Sardinian words in the examples happen to be identical with the proto-forms, but this degree of resemblance would not be maintained in a broader range of data.) In the case of the other Romance languages and changes we have discussed, the most to least conservative are: Portuguese (degemination and voicing) and Rumanian (degemination and vowel reduction); Spanish (degemination, voicing, and frication); and French (degemination, voicing, frication, consonant deletion, vowel reduction, and apocope).

Although there is no reason to expect Proto-Romance to be identical with Classical Latin, close similarity is expected.[6] Accordingly, the fact that our reconstructions are so close to the Latin words gives us confidence in our methods of reconstruction (see table 7.71).

Table 7.71	Comparison of Latin and Proto-Romance forms
Latin	**Proto-Romance form**
rīpa	**ripa*
amīca (c = [k])	**amika*
cuppa	**kuppa*
gutta	**gutta*

Notice that it is sometimes not possible to reconstruct all the characteristics of the proto-language. For example, on the basis of our data we were not able to reconstruct vowel length (Latin had a distinction between long and short vowels) since there was no evidence of this characteristic in the cognate forms.

It is also worth noting that we are not always so fortunate as to have written records of a language we expect to be very close to our reconstructed language. In the case of the Germanic languages, for example, there is no ancient written language equivalent to Latin. We must rely completely on our reconstruction of Proto-Germanic to determine the properties of the language from which the modern-day Germanic languages descended. Furthermore, for many languages of the world we have no written historical records at all and for other languages, such as the Amerindian languages of North America, it is only very recently that we have written records.

In summary, when the forms of two or more languages appear to be related, we can, through a consideration of systematic phonetic correspondences among cognates, reconstruct the common form from which all the forms can be derived by means of phonetically plausible sound changes. Genetically related lexical forms of different languages are called cognates, while the reconstructed forms are proto-forms, and a reconstructed language, a proto-language.

7.3   Internal reconstruction

Sometimes it is possible to reconstruct the earlier form of a language even without reference to comparative data. This technique, known as **internal reconstruction**, relies on the analysis of morphophonemic variation within a single language. The key point is that the sound changes that create allomorphic and allophonic variation can be identified and then used to infer an earlier form of the morpheme. The data in table 7.72 are from French; because of borrowing, English exhibits a parallel set of contrasts involving [k] and [ʃ].

Table 7.72	[k] / [s] correspondence in French		
maʒik	'magic'	maʒis-jɛ̃	'magician'
lɔʒik	'logic'	lɔʒis-jɛ̃	'logician'
myzik	'music'	myzis-jɛ̃	'musician'

The root morpheme in each row exhibits two forms, one ending in [k], the other ending in [s]. The same methods and principles used in comparative reconstruction can be applied here to reconstruct the historically earlier form of the root morpheme. If a root ending in *s is posited, no phonetically plausible change can account for the [k] in the left-hand column. By contrast, if a root-final *k is posited, the [s] can be accounted for by assuming that the *k was fronted under the influence of the high front vowel of the suffix (palatalization) and became an affricate [ts] (affrication) which was later simplified to a fricative [s] (deaffrication). All of these changes are phonetically plausible and listed in the catalogue in table 7.3. Accordingly, internal reconstruction indicates that at an earlier point in the development of French, the root morphemes in table 7.72 contained the consonant *k.

7.4   The discovery of Indo-European

The late eighteenth-century discovery that Sanskrit (an ancient language of India) was related to Latin, Greek, Germanic, and Celtic revolutionized European linguistic studies. Sir

William Jones, a British judge and scholar working in India, summed up the nature and implications of the findings in his 1786 address to the Royal Asiatic Society, a part of which follows:

> The Sanskrit language, whatever be its antiquity, is of a wonderful structure; more perfect than the Greek, more copious [having more cases] than the Latin, and more exquisitely refined than either, yet bearing to both of them a stronger affinity, both in the roots of the verbs and in the forms of the grammar, than could possibly have been produced by accident; so strong indeed, that no philologer could examine them all three, without believing them to have sprung from some common source, which, perhaps, no longer exists; there is a similar reason ... for supposing that both the Gothic and the Celtic ... had the same origin with the Sanskrit; and the old Persian might be added to the same family ...

This discovery led to several decades of intensive historical-comparative work and to important advances in historical linguistics during the nineteenth century. By studying phonetic correspondences from an ever-increasing number of languages, linguists eventually ascertained that most of the languages of Europe, Persia (Iran) and the northern part of India belong to a single family, now called Indo-European. By applying the techniques of the comparative method, they began reconstructing the grammar of the proto-language from which these languages evolved, **Proto-Indo-European (PIE)**.

A number of individuals advanced this research. In 1814, the Danish linguist Rasmus Rask carefully documented the relationships among cognates in a number of Indo-European languages, and at the same time established the methods that would govern the emerging science of historical-comparative linguistics. He wrote:

> When agreement is found in [the most essential] words in two languages, and so frequently that rules may be drawn up for the shift in letters [sounds] from one to the other, then there is a fundamental relationship between the two languages; especially when similarities in the inflectional system and in the general make-up of the languages correspond with them.

Rask worked without access to Sanskrit. The first comparative linguistic analysis of Sanskrit, Greek, Persian and the Germanic languages was done by the German scholar Franz Bopp in 1816. In 1822 another German, Jakob Grimm, extended Rask's observations and became the first person to explain the relationships among the cognates noted by Rask in terms of a **sound shift,** the systematic modification of a series of phonemes. Some of the correspondences on which he based his work are given in table 7.73.

Table 7.73	Some Indo-European phonetic correspondences	
Greek	**Latin**	**English**
patér	pater	father
treîs	trēs	three
hekatón	centum	hundred

The crucial observation is that where English has [f], [θ], and [h] (here, in word-initial position), Greek and Latin have [p], [t] and [k]. Grimm tabulated a series of consonant shifts for Proto-Germanic which differentiated it from other Indo-European languages. **Grimm's**

Law is the name given to the consonant shifts that took place between Proto-Indo-European and Proto-Germanic (see table 7.74).

Table 7.74	The sound shifts underlying Grimm's Law								
Proto-Indo-European p	t	k	b	d	g	bh	dh	gh
Germanic	f	θ	x	p	t	k	b	d	g

Some additional examples of the relationships captured by these shifts are below in table 7.75. The Proto-Indo-European consonants were either maintained in Sanskrit, Greek, and Latin or in some cases underwent changes different from those found in Germanic.

Table 7.75	Some examples of the consonant shifts underlying Grimm's Law			
Shift in Germanic	**Sanskrit**	**Greek**	**Latin**	**English**
p > f	pād-	pod-	ped-	foot
t > θ	tanu-	tanaós	tenuis	thin
k > x	çatam	hekatón	centum	hundred
b > p	–	–	lūbricus	slippery
d > t	daça	déka	decem	ten
g > k	ajras	agrós	ager	acre
bh > b	bhrātā	phrátēr	fráter	brother
dh > d	vidhavā	ēítheos	vidua	widow
gh > g	hansas	khḗn	(h)ānser	goose

Although there appeared to be exceptions to Grimm's Law, they turned out to be systematic and could be traced to specific environments. For example, voiceless stops were not subject to Grimm's Law when they were immediately preceded by *s* (see table 7.76).

Table 7.76	A systematic exception to Grimm's Law
Original s + voiceless stop	
Latin <u>st</u>āre	English <u>st</u>and [st] (not [sθ])

A particularly important discovery was made by Karl Verner, who traced a group of exceptions to Grimm's Law to the original accentual pattern of Proto-Indo-European. In a generalization that came to be known as **Verner's Law**, he proposed that a voiceless fricative resulting from Grimm's Law underwent voicing if the original Proto-Indo-European accent did not immediately precede it. Since stress came to be fixed on the root syllable in Germanic subsequent to the changes covered by Verner's Law, the original environment was obscured. However, Sanskrit provides very direct evidence for Verner's claim since Sanskrit was very conservative in its maintenance of the original Proto-Indo-European accent. Although the English forms are complicated by other developments, the effects of Verner's Law are apparent in the Gothic examples in table 7.77. In the Gothic word for *brother*, PIE *t* becomes [θ] according to Grimm's Law, whereas in the word for *father* it becomes [ð] in accordance with both Grimm's and Verner's Law.

Table 7.77 Verner's Law

PIE	Sanskrit	Grimm's Law	Verner's Law	Gothic	
*t	bhrā́tā	*t > θ	—	[broːθar]	'brother'
*t	pitā́	*t > θ	θ > ð	[faðar]	'father'

It should also be noted here that borrowing is an important factor that must be taken into consideration when comparative reconstruction is being carried out. For example, English has many words that do not show the effects of Grimm's Law (see table 7.78).

Table 7.78 English words not showing the effects of Grimm's Law

Expected by Grimm's Law	Latin	English
p > f	ped-	pedestrian
t > θ	tenuis	tenuous
k > h	canalis	canal

The apparent failure of Grimm's Law here stems from the fact that the English words were borrowed directly from Latin or French many centuries after the sound shifts described by Grimm's Law had taken place. The task of reconstruction can often be complicated by such borrowings.

Subsequent developments

By the middle of the nineteenth century, the study of language had made great strides, especially in the field of phonetics, which opened the way for the detailed comparison of linguistic forms. One influential hypothesis at that time was that sound laws operated without exception. A group of linguists known as the Neogrammarians adopted this idea and made many important contributions to the fledgling science of linguistics by applying it to new and more complicated data. Although such factors as lexical diffusion and social pressures were more or less ignored by the Neogrammarians, their hypothesis represented an important and daring advance in the scientific study of language.

The nineteenth century also saw major advances in the classification of languages. A German scholar, August Schleicher, developed a classification for the Indo-European languages in the form of a genealogical tree. This type of genetic classification is discussed in much more detail in the chapter on language typology that follows.

Work in comparative reconstruction is far from finished. In particular, linguists are now considering the possibility of superfamilies. One such proposed family is Nostratic, which includes Indo-European, Afro-Asiatic (e.g., Arabic, Hebrew), Altaic (e.g., Japanese, Korean, Turkic), and Uralic (e.g., Finnish, Hungarian). (See chapter 8 for further discussion.) Comparative reconstruction is also playing an important role in determining the genetic relationships of the hundreds of North American indigenous languages, a topic that still remains highly controversial.

7.5   Reconstruction and typology

Since the 1800s when the reconstruction of Proto-Indo-European was carried out, linguists have accumulated vast amounts of information on thousands of languages. This is in part due to the explosion of studies in the field of linguistic typology, which is concerned with the investigation of structural similarities among languages that are not genetically related. Even languages that do not belong to the same family can have striking similarities. For example, in addition to shared word order patterns (see section 2.3 in chapter 8), SOV languages commonly exhibit a strong tendency toward agglutinating morphology (a type of complex affixation; see chapter 8) and vowel harmony. Typological studies play an important role in the linguist's search for universals of language—statements that are true for all languages.

The extensive information on the languages of the world available to modern linguists was, of course, not available at the time the original reconstruction of Proto-Indo-European was undertaken. Modern linguists involved in comparative reconstruction now take a keen interest in typological studies and the role of **typological plausibility** in reconstruction has become an important topic. For example, a linguist would be very reluctant to propose a reconstruction that violated a universal property of language or that had no parallel in any known language.

Some linguists have argued that the traditional reconstruction of the PIE consonant system (given in table 7.79) should be rejected on the basis of typological plausibility.

Table 7.79	The traditional reconstruction of the Proto-Indo-European consonants				
p	t	ḱ	k	kʷ	(voiceless stops)
(b)	d	ǵ	g	gʷ	(voiced stops)
bh	dh	ǵh	gh	gʷh	(voiced aspirated stops)
	s				

(*Note*: ḱ, ǵ, and ǵh are palatal stops and ʷ indicates a labialized consonant.)

This reconstruction is typologically questionable in at least two respects. First, reconstructed forms with PIE *b* are extremely rare, almost as if there were a gap in the labial system. Such a gap is very uncommon in the languages of the world. Typically if there is a missing labial stop, it is the voiceless stop that is missing, not the voiced counterpart. Second, the traditional reconstruction posits a series of voiced aspirated stops but no corresponding series of voiceless aspirated stops, even though some typologists have argued that all languages which have a voiced series also have the voiceless one.

Such facts have led some linguists to propose what they believe is a more typologically plausible reconstruction of Proto-Indo-European involving a voiceless stop series, an ejective series, and a voiced stop series (as well as *s* as in the traditional reconstruction) (see table 7.80).[7]

Table 7.80	A recent reconstruction of the Proto-Indo-European consonants				
p	t	ḱ	k	kʷ	(voiceless stops)
(p')	t'	ḱ'	k'	k'ʷ	(ejectives)
b	d	ǵ	g	gʷ	(voiced stops)
	s				

Not only does this reconstruction avoid the problem with aspirates, it is also common for languages with an ejective series to lack the labial. From this perspective, this reconstruction seems much more plausible than the traditional one.

Both reconstructions have their supporters, and it is difficult to come to a definitive decision on the basis of typological considerations since it is common for a proposed universal to have exceptions. For example, a few languages have been found with the characteristics attributed to Proto-Indo-European by the traditional reconstruction. These languages have labial gaps in the voiced series (e.g., Amerindian languages of the Athapaskan and Caddoan families) and a voiced aspirate series but no voiceless counterpart (Madurese, an Indonesian language). Accordingly, as long as the traditional reconstruction is linguistically possible, it would not seem possible to reject it simply because the phonological system proposed would be a rare one.

Typological plausibility will likely continue to play a secondary role in reconstruction until linguists can draw a clear line between what is linguistically possible and what is not possible. Nevertheless, as our knowledge and understanding of language universals continues to improve, it is certain that linguists involved in the reconstruction of proto-languages will maintain an interest in typological plausibility.

8 Language change and naturalness

A striking fact about language change is that the same patterns of change occur repeatedly, not only within the same language at different periods in its history but also across languages. Both the similarity of changes across languages as well as the directionality of language change suggest that some changes are more natural than others. This notion of **naturalness** is implicit in the phonetic plausibility strategy introduced in the section on comparative reconstruction.

If naturalness is a factor in language change, its manifestations should also be found in the language acquisition process and in language universals. This does seem to be the case. As a specific example, let us consider the frequently made claim that the CV syllable is the most natural of all syllable types. At least three different kinds of evidence can be brought forth in support of this claim.

First, in terms of universals, all languages of the world have CV syllables in their syllable type inventory. Second, a variety of sound changes have the effect of reducing less natural syllable types to the more natural CV type (see table 7.81).

Table 7.81 Sound changes yielding CV syllables

Deletion							
CCV	>	CV	Old English	cnēow	English	knee	/ni/
CVC	>	CV	Old Spanish	non	Spanish	no	

Vowel epenthesis						
CCVCV	>	CVCVCV	Italian	croce	Sicilian	kiruci	'cross'

By contrast, note that such changes rarely if ever apply to a CV syllable to yield a different syllable type. Deletion of the C in a word-initial CV syllable is extremely rare, as is vowel epenthesis in a CV syllable or a sequence of CVCV syllables.

Third, in terms of language acquisition, the CV syllable type is one of the first syllable types to be acquired and many phonetic processes found in child language have the effect of yielding CV syllables, just like the sound changes listed above (see chapter 10 on language acquisition; see table 7.82).

Table 7.82	Phonetic processes in language acquisition yielding CV syllables
CCV → CV	tree → [ti] (simplification of consonant clusters)
CVC → CV	dog → [dɑ] (deletion of final consonants)

It is clear, however, that it is inappropriate to take a simplistic view of linguistic naturalness. For example, some sound changes produce less natural syllables. Thus, syncope has the effect of reducing a sequence of CVCVCV syllables to the less natural CVCCV. Usually in such cases, a different motivation can be identified, such as the preference for shorter phonological forms over longer forms. But given the complexity of human language, not to mention human behaviour in general, it should not be surprising that there are many different parameters of linguistic naturalness and that these can, in turn, lead to apparently conflicting changes in language over time. It remains an important task of the linguist to identify, rank, and ultimately explain relations of linguistic naturalness. The study of language change will continue to make an important contribution to this area.

Summing up

Historical linguistics studies the nature and causes of language change. The causes of language change find their roots in the physiological and cognitive makeup of human beings. Sound changes usually involve articulatory simplification as in the case of the most common type, **assimilation**. **Analogy** and **reanalysis** are particularly important factors in morphological change. **Language contact** resulting in **borrowing** is another important source of language change. All components of the grammar, from phonology to semantics, are subject to change over time. A change can simultaneously affect all instances of a particular sound or form, or it can spread through the language word by word by means of **lexical diffusion**. Sociological factors can play an important role in determining whether or not a linguistic innovation is ultimately adopted by the linguistic community at large. Since language change is systematic, it is possible, by identifying the changes that a particular language or dialect has undergone, to reconstruct linguistic history and thereby posit the earlier forms from which later forms have evolved. Using sets of **cognates**, **comparative reconstruction** allows us to reconstruct the properties of the parent or **proto-language** on the basis of **systematic phonetic correspondences**.

Studies in historical linguistics can provide valuable insights into relationships among languages and shed light on prehistoric developments. Furthermore, historical studies of language are of great importance to our understanding of human linguistic competence. In fact, it has often been stated that language change provides one of the most direct windows into the workings of the human mind. Furthermore, the study of language change contributes to our understanding of how social, cultural, and psychological factors interact to shape language. Finally, the integration of studies on language change, language acquisition, and language universals remains one of the most important challenges facing linguists today.

Notes

1 The translation for the passage is as follows:
   Many men say that in dreams
   There is nothing but talk and lies
   But men may see some dreams
   Which are scarcely false
   But afterward come true.
2 In these and other examples throughout this chapter, orthographic forms are given where these clearly reflect the sound change(s) in question. If required, partial or full phonetic transcriptions are provided.
3 Since voicing commonly occurs between voiced segments, it can also be considered a type of assimilation. It is treated here as a weakening since it is often part of a larger pattern of change involving various weakening processes.
4 A fully phonemic contrast between lax and tense vowels appears to be developing in Canadian French. Borrowings from English are contributing to the development of a phonemic contrast between lax and tense vowels in Canadian French (e.g., *poule* 'hen' versus *pool*).
5 We have simplified here in two respects. First, we ignore the fact that the verbs *be* and *have* can undergo Inversion even when they do not function as auxiliaries.
   Are they here?
   Have you no sense?
   Second, we have not traced the emergence of the auxiliary verb do in the formation of questions.
6 Classical Latin was the literary language of ancient Rome whereas Proto-Romance represents an attempt to reconstruct the spoken language spread throughout Europe which was the source of the various Romance languages.
7 Ejectives are produced by a closing of the glottis and raising of the larynx.

Sources

The textbooks (cited under Recommended Reading) by Anttila, Campbell, Hock, Labov, and Trask provide much more detailed discussions of most of the major topics in this chapter. They are also excellent sources for references relating to particular topics. Hock is particularly important for providing detailed discussions of syntactic change and the role of typology in reconstruction.

Overviews of historical linguistics as it applies to the development of English are presented in the books by Blake, Millward, and Smith cited below under Recommended Reading.

The catalogue of sound changes is adapted from catalogues proposed by Theo Vennemann in the article "Linguistic Typologies in Historical Linguistics" in *Società di linguistica italiana* 23:87–91 (1985) and a book entitled *Preference Laws for Syllable Structure and the Explanation of Sound Change* (Amsterdam: Mouton de Gruyter, 1988). Section 2 has also benefited from unpublished material (particularly the manuscript *Linguistic Change*) kindly made available by Theo Vennemann (University of Munich) to the author during his stay in Munich from 1980–85.

The data on vowel laxing in Canadian French are from Douglas C. Walker's book *The Pronunciation of Canadian French* (Ottawa: University of Ottawa Press, 1984). The data on word order in Old and Middle English come from the book by Joseph Williams, *Origins of the English Language: A Social and Linguistic History* (New York: Free Press, 1975). The examples of English loan words in Gwich'in (Loucheux) are given in *Dene* 1 (1): (1985), published by the Dene Language Terminology Committee, Yellowknife, The Northwest Territories. The discussion of borrowing and semantic change in English draws on materials in the book by Williams.

The table depicting lexical diffusion of the stress change in English nouns derived from verbs is taken from the book by Jean Aitchison, *Language Change: Progress or Decay?* (New York: Universe Books, 1985). Aitchison's remarks are based on the article by M. Chen and W. Wang, "Sound Change: Actuation and Implementation" in *Language* 51:255–81 (1975). The data on the realization of [s] as [h] in Spanish were provided by Herbert Izzo of the University of Calgary.

The Germanic cognates used to illustrate family relationships are based on Leonard Bloomfield's classic work, *Language* (New York: Holt, Rinehart and Winston, 1933). Some of the Romance cognates in this section come from *Proto-Romance Phonology* by Robert A. Hall, Jr. (New York: Elsevier, 1976). The quote from Jones is taken from *A Reader in Nineteenth-Century Historical Indo-European Linguistics,* edited and translated by Winfred P. Lehmann (Bloomington, IN: Indiana University Press, 1967) and the quote from Rask is taken from Holger Pedersen's book *The Discovery of Language: Linguistic Science in the Nineteenth Century* (Bloomington, IN: Indiana University Press, 1959).

Question 2 is based on data provided by Dr. George Patterson, whose generosity we hereby acknowledge. The data for questions 3 and 4 are from F. Columbus's *Introductory Workbook in Historical Phonology* (Cambridge, MA: Slavica, 1974). Question 10 is based on data provided by David Bellusci. The data for question 18 are drawn from *Source Book for Linguistics* by W. Cowan and J. Rakusan (Philadelphia: John Benjamins, 1987).

Recommended reading

Anttila, Raimo. 1989. *Historical and Comparative Linguistics.* 2nd ed. Amsterdam: John Benjamins.

Blake, N.F. 1996. *A History of the English Language.* Houndmills, Basingstoke, Hampshire: Macmillan.

Campbell, Lyle. 1999. *Historical Linguistics. An Introduction.* Cambridge, MA: MIT Press.

Hock, Hans Henrich. 1992. *Principles of Historical Linguistics.* 2nd ed. Amsterdam: Mouton de Gruyter.

Hock, Hans Henrich, and Brian D. Joseph. 1996. *Language History, Language Change, and*

Language Relationship: An Introduction to Historical and Comparative Linguistics. New York: Mouton de Gruyter.

Hopper, Paul J., and Elizabeth Closs Traugott. 1993. *Grammaticalization.* Cambridge: Cambridge University Press.

Koerner, E.F., and R.E. Asher, eds. 1995. *Concise History of the Language Sciences: From the Sumerians to the Cognitivists.* New York: Pergamon.

Labov, William. 1994. *Principles of Linguistic Change: Internal Factors.* Oxford: Blackwell.

Lass, Roger. 1997. *Historical Linguistics and Language Change.* Cambridge: Cambridge University Press.

Lehmann, Winfred P. 1992. *Historical Linguistics.* 3rd ed. New York: Routledge.

McMahon, April M.S. 1994. *Understanding Language Change.* Cambridge: Cambridge University Press.

Millward, C.M. 1996. *A Biography of the English Language.* 2nd ed. New York: Holt, Rinehart and Winston.

Smith, Jeremy. 1996. *An Historical Study of English: Function, Form and Change.* New York: Routledge.

Trask, R.L. 1996. *Historical Linguistics.* London: Arnold.

Questions

1. Identify the following sound changes with reference to the catalogue of sound changes provided in table 7.3. In each pair of examples, focus on the segment(s) in bold only. The form on the left indicates the original segment(s) before the change and the form on the right indicates the segment(s) after the change.

a) Sanskrit	**sn**eha	Pali	**sin**eha	'friendship'
b) Old English	**hl**āf	English	**l**oaf	
c) Latin	iu**v**enis [j]	Italian	**gi**ovane [dʒ]	'young'
d) English	triath**l**on	dialect	triath[ə]lon	
e) Latin	vi**du**a [dw]	Spanish	viu**d**a [wd]	'widow'
f) Sanskrit	sa**pt**a	Pali	sa**tt**a	'seven'
g) Latin	turtu**r**	English	turt**le**	
h)	*ven**r**é	Spanish	ven**dr**é	'I will come'
i) Italian	mun**do**	Sicilian	mun**nu**	'world'
j) Old French	cire [ts]	French	cire [s]	'wax'
k) Latin	pā**n**-	French	pai**n** [ɛ̃]	'bread'
l) Latin	mu**lg**ēre	Italian	mu**ng**ere	'to milk'
m) Latin	pa**c**are [k]	Italian	pa**g**are	'to pay'
n) Old Spanish	ni**d**o	Spanish	ni**d**o [ð]	'nest'
o) Latin	pe**cc**ātum [kk]	Spanish	pe**c**ado [k]	'sin'
p)	*hon**ōs**is	Latin	hon**ōr**is	'honor (gen sg)'
q) English	ra**ge**	French	ra**ge** [ʒ]	'rage'
r) English	**co**ffee	Chipewyan	[**ka**θi]	
s) Latin	mar**e**	Portuguese	ma**r**	'sea'
t) Latin	vī**c**īni**tā**s	Spanish	ve**c**inda**d**	'neighbourhood'
u) Gothic	**þl**iuhan [θ]	English	**fl**ee	

v)	Old English	(ic) singe	English	(I) sing	
w)	Latin	su**mm**a	Spanish	suma	'sum, gist'
x)	Latin	ōrn**ā**mentum	Old French	ornement [ə]	'ornament'
y)		*lūsi	Old English	lȳs [y:]	'lice'

2. a) Describe the difference between the two French dialects in the following data. Assume that the data are in phonetic transcription.

    b) What sound change would you posit here? Why?

    c) State the sound change in the form of a rule.

	European French	*Acadian French*	
i)	okyn	otʃyn	'none'
ii)	kør	tʃør	'heart'
iii)	ke	tʃe	'wharf'
iv)	kɛ̃:z	tʃɛ̃:z	'fifteen'
v)	akyze	atʃyze	'accuse'
vi)	ki	tʃi	'who'
vii)	kav	kav	'cave'
viii)	kɔr	kɔr	'body'
ix)	kurir	kurir	'run'
x)	ãkɔ:r	ãkɔ:r	'again'

3. a) What sound changes differentiate Guaraní from its parent language, Proto-Tupí-Guaraní, in the following data?

    b) State these changes in rule form.

	Proto-Tupí-Guaraní	*Guaraní*	
i)	jukɨr	jukɨ	'salt'
ii)	moajan	moajã	'push'
iii)	puʔam	puʔã	'wet'
iv)	meʔeŋ	meʔẽ	'give'
v)	tiŋ	tʃĩ	'white'
vi)	potiʔa	potʃiʔa	'chest'
vii)	tatatiŋ	tatatʃĩ	'smoke'
viii)	kɨb	kɨ	'louse'
ix)	men	mẽ	'husband'

4. a) Describe the three changes that took place between Proto-Slavic and Bulgarian in the following data. (The symbol ˘ over a vowel indicates that it is short.)

    b) State these changes as rules and indicate, as far as possible, the order in which they must have applied.

    c) Apply these rules to the Proto-Slavic word for 'adroit' to show how the Bulgarian form evolved.

	Proto-Slavic	*Bulgarian*	
i)	gladŭka	glatkə	'smooth'
ii)	kratŭka	kratkə	'short'
iii)	blizŭka	bliskə	'near'
iv)	ʒeʒĭka	ʒeʃkə	'scorching'
v)	lovŭka	lofkə	'adroit'
vi)	gorĭka	gorkə	'bitter'

5. Determine all the sound changes required to derive the later form from the proto-form. Where necessary, give the chronology of the sound changes.

   a) *feminam   Old French   femme (final e =[ə])   'woman'
   b) *umine   Spanish   lumbre   'fire'
   b) *tremulare   Spanish   temblar   'tremble'
   c) *stuppam   Spanish   estopa   'tow'
   d) *populu   Rumanian   plop   'poplar'

6. Taking into consideration the Great Vowel Shift, give all the changes necessary to derive the Modern English forms from the Old English forms. (*Note:* Assume, simplifying somewhat, that the Old English forms were pronounced as they are written.)

Old English	*Modern English*
a) brōde (sg acc)	brood
b) cnotta (c = [k])	knot
c) wīse	wise
d) hlæfdige	lady

7. Place names are often subject to spelling pronunciation. Transcribe your pronunciation of the following words and then compare your pronunciation with that recommended by a good dictionary. Do you think any of your pronunciations qualify as spelling pronunciations?

   a) Worcestershire
   b) Thames
   c) Edinburgh (Scotland; compare Edinburgh, Texas)
   d) Cannes (France)
   e) Newfoundland

8. Compare the Old English singular and plural forms:

Singular	*Plural*	
bōc	bēc	'book(s)'
āc	ǣc	'oak(s)'

   Although the Old English words have an umlaut plural (as in Old English gōs/gēs 'goose/geese'), the Modern English forms do not. Explain how the change in plural formation could have come about.

9. As evident in the following sentence, Shona, a modern Bantu language, has SVO word order. (*Note:* The morpheme *ano-* marks present tense.)

   mwana   anotengesa miriwo
   child   sells   vegetables
   'The child sells vegetables'.

   By contrast, Shona's morphology reflects a different pattern as evident in the following examples.

   mwana   ano**mu**ona
   child   **him**+*see*
   'The child sees him'.

mukadzi   ano**va**batsira
woman   **them**+*help*
'The woman helps them'.

What do these examples indicate about earlier Shona or possibly Proto-Bantu word order?

10. All of the following English words at one time had meanings that are quite different from their current ones. Identify each of these semantic changes as an instance of narrowing, broadening, amelioration, pejoration, weakening, or shift.

Word	Earlier meaning
a) moody	'brave'
b) uncouth	'unknown'
c) aunt	'father's sister'
d) butcher	'one who slaughters goats'
e) witch	'male or female sorcerer'
f) sly	'skilful'
g) accident	'an event'
h) argue	'make clear'
i) carry	'transport by cart'
j) grumble	'murmur, make low sounds'
k) shrewd	'depraved, wicked'
l) praise	'set a value on'
m) ordeal	'trial by torture'
n) picture	'a painted likeness'
o) seduce	'persuade someone to desert his or her duty'
p) box	'a small container made of boxwood'
q) baggage	'a worthless person'
r) virtue	'qualities one expected of a man'
s) myth	'story'
t) undertaker	'one who undertakes'
u) hussy	'housewife'
v) astonish	'strike by thunder'
w) write	'scratch'
x) quell	'kill'

11. Look up the following words in a good dictionary. Discuss any semantic changes that have affected the underscored portions since Old English. Do you think speakers of Modern English have reanalyzed any of these forms in terms of folk etymology?
    a) wed<u>lock</u>
    b) witch<u>craft</u>
    c) stead<u>fast</u>
    d) after<u>ward</u>

12. The following line is from *Troilus and Criseyde V* by Geoffrey Chaucer.
    His lighte goost ful blisfully is went.
    [hɪs liçtə gɔːst fʊl blɪsfʊlli ɪs wɛnt] ([ç] is a voiceless palatal fricative.)
    His light spirit has gone very blissfully.

a) How has the meaning of the word *ghost* changed since Chaucer's time?

b) Describe the changes that have taken place in the pronunciation of *light* and *ghost*.

13. Consider the following lyrics from the Middle English song "Sumer is i-cumen in." Compare the Middle English lyrics with the Modern English translation and answer the questions that follow.

Original text
Sumer is i-cumen in;
Lhude sing, cuccu!
Grōweþ sēd, and blōweþ mēd,
And springþ þe wude nū.

Transcription
[sʊmər ɪs ɪkʊmən ɪn
luːdə sɪŋg kʊkku
grɔːwəθ seːd and blɔːwəθ meːd
and sprɪŋgθ ðə wʊdə nuː]

Translation
'Summer has come in;
Loudly sing, cuckoo!
Seed grows and meadow blooms
And the wood grows now.'

a) What affix converted the adjective *loud* into an adverb in Middle English?

b) What accounts for the difference between the Middle English and Modern English pronunciation of the vowel in *loud*?

c) What other words in this poem reflect this general shift?

d) How has the relative ordering of the subject and verb changed since this was written?

e) How has the third person singular present tense suffix changed since Middle English?

14. The following Cree words were borrowed from French as the result of contact between the two groups on the Canadian prairies. (Notice that the French determiner was not treated as a separate morpheme and was carried along with the borrowed word.) What types of considerations could one plausibly assume played a role in the borrowing of these words into Cree?

Cree	French	
a) labutōn	le bouton	'button'
b) lībot	les bottes	'boots'
c) lamilās	la mélasse	'molasses'
d) lapwīl	la poêle	'frying pan'
e) litī	le thé	'tea'

15. The following Latin roots are found in words that have been borrowed into English. Since these words were borrowed after Grimm's Law had applied, they do not show its effects. All of these roots, however, do have Germanic cognates that did undergo Grimm's Law. On the basis of your knowledge of this law and the meaning of the borrowing, try to determine the Modern English (Germanic) cognate for each root. Consult a good dictionary if you need help. (*Note*: Focus on the portion of the Latin word in bold only; vowel changes must also be taken into consideration.)

Latin root	Related borrowing	English cognate
a) **ped**is	pedestrian	foot
b) **nep**os	nepotism	_____
c) **pisc**es	piscine	_____
d) **ten**uis	tenuous	_____

e) **corn**u   cornucopia   _____

f) **duo**   dual   _____

g) **ed**ere   edible   _____

h) **gen**us   genocide   _____

i) **ager**   agriculture   _____

16. Attempt to reconstruct the Proto-Germanic form for each pair of cognates. Focusing on the vowels, describe the changes that affected the Old English forms. (*Note:* y = [y], œ = [ø], and j = [j]).

Gothic	Old English	
a) kuni	cyn	'kin'
b) badi	bed	'bed'
c) dōmjan	dœman	'to judge'
d) sōkjan	sœcan	'to seek'
e) bugjan	bycgan	'to buy'
f) nati	net	'net'

18. Reconstruct the Proto-Romance form for each set of cognates. Give all the changes necessary to derive each of the modern forms from the proto-forms. If you are not sure how to proceed, return to section 7. (*Note:* The Spanish and Rumanian spelling 'ie' represents the sequence /je/, and the Rumanian spelling 'ia' represents the sequence /ja/.)

Spanish	Sardinian	Rumanian	
a) vida	bita	vită (ă = [ə])	'life'
b) sí	si	şi (ş = [ʃ])	'yes'
c) riso	rizu	rís	'laugh'
d) miel	mele	miere	'honey'
e) hierro	ferru	fier	'iron'
f) piedra	pedra	piatră (ă = [ə])	'stone'
g) hierba	erva	iarbă (ă = [ə])	'grass'
h) oso	ursu	urs	'bear'
i) roto	ruttu	rupt	'broken'
j) lecho	lettu	–	'bed'

Aleksandra Steinbergs

The classification of languages

Everything it is possible for us to analyze depends on a
clear method which distinguishes the similar
from the not similar.

LINNEUS GENERA PLANTARUM (1754)

In the world today there are thousands of different languages, each with its own sound patterns, grammar, and vocabulary. Regardless of how different these languages are, they have important similarities that allow linguists to arrange them into a fairly small number of groups. This chapter describes the methods of classification linguists use, and some of the findings which have resulted from this type of research.

1 Some preliminaries

We will begin by considering two topics—the problem of distinguishing between a language and a dialect, and the chief methods of language classification used in linguistics today.

1.1 Dialect and language

It is often difficult to determine whether two linguistic communities speak different languages or merely different dialects of the same language. One test that linguists use to decide this involves the criterion of **mutual intelligibility**. Mutually intelligible varieties of the same language can be understood by speakers of each variety. According to this criterion, the English of Toronto, the English of Milwaukee, and the English of London qualify as dialects of the same language. On the other hand, if two speakers cannot understand one another, then linguists normally conclude that they are speaking different languages. The Italian of Florence and the French of Paris are examples of varieties of speech that are not mutually intelligible.

Political, cultural, social, historical, and religious factors frequently interfere when determining linguistic boundaries. (In fact, it is sometimes said that a language is just a dialect with an army and a navy!) For example, Serbs and Croats, with their different histories, cultures, and religions, often claim that they speak different languages. However, even though they use different alphabets, Serbian and Croatian are actually mutually intelligible dialects of the same language, which linguists call Serbo-Croatian. In contrast, we often speak of Chinese as if it were a single language, even though it is actually a number of individual, mutually unintelligible languages (Cantonese, Mandarin, Hakka, and so on), each with a multitude of dialects of its own.

In addition to the problems presented by these non-linguistic considerations, complications also arise when we try to divide a continuum of mutually intelligible dialects whose two endpoints are not intelligible. Dutch and German, for example, are mutually intelligible around the border area between Germany and Holland; however, the Dutch of Amsterdam and the German of Munich are not. Similarly, Palestinian Arabic and Syrian Arabic are mutually intelligible, but Moroccan Arabic and Saudi Arabian Arabic are not.

Taking these considerations into account, how many languages are there in the world today? The best available estimate places the current figure at about six thousand five hundred. However, many of these languages have only a few hundred speakers and many others are in grave danger of demise as indigenous peoples throughout the world lose their traditional cultures and homelands. Indeed, according to one estimate, only about three hundred of the world's languages have a secure future. The threat of such a massive loss of the world's linguistic diversity is of great concern to linguists, many of whom are actively involved in recording and studying languages on the verge of extinction and in finding ways to improve the prospects for endangered languages.

Section 3 of this chapter presents an overview of a few hundred languages and the families to which they belong. First, however, we will turn our attention to some of the methods that are used for classifying languages into a manageable number of types.

1.2   Types of classification

Within the field of linguistics, three different approaches to language classification are used.

Genetic classification categorizes languages according to their descent. Languages that developed historically from the same ancestor language are grouped together and are said to be **genetically related**. This ancestor may be attested (that is, texts written in this language have been discovered or preserved, as in the case of Latin), or it may be a reconstructed proto-language for which no original texts exist (as is the case for Indo-European). Genetic classification is discussed further in section 3.

Although genetically **related languages** often share structural characteristics, they do not necessarily bear a close structural resemblance. For example, Latvian and English are genetically related (both are descended from Indo-European), but their morphological structure is quite different. An English sentence like *It has to be figured out* can be expressed in Latvian by a single word.

> 1)
> jāizgudro
> (one) must out figure (it)
> 'One must figure it out.'

Of course, Latvian and English are very distantly related, and languages that are more closely related will typically share a larger number of similarities. On the other hand, it is also necessary to recognize that even languages that are totally unrelated may share some structural similarities. Thus, English and Swahili, which are unrelated, both employ subject-verb-object word order in simple declarative sentences.

2)
Maria anapenda Anna
'Maria likes   Anna.'

For this reason, another approach to language classification is useful. Known as **linguistic typology,** it classifies languages only according to their structural characteristics, without regard for genetic relationships. Thus typologists might group together languages with similar sound patterns or, alternatively, those with similar grammatical structures. Typological studies also endeavour to identify **linguistic universals**, that is, structural characteristics that occur in all or most languages. We discuss linguistic typology further in section 2.

Finally, **areal classification** identifies characteristics shared by languages that are in geographical contact. Languages in contact often borrow words, sounds, morphemes, and even syntactic patterns from one another. As a result, neighbouring languages can come to resemble each other, even though they may not be genetically related. Because of space considerations, this chapter will not deal with areal classification specifically; however, borrowing is discussed in sections 1.2 and 5.1 of chapter 7.

2 Typological classification

As just noted, the classification of languages according to their structural characteristics is known as linguistic typology. Typological studies group together languages on the basis of similarities in their syntactic patterns, morphological structure, and/or phonological systems. An important area of research within the study of linguistic typology is the search for linguistic universals. Structural patterns and traits that occur in all languages are called **absolute universals**, while those that simply occur in most languages are known as **universal tendencies**.

Many typological generalizations involve **implicational universals**, which specify that the presence of one trait implies the presence of another (but not vice versa). For instance, languages with fricative phonemes (such as /f/ and /s/) will also have stop phonemes (such as /p/ and /t/), although the reverse is not necessarily true.

Another way to analyze linguistic universals is through **markedness theory**. Within this theory, **marked traits** are considered to be more complex and/or universally rarer than **unmarked** characteristics. In addition, a marked trait is usually found in a particular language only if its unmarked counterpart also occurs. Thus, markedness theory is closely related to the study of implicational universals.

An example can provide some clarification of these terms. Nasalized vowels are said to be marked, while non-nasalized (oral) ones are said to be unmarked. Phonologically, oral vowels can be considered less complex: oral vowels allow the airstream to exit only through the mouth, while nasalized vowels allow air to escape from both the mouth and the nose.

Cross-linguistically, we find that all languages have oral vowels, while only some languages have nasalized vowels. Even in the languages that have both, there are usually fewer nasalized vowels than oral ones. Thus, nasalized vowels (which are considered to be marked) are both rarer and phonologically more complex than (unmarked) oral vowels.

The following sections present some of the typological generalizations and universals that have been proposed in the areas of phonology, morphology, and syntax.

2.1   Phonology

In this section, we represent all vowel and consonant systems phonemically. This simplifies their presentation; note, however, that the exact phonetic realization of these systems may vary in the individual languages.

Vowel systems

Languages are often classified according to the size and pattern of their vowel systems. The most common vowel system has five phonemes—two high vowels, two mid vowels, and one low vowel (see figure 8.1). The front vowels are unrounded, as is the low vowel, and the back vowels are rounded.

Figure 8.1 The most common vowel system

About half the world's languages, including Basque, Hawaiian, Japanese, Spanish, and Swahili, have such a system.

The majority of the world's other languages have vowel systems with three, four, six, seven, eight, or nine different vowels (disregarding contrasts based on length or nasalization, which can double or triple the number of phonemic vowels). Languages with fewer than three, or more than nine distinctive vowels are rare. Some typical vowel systems are presented in figure 8.2.

Figure 8.2 Common vowel systems

Analysis of many languages has led to the discovery of a number of universal tendencies pertaining to vowel systems. Some of these tendencies are listed here, along with a description of the most commonly occurring vowels.

- The most commonly occurring vowel phoneme is /a/, which is found in almost all of the languages of the world. The vowels /i/ and /u/ are almost as common as /a/.

- Front vowel phonemes (/i, e, ɛ, æ/) are generally unrounded, while non-low back vowel phonemes (/ɔ, o, u/) are generally rounded.
- Low vowels (/æ, a, ɑ/) are generally unrounded.

Although English has an above-average number of vowels, they all conform to the above tendencies. Thus, English has only front unrounded vowels, all the low vowel phonemes are unrounded, and all of the back, non-low vowels are rounded. The English vowel system is represented in figure 8.3.

```
i            u

ɪ            ʊ

e            o

ɛ     ʌ     (ɔ)

æ     a     ɑ
```

Figure 8.3 The English vowel system

The relationship between contrasting vowel types (such as oral versus nasal, and long versus short) can also be expressed in terms of implicational universals, since the presence of one vowel phoneme type implies the presence of another (but not vice versa).

- If a language has contrastive nasal vowels, then it will also have contrastive oral vowels. For example, French contrasts different nasal vowels (/lɔ̃/ 'long' and /lã/ 'slow'), and contrasts oral vowels with nasal vowels (/la/ 'weary' and /lã/ 'slow'). Predictably, French also contrasts different oral vowels, as in /klo/ 'shut' and /klu/ 'nail'. English shows contrasts among oral vowels but does not contrast nasal vowels with oral vowels. There are no contrasts in English like /bɑt/ 'bought' and */bɑ̃t/.

- If a language has contrasting long vowels, then it will also have contrasting short vowels. For example, Finnish shows contrasting long vowels, and, predictably, contrasting short vowels (see table 8.1).

Table 8.1	Finnish vowel contrasts	
Long versus long	/viːli/ 'junket'	/vaːli/ 'election'
Short versus short	/suka/ 'bristle'	/suku/ 'family'
Short versus long	/tuli/ 'fire'	/tuːli/ 'wind'

The reverse is not necessarily the case. English has contrasts between short vowels (/bɪt/ vs. /bɛt/) but does not contrast long vowels with short ones, since vowel length in English is predictable.

Consonant systems

It is not particularly useful to classify languages according to the number of consonants that they contain, since languages may have as few as eight consonant phonemes (as in Hawaiian), or more than ninety. (!Kung, a language spoken in Namibia, has ninety-six consonant phonemes.) Nevertheless, typological analysis of consonant systems has produced a number of well-substantiated universals:

- All languages have stops.

- The most common stop phonemes are /p, t, k/. Very few languages lack any one of these, and there are no languages that lack all three. If any one of these three stops is missing, it will probably be /p/; for example, Aleut, Nubian, and Wichita have no /p/ phoneme. The most commonly occurring phoneme of the three is /t/.

- The most commonly occurring fricative phoneme is /s/. If a language has only one fricative, it is most likely to be /s/. It is the only fricative found in Nandi (a language of Kenya) and Weri (a language of New Guinea). The next most common fricative is /f/.

- Almost every known language has at least one nasal phoneme. In cases where a language has only one nasal phoneme, that phoneme is usually /n/ (as in Arapaho, spoken in Wyoming). If there are two contrasting nasals, they are normally /m/ and /n/.

- The majority of languages have at least one phonemic liquid. However, a small number of languages have none at all; for example, Blackfoot, Dakota, Efik (spoken in Nigeria), and Siona (found in Ecuador). English, of course, has two: /l/ and /r/.

Consonant phonemes are also subject to various implicational universals:

- If a language has voiced obstruent phonemes (stops, fricatives, or affricates), then it will also have voiceless obstruent phonemes. The reverse is not necessarily true; for example, Ainu (a language of northern Japan) has only voiceless obstruent phonemes: /p, t, k, tʃ, s/.

- Sonorant consonants are generally voiced. Very few languages have voiceless sonorants; those that do always have voiced sonorants as well. For example, Burmese contrasts voiced and voiceless nasals and laterals.

- If a language has fricative phonemes, then it will also have stop phonemes. There are no languages that lack stops; however, there are some languages that lack fricatives. For example, Gilbertese (Gilbert Islands), Kitabal (eastern Australia), and Nuer (southeastern Sudan) have no fricatives.

- Languages which have affricates will also have fricatives and stops. This is not surprising, since an affricate is, in essence, a sequence of a stop followed by a fricative. However, many languages lack affricates altogether. Note that while European French, for example, has fricatives and stops, but no affricates, English has all three.

Suprasegmental systems

Languages can also be classified according to their suprasegmental (or prosodic) type. Languages that use pitch to make meaning distinctions between words are called **tone languages**. (The phonetics and phonology of tone were introduced in chapters 2 and 3.)

A great many of the world's languages are tone languages. Mandarin Chinese, for instance, has four contrastive tones (see table 8.2).

Table 8.2 Tone contrasts in Mandarin Chinese		
High tone	dā	'build'
Low rising tone	dá	'achieve'
Falling rising tone	dǎ	'hit'
High falling tone	dà	'big'

The other Chinese languages, as well as many languages of Southeast Asia, Africa, and the Americas, are also tone languages. A few tone languages are also found in Europe; for example, one of the dialects of Latvian makes a three-way tonal distinction (see table 8.3).

Table 8.3 Tone contrasts in Latvian			
Falling tone	loks	[lùoks]	'arch, bow'
Level (high) tone	loks	[lūoks]	'green onion'
Rising-falling (broken) tone	loks	[lûoks]	'window'

As noted in the chapter on phonetics, there are two types of tones: level tones and contour tones. Tone languages most often contrast only two tone levels (usually high and low). However, contrasts involving three tone levels (such as high, low, and mid tones) are also relatively common. Five or more levels of tonal contrast are practically unknown.

Tone systems, too, exhibit various universal tendencies:

- If a language has contour tones (such as rising tone or falling tone) then it will also have level tones (such as high, mid, or low tone). Burmese, Crow, Latvian, and Mandarin are examples of languages that fit this pattern. The reverse pattern (languages with contour tones but no level tones) is extremely rare (although Dafla, spoken in northern India, has such a system).

- If a language has complex contour tones (such as rising-falling, or falling-rising), then it will also have simple contour tones (like rising or falling). Both the Mandarin and Latvian examples fit this pattern.

Differences in stress are also useful in classifying languages. **Fixed stress** languages are those in which the position of stress on a word is predictable. For example, in Modern Hebrew and K'iché (a Mayan language), stress always falls on the last syllable of a word; in Polish, Swahili, and Samoan, stress falls on the penultimate (second-to-last) syllable of words, while in Czech, Finnish, and Hungarian, the stressed syllable is always the first syllable of a word. In **free stress** languages, the position of stress is not predictable and must be learned for each word. Free stress is also called phonemic stress because of its role in distinguishing between words. Russian is an example of a language with free stress, as shown in table 8.4.

Table 8.4	Stress contrasts in Russian		
múka	'torture'	muká	'flour'
zámok	'castle'	zamók	'lock'
rúki	'hands'	rukí	'hand's' (genitive singular)

Syllable structure

All languages permit V and CV syllable structures (where V normally stands for a vowel, and C for a consonant). These syllable types are unmarked, in the sense that they are permitted in all languages. They are also simpler than most other syllable structures, such as CVC or VCC. Note, however, that VC is just as simple a structure as CV, but that only the latter is universally permitted. The presence of an onset (as in a CV syllable) is apparently more valued than the presence of a coda (as in a VC syllable), perhaps because an onset may help to signal the beginning of a new syllable.

In any given language, onsets may be structured differently from codas. For example, in English, a nasal + stop sequence is permitted in the coda (in a word like *hand*), but not in the onset (there are no English words that begin with the sequence *nd*). However, Swahili has precisely the opposite restrictions: the *nd* sequence is permitted in onset position (in words like *ndizi* 'banana'), but not in coda position. In fact, Swahili syllables are coda-less—they can only end in vowels.

Differing syllable structure constraints can have interesting consequences when languages come in contact. For example, in Hawaiian only V and CV syllables are permitted. Thus, when a word is borrowed from a language like English, which allows more complicated syllable structures, vowels are inserted to produce the only allowed syllable structures. For example, when the phrase *Merry Christmas* was borrowed into Hawaiian, it was reformulated as follows: *mele kalikimaka*. (Of course, some consonant changes were made as well, since Hawaiian lacks /r/ and /s/ phonemes.)

Two examples of implicational universals for syllable structure are presented below. Both deal with the structure of onsets as opposed to codas.

- If a language permits sequences of consonants in the onset, then it will also permit syllables with single consonant onsets and syllables with no onset at all.

- If a language permits sequences of consonants in the coda, then it will also permit syllables with single consonant codas and syllables with no coda at all.

2.2 Morphology

Both words and morphemes are found in all languages. However, there are clear differences in the ways in which individual languages combine morphemes to form words. Four types of systems can be distinguished.

The isolating type

A language that is purely **isolating** or **analytic** would contain only words that consist of a single (root) morpheme. In such a language there would be no affixes, and categories such as number and tense would therefore have to be expressed by a separate word. In Mandarin Chinese, which is primarily an isolating language, the morpheme *le* is often used to indicate a past or completed action. Although this morpheme is thus semantically similar to a past tense, it acts just like an independent word, since its position in the sentence may vary:

3)
Ta chi fan   le.
he eat meal past
'He ate the meal.'

Ta chi le   fan.
he eat past meal
'He ate the meal.'

Other languages that are primarily isolating include Cantonese, Vietnamese, Laotian, and Cambodian.

The polysynthetic type

In a **polysynthetic** language, single words can consist of long strings of roots and affixes that often express meanings that are associated with entire sentences in other languages. The following word from Inuktitut illustrates this.

4)
Qasuiirsarvigssarsingitluinarnarpuq.
Qasu -iir -sar   -vig -ssar   -si -ngit-luinar   -nar   -puq
tired not cause-to-be place-for suitable find not completely someone 3.sg.
'Someone did not find a completely suitable resting place.'

Polysynthesis is common in many native languages of North America, including Inuktitut, Cree, and Sarcee to name but a few.

The terms *isolating* and *polysynthetic* refer to two extremes: words consisting only of a single morpheme versus words that can be complete sentences. Few if any languages are either purely isolating or purely polysynthetic. Instead, the vast majority of languages are **synthetic**, in that they permit multimorphemic words with non-sentential meanings. There are two types of synthetic languages.

The agglutinating type

An **agglutinating** language has words that can contain several morphemes, but the words are easily divided into their component parts (normally a root and affixes). In such languages, each affix is clearly identifiable and typically represents only a single grammatical category or meaning. The following examples are from Turkish.

5)

a. köj
  'village'

b. köj-ler
  village-pl
  'villages'

c. köj-ler-in
  village-pl gen
  'of the villages'

Turkish words can have a complex morphological structure, but each morpheme has a single, clearly identifiable function. In *5c)*, for instance, *-ler* marks plurality and *-in* marks the genitive case, giving the meaning 'of the villages'.

The fusional type

Words in a **fusional** or **inflectional language** can also consist of several morphemes. However, in contrast to agglutinating systems, the affixes in fusional languages often mark several grammatical categories simultaneously. In Russian, for example, a single inflectional affix simultaneously marks the noun's gender class (masculine, feminine, or neuter), its number (singular or plural), and its grammatical role (subject, direct object, and so on). This is illustrated in *6)* for the suffix *-u*.

6)

mi vid^{j}im ruk-u
we see   hand-fem/sg/Ac
'We see a/the hand.'

The distinction between agglutinating and fusional is sensitive to the number of semantic 'bits' of information normally packed into an affix. In an agglutinating language, each affix normally contains only one element of grammatical or lexical meaning, while in a fusional language, affixes often denote several simultaneous functions.

Mixed types

Many (perhaps most) languages do not belong exclusively to any of the four categories just outlined. For example, English employs isolating patterns in many verbal constructions, where each notion is expressed by a separate word. The future, for instance, is indicated by the independent word *will* (rather than by an affix) in structures such as *I will leave*. On the other hand, English also exhibits considerable agglutination in derived words, such as *re-en-act-ment*, which consist of a series of clearly identifiable morphemes, each with its own unique meaning and function. However, the English pronoun system is largely fusional, since a single form can be used to indicate person, number, gender, and case. The word *him*, for instance, is used to express a third person, singular, masculine direct object.

Since many, if not most, of the world's languages exhibit mixed patterns of this type, it has been suggested that terms like isolating, agglutinating, and fusional should be used to refer not to a language as a whole, but to particular structures within a language.

It is also important to recognize that these classifications do not take into consideration morphological processes such as compounding (e.g., English *greenhouse*), reduplication (e.g., Tagalog *sulat* 'write' versus *susulat* 'will write'), grammatical use of stress or tone (e.g., the noun *présent* versus the verb *presént* in English), and internal word change (e.g., vowel ablaut, as in English *run* versus *ran*).

Implicational universals: morphology

A variety of generalizations can be made about word structure in human language.

- If a language has inflectional affixes, it will also have derivational affixes. For example, English not only has inflectional affixes such as the past tense -*ed* and possessive -*'s*, but it also contains derivational affixes like *un-* (*unhappy*, *unwanted*) and -*ly* (*quickly*, *slowly*).

- If a word has both a derivational and an inflectional affix, the derivational affix is closer to the root (DA = derivational affix; IA = inflectional affix) (see table 8.5).

Table 8.5	The ordering of derivational and inflectional affixes
English	
friend-ship-s	*friend-s -ship
Root DA IA	Root IA DA
Turkish	
iʃ -tʃi -ler	*iʃ -ler-tʃi
work -er -pl	work-pl -er
Root DA IA	Root IA DA

- If a language has only suffixes, it will also have only postpositions. (As noted in chapter 5, postpositions are the equivalent of prepositions in languages that place the head at the end of the phrase.) Turkish, for example, has only suffixes; as expected, it also has postpositions rather than prepositions. This is illustrated in the following sentence.

7)
Ahmet Ajʃe   itʃin kitab-ɨ   al-dɨ.
Ahmet Ayshe for   book-Acc bought
'Ahmet bought a book for Ayshe.'

2.3 Syntax

Because we lack detailed descriptions for most of the world's languages, much of the work on syntactic universals has been restricted to the study of word order in simple declarative sentences such as *The men built the house*. Patterns are classified in terms of the order of the subject (S), direct object (O), and verb (V). The three most common word orders (in descending order of frequency) are SOV, SVO, and VSO. Over 95 percent of the world's languages use one of these patterns as their basic word order.

8)
SOV (Turkish):
Hasan öküz-ü al-dɪ.
Hasan ox-Ac bought
'Hasan bought the ox.'

9)
SVO (English):
The athlete broke the record.

10)
VSO (Welsh):
Lladdodd y   ddraig   y   dyn.
killed   the dragon the man
'The dragon killed the man.'

SOV, SVO, and VSO patterns all have one common trait: the subject appears before the direct object. The prevalence of the S-O pattern may be due to the fact that the subject usually coincides with the topic of the sentence (i.e., what the sentence is about; see chapter 6, section 4.3), and therefore is more useful at an early point in the utterance.

While an overwhelming majority of the world's languages place the subject to the left of the direct object in their basic word order, this pattern is not universal. There are a small number of VOS languages, of which the best-known example is Malagasy.

11)
VOS (Malagasy):
Nahita ny mpianatra ny vehivavy.
saw   the student   the woman
'The woman saw the student.'

As well, there are a very few OVS or OSV languages, all of which seem to be spoken in South America:

12)
OVS (Hixkaryana):
Kana janɪmno bɪrjekomo
fish caught boy
'The boy caught a fish'

13)
OSV (Apuriña)
Anana   nota apa
pineapple I   fetch
'I fetch a pineapple'

Word order universals

Sometimes, the order of elements within one kind of structure has implications for the order of elements in other structures. Many of these implications concern the relationship between the verb and its (direct) object.

- If a language has VO word order, then it will have prepositions rather than postpositions. Languages of this type include Berber (spoken in Morocco), Hebrew, Maori (spoken in New Zealand), Maasai (spoken in Kenya), Welsh, and Irish Gaelic.

14)
Irish Gaelic
a. VSO pattern:
Chonaic mé mo mháthair
saw   I   my mother
'I saw my mother.'

b. Preposition pattern:
sa teach
in house
'in the house'

- If a language has OV word order, then it will probably have postpositions rather than prepositions. Languages with this structural pattern include Basque, Burmese, Hindi, Japanese, Korean, Quechua, Turkish, and Guugu Yimidhirr, an aboriginal language of Australia.

15)
Guugu Yimidhirr
a. S-OV pattern:
Gudaa-ngun jarrga dyindaj
dog-Erg   boy   bit
'The dog bit the boy'

b. Postposition pattern:
juwaal nganh
beach from
'from the beach'

- PPs almost always precede the verb in OV languages, and usually follow the verb in VO languages.

16)
Japanese
a. S-OV pattern:
Gakusei-ga   hon-o   yonda
student-Nom book-Acc read
'The student read a book'

b. PP precedes verb:

Taroo-ga   [$_{PP}$ nitiyoobi ni] tsuita.
Taroo-Nom   Sunday   on arrived
'Taroo arrived on Sunday.'

17)
English
a. S-VO pattern:
  I like candy.

b. PP follows verb:
  George left [$_{PP}$ on Sunday].

• Manner adverbs overwhelmingly precede the verb in OV languages and generally follow the verb in VO languages.

18)
Japanese (S-OV pattern, as seen in *16a*)):
Manner adverb precedes verb:
hayaku hasiru
quickly run
'run quickly'

19)
English (S-VO pattern, as seen in *17a*)):
Manner adverb follows verb:
John runs well.

• With respect to possessive structures, there is an overwhelming preference for Genitive + N order in OV languages, and a (somewhat weaker) preference for N + Genitive order in VO languages.

20)
Japanese (S-OV pattern, as seen in *16a*)):
Genitive structure precedes Head N:
Taroo-no   hon
Taroo-Gen book
'Taroo's book'

21)
French
a. S-VO pattern:
  Pierre aime Marie.
  'Pierre likes Marie.'

b. Genitive structure follows Head N:
  la   maison de   Marie
  the house   of (Gen) Marie
  'Marie's house'

English, although an SVO language, exhibits both Genitive + N and N + Genitive patterns:

22)
 a. Genitive + N pattern:
  the country's laws

 b. N + Genitive pattern:
  the laws of the country

Examples such as this are rare, however, and do not invalidate the universal tendencies we have been considering.

Grammatical hierarchies

Implicational universals are often stated in terms of hierarchies of categories or relations. One of the most important hierarchies of this type refers to the grammatical relations of subject and direct object (see chapter 5).

Least marked

    Subject
    Direct object
    Other

Most marked

Figure 8.4 Hierarchy of grammatical relations

Hierarchies represent degrees of markedness, with the least marked option at the top and the most marked at the bottom. According to the hierarchy in figure 8.4, then, a process that applies only to subjects is less marked than a process that applies to direct objects, and so on. Given the definition of markedness outlined at the beginning of section 2, it follows that if a particular phenomenon applies to direct objects, it should also apply to subjects. The opposite, however, need not be true: it would not be surprising to find a process that applies to subjects but not direct objects.

  Among the many typological phenomena that conform to this hierarchy is verb agreement, first mentioned in chapter 4 (section 6.4). As the following examples show, there are languages in which the verb agrees only with the subject, and there are languages in which it agrees with both the subject and the direct object (3 = 3rd person, Sg = singular, Pl = plural).

 23)
 Agreement with subject only (Spanish):

 Subject
 Juan parti-ó
 Juan leave-3.Sg.Pst
 'Juan left.'

24)

Agreement with subject and direct object (Swahili):

Subject		Direct object		
Juma	a-	li- wa-	piga	watoto
Juma	3.Sg-Pst-3.Pl-hit			children

'Juma hit the children.'

However, as predicted by the hierarchy, there are no languages in which the verb agrees only with the direct object.

2.4 Explaining universals

Linguists are still uncertain about how to explain the existence of many linguistic universals. Nonetheless, a number of interesting proposals have been made, and it is worthwhile to consider some of them here.

Phonology

Perceptual factors play a role in shaping phonological universals. For example, the fact that /s/ is the most commonly occurring fricative may have to do with its acoustic prominence: varieties of /s/ are inherently louder than other kinds of fricatives.

Vowel systems (discussed in section 2.1) develop so as to keep vowel phonemes as different from each other as possible. A three-vowel system such as the following allows for plenty of 'space' around each vowel, which probably makes each vowel easier to distinguish from the others.

i   u

     a

Figure 8.5 A three-vowel system

The same holds true for the distribution of stop phonemes. It may be that /p/, /t/, and /k/ are the three most common stops, because they occur at three maximally distant places of articulation within the supralaryngeal vocal tract. These three stops are much easier to distinguish perceptually than a sequence of dental, alveolar and palatal stops, for example, all of which are produced in the central region of the oral cavity.

It has been recently suggested that consonant systems in general respond to the articulatory pressures that give rise to unmarked sounds and systems. Articulatorily basic obstruents such as [p], [t], and [k] are found much more commonly than more complex articulations such as [tɬ] and [qʷ]. Table 8.7 shows the set of obstruents that is most widely used across human languages.

Languages tend to have consonant systems that consist of about 70 percent obstruents and 30 percent sonorants no matter what the total size of their consonant inventories may be. These figures reflect the articulatory possibilities available for contrast: more distinctions can be made among obstruents than among sonorants. There are, for example, no nasal fricative sonorants, because the air pressure needed to force air through a narrow opening (which is necessary for the production of fricatives) cannot be built up when so much air is flowing through the nasal passage at the same time. For reasons such as this, the number of obstruent consonants in any language is potentially much larger than the number of possible sonorant consonants. This is just one example of how considerations involving articulation can play a role in the shaping of consonant systems.

Table 8.6	Obstruents most often found cross-linguistically		
p	t	k	ʔ
b	d	g	
f	s		h
	tʃ		

Morphology

Other types of explanations are appropriate for morphological universals. For example, the fact that languages with suffixes but no prefixes always have postpositions (section 2.2) may have a historical explanation. In these languages, some postpositions became attached to a preceding word and were thereby converted into suffixes. Because suffixes in such languages evolved from postpositions, the link between the two elements can be traced to their common origin.

An example of this very phenomenon can be seen in the closely related languages, Finnish and Estonian. This ancestor language (Proto-Baltic-Finnic) contained a postposition *kanssa* 'with', which is still evident in Standard Finnish, but has evolved into a suffix in Estonian (see table 8.7).

Table 8.7	Proto-Baltic-Finnic postposition *kanssa* becomes suffix *-ga*
Standard Finnish: postposition *kanssa* 'with'	
poja 'boy' poja-n kanssa 'with the boy' boy+Gen with	
Estonian: case suffix *-ga*	
poja 'boy' poja-ga 'with the boy' boy+Com	

The requirement that derivational affixes occur closer to the root than inflectional affixes has another type of explanation. As noted in the morphology chapter, derivation typically forms new words, while inflection marks the subclass (for example, plural for Ns, past tense for Vs) to which a word belongs. Given that a word must be formed before its subclass can be determined, it follows that derivational processes will precede inflection. This is reflected in word structure, where derivational affixes appear closer to the root than inflectional markers. In figure 8.6, for instance, the verbal root *treat* is converted into a noun by the affix *-ment* before the plural inflectional marker is added.

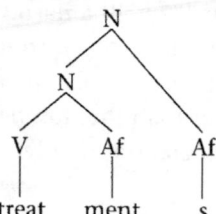

Figure 8.6 The structure of a word containing a derivational affix and an inflectional affix

Syntax

At least some syntactic universals may be explained in terms of the way that the human brain processes sentence structure. Consider the summary of word order patterns in table 8.8, which is based on the implicational universals discussed in section 2.3.

Table 8.8	Word order patterns	
Constituents	**Order in VO language**	**Order in OV language**
P & NP	preposition-NP	NP-postposition
V & PP	verb-PP	PP-verb
V & manner Adv	verb-manner Adv	manner Adv-verb
Gen & N	noun-genitive	genitive-noun

One recent explanation as to why the word order properties in the second and third columns cluster together involves the contrast between right-branching and left-branching languages. In right-branching languages, the more elaborate part of a phrase's structure occurs on its right branch; in left-branching languages, it occurs on the left. Thus, a verb-object pattern is right-branching since a phrasal constituent (an XP) appears on its right branch, but an object-verb pattern is left-branching as shown in figure 8.7.

Figure 8.7 Right-branching and left-branching patterns

As you can easily determine for yourselves, the P-NP, V-PP, V-Adv, and N-Gen patterns commonly associated with VO languages are also all right-branching (both genitives and adverbials are a type of phrase). In contrast, the NP-P, PP-V, Adv-V, and Gen-N patterns typically found in OV languages are all left-branching. In other words, it seems that languages are fairly consistent in using one or the other type of branching structure. This sort of uniformity may make it easier for speakers and hearers to process syntactic structure. Thus, just as some human beings are right-handed and others left-handed, it appears that some languages prefer to use consistently right-branching systems, while others prefer consistently left-branching systems.

The study of linguistic typology and language universals is a relatively new field within linguistics. There is obviously much still to be learned about linguistic universals, and it must be admitted that some of the current work is speculative and incomplete. No doubt many interesting new facts will eventually come to light.

3 Genetic classification

The world's languages can be grouped into a relatively small number of language families. However, genetic classification is sometimes difficult for a number of reasons.

Perhaps the biggest problem is simply the amount of data that must be collected before linguists can be confident about the status of a group of languages. It is only in the last two or three decades, for example, that enough information has been accumulated to propose a detailed classification of the languages of Africa. Moreover, many of the languages of South America, New Guinea, and Australia are still relatively unknown.

In many cases, linguists face the problem of establishing the tests or criteria to be used in proposing genetic relationships. There is some disagreement over the degree of similarity that should exist among languages before a genetic relationship can be proposed. This issue arises because unrelated languages are often typologically similar (that is, share some structural characteristics). This is particularly likely if languages have been in contact long enough to have borrowed a large number of words, sounds, morphemes, or syntactic structures from one another.

Additional difficulties stem from the fact that genetically related languages need not be typologically similar. This is especially true if the relationship is a distant one, as is the case with English and Russian. Russian has numerous inflectional affixes, an extensive case system, and free word order, while English has relatively few inflectional affixes, virtually no case marking, and fixed word order. Yet, both belong to the Indo-European family.

To complicate matters even further, linguists also disagree as to how much evidence is required in order to establish a genetic relationship between languages. The more distant the genetic relationship between languages, the less likely it is that a large number of obvious cognates will be found, especially since sound changes can obscure similarities between cognate words. English and Latin are related (though distantly), but the similarity between cognates like Latin *unda* 'wave' and English *water* is certainly not striking.

Research is also complicated by the fact that words that may be excellent indicators of a genetic relationship can drop out of the lexicon. For example, Old English had a word *leax* 'salmon' (which was cognate with German *Lachs* and Yiddish *lox*), but this lexical item has since been lost from the native English lexicon (although *lox* has, of course, been borrowed back into some varieties of English as the name for a popular delicatessen food).

Since word loss is a common historical event, linguists prefer to use the oldest available form of a language for their research; thus, our knowledge of Proto-Indo-European is drawn from the study of Old English, Sanskrit, Latin, etc., rather than English, Hindi-Urdu, French, and their other modern descendants. Of course, languages that are genetically related do share many similarities, particularly if their common ancestor is not too distant.

Some language families contain many hundreds of languages. In other cases, only one language may remain to represent a family. In still other cases, families have become extinct. The following sections present some information about the makeup and membership of a few of the language families represented in the world today.

3.1   The Indo-European family

With only about a hundred languages, Indo-European is not a large family in terms of the total number of languages. However, it is the largest language family in the world in terms of the total number of speakers: there are about 1.7 billion native speakers of an Indo-European language.

If we consider only living languages, the Indo-European family currently has nine branches, which are listed in table 8.9.

Table 8.9	Main branches of the Indo-European family	
Germanic	Hellenic	Baltic
Celtic	Albanian	Slavic
Italic	Armenian	Indo-Iranian

Germanic

The Germanic branch of Indo-European can be divided into three sub-branches: East, North, and West. The East Germanic branch included Gothic, the oldest Germanic language for which written texts exist (dating from the fourth century AD). Gothic and any other languages belonging to this branch of Germanic have long been extinct.

The North Germanic (or Scandinavian) branch originally included Old Norse (also known as Old Icelandic), which was the language of the Vikings and the ancestor of modern Icelandic, Norwegian, and Faroese (spoken on the Faroe islands, north of Scotland). Swedish and Danish are two other familiar North Germanic languages.

The West Germanic branch includes English, German, Yiddish, Dutch, Frisian, and Afrikaans. Afrikaans is descended from the Dutch spoken by seventeenth-century settlers (known as Boers) in South Africa.

Frisian is the language most closely related to English. It is spoken on the north coast of Holland, and on the Frisian Islands just off the coast, as well as on the northwestern coast of Germany. English descended from the speech of the Angles, Saxons, and Jutes—Germanic tribes who lived in northern Germany and southern Denmark (in an area just east of the Frisians) before invading England in 449 AD and settling there.

The organization of the Germanic family of languages is illustrated in table 8.10. (In this and other tables, parentheses are used to indicate languages that no longer have any native speakers. The tables are intended to illustrate the membership and organization of the families; they do not necessarily provide a complete list of the languages in each family.)

Table 8.10	The Germanic family	
(East Germanic)	**North Germanic**	**West Germanic**
(Gothic)	Icelandic	English
	Faroese	German
	Norwegian	Dutch
	Danish	Frisian
	Swedish	Afrikaans
		Yiddish

Celtic

The Celtic branch of Indo-European (see table 8.11) has two main sub-branches: Insular and Continental (now extinct). Gaulish, a member of the Continental branch, was once spoken in France (the Gauls were the tribe Julius Caesar defeated), but it has long been extinct.

The Insular sub-branch can be subdivided into two groups of languages: Brythonic and Goidelic. Brythonic languages include Welsh and Breton (which is spoken in northwestern France) as well as Cornish, which was formerly spoken in southwest Britain but now no longer has any native speakers. The Goidelic branch contains Irish (or Irish Gaelic), which is still spoken natively in the western parts of Ireland, and Scots Gaelic, which is native to some of the northwestern parts of Scotland (especially the Hebrides Islands) and, to a lesser extent, Cape Breton Island in Nova Scotia.

Table 8.11	The Celtic family	
Insular		**Continental**
Brythonic	***Goidelic***	
Welsh	Irish [=Irish Gaelic]	(Gaulish)
Breton	Scots Gaelic	
(Cornish)		

Italic

The Italic family originally had a number of branches, which included several now-extinct languages spoken in the area corresponding roughly to modern-day Italy. However, the only Italic languages that are presently spoken are all descended from Latin, the language of the Roman Empire (hence the term 'Romance languages').

These languages can be divided into an Eastern group (consisting of Italian and Rumanian), and a Western group, containing all of the other Romance languages with the exception of Sardinian, which stands alone.

The Western group is further divided into Ibero-Romance (Spanish, Portuguese, and Catalan—the latter is spoken in northeastern Spain, around Barcelona) and Gallo-Romance, which includes French, Occitan (spoken in southern France), and Romansch (one of the four official languages of Switzerland). These divisions are illustrated in table 8.12.

Table 8.12	The Romance family		
Eastern	**Western**		
	Ibero-Romance	*Gallo-Romance*	*Sardinian*
Italian	Spanish	French	Sardinian
Rumanian	Portuguese	Occitan	
	Catalan	Romansch	

Hellenic

The Hellenic branch of Indo-European has only one living member, Greek. All modern Greek dialects are descended from the classical dialect known as Attic Greek, which was the speech of Athens during the Golden Age of Greek culture (approximately 500 to 300 BC).

Hellenic Greek, which was used in subsequent centuries, was the language of commerce throughout the Middle East. (Hellenic Greek was also Cleopatra's native language; she was descended from one of Alexander the Great's generals; Egyptian was long extinct by her time.)

Albanian

The Albanian branch of Indo-European has only one member, Albanian, which is spoken not only in Albania, but also in parts of the former Yugoslavia, Greece, and Italy.

Armenian

The Armenian branch also has only one member, Armenian. This language is centred in the Republic of Armenia (formerly part of the USSR), but is also spoken in Turkey, Iran, Syria, Lebanon, and Egypt.

Baltic

The Baltic branch contains only two surviving languages, Latvian (or Lettish) and Lithuanian. They are spoken in Latvia and Lithuania (located just west of Russia and northeast of Poland). Lithuanian has an elaborate case system, which resembles the one proposed for Proto-Indo-European.

Slavic

The Slavic branch of Indo-European can be divided into three sub-branches: East, West, and South. The East Slavic branch is made up of Russian (also called Great Russian), Ukrainian, and Byelorussian (or White Russian). The latter is spoken in Byelorussia, which is just east of northern Poland. The West Slavic branch includes Czech, Slovak, and Polish.

The South Slavic branch consists of Bulgarian, Macedonian, Serbo-Croatian, and Slovene (or Slovenian). The latter three languages are all spoken in the former Yugoslavia. Note that although Alexander the Great was king of Macedonia, he spoke Hellenic Greek, not (Slavic) Macedonian; Slavic-speaking tribes did not move into that area until several centuries later.

The organization of the Slavic group of languages is represented in table 8.13.

Table 8.13 The Slavic family		
East Slavic	**South Slavic**	**West Slavic**
Russian	Slovene	Czech
Ukrainian	Serbo-Croatian	Slovak
Byelorussian	Macedonian	Polish
	Bulgarian	

Indo-Iranian

The Indo-Iranian branch of Indo-European is divided into the Iranian and Indic sub-branches. The Iranian sub-branch contains about two dozen different languages, including Modern Persian (also called Parsi or Farsi, spoken in Iran), Pashto (the principal language of Afghanistan), and Kurdish (found in Iran, Iraq, Turkey, and Syria). Other Iranian languages are spoken in Pakistan, southern parts of the former USSR, and China.

There are about thirty-five different Indic languages. Most of the languages spoken in northern India, Pakistan, and Bangladesh belong to this branch of Indo-European. Some of the most widespread (in terms of number of speakers) are Hindi-Urdu, Bengali, Marathi, and Gujarati. Although Hindi and Urdu are two dialects of the same language, they have totally different writing systems and are associated with different cultures; Urdu is spoken principally in Pakistan by Muslims while Hindi is spoken primarily in India by Hindus.

Less well known as an Indic language is Romany, or Gypsy. It is now believed that the Gypsies (or Roma) fled to Turkey from northwestern India during the Middle Ages, after being defeated by Islamic invaders. Subsequently they spread throughout Europe: gypsies are found as far west as Ireland, and as far east as Russia. Many now also live in North America. Romany contains many borrowed words—particularly from Greek, which was the language primarily spoken in Turkey during the Middle Ages.

Table 8.14 depicts the organization of Indo-Iranian.

Table 8.14 The Indo-Iranian family	
Iranian	**Indic**
Persian [= Farsi]	Hindi-Urdu
Pashto	Bengali
Kurdish	Marathi
	Gujarati
	Romany [= Gypsy]

The map in figure 8.8 illustrates the geographic location of the Indo-European families identified in this chapter.

1   Celtic
2   Germanic
3   Romance
4   Hellenic
5   Slavic
6   Albanian
7   Armenian
8   Indo-Iranian
9   Baltic

Dotted lines indicate
geopolitical boundaries

Solid lines indicate
linguistic boundaries

Figure 8.8   Location of Indo-European languages

3.2   Some other families

Although no introductory text could hope to present a complete survey of all of the world's language families, some further discussion of this topic is worthwhile in order to illustrate the extraordinary variety of human language.

Uralic

The Uralic family (see table 8.15) contains about twenty languages and has approximately twenty-two million speakers. Uralic languages are spoken in a band across the northern part of Europe, all the way from northern Norway to Siberia. Uralic has two major branches: Samoyed and Finno-Ugric. The Samoyed branch contains a handful of languages spoken in northern Russia, particularly in areas around the Ural mountains, and also in Siberia.

The most widely spoken Finno-Ugric language is Hungarian. Other Finno-Ugric languages are Finnish, Lapp (also known as Lappish or Saame, spoken in northern Scandinavia and northwestern Russia), Estonian (Estonia), Livonian (Latvia), Karelian (eastern Finland and northwestern Russia), Erzya, and Cheremis (both spoken in the former USSR).

Table 8.15 The Uralic family		
Finno-Ugric		**Samoyed**
Finnic	*Ugric*	
Finnish	Hungarian	Nganasan
Estonian		Selkup
Lapp [=Saame]		Nenets
Karelian		Enets
Livonian		
Erzya		
Cheremis [=Mari]		

Uralic languages are primarily agglutinating and most have postpositions with SOV or SVO word order. The nouns often have many cases (Finnish has fifteen), which appear to have developed historically from postpositions that became attached to nouns as suffixes.

Altaic

Languages belonging to the Altaic family are spoken in a continuum from Turkey to Siberia, and in China. The membership of the Altaic family (see table 8.16) includes three main branches—Turkic, Mongolian, and Tungusic. Recent scholarship has collected evidence that Korean and Japanese are also members of the Altaic family.

The best-known Turkic language is Turkish, which is spoken by over fifty million people. Other Turkic languages (most of which are spoken in the former USSR) include Uzbek (Uzbekistan), Azeri (Azerbaijan Republic and Iran), Kazakh (Kazakhstan, China, and Mongolia), Uighur (China and Kazakhstan), and Volga Tatar (also called Tatar, in the Tataristan Republic, Kazakhstan, and China).

The Mongolian languages are spoken by around ten million people, primarily in Mongolia and China, while the Tungusic languages are spoken by approximately 50 000 people in central and east Siberia and Mongolia.

Altaic languages are usually agglutinating, often with several suffixes in the same word. They normally employ SOV word order and typically use postpositions rather than prepositions. Many Altaic languages have vowel harmony, a phonological phenomenon in which all vowels of a word share certain features, such as [round] or [back].

Table 8.16 The Altaic family				
Turkic	**Mongolian**	**Tungusic**	**Korean**	**Japanese**
Turkish	Khalkha	Ewenki	Korean	Japanese
Uzbek	Buriat	Manchu		Ryukyuan
Azeri [=Azerbaijani]	Chakhar	Ewen		
Kazakh	Kalmyck	Nanai		
Uighur	Monguor	Orik		
Volga Tatar [=Tatar]				

Caucasian

The languages that are normally grouped together as Caucasian have not yet been assigned to families in a definitive way. These languages are primarily found in northeastern Turkey and in the former USSR (between the Black Sea and the Caspian Sea, in and around the Caucasus Mountains). The best evidence so far points to three distinct language families—Northwest Caucasian, Northeast Caucasian, and South Caucasian (see table 8.17).

South Caucasian (sometimes called Kartvelian) consists of Georgian, Laz (also called Mingrelian), and Svan. Georgian has the largest number of speakers. It was also the native language of Joseph Stalin, dictator of the former Soviet Union in the 1930s and 1940s. Northwest Caucasian contains a handful of languages, including Adyghe and Kabardian (also called West Circassian and East Circassian respectively). Northeast Caucasian consists of about two-dozen languages. Of these Chechen, Lezghian, and Avar have the largest number of speakers.

Altogether there are about thirty-five languages in the three separate families, with a total of approximately five million speakers. Although no genetic relationship has been proven to exist between these three families, they do seem to share a number of areal features (probably brought about through mutual borrowing): many Caucasian languages have glottalized consonants, complex consonant clusters, a very large consonantal inventory, but very few vowel phonemes. It has recently been claimed that the Northwest and Northeast Caucasian languages are part of a single family, but this grouping is not yet widely accepted among Caucasianists.

Table 8.17   The Caucasian languages
The South Caucasian (Kartvelian) family
Georgian Laz [=Mingrelian] Svan
The Northwest Caucasian family
Kabardian [= East Circassian] Adyghe [=West Circassian]
The Northeast Caucasian family
Chechen Lezghian Avar [=Daghestani]

Dravidian

There are twenty-five Dravidian languages (see table 8.18), which are primarily found in the southern half of India, but also in Sri Lanka, Pakistan, and Nepal. About a hundred and seventy-five million people are native speakers of a Dravidian language. The most widely spoken languages in this family are Telugu, Tamil, Kannada, and Malayalam.

Dravidian languages are normally SOV. They are agglutinating and non-tonal, and usually have initial stress.

Table 8.18	The Dravidian family		
North	**Central**	**South-Central**	**South**
Kurux	Kolami	Telugu	Tamil
Malto	Naiki	Savara	Malayalam
Brahui	Parji	Konda	Kannada
	Gadaba	Gondi	Tulu

Austroasiatic

The Austroasiatic family of languages (see table 8.19) consists of about a hundred and fifty languages with approximately fifty million speakers.

Mon-Khmer is the largest branch of Austroasiatic and contains languages such as Cambodian (also called Khmer), Vietnamese, and many other languages of India, Cambodia, Vietnam, Burma, and southern China. The Munda branch of Austroasiatic includes languages spoken in central and northeastern India, such as Mundari and Santali. Other Austroasiatic languages are spoken in Malaysia and on the Nicobar Islands (northwest of Sumatra).

Some Austroasiatic languages are tonal (for example, Vietnamese) and some are characterized by large and complex vowel systems. Word order is generally SVO or SOV.

Table 8.19	The Austroasiatic family
Munda	**Mon-Khmer**
Mundari	Vietnamese
Santali	Cambodian [= Khmer]
	Mon
	Parauk

Tai-Kadai

The Tai-Kadai family includes Thai (formerly called Siamese), Laotian, Shan (spoken in Burma and Thailand), and several other languages of China, Thailand, and Vietnam. Typical salient features of these languages include SVO order, a general lack of inflectional morphemes, and the widespread use of tone (with the number of contrasting tones varying from three to nine).

Sino-Tibetan

In terms of numbers of speakers, the Sino-Tibetan family (see table 8.20) is the largest language family after Indo-European. There are about three hundred Sino-Tibetan languages, with well over a billion native speakers.

Table 8.20	The Sino-Tibetan family						
Tibeto-Burman				**Sinitic**			
	Mandarin	*Wu*	*Min*	*Yue*	*Xiang*	*Hakka*	*Gan*
Burmese	Mandarin	Wu	Amoy	Cantonese	Hunan	Hakka	Gan
Tibetan			Hokkian				
Yi [=Nyi]			Taiwanese				
Sharpa			Fukian				

There are two major branches: Tibeto-Burman and Sinitic. The first branch includes Tibetan, Burmese, and many other languages spoken in northeastern India, Nepal, Burma, Tibet, and China. For the most part, these languages employ SOV word order.

The Sinitic branch contains several different subgroupings, including Mandarin (with major dialects in and around Beijing, Szechuan, and Nanking), Wu (with dialects in Shanghai and Suchow), Min (which includes Taiwanese, Amoy, Hokkian, and Fukian), Yue (Cantonese), Xiang, Hakka, and Gan. The Sinitic languages typically have SVO order and are usually tonal. They are predominantly isolating, having many monomorphemic (and usually monosyllabic) words. Consonant clusters are normally avoided.

The Sinitic family of languages is sometimes referred to as 'Chinese' by non-linguists, as if it were a single language with several dialects rather than a group of related mutually unintelligible languages. This confusion is based on the fact that the same writing system is used across China and can be understood by speakers of different Chinese languages (see chapter 15, section 3.1).

Austronesian

The Austronesian (see table 8.21) family contains approximately one thousand languages, which are spoken from the island of Madagascar halfway across the world to Southeast Asia, Hawaii, Easter Island, and New Zealand. Some of the languages of Formosa (Taiwan) also belong to this family; however, Taiwanese, which is spoken by most of the island's residents, is a Sinitic language (see above).

The largest branch within the Austronesian family is Malayo-Polynesian, which contains all the Austronesian languages outside of Formosa. These include Malagasy (spoken on Madagascar), Malay (and the mutually comprehensible Indonesian), Tagalog (the basis for Pilipino, the official language of the Philippines), Javanese, and many other languages spoken in the Philippines, Malaysia, Indonesia, Vietnam, Cambodia, Formosa, and the islands of the Pacific Ocean.

The Polynesians were intrepid ocean travellers who colonized Hawaii, Easter Island, and New Zealand sometime between 500 and 1000 AD. Well-known Polynesian languages include Samoan, Tahitian, Maori, and Hawaiian (which now has only a few hundred first-language native speakers, although efforts are underway to revive it).

Table 8.21	The Austronesian family	
Formosan	**Malayo-Polynesian**	
	Western	*Oceanic*
Paiwan	Javanese	Samoan
Amis	Malay [=Indonesian]	Fijian
Atayal	Tagalog [=Pilipino]	Tahitian
Seediq	Malagasy	Maori
	Sundanese	Hawaiian
	Balinese	Motu
		Ponapean

A characteristic feature of Austronesian languages is the extensive use of reduplication. Many of these languages also make liberal use of infixes, which are extremely rare in other language families. Word order is usually SVO, although VSO is more prevalent in the Austronesian languages spoken in Formosa, the Philippines, Northern Borneo, and Polynesia.

Some research has attempted to link the Austronesian family with the Austroasiatic family of India and Southeast Asia, forming a larger Austric family. However, this relationship is still very tentative.

Indo-Pacific

Indo-Pacific (or Papuan) languages are all spoken on the island of New Guinea, on nearby islands such as New Britain or Bougainville, or on the Andaman Islands (just southwest of Burma). Little is known about many of these languages, but they appear to be about seven hundred in number, with just under three million speakers.

Two languages with relatively large speaker populations are Enga (a hundred and sixty-five thousand speakers, spoken in the western highlands of New Guinea) and Bunak (fifty thousand speakers, spoken on the island of Timor, west of New Guinea).

Indo-Pacific languages are normally tone languages. Nouns are often marked for case, but not always for number. Word order is usually SOV.

Australian

Recent studies have established that all of the aboriginal languages of Australia belong to the same family. There are about one hundred and seventy such languages, but many have very few speakers. There are currently only about thirty thousand speakers of aboriginal Australian languages.

The majority of Australian languages are spoken in Arnhem Land (north central Australia) and the northern part of Western Australia. The languages with the largest number of speakers are Mabuiag (seven thousand speakers on the Torres Straits Islands, north of Australia) and the Western Desert Language (five thousand speakers in Western Australia).

Australian languages are characterized by simple vowel systems. Nouns are normally marked for case, sometimes in unusual and intricate ways, and word order can be very free.

Afroasiatic

Afroasiatic languages (see table 8.22) are spoken primarily in a band across the northern half of Africa and in the Middle East. There are about two hundred and fifty Afroasiatic languages and a hundred and seventy-five million speakers of these languages.

Afroasiatic has five main branches, one of which—Egyptian—no longer contains any living languages. Although Old Egyptian was spoken from 3000 BC onward (including during the time of Rameses II [1290–1224 BC], who was probably Pharaoh at the time of the Exodus), it has long been extinct. Its descendant, Coptic, is now used only as the liturgical language of the Coptic church.

A second branch of Afroasiatic is Cushitic, whose member languages are spoken in Somalia, Kenya, Ethiopia, and the Sudan. A third branch, Berber, includes several languages of Algeria, Morocco, and Niger, such as Tuareg and Tamazight. Still another branch, Chadic, contains many of the languages of Chad and Nigeria, such as Hausa. Unlike other Afroasiatic languages, Chadic languages are tonal.

The fifth and largest branch of Afroasiatic (in terms of number of speakers) is the Semitic branch. Many (now extinct) languages mentioned in the Bible were of Semitic origin, such as Babylonian, Assyrian, (Old) Canaanite, Moabite, Classical Hebrew, and Biblical Aramaic. Biblical (or Palestinian) Aramaic was spoken in Palestine at the time of Jesus, and may have been his native language.

Classical Hebrew died out several centuries before the birth of Jesus, although it was maintained as a written language within Judaism. Modern Hebrew (or Israeli) is not directly descended from Classical Hebrew; rather, it was created (or re-created) at the beginning of this century by regularizing some aspects of Classical Hebrew and adding new vocabulary. Modern Hebrew has only had a community of native speakers for the past few decades.

Still another Semitic language, Arabic, has various dialects (not all of which are mutually intelligible) spoken across North Africa and throughout the Middle East. All of these are descended from Classical Arabic, which was the language of Mohammed, the founder of Islam, and is the language of the Koran, the holy book of Islam.

The Semitic languages are characterized by a system of consonantal roots. Most roots consist of three (sometimes two) consonants, with vowels being inserted to indicate various inflectional and derivational categories (see chapter 4, section 1.3).

For example, Arabic has the root *k-t-b* (denoting the concept of writing) from which a variety of words can be formed, including *kitaabun* 'book', *kaatibun* 'writer', *kataba* 'he wrote', and *yaktubu* 'he is writing'.

The Semitic languages frequently have complex consonant clusters and pharyngeal or pharyngealized consonants.

Table 8.22   The Afroasiatic family

(Egyptian)	Cushitic	Berber	Chadic	Semitic
(Coptic)	Somali Oromo	Tachelhit Tamazight Kabyle Riff Tuareg	Hausa	(Babylonian) (Old Canaanite) Aramaic (Assyrian) (Moabite) Arabic Modern Hebrew

Niger-Congo

Most of the languages spoken in sub-Saharan Africa belong to the Niger-Congo family of languages (see table 8.23). In all, this family contains over nine hundred languages, with a total of (approximately) one hundred and eighty million speakers. There are three major branches: Kordofanian, Mande, and Atlantic-Congo.

The Kordofanian branch includes only a handful of languages spoken in the Sudan, such as Tegali, Koalib, and Katla. The Mande branch contains a number of families of languages spoken in West Africa such as Maninka, Bambara, and Mende. (Alex Hailey's famous African ancestor, described in the novel *Roots*, was probably a speaker of Maninka.)

Atlantic-Congo, on the other hand, is much larger and can be divided into several branches and numerous sub-branches. One of the largest sub-branches contains the more than one hundred languages of the Bantu family, with about fifty-five million speakers. Some of the principal Bantu languages are Swahili (Tanzania and Kenya), Shona (Zimbabwe and Zambia), KinyaRwanda (Rwanda, Uganda, and Zaire), Zulu (South Africa and Lesotho), and Xhosa (South Africa). Other Atlantic-Congo languages include Yoruba (Nigeria, Togo, and Benin), Igbo (Nigeria), and Wolof (Senegal).

Niger-Congo languages are typically SVO and usually have tone systems (with the notable exception of Swahili). The Bantu languages are usually agglutinating with verb-subject and verb-direct object agreement. Languages in the Bantu group also exhibit a complex system of noun classes, each of which is marked by a separate set of prefixes.

Table 8.23   The Niger-Congo family

Kordofanian	Mande	Atlantic-Congo	
Tegali	Maninka	Swahili	Xhosa
Koalib	Bambara	Shona	Yoruba
Katla	Mende	KinyaRwanda	Igbo
		Zulu	Wolof

Nilo-Saharan

The Nilo-Saharan family is found primarily in eastern and central Africa and includes approximately one hundred and twenty languages, with about thirty million speakers. Languages in this family include Luo and Maasai (both spoken in Kenya), Dinka (Sudan), Kanuri (Nigeria), and Nuer (Sudan and Ethiopia).

Nilo-Saharan languages generally have tonal systems, nouns are usually marked for case, and often use internal change (as in English *foot* vs. *feet*).

Khoisan

The Khoisan family is quite small, containing only about thirty languages, spoken by a hundred and twenty thousand speakers. The majority of Khoisan languages are spoken in the southern and southwestern areas of Africa.

Some Khoisan languages are Hottentot (= Nama), !Kung, and Sandawe (one of only two Khoisan languages spoken in east Africa). Khoisan languages have unusual click sounds in their consonantal systems. These clicks have been borrowed by a few neighbouring Bantu languages, such as Zulu and Xhosa.

1 Indo-European
2 Caucasian
3 Altaic
4 Finno-Ugric (Uralic)
5 Dravidian
6 Austro-Asiatic
7 Sino-Tibetan
8 Austronesian
9 Papuan (Indo-Pacific)
10 Australian
11 Afro-Asiatic
12 Niger-Kordofanian
13 Nilo-Saharan
14 Khoisan

Figure 8.9 Location of some language families

3.3 North, Central, and South America

Contrary to popular belief, not all native American Indian (usually called **Amerindian**) languages belong to the same family. Although many of the genetic relationships are still unclear, it appears that there are well over a dozen different language families in the Americas (see table 8.24).

Table 8.24 North, Central, and South American families	
Language family	**Some member languages**
Eskimo-Aleut	Inuktitut [= Inuit]
Na-Dene	Navajo, Apache, Chipewayan, Dogrib, Slave
Algonquian	Blackfoot, Micmac, Cree, Ojibwa, (Mohican)
Siouan	Dakota, Lakota, Winnebago, Crow
Iroquoian	Cherokee, Mohawk, Cayuga, (Huron)
Caddoan	Caddo, Witchita, Pawnee
Wakashan	Nootka, Kwakiutl, Nitinat
Salish	Flathead, Halkomelem, Okanagan, Shuswap
Klamath-Sahaptin	Yakima, Nez Perce, Sahaptin, Klamath
Penutian	Patwin, Wintu, Nomlaki
Muskogean	Choctaw, Muskogee
Hokan	Diegueno, Yuma, Mohave
Coahuiltecan	Comecrudo, Cotoname, Pakawa, Carrizo
Uto-Aztecan	Hopi, Nahuatl, Papago, (Classical Aztec)
Oto-Manguean	Mazahua, Zapotec, Mixteco, Otomi
Mayan	Yucatec, Kekchi, Maya, Tzeltal, Tojolabal
Andean-Equatorial	Quechua, Aymara, Arawak, Guarani
Ge-Pano-Carib	Carib, Bororo, Witoto, Mataco
Macro-Chibchan	Cuna, Cayapa, Epera, Warao, Talamanca

Figure 8.10 shows the location of groups found in North and Central America.

Since the next chapter describes the native languages of Canada in some detail, it necessarily includes discussion of many of the Amerindian language families of North America. Therefore, we will restrict our focus here to some facts about a few of the indigenous languages of South America.

There are at least six hundred different Amerindian languages spoken in South America, by about eleven million people. However, our knowledge of these languages is often minimal, and some linguists estimate that there may be over a thousand South American Amerindian languages. Most of these languages belong to one of three subfamilies: Andean-Equatorial, Ge-Pano-Carib, and Macro-Chibchan.

The Andean-Equatorial subfamily contains languages that are found throughout South America, and may have as many as ten million speakers all together. The principal language in this family is Quechua, which has over six million speakers. Dialects of Quechua are spoken in Peru, Ecuador, and Bolivia. This was the language of the Inca empire, which reached its height in the sixteenth century AD, before being destroyed by the Spanish conquistadors.

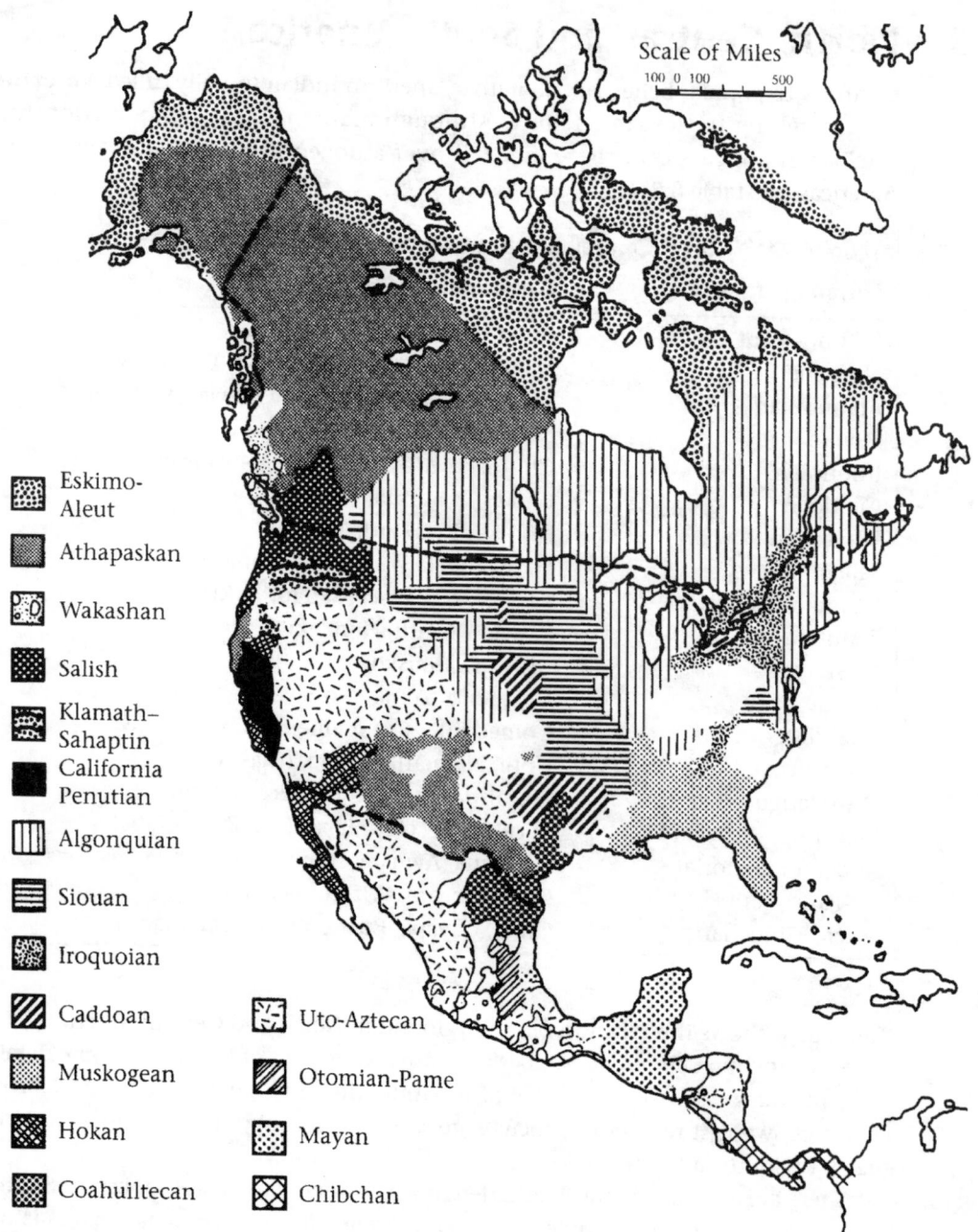

Figure 8.10 North and Central American language groups

Other languages belonging to this family are Aymara (Peru), Arawak (Surinam), and Guarani (the major language of Paraguay). An interesting typological feature of some Andean-Equatorial languages is that they have no lateral consonants whatsoever.

The Ge-Pano-Carib subfamily is also spread over much of South America. Some of the languages belonging to this family are Carib (Surinam), Bororo (Brazil), Witotu (Peru), and

Mataco (Argentina). Languages of the Ge-Pano-Carib family also often lack laterals; the dominant word order in these languages is usually SOV.

Languages of the Macro-Chibchan subfamily are found in Central America and the northwestern part of South America. Some languages belonging to this family are Cuna (Panama), Cayapa (Ecuador), Epera (Colombia), and Warao (Venezuela). Macro-Chibchan languages generally have SOV word order.

3.4   Language phyla

In recent years attempts have been made to group many of the language families presented in sections 3.1, 3.2, and 3.3 into even larger groupings called **phyla** (singular **phylum**) or **macrofamilies**. These attempts are controversial, as they challenge established views within linguistics. However, they also afford a number of intriguing possibilities. In this section we will attempt to provide a balanced view of these ventures into long-range comparison.

One of the best known of the proposed phyla is called Nostratic (also called Eurasiatic). It includes Indo-European, Uralic, Altaic, and (depending on the linguist) various other languages and language families. A number of reconstructed forms have been proposed for this phylum; two of the most convincing are the reconstructed first- and second-person singular pronouns: *m-* 'I' and *t-* 'you (sg)'. These forms are particularly persuasive, since pronoun systems are normally extremely stable, and, thus, are among the most likely forms to have remained constant for the extended period of time since the existence of Proto-Nostratic (about 20 000 years ago).

Another proposed phylum is Dene-Caucasian. It includes Sino-Tibetan, Na-Dené, North Caucasian, and a number of other individual languages. A third proposed phylum is Austric (mentioned in section 3.2), which includes at least Austroasiatic and Austronesian, and perhaps Daic and the Hmong-Mien (Mia-Yiao) group of languages as well.

If all the phyla proposed to date were to be accepted by linguists, the total number of linguistic groupings would be reduced to a mere twelve (as opposed to the fifty or more which have previously been proposed) (see table 8.25).

Table 8.25   Twelve phyla of the world's languages

1. Khoisan
2. Niger-Congo
3. Nilo-Saharan
4. Australian
5. Indo-Pacific
6. Austric:
   a) Austroasiatic
   b) Hmong-Mien
   c) Daic
   d) Austronesian

7. Dene-Caucasian:
   a) Basque
   b) North Caucasian
   c) Burushaski
   d) Nahali
   e) Sino-Tibetan
   f) Yeniseian
   g) Na-Dene
8. Afroasiatic
9. Kartvelian (South Caucasian)
10. Dravidian

11. Nostratic/Eurasiatic:
    a) Indo-European
    b) Uralic
    c) Altaic
    d) Korean-Japanese-Ainu
    e) Gilyak
    f) Chuckchi-Kamchatkan
    g) Eskimo-Aleut
12. Amerind

Venturing still further, some linguists have even gone so far as to reconstruct a single, common ancestor for all human languages, which has been called Proto-World, or Proto-Sapiens. This ancestor language would have been spoken approximately 60 000 to 70 000 years ago. For the sake of interest, we provide a (simplified) example of one of the more than two dozen Proto-World etymologies that have been reconstructed to date:

> **Proto-World *_mena_ 'to think (about)'** Proposed cognates: Latin *men(s)* 'mind', Basque *munak* (pl) 'brains', Hungarian *mon(-d)* 'say', Telugu *manavi* 'prayer, humble request', Shawnee *menw* 'prefer, like', Bambara *mɛ* 'know', Tumale *aiman* 'think', Songhai *ma* 'understand', Masa *min* 'wish'.

It is certainly possible that all human languages have descended from a single ancestor language. It is generally agreed, for example, that all human beings are closely biologically related, and recent genetic studies have even proposed that all living human beings are descended from a particular *Homo sapiens* woman (dubbed 'Eve') who lived in Africa some 200 000 years ago.

Most linguists would probably agree that all human languages must have descended from a small number of languages, if not a single mother language. However, many believe that the tools used for reconstruction (the historical-comparative method) are not able to provide any linguistic evidence for long-range comparisons that go back more than about 8000 or 10 000 years. There are a number of reasons for this.

First, the pronunciation and meaning of words can change so radically over even a much shorter period of time that cognates can become completely unrecognizable. Thus, Latin *aqua* [akwa] 'water' developed into French *eau* [o] 'water' in less than 2000 years, Proto-Indo-European (PIE) **dwo* 'two' developed into Armenian *erku* 'two' in approximately 5000–8000 years, and Old English *hūswīf* 'housewife' radically changed its meaning, to become *hussy* 'a strumpet, or trollop' in less than 1500 years. Of course, as noted in section 3 above, languages also lose words altogether, which can make it all the more difficult to uncover the cognates needed to establish a genetic relationship.

Another argument against long-range comparison has to do with the complications introduced by borrowings. For instance, for many years Thai was thought to be a Sino-Tibetan language, because it contained so many Chinese loan words. However, painstaking research has finally made it clear that Thai is not Sinitic, but that it belongs to the Daic family.

A further difficulty arises when words that appear to be cognates may have evolved independently as instances of onomatopoeia. Since onomatopoeic words (e.g., *cuckoo*, *vroom*) are intended to resemble sounds in the world, it would not be surprising to find that such words would be similar even in unrelated languages.

Another argument against long-range comparison is that certain cross-linguistic similarities among sounds may stem from the fact that all human beings have the same vocal tract configuration. Thus, the presence of universally common sounds like /p t k s i a u/ in suspected cognates may be due not to a shared ancestor, but rather to the fact that these sounds have articulatory and acoustic properties that favour their frequent use.

In defence of their endeavour, supporters of long-range comparison claim that loan words and onomatopoeic words are easily identifiable by the experienced researcher, and can thus be easily discounted. Furthermore, language change need not affect all of the words of a language; some words retain a similar meaning and pronunciation for thousands of years.

Thus, Old English *fisc* [fɪʃ] apparently had the same pronunciation and the same meaning as modern English *fish* [fɪʃ], despite a lapse of 1500 years; the meaning and pronunciation of Latin *aqua* [akwa] 'water' has been maintained in Italian *acqua* [akwa] 'water' (2000 years); Proto-Indo-European **dwo* 'two' changed very little in pronunciation in Latin *duo* 'two' (about 6000 years); and Proto-Indo-European **nepot* 'nephew, grandson' had a meaning and pronunciation almost identical to its descendant *nepot* 'nephew, grandson' in modern Rumanian (about 8000 years).

Supporters of long-range comparison claim that both anthropological and biological evidence show that all human beings are at least distantly related and that it is therefore plausible to believe that all human languages must be related as well. It only remains, they claim, for linguists to determine the degree of relationship among the individual language families.

This controversy is far from being resolved, and it is fair to say that most linguists remain very skeptical about the evidence and conclusions associated with comparative research involving a time depth greater than eight or ten thousand years. Nonetheless, the debate has presented new and intriguing possibilities in the study of linguistic classification.

Summing up

The focus of this chapter is on the criteria that linguists use to classify languages, and on the enormous variety of languages found throughout the world. Linguists sometimes attempt to classify languages solely in terms of their structural similarities and differences (that is, in terms of their **linguistic typology**). Analysis of cross-linguistic data has identified a number of linguistic **universals**, indicating the most common characteristics of human language. The other major type of classificatory work in linguistics is concerned with **genetic relationships**—establishing language families whose members are descended from a common ancestor. While research in this area is hampered both by the large number of languages involved and the scarcity of the available data, a sizable portion of the world's several thousand languages have been placed in families. Finally, we present the controversial work recently done on linguistic **phyla** or **macrofamilies**. Research in these areas can shed light on the nature of language change, as well as the movement of peoples throughout the world.

Sources

The estimate that approximately six thousand five hundred languages are spoken in the world today comes from the website of the Foundation for Endangered Languages (www.bris.ac.uk/Depts/Philosophy/CTL/FEL/; e-mail: nostler@chibcha.demon.co.uk). The suggestion that only three hundred of these languages have a secure future is due to K. Hale, professor of linguistics at MIT, cited in *Time* magazine (23 September 1991, p. 48). For further discussion, see "Endangered Languages" by K. Hale et al., *Language* 68:1–42 (1992).

The section on linguistic typology draws on data from the books by B. Comrie and J. Greenberg cited as Recommended Reading. Other material for this section comes from *Tone: A Linguistic Survey*, edited by V. Fromkin (New York: Academic Press, 1978); J. Hawkins' article "On Implicational and Distributional Universals of Word Order" in *Journal of Linguistics*

16:193–235 (1980); M. Dryer's article "The Greenbergian Word Order Correlations" in *Language* 68:81–138 (1992); *Patterns of Sounds* by I. Maddieson (Cambridge: Cambridge University Press, 1984); M. Ruhlen's book *A Guide to the Languages of the World* (Stanford, CA: Language Universals Project: Stanford University, 1976); *The World's Major Languages*, edited by B. Comrie (Oxford: Oxford University Press, 1990), and the four-volume series *Universals of Human Language*, edited by J. Greenberg (Stanford, CA: Stanford University Press, 1978).

The discussion of morphological typology draws on information presented in B. Comrie's book recommended below. The estimate of the relative frequency of languages in which the subject precedes the direct object is based on information in the book by W. Croft recommended below. The data on OVS and OSV languages is from "Object-Initial Languages" by D. Derbyshire and G. Pullum, *International Journal of American Linguistics* 47:192–214 (1981). The discussion of consonant systems in section 2.4 is based on "Phonetic Universals in Consonant Systems" by B. Lindblom and I. Maddieson in *Language, Speech and Mind: Studies in Honor of Victoria Fromkin*, edited by L. Hyman and C. Li (New York: Routledge & Kegan Paul, 1988), pp. 62–78.

The section on language families is based on B. Comrie's book *The Languages of the Soviet Union* (London: Cambridge University Press, 1981), J. Greenberg's *The Languages of Africa* (Bloomington, IN: Indiana University Press, 1966), the book by M. Ruhlen cited previously and another book by Ruhlen entitled *A Guide to the World's Languages, Volume 1: Classification* (Stanford, CA: Stanford University Press, 1987), and C.F. and F.M. Voegelin's *Classification and Index of the World's Languages* (cited below). Additional data derive from C.D. Buck's book *A Dictionary of Selected Synonyms in the Principal Indo-European Languages* (Chicago: The University of Chicago Press, 1949); *The American Heritage Dictionary of Indo-European Roots*, revised and edited by C. Watkins (Boston: Houghton Mifflin Company, 1985); the three volume *Russisches Etymologisches Wörterbuch* compiled by M. Vasmer (Heidelberg: Carl Winter Universitätsverlag); "Syntactic Reconstruction and Finno-Ugric," an article by L. Campbell in *Historical Linguistics* 1987, edited by H. Andersen and K. Koerner (Amsterdam: John Benjamins, 1990), and the Proto-Baltic Dictionary database developed by the author of this chapter. The maps in figures 8.8 and 8.9 are adapted from *Problems in the Origin and Development of the English Language*, 3rd ed., by John Algeo, copyright © by Harcourt Brace & Company, reprinted by permission of the publisher. The map in figure 8.10 is adapted from *A Guide to the World's Languages, Vol. 1*, by M. Ruhlen (Stanford, CA: Stanford University Press, 1987).

The section on language phyla is based on the book by M. Ruhlen (cited as Recommended Reading), and on *Sprung from Some Common Source*, edited by S. Lamb and E. Mitchell (Stanford, CA: Stanford University Press, 1991).

The data for exercises 1 to 3 are found in *A Guide to the Languages of the World* by M. Ruhlen.

Recommended reading

Comrie, Bernard. 1989. *Language Universals and Linguistic Typology*. 2nd ed. Oxford: Blackwell.
Croft, William. 1990. *Typology and Universals*. New York: Cambridge University Press.
Greenberg, Joseph, ed. 1966. *Universals of Language*. 2nd ed. Cambridge, MA: MIT Press.
Lyovin, Anatole V. 1997. *An Introduction to the Languages of the World*. New York: Oxford University Press.

Ruhlen, Merritt. 1994. *On the Origin of Languages*. Stanford, CA: Stanford University Press.
Voegelin, C.F., and F.M. Voegelin. 1977. *Classification and Index of the World's Languages*. New York: Elsevier.

Questions

1. Which tendencies and universals are manifested in the following vowel systems?
   a) Afrikaans (South Africa) ([y] and [ø] are front rounded vowels)

i	y		u
	ø	ə	o
		e	
ɛ			ɔ
		a	

   b) Squamish (Washington State)

i		u
	ə	
	e	
	a	

2. As noted in section 2.1, the presence of long and nasal vowel phonemes is governed by implicational universals. Do the vowel systems below comply with the implicational universals that make reference to length and nasality?
   a) Maltese Arabic

i		u	iː		uː
e		o	eː		oː
	a			aː	

   b) Awji (North New Guinea)

i		u		ĩ		ũ
e	ə	o		ẽ	ə̃	õ
	a				a	

3. Consider the following consonant systems. Do these consonant systems comply with the implicational universals mentioned in this chapter?
   a) Tahitian (Tahiti)

p	t	ʔ
f		h
v	r	
m	n	

   b) Palauan (Palau Islands)

	t	k	ʔ
b			
	ð		
	s		
m		ŋ	
	l, r		

c) Nengone (Loyalty Islands, South Pacific)—Stop and nasal system only

pʰ	tʰ	t̪ʰ		kʰ	ʔ
b	d	ḍ		g	
m	n		ɲ	ŋ	
m̥	n̥			ŋ̊	

(*Note*: The diacritic [.] indicates a retroflex consonant; [̥] marks a voiceless nasal; [ɲ] represents a palatal nasal.)

d) Mixe (South Mexico)

p	t		k	ʔ
	d		g	
	ts	tʃ		
	s		x	h
v			ɣ	
m	n			

4. Describe the morphological characteristics of each of the following languages in terms of the four-way system of classification outlined in section 2.2 (recip = reciprocal, caus = causative, indic = indicative, statement).

a) Siberian Yupik
Angya-ghlla-ng-yug-tuq
boat -big -get-want-3Sg
'He wants to get a big boat.'

b) Latvian

las-u	las-ām	rakst-u	rakst-ām
read-1sg.Pres	read-1pl.Pres	write-1sg.Pres	write-1pl.Pres
'I read'	'we read'	'I write'	'we write'

c) Japanese
gakusei-wa   homer-are-na- i
student-Topic   praise-Pass-Neg-Pres
'The student is not praised.'

5. Do a morphological analysis of the following data from Latvian. After you have segmented and identified the morphemes, describe how the data reflects the implicational universals in section 2.2.

a) lidotājs   'aviator (nominative)'
b) lidotāju   'aviator (accusative)'
c) lidotājam   'to the aviator (dative)'
d) lidot   'to fly'
e) rakstītājs   'writer (nominative)'
f) rakstītāja   'writer's (genitive)'
g) rakstīt   'to write'

6. Note the following data from Malagasy, an Austronesian language spoken on the island of Madagascar. (The data is from *Malagasy: Introductory Course*, by C. Garvey, Washington: Center for Applied Lingusiics, 1964.) Does Malagasy comply with all the word order tendencies mentioned earlier in section 2.3?

a) amin' ny restauranta
   'to the restaurant'
b) Enti'n ny labiera ny mpiasa.
   brings the beer   the waiter
   'The waiter brings the beer.'
c) Avy any Amerika izy.
   come from America he
   'He comes from America.'

7. For each of the following languages on the left, determine which of the languages on the right is most closely related to it:
   i) Macedonian   a) Albanian
                      b) Ukrainian
                      c) Greek

   ii) Gypsy   a) French
                      b) Old Egyptian
                      c) Egyptian Arabic

   iii) French   a) Spanish
                      b) Italian
                      c) Romansch

   iv) Irish   a) English
                      b) Icelandic
                      c) Breton

   v) Vietnamese   a) Laotian
                      b) Mundari
                      c) Burmese

   vi) Modern Hebrew a) Turkish
                        b) Somali
                        c) Yiddish

8. To which family does each of the following languages belong?
   a) Gujarati   j) Yuma
   b) Hakka   k) Volga Tatar
   c) Lapp   l) Georgian
   d) Uzbek   m) Mohican
   e) Sandawe   n) Aramaic
   f) Quechua   o) Flathead
   g) Faroese   p) Telugu
   h) Maninka   q) Javanese
   i) Santali   r) Navajo

9. Make a list of up to fifteen languages spoken by friends and acquaintances, and identify the language family to which each belongs.

Eung-Do Cook

Amerindian languages of Canada

He who studies only one Indian language and learns
its manifold curious grammatical devices, its wealth
of words, its capacity of expression, is speedily
convinced of its superiority to all other Indian
tongues, and not infrequently to all languages by
whomsoever spoken.

J.W. POWELL, INDIAN LINGUISTIC FAMILIES OF AMERICA NORTH OF MEXICO (1891)

The study of North American Indian (**Amerindian**) languages has made a number of significant contributions to the development of linguistics. In practically every book that the student of linguistics reads, the impact of work in this area is evident. It would be no exaggeration to say that the lasting and profound influence of such eminent pioneers of linguistics as Franz Boas, Edward Sapir, and Leonard Bloomfield is due in large part to the seminal work they did on structurally diverse Amerindian languages.

The value of current research on Amerindian languages stems primarily from the light that it can shed on the nature of human linguistic competence. Besides refuting the popular misconception that the Native languages of North America are somehow primitive, this work has also uncovered certain structural and semantic phenomena that are not found in more widely studied languages such as English, French, Chinese, and so on. Another compelling reason for the study of Amerindian languages is that it can yield clues (sometimes the only ones available) to help resolve problems in archaeology and anthropology (especially ethnohistory) relating to the origin and migration of the indigenous peoples of the Americas.

1   Genetic classification

How many indigenous languages are there? How are they related genetically? How are they distributed? Although definitive answers cannot yet be given to any of these questions, the current tentative consensus is briefly outlined in the next two sections prior to a discussion of the structural characteristics of Amerindian languages.

1.1   Early classification

J.W. Powell's work of 1891, which represents the first attempt at a comprehensive genetic classification of the indigenous languages of North America, recognizes fifty-eight families. Although this classification was preceded by and indebted to many other classifications, it is considered one of the most valuable works in Amerindian linguistics. Powell's classification of hundreds of different languages into fewer than sixty families was a remarkable achievement, but really only a first step toward a final genetic classification.

In the years following Powell's work, many linguists came to assume that all of the indigenous languages of North America ultimately originated from a small number of mother languages (if not a single one). Consequently, they began trying to place the known language families into larger **stocks** and still larger **phyla**. The best-known classification from this perspective was proposed by Edward Sapir in 1929. In this far-reaching analysis, which owes a great deal to earlier work by Alfred Kroeber and Ronald Dixon among others, all Amerindian language families were grouped into stocks which, in turn, were organized into six superstocks or phyla. Although not adequately substantiated in all details, this proposal stimulated a great deal of research aimed at the further classification of Amerindian languages.

1.2   Recent classification

A more realistic and up-to-date classification was proposed in 1964. Following Sapir's scheme, 221 languages were grouped into 42 families and 31 isolates, which were then classified into 9 phyla. A great deal more has been learned since this proposal was made, and some aspects of this work are now out of date. Certain languages that were earlier treated as isolates have since been proven to be related. For example, Yurok and Wiyot of California, originally considered isolates, have not only been found to be related to each other, but have been placed in the Algonquian family (as originally claimed by Sapir as early as 1913). On the other hand, there is also strong evidence that what were formerly considered dialects of one language should be treated as separate languages. For example, Dogrib, Bear Lake, and Hare of the Athapaskan family (see table 9.2) were once believed to be dialects of the same language, but their status has since been reconsidered. The identity of Dogrib as a separate language is now well established and the possibility that Bear Lake and Hare are separate languages is under consideration.

Recently, a new and daring classification of Amerindian languages has been proposed. Highly controversial, this classification places virtually all the indigenous languages of the Americas into a single large group, which is labelled **Amerind**. (Excluded from this group are the Eskimo-Aleut family and Na-Dené, a stock consisting of the Athapaskan family and three isolates.) However, both the methodology and the data underlying this proposal have been subjected to severe criticism, and the Amerind hypothesis is not currently accepted by most specialists in the field. We will therefore not consider it further here.

The map in figure 9.1 shows the geographic distribution of the widely accepted Amerindian language families and isolates of Canada discussed in this chapter. Of course, the political border between Canada and the United States is not a linguistic boundary. As shown in figure 8.10 in the preceding chapter, the traditional homeland of many Native groups includes portions of both countries.

Figure 9.1 Distribution of Amerindian language families in Canada

Of the families shown on the map, Athapaskan and Algonquian are the two largest in terms of the land mass they occupy and perhaps also in terms of speaker population. The Athapaskan people migrated from north to south, so that their languages were once spoken in Alaska, the Canadian northwest (including two territories and four western provinces), Washington, Oregon, California, and the American southwest. The Athapaskan languages in Washington, Oregon, and California are now either extinct or almost extinct.

The Algonquian languages of Canada are spread from the foothills of the Rocky Mountains to the Atlantic coast. While linguistic variation is greatest around the five Great Lakes, dialects of Cree are spoken in almost all localities of the Algonquian territory. Another large family, which is spread from west to east, is Eskimo-Aleut, spoken along the Arctic coast.

1.3 Canadian languages

The population of aboriginal America (north of Mexico) is estimated to have been 1 150 000 at the time of Columbus (the late fifteenth century). The epidemics of the 1830s and 1850s as well as innumerable wars considerably reduced the Native Amerindian population, although recently the number has been growing. The current Native population of Canada is estimated at more than a quarter of a million, including an estimated 150 000 speakers of indigenous languages.

Eleven language families and isolates are represented in Canada, although there are no exact figures on speaker populations and no agreement on the details of genetic classification.

Algonquian

The most widely spoken Amerindian languages in Canada belong to the Algonquian family (see table 9.1). Nine Algonquian languages are found in Canada. (Here and elsewhere, speaker populations for the United States are provided to give an idea of the overall size of the various Amerindian linguistic communities.)

Table 9.1 The Algonquian languages of Canada		
Language	**Estimated number of speakers in Canada**	**Estimated number of speakers in the United States**
Cree	55 000	–
Ojibwa	40 000	10 000–20 000
Montagnais-Niskapi	5 000	–
Blackfoot	4 000	1 000
Micmac	3 000–5 000	–
Malecite	250	300
Potawatomi	100	400
Delaware	5–10	100
Abenaki	10	5

Athapaskan

There are an estimated twenty-nine thousand speakers of the Canadian Athapaskan languages, including Gwich'in, which is also spoken in Alaska (see table 9.2). This language family has the second largest speaker population in Canada and also exhibits the greatest internal diversity, with fifteen distinct languages in this country alone.

Table 9.2 The Athapaskan languages of Canada		
Language	**Estimated number of speakers in Canada**	**Estimated number of speakers in the United States**
Chipewyan	15 000	–
Carrier	2 000	–
Slavey	6 000	–
Gwich'in	500	700
Chilcotin	1 800	–
Tahltan	100	–
Tutchone	450	–

Table 9.2 (continued)	The Athapaskan languages of Canada	
Language	Estimated number of speakers in Canada	Estimated number of speakers in the United States
Dogrib	2 000	–
Hare	600	–
Kaska	200	–
Beaver	200	–
Sekani	200	–
Han	fewer than 50	fewer than 5
Sarcee	50	–
Tagish	extinct	–

Salish

The total speaker population of the ten languages in the Salish family, which is centred in British Columbia, is estimated at twenty-five hundred (see table 9.3).

Table 9.3	The Salish languages of Canada
Language	Estimated number of speakers
Shuswap	500
Thompson	50
Okanagan	500
Lillooet	300–400
Halkomelem	500
Comox	400
Bella Coola	50
Straits	30
Squamish	12
Sechelt	10

Wakashan

The Wakashan family, which is spoken principally on Vancouver Island and the adjacent British Columbia coast, consists of five languages in Canada (see table 9.4). (A sixth Wakashan language, Makah, is spoken in Washington state.)

Table 9.4	The Wakashan languages of Canada
Language	Estimated number of speakers
Nootka	600
Kwakw'ala	250
Haisla	200
Heiltsuk	200–300
Nitinat	60

Iroquoian

Another major group of Amerindian languages represented in Canada is the Iroquoian family, which is found in eastern Canada and the United States (see table 9.5).

Table 9.5	The Iroquoian languages of Canada	
Language	Estimated number of speakers in Canada	Estimated number of speakers in the United States
Mohawk	1 000	2 000
Seneca	25	200
Oneida	200	50
Cayuga	360	10
Onondaga	100	50
Tuscarora	7	30

Other languages

There are a number of other language families represented in Canada, including the Inuit language (of the Eskimo-Aleut family), with about a hundred thousand speakers, of whom sixteen thousand are in Canada; Siouan, with a Canadian population of about five thousand (compared to fifteen thousand in the United States); and the Tsimshian languages of northwestern British Columbia (of which the major representative, Nass-Gitksan, has about thirty-five hundred speakers). There are also three possible language isolates spoken in Canada: Tlingit (five hundred speakers) and Haida (five hundred speakers) in the Queen Charlotte Islands and vicinity; and Kutenai, which is spoken by fewer than two hundred people in the British Columbia interior near the Alberta border. Tlingit is now widely believed to be related to Athapaskan.

Many Native Indian languages have become extinct, and many more are rapidly becoming obsolete under the influence of English, French, and Spanish, which have become the languages of the nursery and the living-room in much of North America thanks in part to the influence of the mass media. Recently, many Native communities have sought to counteract this process. With the help of government agencies, museums, and universities, they have launched programs to retain and promote their languages and cultures. As a result of this renaissance movement, some languages (such as Chilcotin, Kutenai, and Shuswap) have seen the establishment of an orthography for the first time, and others have become part of school curricula or even a medium of instruction in lower grades. The long-term effect of this effort on the survival of Native languages remains to be seen.

2   Structural features

Since there are so many apparently unrelated languages in North America, it is not surprising to find a great deal of typological variation. Although it is impossible to present even a synopsis of the structural characteristics of these languages, a small selection of what the reader might consider strikingly different and interesting will be given.

2.1   Phonology

The Algonquian languages (such as Cree and Blackfoot) and the Athapaskan languages (such as Sarcee and Chipewyan) have long been in contact in the prairie provinces of Canada. However, the phonological differences between these two language families are striking since Algonquian has one of the simplest phonemic inventories in the world, while Athapaskan has one of the most complex.

Cree

Except for /eː/, which is always long, Cree vowels may be either short or long. The Cree consonantal system is also simple and straightforward, with no aspiration or glottalization. Consonant clusters are rare, and the most common syllable types are CV, CVC, and V. The vocalic and consonant systems of Cree are given in table 9.6.

Table 9.6 Vowel and consonant phonemes in Cree					
Vowel phonemes		**Consonant phonemes**			
			Bilabial	*Alveolar*	*Velar*	*Glottal*
i, iː	o, oː	Obstruents	p	t	k	
				ts		
eː	a, aː			s		h
		Sonorants	m	n		
				j	w	

Chipewyan

In Chipewyan, on the other hand, there are five tense vowels, each of which may be either oral or nasal, as well as a lax vowel, which has no nasal counterpart. The Chipewyan consonant system has four times more phonemes than does Cree. It is characterized by a large and symmetrical class of obstruents, particularly affricates, as shown in table 9.7. Another characteristic of Chipewyan phonology is the presence of tone, which, along with nasality, makes for many more syllable types in Chipewyan than in Cree.

Table 9.7 Vowel and consonant phonemes in Chipewyan					
Vowel phonemes					
Oral			*Nasal*		
i		u	ĩ		ũ
e	ə	o	ẽ		õ
	a			ã	

Table 9.7 (continued)		Vowel and consonant phonemes in Chipewyan		
Consonant phonemes				
	Labial	*Interdental*	*Alveolar*	*Alveolar*
Plain	p	tθ	t	ts
Aspirated		tθʰ	tʰ	tsʰ
Glottalized		tθ'	t'	ts'
		ð		z
		θ		s
	m		n	r
	Lateral	*Alveopalatal*	*Velar*	*Labiovelar*	*Glottal*
Plain	tɬ	tʃ	k	(kʷ)	
Aspirated	tɬʰ	tʃʰ	kʰ	(kʷʰ)	
Glottalized	tɬ'	tʃ'	k'	(kʷ')	ʔ
	l	j	ɣ	w	
	ɬ	ʃ	x	(xʷ)	h

Putting aside the elements in parentheses (whose phonemic status is questionable), there are thirty-five consonantal phonemes in Chipewyan, most of which are obstruents. Several sets of stops, affricates, and fricatives constitute the core system. There are two very conspicuous phonological characteristics: a three-way contrast (plain versus aspirated versus glottalized) involving six sets of stops and affricates, and a large inventory of affricates in four series (interdental, alveolar, lateral and alveopalatal). Particularly worthy of note here are the interdental and lateral affricates, which are seldom found in other language families, as well as the paucity of bilabial stops. The syllable structure is either CV or CVC.

The examples in table 9.8 illustrate CV and CVC syllable types as well as a contrast between oral and nasal vowels and between high tone (marked by the diacritic ´) and low tone.

Table 9.8	Vowel and tone contrasts in Chipewyan			
Low tone/high tone	ɬu	'fish'	ɬú	'white fish'
	kʰũe	'house'	kʰũé	'town'
	teskʰoθ	'I cough'	teskʰóθ	'I am wide'
Oral/nasal	ti	'prairie chicken'	tĩ(ɣĩ)	'four'
	tsʰá	'beaver'	tsʰã́	'excrement'
	si	'I'	sĩ	(emphatic particle)

2.2 Morphology

Equally interesting characteristics of Amerindian languages are seen in their morphology, whose complexity has fascinated linguists for a long time. We can illustrate some of these intricacies with the help of several Amerindian languages spoken in Canada.

Polysynthesis

The term *polysynthetic* (see chapter 8, section 2.2) is often used to underscore the morphological complexities that are easily observable in many Amerindian languages. **Polysynthetic languages** are characterized by morphologically complex words whose component morphemes often express meanings that would be expressed by separate words in a European language. In the Inuktitut language, for instance, a typical word consisting of a root followed by one or more well-defined suffixes can be the equivalent of an entire sentence in English. The following utterances are each considered to consist of a single word. (There is allomorphic variation involving the morpheme *gik/rik* meaning 'good'.)

1)
Iglu-gik-tuq.
house-good-he-has
'He has a good house.'

Qayaq-rik-tuq.
canoe-good-he-has
'He has a good canoe.'

In the preceding examples it is relatively easy to identify the individual morphemes. In other languages, it is much more difficult to isolate morphemes because of the complex morphological and phonological processes found there. For this reason, no attempt will be made to provide a morpheme-for-morpheme translation of the following examples of polysynthesis in Slave (an Athapaskan language) and Blackfoot (an Algonquian language).

2)
mewõhníendiʔõ. (Slave)
'I lent it to him.'

3)
máta:kahkajiwa:tsiksi. (Blackfoot)
'He is not going home.'

Number

Most English speakers are familiar with a three-way contrast involving person (first person—speaker; second person—addressee; third person—other party) and a two-way contrast involving number (unmarked singular versus marked plural). In many Amerindian languages, however, a much more elaborate system of contrasts is encountered. As noted in the chapter on morphology, for instance, the Inuit language has three subcategories of number—singular (one), dual (two), and plural (three or more). The following two sets of examples illustrate how these subcategories are marked in nouns and verbs. (In the transcription employed here, the symbol *y* represents a phoneme with the allophones [j] and [ʒ].)

4)

iglu	'an igloo (house)'
iglu-k	'igloos (two)'
iglu-t	'igloos (three or more)'

niriyu-q   'he ate'
niriyu-k   'they (two) ate'
niriyu-t   'they (three or more) ate'

The same number categories that are marked by suffixes in the Inuit language are represented by changing the stem in certain Athapaskan verbs. The following examples are from Chipewyan. (The alternation involving the prefixes *ni-*, *nuh-* and *tuɬ-* involves a separate phenomenon, which need not concern us here.)

5)
ni-tá   'sit down' (singular subject)
nuh-kʰé   'let's (you and I) sit down' (dual subject)
tuɬ-tθ'i   'let's (all of us) sit down' (plural subject)

Cree person and number

The Algonquian languages have an even more elaborate system of person and number marking, as the verb paradigm from Cree in table 9.9 illustrates.

Table 9.9	Person and number marking in Cree	
pimisin 'to lie down'		
1st singular	ni-pimisin-in	'I lie down'
2nd singular	ki-pimisin-in	'you lie down'
3rd singular (proximate)	pimisin	'he or she lies down'
4th singular (obviative)	pimisin-ijiwa	'the other lies down'
1st plural (inclusive)	ki-pimisin-inaw	'we (you and I) lie down'
1st plural (exclusive)	ni-pimisin-ina:n	'we (I and other) lie down'
2nd plural	ki-pimisin-ina:wa:w	'you (pl) lie down'
3rd plural	pimisin-wak	'they lie down'

These examples exhibit a contrast in the first person plural between the so-called **inclusive** and **exclusive**. The inclusive indicates that the addressee is to be included in the interpretation of the morpheme corresponding to English *we*. Thus, *ki-pimisin-inaw*, the inclusive first person plural form, means either 'you and I lie down' or 'you, I, and someone else lie down'. In contrast, the exclusive form (*ni-pimisin-ina:n*) indicates that the addressee is to be excluded. In English, the phrases 'we lie down' is potentially ambiguous because the grammatical distinctions observed in Cree are not made.

The grammatical distinction between **proximate** and **obviative** (sometimes called third person and fourth person, respectively) is not found in English and is not easy to describe. However, an example will help illustrate its function. Suppose we are talking about two people named Steven and Paul and that the sentence *He lay down* is used. In English this sentence could mean either that Steven lay down or that Paul lay down.

Cree speakers avoid this ambiguity by choosing either Steven or Paul as the focus of the conversation and marking this choice grammatically. One of the ways that this choice can be signalled is by using the focused person's name as subject of a proximate form of the verb. Subsequent references to that person can then be made by means of a proximate verb form.

Thus, when a Cree speaker uses the proximate form *pimisin* to express the meaning 'he lay down', listeners know that he or she is talking about the person chosen as the focus of the conversation. Reference to any other person requires use of the obviative form *pimisin-ijiwa*.

Cree noun classes

Cree does not divide nouns into masculine, feminine, and neuter classes in the manner of English (*he, she, it*) and many other Indo-European languages. Instead, grammatical gender in Cree and other Algonquian languages distinguishes between **animate** and **inanimate**. This contrast can be seen in the two different forms of the plural suffix, *-ak* for animate nouns and *-a* for inanimate ones (see table 9.10).

Table 9.10	Animate and inanimate nouns in Cree			
	Singular		**Plural**	
Animate	si:si:p	'duck'	si:si:p-ak	'ducks'
	na:pe:w	'man'	na:pe:w-ak	'men'
	ospwa:kan	'pipe'	ospwa:kan-ak	'pipes'
Inanimate	mi:nis	'berry'	mi:nis-a	'berries'
	astotin	'cap'	astotin-a	'caps'
	a:cimo:win	'story'	a:cimo:win-a	'stories'

Assignment of Cree words to a noun class sometimes seems to lack any natural motivation. The word *ospwa:kan* 'pipe', for instance, belongs to the animate class even though it does not denote a living thing. This practice is somewhat reminiscent of what is found in the gender classification system of English, which can place a few inanimate words (such as those referring to ships and countries) in the feminine class.

Athapaskan classificatory verbs

Another type of classification is found in the verb system of Athapaskan. Every Athapaskan language has up to twelve classificatory verbs, the selection of which is governed by factors such as the shape, texture, and animacy of the referent of the subject or direct object. This set of contrasts may be viewed as a sort of noun classification system within the verb. In the Chipewyan examples in table 9.11, each sentence consists of a verb whose form indicates the type of object undergoing the action it describes. (The variant part of the verb is underlined in these examples; the diacritic ´ marks high tone.)

The classificatory verb stems in the following examples distinguish among eight subcategories of direct object NPs in Chipewyan. In other words, the speaker of Chipewyan must choose one of eight verb forms in accordance with the class of the direct object NP—a phenomenon that has no counterpart in English.

Table 9.11	Classificatory verbs in Chipewyan	
1. round/solid	nijerí-ʔa	'He or she is picking it up (a round solid thing).'
2. animate	nijerí-tʰí	'He or she is picking it up (an animate thing).'
3. long	nijeríɬ-tʰí	'He or she is picking it up (a long thing such as a stick).
4. fabric-like	nijeríɬ-tʃʰuθ	'He or she is picking it up (a fabric-like thing) .'
5. contained in a cup	nijerí-kʰá	'He or she is picking it up (a thing contained in a cup).'
6. grain-like	nijerí-tsah	'He or she is picking it up (a grain-like thing).'
7. messy	nijerí-tɬʰé	'He or she is picking it up (a messy thing).'
8. rope-like	nijerí-le	'He or she is picking it up (a rope-like thing).'

Yana natural gender

An unusual type of natural gender contrast manifests itself in other Amerindian languages, where the sex of the speaker and listener is reflected in the form of individual words. A clear example of this comes from the now extinct Yana language, a member of the Hokan family, once spoken in the American northwest. Words in this language were systematically differentiated phonologically according to the sex of the speaker and addressee (see table 9.12). The male form was used between males (when both the speaker and addressee were male), whereas the female form was used when both or either party was female. This means that the female form was used much more frequently under normal circumstances. Putting details aside, the phonological contrast between the two forms is characterized by two syllable types: one for the male form (sometimes called 'heavy' for expository purposes) and one for the female form (sometimes called 'light').

Table 9.12	Phonological contrasts in Yana	
Male form	**Female form**	
imamba	imampḁ	'deer liver'
gaːgi	gaːki̥	'crow'
ʔija	ʔijḁ	'trail'
ʔina	ʔih	'tree'
bana	bah	'deer'
jaːna	jaːh	'person'

The two sets of forms in table 9.12 show a regular phonological relationship between the male and female forms. In the first three, the last syllable is voiced in the male form and voiceless in the female form. In the last three, on the other hand, the word ends in -*na* in the male form but -*h* in the female form.

Summing up

This chapter outlines several families of **Amerindian** languages spoken in Canada and presents a selection of phonological and grammatical characteristics of these languages. Even this brief discussion should illustrate just how much languages can differ from each other, especially in the area of morphological and phonological contrasts. Although it has sometimes been claimed that languages may differ in unpredictable ways, it should be remembered that there are striking similarities that underlie surface differences and that these differences can be described in terms of universal categories and processes (phonemes, morphemes, inflection, derivation, and so on). For this reason, the structural diversity of Amerindian languages offer the linguist opportunities to reaffirm familiar principles, as well as to discover new insights into the nature of human language.

Sources

The discussion of the genetic relationships among Amerindian languages draws on John Wesley Powell's article "Indian Linguistic Families of America North of Mexico" in the Seventh Annual Report, Bureau of American Ethnology (1891); Edward Sapir's article, "Central and North American Languages" in *Encyclopedia Britannica*, 14th ed., Vol. 5, pp. 138–41 (1929); C.F. and F.M. Voegelin's work, *Map of North American Indian Languages* (Washington, DC: American Ethnology Society, 1966); and the article by Michael Foster cited below. The Sapir article has been reprinted in *Selected Writings of Edward Sapir*, edited by D. Mandelbaum (Berkeley, CA: University of California Press, 1949). The Amerind hypothesis is presented by J. Greenberg in his book, *Language in the Americas* (Stanford, CA: Stanford University Press, 1987). For some sample criticism, see L. Campbell's review of *Language in the Americas* in *Language* 64:591–615 (1988).

The estimates of speaker populations reported here are based primarily on the following sources: M.K. Foster's article "Canadian Indigenous Languages: Past and Present" cited below, *International Encyclopedia of Linguistics* (New York: Oxford University Press, 1992), D.M. Kinkade's article "The Decline of Native Languages in Canada" in *Endangered Languages*, edited by R.H. Robins and E.M. Uhlenbeck (New York: Berg, 1991), pp. 157–76, and E.-D. Cook's article "Aboriginal Languages: A History" in *Language in Canada*, edited by J. Edwards (New York: Cambridge University Press, 1998), pp. 125–43.

The data on Chipewyan vowels comes from F.K. Li's article "Chipewyan" in *Linguistic Structures of Native America,* by H. Hoijer et al. (Viking Fund Publications in Anthropology, No. 6, 1946) and E.-D. Cook's article "Chipewyan Vowels" in *International Journal of American Linguistics* 49:413–27 (1983). The data on Cree are from C.H. Wolfart and J. Carroll's book *Meet Cree: A Guide to the Cree Language*, 2nd rev. ed. (Edmonton: University of Alberta Press, 1981). The data on male and female speech in Yana are drawn from Edward Sapir's 1929 article "Male and Female Forms of Speech in Yana" reprinted in *Selected Writings of Edward Sapir* (cited above).

Recommended reading

Foster, Michael K. 1982. "Canada's Indigenous Languages: Past and Present." *Language and Society* 7:3–16. Ottawa: Commissioner of Official Languages.

Voegelin, C.F., and F.M. Voegelin. 1965. "Classification of American Indian languages." Languages of the World, Native America Fascicle 2, section 1.6, *Anthropological Linguistics* 7:121–50.

William O'Grady
Sook Whan Cho

First language acquisition

*Human brains are so constructed that one brain
responds in much the same way to a given trigger as
does another brain, all things being equal. This is why
a baby can learn any language; it responds to triggers
in the same way as any other baby.*

D. HOFSTADTER

Nothing is more important to a child's development than the acquisition of language.
Most children acquire language quickly and effortlessly—giving the impression that
the entire process is simple and straightforward. However, the true extent of children's
achievement becomes evident when we compare their success with the difficulties encountered by adults who try to learn a second language (see chapter 11). Understanding how children the world over are able to master the complexities of human language in the space of a
few short years has become one of the major goals of contemporary linguistic research.

This chapter provides a brief overview of the progress that has been made in this area.
We will begin by considering the research strategies used by linguists and psychologists in
the study of linguistic development. We will then describe some of the major findings concerning children's acquisition of the various parts of their language—phonology, vocabulary,
morphology, syntax, and semantics. The chapter concludes with a brief examination of the
contribution of the linguistic environment to language acquisition, the relationship between
the emergence of language and cognitive development, and the possible existence of inborn
linguistic knowledge.

1 The study of language acquisition

Although we commonly refer to the emergence of language in children as 'language acquisition', the end result of this process is actually a *grammar*—the mental system that allows people to speak and understand a language. There are at least two reasons for believing that the
development of linguistic skills must involve the acquisition of a grammar.

First, as noted in chapter 1, mature language users are able to produce and understand an
unlimited number of novel sentences. This can only happen if, as children, they have
acquired the grammar for their language. Simple memorization of a fixed inventory of words
and sentences would not equip learners to deal with previously unheard utterances—a basic
requisite of normal language use.

A second indication that children acquire grammatical rules comes from their speech errors, which often provide valuable clues about how the acquisition process works. Even run-of-the-mill errors such as *doed, *runned, and *goed can be informative. Since we know that children don't hear adults produce words like these, such errors tell us that they have formulated a general rule that forms the past tense by adding -ed to the verb stem.

Because language acquisition involves the emergence of a grammar, its study is closely tied to the type of linguistic analysis with which we have been concerned in preceding chapters. Indeed, linguists and psychologists studying language acquisition must often look to the study of phonology, syntax, and other components of the grammar for help in identifying and describing the grammatical system that children acquire during the first years of life.

1.1   Methods

The majority of research on the acquisition of language focuses on children's early utterances, the order in which they emerge, and the kinds of errors they contain. Two complementary methods of data collection are used—naturalistic observation and experimentation.

Two approaches

In the **naturalistic** approach, investigators observe and record children's spontaneous utterances. One type of naturalistic investigation is the so-called **diary** study, in which a researcher (often a parent) keeps daily notes on a child's linguistic progress. Alternatively, a researcher may visit individual children on a regular basis and record (or videotape) a sample of their utterances. In both cases, attention is paid to the context in which children's speech occurs, the toys they are playing with, the pictures they are looking at, and the like.

Naturalistic data collection provides a great deal of information about how the language acquisition process unfolds, but it also has its shortcomings. The most serious of these is that particular structures and phenomena may occur rarely in children's everyday speech, making it difficult to gather enough information from natural speech samples to test hypotheses or draw firm conclusions. This problem is further compounded by the fact that speech samples from individual children capture only a small portion of their utterances at any given point in development. (Because of the amount of time required to transcribe and analyze recordings, researchers typically have to be content with hour-long samples taken at weekly or biweekly intervals.)

In **experimental** studies, researchers typically make use of specially designed tasks to elicit linguistic activity relevant to the phenomenon that they wish to study. The child's performance is then used to formulate hypotheses about the type of grammatical system acquired at that point in time.

Experimental research is typically **cross-sectional** in that it investigates and compares the linguistic knowledge of different children (or groups of children) at a particular point in development. A typical cross-sectional study might involve conducting a single experiment with a group of two year olds, a group of four year olds, and a group of six year olds—taking each of these groups to be representative of a particular stage or 'cross-section' of the developmental process. In contrast, naturalistic studies tend to be **longitudinal** in that they examine language development in a particular child or group over an extended period of time (sometimes as long as several years). As the name suggests, longitudinal studies take a long time to conduct, but unlike cross-sectional studies they have the advantage of permitting researchers to observe development as an ongoing process in individual children.

Type of experimental studies

Experimental studies usually employ tasks that test children's comprehension, production, or imitation skills. One widely used method for testing children's comprehension makes use of a picture selection format. For example, in order to test the interpretation of reflexive pronouns, an experimenter might show children a picture of Big Bird scratching himself as Cookie Monster looks on and a picture of Big Bird scratching Cookie Monster, and then ask which picture goes with the sentence *Big Bird is scratching himself*. A second method involves supplying children with an appropriate set of toys and then asking them to act out the meaning of a sentence—perhaps a passive structure such as *The truck was bumped by the car*. Children's responses can provide valuable clues about the type of grammatical rules being used to interpret sentences at particular stages of development.

In a typical production task, the child is shown a picture and asked to describe it. Although production tasks can be useful for assessing certain types of linguistic knowledge, there are many structures (such as passives) that are hard to elicit even from adults since they are used only in special contexts. Moreover, because children's ability to comprehend language is often more advanced than their ability to produce sentences of their own, production tasks can provide an overly conservative view of linguistic development unless they are accompanied by other types of tests.

Experiments that have children imitate model sentences can also provide important clues about children's grammatical development. Although imitation might appear to be easy, it has been found that children's ability to repeat a particular structure provides a good indication of how well they have mastered it. For instance, a child who has not yet acquired auxiliary verbs can be expected to have difficulty repeating a sentence such as *The doggie has been barking a lot*.

The principal advantage of the experimental approach is that it allows researchers to collect data of a very specific sort about particular phenomena or structures. Experimentation is not without its pitfalls, however. In addition to the difficulty of designing a good experiment, there is always the possibility that children's performance will be affected by extraneous factors, such as inattention, shyness, or a failure to understand what is expected of them. Nonetheless, by using experimental techniques together with naturalistic observation, linguists and psychologists have made significant progress in the study of the language acquisition process. Much of this chapter is devoted to a survey of this progress, beginning with the development of speech sounds.

2 Phonological development

Children seem to be born with a perceptual system that is especially designed for listening to speech. Newborns respond differently to human voices than to other sounds, they show a preference for the language of their parents over other languages by the time they are two days old, and they can recognize their mother's voice within a matter of weeks.

From around one month of age, children exhibit the ability to distinguish among certain speech sounds. In one experiment, infants were presented with a series of identical [ba] syllables. These were followed by an occurrence of the syllable [pa]. A change in the children's sucking rate (measured by a specially designed pacifier) indicated that they perceived the difference between the two syllables, and were therefore able to distinguish between [p] and [b].

Even more amazing is the fact that infants are able to distinguish between sounds in unfamiliar languages. In one experiment, for instance, six- to eight-month-old infants who were being raised in English-speaking homes could hear contrasts among unfamiliar consonants in Hindi and Nthlakampx (an Amerindian language spoken on parts of Canada's west coast). By the time they are ten to twelve months old, though, this ability has begun to diminish.

Despite this early sensitivity to contrasts among speech sounds, children initially cannot distinguish between meaningful words. The emergence of this ability has been examined in a task in which children are presented with two toy animals named *bok* and *pok* (for instance) and are asked to respond to sentences such as *Show me pok*. To respond correctly, children must not only hear the difference between [p] and [b] but also recognize that it is linguistically significant—that it is used to distinguish between words in their language. Children under eighteen months have little success in this type of task.

2.1 Babbling

The ability to produce speech sounds begins to emerge around six months of age, with the onset of babbling. It is likely that babbling provides children with the opportunity to experiment with and begin to gain control over their vocal apparatus—an important prerequisite for later speech. Children who are unable to babble for medical reasons (because of the need for a breathing tube in their throat, for example) can subsequently acquire normal pronunciation, but their speech development is significantly delayed.

Despite obvious differences among the languages to which they are exposed, children from different linguistic communities exhibit significant similarities in their babbling. The tendencies in table 10.1 are based on data from fifteen different languages, including English, Thai, Japanese, Arabic, Hindi, and Mayan. (We focus here on consonant sounds, for which the data is somewhat more reliable than for vowels.)

Table 10.1 Cross-linguistic similarities in babbling	
Frequently found consonants	**Infrequently found consonants**
p b m	f v θ ð
t d n	ʃ ʒ tʃ dʒ
k g	l r ŋ
s h w j	

Such cross-linguistic similarities suggest that early babbling is at least partly independent of the particular language to which children are exposed. In fact, even deaf children babble, although their articulatory activity is somewhat less varied than that of hearing children.

2.2 The developmental order

Babbling increases in frequency until the age of about twelve months, at which time children start to produce their first understandable words. Babbling may overlap with the production of real words for several weeks before dying out. By the time children have acquired fifty words or so, they begin to adopt fairly regular patterns of pronunciation.

Although there is a good deal of variation from child to child in terms of the order in which speech sounds are mastered in production and perception, the following general tendencies seem to exist.

- As a group, vowels are generally acquired before consonants (by age three).

- Stops tend to be acquired before other consonants.

- In terms of place of articulation, labials are often acquired first, followed (with some variation) by alveolars, velars, and alveopalatals. Interdentals (such as [θ] and [ð]) are acquired last.

- New phonemic contrasts manifest themselves first in word-initial position. Thus, the /p/-/b/ contrast, for instance, will be manifested in pairs such as *pat-bat* before *mop-mob*.

By age two, a typical English-speaking child has the inventory of consonant phonemes shown in table 10.2.

Table 10.2	Typical consonant inventory at age two			
Stops			**Fricatives**	**Other**
p	b	m	f	w
t	d	n	s	
k	g			

By age four, this inventory is considerably larger and typically includes the sounds shown in table 10.3.

Table 10.3	Typical consonant inventory at age four					
Stops			**Fricatives**	**Affricates**	**Other**	
p	b	m	f v	tʃ dʒ	w j	
t	d	n	s z		l r	
k	g	ŋ	ʃ			

Still to be acquired at this age are the interdental fricatives [θ] and [ð] and the voiced alveopalatal fricative [ʒ].

In general, the relative order in which sounds are acquired reflects their distribution in languages of the world (see chapter 8). The sounds that are acquired early are generally found most widely in the world's languages while the sounds that are acquired late tend to be less common across languages.

2.3   Early phonetic processes

Children's ability to perceive the phonemic contrasts of their language develops well in advance of their ability to produce them. So even children who are unable to produce the difference between words like *mouse* and *mouth*, *cart* and *card*, or *jug* and *duck* may nonetheless be able to point to pictures of the correct objects in a comprehension task. Moreover, as the following experimenter's report vividly illustrates, children even seem to know that their pronunciations are not yet 'right'.

> One of us, for instance, spoke to a child who called his inflated plastic fish a *fis*. In imitation of the child's pronunciation, the observer said: "This is your fis?" "No," said the child, "my fis." He continued to reject the adult's imitation until he was told, "That is your fish." "Yes," he said, "my fis."

The child's reaction to the adult's initial pronunciation of *fish* shows that he could perceive the difference between /s/ and /ʃ/ and that he had correctly represented the word as /fɪʃ/ in his lexicon even though he could not yet produce it himself.

What precisely is responsible for the special character of the sound patterns in children's early speech? The key seems to lie in the operation of a limited number of universal phonetic processes that replace certain sounds with others that children find easier to produce and/or perceive.

Syllable deletion

Because syllables bearing primary or secondary stress are more noticeable than their unstressed counterparts, they tend to be more salient to children in the early stages of the language acquisition process. As a result, they are retained in children's pronunciation while unstressed syllables are often deleted (see table 10.4).

Table 10.4 Deletion of unstressed syllables	
Word	**Child's pronunciation**
hip po pó ta mus	[pɑs]
spa ghé tti	[gɛ]
hé li còp ter	[ɛlkɑt]
kan ga róo	[wu]
té le phòne	[fow]

However, unstressed syllables in final position tend to be retained, probably because the ends of words are easier to notice and remember (see table 10.5).

Table 10.5 Retention of unstressed syllables in final position	
Word	**Child's pronunciation**
po tá to	[tejdo]
ba ná na	[ænə]
to má to	[mejdo]
él e phant	[ɛlfən]

Syllable simplification

Another frequent process in children's speech involves the systematic deletion of certain sounds in order to simplify syllable structure. In the data in table 10.6, typical of the speech of two- and three-year-old children, consonant clusters are reduced by deleting one or more segments.

Table 10.6   Reduction of consonant clusters
[s] + stop (strategy: delete [s])
stop → [tɑp]
small → [mɑ]
desk → [dɛk]
stop + liquid (strategy: delete liquid)
try → [taj]
crumb → [gʌm]
bring → [bɪ ŋ]
fricative + liquid (strategy: delete liquid)
from → [fʌm]
sleep → [sip]
nasal + voiceless stop (strategy: delete nasal)
bump → [bʌp]
tent → [dɛt]

Yet another common deletion process in early child language involves the elimination of final consonants, as in the following examples.

1)
dog	[dɑ]
bus	[bʌ]
boot	[bu]

Both the reduction of consonant clusters and the deletion of final consonants have the effect of simplifying syllable structure, bringing it closer to the CV template that is universally favoured by children and that is the most widely found pattern in human language in general.

Substitution

One of the most widespread phonetic processes in early language involves substitution—the systematic replacement of one sound by an alternative that the child finds easier to articulate (see table 10.7). Common substitution processes include **stopping**, the replacement of a fricative by a corresponding stop; **fronting**, the moving forward of a sound's place of articulation; **gliding**, the replacement of a liquid by a glide; and **denasalization**, the replacement of a nasal stop by a non-nasal counterpart.

Table 10.7	Substitution in early speech	
Process	**Example**	**Change**
Stopping (continuant → stop)	sing → [tɪŋ]	s → t
	sea → [ti]	s → t
	zebra → [dibrə]	z → d
	thing → [tɪŋ]	θ → t
	this → [dɪt]	ð → d, s → t
	shoes → [tud]	ʃ → t, z → d
Fronting	ship → [sɪp]	ʃ → s
	jump → [dzʌmp]	dʒ → dz
	chalk → [tsɑːk]	tʃ → ts
	go → [dow]	g → d
Gliding	lion → [jajn]	l → j
	laughing → [jæfɪŋ]	l → j
	look → [wʊk]	l → w
	rock → [wɑk]	r → w
	story → [stowi]	r → w
Denasalization	spoon → [bud]	n → d
	jam → [dæb]	m → b
	room → [wub]	m → b

Assimilation

Still another widespread phonetic process in child language is assimilation—the modification of one or more features of a segment under the influence of neighbouring sounds. In the following examples, initial consonants have been voiced in anticipation of the following vowel.

2)

tell	[dɛl]
pig	[bɪg]
push	[bʊs]
soup	[zup]

Assimilation is also observed in children's tendency to maintain the same place of articulation for all of the consonants or vowels in a word. This can lead to the pronunciation of *doggy* as [gɑgi] (with two velar stops). Other examples include [fɛlf] for *self* (with identical consonants), [bibi] for *baby* (with identical vowels in both syllables), [kæklin] for *Cathleen* (with identical velar stops), and [næns] for *dance* (with identical nasal consonants).

3 Vocabulary development

By age eighteen months or so, the average child has a vocabulary of fifty words or more. Common items include the words listed in table 10.8.

Table 10.8   Common items in the first fifty words
Entities

Words referring to
      people: *daddy, mommy, baby*
      food/drink: *juice, milk, cookie, water, toast, apple, cake*
      animals: *dog, cat, duck, horse*
      clothes: *shoes, hat*
      toys: *ball, blocks*
      vehicles: *car, boat, truck*
      other: *bottle, key, book*

Properties
hot, allgone, more, dirty, cold, here, there
Actions
up, sit, see, eat, go, down
Personal-social
hi, bye, no, yes, please, thank-you

As this table shows, noun-like words make up the single largest class in the child's early vocabulary, with verb- and adjective-like words being the next most frequent category types. Among the most frequent individual words are expressions for displeasure or rejection (such as *no*) and various types of social interaction (such as *please* and *bye*). Over the next months this vocabulary grows rapidly, sometimes by as much as ten or twelve words a day. By age six, most children have mastered about thirteen thousand words.

Children seem to differ somewhat in the types of words that they focus on, especially in the early stages of language acquisition. One of these differences is reflected in the number of nouns in early vocabulary. Whereas some children have a relatively high proportion of such words (75 percent or more) by age two, other learners exhibit a much lower percentage of nouns (50 percent or less). Making up for the smaller number of nouns is a larger vocabulary of socially useful expressions such as *bye, go-away, stop-it, thank-you, I-want-it*, and so on. (Hyphens are used here to indicate that these expressions are not yet segmented into their component words.)

3.1 Strategies for acquiring word meaning

Children seem to draw on special strategies when trying to determine the meaning of a new word. This is perhaps easiest to illustrate in the case of noun-type meanings, for which the following strategies seem to be employed.

3)
Three strategies for learning the meanings of new words.

The Whole Object Assumption
A new word refers to a whole object.

The Type Assumption
A new word refers to a type of thing, not just to a particular thing.

The Basic Level Assumption
A new word refers to types of objects that are alike in basic ways.

To see how these strategies work, imagine that a mother and her eighteen-month-old daughter are driving through the countryside and they encounter a sheep munching on the grass. The mother points to the animal and says 'sheep'. What does the child think that the word means? Does it mean 'white'? Or does it mean 'woolly'? Does it refer to the animal? Or to parts of the animal? Or does it refer to the fact that a particular animal is munching on grass?

The Whole Object Assumption allows the child to infer that the word *sheep* refers to the animal itself, not to its parts, not to whiteness, and not to wooliness. The Type Assumption allows her to infer that *sheep* refers to a type of animal, not to just one particular sheep. And the Basic Level Assumption leads her to guess that *sheep* is used to refer just to white, four-legged, woolly animals, and not animals in general.

The fact that so many of children's first words are names for types of whole objects suggests that language learners rely heavily on strategies such as these in the early stages of word learning. Of course, these strategies don't always give the right result. Some words do in fact refer to parts of things (*toe, fingernail, eyeball*), to properties (*white, woolly*), to individuals (*Susie, Mr. Jones*) and to broad classes (*animal, plant*). Nonetheless, the strategies we have been considering provide children with a good way to get started, postponing the acquisition of certain types of words in favour of more basic vocabulary items.

Contextual clues

Another major factor in vocabulary development is the child's ability to make use of contextual clues to draw inferences about the category and meaning of new words. For instance, from early in the language acquisition process, children can use the presence or absence of determiners to distinguish between names and ordinary nouns. Two-year-old children who are told that a new doll is a *dax* will apply this label to similar-looking dolls as well. However, if they are told that the new doll is *Dax*, they will restrict use of the new word to the doll they have actually been shown. Like adults, these children treat *dax* as an ordinary noun when it is preceded by *a*, but as a name when there is no determiner.

In another experiment, three- and four-year-old children were asked to act out the meaning of sentences such as 'Make it so there is *tiv* to drink in this glass (of water)'. The only clues about the interpretation of the nonsense word *tiv* came from the meaning of the rest of the sentence and from the child's understanding of the types of changes that can be made to a glass of water. Not only did more than half the children respond by either adding or removing water, some even remembered what *tiv* meant two weeks later!

3.2   Meaning errors

The meanings that children associate with their early words sometimes correspond closely to the meanings employed by adults. In many cases, however, the match is less than perfect. The two most typical semantic errors involve overextension and underextension.

Overextensions

In cases of **overextension**, the meaning of the child's word is more general or inclusive than that of the corresponding adult form. The word *dog*, for example, is frequently overextended to include horses, cows, and other four-legged animals. Similarly, *ball* is sometimes used for any round object, including a balloon, an Easter egg, a small stone, and so on. As many as one-third of children's words may be overextended at the fifty-word stage of vocabulary development (see table 10.9).

Table 10.9 Additional examples of overextension		
Word	**First referent**	**Subsequent extensions**
tick tock	watch	clocks, gas-meter, fire hose on a spool, scale with round dial
fly	fly	specks of dirt, dust, small insects, child's toes, crumbs of bread
quack	duck	all birds and insects, flies, coins (with an eagle on the face)
candy	candy	cherries, anything sweet
apple	apples	balls, tomatoes, cherries, onions, biscuits
turtle	turtles	fish, seals
cookie	cookies	crackers, any dessert
kitty	cats	rabbits, any small furry animal
box	boxes	elevators
belt	belts	watch strap

The evidence collected to date suggests that perceptual properties are the critical factor in children's first hypotheses about word meanings. As a result, children often overextend a word to include a set of perceptually similar objects that they know to have diverse functions. For example, one child used the word *moon* for the moon, grapefruit halves, and a crescent-shaped car light. Another child used the word *money* for a set of objects ranging from pennies to buttons and beads. If you reconsider the examples of overextension given in table 10.9, you will see that they too are more plausibly explained in terms of perceptual similarities than a shared function.

There is reason to believe that many overextensions may be deliberate attempts to compensate for vocabulary limitations. One indication of this is that particular overextensions often disappear as soon as children learn the right word for the objects that they have been mislabelling. For example, two-year-old Allen was using the word *dog* for dogs, cats, sheep, and other four-legged mammals, but he stopped doing so as soon as he learned the words *cat* and *sheep*. If he thought that *dog* meant 'animal', he could still have sometimes referred to cats and sheep as *dogs* (just as adults sometimes refer to them as animals). The fact that he didn't suggests that he never thought *dog* meant 'animal'; he had just been 'borrowing' it until the right word came along.

A further indication that many overextensions are designed to compensate for vocabulary limitations comes from the fact that children seem to overextend more in their production than in their comprehension. In one study, for instance, five children who were overextending words were given a naming task in which they were shown pictures and asked to name them. Overextensions were identified and then used to design a comprehension test. For example, if the child overextended *doggie* to include cows and horses on the naming test, the comprehension test would include pictures of these animals as well as a dog. The child would then be asked 'Show me the doggie', 'Show me the cow', and so on. The results were quite dramatic, revealing that overextensions in comprehension were much less frequent than in production. This is not the result that one would expect if children thought that *doggie* meant 'animal'.

Underextensions

Another possible type of word-meaning error in early language involves **underextension**, the use of lexical items in an overly restrictive fashion. Thus, *kitty* might be used to refer to the family pet, but not to any other cats. Or the word *dog* might be used for collies, spaniels, and beagles, but not for Chihuahuas.

Underextension errors often reflect children's propensity to focus on prototypical or core members of a category. As noted in section 1.3 of chapter 6, the potential referents of many words differ in terms of how well they exemplify the properties associated with a particular concept. For example, among the potential referents of the word *dog*, collies and spaniels have more of the properties associated with the concept 'dog' (long hair, relative size, type of bark, and so on) than do Chihuahuas. While the preference for a prototype can be overruled by factors such as the presence of a non-typical category member in the child's everyday experience (e.g., a Chihuahua as a family pet), the internal structure of concepts can have an important influence on semantic development.

Verb meanings

Meaning errors are also common for verbs. For example, many preschool children believe that *fill* means 'pour' rather than 'make full'. So, when asked to decide which of the two series of pictures in figure 10.1 is an example of filling, they choose the second series—even though the glass ends up empty!

Not surprisingly, there is a tendency for children who make this sort of mistake to use *fill* in the wrong syntactic patterns as well.

4)
I filled the grain up. (Adam, at age 4 yrs., 11 mos.)
And fill the little sugars up in the bowl ... (Mark, at age 4 yrs., 7 mos.)
I didn't fill water up to drink it. (E, at age 4 yrs., 1 mo.)
Can I fill some salt into the [salt shaker]? (E, at age 5 yrs.)

Figure 10.1 Sample pictures used to test children's understanding of *fill*. Some children believe that the action depicted in the bottom series of pictures involves filling, even though the glass remains empty.

These errors disappear as children come to realize that *fill* means 'make full' rather than 'pour into'.

Dimensional terms

Terms describing size and dimensions are acquired in a relatively fixed order, depending on their generality (see table 10.10). The first adjectives of this type to be acquired, *big* and *small*, are the most general in that they can be used for talking about any aspect of size (height, area, volume, and so on). In contrast, the second group of adjectives to emerge—*tall, long, short, high,* and *low*—can only be used for a single dimension (height-length). The remaining modifiers (*thick-thin, wide-narrow,* and *deep-shallow*) are still more restricted in their use since they describe the secondary or less extended dimension of an object. For instance, the dimension of a stick that we describe in terms of width or thickness is almost always less extended than the dimension that we describe in terms of height or length, which tends also to be perceptually more salient.

Table 10.10 Order of acquisition for dimensional adjectives

Step	Words	What they describe
1	*big-small*	any aspect of size
2	*tall-short, long-short, high-low*	a single dimension
3	*thick-thin, wide-narrow, deep-shallow*	a secondary dimension

The difficulty of dimensional adjectives for children is also evident on experimental tasks. For instance, in one experiment children aged three to five were shown pairs of objects—sometimes a big one and a tall one and sometimes a big one and long one (see figure 10.2).

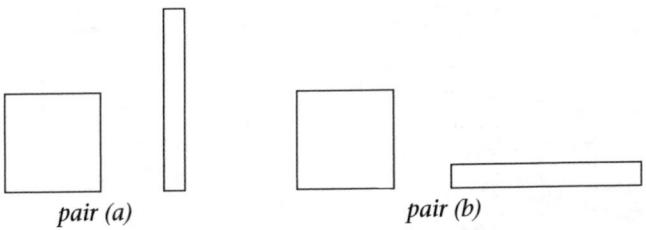

pair (a)   *pair (b)*

Figure 10.2 'big'-'tall' versus 'big'-'long'

Younger children do well when asked to choose 'the big one'. However, when asked to choose 'the tall one' or 'the long one', they often pick the big one instead. This suggests that they are initially more sensitive to overall size than to a single dimension like height or length.

4   Morphological development

As is the case with the sound pattern of language and with vocabulary, the details of morphological structure emerge over a period of several years. Initially, the words produced by English-speaking children seem to lack any internal morphological structure. Affixes are systematically absent and most words consist of a single root morpheme.

4.1   Overgeneralization

Because English has many examples of irregular inflection (*men* as the plural of *man*, *ran* as the past of *run*), children sometimes begin by simply memorizing inflected words on a case-by-case basis without regard for general patterns or rules. As a result, they may initially use irregular forms such as *men* and *ran* correctly. However, when they subsequently observe the generality of *-s* as a plural marker and *-ed* as a past tense marker (usually around age two and a half), they sometimes use these suffixes for the irregular forms—producing words such as *mans* and *runned*. (Errors that result from the overly broad application of a rule are called **overgeneralizations** or **overregularizations**.) Even occasional mixed forms such as *felled*, a blend of *fell* and *falled*, may occur during this period (see table 10.11).

Table 10.11 The development of affixes	
Stage 1:	case-by-case learning
Stage 2:	overuse of general rule
Stage 3:	mastery of exceptions to the general rule

One of the best indications that children have mastered an inflectional rule comes from their ability to apply it to forms they have not heard before. In a classic experiment, children were shown a picture of a strange creature and told, "This is a wug." A second picture was then presented and the children were given the following type of question (see figure 10.3).

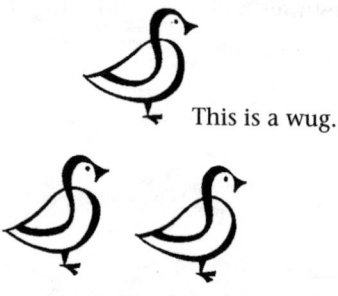

This is a wug.

Now, there's another wug.
There are two of them.
Now, there are two . . .?

Figure 10.3 The 'wug test'

Even four- and five-year-old children did well with the plural forms of '*wug* words', demonstrating that the general rules for inflection have been learned by that time, despite the occurrence of occasional errors.

Recent work has shown that inflectional overgeneralization, which can last into the school years, is much less frequent than previously thought: preschool children seem to overregularize verbs less than 25 percent of the time at any point in development. This suggests that the overgeneralization errors observed in early speech reflect lapses in accessing the appropriate irregular form from the lexicon rather than the failure to learn irregular forms per se.

4.2 A developmental sequence

An important result of child language research during the 1970s was the discovery that the development of bound morphemes and functional categories (such as determiners and auxiliaries) takes place in an orderly fashion that is quite similar across children. In a pioneering study of three children between the ages of twenty and thirty-six months, the developmental sequence in table 10.12 was found to be typical.

Table 10.12 Typical developmental sequence for non-lexical morphemes	
1. *-ing*	5. past tense *-ed*
2. plural *-s*	6. third person singular *-s*
3. possessive *-'s*	7. auxiliary *be*
4. *the, a*	

An interesting feature of this developmental sequence is that it seems to be largely unrelated to the frequency of the different morphemes in the speech heard by children (see table 10.13). For example, the determiners *the* and *a* are the most frequent morphemes in the children's environments even though they are acquired relatively late.

Table 10.13 Typical relative frequency of morphemes in parental speech	
1. *the, a*	5. possessive *-'s*
2. *-ing*	6. third person singular *-s*
3. plural *-s*	7. past tense *-ed*
4. auxiliary *be*	

This shows that frequency by itself cannot explain developmental order, although it may have some role to play in conjunction with other factors. (It's also clear that pronunciation by itself is not the key factor either, since the three '*-s*' morphemes are acquired at different times.)

Some determining factors

What, then, determines the order of acquisition of non-lexical categories and bound morphemes? Research on a variety of languages suggests that several factors are involved.

1. ***Frequent occurrence in utterance-final position*** Children show a greater tendency to notice and remember elements that occur at the end of the utterance than those found in any other position.

2. ***Syllabicity*** Children seem to take greater notice of morphemes such as *-ing*, which can constitute syllables on their own, than the plural or possessive suffix *-'s*, whose principal allomorphs (/s/ and /z/) are single consonants.

3. ***Absence of homophony*** Whereas the word *the* functions only as a determiner in English, the suffix *-s* can be used to mark any one of three things: plural number in nouns, third person singular in verbs, or possession. The resulting complication in the relationship between form and meaning may impede acquisition.

4. ***Few or no exceptions in the way it is used*** Whereas all singular nouns form the possessive with *-'s*, not all verbs use *-ed* to mark the past tense (*saw, read, drove*). Such exceptions hinder the language acquisition process.

5. ***Allomorphic invariance*** Whereas the affix *-ing* has the same form for all verbs, the past tense ending *-ed* has three major allomorphs—/t/ for verbs such as *chase*, /d/ for forms such as *crave* and /əd/ for verbs such as *recite*. This type of allomorphic variation, which also occurs with the plural, possessive, and third person singular affixes in English, slows morphological development.

6. **Clearly discernible semantic function** Whereas morphemes such as plural *-s* express easily identifiable meanings, some morphemes (such as the third person singular *-s*) make no obvious contribution to the meaning of the sentence. Acquisition of this latter type of morpheme is relatively slow.

The status of the English morphemes whose developmental order we have been considering is indicated in table 10.14; as before, morphemes are listed in typical order of emergence. (The ± symbol in the second column indicates that the morphemes in question have both syllabic and non-syllabic allomorphs. The plural suffix, for example, is realized as /s/ in some contexts but as /əz/ in others.)

Table 10.14 Factors affecting development

Morphemes	Factors					
	1	*2*	*3*	*4*	*5*	*6*
-ing	+	+	+	+	+	+
plural *-s*	+	±	+	+	-	+
possessive *-'s*	-	±	+	+	-	+
the, a	-	+	+	+	-	-
past tense *-ed*	+	±	+	-	-	+
third person singular *-s*	-	±	-	+	-	-
auxiliary *be*	-	±	-	+	-	-

As table 10.14 helps show, the morphemes that are acquired first generally exhibit more of the properties just outlined than those that emerge at a later point.

4.3 Word formation processes

The major word formation processes in English—derivation and compounding—both emerge early in the acquisition of English. The first derivational suffixes to show up in children's speech are the ones that are most common in the adult language (see table 10.15).

Table 10.15 Suffixes in the speech of Damon prior to age four

Ending	Meaning	Example
-er	'doer'*	walk<u>er</u>
-ie	'diminutive'	dogg<u>ie</u>
-ing	'activity'	Runn<u>ing</u> is fun.
-ness	'state'	big<u>ness</u>

(*Note:* *-er* also has an 'instrument' meaning [as in *cutter* 'something used for cutting'], but this is less frequent in children's early speech.)

Moreover, children as young as three demonstrate an ability to use derivation to make up names for agents and instruments when presented with questions such as the following.

'I've got a picture here of someone who crushes things. What could we call someone who crushes things? Someone who crushes things is called a ...'

'I've got a picture here of something that cuts things. What could we call something that cuts things? Something that cuts things is called a ...'

Children also exhibit a propensity for forming compounds, especially of the N–N type, both in experimental settings where they are asked to make up words (e.g., 'What would you call a boy who rips paper?') and in their own spontaneous speech. Some of the compounds found in the speech of three and four year olds do not follow the usual pattern for English compounds (e.g., *open man* for someone who opens things and *cutter grass* for 'grass cutter'), but these disappear by age five. Other early compounds have the right structure, but are inappropriate because English already has words with the intended meaning (see table 10.16).

Table 10.16 Some innovative compounds	
Child's word	**Intended meaning**
car-smoke	'exhaust'
cup-egg	'boiled egg'
firetruck-man	'fire fighter'
plant-man	'gardener'
store-man	'clerk'

Children's creativity with compounds points to a preference for building words from other words, perhaps because this places less demand on memory than does learning a new simple word for each concept.

Even the subtlest properties of word formation seem to be acquired in the preschool years. One such property, first discussed in section 3.1 of chapter 4, involves the fact that an inflectional suffix such as the plural cannot occur inside compounds (compare *dogs catcher* with *dog catcher*). In one study, children as young as three years of age produced compounds that obeyed this constraint. Thus, when asked a question such as "What do you call someone who eats cookies?", they responded by saying *cookie eater* rather than *cookies eater*.

5 Syntactic development

Like phonological and morphological development, the emergence of syntactic structure takes place in an orderly manner and reveals much about the nature of the language acquisition process. We will briefly survey some of the milestones in this developmental process here.

5.1 The one-word stage

As noted earlier, children begin to produce one-word utterances between the ages of twelve and eighteen months. A basic property of these one-word utterances is that they can be used to express the type of meaning that is associated with an entire sentence in adult speech.

Thus, a child might use the word *dada* to assert 'I see Daddy', *more* to mean 'Give me more candy', and *up* to mean 'I want up'. Such utterances are called **holophrases** (literally 'whole sentences').

In forming holophrastic utterances, children seem to choose the most informative word that applies to the situation at hand. A child who wanted a candy, for example, would say *candy* rather than *want* since the former word is more informative in this situation. Similarly, a child who notices a new doll would be more likely to say *doll* than *see*, thereby referring to the most novel feature of the situation he or she is trying to describe.

Table 10.17 lists some of the semantic relations that children commonly express during the one-word stage.

Table 10.17 Semantic relations in children's one-word utterances

Semantic relation	Utterance	Situation
Agent of an action	*dada*	as father enters the room
Action or state	*down*	as child sits down
Theme	*door*	as father closes the door
Location	*here*	as child points
Recipient	*mama*	as child gives mother something
Recurrence	*again*	as child watches lighting of a match

5.2   The two-word stage

Within a few months of their first one-word utterances, children begin to produce two-word 'mini-sentences'. Table 10.18 provides a sampling of these utterances and the types of meaning they are commonly used to express. (Although these examples are from English, similar patterns are found in the early development of all languages.)

Table 10.18 Some patterns in children's two-word speech

Utterance	Intended meaning	Semantic relation
Baby chair	'The baby is sitting on the chair.'	agent-location
Doggie bark	'The dog is barking.'	agent-action
Ken water	'Ken is drinking water.'	agent-theme
Hit doggie	'I hit the doggie.'	action-theme
Daddy hat	'Daddy's hat'	possessor-possessed

It is unclear whether children have acquired syntactic categories such as noun, verb, and adjective at this point in their development. This is because the markers that help distinguish among syntactic categories in adult English (e.g., inflection such as the past tense suffix and minor categories such as determiners and auxiliary verbs) are absent during this period. To complicate matters still further, the relative shortness of the utterances produced during the two-word stage means that the positional differences associated with category distinctions in adult speech are often not manifested. Thus, words such as *busy* (an adjective in adult speech) and *push* (a verb) may appear in identical patterns.

5)
Mommy busy.
Mommy push.

While this does not show that children lack syntactic categories, it makes it difficult to demonstrate that they possess them. For this reason, linguists and psychologists are split over whether to describe children's utterances in terms of the semantic relations that they express (as in table 10.18) or the syntactic categories of adult speech.

A notable feature of children's two-word utterances is that they almost always exhibit the appropriate word order. This suggests a very early sensitivity to this feature of sentence structure, but there is reason to believe that children do not initially have a general word order rule. Rather, they may have a separate rule for each verb (e.g., 'Put the subject in front of *push*'; 'Put the subject in front of *read*'; and so on). In one experiment, for instance, children aged two to four were taught made-up verbs (such as *tam, gop,* and *dack*) for novel actions involving puppet characters. Each verb was presented in one of the following orders:

6)
subject-verb-object order: Elmo tammed the apple.
subject-object-verb order: Elmo the apple gopped.
verb-subject-object order: Dacked the apple Elmo.

The two- and three-year-old children were willing to learn word order patterns not found in English and would often employ the subject-object-verb and verb-subject-object order for new verbs if that was what they had been exposed to. In contrast, the four year olds used the subject-verb-object order regardless of what the experimenter had said, which suggests that they had acquired a general word order rule for English that they automatically extended to new verbs.

5.3 The telegraphic stage

After a period of several months, during which their speech is limited to one- and two-word utterances, children begin to produce longer and more complex grammatical structures (see table 10.19). Some representative utterances from the first part of this period are given in *7)*.

7)
Chair broken.
Daddy like book.
What her name?
Man ride bus today.
Car make noise.
Me wanna show Mommy.
I good boy.

At first, these utterances lack bound morphemes and most non-lexical categories. Because of the resemblance to the style of language found in telegrams, this acquisitional stage is often dubbed **telegraphic**.

The telegraphic stage is characterized by the emergence of phrase structure. As the examples in *7)* help show, the Merge operation can form phrases consisting of a head and a complement (*like book, ride bus, show mommy*), phrases that include a modifier (such as *today* and *good*), and even full-fledged sentences.

Table 10.19 The development of phrase structure		
Stage	**Approx. Age**	**Developments**
Holophrastic	1–1.5 yrs.	single word utterances; no structure
Two-word	1.5–2 yrs.	early word combinations; presence of syntactic categories unclear
Telegraphic	2–2.5 yrs.	emergence of phrase structure, especially head-complement and subject-VP patterns

Language development from this point onward is rapid. As the examples in table 10.20 help illustrate, children move from relatively primitive two- and three-word utterances at the beginning of the telegraphic stage to a broad range of syntactically intricate sentence types that include affixes and non-lexical categories in the space of just a few months.

Table 10.20 Sample utterances from a child's speech over a 12-month period	
Age	**Sample utterances**
28 mos.	Play checkers. Big drum. I got horn. A bunny-rabbit walk.
30 mos.	Write a piece of paper. What that egg doing? I lost a shoe. No, I don't want to sit seat.
32 mos.	Let me get down with the boots on. Don't be afraid of horses. How tiger be so healthy and fly like kite? Joshua throw like penguin.
34 mos.	Look at that train Ursula brought. I simply don't want put in chair. Don't have paper. Do you want little bit, Cromer? I can't wear it tomorrow.
36 mos.	I going come in fourteen minutes. I going wear that to wedding. I see what happens. I have to save them now. Those are not strong mens. They are going sleep in wintertime. You dress me up like a baby elephant.

Table 10.20 **(continued)**   Sample utterances
38 mos.	So it can't be cleaned?
	I broke my racing car.
	Do you know the lights went off?
	What happened to the bridge?
	Can I put my head in the mailbox so the mailman can know where I are and put me in the mailbox?

5.4   Later development

In the years following the telegraphic stage, children continue to acquire the complex grammar that underlies adult linguistic competence, including the Move operations outlined in chapter 5.

Inversion

In the very early stages of language acquisition, children signal *yes-no* questions by means of rising intonation alone. (Recall that auxiliary verbs are a relatively late development.)

> 8)
> See hole?
> I ride train?
> Ball go?
> Sit chair?

Even after individual auxiliary verbs appear in child language, there is often a delay of a few months before they appear at the beginning of the sentence in *yes-no* questions. In one study, for example, a young boy began using the auxiliary verb *can* at age two years, five months, but it did not undergo Inversion in questions until six months later.

An interesting—but infrequent—error in children's early use of Inversion in both *yes-no* and *wh* questions is exemplified in 9).

> 9)
> *Can* he *can* look?
> What *shall* we *shall* have?
> *Did* you *did* came home?

In these sentences, the auxiliary verb occurs twice—once to the left of the subject (in the position that it occupies after Inversion) and once to the right (in the position it occupies in deep structure). It has been suggested that this pattern reflects an error in the application of the Inversion transformation in that a copy of the moved auxiliary is left behind in its original position.

Wh questions

Wh questions emerge gradually between the ages of two and four. The first *wh* words to be acquired are typically *what* and *where*, followed by *who, how,* and *why; when, which,* and *whose* are relatively late acquisitions.

10)
Where that?
What me think?
Why you smiling?
Why not me drink it?

With the acquisition of auxiliary verbs, Inversion becomes possible. Interestingly, some children appear to find it easier to carry out the Inversion operation in *yes-no* questions, where it is the only Move operation, than in *wh* questions, where *Wh* Movement must also apply. They go through a stage where Inversion is more common in the former pattern than in the latter.

11)
Yes-no questions (with Inversion):
Did Mommy pinch her finger?
Can't you fix it?
Do I have it?
Will you help me?
Is Mommy talking to Robin's grandmother?

12)
Wh questions (no Inversion):
What I did yesterday?
Why Kitty can't stand up?
Where I should put it?
Where I should sleep?
Why you are smiling?

5.5   The interpretation of sentence structure

As noted in chapter 6, the interpretation of sentences draws heavily on various features of syntactic structure. In this section we will briefly consider some aspects of the acquisition of two interpretive phenomena that rely on information about syntactic structure.

Passives

Children learning English are able to associate thematic roles with particular structural positions at a very early point in the acquisition process. By the time their average utterance length is two words, they are able to respond correctly about 75 percent of the time to comprehension tests involving simple active sentences such as *13*), in which *the truck* is the agent and *the car* is the theme.

13)
The truck bumped the car.

However, children find it much harder to interpret certain other types of sentences correctly. This is especially true for passive sentences such as the one in *14*), which contains no semantic clues about which NP is agent and which one is theme. (Note that it makes just as much sense for the car to bump the truck as it does for the truck to bump the car. Such sentences are said to be 'reversible'.)

14)
The car was bumped by the truck.

Although children produce passive sentences in their own speech from around age three, they have continuing difficulty responding appropriately to passive constructions in comprehension tests (see table 10.21).

Table 10.21 Comprehension of reversible passive constructions	
Group	Percentage correct
Nursery School	20
Kindergarten	35
Grade 1	48
Grade 2	63
Grade 3	88

Why should this be so? One possibility is that children expect the first NP in a sentence to bear the agent role and the second NP to bear the theme role. This is sometimes called the **Canonical Sentence Strategy** (see figure 10.4).

NP   ...   V   ...   NP   is interpreted as:
agent – action – theme

Figure 10.4 The Canonical Sentence Strategy

The Canonical Sentence Strategy works for active, transitive sentences, but not for passive sentences, where the first NP is the theme and the second NP is the agent.

15)
Active sentence: The truck bumped the car.
              agent   *theme*

Passive sentence: The car was bumped by the truck
               theme   *agent*

Not surprisingly, the most common error made by children employing this strategy is to treat the first NP in passive sentences as the agent and the second NP as the theme.

As the data in table 10.21 show, this strategy is applied much less consistently by first graders, who have evidently begun to realize that there is no simple correlation between linear position and thematic role. A year or so later, children's scores start to rise dramatically, indicating that they have come to recognize the special properties of the passive construction.

Pronominals and reflexives

In chapter 6, we saw that a reflexive pronoun (*myself, himself, herself,* and so on) must have a 'higher' (i.e., c-commanding) antecedent in the minimal clause containing it.

16)

a. Reflexive pronoun with a higher antecedent in the same clause
I hurt *myself* with the knife.

b. Reflexive pronoun without a higher antecedent in the same clause
*You hurt *myself* with the knife.

In contrast, a pronominal (*me, him, her*) cannot have a higher antecedent in the same minimal clause.

17)

a. Pronominal with a higher antecedent in the same clause
*I hurt *me* with the knife.

b. Pronominal without a higher antecedent in the same clause
You hurt *me* with the knife.

Despite the intricacy of the principles involved here, children appear not to have trouble distinguishing between pronominals and reflexive pronouns in their own speech. In one study of the use of *me* and *myself* in speech transcripts from three children aged two to five, researchers found a few errors of the following type.

18)
Sample pronoun errors:
Mistake involving *me*: I see *me*. (Adam, age 34 mos., looking through a telescope)

Mistake involving *myself*: Don't you drop me... you hurt *myself*. (Abe, age 34 mos.)

Overall though, the children misused *me* only about 5 percent of the time and made mistakes on *myself* less than 1 percent of the time. We will return to this point in section 6.4.

6 What makes language acquisition possible?

In the preceding sections, we have seen that the language acquisition process extends over a period of several years. It is relatively easy to describe what takes place during these years, but it is much more difficult to explain *how* it happens. The sections that follow focus on some of the factors that may contribute to an eventual understanding of how the language acquisition process works.

6.1 The role of adult speech

At one time, it was widely believed that children learn language simply by imitating the speech of those around them. This cannot be right, however. Not only do children tend not to repeat the speech of others, they are typically unable to imitate structures that they have not yet learned. For instance, a child who has not yet acquired the Inversion operation will imitate sentence *19a)* by producing *19b)*.

19)
a. *Model sentence*: What can you see?
b. *Child's imitation*: What you can see?

A child's own grammar, not the model provided by adult speech, determines what she or he will say at any given point of development.

Of course, language learners must be sensitive in some way to the language in their environment. After all, children who are exposed to English learn to speak English, those exposed to Cree learn Cree, and so forth. It seems, though, that the relationship between input (the language children hear) and acquisition is subtler and more complicated than one might think.

Caregiver speech

A good deal of recent work has been devoted to the search for a possible relationship between language acquisition and the type of speech that is typically addressed to young language learners. Such speech is often called **motherese** or **caregiver speech**. Table 10.22 summarizes the principal features of the caregiver speech used by middle-class English-speaking mothers with their children.

Table 10.22 Some features of English caregiver speech
Phonetic
Slow, carefully articulated speech Higher pitch Exaggerated intonation and stress Longer pauses
Lexical and semantic
More restricted vocabulary Concrete reference to here and now
Syntactic
Few incomplete sentences Short sentences More imperatives and questions
Conversational
More repetitions Few utterances per conversational turn

Caregiver speech could be helpful to children in a variety of ways. For example, exposure to slow, carefully articulated speech may make it easier for children to pick out words and to learn their pronunciation. (Remember that sentences consist of a continuous stream of speech sounds; there are no pauses between words.) Moreover, the acquisition of meaning may be facilitated by the fact that maternal speech tends to concentrate on the here and now, especially the child's surroundings, activities, and needs. The examples in table 10.23 help illustrate this.

Table 10.23 Some examples of maternal speech	
Mother's utterance	**Context**
That's right, pick up the blocks	the child is picking up a box of building blocks
That's a puppy.	the child is looking at a young dog
The puppy's in the basket.	the child is examining a puppy in a basket

Exposure to language of this type may well make it easier to match morphemes, words, and phrases with meanings—a major part of the language acquisition process.

Although potentially *helpful*, caregiver speech may not actually be *necessary* to the language acquisition process. In some cultures, for instance, children are not considered to be potential conversational partners until they are fluent speakers. Little speech is addressed directly to them, although they do spend a lot of time with their mothers and are exposed to a good deal of conversation among adults. The fact that these children learn language in a normal fashion indicates that exposure to the speech style typical of middle-class mothers in North American society is not necessary for language acquisition.

Moreover, even in cultures where it is common, caregiver speech seems to have very selective effects on child language. For instance, the number of *yes-no* questions in maternal speech seems to be correlated with the rate at which auxiliary verbs develop—apparently because auxiliaries occur in the salient sentence-initial position in *yes-no* questions (*Can Jennifer go?*). At the same time, though, many other features of maternal speech seem not to affect child language. As we saw earlier (section 3.1), for example, the relative frequency of bound morphemes and non-lexical categories in maternal speech apparently does not determine their order of acquisition.

In and of itself, then, caregiver speech cannot explain how language acquisition occurs. However, research into this subject may contribute to this goal in less direct ways by helping determine the types of linguistic experience that are most valuable to children. This in turn could help linguists identify the types of mechanisms and strategies involved in language acquisition.

6.2 The role of feedback

It is sometimes suggested that parents provide children with direct linguistic training by correcting ill-formed utterances. However, studies of actual interactions between parents and children point in a quite different direction. In general, parents tend to be more concerned with the truth of children's utterances than with their grammaticality—one transcript of a parent-child conversation includes *That's right* as a response to the grammatical monstrosity *Mama isn't boy, he's a girl!*

Moreover, even when adults do attempt to correct children's grammatical errors, their efforts often have little effect. The following exchange between a child and his father is typical in this regard.

20)

Child: Want other one spoon, daddy.
Father: You mean, you want the other spoon.
Child: Yes, I want other one spoon, please Daddy.
Father: Can you say 'the other spoon'?
Child: other . . . one . . . spoon.
Father: Say 'other'.
Child: other.
Father: 'spoon.'
Child: spoon.
Father: 'other spoon.'
Child: other . . . spoon. Now give me other one spoon?

Interestingly, however, some research suggests that subtler forms of feedback may have a role to play in the language acquisition process.

Recasts

Adults often respond to a child's utterance by repeating it, making adjustments to its form and/or content. (Responses of this sort are called **recasts**.)

21)

Child: Daddy here.
Mother: Yes, Daddy is here.

Child: Him go.
Mother: Yes, he is going.

Child: Boy chasing dog.
Mother: Yes, the boy is chasing the dog.

Child: The dog is barking.
Mother: Yes, he is barking at the kitty.

Recasts provide children with potentially useful information—adding a missing verb (*is* in the first example), changing the form of a pronoun (*him* to *he* in the second example), and so on. On the other hand, parents sometimes modify their children's grammatical utterances too (as in the final example), so recasts also have the potential to be misleading.

It is not yet clear what role recasts play in language learning, and studies to date have yielded conflicting results. For instance, a study of the acquisition of *the* and *a* by three children revealed no link between the frequency of recasts and the rate at which their use of determiners increased—no matter how many recasts children heard, it didn't seem to speed up their learning.

On the other hand, a quite different result emerged from an experiment in which four and five year olds were taught made-up verbs that have irregular past tense forms—for example, *pell* (with *pold* as its past tense). When the children first learned what the verbs meant (they were linked to various funny actions, such as hitting someone with a beanbag attached to a string), they heard only the '-*ing*' forms ('This is called *pelling*'). They therefore had no idea what the past tense forms should be and often produced 'mistakes' such as *pelled* when using the new verbs to describe actions in the past tense. Interestingly, a single recast was often enough to permit learning of the 'correct' form—which suggests that feedback of this type may have a role to play in the language acquisition process after all.

6.3   The role of cognitive development

Because there are dramatic changes in both linguistic and non-linguistic abilities during the first years of life, it is tempting to think that the two are somehow linked. Indeed, prominent psychologists have suggested both that general cognitive development shapes language acquisition (a view put forward by the late Swiss psychologist Jean Piaget) and that language acquisition is crucial to other aspects of cognitive development (a position associated with the late Russian psychologist Lev Vygotsky).

There are many suggestive similarities between language acquisition and cognitive development. During the first two years of life, for example, several cognitive advances that could facilitate language acquisition take place. One of these involves the development of **object permanence**, the ability to recognize that objects have an existence independent of one's interaction with them. Prior to the development of this ability, children seem to assume that an object ceases to exist when it moves out of sight, and that it is a different entity when it reappears. They therefore do not know where to look for an object that they observe being hidden; from their perspective, it has apparently simply ceased to exist. Object permanence emerges around age eighteen months, just prior to a period of rapid growth in the child's vocabulary. The relative timing of these two events suggests a possible connection: children's ability to learn the names for objects increases dramatically once they understand that those objects have an independent existence.

Another possible link between cognitive development and language acquisition involves seriation, the ability to arrange elements (such as sticks) in order of increasing or decreasing size. Children who are unable to perform this type of task typically describe the objects on which they are working simply as *long* or *short*. In contrast, children who are capable of seriation (age five and older) use comparative terms such as *longer* and *shorter*. Here again, there is an apparent connection between an aspect of language (the *-er* suffix for adjectives) and a more general cognitive skill (seriation).

Just as cognitive development may influence language acquisition, so the emergence of linguistic skills may have an effect on cognition. At the very least, language seems to provide its users with an enhanced capacity for complex reasoning. It is also conceivable that language may help draw children's attention to certain conceptual distinctions that would otherwise develop more slowly. For instance, in the course of learning words such as *father, mother, brother, uncle,* and so on, children may make discoveries about family relationships that would otherwise develop more slowly.

Selective impairment

These examples notwithstanding, there is good reason to believe that language acquisition is to a large extent independent of other types of cognitive development. One source of evidence for this conclusion comes from the study of individuals whose general cognitive development is deficient but whose language is highly developed.

One important study of this type focused on Rick, a severely retarded fifteen year old whose performance on a variety of non-linguistic tasks suggests that his general cognitive level is that of a preschool child. Yet, as the following examples illustrate, Rick's speech shows signs of syntactic and morphological sophistication—with appropriate use of affixes, non-lexical categories, and word order.

22)
She must've got me up and thrown me out of bed.
She keeps both of the ribbons on her hair.
If they get in trouble, they'd have a pillow fight.
She's the one that walks back and forth to school.
I wanna hear one more just for a change.

Another celebrated case involves Christopher, a linguistic savant. Although mentally impaired due to early brain damage (his IQ is 56) and unable to care for himself, he has shown an obsession for language since he was six years old. Thanks solely to his own efforts, he is able to read, write, and communicate in fifteen to twenty different languages, taking particular delight in learning complex morphological paradigms.

On the other hand, there are also documented cases of people whose IQ is perfectly normal but who nonetheless have great difficulty with inflection for the past tense and plural, as illustrated by the examples in *23)*. (There is reason to believe that this particular disorder is inherited, since it has been observed in some, but not all, members of three generations within a single family.)

23)
The boys eat four cookie.
It's a flying finches, they are.
The neighbors phone the ambulance because the man fall of the tree.

Case studies such as these suggest that certain aspects of language (in particular, morphology and syntax) are independent of non-linguistic types of cognitive development. This in turn implies that the mental mechanisms responsible for the acquisition of those parts of the grammar are relatively autonomous and that their operation neither follows from nor guarantees general cognitive development.

6.4   The role of inborn knowledge

There can be no doubt that there is something special about the human mind that equips it to acquire language. The only real question has to do with precisely what that special thing is. A very influential view among linguists is that children are born with prior knowledge of the type of categories, operations, and principles that are found in the grammar of any human language. They therefore know, for example, that the words in the language they are acquiring will belong to a small set of syntactic categories (N, V, and so on) and that they can be combined in particular ways to create larger phrases (NP, VP, S, etc.). The set of inborn categories, operations, and principles common to all human languages makes up Universal Grammar (UG), first mentioned in chapter 5.

The view that certain grammatical knowledge is inborn is known as **nativism**. Although nativism has roots in philosophy that date back thousands of years, its popularity in linguistics is due largely to the influence of Noam Chomsky, a linguist at the Massachusetts Institute of Technology. Chomsky's basic claim is that the grammars for human language are too complex and abstract to be learned on the basis of the type of experience to which children have access. Therefore, he argues, significant components of the grammar must be inborn. To illustrate this, we must consider a relatively complex example involving the notion of c-command introduced in chapter 6 (section 3.3).

Principle A (*Advanced*)

The interpretation of pronouns such as *himself* and *him* is regulated by the following two principles.

> **24)**
> *Principle A*
> A reflexive pronoun must have an antecedent that c-commands it in the same minimal S.
>
> *Principle B*
> A pronominal must not have an antecedent that c-commands it in the same minimal S.

These principles have played an important role in the study of language acquisition, and three arguments have been put forward in support of the claim that they are inborn.

First, the notion of c-command is quite abstract. It is not the type of concept that we would expect young children to discover simply by listening to sentences. Since we also know that no one teaches them about c-command, it makes sense to think that this notion is inborn and therefore does not have to be discovered or taught.

Second, the c-command relation seems to be universally relevant to pronoun interpretation. Thus, there appears to be no language in which the equivalent of English *himself* can refer to the boy rather than the boy's father in sentences such as the following (see chapter 6 for discussion).

> **25)**
> The boy's father overestimates himself.

The universality of this restriction would be explained if Principles A and B were innate and hence part of the inborn linguistic knowledge of all human beings.

Third, as we saw earlier in this chapter, Principles A and B seem to be available to children from a very early stage in their development—even three-year-olds appear to have mastered the distinction between reflexives and pronominals. Given the complexity of these principles, this provides additional evidence for the claim that they are inborn.

Parameters

Of course, not every feature of a language's grammar can be inborn. Its vocabulary and morphology must be learned, and so must at least part of its syntax. In the case of phrase structure, for example, UG stipulates that an XP constituent can include a head and its complements, but it does not specify the relative order of these elements. This differs from language to language, so that a child acquiring English must learn that heads precede their complements whereas a child acquiring Japanese must learn the reverse order. As noted in section 4.1 of chapter 5, UG includes a parameter for word order that offers a choice between head-initial and head-final order. (We ignore the positioning of specifiers for the purposes of this illustration in table 10.24.)

Table 10.24 The word order parameter	
Stipulated by UG	**Resulting options**
XP → X, Complement	XP → X Complement [head-initial]
	XP → Complement X [head-final]

There are also phonological parameters: for example, languages can differ from each other in terms of whether they allow a branching syllable onset—English does (e.g., *gleam, print*) whereas Japanese does not.

Part of the language acquisition process involves **parameter setting**—that is, determining which of the options permitted by a particular parameter is appropriate for the language being learned.

6.5   Is there a critical period?

One of the most intriguing issues in the study of language acquisition has to do with the possibility that normal linguistic development is possible only if children are exposed to language during a particular time frame or **critical period**. Evidence for the existence of such a period comes from the study of individuals who do not experience language during the early part of their lives.

One such individual is the much-discussed Genie, who was kept in a small room with virtually no opportunity to hear human speech from around age two to age thirteen. After many years of therapy and care, Genie's non-linguistic cognitive functioning was described as 'relatively normal' and her lexical and semantic abilities as 'good'. In terms of syntax and morphology, however, many problems remained, as evidenced in the sample utterances in table 10.25.

Table 10.25 Some of Genie's utterances	
Utterance	**Meaning**
Applesauce buy store	'Buy applesauce at the store.'
Man motorcycle have	'The man has a motorcycle.'
Want go ride Miss F. car	'I want to go ride in Miss F.'s car.'
Genie have full stomach	'I have a full stomach.'
Mama have baby grow up	'Mama has a baby who grew up.'

As these examples show, Genie makes word order errors (the first two examples) and her speech does not contain non-lexical categories or affixes.

Another revealing case study involved Chelsea, a deaf child who was misdiagnosed as retarded and emotionally disturbed. Chelsea grew up without language and was not exposed to speech until the age of thirty-one, when she was finally fitted with hearing aids. After intensive therapy, she is able to hold a job and to live independently. However, her vocabulary consists of only 2000 words and her sentences are badly ill formed, as the following examples help show.

26)
The woman is bus the going.
Combing hair the boy.
Orange Tim car in.
The girl is gone the ice cream shopping buying the man.

Based on case studies such as these, it is now widely believed that the ability to acquire a first language in an effortless and ultimately successful way begins to decline from age six and is severely compromised by the onset of puberty.

Summing up

This chapter has been concerned with the problem of how children acquire the **grammar** of their first language. Research in this area deals with two major issues: the nature of the developmental sequence leading to the emergence of mature linguistic competence in the areas of phonology, vocabulary, morphology, and syntax, and the factors that make it possible for children to acquire a complex grammar. A number of factors may contribute to the child's acquisition of language, including the properties of **caregiver speech, recasts,** the effects of general cognitive development, and inborn linguistic knowledge (**Universal Grammar**). We look to future research for deeper insights into the precise role of these and other factors.

Sources

Pioneering work on infant perception is reported in "Developmental Studies of Speech Perception" by P. Eimas in *Infant Perception*, edited by L. Cohen and P. Salapatek (New York: Academic Press, 1975). More recent work is reported by J. Mehler, E. Dupoux, T. Nazzi, and G. Dehaene-Lambertz in "Coping with Linguistic Diversity: The Infant's Viewpoint" and by J. Werker, V. Lloyd, J. Pegg, and Linda Polka in "Putting the Baby in the Bootstraps: Toward a More Complete Understanding of the Role of the Input in Infant Speech Processing," both in *Signal to Syntax*, edited by J. Morgan and K. Demuth (Mahwah, NJ: Erlbaum, 1996). The ability to use phonetic contrasts to distinguish between words is examined in "Perception and Production in Child Phonology: The Testing of Four Hypotheses" by M. Edwards in *Journal of Child Language* 1:205–19 (1974). The cross-linguistic data on babbling are summarized and discussed on pp. 9–11 of *Phonological Acquisition and Change* by J. Locke (San Diego: Academic Press, 1983); see also "Adaptation to Language: Evidence from Babbling and First Words in Four Languages" by B. de Boysson-Bardies and M. Vihman in *Language* 67:297–319 (1991). For a recent discussion of the relevance of babbling to the development of control over the vocal tract, see S. Pinker's *The Language Instinct* (New York: Morrow, 1994), p. 266. Differences between children's production and perception of speech sounds are found in *The Acquisition of Phonology: A Case Study* by N. Smith (New York: Cambridge University Press, 1973); the "*fis* phenomenon" is reported in "Psycholinguistic Research Methods" by J. Berko and R. Brown in *Handbook of Research Methods in Child Development*, edited by P. Mussen (New York: John Wiley & Sons, 1960). David Ingram's *Phonological Disability in Children* (London: Edward Arnold, 1976) contains many useful examples of early phonetic processes. The discussion of syllable deletion draws on information in "A Role for Stress in Early Speech Segmentation" by C. Echols, in *Signal to Syntax*, edited by J. Morgan and K. Demuth (Mahwah, NJ: Erlbaum, 1996) and in "The Acquisition of Prosodic Structure: An Investigation of Current Accounts of Children's Prosodic Development" by M. Kehoe and C. Stoel-Gammon in *Language* 73:13–44 (1997). The data on developmental order for speech sounds comes from chapter 8 of *First Language Acquisition* by D. Ingram, cited below.

The sample fifty-word vocabulary in section 3 is from p. 149 of the book by Ingram, cited below. Differences among children in terms of the types of words in their early vocabulary were first noted by K. Nelson in "Structure and Strategy in Learning to Talk" in *Monographs of the Society for Research in Child Development* 38 (149): 1–135 (1973). The '*dax* experiment' on proper and common nouns is reported by N. Katz, E. Baker, and J. Macnamara in their article, "What's in a Name? A Study of How Children Learn Common and Proper Nouns" in *Child Development* 45:469–73 (1974); the '*tiv* experiment' is from "The Child as Word Learner" by S. Carey in *Linguistic Theory and Psychological Reality*, edited by M. Halle, J. Bresnan, and G. Miller (Cambridge, MA: MIT Press, 1978). The discussion of strategies for learning word meaning is based on the proposals outlined in *Categorization and Naming in Children: Problems of Induction* by E. Markman (Cambridge, MA: MIT Press, 1989). The contrast between overextension in production and comprehension is described on pp. 152–53 of the book by Ingram cited below. The report of overextension in the speech of Allen is based on the discussion on p. 92 of the book by Eve Clark recommended below. The experimental study on overextension was carried out by J. Thomson and R. Chapman and reported in "Who is 'Daddy' Revisited: The Status of Two-Year-Olds' Over-extended Words in Use and Comprehension" in *Journal of Child Language* 4:359–75 (1977). The experiment on *pour* and *fill* can be found in "Syntax and Semantics in the Acquisition of Locative Verbs" by J. Gropen, S. Pinker, M. Hollander, and R. Goldberg in *Journal of Child Language* 18:115–51 (1991). The experiment on dimensional terms was carried out by P. Harris and J. Morris and is reported in "The Early Acquisition of Spatial Adjectives: A Cross-linguistic Study" in *Journal of Child Language* 13:335–52 (1986).

The remarks on inflectional overgeneralization are based in part on *Overregularization in Language Acquisition* by G. Marcus, S. Pinker, M. Ullman, M. Hollander, T. Rosen, and F. Xu, *Monographs of the Society for Research in Child Development*, Serial No. 228, Vol. 57, No. 4 (1992). The pioneering work on the developmental order for English bound morphemes and lexical categories was done by R. Brown and reported in his book *A First Language: The Early Stages* (Cambridge, MA: Harvard University Press, 1973); see also "Universal and Particular in the Acquisition of Language" by D. Slobin in *Language Acquisition: The State of the Art*, edited by E. Wanner and L. Gleitman (New York: Cambridge University Press, 1982). The original '*wug* test' was done by J. Berko and is reported in her article "The Child's Learning of English Morphology" in *Word* 14:150–77 (1958). The work on the development of derivational affixes and compounding in English is based on information reported in the book by Eve Clark recommended below and in the article by E. Clark and B. Hecht, "Learning to Coin Agent and Instrument Nouns" in *Cognition* 12:1–24 (1982). The data on the acquisition of the prohibition against inflection within compounds is from "Level-Ordering in Lexical Development" by P. Gordon in *Cognition* 21:73–93 (1985). Word order errors within compounds are reported in "Coining Complex Compounds in English: Affixes and Word Order in Acquisition" by E. Clark, B. Hecht, and R. Mulford in *Linguistics* 24:7–29 (1986).

The data in table 10.14 in section 4.3 is taken from S. Pinker, *The Language Instinct* (New York: Morrow, 1994), pp. 269–70. The data on the development of question structures is based on the classic article by E. Klima and U. Bellugi, "Syntactic Regularities in the Speech of Children" in *Psycholinguistic Papers*, edited by J. Lyons and R. Wales (Edinburgh: Edinburgh University Press, 1966). The auxiliary copying error in question structures is the subject of an experiment reported by M. Nakayama, "Performance Factors in Subject-Auxiliary Inversion," *Journal of Child Language* 14:113–26 (1987). The developmental order for *Wh* words is documented by L. Bloom, S. Merkin, and J. Wootten, "*Wh* Questions: Linguistic Factors That Contribute to the Sequence of Acquisition," *Child Development* 53:1084–92 (1982). Other descriptions confirming the main points of this account can be found in chapter 9 of the book by Ingram cited below. The data on the acquisition of passive structures come from a study by E. Turner and R. Rommetveit, reported in their article "The Acquisition of Sentence Voice and Reversibility" in *Child Development* 38:650–60 (1967). The data on children's use of *me* and *myself* comes from "Children's Knowledge of Binding and Coreference: Evidence from Spontaneous Speech" by P. Bloom, A. Barss, J. Nicol, and L. Conway in *Language* 70:53–71 (1994).

The role of correction in language development is examined in "Derivational Complexity and the Order of Acquisition in Child Speech" by R. Brown and C. Hanlon in *Cognition and the Development of Language*, edited by J. Hayes (New York: John Wiley & Sons, 1970). The data on mothers' reactions to children's ungrammatical and grammatical utterances comes from "Brown and Hanlon Revisited: Mothers' Sensitivity to Ungrammatical Forms" by K. Hirsh-Pasek, R. Treiman, and M. Schneiderman in *Journal of Child Language* 11:81–88 (1984). The relationship between *yes-no* questions in maternal speech and the development of auxiliaries is discussed by E. Newport, H. Gleitman, and L. Gleitman in their article, "Mother, I'd Rather Do It Myself: Some Effects and Noneffects of Maternal Speech Style" in *Talking to Children*, edited by C. Snow and C. Ferguson (New York: Cambridge University Press, 1977); see also the discussion in the book by Gallaway and Richards recommended below. The 'other one spoon' example is reported on p. 161 of an article by M. Braine, "The Acquisition of Language in Infant and Child," in *The Learning of Language*, edited by C. E. Reed (New York: Appleton-Century-Crofts, 1971). The recast experiment involving nonsense verbs is from "The Contrast Theory of Negative Evidence" by M. Saxton in *Journal of Child Language* 24:139–61 (1997).

General reviews of the role of the cognitive development in language acquisition can be found in the book by D. Ingram cited below and in "Cognitive Prerequisites: The Evidence from Children Learning English" by J. Johnston in *The Crosslinguistic Study of Language Acquisition*, Vol. 2, edited by D. Slobin (Hillsdale, NJ: Erlbaum, 1985), pp. 961–1004. The description of Genie and of Rick is based on "Abnormal Language Acquisition and the Modularity of Language" by S. Curtiss in *Linguistics: The Cambridge Survey*, Vol. 2, edited by F. Newmeyer (New York: Cambridge University Press, 1988), pp. 96–116. Chelsea's case is discussed by S. Curtiss in "The Independence and Task-Specificity of Language" in *Interaction in Human Development*, edited by A. Bornstein and J. Bruner (Hillsdale, NJ: Erlbaum, 1989). Christopher is the subject of a book by N. Smith and I. Tsimpli, *The Mind of a Savant: Language Learning and Modularity* (Cambridge, MA: Blackwell, 1995). The examples of sentences produced by speakers who have problems with inflection are from p. 49 of *The Language Instinct* by S. Pinker, cited above.

Figure 10.1 is adapted from "Syntax and Semantics in the Acquistion of Locative Verbs" by Jess Gropen, Steven Pinker, Michelle Hollander, and Richard Goldberg in *Journal of Child Language* 18:115–51. Figure 10.3 is adapted from *A First Language* by Roger Brown (Cambridge, MA: Harvard University Press). Exercises for this chapter were prepared by Joyce Hildebrand.

Recommended reading

Clark, Eve. 1993. *The Lexicon in Acquisition*. New York: Cambridge University Press.
Gallaway, Clare, and Brian Richards. 1994. *Input and Interaction in Language Acquisition*. New York: Cambridge University Press.
Ingram, David. 1989. *First Language Acquisition: Method, Description and Explanation*. New York: Cambridge University Press.
O'Grady, William. 1997. *Syntactic Development*. Chicago: University of Chicago Press.
Piattelli-Palmarini, Massimo, ed. 1980. *Language and Learning: The Debate between Jean Piaget and Noam Chomsky*. Cambridge, MA: Harvard University Press.
Vihman, Marilyn. 1996. *Phonological Development: The Origins of Language in the Child*. Cambridge, MA: Blackwell.

Questions

1. One piece of evidence that children acquire a grammar is their production of forms like *doed, leaved,* and *goed*. From recollections of your experience with children, what are some other forms (not related to the past tense rule) that children produce that indicate they are acquiring and overgeneralizing grammatical rules?

2. In one naturalistic study, a search for passive structures in a sample of 18 000 utterances from sixty children yielded only nineteen examples produced by twelve of the children.
   a) Does this mean that the other forty-eight children had not yet learned the passive structure?
   b) How are the disadvantages of the naturalistic method exemplified here?

3. The following transcriptions represent the pronunciation of a two-year-old child. Indicate which phonetic processes have applied in each case.
   a) skin [kɪd]
   b) spoon [bun]
   c) zoo [du]
   d) John [dɑn]
   e) bath [bæt]
   f) other [ʌdə]
   g) Smith [mɪt]
   h) tent [dɛt]
   i) teddy [dɛdi]
   j) brush [bʌt]
   k) bump [bʌp]
   l) play [pwej]
   m) breakfast [brɛkpəst]

4. Drawing on the phonetic processes posited for the preceding exercise, predict one or more plausible immature pronunciations for each of the following words.
   a) show
   b) please
   c) spit
   d) under
   e) juice
   f) thumb
   g) zebra
   h) ring

5. Consider the following examples of overextensions, all of which have actually been observed in children's speech. What is the basis for each of these overextensions?

Word	First Referent	Overextensions
a) sch	sound of a train	music, noise of wheels, sound of rain
b) bow-wow	dog	sheep, rabbit fur, puppet
c) baby	baby	people in pictures
d) sizo	scissors	nail file, knife, screwdriver, spoon
e) policeman	policeman	mailman, sailor, doctor
f) strawberry	strawberry	grapes, raspberry
g) fireworks	fireworks	matches, light, cigarette
h) Batman	Batman logo on a T-shirt	any logo on a T-shirt

6. Since children have a tendency to focus on the prototypical members of categories in the acquisition of words, how might you expect children to underextend the following words? What members of the category might you expect children not to include?
   a) car
   b) tree
   c) ball

7. Children acquire certain spatial terms like *behind* and *in front of* relatively late. They also acquire words like *those, this, here*, and *there* relatively late. What do all of these words have in common that delays their acquisition?

8. The allomorphic variation associated with the 3rd person singular verbal ending -*s* is identical to that found with plural -*s*.
   a) Make up a test parallel to the '*wug* test' discussed in section 4.1.
   b) If possible, give your test to children between the ages of three and seven. Are your results similar to the ones discussed in the chapter?

9. Based on the discussion in section 4.2 about the developmental sequence of morpheme acquisition, consider the acquisition in other languages of the morphemes corresponding to those listed in table 10.14. Would you predict that these morphemes would be acquired in exactly the same order as their English equivalents? Why or why not?

10. Considering children's tendency to overgeneralize morphological rules, what might we expect a young child to use in the place of the following adult words? Justify your choice in each case.
    a) fish (plural)   f) geese
    b) went   g) brought
    c) mice   h) hit (past tense)
    d) ate   i) himself
    e) has   j) women

11. Each of the following utterances is from the speech of a child in the two-word stage. Identify the semantic relation expressed by each of these utterances.

Intended meaning	Child's utterance
a) Jimmy is swimming.	Jimmy swim.

b) Ken's book   Ken book
c) Daddy is at his office.   Daddy office
d) You push the baby.   push baby
e) Mommy is reading.   Mommy read

12. Consider the following data from Jordie, a two-and-a-half-year-old child, in light of the list of morphemes in table 10.14.

Intended meaning	*Jordie's utterance*
a) Where's my blanket?	Where my blanket?
b) Does it go right here, Mommy?	Go right here, Mommy?
c) It's running over.	Running over.
d) Here, it goes here.	Here, go here.
e) No, that's mine.	No, that mine.
f) Dinosaurs say gronk.	Dinosaur say gronk.
g) There's more.	There more.

i) Which of the morphemes in table 10.14 are missing in Jordie's sentences but present in the equivalent adult utterance?

ii) List the morphemes that are present in both the adult interpretations and in Jordie's speech.

13. Now consider the following utterances from a child named Krista.

Intended meaning	*Krista's utterance*
a) My name is Krista.	Mine name Krista.
b) My last name is Pegit.	Last name Pegit.
c) The tape is right there.	Tape right there.
d) Daddy's book	Daddy book.
e) I've got a book.	I'm got a book.
f) Read me a story.	Read me story.
g) I'll do it.	I'm do it.
h) He went outside.	He went outside.
i) Open the gate, please.	Open a gate, please.
j) Gramma's house.	Gramma's house.
k) Smell the flowers.	Smell flowers.
l) Shoes on.	Shoes on.
m) The wee boy fell down.	Wee boy fell down.
n) That's my ball.	That's mines ball.

i) Which morphemes are missing in Krista's speech, but present in the adult interpretations?

ii) Krista uses the past tense twice in the above utterances. Do you think this is evidence that she has acquired the past tense morpheme? Why or why not?

iii) Comment on Krista's difficulty with possessive pronouns.

iv) Do you think she has acquired possessive -'s? Why or why not?

14. The following utterances were produced spontaneously by Holly, age three years.
    a) I learned about loving moms.
    b) Put him in the bathtub.

    c) We eated gummy snakes.

    d) Thank you for giving these books us.

    e) I don't know.

    f) He bited my finger. (when corrected, she said: He bitted my finger.)

    g) I runned in the water.

    h) I rided on a elephant.

    i) Has Holly acquired the past tense morpheme? How do you know?

    ii) What is the evidence in Holly's speech that she has learned the XP rule? the S rule?

    iii) What is the evidence that she has acquired the category noun? the category verb?

15. The following sentences were uttered by a child aged two and a half.

    a) What's this is called?

    b) Mom, what these is called?

    c) Did you don't go to school today?

    d) You gonna don't go to school?

    Considering these four sentences, describe the child's current knowledge of the Inversion transformation.

16. Consider the following speech sample from a child.

    a) What Evan will read?

    b) Where Evan will read?

    c) Why you see seal?

    d) Why she want to?

    i) Determine the stage of development of this child in terms of his acquisition of question structures.

    ii) What do we expect to happen next?

17. It has been reported that hearing children growing up in homes with non-speaking deaf parents cannot learn language from radio or even television (see p. 278 of *The Language Instinct* by S. Pinker [New York: Morrow, 1994]).

    i) Can you think of any reasons for this?

    ii) What are the implications of these findings for our understanding of the type of experience that is required for language acquisition?

CHAPTER Eleven

John Archibald

Second language acquisition

When we talk about acquisition in SLA research,
we are not talking about acquisition in the sense
that one acquires polo ponies, Lladró figurines, or
CBS, but rather in the sense that one acquires
vicious habits, a taste for Brie, or a potbelly.

KEVIN R. GREGG

The field of **second language acquisition** (SLA) research investigates how people attain proficiency in a language that is not their mother tongue. Whether we are looking at someone learning to read Greek in university, or someone becoming fluent in a fifth language in their forties, or a child acquiring a new language after moving to a new country, we refer to it as second language acquisition. The interesting phenomenon of children simultaneously acquiring two languages is generally investigated in the field known as **bilingualism** (which may be thought of as a subdiscipline of SLA research). In this chapter, we will primarily be concerned with second language acquisition in adults.

Over the years, the study of second language acquisition has been undertaken from a variety of different perspectives. In the 1950s and 1960s the primary objective was pedagogic. Researchers were interested in trying to improve the way in which second languages were taught. Hence, they were interested in discovering how those languages were learned. From the 1970s on, the focus shifted from the teacher to the learner and the field of L2 instruction became somewhat separate.

The reason for this has something to do with what was going on in linguistics, psychology, and first language acquisition research. All three of these areas shifted focus from the external to the internal in the 1960s. Linguistics became concerned with the mental grammar of the speaker, not just the description of the linguistic structures of a given language. Psychology shifted from behaviourism (which denied the importance of mental representations) to cognitive psychology. And research on first language acquisition focused on children's internal grammars. These fields are also crucial to the study of SLA. Linguistics gives us a sophisticated and accurate description of what people are trying to learn (the second language), and what they already know (the first language). Psychology can provide us with a learning theory to account for how people acquire knowledge. Finally, the field of first language acquisition (which has been around longer than the field of second language acquisition) offers various findings that can be productively applied to SLA. For example, we know that children who are acquiring their first language (L1) have grammars that are systematic and that their utterances are not just bad imitations of the adult target. As we will see, second language learners, too, are developing a grammar that is systematic even if it is not nativelike.

1 The study of second language acquisition

In the case of first language acquisition, we may ascribe the difference between child and adult grammars to either cognitive or biological immaturity in the child. In the case of second language learning by adults, however, we cannot say that the learners are either cognitively or biologically immature. Rather, they are subject to an influence that is absent from the child's situation: the first language itself. Let us diagram the situation as shown in figure 11.1.

L1 → Interlanguage Grammar ← L2

Figure 11.1 Influences on an interlanguage grammar

This diagram illustrates the fact that second language learners have a systematic interlanguage (IL) grammar—so-called because it is a system of mental representations influenced by both the first and the second language and has features of each.

1.1 The role of the first language

One of the most easily recognizable traits of a second language learner's speech is that it bears a certain resemblance to the first language. Thus, someone whose first language is French is likely to sound different from someone whose first language is German when they both speak English. Consider in this regard the typical pronunciation of the English word *have* by speakers of French and German shown in table 11.1.

Table 11.1	Phonological transfer	
English target	**French speaker**	**German speaker**
have [hæv]	[æv]	[hæf]

Table 11.2	More phonological transfer		
L1	**L2**	**Example**	**Comment**
Spanish	English	I espeak Espanish.	Spanish does not allow s + consonant sequences word-initially.
English	French	[ty] (you) → [tu]	English does not have the front, rounded vowel [y]. The English speaker substitutes the [u] sound.
Quebec French	English	Over dere.	The [ð] sound is replaced by [d].
European French	English	Over zere.	The [ð] sound is replaced by [z].
English	Spanish	[paɾa] 'for' → [para]	As English does not have the tapped [ɾ], a [r] is substituted.

The form in table 11.1 produced by the French speakers reflects the fact that French lacks the phoneme /h/ while the pronunciation associated with German speakers can be traced to the fact that German includes a rule of Syllable Final Obstruent Devoicing (which changes the [v] to a [f]). The term **transfer** is used to describe the process whereby a feature or rule from a learner's first language is carried over to the IL grammar. Other examples can be seen in table 11.2.

1.2   The role of the L2

The first language is not the only influence on the interlanguage grammar, since some properties of the IL can be traced to aspects of the L2. In the case of a German speaker who is learning English, for example, the IL grammar will contain some features of both German and English. Consider how a German speaker learning Canadian English might pronounce the word *eyes* (see table 11.3).

Table 11.3 One possible pronunciation of the English word *eyes* by a German-speaking learner		
Target form	Result of Final Obstruent Devoicing	Result of Canadian Vowel Raising
/ajz/	[ajs]	[ʌjs]

Here, the learner first applies the rule of Syllable Final Obstruent Devoicing (transferred from German), changing /ajz/ to [ajs]. But the learner also has acquired some knowledge of the target language—in this case, the rule of Canadian Vowel Raising (discussed in chapter 3), which states that [aj] becomes [ʌj] before a voiceless consonant in the same syllable. Thanks to application of the Syllable Final Obstruent Devoicing Rule, the input form now ends in a voiceless consonant ([s]) which triggers Canadian Raising. This example serves to show us something about the nature of an interlanguage: it contains features of both the L1 and the L2.

1.3   The nature of an interlanguage

The dual nature of IL grammars is captured in the **Ontogeny Model** of second language acquisition. According to this model, there are two types of error in an IL grammar: **transfer errors** and **developmental errors**. As we have seen, the former type of error reflects transfer from the L1. In contrast, developmental errors involve the same sort of mistakes that children make in acquiring their L1. For example, as we saw in chapter 10, children learning English as a first language sometimes produce forms like *goed* and *breaked*, apparently overgeneralizing the regular rule for past tense formation. A similar developmental error has been observed in second language learners, who also overgeneralize rules as they acquire a grammar.

It is possible that the processes of transfer and overgeneralization in L2 learning are the result of a single cognitive strategy that could be informally stated as 'use what you know'. This predicts that the kind of errors made by second language learners will be dependent on their level of proficiency. Beginning learners may have nothing to draw on but their L1. However, more advanced learners have acquired a certain amount of knowledge about the L2 and this knowledge becomes a potential source of errors. This is illustrated in table 11.4.

Table 11.4 Error patterns in L2 acquisition		
Level of proficiency	**Transfer errors**	**Developmental errors**
Beginner	high	low
Intermediate	medium	high
Advanced	low	low

Graphically, the predictions of the Ontogeny Model are illustrated in figure 11.2. The number of transfer errors should decrease over time while the number of developmental errors should initially be small, but then should increase before finally decreasing.

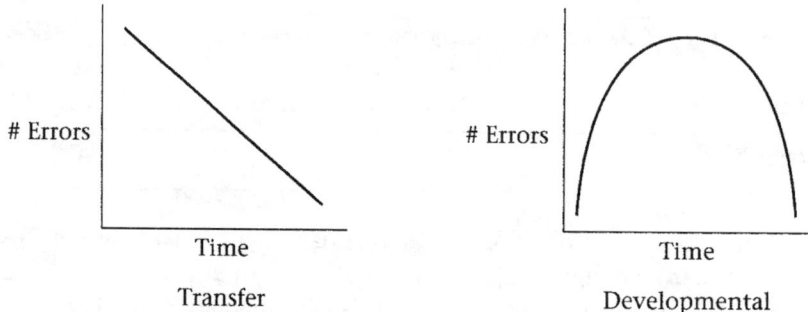

Figure 11.2 Error patterns predicted by the Ontogeny Model

The IL grammar, then, is influenced by both the L1 and the L2, though the proportion of influence is dependent on the learner's level of overall proficiency. Note that advanced learners have low numbers of both transfer and developmental errors. Not all learners, however, reach this advanced stage. It is common in second language acquisition for learners to reach a plateau in their development. For example, even after many years of exposure to English, a second language learner may still produce sentences like *I don't know what should I do* (meaning 'I don't know what I should do') in spite of hearing the grammatical version from native speakers and perhaps being corrected. When the interlanguage grammar stops changing, it is said to have **fossilized**.

Second language learners can exhibit non-nativelike characteristics in any linguistic domain, as can be seen in table 11.5.

Table 11.5 Types of errors found in the acquisition of English			
L1	**Example**	**Error type**	**Comment**
Spanish	My wife is <u>embarrassed.</u> (meaning 'pregnant')	lexical	Spanish *embarasado* = 'pregnant'
Various	I live in a two bedroom <u>department</u>.	lexical	Sometimes the wrong word can be chosen

Table 11.5 (continued) Types of errors found in the acquisition of English			
L1	**Example**	**Error type**	**Comment**
Various	I <u>didn't took</u> the car.	morphological	English doesn't mark the past tense on both auxiliary and main verbs.
Various	She <u>get ups</u> late.	morphological	The speaker adds the agreement marker to the particle not the verb.
French	He <u>drinks frequently</u> beer.	syntactic	French places the main verb before the adverb.
Various (e.g., Turkish, Arabic)	There's the man that I saw <u>him</u>.	syntactic	Some languages allow pronouns in this position in a relative clause.

1.4   The final state

So far we have been talking about the characteristics of the intermediate grammar. But a discussion of what an IL grammar looks like must consider the **target**, that is, what is to be acquired. The field of SLA, then, must address the issue of actual proficiency or **communicative competence**. While knowledge of a language's grammar allows us to distinguish between grammatical and ungrammatical sentences, successful communication requires much more than this. The learner must also be able to use the language in a way that is appropriate to the situation or context. As figure 11.3 helps illustrate, both grammatical accuracy and communicative ability are part of communicative competence.

Let us now briefly consider each of the major subparts of the model.

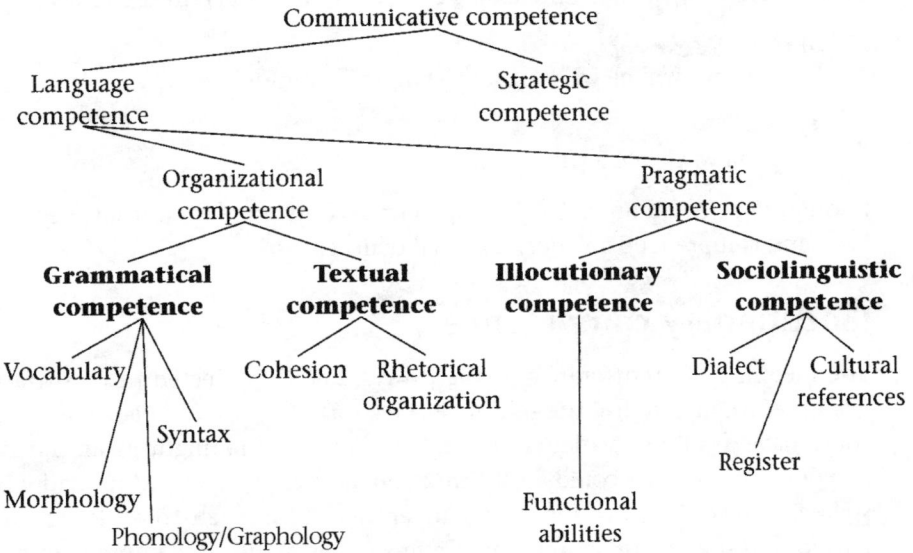

Figure 11.3 A model of communicative competence

Grammatical competence

Grammatical competence has to do with knowledge of the core components of the grammar: phonetics, phonology, morphology, syntax, and semantics. We will address these areas in detail in section 2.

Textual competence

Textual competence involves knowledge of well-formedness above the sentence level, including the rules that string sentences together to make a well-formed text in the spoken or written language. As the following examples help show, a text is not just a sequence of grammatical utterances.

> 1)
> MGs can be very temperamental. MGs won't start if they are wet. When they work, MGs are fun to drive. They do not work often.

> 2)
> Like most roadsters, MGs can be very temperamental. For example, they won't start if they are wet. However, on the rare days when they work, they are fun to drive.

The difference between the two texts does not involve the grammaticality of individual sentences, but rather relates to differences in the use of linking words such as *like*, *for example*, and *however*. To be proficient, second language learners have to acquire the ability to organize and link sentences in this way.

Sociolinguistic competence

As we will see in chapter 14, language use can vary according to the context. For example, we use a different style of language in informal situations than we do in formal ones. This can affect phonology, syntax, and lexical choice, as can be seen in the following two utterances.

> 3)
> I assume we will be working late again this evening? What a shame!

> 4)
> We gotta work late again? Dammit!

In order to be communicatively competent, second language learners need to be able to produce and comprehend a variety of social dialects.

Illocutionary competence

The meaning of an utterance is not always directly reflected in its surface structure. For example, when uttering the sentence *Have you ever considered professional help?*, a speaker could have in mind a variety of intended meanings. He might mean 'I can't help you, but maybe somebody else could' or 'I think you are a truly disturbed individual; seek help.' The speaker's intent in producing an utterance is referred to as **illocutionary force.** **Illocutionary competence**, then, refers to the ability to comprehend a speaker's intent, and to produce a variety of syntactic structures to convey a particular intent in various circumstances (e.g., *Are you cold?*, *Could I close the window?*, *Why on earth is the window open?*). This, too, is something that second language learners need to acquire.

In sum, communicative competence is a model of proficiency that allows us to measure second language knowledge and ability, to construct second language proficiency tests, and to design balanced second language courses.

1.5 Variation in performance

An important goal of L2 research is to integrate the study of competence (linguistic knowledge) and **performance** (actual language use in particular situations). One of the characteristics of the output of second language learners is that it is quite variable. For example, a learner might well produce the following sentence:

> 5)
> I **didn't** like **th**at movie so I told her I **no** want to go **d**ere.

In the preceding (hypothetical) example, the learner is inconsistent, getting one of the two negatives right and correctly pronouncing one of the interdental fricatives. The question that intrigues researchers has to do with what causes this sort of variation. We usually think of knowledge as fairly stable within an individual. So, for example, if you make a mistake while speaking in your native language, you tend not to question your competence in that language, but rather to assume that you made some kind of performance error. So how do we account for learners who behave as if they know how to negate a verb or pronounce [ð] on some occasions, but not others? Do they have the knowledge or don't they?

It is difficult to answer this question, in part because of considerations involving error frequency. If a second language learner gets something wrong 10 percent of the time, is it the same (in terms of competence) as getting it wrong 60 percent of the time? We would probably say that a non-native speaker who gets the English past tense correct 10 percent of the time doesn't know it, and that someone who gets it right 90 percent of the time does. But what of someone who gets it right somewhere between those two scores? This is a complex research question. The (admittedly simplistic) view adopted in this chapter is that variation falls into the realm of linguistic performance.

Linguistic performance clearly involves the interaction of a number of cognitive systems and has much in common with other skills. A crucial notion for the study of how skills develop involves the distinction between controlled and automatic processing. When acquiring a new skill (e.g., playing golf) we begin by having to devote a lot of conscious or controlled processing to the activity. Feet apart, head down, elbow straight, white shoes, etc. Once we become proficient, we 'just' hit the ball; the activity has become automatic.

We need to shift processing from controlled to automatic because, as humans, we have a fixed processing capacity. We can't consciously process everything at once. Shifting some material into automatic processing frees up space for more controlled processing. Consider an example from reading. When we first learn how to read, we devote much of our cognitive processing to determining what the written symbols stand for. When we are focusing on decoding the letters, we do not have the processing capacity to deal with things like reading for prejudice or bias. After a time, though, letter recognition happens automatically in our first language and learners can devote more of their cognitive capacity to higher level skills.

That native speakers do this kind of thing automatically can be seen by the difficulty we have in proofreading. It is hard to suppress the information we're getting from the context since the mind tries to make sense of what it's reading. Conversely, when we are forced by exceptional circumstances to devote a lot of energy to decoding the print (e.g., a bad photocopy or fax), our higher-level processing slows down; we can't focus as much on the message when we are focusing on the form.

All this is relevant to second language acquisition in that it can help explain the variable performance of L2 learners. When learners are focusing on the form of the L2 utterance, they may be able to produce it accurately. However, when there are extra demands, such as trying to communicate a complex thought or carry on a conversation in a noisy room, errors may occur. This suggests that the learner has a mental representation of the form in question (say a negated verb or a [ð]) but can have difficulty implementing or accessing it under certain conditions.

2   Interlanguage grammars

Let us turn now to a discussion of the specifics of what is acquired when learning the phonology, morphology, and syntax of a second language. The general question we are trying to answer here is "What is the structure of an interlanguage?" Second language learners are acquiring grammars, and those grammars involve mental representations. Therefore we can investigate the nature of those representations within the various subdomains of linguistic theory. We begin with phonology.

2.1   L2 phonology

Let us consider what is to be acquired in the domain of phonology. Broadly speaking, we can distinguish between segmental and prosodic phonology. Segmental phonology has to do with the characteristics of phonological segments, like consonants (C) and vowels (V). Prosodic phonology, on the other hand, has to do with phonological phenomena that affect more than a single segment (e.g., syllables and stress).

Segmental phonology

As we saw in chapter 3, languages vary in their segmental inventory in that they choose a subset of the sounds found in human languages. There is thus a good chance that a second language learner will have to learn to produce and perceive some new sounds when acquiring a second language.

One of the most obvious characteristics of adult second language speech is that it is 'accented' as the result of phonological and phonetic transfer from the native language. This is why native speakers of English can usually distinguish French-accented English from German-accented English. Consider the examples in table 11.6.

Table 11.6   French- and German-accented English

English target	Quebec French speaker	German speaker
[ðə] 'the'	[də]	[zə]

As both French and German lack the interdental fricative [ð], native speakers of those languages substitute a sound from their L1 wherever English has that sound. Generally, the learners substitute a sound that shares some features with the target sound. In table 11.6, the French speaker substituted a voiced alveolar (coronal) stop, while the German speaker substituted a voiced alveolar (coronal) fricative for the English voiced, interdental (coronal) fricative. Particularly at a beginning level of proficiency, L2 learners pronounce words using their L1 phonological system.

A similar phenomenon can be seen in the phonology of loan words. When a language borrows a word from another language, it makes the word fit into its own phonological system. For example, as we saw in chapter 3, when English borrowed the word *pterodactyl* from Greek, it reduced the onset cluster [pt], which is well-formed in Greek but not English. However, no such change was made in the word *helicopter* (also from Greek) since it already complied with the phonological pattern of English.

Markedness

One question that has received a lot of attention in SLA research is whether some sounds are harder to acquire in a second language than others. Perhaps some sounds are simpler than others. Or perhaps some sound systems are easier for speakers of a certain language to acquire. Would it be easier for a Japanese speaker to acquire English or Vietnamese? As might be expected, these are not simple issues. We cannot talk about the ease or difficulty of entire languages, but we may have something to say about individual sounds.

When linguists try to deal with the notions of ease or simplicity, they make use of the notion of *markedness*. Structures that are simple and/or especially common in human language are said to be **unmarked**, while structures that are complex or less common are said to be **marked**. So, we might say that a sound that is found in relatively few of the world's languages (e.g., [θ]) is marked while a sound that occurs in many of the world's languages (e.g., [t]) is unmarked.

Markedness is commonly approached from the perspective of language typology, which is concerned with the comparative study of similarities and differences among languages. As noted in chapter 8, researchers have discovered certain implicational universals of the form 'if a language has *x*, it will also have *y*'. For example, if a language has nasal vowels (e.g., [ã]), then it will also have oral vowels (e.g., [a]). Crucial to the understanding of implicational universals is the fact that the implication is unidirectional. Thus a language that has oral vowels does not necessarily have nasal vowels. This allows us to identify [a] as less marked than [ã], in accordance with the following generalization.

6)
  X is more marked than *y* if the presence of *x* implies the presence of *y*, *but not vice versa*.

It is interesting to ask whether IL grammars obey such implicational universals and whether this can tell us something about the question of ease and difficulty of learning.

The **Markedness Differential Hypothesis** investigates second language acquisition by comparing the relative markedness of structures in the L1 and the L2. Remember the earlier example of Syllable Final Obstruent Devoicing in German, which explains why a word like *hund* 'dog' is pronounced with a [t] at the end. German speakers learning English typically transfer Syllable Final Obstruent Devoicing into their IL (producing [hæt] for [hæd] 'had') and must learn to make the contrast between [t] and [d] at the ends of words. We might be tempted to think that the principle underlying this phenomenon is something like 'it's hard to learn to make contrasts that your L1 doesn't make'. But when we look at another set of data we see that this is not the case.

French makes a contrast between [ʃ] and [ʒ] in places where English does not, as table 11.7 indicates.

Table 11.7 The [ʃ]/[ʒ] contrast in English and French	
English [ʃ]/[ʒ]	**French [ʃ]/[ʒ]**
Initial <u>s</u>ure [ʃ]/* [ʒ]¹	<u>ch</u>ant ([ʃ])/<u>g</u>ens ([ʒ]) 'song' 'people'
Medial as<u>s</u>ure ([ʃ])/a<u>z</u>ure ([ʒ])	bou<u>ch</u>er ([ʃ])/bou<u>g</u>er ([ʒ]) 'to fill up' 'to budge'
Final lea<u>sh</u> ([ʃ])/lie<u>g</u>e ([ʒ])	ha<u>ch</u>e ([ʃ])/a<u>g</u>e ([ʒ]) 'h' 'age'

If it were invariably difficult for second language learners to make contrasts that are not found in their L1, we would expect English speakers to have difficulty learning to produce [ʒ] at the beginning of words. But they don't. English speakers seem able to learn to pronounce French words like *jaune* 'yellow' and *jeudi* 'Thursday' without trouble.

The notion of *markedness* can be used to explain why German speakers have difficulty making a new contrast in English, while English speakers don't have difficulty making a new contrast in French. The typological situation is as follows:

- There are languages that have a voicing contrast initially, medially, and finally (e.g., English).
- There are languages that have a voicing contrast initially, and medially, but not finally (e.g., German).
- There are languages that have a voicing contrast initially, but not medially or finally (e.g., Sardinian).

These generalizations allow us to formulate the following implicational universal.

7)
The presence of a voicing contrast in final position implies the presence of a voicing contrast in medial position, which in turn implies the presence of a voicing contrast in initial position.

We can represent this universal graphically as follows:

8)
initial < medial < final
   C   B   A

The presence of A implies the presence of B (but not vice versa), and the presence of B implies the presence of C (but not vice versa). Therefore A is the most marked and C is the least marked. This markedness differential explains the differing degrees of difficulty exhibited by the German and English L2 learners. The German speakers learning English are attempting to acquire a contrast in a universally more marked position (final) whereas the English speakers learning French are attempting to acquire a contrast in a universally unmarked position (initial).[2]

Another way of looking at the similarity/difference question, though, is not in terms of ease or difficulty of acquisition but rather in terms of *rate* of acquisition. The **Similarity Differential Rate Hypothesis** (SDRH) makes the claim that the rates of acquisition for dissimilar phenomena are faster than for similar phenomena. In other words, all other things being equal, learners will learn something that is unlike their first language structure *faster* than something that is similar to (and hence could be confused with) a first language structure. The data shown in figure 11.4 describe the acquisition of English [r] (in word-initial position) and English velarised [ɫ] (in word-final position) by a native speaker of Haitian creole that has a uvular [ʁ] and only a clear alveolar [l]. Note that there is virtually no acquisition of the velarised [ɫ] and little change in rate, whereas the rate of change for [r] is much more dramatic. The dissimilar [r] is acquired at a faster rate than the similar [l].

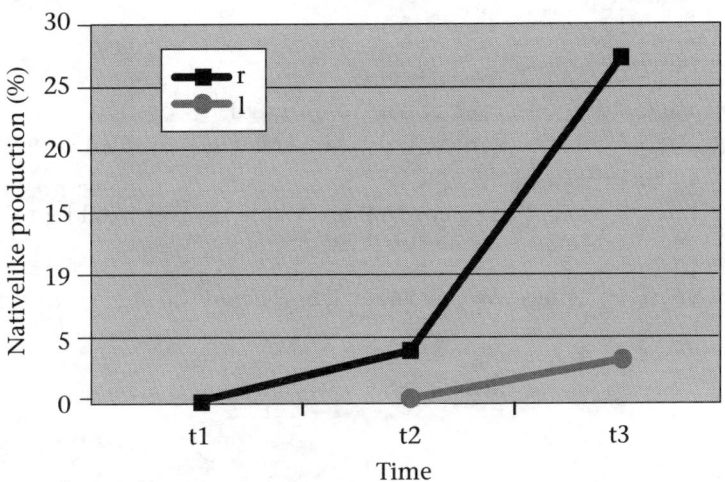

Figure 11.4 Differential rates of acquisition

Of course, the question of how to determine whether two features are similar or dissimilar is not always straightforward. To really test this hypothesis, we would need to look at perceptual, phonetic, phonological, and even orthographic factors that could affect this judgment. Here we will just accept that the two *l*'s are more similar than the two *r*'s.

In addition to the segmental inventory, second language learners also have to acquire the prosodic phonology of the target language. For example, they have to acquire the principles of syllabification and stress assignment. We will now look at each in turn.

L2 syllabification

We saw in chapter 3 that syllables have the hierarchical structure shown in figure 11.5.

Figure 11.5 The internal structure of the syllable

The languages of the world vary according to such things as whether syllabic nodes can branch. Some languages (e.g., Japanese) do not allow branching onsets or codas. Ignoring some complexities, let us assume that all syllables must be CV or CVC. More complex syllables such as CCVCC are not allowed. A common phenomenon in second language learning involves modifying an L2 word so that it fits the L1 syllable structure. Consider the following words spoken by someone whose L1 is Arabic:

9)

English target	*Non-native speaker's version*
plant	pilanti
Fred	Fired
translate	tiransilet

Arabic does not allow branching onsets or codas, so an English word like *plant* cannot be mapped onto a single Arabic syllable. A characteristic of Arabic is that illicit consonant clusters are broken up by an epenthetic [i].[3]

With this in mind, let us look at the steps that an Arabic speaker would go through in syllabifying 'plant'.

Step 1 ***Initial syllabifiation:*** Assign vowels to a nucleus (N) and the nucleus to a rhyme (R).

Step 2 Assign allowable onset (O) consonants (in Arabic, one).

Step 3 Assign allowable coda (Co) consonants (in Arabic, one).

Step 4 Insert an epenthetic [i] to the right of an unsyllabified consonant.

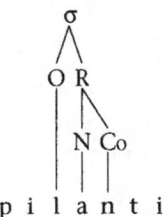

Step 5 Assign vowels to a nucleus and the nucleus to a rhyme.

Step 6 Assign allowable onset consonants (in Arabic, one).

As this example helps show, we can explain why Arabic speakers pronounce English words in the way that they do by investigating the principles of syllabification in the L1. Especially at the beginning levels of proficiency, the structure of the IL is influenced by the structure of the L1.

Stress assignment

L2 learners also have to acquire the stress patterns of the language they are trying to learn. Consider an example from Polish. Polish is a language in which word-level stress is assigned to the penultimate syllable (regardless of syllable weight). These metrical principles transfer and result in one of the characteristics of a Polish accent in English: the tendency to place stress on the penultimate syllable regardless of syllable weight. Remember from chapter 3 that in English, heavy syllables tend to attract stress (e.g., *aróma, agénda*). The following examples illustrate a non-native stress pattern in which the second-to-last syllable is always stressed.

10)

English target	*Non-native form*
astónish	astónish
maintáin	máintain
cábinet	cabínet

2.2   L2 syntax

L2 learners also have to acquire the syntax of their new language. In this section, we will look at two facets of syntactic structure: the null subject parameter and verb movement.

Null subjects

As we saw in chapter 5, Universal Grammar includes universal principles (that account for what all natural languages have in common) as well as parameters (that account for cross-linguistic variation). Parameters are like linguistic switches (often binary) that can be set to a particular value as a result of the linguistic input. One of the first parameters to be proposed was the Null Subject (or pronoun-drop) Parameter. Essentially, this parameter is designed to account for the contrast between languages like French and English, which require overt grammatical subjects (e.g., *He speaks French/*Speaks French*), and languages like Spanish and Italian, which allow subjects to be omitted (e.g., Spanish *El habla español/Habla español* '[S/he] speaks Spanish').

11)
The Null Subject Parameter
The subject of a clause with a verb marked for tense {may/may not} be null.

Languages that allow null subjects tend to have other grammatical traits associated with them. For one, they tend to allow declarative sentences with the word order Verb + Subject as well as Subject + Verb, as in the following examples from Spanish.

12)
a.   Juan llegó.
      John arrived.

b.   Llegó Juan
      arrived John.

Secondly, they tend to allow sentences like the following, in which a complementizer (here *que* 'that') is immediately followed by the trace of a moved *wh* word.

13)
Quién dijo usted que *t* llegó?
who   said you   that arrived?
'Who did you say that arrived?'

As the following example shows, such sentences are unacceptable in English.

14)
*Who did you say [$_{CP}$ that [$_S$ *t* arrived]]?
(deep structure = *you did say that who arrived*)

In other words, languages like English ([-null subject]) do not allow *that*-trace sequences, whereas languages like Spanish ([+null subject]) do.

Studies on L2 learners of English show that Spanish speakers are more likely to judge subjectless English sentences to be grammatical than are French speakers. This is consistent with the assumption that L1 parameter settings are transferred into the IL grammar, at least in the early stages. Learning a second language can be seen as involving the resetting of parameters that have different values in the L1 and the L2.

Moreover, when Spanish subjects are given a task that requires them to change a declarative sentence into a question, they are more likely to produce a sentence that contains a *that*-trace sequence than are French subjects. For example, if Spanish subjects are given a sentence like *Joshua believed that <u>his father</u> would be late* and have to form a question asking about the underlined element, they are more likely than French subjects to produce a sentence like *Who did Joshua believe that t would be late?* This points toward the possibility that the admissibility of null subjects and the acceptability of *that*-trace sequences are somehow both related to the Null Subject Parameter (i.e., speakers of null subject languages are more likely to permit *that*-trace sequences).

However, there are complications. Remember that the study just described had the Spanish and French speakers form new sentences. Another study had both French and Spanish subjects judge the grammaticality of English sentences with a *that*-trace violation. Both groups were quite able to reject those sentences as ungrammatical. For some reason, there is a stronger L1 influence when learners have to form new sentences themselves.

Verb movement

French and English differ in the setting of the Verb Movement Parameter.

15)
The Verb Movement Parameter
V {raises/does not raise} to I.

We saw in chapter 5 that the transformation of verb movement takes a verb from within the VP and moves it to I (see figure 11.6). Simplifying slightly, let us say that English does not allow verb movement but French does. Thus, in French the verb raises to I past a preverbal adverb, but in English it does not. This difference can be seen in the following sentences, in which movement of the verb over the adverb separating it from the I position gives a bad result in English but a good result in French.

16)
a. *Marie watches often *t* television.
b. Marie regarde souvent *t* la télévision.

Studies have shown that French speakers learning English initially assume that English allows verb raising. In order to learn English they have to reset the value of their verb-raising parameter.

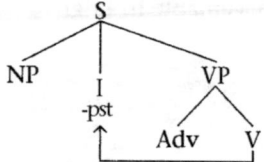

Figure 11.6 Verb movement

Markedness and the Subset Principle

Another interesting facet of a parameter-setting approach to SLA has to do with whether adult L2 learners can reset their parameters, and whether the notion of directionality of difficulty captured by the Markedness Differential Hypothesis (see section 2.1) can be captured in a parameter-setting model. The Null Subject Parameter can be used to address these questions. To understand how, we must first consider how a parameter-setting model instantiates the notion of markedness.

If we consider the two settings of the null subject parameter (+/-), we can see that the different values generate different grammars, as shown in the following sentences from English and Spanish.

17)
[-null subject]: I   speak Spanish.
[+null subject]: Yo hablo español.
                  Hablo español.

As you can see, the [+null subject] setting generates more grammatical utterances than the [-null subject] setting does. Therefore the [-] setting is said to be a subset of the [+] setting. Graphically, this can be represented as shown in figure 11.7.

The **Subset Principle** stipulates that for first language learners, the initial or default setting will be the subset value (i.e., [-null subject] in the case of the Null Subject Parameter.[4]

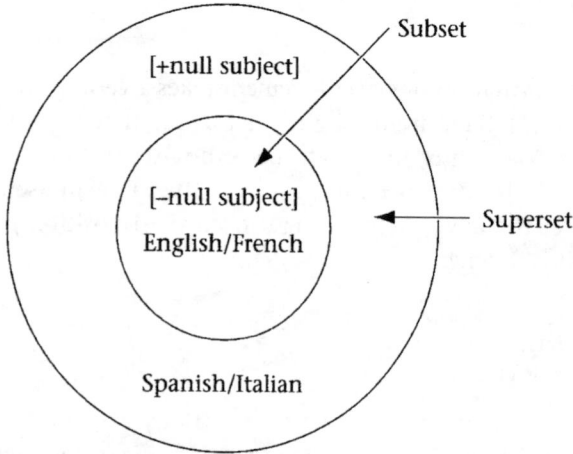

Figure 11.7 Subset/superset relation for the Null Subject Parameter

Second language learners may have to reset their parameters. When attempting to reset from subset to superset or from superset to subset, learners have access to different types of evidence. Imagine a learner of English (who has the [-] setting) trying to learn Spanish. The learner's initial assumption will be the L1 parameter setting, which leads to the expectation that all sentences will have overt subjects. When faced with Spanish input, the learner will be exposed to grammatical utterances in the L2 that do not have overt subjects (e.g., *Hablo español* '[I] speak Spanish'), which indicates that the L1 setting is incorrect and needs to be reset. Data like this, which involves grammatical utterances to which one is actually exposed, is referred to as **positive evidence**.

Now imagine a learner whose L1 is Spanish ([+]) who is trying to learn English ([-]). The learner's initial assumption will be that English should be [+null subject], like the L1. The learner's IL grammar will allow both sentences with overt subjects and sentences without. Crucially, there will be no positive evidence in the English input directed at this learner to show that the L1 parameter setting is wrong. The learner will hear sentences with overt subjects, which are sanctioned by the current IL grammar, but there will be no direct indication that sentences with null subjects are not allowed. There is no pressure to reset the parameter. In this case, the learner will have to rely on **negative evidence** (i.e., observations about what is missing or ungrammatical in the data) to reset the parameter. In particular, the learner would either have to be explicitly told what is ungrammatical (**direct** negative evidence), or infer that it is ungrammatical on the basis of the fact that no one else ever says it (**indirect** negative evidence).

Given that direct positive evidence is available in one case (English → Spanish), and negative evidence is required in the other (Spanish → English), we might predict that it is harder for Spanish speakers to learn the English value of the Null Subject Parameter than vice versa. In fact, the prediction is borne out. Studies have shown that it is easier for English speakers to reset to the Spanish value of the Null Subject Parameter, than it is for Spanish subjects to reset to the English setting.

Let us now consider how an approach based on typological universals would treat the same phenomenon. The presence of null subjects implies the presence of overt subjects, but not vice versa.

18)
overt subjects > null subjects

Therefore, null subjects would be thought of as more marked, and, consequently, more difficult to acquire. The Markedness Differential Hypothesis predicts that structures that are more marked typologically will cause difficulty in SLA because they are more marked. The Subset Principle, on the other hand, predicts that structures that are more marked will not cause difficulty because there will be clear evidence that the L1 setting is wrong. Although only the Subset Principle seems to make the correct prediction in the case of the null subjects, further research is necessary in order to see which approach is better able to handle a wider range of data.

2.3　L2 morphology

The study of second language morphology has a slightly different flavour than the study of either L2 phonology or syntax. L2 phonology has been studied for a long time, though the analyses have changed to reflect changes in linguistic theory. L2 syntax is a much younger field, and much of it has been informed by current linguistic theory. By contrast, L2 morphology has been studied more or less in a theoretical vacuum. In the 1970s, a number of studies collected data on the accuracy of second language learners on a variety of morphemes. This research drew on previous studies in the field of first language acquisition that had attempted to determine the order of acquisition of morphemes in L1 development. The developmental sequence in table 11.8 was found.

Table 11.8   Developmental order for first language acquisition

1. *–ing*	The present participle affix (e.g., she is work*ing*)
2. Plural *–s*	(e.g., bottle*s*)
3. Irregular past	(e.g., she *taught* French)
4. Possessive *–s*	(e.g., a child*'s* toy)
5. Copula *be*	(e.g., I *am* happy)
6. Articles	(e.g., *a, the*)
7. Regular past	(e.g., she walk*ed* quickly)
8. 3rd person *–s*	(e.g., she walk*s* quickly)
9. Auxiliary *be*	(e.g., she *is* working)

Research on second language acquisition focused on whether the developmental sequence in L2 learning was the same as for L1 learning. The order in table 11.9 was found.

Table 11.9   Developmental order for second language acquisition

1. *-ing*	4. Auxiliary *be*	7. Regular past
2. Copula *be*	5. Plural *-s*	8. 3rd person *-s*
3. Articles	6. Irregular past	9. Possessive *-s*

There are many similarities but there are also some differences. For example, note that auxiliary and copula *be* are acquired at a relatively earlier point in L2 than in L1, and that the possessive morpheme *-'s* is acquired later in L2 than in L1. To attempt to explain these patterns, we need to look a little more closely at the structures that implement inflectional morphology.

In the syntax section we saw that in English, main verbs do not raise to I. Now we note that the verb *be* does raise to I if no modal is present (see section 4.2 in chapter 5).

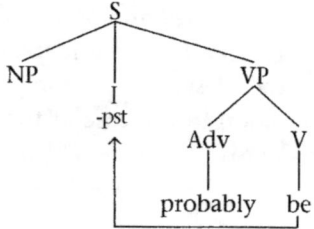

Figure 11.8 Raising of *be* to I

19)
    a. No modal is present: the auxiliary verb moves from inside the VP to I.
       He is [$_{VP}$ probably *t* eating].

b. A modal is present: the auxiliary verb does not raise.
He should [$_{VP}$ probably be eating].

c. Regular verbs do not raise.
He [$_{VP}$ probably likes eating] vs. *He likes [$_{VP}$ probably *t* eating].

Children acquire *be* as a main verb before they acquire *be* as an auxiliary verb. So, children start by producing sentences that are simpler in that they have only a copula verb (e.g., *He is hungry*) before they produce sentences that include an auxiliary plus a main verb (e.g., *He was working*) as shown in the following trees:

Figure 11.9 Copula versus auxiliary *be*

The structure in *b* has an extra level of complexity in that it has a complex verb phrase (one VP within another). Adults, on the other hand, appear to be able to use both the simple copula and auxiliary verbs quite early on. Whether this difference is because of the adult's greater ability to handle complexity in general cognitive terms or because children's linguistic systems are maturing remains a controversial and unresolved issue.

In addition, note that children acquire the three -*s* morphemes in the order plural, possessive, third person in their first language. Phonetically, these morphemes have the same realization, so we can't say that the order reflects phonological complexity. The order might be explained by noting that plural is a word-level phenomenon (e.g., *dogs*), possessive is a phrase-level phenomenon (e.g., [*the king of England*]'s *horse*, not *[*the king*]'s *of England horse*), and third person marking involves a relation between the verb and a phrase (the subject) elsewhere in the sentence (e.g., [*That man*] *usually thinks too much*). Like the pattern noted for the development of copula and auxiliary *be*, children seem to be acquiring structures in order of complexity, as shown in the following trees:

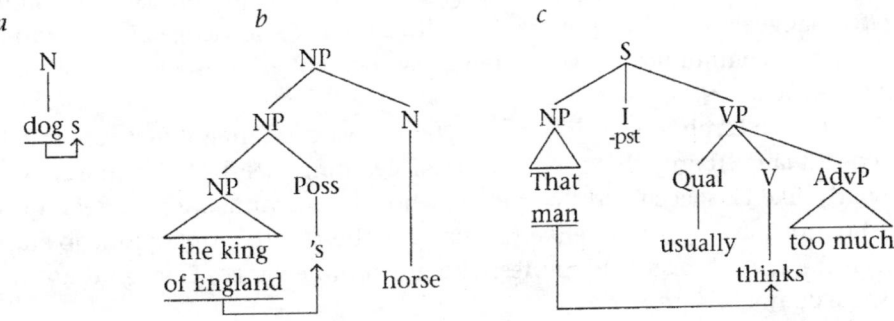

Figure 11.10 Three types of /s/ affix

In contrast, adults acquire the plural quite early, but then seem to get both the possessive and the third person marking quite late—perhaps for reasons involving processing. (When concentrating on getting the words right, we do not always have the processing capacity to produce well-formed higher-level structures.) Interestingly, the adults do not seem to find interphrasal morphology (like *c* above) more difficult than phrasal morphology (like *b* above). This may be because the adults have already acquired the grammar for their first language and that grammar most likely has both phrase-level and interphrasal morphological phenomena. In contrast, children have to set up hierarchical structure of a grammar for the first time, and could conceivably be building the structure from the bottom up (words → phrases → sentences).

In summary, we note that the order of acquisition data are intriguing in both first and second language acquisition, even though we await a conclusive explanation of the facts.

3   Factors affecting SLA

So far, we've looked at some of the characteristics of an IL grammar. Now let's turn to a variety of factors that can influence second language acquisition. It is clear that there is much more variation in the grammars of people learning second languages than in the grammars of people learning first languages.   This brings us to the question of what factors might help to account for that variation.

3.1   Age

One of the obvious ways that language learners vary is in their age. People start learning second languages at different points in their lives. Could the age of onset of L2 learning cause different levels of final proficiency?

This is a question usually considered under what is known as the *critical period hypothesis* (see chapter 10, section 6.5). We know that biologically based critical periods exist in other species. For example, some birds can learn the song of their species only if exposed to it during a particular window of opportunity. If they only hear the song too early or too late, then learning will not take place. (See chapter 16 for further discussion.)

Is second language learning like this? Is there an optimal time (or critical period) to acquire a second language? The answer appears to be 'yes and no'. Proficiency in a language is a remarkably complex thing (see the discussion of communicative competence in section 1.4). Usually, discussion of a possible critical period focuses on the area of phonological competence. While people who begin SLA as adults tend to retain non-nativelike phonology in the target language, it is much more difficult to predict knowledge or ability in any of the other areas of communicative competence (syntax, cohesion, sociolinguistics, etc.) based upon age of acquisition.

In fact, even L2 phonology is not so straightforward as it might first appear to be. We can predict with fair certainty that people who start learning their L2 before the age of seven will have nativelike L2 speech and that people who start learning after fourteen or fifteen will probably not have non-nativelike speech. But the results of people who start learning between the ages of seven and fourteen are much more varied. Some end up with accents, and some do not.

There is no current evidence of anything biological that prevents adults from acquiring proficiency in a second language. Factors that have been considered in the past (like brain lateralization; see chapter 13) are now thought to be of little predictive value in determining L2 ability. The question of 'ultimate attainment' in L2 acquisition is still hotly debated, and the literature has cited cases of adult L2 learners who apparently perform virtually identically to native speakers in a variety of domains (including phonology).

Currently, the critical period debate in SLA research is usually couched in terms of the question, "Do adults have access to Universal Grammar?" Rather than looking for changes in the brain that coincide with aging, researchers now look to see whether IL grammars are governed by the same constraints as primary languages (e.g., Swahili, Yoruba). If adults are engaged in the same kind of development process as children, then we would expect their IL grammars to be describable in terms of the same principles and parameters of UG that we use to describe primary languages. Conversely, if adults are acquiring their second languages using qualitatively different learning mechanisms than are used to acquire an L1 (e.g., if they use general problem-solving abilities), then we might expect them to adopt hypotheses that are not sanctioned by Universal Grammar. Something like this may in fact happen in the acquisition of gender in French. Children learning French as a first language seem to have very little trouble learning gender as they learn the words themselves (e.g., *le livre*, 'the book' is masculine; *la table*, 'the table' is feminine) and so on. On the other hand, adults whose first language does not have gender often have great difficulty learning French gender. They seem to set up complex (but incorrect) rules for predicting the gender of a given noun. For example, they may assume that words naming colours (or some other semantic category) are of one gender, or that words that end with a certain sound sequence are of another. Rules like this sometimes allow non-native speakers to guess the gender correctly, but they still perform significantly differently from native speakers. This is an example of how adults' greater capacity to formulate general rules can sometimes lead them down the wrong path.

3.2   Individual differences

Learners vary in ways other than age. Broadly speaking, the researcher asks the question, "If learners have a particular quality x, does this make them better at second language acquisition?" For example, we might look at the effect of inhibition, left-handedness, or some other individual trait on L2 ability. As intuitively appealing as this avenue is, it is one that must be taken carefully. In particular, there are three points on which we must be explicit:

1. how we define and measure x;
2. what it means to be *better*;
3. what aspect of communicative competence we are referring to.

Consider in this regard a trait like empathy. It has been argued that people who are empathetic are better language learners. This is an intuitively appealing notion. People who are empathetic can imagine what it feels like to be in someone else's shoes and they can look at things from another perspective. And second language learning certainly involves looking at things from a different perspective. But in SLA research, we need to find a more precise way to evaluate this hypothesis.

There are tests that claim to measure a person's empathy, but is this notion really a well-defined construct? Is one simply empathetic or not, or are there degrees of empathy? If there are degrees, do we see a correlation between degree of empathy and degree of success? And what does it mean for empathetic learners to be better language learners than people who aren't empathetic? Do they make fewer errors? Less serious errors? Should we expect people with greater empathy to be better at everything in the L2? Or maybe just at phonology and sociolinguistic competence? On what basis could we make a prediction? These are not simple issues. We raise them not to argue that research in individual variation is misguided, but to show some of the complex areas that need to be addressed before we can hope to establish a causal connection between a particular personality trait and success at second language learning.

We can distinguish between two kinds of factors in terms of which individuals can vary: affective factors and cognitive factors. First we will look at the role of affect.

Affective factors

Affective factors have to do with the emotional side of learning a second language. Clearly there can be a great deal at stake emotionally when learning a second language, and it is possible that emotions affect how successful a second language learner is. Affective factors that have been studied include empathy, anxiety, inhibition, and risk-taking. In this section we will look at one such factor: motivation.

Learners can vary with respect to the amount or type of motivation they have to learn a second language. If someone is highly motivated to learn, will that person do better at learning? In order to answer this question, we need to say a bit more about what it means to be motivated.

Traditionally, two types of motivation have been proposed: **instrumental** and **integrative**. Instrumental motivation involves wanting to learn the L2 for a specific goal or reason. For example, someone might need to pass a language requirement in order to get a graduate degree, or a job with a government agency. Integrative motivation, on the other hand, involves wanting to learn the L2 in order to learn more about a particular culture or fit into it better. For instance, someone might want to learn Japanese in order to learn more about a fascinating culture.

Studies have shown that the degree of integrative motivation correlates with the degree of success in language learning. That is to say, subjects who score highly on tests of integrative motivation do better on certain language tests than comparable subjects who score poorly on the same tests. However, subjects with instrumental rather than integrative motivation can also do well if their level of motivation is high. One study found that subjects who were offered a cash reward if they obtained a certain score on a language test performed much the same as subjects with high integrative motivation. All this seems to suggest that degree of motivation is a better predictor of future learning success than is type of motivation.

Cognitive factors

While affective factors have something to do with the emotional side of learning, cognitive factors involve the mechanics of how an individual learns something. Different people seem to learn via different cognitive styles and different learning strategies. We will first address cognitive style.

As individuals, we tend to tackle mental tasks using a particular 'cognitive style'. In contrast with an affective factor like motivation, which may vary from domain to domain (e.g., someone might be more motivated to learn French cooking than to learn the French language), cognitive style is a stable trait across domains.

The study of cognitive style often focuses on a contrast between field dependence and field independence. Learners who are **field independent** are not distracted by irrelevant background information when trying to learn something. These are people who can see the trees without being distracted by the forest. On the other hand, learners who are **field dependent** tend to see the forest but may miss the characteristics of individual trees. Of course, this is not to say that, overall, one trait is good and the other is bad. Field-dependent learners probably are able to synthesize the overall picture better than field-independent learners, but field-independent learners are probably better able to pick out relevant facts.

In terms of second language acquisition, it seems that field independent learners do better on language tests that focus on analytic tasks such as providing the correct grammatical form in a given sentence:

20)
Yesterday, we ___ the kids to the zoo. (take)

In contrast, field-dependent learners tend to do better on tasks that involve synthesizing their knowledge. For example, they may demonstrate broader communicative competence in that they are more concerned with getting the message across than with the grammatical accuracy of the sentences they use to form their message.

Ultimately, the proficient L2 learner needs to be concerned with both **accuracy** and **fluency**. Broadly speaking, accuracy has to do with whether the learner has the correct representation of a particular linguistic structure (i.e., it involves *knowledge*). Fluency, on the other hand, has to do with the rapid retrieval or processing of those representations (i.e., it involves *skills*). Someone who is not fluent may well have accurate representations, but take considerable time and energy to retrieve them. Different learners, though, are probably going to have a natural affinity to emphasize either accuracy or fluency, depending perhaps on their individual cognitive style.

While cognitive styles appear to be relatively stable traits in an individual, there are elements of learning that we have some control over. Each of us has certain **learning strategies** that we can employ to try to fill gaps in our linguistic knowledge. These strategies can be contrasted with **communication strategies**, which are designed to keep communication happening in spite of gaps in knowledge—as when someone uses paraphrase to describe an object for which he or she has no vocabulary item (e.g., *Could you pass me the thing you use for hitting nails?*). In contrast, a learning strategy is used to discover something new about the L2.

Many different learning strategies have been proposed. For example, using the strategy of directed attention, learners may decide in advance to focus on particular aspects of a task and to ignore others. So, when reading a text or listening to a lecture, they might decide to focus only on the main points. Another strategy involves repetition: to retain a lexical item or to improve the pronunciation of a sequence of sounds, the learner may repeat a word or phrase over and over. A third strategy makes use of clarification requests (to the teacher, a peer, or the others in a conversation) about something that is not understood (e.g., How come *stood* doesn't rhyme with *food*? What's a *liege*?). Under this view, learners have a variety of strategies at their disposal and have to discover which ones work best for them.

3.3   The good language learner

The question of individual variation in second language learning has received quite a bit of attention under the heading 'the good language learner'.

What makes a good language learner? One researcher has presented the following list of characteristics. (For the most part, this list is concerned with the learning strategies that people invoke in an attempt to acquire L2 knowledge and ability.)

Table 11.10 Characteristics of the 'good language learner'

1. Has an effective personal learning style or positive learning strategies.
2. Has an active approach to the learning task.
3. Has a tolerant and outgoing approach to the target language and empathy with its speakers.
4. Has technical know-how about how to tackle a language.
5. Has strategies of experimentation and planning with the object of developing the new language into an ordered system and revising this system progressively.
6. Is consistently searching for meaning.
7. Is willing to practise.
8. Is willing to use the language in real communication.
9. Has self-monitoring ability and critical sensitivity to language use.
10. Is able to develop the target language more and more as a separate reference system and is able to learn to think in it.

By focusing on such characteristics, the learning strategy approach seeks to account for differences in L2 proficiency by referring to the way in which individuals try to acquire new knowledge. Some people have gone so far as to suggest that this type of research will make it possible to teach not-so-good language learners the learning strategies necessary to be good language learners.

This brings us to the interesting question of second language learning in classrooms and the effect that instruction has on L2 learning. Is it really possible to teach someone a second language? Or can you just create an environment in which second language learning can take place? We turn now to the research that has looked specifically at L2 classrooms.

4   The L2 classroom

It has been flippantly said that people have been successfully acquiring second languages for thousands of years, but when teachers get involved, the success rate plummets. This comment is probably more a reflection of people's unfortunate experience in certain types of language classrooms (that may have been dull or even physically threatening, depending on the century) than it is a statement about general pedagogic utility. However, the fact remains that language classrooms can be sheltered environments where students can benefit from being given the opportunity to learn and practise without being subject to the penalties for failure that can be imposed outside the classroom.

We should acknowledge at this point that there is really no such thing as *the* second language classroom. In reality, all classrooms are different because they have different people in them (both students and teachers). Nevertheless, there are certain statements that can be made. There are three relevant characteristics of a second language classroom that we wish to explore:

1. modified input;
2. modified interaction;
3. focus on form.

4.1 Modified input

In chapter 10 it was noted that adults do not talk to children in the same way that they talk to other adults. Just as the input directed to children has certain simplifying characteristics, so speech directed at non-native speakers tends to be simplified compared to the speech directed at native speakers. In all communicative situations—whether dealing with a child or an adult, a non-native speaker or a native speaker—we seem to make a rapid assessment of the level of proficiency or background knowledge of the listener, and adjust the input accordingly.

The input aimed at non-native speakers is referred to as **foreigner talk**. The subset of this speech that takes place in classrooms is known as **teacher talk**. Teacher talk (or teacher language) tends not to be as evenly matched to the proficiency of the listener as foreigner talk is, for the simple reason that teachers are usually addressing a class rather than an individual. As a result, some learners may find the modified speech too hard or too easy.

The pedagogic goal of teacher talk is crystal clear: make sure the students know what is being talked about by providing **comprehensible input**. Perhaps surprisingly, this idea has generated an extraordinary amount of conflict in the field of SLA research. Although it seems to be useful to provide learners with comprehensible input, teachers must guard against simplifying too much, which might give the appearance of patronizing the learners or talking to them as if they were stupid rather than on the way to becoming bilingual.

4.2 Modified interaction

Second language classrooms also differ from the outside world in terms of the kind of interactions that go on there. However, the difference appears to be mainly one of degree, not quality. Inside a classroom, the teacher may engage in the following kinds of strategies:

- more comprehension checks, e.g., *Do you understand?; OK?*

- more prompting, e.g., *Who knows where Moose Jaw is?*

- more expansions, e.g., *Student*: Me red sweater.

    Teacher: Yes, you're wearing a red sweater, aren't you?

This modified interaction appears to be one of the characteristics that differentiates classrooms from other communicative settings. While all these devices (e.g., comprehension checks) occur in non-classroom discourse as well, they appear to occur more frequently in second language classrooms. Assuming that the teacher realizes that the purpose of the classroom is to prepare the student to understand input and interaction outside of the classroom as well, modified interaction is beneficial.

4.3   Focus on form

The final characteristic of the second language classroom to be discussed here involves focus on form. The term *focus on form* encompasses two distinct practices that tend to occur in most L2 classrooms: instruction about the language and explicit correction.

Most second language classes present the students with some sort of information about the language—noting, for example, that 'English has voiced and voiceless interdental fricatives' or that 'French has nasal vowels'. Instruction of this type is designed to improve the form (or accuracy) of the student's L2. In all likelihood, other activities that happen in the class will focus on giving the student a chance to improve fluency or particular sociolinguistic skills.

Error correction is also designed to improve the form of the student's L2. Regardless of the methodology used in most classes today there is some focus on form and some error correction. The interesting research question is whether either of these practices can be shown to have a positive effect on the learner. Do students who get corrected do better than students who don't?

The question may not be as straightforward as it appears. Remember that it has frequently been argued in first language acquisition research that attempts at error correction are relatively infrequent and don't really affect children's grammars. Could it be different for adult second language learners? The learning environment is different in that adult learners (unlike children) are usually exposed to a fair amount of error correction. But does that make a difference? Not surprisingly, this question is difficult to answer. Some studies have argued that second language learners who receive correction develop at about the same pace as those who do not. Other studies have shown certain increases in accuracy as the result of correction.

These results may not be as contradictory as they seem, though. The areas where correction seems to be most useful involve lexical items. When someone tries to learn the properties of a certain lexical item, they benefit from feedback. However, feedback concerning certain structural phenomena may not be as effective. For example, the previously mentioned study of French speakers learning about the lack of verb movement in English (see section 2.2) found that while there were short-term improvements in the subjects who were explicitly taught the relevant facts, there were no significant long-term effects. When the subjects were tested a year later, they were found to have reverted to their pre-instructional performance.

This doesn't necessarily mean either that students should not be corrected or that there should be no focus on form in the second language classroom. If a balance is struck between classroom activities that focus on form and those that focus on meaningful communication, then there is certainly no evidence that feedback causes any problems. Indeed, to the contrary, there is evidence that students in classes that focus primarily on communication but also include some instruction on form are significantly more accurate than students who are exposed only to instruction that focuses on communication.

Most of the studies to date have considered focus on form within a pedagogical framework (i.e., how does it affect the learner or the classroom) but there are more recent studies that are couched within a cognitive framework. Under this approach, the following questions could be asked:

1. ***The noticing issue***: Do learners have the cognitive resources to notice the gap between their IL utterances and the TL utterances around them?

   This is a very complex question that involves the details of how memory (working, short-term, and long-term) works. Learners would have to have the coordinated working and long-term memory resources to enable the cognitive comparison of the IL and TL sentences. This sort of comparison eventually leads to knowledge restructuring. Studies suggest that learners do have the cognitive resources to engage in this type of comparison especially if they are comparing TL utterances that have occurred recently in the discourse.

2. ***The interruption issue***: Is pedagogical intervention that does not interrupt the learner's own processing for language learning even possible?

   Focus on form should be carried out in response to the learners needs. If (a) the primary focus of the lesson is on meaning, (b) the focus-on-form targets arise incidentally, and (c) the learner shifts attention briefly, then the focus-on-form activity will be relatively unobtrusive. Indeed rather than being an unwanted interruption, focus-on-form may allow the learner to pay selective attention to a structure for a short period of time which would be beneficial.

3. ***The timing issue***: If so, then precisely 'when', in cognitive terms, should the pedagogical intervention occur?

   Learners appear to benefit from being prepared in advance for some focus-on-form activities. If they know what is coming, it helps them to notice the relevant features in the input. One of the most promising types of intervention is an immediate recast. A corrective recasting involves the repetition of an error plus a recast, as shown below:
   Student: I think that the worm will go under the soil.
   Teacher: I <u>think</u> that the worm <u>will</u> go under the soil?…I <u>thought</u> that the worm <u>would</u> go under the soil.

In sum, adult students usually expect error correction, and teachers are accustomed to providing it. Assuming that the class is not devoted entirely to instruction that focuses on form (with no opportunity for meaningful practice), error correction doesn't seem to cause any harm. In a class with activities that focus on both form and fluency, the students tend to emerge with greater accuracy. Certain types of classroom activities seem to be able to engage the cognitive abilities of adult second language learners and allow them to continue to advance their L2 proficiency.

4.4   Bilingual education

We will conclude this chapter with a discussion of two types of bilingual education program: minority language maintenance programs and French **immersion** programs. Both are designed to produce bilingual children, but there are important differences. French immersion programs involve children from a majority language (English) being immersed in a minority language (French). As English-speaking children in Canada, they are in no danger of losing their first language since it is so dominant in the culture. Their situation is clearly different from that of children who speak a minority language (e.g., Greek or Italian) and who are submersed in the majority language (English). Not only are these children in some danger of losing their first language, the sink-or-swim approach can have strongly negative consequences on their future in school. For these reasons, it should be emphasized that even if we argue for the benefits of immersing English-speaking children in French classrooms, it does not follow that we should submerse speakers of other languages in English classrooms.

Let us look in more detail at some of the issues surrounding bilingual education. We begin with minority language maintenance programs.

Minority language maintenance programs

Minority language maintenance programs, which are also known as 'heritage language programs' or 'L1 maintenance programs', have been introduced around the world to try to address the fact that minority language children often have difficulty in majority-language schools. Even with separate classes of instruction, they tend to have more than their share of problems later in school (including a higher-than-expected drop-out rate). One reason for this becomes evident when one thinks of the challenge these children face. Up until the age of five, they are exposed to a language at home (say, Greek). Then at age five, they are put into an English-speaking school in a class of primarily native English speakers. Typically, they do not understand everything that the teacher is saying, and they do not have the opportunity to develop the basic cognitive skills necessary for functioning in school. These children may thus suffer a setback from which they will never recover.

This poor beginning can lead to minority language students being placed in classes not designed for students intending to pursue post-secondary education, which in turn can lead to an exit from the educational system. To try to change this recurring pattern, a number of bilingual education programs have been set up in places like Canada, Finland, England, and the United States. In all of these programs the children of minority language background receive their initial instruction in the minority language. Over the years of their elementary education, instruction in the majority language is gradually introduced so that by grades three to six, the children receive about half of their instruction in the majority language as well.

The question raised in evaluating these programs (and indeed the question that led policymakers to adopt the competing sink-or-swim approach to minority language education) is "What is the effect on the children's English?" Obviously, knowledge of English in places like Canada and the United States is essential. But is submersion in English the only way to acquire proficiency in English? It would seem that the answer is no, since children can become bilingual with relative ease. In virtually all of the bilingual education programs studied, the subjects ended up performing as well as their monolingual L1 and L2 peers by the end of grade six. So, for example, a child who received all instruction in Cree for the first couple of years of schooling and was getting 50 percent English and 50 percent Cree instruction by the end of grade six would be performing in Cree like a monolingual Cree speaker and in English just like a monolingual English speaker.

Thus, receiving instruction in the L1 does not have negative consequences on the L2. On the contrary, it seems to have significant positive effects on success in school, on linguistic proficiency, and even on the family situation of the students. The students can understand the teacher (which helps them at school), and they can understand their parents and grand-parents (which helps them at home).

French immersion programs

French immersion programs in Canada involve immersing a majority language student in a minority language class. While any second language can be involved, we will refer to these as 'French immersion programs'. Table 11.11 shows recent enrolments throughout Canada.

Table 11.11 French immersion enrolments in Canada

PROVINCE/ TERRITORY	Dates	Total school population	Total second language	FRENCH IMMERSION	
				Enrolment	Schools offering immersion
Newfoundland	1977–78	156 168	67 791	95	3
	1996–97	106 212	61 576	4 615	47
	1997–98	102 594	60 506	4 533	46
Prince Edward Island	1977–78	27 628	16 495	541	7
	1996–97	24 537	14 517	3 431	27
	1997–98	24 390	14 514	3 423	27
Nova Scotia	1977–78	198 097	88 991	127	3
	1996–97	163 232	91 691	11 599	108
	1997–98	163 478	91 888	11 626	108
New Brunswick *students taking English as a second language*	1977–78	60 679	n.a.		
	1996–97	43 259	28 882		
	1997–98	42 187	28 418		
New Brunswick *students taking French as a second language*	1977–78	101 550	70 629	3 179	34
	1996–97	90 127	73 623	18 363	117
	1997–98	89 351	73 328	18 294	117
Quebec *students taking English as a second language*	1977–78	1 260 983	678 664		
	1996–97	940 563	600 678		
	1997–98	938 814	596 169		
Quebec *students taking French as a second language*	1977–78	207 230	17 754	17 754	n.a.
	1996–97	101 005	32 968	32 968	154
	1997–98	101 325	33 072	33 072	155

Table 11.11 (continued)			French immersion enrolments in Canada	**FRENCH IMMERSION**	
PROVINCE/ TERRITORY	Dates	Total school population	Total second language	Enrolment	Schools offering immersion
Ontario	1977–78	1 950 308	883 269	12 764	160
	1996–97	2 149 472	1 170 556	154 787	1 061
	1997–98	2 184 501	1 196 490	158 198	1 084
Manitoba	1977–78	221 408	85 619	1 667	13
	1996–97	195 032	94 910	18 674	102
	1997–98	196 523	95 757	18 848	103
Saskatchewan	1977–78	216 248	53 804	407	2
	1996–97	196 391	102 635	10 325	77
	1997–98	196 730	102 803	10 332	77
Alberta	1977–78	439 804	111 338	n.a.	n.a.
	1996–97	523 879	174 112	27 147	173
	1997–98	531 710	177 117	27 592	178
British Columbia	1977–78	527 769	161 110	1 301	15
	1996–97	607 905	283 646	29 729	234
	1997–98	618 945	288 582	30 193	238
Yukon	1977–78	5 394	2 285	n.a.	n.a.
	1996–97	6 372	4 167	429	3
	1997–98	6 423	4 182	432	3
Northwest Territories	1977–78	12 717	3 200	n.a.	n.a.
	1996–97	17 838	3 357	486	5
	1997–98	18 103	3 406	493	5
TOTAL	**1977–78**	**5 178 753**	**2 240 949**	**37 835**	**237**
	1996–97	**5 165 823**	**2 708 137**	**312 553**	**2 110**
	1997–98	**5 215 074**	**2 737 814**	**317 036**	**2 141**

Clearly, French immersion programs have maintained their popularity in Canada. French immersion differs from traditional French instruction (also known as Core French) and from submersion programs. It is different from a Core French course in that French is the medium of communication, not the subject of the course. It is teaching *in* French, not teaching *of* French. In a Core French course, French is just another subject (say 40 minutes a day). In French immersion, all of the instruction is in French, even when the content is geography or music.

French immersion is different from submersion programs in that no student in the class is a native speaker of the medium of instruction. Native speakers of French do not enrol in French immersion classes, so all the students are starting from approximately the same place.

Contrast this with a native Cree speaker who is thrown into an English-only class with a large number of native speakers of English.

Probably the two biggest questions that get asked about immersion programs are (1) What effect does such a program have on the students' English? and (2) How good is their French? The answer to the first question is remarkably similar to the answer provided by the heritage language programs. Children can become bilingual, and instruction in one language does not necessarily mean a diminished capacity for the other language. Often, though, children in French immersion programs exhibit a delay in productive skills (talking and writing) in English in the early years. However, by grade six, on average they are outperforming their monolingual English peers. Boldly stated, children in French immersion learn English.

So how good is their French? Concerns are often expressed that the children who come out of French immersion programs end up speaking a kind of mixed language (that has been called *Frenglish*, or *Franglais*). It is true that immersion students tend to make mistakes in things like French gender, the *tu/vous* distinction (where *vous* is used as an honorific second person singular pronoun), and polite conditionals such as *Je voudrais un crayon* 'I would like a pencil' versus the somewhat less polite simple present form *Je veux un crayon* 'I want a pencil'. Overall however, their receptive skills (reading and listening) end up virtually nativelike and their productive skills, while not nativelike, are at an advanced level.

In sum, the positive features of French immersion programs can be stated as follows. Children who emerge from French immersion suffer no negative effects on their English, do well in school, outperform their monolingual counterparts in a number of ways, and know a heck of a lot of French.

Summing up

This chapter has dealt with a number of issues in the field of second language acquisition. We investigated the notion of an **interlanguage grammar** and the influence of both the source and target languages on this grammar in terms of **transfer** and **developmental errors**. Proficiency in a second language requires both knowledge and ability, something captured in a model of **communicative competence**. Someone must acquire knowledge in all linguistic domains (phonetics, phonology, morphology, syntax, and semantics) as well as the ability to use that knowledge in a variety of social contexts.

What is easy or difficult to acquire in a second language has been investigated from a variety of perspectives. We focused on **Universal Grammar** (the **Subset Principle**) and **typological universals** (the **Markedness Differential Hypothesis**). However, it is not just universals that influence second language learning; the specific characteristics of an individual can also affect the process. Affective factors and cognitive factors both influence second language learning. So too do factors such as modified input, modified interaction, focus on form and bilingual education.

The field of second language acquisition is remarkably diverse, in part because of what is involved in L2 learning. Someone who is attempting to learn an additional language must develop new mental representations, and develop facility at accessing those representations in a variety of circumstances. The field of SLA research must therefore draw on philosophy (theories of mind), psychology (theories of learning, theories of performance), linguistics (theories of linguistic structure), and pedagogy (theories of instruction). This is probably the main reason why we have not established anything like a comprehensive theory of how second languages are learned. But bit by bit, piece by piece, we're starting to put together some pieces of the puzzle.

Notes

[1] The asterisk indicates that this sound is not allowed in initial position (except in a few words that have been borrowed from French—e.g., *genre, gendarmes,* and so forth).

[2] Note that English phonology in general respects the implicational universal given in *7),* as can be seen in pairs such as *sip/zip.* The lack of contrast of [ʃ]/[ʒ] in initial position is an accidental gap. Even with this gap, however, it seems that English speakers respect the universal when learning the phonology of a second language. The voicing contrast is easier to acquire in the universally unmarked position.

[3] This might happen in a native Arabic word if two morphemes are put together and, as a result, two consonants occur adjacent to each other.

[4] As we will see, linguists infer the initial setting of a parameter on the basis of the kind of input or evidence available to the language learner. It is a separate question to determine whether children's early grammars actually have the [+] or [-] setting of the Null Subject parameter. For example, children's early sentences in English often lack overt subjects, which might lead us to believe that the grammars have the [+] setting. However, the early sentences of English-speaking children do not contain the other structures associated with the [+null subject] parameter setting: *that*-trace patterns and VS order in declaratives. Given the complexity of this issue, we will assume the relationship shown in figure 11.7 when discussing second language learners.

Sources

The Ontogeny Model was proposed by R. Major in "A Model for Interlanguage Phonology" in *Interlanguage Phonology,* edited by G. Ioup and S. Weinberger (New York: Newbury House/Harper & Row), pp. 101–24. The model of communicative competence is an adaptation of L. Bachman's, *Fundamental Considerations in Language Testing* (Oxford: Oxford University Press, 1990). The Markedness Differential Hypothesis was developed by F. Eckman in "Markedness and the Contrastive Analysis Hypothesis" in *Language Learning* 27:315–30 (1977). The discussion of the Similarity Differential Rate Hypothesis comes from R. Major, "Further Evidence for the Similarity Differential Rate Hypothesis" in J. Leather and A. James, eds., *New Sounds 97* (Klagenfurt, Austria: University of Klagenfurt).

The data from Arabic syllabification come from E. Broselow, "Prosodic Phonology and the Acquisition of a Second Language" in S. Flynn and W. O'Neil, eds., *Linguistic Theory in Second Language Acquisition* (Dordrecht: Kluwer, 1988). The stress data were reported in J. Archibald, *Language Learnability and L2 Phonology* (Dordrecht: Kluwer, 1993). The Null Subject analysis is drawn from L. White, *Universal Grammar and Second Language Acquisition* (Amsterdam: John Benjamins, 1989). The Verb Movement study can be found in L. White, "Adverb Placement in Second Language Acquisition: Some Effects of Positive and Negative Evidence in the Classroom" in *Second Language Research* 7:133–61 (1991).

The L2 morphology data can be found in H. Zobl and J. Liceras, "Functional Categories and Acquisition Order" in *Language Learning* 44(1): 159–80 (1994). The French gender information is discussed in S. Carroll, "Second-Language Acquisition and the Computational Paradigm" in *Language Learning* 39(4): 535–94 (1989). The instrumental/integrative distinction comes from R. Gardner, J.B. Day, and P.D. MacIntyre, "Integrative Motivation, Induced Anxiety and Language Learning in a Controlled Environment" in *Studies in Second Language Acquisition* 14(2): 197–214 (1992).

The good language learner profile of table 11.10 can be found in H.H. Stern, "What Can We Learn from the Good Language Learner?" in *The Canadian Modern Language Review* 34:304–18 (1975), but see also J. Rubin, "What the 'Good Language Learner' Can Teach Us" in *TESOL Quarterly* 9(1): 41–51 (1975), and R. Ellis, *Understanding Second Language Acquisition* (Oxford: Oxford University Press, 1986). The L2 classroom discussion owes much to R. Allwright and K. Bailey, *Focus on the Language Classroom: An Introduction to Classroom Research for Language Teachers* (Cambridge: Cambridge University Press, 1991). The evidence from focus on form was presented by P. Lightbown and N. Spada, "Focus-on-Form and Corrective Feedback in Communicative Language Teaching: Effects on Second Language Learning," in *Studies in Second Language Acquisition* 12(4): 429–48 (1990). The discussion of focus-on-form draws on C. Doughty, "Cognitive Underpinnings of Focus on Form," in *Cognition and Second Language Instruction*, Cambridge Applied Linguistics Series (Cambridge: Cambridge University Press, forthcoming). Bilingual education and French immersion programs are discussed in J. Cummins and M. Swain, *Bilingual Education* (New York: Longman, 1986). Figure 11.4 and the data on enrolments in programs come from the Canadian Parents for French.

Recommended reading

Archibald, J., ed. 1999. *Second Language Acquisition and Linguistic Theory*. Oxford: Blackwell.

Cummins, J., and M. Swain. 1986. *Bilingual Education*. London: Longman.

Flynn, S., G. Martohardjono, and W. O'Neil, eds. 1998. *The Generative Study of Second Language Acquisition*. Mahweh, NJ: Lawrence Erlbaum.

Leather, J., and A. James. 1997. *New Sounds 97*. Klagenfurt, Austria: University of Klagenfurt.

Long, M., and D. Larsen-Freeman. 1991. *Second Language Acquisition Research*. London: Longman.

Sharwood Smith, M. 1994. *Second Language Learning: Theoretical Foundations*. London: Longman.

White, L. 1989. *Universal Grammar and Second Language Acquisition*. Philadelphia: John Benjamins.

Appendix: L2 pedagogy

It has probably become clear that this chapter (and the field of second language acquisition research) is not directly concerned with second language *teaching*. Anyone interested in a catalogue of approaches to language teaching could consult *Approaches and Methods in Language Teaching* by J.C. Richards and T.S. Rodgers (Cambridge: Cambridge University Press, 1986).

Historically, there have been a number of specific methods proposed as the best way to teach a language. There have been methods that emphasize physical activity (Total Physical

Response), and methods that emphasize relaxed learning (Suggestopedia). Some methods encourage translation (Grammar-Translation) while others discourage it (Direct Method). There are approaches that encourage repetitive drilling (Audiolingualism) and others that discourage it (Communicative Language Teaching).

Recent trends in second language pedagogy have tended to downplay the idea that a single method of instruction will work for all people. As second language acquisition research identified the large number of ways in which second language learners can vary, it became evident that not everybody learns in the same way. Therefore, not everybody can be taught in the same way.

Currently, teachers tend to adopt an eclectic approach to second language instruction. What this means is that a variety of methods and approaches are utilized. A class may include some time for drilling and some time for physical activity (just to name two possibilities). The metaphor of multiple bridges may help to explain the rationale of this eclectic approach. If teachers want to get as many students as possible to a particular destination (call it proficiency) then they have a better chance if there are multiple bridges (i.e., techniques) than if there is only one bridge (i.e., a single methodology).

The activities that make up a class will be determined by the needs and preferences of the learners, as well as by the experience and preferences of the teacher. Together they attempt to negotiate a program of instruction that is best-suited for all concerned.

Questions

1. Some dialects of Arabic break up clusters by inserting an epenthetic vowel to the *left* of an unsyllabified consonant (unlike the dialect discussed in this chapter). How would a speaker of this dialect pronounce the words *plant*, *transport*, and *translate*? Draw the necessary syllable structures.

2. The following is a sample of non-native writing. The assignment was to write about whether you prefer to live in the city or the country. Look through the sample and 'correct' the errors. Do you have any idea what the student's first language might be? Compare your corrected copy with that of someone else in the class and see if you agree on the corrections.

> *Are you among the number of people who have to choose their place to live? Whenever they have to move from another country, they even change the profession, they want to have a house outside the big city, or they can't find a place in Downtown.*
>
> *Its possible to move as well as you are supported by some essential condition of life I've mention in the following lines.*
>
> *Most of people are living in the Big city to have many of the opportunities that offer the Downtown lifestyle, jobs, studies, activities or whatever but nowadays for instance in TO [Toronto] its really difficult to find a place to live because the percentage of vacancy is slightly under 0% so many people are constrained to move on the suburb, by this way some of these get along this phenomene because they want to avoid the noise, the smog of the city and even they try to find their own place to live with garden and everything, actually to invest money to owe their house which is better than to rent an apartment in downtown, therefore they have to consider the transportation problem to reach the city even to have a car or use the public transportation.*

to have your own house outside the city required a great initial capital that you have to draft from any bank or you dispose in your account but afterwhat the house become your possession with the years and couple of more will increase the house value, although it is expensive furthermore it should be a great benefit for the owner even though he decided to rent the unoccupied room into the house.

Moreless the frienship beetween the person in the subrub is closer they are ore contact with each other and maybe can meet themselves doing yardwork or other kind of activities belong to the suburb lifestyle.

But in another (illegible) it should be difficult for the people who haven't ever lived in the suburb to move from th big city because they have to adapt their habits but they can fin amonst a great number of things that they use to have in the city. Otherwise during the last 15 years the business activites has developing around the city quickly in the North America also the supermarket company, manufacture and so on offered the job opportunity to the people outside the big aglomeration in that way it was created some apartments vacaint in the city.

For me I don't even care where I have to live but I will observe which part could be the less expensive as well as transportation to reach my job but I will be sure that I'd like to live outside the downtown.

3. Given what you know about implicational universals, do you think it would be easier for an English speaker to acquire French nasal vowels (e.g., *gant* [gã], 'glove') or for French speakers to acquire English oral vowels?

4. What explanation would you give for a native speaker of French who produced the English sentence *I drink frequently coffee*? How could you explain the fact that when the same speaker produces the sentence *He is frequently late*, it is grammatical? Do any other English verbs have the same properties as *be*?

5. Which of the following sentences would you classify as positive evidence and which as negative evidence for the learner:
   a) *Non-Native Speaker (NNS):* He study a lot.
      Native Speaker (NS): He *studies* a lot.
   b) *NS:* What kind of books do you like to read?
      NNS: Mysteries.
   c) *NNS:* I was born in Munich.
      NS: Pardon me?
   d) *NNS:* I goed to Montreal on the weekend.
      NS: Remember that *go* has an irregular past.

6. Discuss why second language learners, regardless of their first language, might produce forms such as *goed, sheeps,* and *coulds* given that they never hear these forms in input from native speakers of English. Give some other forms analogous to the above that might be generated.

7. What factors can you think of that might influence fossilization? In other words, do you think that some people are more likely to fossilize than others? Do you think it can be reversed? How?

8. Acquiring a second language involves both knowing something about the language, and

being able to do something with the language. Do you think that knowledge and skills are related? Can you see any trade-off between accuracy and fluency?

9. Why do you think that non-native speakers of English would be more at risk of leaving the education system than native speakers?

10. Respond to the following statement:

> *It's the school system's job to make sure that non-native speakers of English learn English. They need English in order to be able to suceed in this country. We want them to succeed. If we encourage them to speak their own language, then ghettoes will form and they'll never learn English. And if we want them to learn English, then obviously they need to be exposed to more English. What good is it knowing how to speak another language in North America? What they need is English, English and more English.*

Twelve

Gary Libben

Psycholinguistics: the study of language processing

Leaving one still with the intolerable wrestle
With words and meanings

T.S. ELIOT

We engage in language processing most every day of our lives. This processing takes place when we watch television, listen to the radio, read a passing billboard while driving, or discuss the weather. Usually these language activities are carried out with great ease and in a completely subconscious manner. We might sometimes be aware that we are searching for a word, composing a sentence or straining to understand someone else, but we are never aware of the actual mechanisms and operations involved in producing and understanding language.

Psycholinguistics is the study of these language processing mechanisms. Psycholinguists study how word meaning, sentence meaning, and discourse meaning are computed and represented in the mind. They study how complex words and sentences are composed in speech and how they are broken down into their constituents in the acts of listening and reading. In short, psycholinguists seek to understand how language is done.

This chapter introduces the field of psycholinguistics by first discussing some methods used by psycholinguists to probe language representation and processing in the mind. This is followed by a summary of recent research on language processing in the domains of phonetics, phonology, morphology, and syntax. Finally, we will discuss how these various aspects of linguistic processing work together to make the everyday acts of speaking, listening, and reading appear so simple and effortless.

1 Methods of psycholinguistic research

As was noted, language users are not able to introspect on the details of language processing. Simply paying attention to what you are doing will not provide reliable insights into how you access words or build sentences. Perhaps the reason for this is that, in normal use, language processing must occur very quickly. By shielding mental linguistic operations from the conscious mind, it is possible that the language processing system is maximizing its ability to operate with speed and efficiency.

In order to get a sense for just how subconscious language processing is, you might try the following exercise: Give a friend a page of text to read silently and sit opposite him or her. Carefully observe your friend's eyes as they move across the text. You will notice that the eyes do not move smoothly form left to right but rather proceed in a series of jerks called **saccades**. Like most of us, your friend probably has the subjective impression that his or her eyes are moving very evenly across the page. But that subjective impression is incorrect. It seems that we are simply not constructed to be able to monitor many of our automatic activities, including language processing.

A substantial additional challenge for the psycholinguistic researcher is presented by the fact that most of language processing does not involve observable physical events such as eye movement, but rather involves mental events that cannot be observed directly. Research in this field therefore requires that mental language-processing events be inferred from observable behaviour. Consequently, a large part of psycholinguistic research is concerned with the development of new (and often very clever) techniques to uncover how language processing is accomplished. Some of these techniques are presented in the following sections.

1.1   Slips of the tongue

Some of the earliest and most influential studies of language processing examined the spontaneous slips of the tongue produced during speech. Slips of the tongue are also known as **Spoonerisms** after Reverend William A. Spooner who was head of New College Oxford between 1903 and 1924. Reverend Spooner was famous for producing a great many, often humorous, speech errors. Some of his more well-known mistakes are presented below.

1)
What he intended: You have missed all my history lectures.
What he said: You have hissed all my mystery lectures.

2)
What he intended: Noble sons of toil
What he said: Noble tons of soil

3)
What he intended: You have wasted the whole term.
What he said: You have tasted the whole worm.

4)
What he intended: The dear old Queen
What he said: The queer old dean

Beginning in the 1960s Victoria Fromkin began to study these and other naturally occurring slips of the tongue and noted that they can be very revealing of the manner in which sentences are created in speech. For instance, as can be seen in the examples, the characteristic pattern in Reverend Spooner's errors is a tendency to exchange the initial consonants of words in the utterance. When these segment exchanges create new words (as opposed to non-words as in *fire and brimstone → bire and frimstone*), the result is often humorous. But here's the important psycholinguistic point: In order for these exchanges to occur, the entire sentence would have to be planned out before the person begins to say it. Otherwise, how would it be possible in example *1)* for the first segment of the sixth word *history* to be transported backwards so that it becomes the first segment of the third word (*missed* → *hissed*)?

Another important observation that Fromkin made was that speech errors also often involve 'mixing and matching' morphemes within words. Consider the following slips of the tongue from Fromkin (1993):

5)
Intended: rules of word formation
Produced: words of rule formation

6)
Intended: I'd forgotten about that.
Produced: I'd forgot aboutten that.

7)
Intended: easily enough
Produced: easy enoughly

All these errors involve morphemes being exchanged within a sentence. As is the case for sound exchange errors, these slips of the tongue provide evidence that a sentence must be planned out before speech begins. They also provide evidence that the morpheme, rather than the word is the fundamental building block of English sentence production. Note how in example *5)*, although the nouns *rule* and *word* are exchanged in the sentence, the inflectional suffix -*s* remains in its original position. In examples *6)* and *7)*, it is the suffixes that move while the stems remain in their original positions. These examples all suggest that morphological components of words can function independently during sentence planning (and of course also in sentence mis-planning).

As can be seen from these examples, slips of the tongue can offer a fascinating window to the mechanisms involved in language production and to the role that linguistic units such as phonemes and morphemes play in that production. But because slips of the tongue are naturally occurring events, the researcher has no control over when and where they will occur and must simply wait for them to happen. In this way, the analysis of slips of the tongue is a **field technique** and differs from the **experimental paradigms** discussed in the following sections. In these experimental paradigms, the researcher takes an active role in controlling the circumstances under which language is processed, the stimuli to which the experimental subjects are exposed, and in controlling the ways in which subjects may respond to these stimuli.

1.2   Experimental methods: words in the mind

One of the most intense areas of psycholinguistic research has been the investigation of how words are organized in the mind. We are all in possession of a vocabulary that forms the backbone of our ability to communicate in a language. In many ways, this vocabulary must be used as a normal dictionary is used. It is consulted to determine what words mean, how they are spelled, and what they sound like. But the dictionary in our minds, our mental lexicon, must also be substantially different from a desktop dictionary. It must be much more flexible, accommodating the new words that we learn with ease. It must be organized so that words can be looked up extremely quickly—word recognition takes less than one-third of a second and the average adult reads at a rate of about 250 words per minute. It must allow us to access entries in terms of a wide variety of characteristics. 'Tip-of-the-tongue' phenomena, in which we are temporarily unable to access a word, are particularly revealing of how flexible access to the mental lexicon can be—we have all experienced episodes in which we eventually retrieve words on the basis of their meaning, sound, spelling, first letter, or even what they rhyme with.

Many psycholinguists conceive of the mental lexicon as a collection of individual units as in figure 12.1. In this figure, the lexicon is shown as a space in which entries of different types are stored and linked together. The main questions that are asked about the mental lexicon are: (1) How are entries linked? (2) How are entries accessed? (3) What information is contained in an entry?

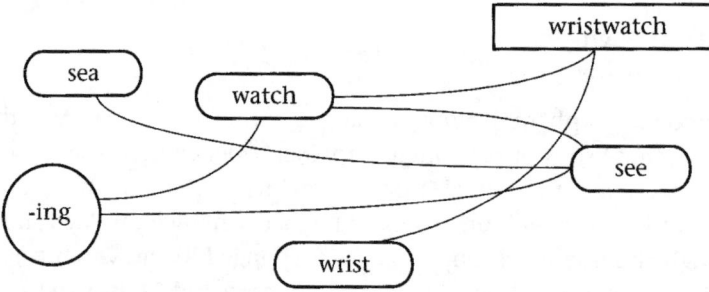

Figure 12.1 Units in the mental lexicon

Although these questions are simple and straightforward, there is no way to answer them directly because the human mental lexicon cannot be observed. So the psycholinguist must use special experimental methods to understand how words are organized, accessed and represented in the mind. We will briefly discuss the two most common of these methods—**lexical decision** and **priming**.

Lexical decision

In the lexical decision paradigm, the experimental subject (in this example, a native speaker of English) is seated in front of a computer screen. A word appears in the middle of the screen and the subject must judge as quickly as possible whether or not the word is a real English word by pressing a button labelled 'yes' or a button labelled 'no' (see figure 12.2).

This task is very easy for subjects to carry out. They typically see and judge hundreds of words in a single fifteen-minute lexical decision experiment. In most lexical decision experiments there are two **dependent variables**, that is, things that are being measured: the time that it takes for a subject to respond (**response latency**) and whether or not the subject's judgment is correct (**response accuracy**). A response is judged as correct if a subject responds 'yes' to a real word such as *glove* or *sadness* and 'no' to a non-word such as *blove* or *sadding*.

Figure 12.2   A lexical decision experiment

Lexical decision experiments usually involve comparing subjects' performance on one set of stimuli (e.g., nouns) to their performance on another set of stimuli (e.g., verbs). The key to the importance of the experimental paradigm is that, in order for a subject to respond 'no' to a stimulus such as *blove* or 'yes' to a real word such as *glove*, the subject's mental lexicon must be accessed. The lexical decision task can therefore be used to measure the speed and accuracy with which words in the mental lexicon are accessed. It has been found in many experiments, for example, that subjects take about half a second (500 milliseconds) to press the *yes* button for frequently used words such as *free*, but almost three-quarters of a second to press the *yes* button for less common words such as *fret*. This finding has been called the **frequency effect**. Assuming that longer response times reflect processing that is more difficult or complex, this finding suggests that our mental dictionaries are organized so that words that we typically need more often (the frequent words) are more easily and quickly available to us.

Another way in which the lexical decision task can be used to explore language representation and processing is to investigate the speed and accuracy with which subjects press the *no* button for different types of stimuli. It has been found, for example, that pronounceable non-words such as *plib* show slower 'no' response times than unpronounceable non-words such as *nlib*. Thus subjects' lexical decisions seem to take into account the phonotactic constraints of the language. It has also been found that non-words that sound like real words (e.g., *blud*, *phocks*) take longer to reject than stimuli that are non-words both visually and phonologically. Again this tells us that aspects of phonology are automatically activated during word reading (note that in the lexical decision task, the subject never has to pronounce the word aloud).

The priming paradigm

The priming paradigm very often involves the lexical decision task and can be considered an extension of it. Recall that in lexical decision tasks different categories of stimuli (e.g., concrete versus abstract words) are compared in terms of subjects' response latency and accuracy. Priming experiments typically involve the same procedure as the lexical decision task except that the word to be judged (now called the **target**) is preceded by another stimulus (called the **prime**). What is measured is the extent to which the 'prime' influences the subject's lexical decision performance on the target stimulus.

The priming paradigm is an excellent technique for probing how words are related in the mind. One of the first experiments using this paradigm showed that response time is faster when a target is preceded by a semantically related prime (e.g., *cat-dog*) as compared to when it is preceded by an unrelated prime (e.g., *cat-pen*). Results of this sort lead us to the view that words are related in the mind in terms of networks. On the basis of evidence from these priming experiments, psycholinguists reason that when a word such as *cat* is seen, its image is activated in the mind and that activation spreads to other words in the lexical network that are semantically related (e.g., *dog*). Now, because the mental representation for *dog* has already been activated through the prime, it is in a sense 'warmed up' so that when the subject later sees it on the screen as the target, response time is faster than it otherwise would have been. This is called the **priming effect**.

In recent years, the priming paradigm has been used to explore many aspects of the representation of words in the mind, and researchers have explored many types of priming in addition to the semantic priming above. For example, priming effects have been found for orthographically related words (e.g., *couch-touch*), phonologically related words (e.g., *light-bite*), and between word roots and complex forms (e.g., *legal-illegality*). This last finding suggests that words are represented in the mind in terms of their constituent morphemes and will be discussed further in section 2.2.

1.3   Experimental methods: sentence processing

The lexical decision and priming paradigms discussed above offer interesting insights into how words are processed, but are of limited use in exploring the processing of sentences. The main reason for this is that the types of questions asked about sentence processing tend to be different from those asked about the mental lexicon. The vast majority of the sentences that we hear are unique events. Therefore, sentence processing must be fundamentally a process that relies on a particular type of computation (as opposed to a particular type of storage in the case of words in the mind). It is presumed that in sentence processing (i.e., in reading or listening) a sentence is understood through the analysis of the meanings of its words and through the analysis of its syntactic structure. Psycholinguists refer to this type of unconscious automatic analysis as **parsing**. Much of the research on sentence processing is concerned with the principles and steps in sentence parsing, the speed of parsing, and the manner and conditions under which parsing can break down.

In this section, we review two groups of experimental paradigms that have been used extensively to study sentence processing. These are timed-reading experiments and eye-movement experiments.

Timed-reading experiments

Timed-reading experiments begin with the assumption that the more difficult sentence processing is, the longer it should take. Therefore by timing how long it takes subjects to read particular sentence types or parts of sentences, we can study the determinants of sentence-processing difficulty.

One of the more common and revealing timed-reading experimental paradigms is the bar-pressing paradigm in which subjects are seated in front of a computer screen and read a sentence one word at a time. The subject begins by seeing the first word of the sentence in the middle of the screen. When the subject presses a bar on the keyboard, the first word disappears and the second word of the sentence appears in its place. This process continues until the subject has read all the words in the sentence.

The dependent variable in these experiments is the amount of time it takes subjects to press the bar after seeing a particular word (i.e., the amount of time they need to process that word in the sentence).

Bar-pressing experiments can be very revealing of the manner in which sentence processing occurs. Subjects do not show equal bar-pressing times across a sentence, but rather a pattern that reflects the syntactic structure of the sentence. An example of such a pattern for the sentence is shown in figure 12.3, which displays bar-pressing times for the sentence *The Chinese, who used to produce kites, used them in order to carry ropes across the rivers.*

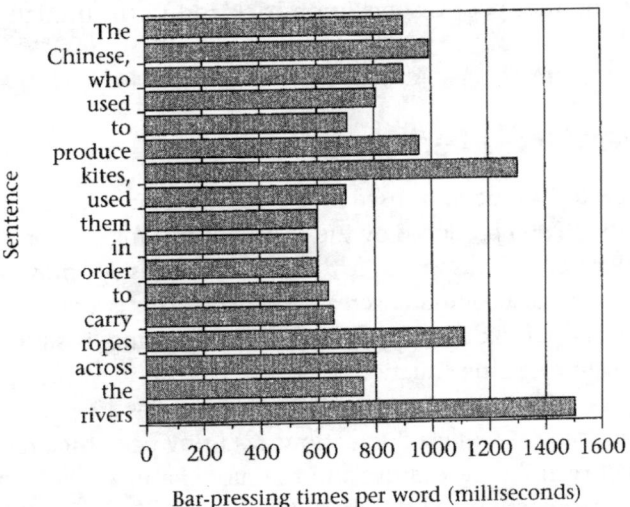

Figure 12.3 Bar-pressing times in sentence reading (adapted from Stine 1990)

As can be seen in figure 12.3, subjects show longer bar-pressing times for processing content words such as nouns and verbs and relatively less time for function words such as determiners, conjunctions and prepositions. What is particularly interesting is how subjects pause at the end of clause boundaries. This increased processing time is interpreted as reflecting the extra amount of time required to integrate preceding information into a complete clause structure. Thus the greatest bar-pressing time is required for *rivers*, the final noun in the sentence.

Eye movements

We have already noted that sentence reading involves a series of jerky eye movements called saccades. A number of events occur during these jerky movements. When the eyes are at rest they take a 'snapshot' of two or three words. These snapshots usually last from 200 to 250 milliseconds. While the snapshot is being taken, the language-processing system calculates where to jump to next. During a jump to the next fixation location (usually about eight letters to the right), the subject is essentially blind.

The details of eye movements in sentence reading are studied with sophisticated laboratory procedures in which a subject is seated in front of a computer screen on which text is displayed. A low-intensity infra-red beam of light is bounced off the subject's eyeball and registered on a video camera. The image from the video camera is fed to a computer that calculates where on the screen the subject is currently fixating.

This technique has revealed that fixation times are typically longer for less-frequent words and the points of fixation are typically centered on content words such as nouns and verbs rather than function words such as determiners and conjunctions. Difficult sentence structures create longer fixation times as well as many more **regressive** (backward) **saccades**. Regressive saccades are backward jumps in a sentence and are usually associated with mis-parsing or miscomprehension. On average, backward saccades make up 10 to 15 percent of the saccades in sentence reading. But syntactically complex sentences and semantically anomalous sentences (e.g., *The pizza was too hot to drink*) create many more regressive saccades. It has also been found that poor readers jump back and forth through sentences much more often than good readers do.

1.4   Brain activity: event-related potentials

Perhaps the most exciting new technique to be used in psycholinguistic research is the study of **event-related potentials** (**ERPs**) produced by the brain during language processing. As a research technique, the ERP paradigm has the same basic advantage as eye-movement studies. The subject simply sits in front of a computer screen and reads. This is a relatively natural language processing activity that, unlike lexical decision or bar pressing, is similar to what subjects do in normal language-processing situations.

ERP experiments measure electrical activity in the brain. Electrodes are placed on a subject's scalp and recordings are made of voltage fluctuations resulting from the brain's electrical activity. The difference between ERP recordings and the more familiar EEG recordings is that, in the EEG, all the electrical activity of the brain is recorded. This electrical activity results from a very large number of background brain activities that are always going on. The advantage of the ERP approach is that it uses a computer to calculate what part of the electrical brain activity is related to a stimulus event (in our case words or sentences on a screen). This is done by a process of averaging. The computer records the instant at which a stimulus is presented and compares the voltage fluctuation immediately following the stimulus presentation to the random background 'noise' of the ongoing EEG. By repeating this process many times with stimuli of a particular type, random voltage fluctuations are averaged out and the electrical potentials related to that stimulus type can be extracted. The resulting wave forms are called the event-related potentials.

The ERP pattern is typically shown in terms of a line graph in which time is shown from left to right and voltage is shown on the vertical axis with negative values on top and positive values on the bottom. An example of an ERP graph is provided in figure 12.4. This figure also displays one of the most interesting psycholinguistic findings using ERPs. It turns out that in the processing of sentences, the brain displays a characteristic ERP sign of surprise. Consider the following sentences:

8)
- *a.* The pizza was too hot to eat.
- *b.* The pizza was too hot to drink.
- *c.* The pizza was too hot to cry.

The sentences in *8)* are arranged in order of semantic plausibility. In the first case, the last word fits in perfectly well with the sentence and would typically be expected by the reader. As can be seen in figure 12.4, the ERP for this sentence shows a positive voltage associated with the last word. In the case of *8b),* however, in which the last word does not make sense (people do not drink pizza), the ERP is much more negative. As is shown in the horizontal axis, this negative spike occurs 400 milliseconds after the onset of the word. For this reason, this signal of semantic anomaly is called the N400 (negative spike at 400 milliseconds after stimulus presentation). Note how the N400 is even stronger in the case of sentence *8c)* which is less congruent with the sentence context ('drink' is at least associated with food).

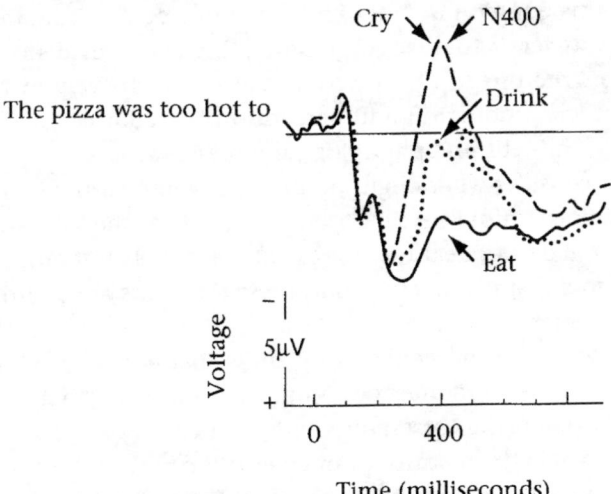

Figure 12.4 ERPs elicited by sentence-final words that are congruent, incongruent, and very incongruent with the sentence context

The N400 effect can be obtained not only at the ends of sentences but in any sentence position. This fact suggests that sentence processing is immediate and on-line. When reading a sentence we do not wait until the entire string is complete, but are rather constantly building interpretations of the sentence as it unfolds. Whenever what we see or hear contradicts our expectations based on our ongoing interpretative processes, a N400 ERP spike is observed.

2   Language processing and linguistics

In the preceding sections we discussed some of the methods that psycholinguists use to investigate the manner in which language is processed. One of the most important results of such psycholinguistic investigations has been that many of the concepts and principles used by linguists to describe and understand the structure of language in terms of phonetics, phonology, morphology, and syntax have been found to also play an important role in the understanding of how language is produced and comprehended during activities such as speaking, listening, reading and writing. In this section we will focus on these points of contact between theoretical linguistics and psycholinguistics. In doing so, we will also highlight the correspondence between the study of language processing and the concepts discussed in chapters 1 to 5 of this book.

2.1   Phonetics and phonology

The study of phonetics and phonology reveals that the sound system of language is richly structured and contains different levels of representation. Thus, as is discussed in chapters 2 and 3, individual segments can be characterized in terms of place and manner of articulation or with respect to a matrix of phonological features. Sequences of sounds can be grouped into syllabic structures, and allophonic variation can be described in terms of underlying phonemes and surface allophones. How much of this structure plays a role in language processing? The simple answer to this question is: "All of it!" The more complex answer, and of course also the more accurate answer, is that language processing shows evidence that features, phonemes, and syllable structure all capture some aspects of the way in which we process language, but that speech production and perception is a complex activity that involves much more than these phonetic and phonological representations.

To see why this is the case, consider what might occur when you hear the sentence *The dog bit the cat*. Because the utterance unfolds in time, you will first hear the segment /ð/ and then the segment /ə/. (In fact, you do not hear these segments separately but rather you create them out of a continuous sound stream.) As soon as these segments are identified, you have already accessed the representation for the word *the* in your mental lexicon. When the next segment comes up in the sound stream, you already know that it is the beginning of a new word and you also know that this word must be a noun. The phonetic analysis that follows identifies the segments *d-o-g* and the corresponding lexical entry. Now come the first segments of the word *bit*. In principle the first two phonemes /bɪ/ could be the first two segments of the word *believe*, but you are not likely to consider this possibility because your developing interpretation of the sentence is biasing you toward the word *bit* which is associated in your mind with *dog*.

As can be appreciated from this example, language processing involves the interplay of information that develops simultaneously at many different levels of analysis. The person hearing the sentence *The dog bit the cat* is performing a phonetic analysis to isolate phonemes and word boundaries, and to relate these to representations in the mental lexicon. This inductive analysis is referred to as **bottom-up processing**. But we do not wait until we have analyzed all the phonemes in a sentence before we begin to try to understand it. Rather, we begin interpretation of a sentence spontaneously and automatically on the basis of whatever information is available to us. For this reason, by the time we get to the word *bit* in the sentence, we are not only recognizing it using bottom-up processing but are also employing a set of expectations to guide phonetic processing and word recognition. This is called **top-down processing**. In normal language use we are always engaged in both bottom-up and top-down activities. We never just process features, or phonemes, or syllables. We process language for the purposes of understanding each other.

In section 3 of this chapter, we will discuss how phonetic and phonological analysis fits into other processes involved in speaking and listening. For now, however, we will concentrate on three levels of linguistic structure that seem fundamental to phonetic and phonological representation: features, phonemes, and syllables.

Features

In both linguistics and psycholinguistics, the term *feature* is used to refer to the most basic level of representation. It is therefore always associated with bottom-up processing in language. In the processing of sound, it refers to characteristics of individual phonemes (e.g., ± voice, ± stop, etc.). The most straightforward evidence concerning the role of such features comes from the analysis of slips of the tongue. Some examples of these slips are presented in table 12.1.

Table 12.1 The role of features in speech errors	
Intended	**Actually produced**
a. big and fat	pig and vat
b. Is Pat a girl?	Is bat a curl?
c. Cedars of Lebanon	Cedars of Lemmanon

The errors in table 12.1 follow a pattern. But that pattern can only be understood with reference to a system of phonological features. In all three examples in this table, the errors involve a phonological feature. In example *a* the feature [voice] has been exchanged between the words *big* and *fat* to create the new words *pig* and *vat* (note that /b-p/ and /f-v/ only differ in the feature [voice]).

This same pattern of voice feature exchange can be seen in example *b*, where *Pat* becomes *bat* and *girl* becomes *curl*. Finally, the error in *c* is particularly intriguing because we normally think of /b/ and /m/ as completely different phonemes. In fact, however, they are both voiced bilabial stops that only differ in terms of the feature ± nasal. Changing the /b/ in *Lebanon* from [−nasal] to [+nasal] creates the error *Lemmanon*. These examples offer evidence that language production makes use of the individual feature components of phonemes and that the phonemes that we produce in speech may actually be put together 'on the fly' out of bundles of such features.

Phonemes

We have seen in section 1.1 that Spoonerisms show evidence of entire phonemes being misplaced during sentence planning. The phonemic unit of representation also plays a central role in psycholinguistic models of speech processing such as the **cohort model**, proposed by William Marslen-Wilson. This model states that, in word comprehension, words are analyzed by hearers from beginning to end. So, for example, when we hear the word *glass*, we initially consider all the words that begin with the sound [g]. When the next sound [l] is recognized, the number of possible words (the **cohort**), is reduced to those words that begin with [gl]. This process continues until the cohort of possible words is reduced to one—the word that is being recognized. In a number of experiments, Marslen-Wilson investigated whether this beginning-to-end analysis of spoken words proceeds one phoneme at a time, one cluster at a time, or one syllable at a time. He and his colleagues found that the phoneme seems to be the fundamental unit of auditory word recognition.

Syllables

Although in the *cohort model*, the phoneme rather than the syllable seems to be the fundamental unit of auditory word recognition, there is other evidence that the syllable plays an important role in speech perception. In one study, subjects were presented with disyllabic words (e.g., *bullet*) and disyllabic non-words (e.g., *sullet*) and were asked to press a button if a particular target unit was in the stimulus. The target units were either syllables (e.g., *let*) or segments (e.g., *t*). It was found for both words and non-words that subjects were significantly faster at identifying syllable targets than at identifying single segment targets. It was concluded that syllable identification was faster because, in normal auditory analysis, subjects first break down stimuli into syllables and then into individual segments as the situation demands.

Another source of evidence on the role of the syllable in language processing comes from observing subjects' performance on word blending tasks. In such a task, subjects are given two words such as *bug* and *cat* and are required to blend the words together to make a new word. Now, what sounds better: (*bug* + *cat* = *bat*) or (*bug* + *cat* = *but*)? The difference between these two possibilities is that the first one takes the onset of the first syllable and combines it with the rhyme of the second syllable. The other possibility does not split the words in a natural point of English syllable structure. As you might expect, subjects are much better at creating word blends that correspond to the syllable structure of their language and prefer such blends when presented with a choice. The fact that English speakers find such onset-rhyme divisions easier and more natural suggest that the sound of words is represented in speakers' minds in terms of their syllables and syllable constituents (e.g., onset and rhyme).

2.2 Morphological processing

Morphology is the study of word structure. It seeks to characterize the system of categories and rules involved in word formation and interpretation. The psycholinguistic study of mor-

a   *b*

Figure 12.5 Speakers of English find the word blend in *a* easier and more natural than the word blend in *b* because the former involves breaking the words at natural syllable-structure boundaries.

phological processing seeks to understand how this word structure plays a role in language processing. In the following sections, we will summarize some psycholinguistic research that reveals how morphological structures and principles play a substantial role in the representation of words in the mind and in word recognition.

Morpheme activation

Words such as *blackboard*, *happiness*, and *watching* are made up of two morphemes. In the case of the compound *blackboard*, both these morphemes are roots. In the case of *happiness*, one morpheme is a root and the other is a derivational suffix. Finally, in the case of *watching*, one morpheme is a root and the other is an inflectional affix. The first question we will address is whether the individual morphological components of words play a role in processing.

The answer to this question seems to be a straightforward 'yes.' For most multimorphemic words, individual morphemes are automatically activated during word recognition. One source of evidence for this conclusion comes from priming experiments in which it is found that words like *happiness* will prime their constituents and vice versa in a lexical decision experiment. In other words, when a subject is exposed to a multimorphemic word such as *happiness*, the activation of that word in the mind automatically activates the lexical entry for its root *happy*, which results in its showing a faster response time as the target in a lexical decision task.

Another source of evidence for this view comes from semantic priming lexical decision experiments with compounds in which it is found that presentation of a compound such as *crowbar* will produce a priming effect for the subsequent lexical decision time for a word such as *bird*. For this priming effect to take place, the morpheme *crow* would have to be individually activated during word recognition because as a whole, the compound *crowbar* has nothing to do with birds.

Selectional restrictions

As discussed in chapter 4, one of the properties of English morphology is that not all affixes can attach to all stems. So, for example, the suffix *-ize* attaches to adjectives or nouns to form verbs. For this reason, English morphological constraints would not allow a word such as **understandize* because *understand* is already a verb. Now the question for psycholinguistic research is: Do these formal restrictions play a role in the way in which native speakers of English process new words?

In a recent experiment in morphological processing, subjects were presented with nonsense roots (e.g., *birm*) that had prefixes and suffixes attached to them. Because they contained nonsense roots, none of these words made much sense (e.g., *re-birmable*, *re-birmize*, *re-birmity*). But notice that as is shown in figure 12.6, *re-birmable* and *re-birmize* are morphologically legal whereas *re-birmity* violates a morphological constraint—the prefix *re-* must attach to a verb and the suffix *-ity* must attach to a noun. The construction is illegal because the nonsense root *birm* cannot be both at the same time. In experiments with these sorts of stimuli, it was found that processing times were significantly longer for the illegal nonsense than for the morphologically legal words. These results suggest that knowledge of the selectional restrictions of affixes does indeed form part of the word-processing system.

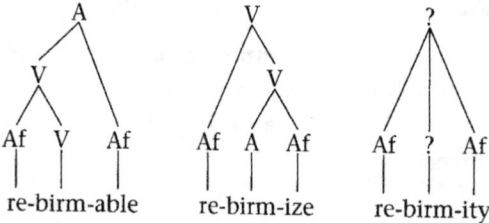

Figure 12.6 Morphologically legal and illegal affixed nonsense roots

Hierarchical structure

In figure 12.6, trimorphemic words are represented in terms of a tree diagram in which constituent morphemes are arranged in a hierarchy. The last question we will consider in our discussion of morphological processing is whether there is evidence that the representation of multimorphemic words in the mind includes a representation of hierarchical structure.

This question has been investigated in priming experiments that use lexical decision response times as the dependent variable. These experiments compare stimuli such as *refillable,* which have a left-branching structure, to stimuli such as *unbearable,* which have a right-branching structure (see figure 12.7). This means that for the word *refillable,* the substring *fillable* is not a morphological component of the tree structure (even though it is a real word of English). However, because the word *unbearable* is right-branching, its final two morphemes (*bear* and *-able*) make up a component of the morphological tree.

In the priming experiments, subjects were first shown the right substrings such as *fillable* and then the full trimorphemic word (e.g., *re-fillable*). Priming effects were measured in terms of the lexical decision response times for the full word. It was found that those substrings that were real morphological constituents produced a significantly larger priming effect than those that were not.

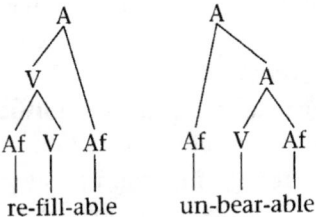

Figure 12.7 Left-branching and right-branching trimorphemic words

Note that if hierarchical structure were not part of the representation of multimorphemic words in the mind, that is, if these words were simply strings of morphemes (e.g., *re* + *fill* + *able*), then there should be no difference between the priming effects for right-branching versus left-branching stimuli. The fact that such priming effects were observed is evidence that our representation of complex words is organized in terms of hierarchical morphological structure.

2.3   Syntax

Syntax is the system of rules and categories that underlies sentence formation in human language. One of the fundamental insights in the study of syntax is that sentences are unique events. That means that virtually all of the sentences that you read in this chapter are sentences that you have never encountered before. They are typically made up of familiar words, but the arrangement of those words into a syntactic structure is unique to each sentence. The question that we will consider in this section is: How are these syntactic structures created during sentence processing?

The syntax module

One very simple possibility for how sentences are processed is that production and comprehension employ the system of rules that are used by syntacticians to describe sentence structure. This possibility suggests that speakers would begin with deep structure representations and employ a series of transformations to derive the surface structure characteristics of a sentence. Many psycholinguistic experiments examined this possibility by testing, for example, whether sentences with many transformations take longer to process than sentences with fewer transformations. It turned out that the number of transformations in a sentence did not predict processing time. Researchers concluded that there is at least some difference between the rules that native speakers use to generate and comprehend sentences and the rules that linguists use to characterize the linguistic knowledge of native speakers. It was therefore necessary to postulate a special module for sentence processing and another for grammatical knowledge. This processing module is called the **syntactic parser**.

The parser is understood to be the system that makes use of grammatical knowledge but also contains special procedures and principles that guide the order in which elements of a sentence are processed and the manner in which syntactic structure is built up. Because our parsing ability is based on our grammatical knowledge of our language, it is usually the case that there is a close correspondence between sentence parsing and grammatical structure.

However, because the parsing module has its own set of principles, sentences that are grammatically complex are not necessarily difficult to parse and some sentences with relatively simple syntactic structure can create substantial parsing problems.

It should be noted that in discussing how processing takes place, the term **module** has a special meaning. It refers to a unit of processing that is relatively autonomous from other processing units. The idea of processing modules has been very important and controversial in many domains of human information processing. To get a sense of how processing may involve the coordination of separate modules, consider what occurs when you watch a movie. The movie director, in order to obtain a variety of effects, relies on processing modularity. The director knows that in watching an adventure film, your stomach will take a dip when the airplane on the screen goes into a dive or when the canoe goes over the falls. He or she knows that you cannot stop this from happening even though you are aware that you are sitting in a chair that is not moving. Similarly, you will be frightened by the sudden appearance of a monster, even though you know that you are really in no danger. All these effects result from processing modularity. The bottom-up information that comes from processing modules cannot be turned-off by the top-down information that you are seated in a stationary and safe movie-theatre environment.

A variety of psycholinguistic studies have investigated whether this same sort of modularity is present in syntactic processing. In other words, they look at whether syntactic parsing operates in an automatic and obligatory manner that is relatively independent of the activity of other processing systems. Two sources of evidence have been very important in the exploration of the principles of modularity of sentence processing. These are garden path sentences and sentence ambiguity, which are discussed below.

Garden path sentences

Some sentences are extraordinarily difficult to understand even though they are not very complex syntactically. These sentences are called **garden path sentences** because they lead the syntactic parser down the garden path to the wrong analysis. Perhaps the most famous garden path sentence is the one given in *9)* below.

9)
The horse raced past the barn fell.

This sentence is perfectly grammatical, but almost impossible to understand. The reason for this is that as we read the sentence, we build up a syntactic structure in which *the horse* is the subject of the sentence and *raced past the barn* is the main VP. When we get to the word *fell*, we are surprised because the sentence we have built up has no room for an extra VP. The correct interpretation for the sentence requires that *fell* be the head of the main VP and that *raced past the barn* be a clause that attaches to the NP *the horse* (see figure 12.8).

The ways in which native speakers misunderstand garden path sentences reveals how the parser might work. It seems that we construct syntactic representations from the beginning of the sentences to the end and that our sentence parsers are organized so that we make a number of assumptions about how a sentence will proceed. This can be seen by considering the garden path sentence in *10)*.

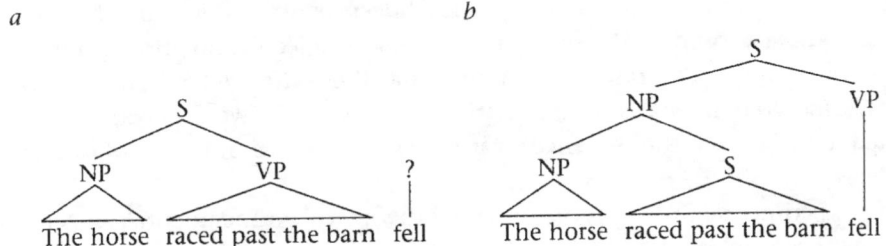

Figure 12.8 A garden path sentence. The garden path effect is shown in *a*. The correct interpretation is represented in *b*.

10)
Since Jay always walks a mile seems like a short distance to him.

This sentence is not as difficult to process as the sentence in *9)*, but you probably noticed yourself having to backtrack after an initial mis-analysis. Your parser is inclined to build a single VP out of the string *walks a mile*, when in fact they belong to different clauses. This tendency has been extensively studied by psycholinguists. The backtracking that you might have noticed in your own reading shows up significantly in eye-movement studies in which it is found that subjects show more regressive saccades for these sentences as well as longer fixation times.

It has been claimed by Lynn Frazier and her colleagues that the garden path effect results from two principles of parsing. These are **minimal attachment** and **late closure**. The principle of minimal attachment states that we do not postulate new syntactic nodes (like the extra embedded S in figure 12.8b), unless it is clear that we absolutely have to. The principle of late closure states that we prefer to attach new words to the clause currently being processed as we proceed through a sentence from beginning to end. The result of late closure can be discerned in sentence *10)*, where we are inclined to add the NP *a mile* to the VP headed by *walk* rather than beginning a new clause.

Now, there is one last point to be made concerning what garden path sentences can tell us about how people process sentences. Try reading the sentence in *10)* again. You should find that although you now know the correct analysis for the sentence, you misread it the second time just as you did the first time. This suggests that the parsing system is in fact a module that operates automatically and independently.

Sentence ambiguity

Another important clue to how syntactic processing is accomplished comes from the study of ambiguity. Consider the sentence in *11)*.

11)
They all rose.

In fact the last word in *11)* is ambiguous. The word *rose* can either be related to *stand* or related to *flower*. However, the sentence context leads us clearly to favour the *stand* version of the word. Does the sentence context therefore inhibit activation of the other meaning of *rose?* This question was investigated in a lexical decision experiment in which the sentence in *11)* served as the prime. After seeing the sentence, subjects were presented with either the word *flower* or *stand*. The researchers found that the sentence facilitated lexical decision response times to both words. That is, both meanings for the word *rose* in the sentence were activated, even though the sentence clearly presented a bias in favour of one reading over the other.

This experimental finding is one of many that reveal a fundamental property of human language processing. We create all representations possible and then discard the ones that are either incorrect or unnecessary. This last characteristic was found in a follow-up priming experiment which was identical to the one just described except that there was a pause of several hundred milliseconds between the prime and the target. When the pause was present, the priming effect disappeared for the meaning that was unrelated to the sentence context (i.e., *flower*). This suggests that, in fact, sentence processing proceeds in two stages. In the first stage, all possible representations and structures are computed. In the second stage one of these structures is selected and all others are abandoned. Of course all this happens very quickly and subconsciously so that we as native speakers of a language are never aware that for a sentence such as *12)*, we compute two possible interpretations.

12)
The tuna can hit the boat.

In reading this sentence, you either ended up imagining:

a. tuna meat that is packed in a small round can
b. a large fish swimming toward a boat.

The point of the psycholinguistic experiments just described is this: No matter which interpretation you arrived at (*a* or *b*), you probably considered both of them, chose one, discarded the other, and forgot about the whole thing in less than a second.

3 Putting it all together: psycholinguistic modelling

Up to this point, our discussion of psycholinguistic research has been restricted to examining characteristics of phonetic, phonological, morphological and syntactic processing and the relation between the concepts used in theoretical linguistics and in psycholinguistics. It is important to note however that research in language processing seeks not only to discover which types of representations play a role in language processing, but also how these representations and processes fit together to make activities such as speaking, listening, reading, and writing possible.

Psycholinguistic researchers present their ideas of how *language is done* in terms of models. A psycholinguistic model incorporates the results of experiments into a proposal of how processing takes place. In other words, it is a statement of what happens when.

Suppose, for example, we wished to present the finding discussed in section 2.3 that a sentence such as *They all rose* will prime both the words *flower* and *stand*. The model might look like figure 12.9.

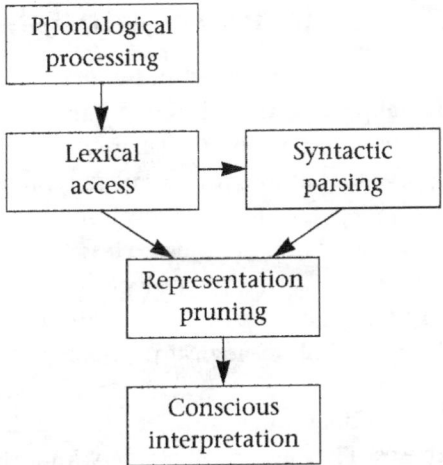

Figure 12.9 A serial psycholinguistic model of sentence processing

For our present purposes, it is not important whether this model is actually correct. The purpose of the model is simply to illustrate how psycholinguistic statements can be represented. This model, which looks very much like a computer flow chart, 'says' that when processing a sentence such as *They all rose,* we first perform phonological analysis. This is followed by lexical access, in which all words with matching phonological representations are accessed (including the two words *rose*). Information from lexical access 'feeds' the syntactic parsing module, and information from both the lexical access module and the parsing module are fed to the representation pruning module (the module that discards multiple representations). Finally, the model states that interpretation becomes conscious only in the final stage of analysis and that there is only one-way information flow to conscious interpretation (in other words, the conscious mind cannot 'peek' at how things are going).

You will note that in creating this model, we have taken two kinds of shortcuts. First, we have created a novel name (e.g., pruning) to describe an operation that has been deduced from the results of psycholinguistic experimentation. Second, our model uses the box notation as a shorthand for a constellation of processes. Thus, it is understood that as the model becomes more elaborated, each one of the boxes in figure 12.9 would be expanded into a flow chart of its own.

As you inspect the model in figure 12.9 you should find that it is really very inadequate. It is missing much important detail, it seems to characterize only one aspect of sentence processing, and it avoids any mention of how meaning is accessed or how sentence interpretation actually takes place. In other words, to be a model of any real value, it would have to be much more elaborate.

Indeed, the types of psycholinguistic models that have been proposed in recent years are very elaborate. This is a good thing. We want models to be as detailed and comprehensive as possible, to take a great deal of experimentation into account and, perhaps most importantly, to show how linguistic and non-linguistic operations work together in the processing of language.

3.1   The use of metaphors in psycholinguistic modelling

Perhaps the most important characteristic of the model presented in figure 12.9 is the fact that it obviously could not reflect what really happens in the mind of a language user. It is exceedingly unlikely that our minds possess boxes and arrows (or their equivalents). This model, like all psycholinguistic models, employs metaphors for language representations and language processing. The value of these metaphors is that they allow researchers to make specific claims about how language processing works, which can then be tested. For example, through its architecture, the model in figure 12.9 claims that phonological processing precedes lexical access, which in turn precedes syntactic processing. This claim can easily be tested in an experiment that investigates whether all phonological processing is complete before syntactic processing begins.

We see then that psycholinguistic models have dual functions. They summarize specific research findings and generate specific hypotheses. They also have the very important function of embodying general perspectives on how language processing works. This is again accomplished through the use of metaphors. These metaphors have the effect of shaping how we conceive of language in the mind and what kinds of questions are asked by psycholinguistic researchers. Finally, these metaphors provide the means by which major families of models can be contrasted in order to test which most accurately describes language processing. In the following sections, we review three of the most important current contrasts in psycholinguistic modelling: serial versus parallel processing models; single-route versus dual-route models, and finally, symbolic versus connectionist models.

Serial versus parallel processing models

Let us return to figure 12.9. By employing the metaphor of a computer program that operates sequentially, the **serial processing model** in figure 12.9 not only makes a claim about sentence processing, but also claims that language processing proceeds in a step by step manner. In contrast, a **parallel processing model** would claim that phonological, lexical, and syntactic processes are carried out simultaneously. Figure 12.10 represents an example of a parallel processing model. Here information does not flow in a sequential manner. Rather all modules operate simultaneously and share information. The model in figure 12.10 claims, therefore, that when we hear a sentence, we begin phonological, lexical, and syntactic processes at the same time. As each type of processing proceeds it informs the other.

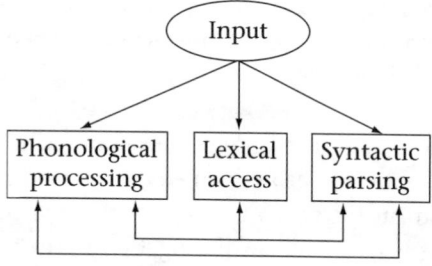

Figure 12.10 A parallel psycholinguistic model of sentence processing

In recent research, serial and parallel processing models have been central in our ability to understand the extent to which bottom-up and top-down processing interact. Serial models correctly characterize those aspects of language processing that are modular and are driven by strict bottom-up procedures. Parallel processing models, on the other hand, are more effective than serial models at characterizing complex processes such as sentence comprehension.

Single-route versus dual-route models

Put most directly, **single-route models** claim that a particular type of language processing is accomplished in one manner only. Dual-route models, on the other hand, claim that a language-processing task is accomplished through (usually two) competing mechanisms. Consider, for example, the task of reading English words. Here there are three possibilities: (1) we always read a word by looking it up in our mental lexicon directly based on its visual characteristics; (2) we convert a visual input into phonological representations first and this phonological representation becomes the basis for comprehension; and (3) we do both at the same time. Options (1) and (2) represent single-route models in the sense that they claim that reading is accomplished in one way. Option (3), which is represented in figure 12.11, represents a **dual-route model** in that it claims that both mechanisms are employed. Usually such dual-route models employ the additional metaphor of a horse race by claiming that for some words (e.g., very frequent short words) the direct route is faster but for others (e.g., rare words) the phonological conversion route is faster and 'wins the horse race.'

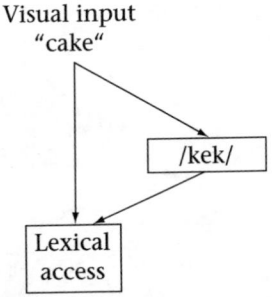

Figure 12.11 A dual-route model of word reading

In recent psycholinguistic investigations, the dual-route model has been very influential in modelling whether multimorphemic words are decomposed into their constituent morphemes during word recognition or are accessed as whole words. It has been found that although both procedures are active all the time, the whole-word recognition route wins the race for frequent bimorphemic words such as *blackboard*. However, in the case of less frequent words such as *breadboard* or novel multimorphemic forms such as *blueboard*, the morphological decomposition route is the one that provides the basis for comprehension.

Symbolic versus connectionist models

The final modelling contrast that we review in this section is the contrast between symbolic and connectionist models. These types of models represent fundamentally different views about the nature of mental representations. **Symbolic models** (which include all the ones we have discussed so far) claim that models of linguistics knowledge must make reference to rules and representations consisting of symbols, such as phonemes, words, syntactic category labels, and so forth. **Connectionist models**, on the other hand, claim that the mind can be best modelled by reference to large associations of very simple units (often called **nodes**) which more closely approximate the kinds of processing units (i.e., neurons) that we know the brain to be composed of. Connectionist models typically do not contain direct representations for language units such as words, but rather represent these as an association of nodes. This difference is exemplified in figure 12.12.

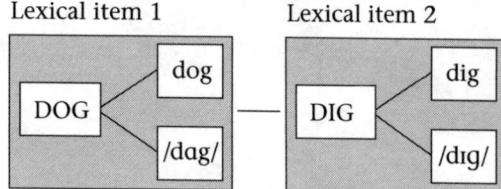

Figure 12.12 Symbolic versus connectionist representations for the words *dog* and *dig* in the mind

In one sense, the two kinds of representations in figure 12.12 represent exactly the same information—namely the graphemic and phonological makeup for the words *dog* and *dig*. In another sense, however, they are very different. The connectionist representation shows words as having 'reality' only in the sense that they are bundles of associations between phonological and graphemic nodes. (In some connectionist approaches, the word nodes would not exist at all.) In the symbolic representation, on the other hand, words do indeed have discrete representations in the mind and each representation contains information regarding the word's sound and spelling.

3.2 Which model is right?

Almost certainly, none of the models that we have discussed is correct. All models represent a researcher's claim about the most current version of the truth. Because psycholinguistics is a very young field, we can expect that any 'current version of the truth' will be very far from the real truth (if there is one). Perhaps this is the reason that psycholinguistic models are so important. They give us the vocabulary with which to ask major questions about mental processing. For example, do our representations consist of symbols corresponding to phonemes, words, and phrases, or are mental representations distributed over a large number of nodes? Does the mind settle into a best way to perform a task, or are all processes horse races between alternative ways to solve a problem? Do mental operations proceed in a step-by-step manner?

These are all big questions and big issues. Language research is at the centre of them. The more we investigate the details of language processing, the more we realize that it offers our best clues to the secrets of human cognition and the more we appreciate how well guarded those secrets are. In the past quarter-century of psycholinguistic research we have learned a great deal about language representation and processing. In the first part of this chapter, we concentrated on the research techniques that have made these advances possible. In this final section of the chapter we have focused on the yet unresolved major issues. Although we do not yet know which models are right or which hybrids will be most effective in our evolving understanding of human cognition, one thing is certain: psycholinguistic research has been and will continue to be critical to that understanding.

Summing up

Psycholinguistics is the study of language processing. The field is defined both by an area of subject matter and a particular methodology. Psycholinguists study how people perform the functions of language comprehension and production. They seek to discover the nature of the mental representations that serve these functions and the nature of the cognitive operations and computations that are employed when we understand and produce language.

Because language processing involves computations and representations that cannot be observed and measured directly, psycholinguists have devised special experimental techniques to investigate language processing. Some of these techniques, such as **lexical decision** and **priming**, measure a subject's response time and response accuracy to linguistic stimuli. Other techniques measure eye movement while subjects are reading silently and yet others measure electrical activity in the brain during language processing.

Language processing involves many processing modules that are specialized for a particular language processing task and interact with other modules in restricted ways. Thus, language processing involves a constant interplay between bottom-up and top-down processing. We process phonetic features, phonemes, and words all at the same time. We construct syllable representations, morphological representations, and syntactic representations in a spontaneous and obligatory manner. As conscious beings we are aware of the results of our processing but not of the processing itself.

In general, psycholinguistic studies have revealed that many of the concepts employed in the analysis of sound structure, word structure, and sentence structure also play a role in language processing. However, an account of language processing also requires that we understand how these linguistic concepts interact with other aspects of human processing to enable language production and comprehension.

Psycholinguists typically present their views of how language production and comprehension are achieved in terms of processing models. These models are at the heart of research in psycholinguistics and allow researchers to express the significance of particular research findings, to predict the outcomes of future experiments and to debate the fundamental characteristics of human cognition.

Sources

In recent years, many new books on psycholinguistics have appeared. These include *Psycholinguistics* by Joseph Kess (Philadelphia: John Benjamins, 1992) and *Psycholinguistics* by Jean Berko-Gleason and Nan Bernstein Ratner (Philadelphia: Harcourt Brace, 1993). Another excellent source is the *Handbook of Psycholinguistics,* edited by Morton Ann Gernsbacher (New York: Academic Press, 1994). Some of the 'slip of the tongue' material in section 1.1 is drawn from Victoria Fromkin's chapter on speech production (pp. 272–300) in the Berko-Gleason and Ratner volume cited above.

The experiment in which bar-pressing times were found to correspond to clause boundaries was reported by E.A. Stine in an article titled "On-Line Processing of Written Text by Younger and Older Children" in *Psychology and Aging*, 5:68–78 (1990) and is discussed in Arthur Wingfield's chapter "Sentence Processing" in the Berko-Gleason and Ratner text. Copyright © (1990) by the American Psychological Association. Adapted with permission.

The discussion of eye-movement data in psycholinguistics was based on the article by K. Rayner and S. Sereno, "Eye Movements in Reading" in the *Handbook of Psycholinguistics,* edited by M.A. Gernsbacher, as well as in the book by K. Rayner and A. Pollatsek, *The Psychology of Reading* (Englewood Cliffs, NJ: Prentice-Hall, 1989).

The material on event-related potentials is discussed in an excellent review article by Marta Kutas and Cyma Van Petten in the Gernsbacher's *Handbook of Psycholinguistics* cited above (pp. 83–133); see p. 103 for a discussion of figure 12.4. The syllable-processing experiment cited in the syllable section was reported in "Phoneme Monitoring, Syllable Monitoring, and Lexical Access" by J. Segui, U. Frauenfelder, and J. Mehler in the *British Journal of Psychology* 72:471–77 (1981) and is discussed by R.E. Remes in "On the Perception of Speech" in the Gernsbacher *Handbook*.

The word-blending studies are reported in a series of studies conducted by Rebecca Treiman; see "The Structure of Spoken Syllables: Evidence from Novel Word Games" in *Cognition* 15:49–74 (1983). A cross-linguistic study using a forced-choice version of these word games is reported in G.E. Wiebe and B.L. Derwing's paper, "A Forced-Choice Blending Task for Testing Intra-syllabic Break Points in English, Korean, and Taiwanese," in *The Twenty-First LACUS Forum* (Chapel Hill, NC: LACUS, 1994).

The morphological priming experiments are summarized in an article by William Marslen-Wilson, Lorraine Komisarjevsky Tyler, Rachelle Waksler, and Lianne Older, "Morphology and Meaning in the English Mental Lexicon" in *Psychological Review* 101:3-33 (1994). The experiments on selectional restrictions and hierarchical structure are reported in Libben's article, "Are Morphological Structures Computed During Word Recognition?" in

Journal of Psycholinguistic Research 22:535–44 (1993) and in Libben's article "Computing Hierarchical Morphological Structure: A Case Study" in *Journal of Neurolinguistics*, 8:49–55 (1994).

The section on the processing of garden path sentences is taken from Lynn Frazier's article, "Sentence Processing: A Tutorial Review," in *Attention and Performance (XII): The Psychology of Reading*, edited by M. Coltheart (London: Lawrence Erlbaum, 1987), 559–96. These sentence types are also discussed in David Caplan's book, *Language: Structure Processing and Disorders* (Cambridge, MA: MIT Press, 1994).

The study of sentence ambiguity was conducted by M.K. Tannenhaus, G.N. Carson, and M.S. Seidenberg in "Do Listeners Compute Linguistic Representations?" in *Natural Language Parsing*, edited by D.R. Dowty, L. Karttunen, and A.M. Zwicky (New York: Cambridge University Press, 1985).

Recommended reading

Berko Gleason, J., and Nan Bernstein Ratner. 1993. *Psycholinguistics*. Philadelphia: Harcourt Brace.

Gernsbacher, M.A. 1994. *Handbook of Psycholinguistics*. New York: Academic Press.

Kess, J. 1992. *Psycholinguistics*. Philadelphia: John Benjamins.

Questions

1. How do psycholinguistic investigations of language differ from theoretical linguistic investigations?

2. Consider the following slips of the tongue. What does each reveal about the process of language production?
   a) They *laked* across the *swim*.
   b) The spy was *gound* and *bagged*.
   c) I will *zee* you in the *bark*.

3. Imagine that you read that a psycholinguist has reported an experiment in which a priming effect was found for morphological roots on suffixed past tense forms in a lexical decision task.
   a) State the dependent variable in the experiment.
   b) Give an example of a prime stimulus.
   c) Give an example of a target stimulus.

4. Imagine that ERP researchers find that a positive spike is consistently observed half a second after the presentation of a particular sentence type. What do you think this new ERP spike would be called?

5. Complete the following sentences by filling in the blanks. In each case, what type of top-down processing and bottom-up processing guided your decision?
   a) The children _____ running in the park.
   b) All _____ movies I like have happy endings.
   c) He tends to see everything as _____ and white.

6. Recall that according to the cohort model a word is recognized from beginning to end, one phoneme at a time. According to the cohort model, how many phonemes of each of the following words would have to be processed before a hearer would be sure which word had been spoken?
   a) giraffe
   b) splat
   c) computerize

7. Write the garden path sentences in examples *9)* and *10)* of this chapter on separate index cards. Take a few other cards and write a normal sentence on each of them. Now, have some friends try to read aloud the sentences on the cards. Do they show evidence that the garden path sentences are more difficult to process?

8. What is a processing model? Try to describe the process of reading single words in terms of a processing model that contains specific modules.

9. In this chapter, parsing has been discussed in the context of sentence processing. The notion of parsing, however, can also be used to describe how morphologically complex words are parsed. Describe, in terms of parsing, how you think the following multimorphemic words would be processed.
   a) bookmark
   b) unredoable
   c) overbearing

10. Imagine yourself as a psycholinguist trying to devise experiments to investigate how people do language. What experiments would you make up to address the following questions? Be as specific as possible about how you would interpret the question and about what you would do to try to find an answer through psycholinguistic experiment.
    a) Are semantically abstract words easier to process than semantically concrete ones?
    b) Are simple clauses more difficult to understand than conjoined clauses?
    c) Do people read words from beginning to end?
    d) Do people with different degrees of education process language in fundamentally different ways?
    e) Does the way you parse a sentence depend on what language you speak?

CHAPTER

Thirteen   Gary Libben

Brain and language

The goal of neurology is to understand humanity

WILDER PENFIELD

In this chapter we will be concerned with the branch of neuroscience that has as its goal the understanding of how language is represented and processed in the brain. This field of study is called **neurolinguistics**. Although the study of the relationship between brain and language is still in its infancy, much has already been learned about which parts of the brain are involved in various aspects of language production and comprehension. The field of neurolinguistics has also done much to deepen the way we think about the nature of linguistic competence.

The chapter provides a brief survey of brain structure and the methods that are currently available to study the brain. This is followed by a discussion of the different types of language disturbance that result from brain damage and by a discussion of how phonology, morphology, syntax, and semantics may be represented in the brain. The chapter concludes by reviewing the current answers to the important neurolinguistic question: Where is language?

1   The human brain

Contained within your skull is about 1400 grams of pinkish-white matter. It may be the most complex 1400 grams in the galaxy. For most of human history, however, the role of the brain as the centre of mental life remained completely unknown. Even the Greek philosopher Aristotle believed that its primary function was to cool the blood.

We now know much more about the structure and functioning of the brain. But in many ways we are still quite like Aristotle, finding it hard to believe that this wrinkled mass of nerve cells could be the stuff that dreams, fears, and knowledge are made of. Nevertheless, it is, and the task of brain science (or **neuroscience**) is to understand how the breadth and depth of human experience is coded in brain matter.

The brain is composed of nerve cells or **neurons** that are the basic information-processing units of the nervous system. The human brain contains about 10 billion neurons that are organized into networks of almost unimaginable complexity. This complexity results from the fact that each neuron can be directly linked with up to 10 thousand other neurons. But the brain is not simply a mass of interconnected neurons. It is composed of structures that seem to play specific roles in the integrated functioning of the brain. The following sections provide a brief overview of these structures.

1.1   The cerebral cortex

The brain encompasses all the neurological structures above the spinal cord and appears to have evolved from the bottom up. The lower brain structures are shared by almost all animals. These structures are responsible for the maintenance of functions such as respiration, heart rate, and muscle coordination that are essential to the survival of all animals. As we move farther away from the spinal cord, however, we begin to find structures that have developed differently in different species. At the highest level of the brain, the **cerebral cortex**, the differences are most pronounced. Reptiles and amphibians have no cortex at all, and the progression from lower to higher mammals is marked by dramatic increases in the proportion of cortex to total amount of brain tissue. The human brain has the greatest proportion of cortex to brain mass of all animals.

In humans, the cortex is a grey wrinkled mass that sits like a cap over the rest of the brain. The wrinkled appearance results from the cortex being folded in upon itself. This folding allows a great amount of cortical matter to be compressed into the limited space provided by the human skull (in much the same way as the folding of a handkerchief allows it to fit into a jacket pocket). It has been estimated that up to 65 percent of the cortex is hidden within its folds.

It is the human cortex that accounts for our distinctness in the animal world and it is within the human cortex that the secrets of language representation and processing are to be found. The remainder of our discussion of brain structure, therefore, will focus on the features of the cerebral cortex.

1.2   The cerebral hemispheres

The most important orientation points in mapping the cortex are the folds on its surface. The folds of the cortex have two parts: **sulci** (pronounced /sʊlsaj/; singular: **sulcus**), which are areas where the cortex is folded in, and **gyri** (singular: **gyrus**), which are areas where the cortex is folded out toward the surface.

Figure 13.1 shows a human brain as seen from above, illustrating the many sulci and gyri of the cortex. A very prominent feature is the deep sulcus (in this case called a **fissure** because of its size) which extends from the front of the brain to the back. This fissure, which is known as the **longitudinal fissure**, separates the left and right **cerebral hemispheres**. In many ways, the cerebral hemispheres can be considered to be separate brains and indeed are often referred to as the left brain and the right brain. There are two main reasons for this.

First, the hemispheres are almost completely anatomically separate. The main connection between them is a bundle of nerve fibres known as the **corpus callosum**, whose primary function is to allow the two hemispheres to communicate with one another.

The other reason for considering the hemispheres to be separate brains is that they show considerable functional distinctness. In terms of muscle movement and sensation, each hemisphere is responsible for half the body—oddly enough, the opposite half. Thus the left hemisphere controls the right side of the body and the right hemisphere controls the left side of the body. These **contralateral** (contra = opposite, lateral = side) responsibilities of the cerebral hemispheres account for the fact that people who suffer damage to one hemi-

Figure 13.1 The cerebral hemispheres seen from above the head. Note the many fissures and gyri of the cortex and the prominence of the longitudinal fissure that separates the left and right hemispheres.

sphere of the brain (as a result of a stroke or accident) will exhibit paralysis on the opposite side of the body.

The hemispheres also show functional distinctness with respect to higher cognitive functions. In general, the left hemisphere seems to excel in analytic tasks such as arithmetic, whereas the right hemisphere excels in tasks that require an overall appreciation of complex patterns such as the recognition of familiar faces and melodies.

Despite the fact that the hemispheres show such specialization, we should be cautioned against sweeping generalizations about left brain versus right brain abilities or strategies. In all probability, complex mental activities involve the coordinated functioning of both hemispheres. The representation of language in the brain provides a useful example of this.

Most right-handed individuals have language represented in the left cerebral hemisphere and are therefore said to be left **lateralized** for language. But not every aspect of language is represented in the left hemisphere of right-handers. Adults who have had their left cerebral hemispheres surgically removed lose most, but not all, of their linguistic competence. They typically lose the ability to speak and process complex syntactic patterns but retain some language comprehension ability. Clearly, it must be the right hemisphere that is responsible for whatever language-processing ability remains (see figure 13.2).

It has also been reported that right-handed patients who suffer damage to the right cerebral hemisphere exhibit difficulty in understanding jokes and metaphors in everyday conversation. These patients are able to provide only a literal or concrete interpretation of figurative sentences such as *He was wearing a loud tie.* They frequently misunderstand people

Figure 13.2 The right hemisphere seen from the inside. In this picture the corpus callosum has been cut so that one hemisphere may be separated from the other. Note how the grey cortex caps the lower structures (the brain stem and cerebellum) which are whitish in colour.

because they cannot use loudness and intonation as cues to whether a speaker is angry, excited, or merely joking. Thus the right hemisphere has a distinct role to play in normal language use.

Finally, consideration of language representation in the brains of left-handers makes matters even more complex. Contrary to what might be expected, few left-handers have a mirror image representation for language (that is, language localization in the right hemisphere). Rather, they tend to show significant language representation in both hemispheres. Thus, left-handers are generally less lateralized for language.

To sum up, although the left and right hemispheres have different abilities and different responsibilities, complex skills such as language do not always fall neatly into one hemisphere or the other. Research into why this is the case constitutes an important part of neuroscience. This research promises to reveal much about the cerebral hemispheres and about the individual representations and processes that comprise language.

1.3   The lobes of the cortex

We have seen that the cerebral hemispheres make distinct contributions to the overall functioning of the brain. In addition, each hemisphere contains substructures that appear to have distinct responsibilities. The substructures of the cortex in each hemisphere are called **lobes**. Like the hemispheres, the lobes of the cortex can be located with reference to prominent fissures, sulci, and gyri, which are useful as orientation points in much the same way that rivers and mountain ranges are useful in finding particular locations on a map. As can be seen in figure 13.3, the **central sulcus** (also called the fissure of Rolando) extends from the top of the cortex to another groove known as the **lateral fissure** (also called the Sylvian fissure). These two features are important in the delineation of the cerebral lobes. The

Frontal lobe
Planning
Prediction
Speech
Discrete movements
of the body

Central
sulcus

Parietal lobe
Reading ability
Sensation of
–pain
–temperature
–touch
–pressure
–taste

Angular
gyrus

Lateral
fissure

Temporal lobe
Audition
Memory processing
Sensory integration

Occipital lobe
Visual processing

Figure 13.3 The left hemisphere seen from the outside

frontal lobe lies in front of the central sulcus and the **parietal lobe** lies behind it. The **temporal lobe** is the area beneath the lateral fissure. The fourth lobe, the **occipital lobe**, is not clearly marked by an infolding of the cortex, but can be identified as the area to the rear of the **angular gyrus** (which has been found to play an important role in reading).

Figure 13.3 shows the left hemisphere of the brain. It indicates the location of each lobe and its specialized functions. Assuming that this is the brain of a right-hander, it is also possible to identify those areas of the cortex that have a particular role to play in language processing, as we will see.

2 Investigating the brain

Imagine that you could open the top of a living human being's skull and observe the brain while the individual is engaged in activities such as reading, writing, watching a hockey game, or having a heated argument. What would you see? The answer is—nothing! To the outside observer, the working brain shows no evidence of its activity. This is clearly a problem for the field of neurolinguistics, which requires the use of special investigative techniques to uncover the secrets of where and how language is processed in the brain. In addition, these special techniques must meet the ethical requirements of research with human subjects. While other neuroscientists are able to do much of their research using animal subjects, this option is not available to neurolinguists.

Imposing as they may be, the problems of investigating the processing of language in the brain are not insurmountable. Recent decades have seen a number of technological advances that have greatly facilitated the investigation of the question: What is going on in the brain when people are engaged in language behaviour? In the following sections, we discuss some of the techniques of neurolinguistic investigation.

2.1   Autopsy studies

Until recently the only way to study the brain was through **autopsy studies**. This technique was most often carried out with patients who were admitted to hospitals displaying a neurological disorder. Careful observations were made of a patient's behaviour, and subsequent to his or her death, the brain was examined to determine which areas were damaged. By comparing the area of brain damage and the type of disorder the patient displayed while alive, neurologists could develop theories about the role of the damaged brain parts in normal brain functioning.

A famous example of this type of analysis comes from the work of Paul Broca, a nineteenth-century French neurologist. In 1860, Broca observed a patient who had been hospitalized for over twenty years in Paris. For most of his hospitalization, the patient was almost completely unable to speak, but appeared to understand everything that was said to him. Toward the end of his life (he died at age fifty-seven), he also developed a paralysis of the right arm and leg. Immediately after the patient's death (as a result of an unrelated infection), Broca examined the brain. It showed severe damage (called a **lesion**) in the lower rear area of the left frontal lobe. Broca concluded that because the patient was unable to speak, this part of the frontal lobe must normally be responsible for speech production. Since that time, many other autopsy studies have supported Broca's conclusions. This lower rear portion of the left frontal lobe is now called **Broca's area** (see figure 13.4 which shows this and

Figure 13.4 Language processes in the left hemisphere. Damage to Broca's area is usually associated with non-fluent speech and difficulty processing complex syntactic patterns. Damage to Wernicke's area (see section 3.2) is usually associated with comprehension disturbances. Damage to the area around the angular gyrus results in reading impairment

other language-processing areas of the left hemisphere). As will be discussed in section 3.1, the impairment of the ability to speak as a result of brain damage is called **Broca's aphasia**.

2.2   Images of the living brain

Autopsy analysis has been and continues to be an important tool in the understanding of the brain. But an autopsy can be carried out only after the patient's death. Therefore, whatever information it reveals about the nature and extent of the patient's brain damage can no longer be of any use in treatment of that patient.

Computerized Axial Tomography (also called **CT scanning**) is a relatively new technique which uses a narrow beam of X-rays to create brain images that take the form of a series of brain slices. CT scans have offered neuroscientists their first opportunity to look inside a living brain. However, like autopsy, CT scanning provides a static image of the brain. It is most useful in identifying brain lesions and tumors.

Recently a number of new techniques have emerged that also make it possible to study the brain in action. One such technique is **Positron Emission Tomography** (also called PET). The technique capitalizes on one of the brain's many interesting properties—it is extremely hungry for glucose and oxygen. Although the brain accounts for only about 2 percent of total body weight, it consumes about 20 percent of the oxygen the body uses while at rest. This oxygen is, of course, carried to the brain by the blood.

In the PET technique, positron-emitting isotopes, which function as radioactive tracers, are injected into the arteries in combination with glucose. The rate at which the radioactive glucose is used by specific regions of the brain is recorded while the subject is engaged in various sorts of cognitive activities. These recordings are used to produce maps of areas of high brain activity associated with particular cognitive functions. Examples of such PET maps are represented in figure 13.5.

Another dynamic brain imaging technique that has become increasingly important over the past few years is **functional magnetic resonance imaging** (fMRI). This technique yields information on areas of high brain activity during the performance of cognitive tasks but is somewhat less invasive than PET because it does not require the injection of radioactive compounds. The fMRI technique allows many measurements to be taken in a single testing session and offers a good measure of how brain activity changes during language comprehension and production. At present, however, the best fMRI machines employ high-field permanent magnets and require expensive installations not currently available at most research centres.

PET and fMRI studies have greatly increased our knowledge of where language processing takes place in the brain. It has been found, for example, that when subjects speak, much blood flows to the left hemisphere of the cortex and to Broca's area in particular. When subjects read, much blood flows to the occipital lobe (because it is responsible for visual processing), to the angular gyrus (which has a special role to play in reading), and to other areas of the left hemisphere. These observations support the view that the left hemisphere is primarily responsible for language and that there are specific language areas within the left hemisphere.

Finally, fMRI studies are playing an important role in increasing our understanding of the differences that might exist between language processing in a mother tongue and language processing in a second language. Second language processing has been shown to

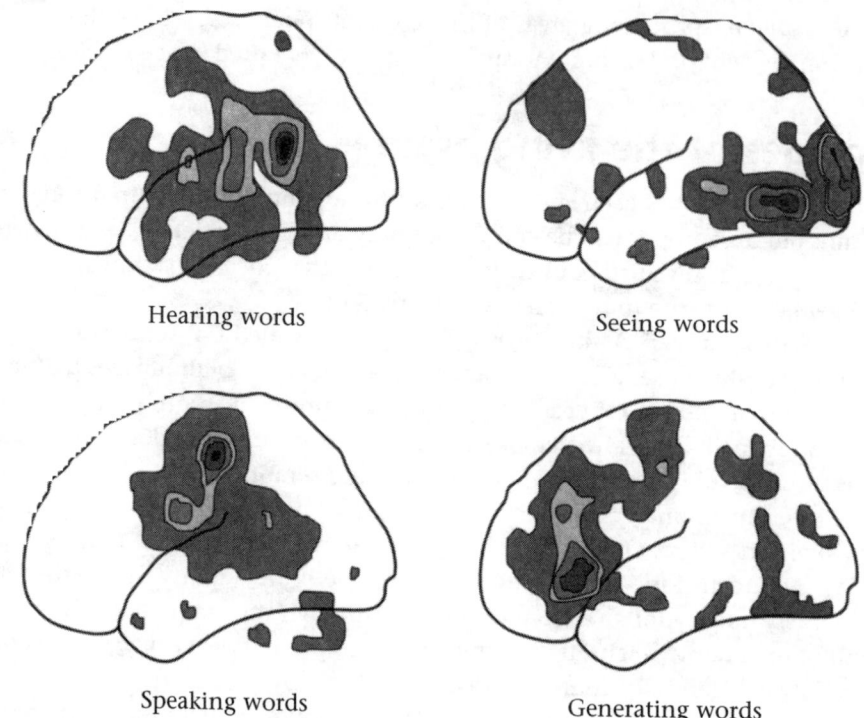

Hearing words

Seeing words

Speaking words

Generating words

Figure 13.5 PET scans show how blood flow to the brain shifts to different locations depending on which task is being performed.

involve a wider variety of cortical sites, which supports the view that the less automatic nature of language use in a second language requires the involvement of diverse mental processes in addition to those specifically dedicated to language.

2.3   Learning from hemispheric connections and disconnections

In the techniques that have been described, information about language representation in the brain is gained through an investigation of the brain itself. In this section, we review an alternate approach—one which examines behaviour that can be associated with a particular brain hemisphere.

Dichotic listening studies

Dichotic listening studies have been extremely important in the accumulation of the knowledge we possess about the specialization of the cerebral hemispheres. The technique capitalizes on the property of the brain that we have discussed in section 1.2—namely that each hemisphere is primarily wired to the opposite side of the body (including the head). So, most of the input to your right ear goes to the left hemisphere of your brain. Now, if the left cerebral hemisphere is indeed specialized for language processing in right-handers, these individuals should process language better through the right ear.

If you are right-handed, you will most probably be able to verify this by observing the difference between holding a telephone receiver to your right ear and holding it to your left ear during a conversation. When the receiver is held to the right ear, it will appear that the speech is louder and clearer. This phenomenon is known as the **right ear advantage (REA)**. In the laboratory technique, stereo earphones are used and different types of stimuli are presented to each ear. In general, the right ear shows an advantage for words, numbers, and Morse code, whereas the left ear shows an advantage for the perception of melodies and environmental sounds such as bird songs.

Split brain studies

If the left hemisphere is wired to the right ear, why is it possible to understand speech presented to the left ear? There are two reasons for this. The first is that the auditory pathways to the brain are not completely crossed—there are also secondary links between each hemisphere and the ear on the same side of the body. The second is that after the right hemisphere receives information from the left ear, that information can be transferred to the left hemisphere via the corpus callosum—the bundle of fibres that connects the two hemispheres.

Evidence concerning the crucial role that the corpus callosum plays in normal brain functioning is from the study of patients who have had this pathway surgically severed.[1] Studies that have investigated the effects of this surgery on cognition are referred to as **split brain experiments**. They have provided dramatic illustrations of what happens when the hemispheres cannot communicate with one another.

It appears from the behaviour of split brain patients that although the right hemisphere does show some language understanding, it is mute. In one of the many split brain experiments, a patient is blindfolded and an object (e.g., a key) is placed in one hand. When the key is held in the right hand, the patient can easily name it, because the right hand is connected to the left hemisphere which can compute speech output. However, when the key is placed in the left hand, the patient cannot say what it is. The right hemisphere, which receives information from the left hand, knows what is there, but it can neither put this into words nor transfer the information across the severed corpus callosum to the left brain.

Split brain experiments have presented new and important knowledge about the functioning of the brain. In terms of overall investigative methodology, however, they are not quite as exotic as they seem. In fact, the logic of split brain experiments is identical to the logic employed by Broca in 1860. In both cases the researcher endeavors to learn how the normal brain works by examining which functions are lost as a result of the brain damage. In the case of split brain studies, the damage is surgically induced. In the case of Broca's aphasia, disease caused an 'experiment in nature'. In the following section, we return to these experiments in nature and examine what they reveal about language representation in the brain.

3 Aphasia

Occasionally, humans suffer damage to particular parts of their brains. The most common cause of such brain damage is a **stroke** (also called a **cerebrovascular accident**). A language deficit caused by damage to the brain is called **aphasia**. The study of aphasia is by far the most important tool in the investigation of language in the brain. By observing and documenting the varieties of aphasic symptoms, neurolinguists have the best chance of identifying the major components of language in the brain.

In general, the amount and type of aphasic disturbance that a patient will exhibit depends on how much the brain is damaged and where it is damaged. There are many varieties of aphasia. In the following sections, we will describe some of the more important types.

C.S. Moss was a psychologist who became aphasic subsequent to a stroke. He later wrote a book about the experience entitled *Recovering with Aphasia*. The following is an excerpt from that book:

> *I recollect trying to read the headlines of the* Chicago Tribune *but they didn't make any sense to me at all. I didn't have any difficulty focusing; it was simply that the words, individually or in combination, didn't have meaning, and even more amazing, I was only a trifle bothered by that fact.*
>
> *The second week I ran into a colleague who happened to mention that it must be very frustrating for me to be aphasic since prior to that I had been so verbally facile. [I] later found myself wondering why it was not. I think part of the explanation was relatively simple. If I had lost the ability to converse with others, I had also lost the ability to engage in self-talk. In other words, I did not have the ability to think about the future—to worry, to anticipate or perceive it—at least not with words.*
>
> *It took a great deal of effort to keep an abstraction in mind. For example, in talking with the speech therapist I would begin to give a definition of an abstract concern, but as I held it in mind it would sort of fade, and chances were that I would end up giving a simplified version rather than the one at the original level of conception. It was as though giving an abstraction required so much of my added intelligence that halfway through the definition I would run out of energy available to me and regress to a more concrete answer.*

A consideration of Moss's recollections leads to some provocative questions about the relationship between language and thought. Is it possible that the ability to think about the future is dependent on language? Does language support abstract thought?

The type of aphasia that Moss reports involves a mixture of deficits—speaking, listening, reading, and writing. Some other forms of aphasia, however, are much more specific. In these more specific forms, particular skills are lost, and others remain intact. The study of the specific aphasias can tell us much about the building blocks of language in the brain. Sections 3.1 and 3.2 discuss the two most important specific aphasias.

3.1   Non-fluent aphasia

Non-fluent aphasia (also called **motor aphasia**) results from damage to parts of the brain in front of the central sulcus. Recall that an important part of the frontal lobe is concerned with motor activity and that the bottom rear portion of the frontal lobe (Broca's area) is responsible for the articulation of speech (see figure 13.4). Not surprisingly, therefore, non-fluent patients show slow effortful speech production (hence the term *non-fluent*). The most severe form of non-fluent aphasia is **global aphasia**. In this type of aphasia, the patient is completely mute. Of the less severe forms, **Broca's aphasia** is the most important.

The speech of Broca's aphasics is very halting. Patients have great difficulty in accurately producing the needed phonemes to say a word. For example, a patient who wishes to produce the sentence in *1a)* would be likely to produce the utterance in *1b)*.

1)
a. It's hard to eat with a spoon.
b. ... har eat ... wɪt ... pun

The ellipsis dots (...) between the words in *1b)* indicate periods of silence in the production of the utterance. Sentences produced at this slow rate tend to also lack normal sentence intonation. This is a common characteristic of the speech of Broca's aphasics and is called **dysprosody**. Note how the patient simplifies the consonant clusters in the words *hard* and *spoon* and changes the /θ/ to /t/ in the word *with*. The speech errors that result from these sorts of phonemic errors are called **phonemic paraphasias**.

It is tempting to think that the impairment of speech production in Broca's aphasia is caused by the fact that Broca's area is adjacent to the motor strip that controls movement of the facial muscles. The problem with this hypothesis is that damage to Broca's area usually produces only mild weakness of the muscles on the opposite side of the face and no permanent damage. Yet, for some reason, even people who can still control the muscles used in speech cannot use language properly after damage to Broca's area. This suggests that Broca's area has a language-specific responsibility.

Broca's aphasia as a syntactic disorder

Returning to the utterance in *1b)*, note that the patient also omits a number of words that would normally be used in this utterance. The words that are omitted are *it, is, to, a*—the sorts of words that we too would be likely to omit if we were writing a telegram (for example, *I will meet you in the airport lounge* → *Meet you in airport lounge*). These 'little words' are often called **function words** and their omission in the speech of Broca's aphasics has been referred to as **telegraphic speech**. (We will return to the problem of determining which items belong to the set of function words in section 5.)

One possible account of the speech of Broca's aphasics is that it results from an economy of effort. Speech production is very effortful for these patients so they use as few words as possible because, like telegram writers, they are 'paying' by the word. But there are other characteristics of their linguistic abilities that point to a deeper cause—the disturbance of syntactic competence.

In addition to omitting function words, Broca's aphasics tend to omit inflectional affixes such as *-ing*, *-ed*, and *-en* in words such as *running*, *chased*, and *broken*. They also show difficulty judging the grammaticality of sentences. For example, given sentences such as the ones in *2)*, Broca's aphasics will not always be able to determine which ones are grammatical and which ones are not.

2)
a. The boy ate it up.
b. *The boy ate up it.
c. *Boy ate it up.
d. The boy ate up the cake.

Finally, a close examination of the comprehension of Broca's aphasics offers further support to the view that there is a syntactic component to the disorder.

3)
a. The mouse was chased by the cat.
b. The dog was chased by the cat.
c. The cat was chased by the mouse.

Broca's aphasics tend to interpret sentences such as *3a)* correctly. In a sentence such as this, knowledge about the behaviour of cats and mice helps the patient to guess correctly at the meaning of the sentence. For sentences such as *3b)*, however, in which knowledge of the world is not a reliable guide to comprehension, patients are unsure about the meaning. Finally, Broca's aphasics tend to interpret a sentence such as *3c)* as though it had the same meaning as *3a)*. When we read a sentence like *3c)*, we recognize it as describing an unlikely event, but our interpretation is driven by the syntax of the sentence, not by our knowledge of the world. Many Broca's aphasics appear not to have this ability.

These sorts of observations have led many neurolinguists to reconsider the traditional view that Broca's aphasia is simply a production deficit. The possibility that Broca's aphasia also involves some central disturbance of syntactic competence is intriguing and may lead to a deeper understanding of how syntactic knowledge is represented in the brain. We will return to this question in section 4.

A final point about Broca's aphasia is of a less technical nature but is of great importance to the understanding of the syndrome as a whole. Unlike patients such as C.S. Moss, Broca's aphasics are acutely aware of their language deficit and are typically very frustrated by it. It is as though they have complete understanding of what they should say, but to their constant dismay, find themselves unable to say it. This plight of Broca's aphasics is consistent with our understanding of the role of the frontal lobe, which is usually the site of lesion in the syndrome. Broca's area of the frontal lobe plays an extremely important role in language; however, it does not seem to be involved in the semantic relationships between words and the relationship between units of language and units of thought. The neurological basis of these meaning relationships remains almost entirely unknown. From the analysis of non-fluent aphasia in general and Broca's aphasia in particular, however, we suspect that these semantic relationships are the responsibility of areas of the brain that lie behind the central sulcus—in the temporal and parietal lobes of the brain (see figure 13.3). This suspicion is supported by the type of language deficits associated with damage to the temporal-parietal lobes.

3.2   Fluent aphasia

The type of aphasia that results from damage to parts of the left cortex behind the central sulcus is referred to as **fluent aphasia** (or **sensory aphasia**). This type of aphasia stands in sharp contrast to non-fluent aphasia. Fluent aphasics have no difficulty producing language, but have a great deal of difficulty selecting, organizing, and monitoring their language production.

The most important type of fluent aphasia is called **Wernicke's aphasia**. The syndrome is named after the German physiologist Carl Wernicke, who, in 1874, published a now famous report of a kind of aphasia that was almost the complete opposite of Broca's aphasia. It was determined from autopsy data that this type of aphasia was associated with a lesion in the temporal lobe just below the most posterior (rear) portion of the lateral fissure. In severe cases, the lesion could also extend upward into the lower portion of the parietal lobe. This area of the brain is now known as Wernicke's area (see figure 13.4).

In contrast to Broca's aphasics, Wernicke's aphasics are generally unaware of their deficit. Their speech typically sounds very good: there are no long pauses; sentence intonation is normal; function words are used appropriately; word order is usually syntactically correct. The problem is that the patient rarely makes any sense. The following is a conversation between an examiner (E) and a Wernicke's patient (P).

4)
E: How are you today, Mrs. A?
P: Yes.
E: Have I ever tested you before?
P: No. I mean I haven't.
E: Can you tell me what your name is?
P: No, I don't I ... right I'm right now here.
E: What is your address?
P: I cud /kʌd/ if I can help these this like you know ... to make it.
   We are seeing for him. That is my father.

The patient in this conversation produces a number of errors. But note that most of these errors are different from the kinds of errors made by Broca's aphasics. While the patient is able to produce some well-formed structures (e.g., *no I don't*), these structures appear intermittently amidst various unrelated fragments. Not only are these constructions unrelated to each other, but they are also unrelated to the examiner's questions. It appears that the patient has no understanding of the questions being asked.

This patient displays a significant but not severe form of Wernicke's aphasia. Her speech appears to result from a semi-random selection of words and short phrases. In very severe cases of this syndrome, phonemes are also randomly selected and the result is speech that has the intonational characteristics of English but actually contains very few real words of the language. This is termed **jargonaphasia**.

The type of deficit found in Wernicke's aphasia leads us to a greater understanding of the role of the temporal-parietal area of the brain known as Wernicke's area and to a deeper consideration of the nature of language comprehension. Wernicke's aphasia is primarily a comprehension deficit. But as we have seen, when comprehension breaks down, most of what we call language ability breaks down with it. Patients cannot express themselves because they cannot understand what they have just said and use that understanding in the planning of what to say next. In a very real sense, these patients have lost contact with themselves (and therefore with the rest of the world). Wernicke's patients cannot have coherent trains of thought—the brain damage does not allow the elements of the train to be connected.[2]

In summary, our discussion of fluent and non-fluent aphasia has demonstrated how normal language use is a marriage of content and form. In the case of non-fluent aphasia, form is compromised but the content of language remains relatively intact. In contrast, fluent aphasia is characterized by a rapid flow of form with little content.

4 Acquired dyslexia and dysgraphia

Reading and writing skills involve a complex array of perceptual and motor skills. In this section we will consider impairments of reading and writing that are caused by damage to the brain. The impairment of reading ability is called **acquired dyslexia** (or **acquired alexia**). The impairment of writing ability is called **acquired dysgraphia** (or **acquired agraphia**). In both cases the term *acquired* indicates that the patient possessed normal reading and/or writing ability prior to brain damage and distinguishes the syndromes from developmental dyslexia and developmental dysgraphia, which deal with disturbances of reading and writing development in children.

4.1 Reading and writing disturbances in aphasia

Acquired dyslexia and dysgraphia typically accompany the aphasic syndromes that we considered in section 3. Most Broca's aphasics show writing disturbances that are comparable to their speaking deficits. In other words, a patient who cannot pronounce the word *spoon* will also not be able to write it correctly. The resulting error in writing (e.g., *poon*) is called a **paragraphia**. In spontaneous writing, Broca's aphasics also tend to omit function words and inflectional affixes. Finally, while the silent reading of Broca's aphasics is very good, their reading aloud shows the same telegraphic style as their spontaneous speech. These observations reinforce the view that the deficit in Broca's aphasia is much more than a speech articulation deficit. It is a production deficit at a very deep level of language planning.

Wernicke's aphasics also show reading and writing deficits that match their deficits in speaking and listening. The writing of Wernicke's aphasics is formally very good. They typically retain good spelling and handwriting. However, like their speaking, what they write makes little sense. Reading comprehension is also severely impaired in Wernicke's aphasia. Like C.S. Moss, patients can see the letters and words, but cannot make any sense of them. Again the conclusion to be drawn is that Wernicke's aphasia, like Broca's aphasia, involves a central disturbance of language competence—the knowledge that underlies language functioning. In such cases of central language disturbance, whatever impairment the patient has in listening and speaking will be matched in reading and writing.

4.2 Acquired dyslexia as the dominant language deficit

In addition to the reading and writing deficits that accompany aphasia, there are many cases in which the disruption of reading and writing ability is the dominant symptom. This typically follows damage in and around the angular gyrus of the parietal lobe. An analysis of these types of disabilities has led to some very interesting theories about the nature of reading (at least in English).

Before we proceed to discuss two contrasting types of acquired dyslexia, it might be worthwhile to reflect on the abilities involved in the reading of words. Up to this point in the chapter you have read over five thousand words. Some of these words (such as the function words) are very familiar to you and you probably recognized them as wholes. But others, such as *angular gyrus*, are words that you probably read for the first time. How then could you know how to pronounce them? Many theorists believe that readers maintain a set of spelling-to-sound rules that enables them to read new words aloud. These rules are important in the development of reading ability and in the addition of new words to our reading vocabulary.

Phonological dyslexia is a type of acquired dyslexia in which the patient seems to have lost the ability to use spelling-to-sound rules. Phonological dyslexics can only read words that they have seen before. Asked to read a word such as *blug* aloud, they either say nothing or produce a known word that is visually similar to the target (e.g., *blue* or *bug*).

Surface dyslexia is the opposite of phonological dyslexia. Surface dyslexics seem unable to recognize words as wholes. Instead they must process all words through a set of spelling-to-sound rules. This is shown by the kinds of errors they make. Surface dyslexics do not have difficulty reading words such as *bat* that are regularly spelled. They read irregularly spelled words such as *yacht*, however, by applying regular rules and thus producing /jɑtʃt/. The most interesting aspect of surface dyslexics' reading ability is that they understand what they produce, not what they see. For example, a surface dyslexic would be likely to read the word *worm* as /warm/ (and not /wərm/). When asked what the word means, the patient would answer: the opposite of *cold*.

Data from acquired dyslexia allow researchers to build models that specify the components of normal reading ability and their relationship to each other. Clearly, this type of analysis plays a very important role in the development of our understanding of language, the mind, and the brain.

5 Linguistic theory and aphasia

Looking at aphasia in terms of linguistic theory gives us a new perspective on language in the brain. Linguistic theory has been traditionally concerned with the structure of language, not with how it is used in the processes of listening, speaking, reading and writing. In contrast, the traditional way of looking at aphasia has been in terms of what the patient can and cannot do. The involvement of theoretical linguists in the study of aphasia has caused a minor revolution in the field. Aphasia researchers have begun to think about the deficit in terms of the loss of semantic features, phonological rules and perhaps syntactic tree structures. Theoretical linguists have also found that the study of aphasia offers an important area for testing theoretical distinctions such as the one between derivational suffixes and inflectional suffixes. In this section, we will look at some of the areas in which the marriage of theoretical linguistics and neurolinguistics has been most fruitful. This fruitfulness has usually meant an increase in the sophistication of the questions which are asked about aphasia. It has also meant the discovery of new and often bizarre aphasic phenomena.

5.1   Features, rules, and underlying forms

In the area of phonology, we have found that the phonemic paraphasias of Broca's aphasics usually differ from the target phoneme by only one distinctive feature (recall example *1*) in section 3.1): *with* → /wɪt/) and can therefore be easily described by phonological rules. Observations such as these lead us to believe that phonological features and rules might be good tools to characterize how language is represented and produced.

In the area of morphology, the study of aphasia has offered empirical support for the theoretical distinction between inflection and derivation. As we have discussed, Broca's aphasics show a sensitivity to this distinction in their omission of affixes in speech. Inflectional affixes are commonly dropped, but derivational affixes are usually retained. Perhaps most interesting is the tendency of some aphasics to produce underlying forms of morphemes in reading and repetition. Asked to repeat the word *illegal* for example, some aphasics will produce *inlegal*, using the underlying form of the negative prefix rather than the allomorph that should occur before a base beginning with /l/. Again, errors such as these point to the possibility that phonological processes such as nasal assimilation and the notion of underlying form are not only an elegant way to represent linguistic competence but are also relevant to the processing of language in the brain.

The study of aphasia also stands to shed light on the nature of semantic representations. Most of the work in this area has concentrated on the many subvarieties of acquired dyslexia. In a syndrome known as **deep dyslexia**, patients produce reading errors that are systematically related to the word that they are asked to read (in the sense that they share some semantic features but not others). Given the word *mother*, for example, a deep dyslexic is likely to read *father*.

The detailed study of semantic deficits associated with brain damage has also led to some very surprising discoveries. Most aphasics and dyslexics find abstract words much more difficult to process than concrete words. But there have been reports of concrete word dyslexia in which the patient shows exactly the opposite problem (having difficulty with concrete words such as *table)*. There has even been a report of a patient who shows a selective inability to read words that refer to fruits and vegetables.

5.2   Agrammatism

In section 3.1, we observed that many theorists now believe that Broca's aphasia involves a central syntactic deficit. The syndrome that is characterized by telegraphic speech has been given the name **agrammatism**—to indicate that grammatical ability has been lost. Agrammatism is the aphasic disturbance that has been most studied by linguists. As was discussed in section 3.1, it is characterized by the omission of function words such as *it, is, to,* and *a,* the omission of inflectional affixes, and by comprehension deficits in cases where the correct interpretation of a sentence is dependent on syntax alone.

In recent years, many linguists have become involved in the problems of characterizing the agrammatic deficit. These problems have raised both specific questions such as: What exactly is a function word? and general questions such as: Is it possible to lose syntax? The involvement of linguists has also generated cross-linguistic studies of agrammatism that provide interesting insights into the interaction between characteristics of the syndrome and characteristics of particular languages.

5.3   Function words

Intuitively, function words are grammatical words that can be distinguished from content words such as nouns, verbs, and adjectives. In terms of formal syntax, however, they are quite heterogeneous. They include pronouns, auxiliaries, determiners, and prepositions—

items that do not fall into any single syntactic category. Much of the recent work in this area by linguists has concentrated on working out what exactly the so-called function words have in common. Some researchers have suggested that they form a phonological group—they are all words that do not normally take stress. Others have pointed to the fact that function words do not normally take affixes and therefore form a morphological group. Still others have suggested that syntactic theory should be modified so that all the words that are lost in agrammatism fall under the heading functional category (this would involve changing the status of prepositions, which are currently treated as lexical categories—see chapter 5).

Whatever the outcome of this debate, it is clear that neurolinguistic evidence has presented a new set of challenges to the field of formal linguistics. One of these challenges is to build bridges between normal and pathological linguistic competence by finding units of analysis that are appropriate to both.

5.4 The loss of syntactic competence

Another, much more general, challenge is to define what it means to possess syntactic competence such that we can speak of its loss. This challenge has forced researchers to address the question: What is the essence of syntactic knowledge? Is it the hierarchical arrangement of elements? Is it the representation of abstract entities such as empty categories and traces?

Some researchers have suggested that agrammatism involves the loss of the ability to form hierarchical representations. They claim that agrammatics interpret sentences as strings of content words and assign thematic roles to nouns (as opposed to NPs) according to a default strategy that treats the first noun as the agent (for example). This strategy works reasonably well for simple sentences in which the first noun can be assigned the thematic role of agent and the second noun can be assigned the role of theme as in sentence *5a)*. It results in miscomprehension, however, for sentences such as *5b)* and *5c)*, where the first noun does not have the role of agent.

> **5)**
> *a.* The girl kissed the boy.
> *b.* The girl was kissed.
> *c.* It was the girl that the boy kissed.

Other researchers have argued that agrammatism does not involve the loss of syntactic competence, but rather an alteration of that competence. They have claimed that agrammatics have hierarchical syntactic structures but can no longer represent the traces that indicate an NP's position in deep structure. As a result, they are unable to recognize that the subject NP bears the theme role since they do not realize that it is the complement of the verb in deep structure (see section 3 of chapter 6).

5.5 Agrammatism in other languages

Data from other languages has suggested that the original characterization of agrammatism as a syndrome in which function words and inflectional affixes are lost may not reflect the true nature of the deficit but rather reflects the fact that the English language normally allows such deletions.

In English, affixes are typically attached to a base that is itself a free form. The past form of the verb *watch*, for example, is created by the addition of *-ed*; the third person singular is created by the addition of *-s*. However, not all languages work this way. In Semitic languages, such as Hebrew, the base is typically a string of three consonants, which is unpronounceable in its uninflected form. Inflections are produced by inserting vowels into this triconsonantal 'skeleton'. For example, the Hebrew root for the verb *to write* is /ktv/. The masculine third person present form of the verb is /kɔtɛv/ and the masculine third person past form is /katav/. If Hebrew agrammatics simply 'lose' inflectional affixes the way they do in English, they should not be able to produce any verbs. As it turns out, Hebrew agrammatics do produce verbs, but instead of dropping inflectional forms, they choose randomly among them. This sort of evidence has provided a convincing argument against the view that agrammatic language results from a simple economy of effort. Rather, it seems that it is a linguistic deficit that involves the mis-selection of linguistic forms. It is only in languages such as English, where the base is also a legal free form, that the agrammatism is characterized by affix omission.

6 Where is language?

In this chapter we have outlined some important findings that have greatly increased our understanding of the types of language disturbances that result from damage to the brain, as well as our understanding of the association between specific areas of the brain and particular language functions. We have seen that Broca's area plays a crucial role in the articulation of speech and in the ability to create syntactic representations. Wernicke's area plays a key role in language comprehension, and the area surrounding the angular gyrus plays a special role in reading.

On the other hand, we have seen that, in an important sense, normal language use involves the integrated functioning of the entire cortex. Even right-handers who are strongly left lateralized for language show some language deficit in cases of damage to the right hemisphere. Finally, virtually all forms of aphasia are accompanied by word-finding difficulties. This observation suggests that the storage and retrieval of word forms may be diffusely represented in the brain.

There is, therefore, no simple answer to the question: Where is language? Even if there were, the task of neurolinguistics would be far from done, for the truly important question concerning language in the brain is not Where is it? but What is it? Indeed, the answer to the first question may have little to do with the answer to the second question. Consider, by analogy, the goal of understanding the Canadian parliamentary system: to what extent does the knowledge that Parliament is to be found in Ottawa advance the understanding of how Parliament works?

Ultimately, the goal of neurolinguistics is to understand, in neurological terms, what language is. The field of neurolinguistics is still a long way from being able to specify how syntax is coded in brain matter, or even how a word is represented. Nevertheless, as our discussion of agrammatism has revealed, recent work by neurolinguists has resulted in important new perspectives on the nature of language competence.

Summing up

This chapter is concerned with how language is represented and processed in the human **brain**. **Dichotic listening** studies and **split brain** studies have shown that the **left hemisphere** of the brain carries most of the responsibility for language processing in right-handed individuals. Neuroscientists have also used **autopsy** studies, **computerized axial tomography**, **positron emission tomography**, and **functional magnetic resonance imaging**, to determine the relationship between particular areas of the left hemisphere and specific language functions. It has been found that **Broca's area** is primarily responsible for speech production, **Wernicke's area** is primarily responsible for language comprehension, and the area surrounding the **angular gyrus** plays an important role in reading. Most of our knowledge concerning language representation in the brain comes from the study of **aphasia**—language disturbance resulting from damage to the brain. Neurolinguists, trained in both linguistics and neuroscience, carefully examine the manner in which linguistic competence is affected by brain damage. Their goal is to increase our understanding of how linguistic knowledge is coded in brain matter and how this knowledge is used in the processes of language comprehension and production.

Notes

1 The callosumectomy is a rare surgical procedure used to treat severe forms of epilepsy. It prevents epileptic seizures from spreading to both hemispheres.
2 It is interesting to note that Wernicke patients have difficulty planning and executing many types of sequenced behaviour such as purchasing groceries, getting home by bus, or washing laundry.

Sources

David Caplan's 1996 book *Language: Structure, Processing and Disorders* (Cambridge, MA: MIT Press) offers a comprehensive overview of the breakdown of language in aphasia and its relation to normal processing. His 1987 book *Neurolinguistics and Linguistic Aphasiology: An Introduction* is an excellent introduction to the field and provides important historical background. A more practical approach to aphasia and its treatment is to be found in J. C. Rosenbek, L.L. Lapointe, and R.T. Wertz's book *Aphasia: A Clinical Approach* (Austin, TX: PRO-ED). The discussion of agrammatism was drawn from the rich literature that includes M.-L. Kean's edited volume *Agrammatism* (New York: Academic Press, 1985) and Yosef Grodzinsky's challenging proposals in *Theoretical Perspectives on Language Deficits* (Cambridge, MA: MIT Press, 1990). An alternative approach to Grodzinsky's is well represented by David Caplan and Nancy Hildebrandt's book, *Disorders of Syntactic Comprehension* (Cambridge, MA: MIT Press, 1988).

C.S. Moss's autobiographical account of his aphasic experience is to be found in *Recovery with Aphasia* (Urbana, IL: University of Illinois Press, 1972). Another book that offers an experiential perspective on aphasic disturbance is Howard Gardner's *The Shattered Mind* (New York: Knopf, 1975).

The material on acquired dyslexia is drawn from the volumes *Deep Dyslexia* and *Surface Dyslexia* (see Recommended Reading) as well as Y. Zotterman's book *Dyslexia: Neuronal, Cognitive, and Linguistic Aspects* (Oxford: Pergamon Press, 1982). Figure 13.5 is adapted from Gerald D. Fischbach's "Mind and Brain" in *Scientific American* (September, 1992).

Finally, an excellent overview of recent developments in the field of neurolinguistics as a whole is available in the *Handbook of Neurolinguistics*, edited by B. Stremmer and H. Whitaker (New York: Academic Press, 1998).

Recommended reading

Caplan, D. 1987. *Neurolinguistics and Linguistic Aphasiology.* New York: Cambridge University Press.

Caplan, D. 1993. *Language: Structure, Processing, and Disorders.* Cambridge, MA: MIT Press.

Coltheart, M., J. Patterson, and J.C. Marshall. (eds.). 1980. *Deep Dyslexia.* London: Routledge & Kegan Paul.

Patterson, K.E., J.C. Marshall, and M. Coltheart (eds.). 1986. *Surface Dyslexia.* Hillsdale, NJ: Lawrence Erlbaum.

Rosenbek, J.C., L.L. Lapointe, and R.T. Wertz. 1989. *Aphasia: A Clinical Approach.* Boston: College-Hill Press.

Segalowitz, S. 1983. *Two Sides of the Brain.* Englewood Cliffs, NJ: Prentice-Hall.

Questions

1. What distinguishes the human brain from a non-human brain?

2. In what ways can the cerebral hemispheres be considered to be two separate brains?

3. Below is an unlabelled diagram of the left hemisphere. Choose four contrasting colours and colour each lobe of the cortex. Use arrows to point to the central sulcus, the lateral fissure, and the angular gyrus. Finally, use a pencil to indicate areas of lesion that would result in Broca's aphasia, Wernicke's aphasia, and acquired dyslexia. Label these lesions.

Front

Back

4. What are the relative advantages and disadvantages of the various techniques used to investigate the brain? Consider ethics, cost, intrusiveness, and type of information yielded.

5. What do dichotic listening tests tell us about the specialization of the cerebral hemispheres? Can you think of types of stimuli that would be interesting to present dichotically?

6. Do you think it is possible to learn how the normal brain functions by studying brain-damaged patients? What can the study of aphasia tell us about normal language competence?

7. Contrast the differences in behaviour between fluent and non-fluent aphasics. What could explain these differences?

8. Describe the differences between phonological and surface dyslexia.

9. Re-read section 3. What do you think Moss's account tells us about the relationship between language and thought?

10. Many researchers have claimed that agrammatism involves a loss of syntactic knowledge. Imagine a type of aphasia that involves a loss of *phonological* knowledge. How would patients with this type of aphasia behave?

Fourteen

Marjory Meechan

Language in social contexts

The real linguistic fact is the full utterance within its context of situation.
BRONISLAW MALINOWSKI

Language is a tool for social interaction and it should not be surprising to learn that it can be affected by different social contexts. The study of language in social contexts, termed **sociolinguistics**, focuses on the relationship between linguistic behaviour and social situations, roles, and functions. Rather than concentrating on individuals, sociolinguistics is centred on the **speech community**; defined as any group of people who share some set of social conventions, or **sociolinguistic norms**, regarding language use.

Speech communities may be distinguished by differing sociolinguistic norms at almost any level of language. Distinctions may be limited to minor phonetic differences in pronunciation as when two groups have different **accents**, or when differences in grammatical structure may be evident. For example, in some parts of the eastern United States, the words *caught* and *cot* contain two different vowel phonemes while in Canada and most of the western United States, they are homophones. In other words, where the phoneme inventory of one community has two vowels, the other has only one. Differences in norms between communities may also show up as different preferences for particular morphemes or words or even different orderings of words. Where there is a systematic difference between varieties, the two varieties are generally considered to be different **dialects**.

There are cases where the degree of structural difference between dialects is so extensive that speakers from each community no longer have **mutual intelligibility**. In other words, they can no longer understand one another. Although it might seem that in these cases, the dialects should then be classified as different languages, their speakers may still consider themselves to speak the same language as, for example, when they all are citizens of the same country or members of the same ethnic group. In these cases, even radically distinct varieties may also be classified as dialects of the same language. This situation holds for many varieties of Chinese.

Of course, groups will vary widely as to the degree to which they differ and where it is not clear whether their speech involves an accentual, dialectal or even language difference, the term speech **variety** is used as a cover term merely to indicate that some set of sociolinguistic norms are present. It can refer to accentual differences, dialect differences or language differences. Essentially, a **dialect** shows systematic linguistic distinctions from some other variety of the same language and is spoken by a socially identifiable subgroup of some larger speech community. Dialects that are strongly associated with some social group are referred to as **sociolects**. An **ethnic dialect**, where the accent is associated with a particular ethnic group, is a type of sociolect. **Regional dialects** occur when the speakers are associated with a particular geographical area.

Sociolinguistic norms are not only important for distinguishing speech communities but may also be relevant to language behaviour within the community. There are two aspects of the social context that are important. On the one hand, differing sociolinguistic norms can serve to express a speaker's social identity or membership in the community. This can be referred to as the **sociolinguistics of society**. On the other hand, sociolinguistic norms can determine how language is structured depending on the social circumstances in which it is used. This can be referred to as the **sociolinguistics of language**.

1 Sociolinguistics of language

Conventions associated with social situations can have an influence on the structure of individual speech interactions. These can include anything from conventions for beginning a casual conversation to asking a question of a teacher in a formal classroom setting or even the conventions for writing a technical manual or a novel. Almost any interaction can be the focus of sociolinguistic study. No matter what sort of interaction is involved it is a representation of some type of **discourse**.

1.1   Discourse analysis

Analysis of the structure of discourse concentrates on how **utterances** are put together by speakers in individual interactions. Language in natural conversations is not always produced in complete sentences (*Do you want a cookie?*), so elliptical sentences (*Want a cookie?*) and even single words (*Cookie?*) can also be considered utterances. Both written and spoken discourse can be subjected to **discourse analysis** using one of various methods. Among these are analyses using speech act theory and the study of pragmatics, which have been described in previous chapters and will not be expanded on here. Other methods include **ethnography of communication, ethnomethodology**, and **text analysis**.

Ethnography of communication

The ethnography of communication method analyzes discourse using the same approach as anthropologists might use to study other cultural institutions like medical practices or religious practices. Discourse studied using this approach is called a **speech event** and appears within a **speech situation**, which is any circumstance that may involve the use of speech. Speech events are subject to cultural rules of usage that are determined by the speech situation.

Ethnography of communication analysis involves the identification of individual components of the speech event and how they are realized. Eight basic components relevant to every speech event have been identified using the mnemonic SPEAKING, as shown in table 14.1, which also includes a sample analysis of a local telephone call.

Table 14.1   SPEAKING mnemonic indicating components of a speech event

Component	Explanation	Sample analysis
Setting or locale	Specific information about when and where it occurred (place, time)	Calgary, Alberta at ten AM on May 3rd, 2001
Scene or situation	Generic information about the social occasion	Telephone call
Participants	Who was there (addressor/ addressee, performer/audience, questioner/answerer)	Caller – Mrs. J. Smith Receiver – Mrs. E. Jones, manager of *The Bay* department store
Ends Outcomes –	Purpose of the event (transfer of knowledge, exchange of goods)	Complaint
Goals –	Purpose of the participants (impart knowledge, minimize price)	Caller – to register a complaint Receiver – to appease the caller
Act sequences	Content and forms particular to its use	Content: complaint about a mal-functioning toaster Form: tirade
Key	Tone or mood	Angry, sarcastic
Instrumentalities	Type of discourse or channel (spoken, written, recitation, etc.)	Spoken over a telephone line (only speech communication cues)
	Types of speech (dialect, style)	Formal standard business English
Norms Interaction –	Conventions of the interaction	After the conventional greeting, the caller speaks first giving complaint, receiver says she is sorry and offers to refund the money, etc.
Interpretation –	Normal interpretation	Receiver recognizes that the caller is angry and must be appeased while the caller recognizes that the receiver is making an attempt to do so.
Genres	Category of event (poem, story, conversation)	Conversation

Comparisons of these components across speech events shows that, in order for speakers to function effectively in any speech situation, they must be aware of more than just the grammatical rules for language. They must also have access to all the rules of communication, or **communicative competence** (as discussed in chapter 11). For example, if the receiver in the example in table 14.1 had failed to answer the caller's complaint with an apology, the goal of the receiver would have been compromised. Conversely, if the receiver's goal had been to get rid of the caller in the most expeditious way, an apology might not have been indicated.

Instrumentalities can also be important for achieving specific outcomes and goals. For example, if the receiver wishes to appease the caller, it is important for her to show the caller that she views her with respect and takes her concerns seriously. To achieve this in North American society, she adopts a formal **style** or **register** during the conversation. Although these two terms are very similar in meaning and are often used interchangeably, they do differ. A speech style is defined in terms of formality of situation and its values range along a continuum from relatively informal to formal. A register is more often directly associated with a specific speech situation that may or may not also be associated with some specific degree of formality. In both cases, they are characterized by a range of phonological, lexical and syntactic properties. As example *1a)* shows, the register used in newspaper headlines tends to omit small function words such as the determiners *the* or *a* and the copula *be*. Ritualistic register, as in *1b)*, often includes archaic forms such as *ye* and *thou*. Recipes, as in *1c)*, also have a recognizable structure with frequent omission of both subject and object pronouns as well as omission of determiners. All these contrast with more formal registers, such as the technical writing in *1d)*.

1)

a. *Newspaper headlines*
T.O. psychics 'scared' after murder
Drink helps active dogs replace bodily fluids
Natives allegedly paid to protest in Manitoba

b. *Rituals*
With this ring, I thee wed.
Hear ye, hear ye, the court of Judge John Smith is now in session.

c. *Recipes*
DINO-GETTI ON TOAST:
INGREDIENTS:
2 slices bread (white or brown, must fit in toaster)
butter or margarine
1 can 16 oz dino-getti
INSTRUCTIONS:
Pour contents of dino-getti tin into medium size saucepan. Place on medium heat. Stir ever so gently, so as not to disfigure any of the dinosaur pasta shapes. Taste occasionally, and remove from heat when desired temperature is reached. While the dino-getti is being heated, carefully place bread in the toaster and press down on the handle. Bread will automatically pop up when done. At this time delicately spread a small amount of butter *one* side of the toast. Place toast on plate (butter side up), and gingerly pour dino-getti on top.

d. *Technical writing*
Developers used several different languages to generate project code.

Patients who recovered either through cognitive-behaviour therapy (CBT; N = 25) or through pharmacotherapy (PT; N = 29) completed self-reported ratings of dysfunctional attitudes before and after a negative mood induction procedure.

When a register is connected to a particular profession or activity, it may also be characterized by specific vocabulary items known as **jargon**. Jargon may involve specialized meanings for existing lexical items as in the specialized use of the word *language* to mean programming language in *1d*). There also may be new terms coined specifically for that register as in the psychological term *pharmacotherapy* for a treatment involving drugs. Jargon is interesting because although it is generally developed to facilitate communication within the group, it can also be used to indicate membership in the group. Jargon is not always viewed positively by all members of the community. For example, in the computer field, advanced developers will often dismiss jargon-filled sales and managerial reports with little real technical content as *technobabble*.

Slang, a common register found in a number of languages, is also a well-known vehicle for demarking group membership. The term *slang* refers to the use of faddish or nonstandard lexical items. Since slang is sensitive to current styles, it changes rapidly. Most slang terms like those in table 14.2 will either disappear from use within a generation or become standardized and therefore, no longer slang. Words like *dwindle, fan,* and *mob* were all once slang terms.

Table 14.2	Selected slang terms
Term	**Definition**
to beagle	to leave in a hurry without attracting attention
cherry	cool, hip, retro
full	expression of confirmation or agreement
hot	attractive
to jack	to stab or punch
kickass	very good
to scrape	to understand (in sixties slang, to dig)
skid	someone who drinks, smokes and/or talks grungy
stick	someone who lives in a rural area
welfare	bad, ugly

Slang is generally considered to be a low or vulgar form of the language and is most consistently associated with younger speakers. The form of any particular slang will differ according to the interests of the group that employs it. For example, high school students usually group themselves according to their interests and goals. Most high school communities include a popular group sometimes called Jocks (or also Preppies, Collegiates, or Soc's [sowʃəz]) and a rebellious group sometimes called Burnouts (or Hoods or Greasers). Anyone not falling into either group can be considered a Lame. Of course, some high schools are not necessarily limited to these three although, in some sense, they do tend to be universal.

For example, in one Calgary high school in the early 1980s, as many as seven groups could be identified (Jocks, Freaks or Heads, Punks or Rockers, Snobs, Preppies, Brown-noses or Homework Gang, and Nerds or Hosers). Some groups were more closely linked than others and shared some slang features. Freaks and Punks both used many terms for drugs. Jocks and Preppies employed a kind of California 'Valley Girl' speech (for example, extreme shifts in pitch or frequent use of *like*) in their slang. Special high school cliques can be formed on the basis of whatever brings the group together and in most cases, they will employ some slang. Slang is always an informal register and its use in a speech situation requiring a more formal register would be viewed negatively by other participants in the speech event.

Ethnography of communication can be an important tool for those who need to translate speech situations across cultures. For example, second language teachers want to educate students in both the grammatical and communicative rules of the language in question if the students are to function effectively in the second language society. Even where the participants are all native speakers of the same language, differences in communicative competence can lead to difficulties. English speakers with only one register or who lack the knowledge of where each register is appropriate would find it difficult to function in a wide variety of speech situations. Furthermore, the rules may change across cultures.

A great deal of international business is now carried out in English and yet, there is no guarantee that characteristics of the components of a speech event conducted in a Canadian setting will necessarily be the same as those occurring in other English-speaking regions such as Ghana, West Africa or England. For example, the standard response to *thank you* is *you're welcome* but in parts of the United States, a convenience store clerk may give the reply *uh huh*. In Barbados, in the West Indies, the response is frequently *alright*. A Canadian travelling in areas where other responses besides *you're welcome* are perfectly acceptable may get the erroneous impression that people in this place are rude and respond in kind. It is obvious that violating the often unspoken rules of communication can lead to errors in interpretation which can have embarrassing and even, costly, consequences.

Ethnomethodology

Ethnomethodology, also called **conversation analysis**, is another approach to the study of discourse interactions. By identifying different types of utterances and isolating recurring patterns for their distribution in large corpora of tape-recorded natural conversations, many rules for the organization of conversation have been discovered. One very common structure that has been identified is the **adjacency pair**. This is an ordered pair of adjacent utterances spoken by two different speakers. Once the first utterance is spoken, the second is then required. A few of the many adjacency pairs that have been identified are shown in *2)*.

2)
Summons – answer
Can I get some help here?
On my way.

Offer – refusal
Sales clerk: May I help you find something?
No thank you, I'm just looking.

Compliment – acceptance
Your hair looks lovely today.
Thank you. I just had it cut.

Conversation analysis also tries to identify discourse units within a conversation. For example, most conversations will include an **opening**, or a beginning section and these frequently include the 'greeting – response' adjacency pair as in example *3)*.

3)
How are you?
Fine, thank you.

How these are structured can determine if the conversation will proceed. It affects which participant will introduce the first topic of conversation and even if the conversation will proceed at all. For example, conventionally, speakers will respond by saying they are 'fine' even if they are not. Someone who responds with a detailed description of their health has taken control over the conversation. Another common part of conversations is a **closing** section that signals the end of the conversation.

Between the opening and closing, speakers participate in the conversation in turns. The study of **turn-taking** is a central interest in conversation analysis. Three basic rules for turn-taking have been isolated based on the observation that at the end of a turn, a speaker may either select the next speaker (for example, by asking him or her a question) or may not.

4)
a. If the next speaker in the conversation is selected, then only that person has either a 'right' or 'obligation' to speak.

b. If no particular speaker is selected, then any other participant in the conversation may 'self-select'.

c. If no other speaker opts to take a turn, then the original speaker may continue.

Conversation analyses have shown that there are cues in the discourse that tell speakers where potential transition points occur in conversation. Besides direct questions, transition points can also be identified by intonational cues and even pause durations. For example, in *5)*, the tag question, *don't you think* followed by a pause invites other participants to take a turn. If the discourse marker *but* occurs before another speaker takes a turn, the speaker shows that she is continuing the turn.

5)
He's a nice guy, don't you think, … but I don't think I'll go out with him.

Interestingly, cross-linguistic studies have shown that there are culture-specific conventions for turn-taking. For example, in some communities as is generally the case for standard North American varieties of English, turns generally do not overlap. In other communities, where speakers show a **high involvement style**, such as Eastern European Jews in New York, beginning a turn before the previous speaker is finished is not only acceptable but desired. In these cases, turns are not so much offered but rather, are taken using strategies such as finishing another's sentence or other **cooperative overlaps**. Failure to do so may give the initial speaker the impression that the other participants are not involved or interested in the conversation.

Even where overlaps are desired, there are culture-specific differences in the meaning of transition point cues. For example, the pause signalling a transition point in Cree discourse is far longer than that found in standard English. Someone using standard English pause lengths as cues for transition points in other communities would either fail to take their turn when obligated (as in New York conversation) or would be constantly interrupting other speakers' turns (as in Cree conversation). In both of these cases, the conversational flow would be disrupted.

Text analysis

The types of discourse analysis mentioned so far focus on the roles and obligations of speakers in conversation as controlled by aspects of their social and cultural environments. Text analysis, both written and oral, concentrates on the linguistic structure of discourse; both within and between utterances. These kinds of studies include analyses of pragmatics and speech act theory discussed in earlier chapters. A prominent sociolinguistic approach to text analysis uses variationist methodology. The variationist approach to discourse operates under the assumption that although a variety of structures may be used to fulfill any one discourse function, patterns in the variation found in natural conversational speech show that there is structure in discourse.

An important tool in variationist analysis is the sociolinguistic variable which, roughly speaking, is an alternative way of saying the same thing. For example, in *6)* the variable is a question, and to show that it is a variable it is enclosed in parentheses. This is a standard convention of variationist sociolinguistics. Any form put into parentheses is a variable.

6)
(Questions)
Wanna drive?
Do you want to drive?
You want to drive?

In the study of structure in discourse, any set of utterances with equivalent discourse functions can constitute a variable. To determine which utterances are functionally equivalent, utterances in specific types of discourse units, such as narratives or lists, are analyzed to isolate their function. For example, **narratives** are composed of several different clause types. **Abstract clauses**, which contain a general summary of the experience to be narrated, will sometimes appear at the beginning of the narrative. More often, **orientation clauses** will begin the narrative giving the background to the story such as who was involved as well as where and when it took place. **Complicating action clauses** describe the events of the story and each event generally appears in the order it took place. **Evaluation clauses** consist of comments regarding the events. Finally, the narrative may end with a **coda clause** that serves to shift the time of the narrative back into present time. Example *7)* shows a narrative analysis with most of these elements.

7)
Narrative example from southern Alberta English corpus (Cass 12, Spkr 011, 1.01.00)

a. Abstract	**Well**, there was one time
b. Orientation	when I was driving with my mom.
c. Orientation	I just— just got my learners,
d. Orientation	we're going to my— had a banquet— hockey banquet
e. Orientation	**and** it was snowing outside, everything
f. Complicating action	**and all of a sudden**, I just lost control of the car going down into a coulee.
g. Orientation	Car's slowly going over
h. Orientation	**and** I'm just turning it this way,
i. Complicating action	slammed on the brakes.
j. Orientation	There's my mom

k. Orientation	just looking,
l. Orientation	just praying, **eh**
m. Complicating action	**and** I w— I just— I missed the barricade by this much
n. Complicating action	**and then** I came to a complete stop in an in— into a— an approach.
o. Evaluation	It was close.
p. Complicating action	I sa— I got out of the car,
q. Complicating action	I said, "mom, you're driving now".
r. Evaluation	I think that was the closest thing
s. Evaluation	that I came to even experiencing anything
t. Evaluation	that would be— even be close to death.

This approach to discourse can be very valuable for examining the role of **discourse markers**. These are elements that bracket utterances and organize the sequence and relationship between events and participants in the discourse. In *7)*, there are numerous examples of discourse markers (shown in bold). For example, the word *well* in utterance *7a)*, *eh* in *7l)*, and *then* in *7n)* are all discourse markers and there are numerous other examples in this short narrative such as *just, and, all of a sudden,* etc. Speakers are not generally aware of discourse markers but they are important signals in discourse. For example, the discourse in *7)* was given in response to a question asking if the speaker had ever been in serious danger of death. Speakers will often use *well* to soften responses to questions. In *7a)*, the speaker's use of *well* may be expressing the feeling that while the experience was harrowing, there was never really any strong danger of death.

The study of discourse markers is closely connected to a central interest of many variationist analyses of discourse. One frequently noted function of discourse markers is to provide additional temporal organization or cohesion to clauses. The discourse marker *then* has been shown to signal some point of achievement in discourse. In *7)*, the speaker is describing the experience while the car was out of control and uses *then* to signal how it ended. This shows the importance of **cohesive devices** in discourse. For example, discourse markers like *well, then* and *and* link utterances in discourse and provide information about how they relate to one another. This gives coherence to the discourse. To see this, try removing the discourse markers from the example in *7)* and it is obvious that the flow of discourse is interrupted.

Cohesive devices are also important for tracking participants and events in discourse, as an examination of temporal and spatial **reference** clearly shows. For example, in *7)*, there is variation in the speaker's reference to the car. In *7e)*, it is referred to as *the car*, in *7g)*, the speaker just says *car*, in *7h)*, the car is designated by the pronoun *it* and in *7p)*, the speaker again refers to *the car*. Pragmatic and discourse analysis of this has revealed that speakers have conventions for reference in discourse. For example, the pronoun *it* is generally found after the full noun phrase *the car* in discourse. This is called **anaphoric** reference. In less frequent cases, a pronoun may precede the full noun phrase and is then called **cataphoric** reference. For example, in *7g)*, the speaker might have used the clause in *8)*.

8)
It's slowly going over, **the car**.

The function and structure of discourse marking is still not very well understood. For example, the study of *eh* in Canadian English has focused almost completely on its use as a questioning form although its use in example *7l)* is clearly not of this type. As this shows, one of the problems of studying discourse markers is the fact that they often perform multiple functions depending on the type of clause or adjacency pair where they are found and their position in the clause. For example, the use of *then* depends on the type of discourse, in what kind of clause it appears and its position in relation to the clause—initial or final. Quantitative variationist analysis takes these factors into account and avoids the dangers of ad hoc explanations as found in many anecdotal studies. It also recognizes the fact that choice of discourse markers can be a signal of group identity, which explains why a particular marker may occur less often and in a more restricted number of positions in the speech of one speaker as opposed to another. For example, the use of *eh* in New Zealand English is most frequent among Maori men and operates as a mark of Maori identity for these speakers. In fact, discourse markers are just one device that speakers may use to mark relationships of solidarity and power.

1.2   Solidarity and power

Language use can reflect not only the identity of a speaker but also relationships between speakers. For example, language behaviour can reflect differences in **power** between speakers in that some individuals have some degree of control over the behaviour of others. In addition, speakers can either show **solidarity** by using forms of language that emphasize some degree of closeness or intimacy, or register difference by avoiding them. Solidarity and power are frequently invoked as explanations for linguistic behaviour. Examination of politeness in language can illustrate how this occurs.

Politeness

Politeness can be expressed in many ways in language and is culture-specific. This is illustrated very clearly in ethnomethodology studies of the compliment-response adjacency pair. In North American culture, one polite response to a compliment is **self-praise avoidance** as in example *9)*.

> 9)
> *a.* What a nice dress!
> *b.* This old thing?

In other cultures, avoidance of self-praise may be considered rude. There may also be other responses unrelated to self-praise. For example, in some cultures, the response to *9a)* is to offer the item which was praised as a gift, as is the case in traditional Cree society and in some African societies.

Politeness is related to the notions of solidarity and power. Standards of politeness are determined by both the power relationship between speakers and the degree of solidarity between them. Speakers with a high degree of solidarity are most likely to observe the conventions of politeness as determined by relative differences of power between speakers since this emphasizes shared attitudes and values. Where these are used to express regard and consideration for other participants it can be considered **positive politeness**. Speakers wishing to show distance and/or lack of regard will employ these conventions to show rudeness or **negative politeness**. For example, a Cree speaker who overtly compliments someone on an expensive or otherwise valued item which they know the recipient would not like to give up, would be expressing negative politeness. Another example of this involves register choice in speaker interactions. If standards of politeness require a formal register and a speaker with control over both formal and informal registers chooses to be informal, he is using politeness conventions to deliberately be impolite. Notice that this is different from incorrect use or failure to use conventions due to ignorance or other reasons. In these cases, the speaker is not employing politeness conventions at all.

Another effect of politeness on language use is the avoidance of certain topics of conversation that are deemed by societal convention to be impolite. Words used to refer to these are frequently considered **taboo** by some or all members of the community. What is considered taboo is culture-specific. For example, in Western society, speakers will frequently avoid words relating to bodily functions. This results in the use of **euphemisms** as in *10)* where the top word is the most taboo and the bottom is the least.

10)
piss
pee
urinate

Euphemisms are also used when the common word for some item or activity has possible negative associations which the speaker wishes to avoid. For example, a spokesman for a Calgary company in the 1980s referred to a gas leak at their plant as an *operational anomaly* rather than an *accident*, presumably to avoid the notion that neglect or incompetence was involved. After a Stealth fighter crashed during the NATO bombing of Belgrade, U.S. military spokesmen suggested that at the time when the airplane went down, the pilot was *task saturated*. In fact, special care needed to be taken during operation of the aircraft due to its sophisticated and complicated engineering and the pilot was merely busy.

Perhaps a more obvious example of the role of politeness and avoidance strategies in discourse is found in the employment of different forms of address.

Forms of address

Address terms are the forms which speakers use to address and refer to each other. Some types of address in English are shown in table 14.3.

Table 14.3 Types of address terms in English	
Term	**Example**
First name (N)	Mary
Title + last name (TLN)	Mr. Jones
Title alone (T)	Nurse
Last name (LN)	Jones

Which form of address is chosen is heavily dependent on both the power and solidarity relationship between speakers as well as conventions for usage in each culture. For example, the use of a particular form indicates the degree of solidarity the speaker feels with the addressee (person spoken to). With a friend, speakers are more likely to be on a first name basis while more distant relationships involve the use of a title and last name. In the case of a friendship, speakers are likely to address each other reciprocally, each using the other's first name. In relationships where there is a perceived power distinction such as between age groups or work associates, addressing may be non-reciprocal. For example, students will usually refer to their teachers as Miss Smith or Professor Smith whereas the teacher will use the students' first names. In some cases, power and solidarity relationships between individuals can conflict for the use of address forms. For example, newlyweds will often have difficulty deciding what to call their in-laws. *Mother* may seem too familiar while the use of a first name might seem disrespectful. However, title and last name is too formal. It implies that the speaker is unwilling to form a close relationship. In this situation, the speaker may engage in what is called **no-naming**. They avoid naming their in-laws at all.

In English, it is possible to avoid directly naming someone because unlike other European languages, English has lost a formality distinction in the pronoun system. In languages where distinctions in pronouns still exist, no-naming is more difficult. For example, in most French communities the standard rule is that between speakers of roughly equal status, reciprocal pronouns are used. To express solidarity, as in relationships between family members and friends, the form *tu* is used. If the addressee is someone of roughly equal status with whom the speaker shares no feeling of solidarity, then the form *vous* is used. Where one speaker is in a position of power over another, pronouns are employed non-reciprocally with the more powerful participant addressed as *vous* and the less powerful as *tu*.

Studies of *tu/vous* usage patterns in Quebec French found that rural areas showed more usage of non-reciprocal *vous* within the family than urban areas. In other words, in rural families, elders were more likely to be addressed as *vous* and younger people as *tu*. It has been suggested that increased use of pronouns as solidarity markers rather than markers of power in urban areas may indicate that there is a de-emphasis of the power relationship in modern society. However, variationist studies comparing *tu/vous* use in Montreal over a period of thirteen years found that there was no clear evidence that *vous* was disappearing, indicating the continued use of *tu/vous* as markers of both power and solidarity.

Pronoun usage to express solidarity is not restricted to Indo-European languages. In Bislama, a creole spoken in the Republic of Vanuatu, there is a distinction between inclusive and exclusive first person pronouns like those found in Cree (as discussed in chapter 9) shown in table 14.4.

Table 14.4	Some pronoun contrasts in Bislama	
	Singular	**Plural**
1st (exclusive)	mi	mifala
1st (inclusive)	–	yumi
2nd	yu	yufala

In addition to marking addressee participation in the event described, these pronouns are also used as signals of solidarity between the speaker and addressee. Speakers of Bislama will use the inclusive forms like *yumi* in the presence of someone with whom they want to show solidarity, even if they were not actually a participant in the activity described, and an exclusive form like *mifala* to express distance.

In Javanese discourse, solidarity marking is not limited to address terms or pronoun choice but also involves sharp morphological and lexical differences across registers. Table

14.5 shows examples of high and low registers found in the most standard dialect. In fact, these do not exhaust all of the distinctions available to a speaker of Javanese for indicating differences of solidarity and power.

Table 14.5	Dialect of the Prijajis (Javanese)							
Level	*are*	*you*	*going*	*to eat*	*rice*	*and*	*cassava*	*now*
High	menapa	pandjenengan	badé	ḍahar	sekul	kalijan	kaspé	semanika
Low	apa	sampéjan	arep	neda	sega	lan	kaspé	saiki

As with address terms, speakers can either show reciprocal use of the low register (indicating strong solidarity and equivalent status) reciprocal use of higher registers (showing distance but equivalent status) or non-reciprocal use (where each speaker uses forms that reflect the status of the addressee). In other words, a lower status person would address a higher status person using the higher form and would be answered in the lower form.

Address forms are also a commonly noted source of distinction between the sexes in a number of societies. For example, in Japanese, there are differences in the pronoun systems of the speech of men and women as shown in table 14.6.

Table 14.6	Japanese non-formal personal pronouns	
	Men's speech	**Women's speech**
First person	boku	watasi
Second person	kimi	anata

Language and sex

In most societies, the language of men and women differs. Among the Gros Ventre tribe in Montana, women consistently pronounce some words differently than men. For example, the word for *bread* is pronounced /kjá tsa/ by the women and /dʒá tsa/ by the men. In Koasati, a Muskogean language found in Louisiana, verb forms differ depending on the sex of the speaker as shown in table 14.7.

Table 14.7	Gender-exclusive verb forms in Koasati	
Women	**Men**	**Gloss**
lakawwíl	lakawwís	'I am lifting it'
lakáwtʃ	lakáwtʃ	'You are lifting it'
lakáw	lakáws	'He is lifting it'
lakáwwilit	lakáwwilitʃ	'I lifted it'

Types of differences such as those found in Koasati and Japanese are considered **gender-exclusive** in that there are strong social prohibitions against using forms associated with the opposite sex.

Although most examples of gender-exclusive differentiation come from non-European languages, differences between sexes have also been noted in European languages. In most cases, these are exhibited as tendencies rather than categorical distinctions. For example, women in North American society tend to possess a wider variety of colour terms than men. Men, on the other hand, tend to have more terms relating to sports. Men and women may also differ in rates of usage of variable grammatical forms as discussed later in the chapter. This kind of differentiation is called **gender-variable** because it involves overall rates rather than absolute distinctions.

Despite the strong correlation between sex of the speaker and language differences, the wide variety of distinctions argues against a biological explanation. There is no genetic reason for men and women to be different in terms of how they use language. Clearly these differences are related to **gender roles** in these societies. There are two basic views for explaining the relationship between language and gender. One claims that these differences reflect the inherent differences between the sexes in society. On the other hand, these differences may indicate that language operates as a tool for one group to establish and maintain power over another group. This latter view is often held by feminists.

This is a classic point of contention in linguistics. Does language determine society or does society determine language? Some linguists have found that women are more likely to use **verbal hedges** such as *perhaps, you know, sort of,* etc. than are men. It has been suggested that this indicates unassertiveness of women as a result of their relatively powerless position in society. However, a study of the verbal hedge *you know,* which distinguished between its use as an expression of uncertainty as in example *11a)* where there is rising intonation (´) as well, as opposed to its use as a mark of confidence as in *11b)* with falling intonation (`), found that women are more likely to use *you know* to express confidence than are men.

11)
a. well it was all very embarrassing *you knów.*
b. and that way we'd get rid of exploitation of many by many all that stuff *you knòw* you've heard it before.

Thus, the existence of increased amounts of verbal hedges in women's speech is not necessarily proof that they are unassertive. Furthermore, other studies of gender-variable differences in language have found that upper-middle-class speakers tend to show the greatest differences across genders. Since upper-middle-class women are arguably the *most* powerful in society, power differential as an explanation for gender difference is probably an overly simplistic explanation.

Even so, it is undoubtedly the case that women, as a group, *do* occupy less powerful positions in most societies. For example, in Canada, women in full-time employment, on average, earn about $7,000 per year less than men and while 14 percent of men hold managerial positions, only 10 percent of women do. This difference between the sexes is reflected in both the way women's speech is described and in how men and women are referenced. In English, what is considered 'correct' can frequently be traced back to an androcentric bias on the part of grammarians in that characteristics of men's speech have been considered desirable and those of women are traditionally denigrated. A fourteenth-century grammar of English noted that the noun phrase in *12a)* which places the woman before the man should be considered less 'correct' than that in *12b)*.

12)
a. My mother and father
b. My father and mother

Difference in speech as it correlates with gender of the speaker is only one side of the coin. There are numerous examples in language relating to differences between how men and women are referred to.

Correlation of language behaviour with gender roles is also connected to another kind of gender in language, that of grammatical gender. In particular, the use of masculine gender as a generic or unmarked form shows a male bias. As mentioned in earlier chapters, many languages use a noun classification system that puts nouns into different classes which, in European languages, is called gender partly because nouns with female referents take one grammatical gender and those with male referents take another although as the Spanish data in *13)* shows, sex is not the only consideration.

13)

Feminine		*Masculine*	
la mujer	'the woman'	**el** hombre	'the man'
la casa	'the house'	**el** edificio	'the building'

English has lost most of its grammatical gender with only a few vestiges of the system remaining, particularly in the pronoun system. However, androcentric grammatical 'correctness' influences pronoun choice in situations where the sex of the referent is not specified. For instance *14a)*, which uses the masculine pronoun, is traditionally considered more correct by prescriptive grammarians than *b*, which uses a gender-neutral pronoun.

14)
a. Someone left a message but he forgot to leave his name.
b. Someone left a message but they forgot to leave their name.

Of course, not all gender distinction in language is the result of androcentric bias. Gender differences in many languages may have also arisen due to differences in what was considered taboo for each sex. The avoidance of taboo words by one sex and not the other may have led to differences in word choice. In any case, the study of gender differences in language can provide a revealing glimpse into the structure of any society.

Accommodation

Another important aspect of interpersonal relationships related to solidarity and power is that of linguistic **accommodation,** where speakers will modify their language patterns in interactions to make them more like those of the people with whom they are speaking. Speakers' language may **converge** syntactically, morphologically, and even phonologically during the course of the conversation. For example, a study comparing conversations between a travel assistant in Wales and several of her clients according to the social class of the client to whom she was speaking found that the assistant tended to use phonological characteristics such as /h/ deletion, *-in'* versus *-ing,* etc., more often when speaking to clients of lower socioeconomic classes whose speech is also characterized by these forms. In other words, her speech became more like that of the client with whom she was speaking.

Conversely, speakers may also make modifications that cause their language patterns to **diverge** or become more unlike each other. Studies in Catalonia (in Spain) and in Japan have found that some speakers, when addressed in their native language by foreigners, will often shift into the foreigner's language even though their speech may be perfectly understandable and even technically 'correct'. Accommodation theory suggests that speakers converge in order to show solidarity and diverge to show distance. This is important for analyzing style differences between speakers but may also be related to how they express their identity linguistically in relation to others in society.

2 Sociolinguistics of society

Sociolinguistics of society relates to the way language behaviour operates as a mark of a speaker's social identity. Since any individual speaker may at the same time have any number of identities related to her sex, age, ethnic background, or social class, the investigation of the sociolinguistics of society can be complex. A central issue is the notion of what sociolinguistic norms are guiding speakers with respect to their choices for linguistic behaviour.

2.1 Sociolinguistic norms

Numerous studies have found that patterns within individual social groups reflect perceived societal norms for the entire community. How subgroups pattern for mainstream norms may reflect their participation (or lack of it) in the society. Linguistic patterns across social groups form an **orderly heterogeneity** in that even though subgroups show varying degrees of use of particular variants, similar overall patterns of variability within each group reveal shared linguistic systems and social norms. Distinct behaviour can reveal both distinctions in linguistic systems as well as the ways language use can construct social barriers.

Standard varieties

Most speech communities feature more than one language variety. In a number of situations, prescriptive grammarians and other language purists may hold up one variety as the 'correct' or **standard** way of speaking. Language standardization is largely limited to international and colonial languages like English or French and classical languages such as Arabic. Despite the strong belief in the 'correctness' of the standard, it is an idealization created as a result of social and historical pressures associated with the growth of nation states and colonial empires.

The intangibility of the standard is most clearly shown by the fact that in both Canada and the United States, when linguists have come together to define standard American and Canadian English, the attempt has failed because of lack of agreement on how a standard variety arises and how it should be defined. This situation also holds with French in North America where the principal debate concerns the existence of a standard form of Quebec French that is distinct from standard European French. Is the standard merely the most frequent form, or that which most people consider most prestigious, or is it some collection of grammatical rules imposed on a community by 'experts'?

In fact, the standard variety, as defined by grammarians, does not really exist. Speakers in any community will adopt more or less of its features according to their social status, education, and the situation in which they find themselves and even in the written form, any sizeable stretch of discourse may violate someone's idea of correct or standard language since grammarians often disagree. For example, a survey of English professors found that there was quite a bit of disagreement about the acceptability of some commonly noted grammatical 'errors' as shown in table 14.8.

Table 14.8   Sample results: survey of English professors

	Frequency (%) (as estimated by the English professors)				Acceptability (%)		
	Rare	*Moderately frequent*	*Very frequent*	*Can't say*	*Yes*	*No*	*Can't say*
Everyone volunteered but they all failed to appear. (agreement error)	0	25	63	13	19	81	0
Jane Austen now feels that it is necessary to partially clarify Frank Churchill's relationship to Jane. (split infinitive)	0	16	74	10	17	72	11
Considering how little satisfaction she obtained from it, it was just a waste. (dangling participle)	12	47	35	6	35	59	6

A more reasonable way of thinking of the standard is to consider it to be that variety which has the most features that are conventionally believed in society to be prestigious. In fact, in popular use the standard variety is usually the one that is taught in the schools and its features are found more frequently in the speech of the upper classes, politicians, and the news media. In this sense, there are a number of ways of establishing what features characterize the standard of any given speech community since these may vary.

Language attitudes

One way of determining which variety is looked on as more standard in any community is through attitude studies. For example, a study of **linguistic insecurity** in Winnipeg used a list of words with variable pronunciations in Canadian English to test the relationship between usage and speakers' intuitions of correctness or standard language. Table 14.9 shows a partial list of the items tested.

Participants were asked to listen to two possible pronunciations of each word and then to mark on a questionnaire which was the one they usually used and if they thought their pronunciation was correct. The study found that common usage was not always a good indicator of standard language since, although forms associated with American usage were more often reported as being used in Winnipeg as well, pronunciations considered to be those of British English were considered more 'correct'. Interestingly, they also found that lower-middle-class speakers were most likely to show high linguistic insecurity in that they most often judged their own responses to be 'incorrect'.

Table 14.9   Items on the Canadian index of linguistic insecurity test

Token	Form 1	Form 2	Token	Form 1	Form 2
new	[nu]	[nju]	avenue	[ævənju]	[ævənu]
lever	[livɚ]	[lɛvɚ]	leisure	[lɛʒɚ]	[liʒɚ]
student	[stjuːdənt]	[stuːdənt]	either	[ajðɚ]	[iðɚ]
apricot	[ejprəkɑt]	[æprəkɑt]	missile	[mɪsəl]	[mɪsajl]
schedule	[skɛdʒul]	[ʃɛdʄul]	film	[fɪlm]	[fɪləm]
genuine	[dʒɛnjuɪn]	[dʒɛnjuajn]	almond	[ɑlmənd]	[amənd]
butter	[bʌrɚ]	[buʈɚ]	progress	[prowgrɛs]	[prɑgrɛs]
arctic	[arktɪk]	[artɪk]	route	[rut]	[rʌwt]
lieutenant	[lɛftɛnənt]	[lutɛnənt]	whine	[wajn]	[ʍajn]

Another method for determining speakers' attitudes to particular varieties and languages is the **matched guise test**. In this test, participants are asked to listen to recordings of two speakers and then give the speakers ratings according to characteristics like intelligence, likeability and social class. In reality, the participants are listening to the same speaker speaking two different varieties. Studies in Britain found that, as expected, the variety taught in school, 'received pronunciation' (RP), was ranked as most standard. The RP-accented speaker was felt to have had more characteristics associated with success such as intelligence, height, and high socioeconomic status. Matched guise tests have been used extensively since the early sixties to investigate attitudes towards French and English in Quebec. Early studies found that both anglophone and francophone Canadians ranked speakers more positively when they were speaking English.

Another type of attitude test that originated in the Netherlands and Japan but is also used in both the United States and Canada asks participants to rate the accents of different geographical areas according to perceptual categories such as 'pleasantness', 'correctness', and 'similarity' to the participants' own speech. In the United States, residents of Michigan rated their own speech highest with respect to values connected to 'correctness' but ranked the speech of Southerners higher for categories connected to 'pleasantness'.

A similar study in Canada also revealed interesting results especially since, unlike the situation in the United States, in most provinces of Canada the same dialect is spoken with the exception of Newfoundland and the Maritimes. Not surprisingly, a study of the attitudes of Albertans and Ontarians found that both groups considered speakers from Newfoundland to be less similar, less correct, and less pleasant than all other provinces except Quebec. Both groups also agreed that speakers in British Columbia have the most 'correct' English. However, it is clear that Canadians make far fewer distinctions on this basis than have been found in the United States. Many of the respondents (about 22 percent) could make no distinction between provinces as to dialect characteristics.

Non-standard varieties

The existence of standard forms of a language implies that all other forms are somehow not standard or even *substandard*. However, this is not the case. There are many forms that are proscribed by grammarians but are commonly used throughout the community without stigma. An excellent example is the use of the pronoun *they* discussed in the section on language and gender to refer to referents that are unspecified for gender. Widely used forms that carry no negative connotations are not necessarily **non-standard**. The use of the term *non-standard* merely indicates that the form lacks positive prestige in the community. However, in no way does it mean that the forms are somehow defective.

Prescriptivists often claim that non-standard forms show an inherent illogic or lack of systematicity. The so-called double negative, seen in *15a)* is a prime example.

15)
a. She didn't see nobody.   *c.* She saw somebody.
b. She didn't see anybody.   *d.* She saw nobody.

From a prescriptivist point of view, where a sentence is marked for negation twice as in *15a)*, the *double negative* will give the sentence an affirmative meaning as in *15c)*. However, as everyone knows, this is patently false. Both *15a)* and *15b)* are universally recognized by even highly standard speakers as having the meaning in *15d)*. In fact, both negative sentences, standard and non-standard, show parallel grammatical marking. It is just the form which differs. In *15a)*, the pronoun is marked with *no-* and in *15b)*, it is marked with *any-*. In both cases, the negative pronoun differs from that found in an affirmative sentence such as *15c)*. Neither *15a)* nor *15b)* is any more or less logical than the other. Furthermore, while the double negative construction is considered non-standard in modern English, it is the standard form in many other languages, such as Spanish, as shown in *16a)*.

16)
Ella no   vio   nada.
She neg saw nothing
'She didn't see anything.'

In other words, non-standard varieties are not *grammatically* less valued, but since they generally represent the speech of a politically less powerful group, they may be *socially* less valued. However, it is possible that two relatively standard varieties can co-exist in one community.

Where two varieties are used in sharply distinguished situations or **domains of use** in a particular speech community, the relationship between varieties is known as **diglossia**. One variety is used in more formal situations or in the written form and is called the high variety while the other is used in less formal situations and is referred to as the low variety. Table 14.10 shows some uncontroversial cases of diglossia.

Table 14.10 Recognized situations of diglossia		
Country	**High**	**Low**
Switzerland	Standard German	Sweitzerdeutche
Haiti	French	Haitian creole
Greece	Katharévusa	Demotic Greek

In most communities, use of informal language features is restricted in formal situations. This differs from what is generally considered diglossia in that the differences in features between formal and informal registers indicates a clear difference in varieties. Furthermore, in situations of diglossia, each variety can be considered the standard or correct variety for its particular domain of use.

Official languages and language planning

The issue of standard and non-standard varieties is also connected to the notion of **official language**. An official language differs from a standard language in that it has been declared the language of a particular region or country as a result of legislation. Designation of an official language has implications for the political and economic power of ethnic groups and is often a reaction to a perceived increase in power of a minority group by the majority. Currently, about half of the U.S. have some sort of law giving English official status. In Canada, there are two designated official languages at the federal level—English and French. However, most individual provinces conduct official business in one or the other. Governments are not the only institutions concerned with language use. Use of particular languages can be dictated by the official policies of any organization; determining what policies are to be followed is called **language planning**.

Official language designation usually puts speakers of non-official languages at a disadvantage because their access to legal or other documents and their participation during official business may be restricted if they have a reduced ability in the official language. They may have less access to educational opportunities and hence, advancement in society. In the past, language planning has even resulted in speakers being **banned** from using their languages at all. This was the case in the earlier part of the twentieth century when native languages such as Cree or Blackfoot were banned at residential schools for native Canadians, with harsh punishments dealt out to offenders. In the 1950s, many large corporations operating in Quebec banned the use of French in the workplace even though most of their employees were native francophones. However, restricting language use is not the only possible outcome of language planning. For example, regulations can also be enacted to increase minority language rights such as access in the minority language to education as well as to official government processes like drivers' licence examinations.

Language planning is not restricted to multilingual situations. It also can have an effect on which variety of a language is deemed acceptable for official use. For example, in 1961, the *Office de la langue française* was formed in Quebec to regulate the use of Quebec French. Its goal was to establish and protect a standardized Quebec French from contamination by both non-standard varieties of French and English. The mission statement is shown in *17)*.

17)
L'office de la language française a été créé pour veiller à l'application de la Charte de la langue française. Dans les faits, il joue surtout le rôle de conseiller et offre à l'ensemble de la population et plus particulièrement aux entreprises de nombreux services visant la généralisation de l'usage du français ainsi que l'amélioration de sa qualité.

In essence, they give advice to Quebecers and others on the correct use of the language. As well, when new technologies or products are introduced into the society, they will decide on what the product is to be called in Quebec French and issue press releases advising the public of the new term. A similar watchdog on the French language also exists in France. Although there are no equivalent government regulators on the quality of the English language, recognized authorities on English such as the *Oxford English Dictionary* and numerous published grammars and style manuals serve a similar purpose.

Language planning can be a particularly hot issue in the field of education. There has been a great deal of debate over whether it is preferable to educate minority groups using their native languages, at least at the primary levels, or to force assimilation of the group by eliminating minority language education. This is the main issue surrounding the debate over the use of **ebonics**, or African American Vernacular English, as a tool for minority education in the Oakland, California, school system. Many people mistakenly believed that the Oakland school system was considering *teaching* students to speak ebonics rather than merely *recognizing* the variety and incorporating it into the teaching of standard English (among other topics). In other words, they were proposing an attempt to reduce the disadvantage of speaking a non-standard variety. A portion of the official statement of the Linguistic Society of America on the issue is shown in *18)*.

18)

There is evidence from Sweden, the US, and other countries that speakers of other varieties can be aided in their learning of the standard variety by pedagogical approaches which recognize the legitimacy of the other varieties of a language. From this perspective, the Oakland School Board's decision to recognize the vernacular of African American students in teaching them Standard English is linguistically and pedagogically sound.

Wherever non-standard or non-official languages exist side-by-side with a standard national language, this issue arises. For example, many African nations have adopted a colonial language such as English or French as their official language, partly because of access to international trade and partly because, in many of these countries, there are a number of ethnic languages and by choosing an international language, they avoid ethnic disputes. Despite the fact that most of their citizens are native speakers of an indigenous language, in many countries, most education takes place in the colonial language. This issue is also highly relevant to addressing possible education problems among native Canadians who may speak Cree, Blackfoot, or any one of a number of indigenous languages as their first language.

Identification and status of a language variety can affect what form of the language will be spoken in any one situation and if it will be considered as standard. What is considered prestigious for one community may not be so considered for another and speakers will vary their language depending on the situation and their need to express their social identity. In order to properly determine how language is structured as a function of these social considerations, special methodologies have been developed for the study of variation.

2.2   Methods of studying variation

One problem in determining the relationship between form, function, and social identity in language is that it is highly variable. The claim that language is variable is relatively uncontroversial. Any short discourse will reveal variability. For example, in *19)* there are five words ending in -*ing*. Two are pronounced [ɪŋ], two are pronounced [ən], and one is pronounced [in].

19)
Stocks and investments and stuff like that in math but no, they don't do noth*en'*. Like, I don't do anyth*ing*. We were talk*en'* about school and I don't do anyth*ing* that I've learned from school. Noth*een*. (Alberta English Corpus; Cass 26, Spkr 023, 22.08)

Where fields of linguistics differ is in how this variation is to be interpreted and even if it is to be interpreted at all. Most studies of the rules governing phonology, morphology and syntax attempt to factor out unexplained variation. The variationist approach to language is unique in that it takes as its starting point the tenet that language is **inherently variable**. Variation like this, where the appearance of different variants is regulated by one variable linguistic system, is a classic example of inherent variability.

As noted in the section on discourse, the central focus of interest to variationist analysis is the sociolinguistic variable. This is a set of forms or **variants** that can all be used to say the same thing. A phoneme, a morpheme, or a set of syntactic structures operating over some semantic or functional domain can each be considered a variable if at least some of their surface structures cannot be explained using **categorical**, or invariant, rules. By counting each possible variant of a variable and finding out what percentage occur in each possible conditioning environment, patterns in the variation can be discovered. For example, variationist analyses of the example in *19)* comparing the percentage of *-in'* versus *-ing* in casual registers to that found in formal registers in a number of communities have usually found that formality is a factor in determining which variant is used.

Data culled from speaker intuitions is prohibited in variationist study of the sociolinguistics of society because the researcher can never be sure what speaker intuitions about variable patterns represent. Some people have very strong attitudes about language. The *Letters to the Editor* column in the magazine *Organic Gardening* provides an excellent example. When the magazine hired a new editor who adopted a more casual style, a controversy began that ran for well over three years with many readers voicing strong objections as shown in *20)*.

20)
I suspect you view yourself as a breath of fresh air to this encrusted old publication. I view your insistence on fracturing the written English language as a blast of pollution. (January, 1992, p. 14)

Sociolinguistic studies have found that speakers who believe a particular form to be 'slang' or 'incorrect' will often deny using it even though subsequent examination of their recorded speech shows that they do. Thus, only corpora of natural conversational speech are acceptable for examining variation.

Since the rarity of some variant may merely reflect the rarity of the structure where it is most likely to occur, there is no infallible way, using conversational data, to determine when a form is completely prohibited. Instead, variation studies compare overall rates of occurrence and co-occurrence of variants to determine which linguistic or social contexts favour or disfavour any one form. To obtain this information, a quantitative analysis is required.

Indexing analysis

When a variable is continuous, one method of quantifying the variation is by assigning an index value to points along the continuum. Each **token** or instance of the variable uttered by the speaker is given a value based on how close to each point it comes. Fronting of /aw/, shown in *21)*, where the initial portion of the diphthong is sometimes pronounced using a more forward articulation than other times is an example of a continuous variable.

21)
There's a whole *new crowd* [aw] *out* [ɔw] there *now* [æəw].

Table 14.11 shows individual vowel values for /aw/ fronting used in indexing studies of Canadian English. Notice that the height of the diphthong is ignored and only the relative position along the front-back dimension is taken into account.

Table 14.11 Fronting index	
Value	**Phonetic form**
Ø	[ɑw], [ʌw], [ɒw], [ɔw]
1	[aw], [ɐw]
2	[æw], [ɛw]

To arrive at an individual score for each speaker, their scores are added and divided by the total number of vowels sampled. So, in *21)*, the first token, *crowd*, receives a score of 1. The second token gets Ø and the third has a score of 2. The overall index score for this utterance is shown in *22)*.

22)

$$\frac{1 + \varnothing + 2}{3} = 1$$

So, even though this utterance contains one fronted variant, the back rounded variant offsets this and gives the speaker a score of 1. A speaker who always fronts would receive an overall score of 2 and one who produces only back variants would receive a score of Ø. Of course, an actual analysis would involve far more tokens than three. Table 14.12 shows index scores for different age groups from a study of /aw/ fronting in Toronto and Vancouver which shows younger speakers to be more advanced than older.

Table 14.12 Index scores for /aw/ fronting by age group in Toronto and Vancouver in interview style		
Age group	**Toronto index**	**Vancouver index**
12	81	76
22	58	58
46+	24	32

This methodology is most valuable where the variation operates along a continuum to evaluate degree and direction of vowel movement. In other cases, however, where the variation involves a choice between discrete categories, such as syntactic structures as in active or passive sentences in *23a)* or where the opposition is between presence and absence as in *23b)*, where the final [t] of *past* may be deleted, indexing is not appropriate.

23)
  a. The cat bit the dog.
  The dog was bitten by the cat.

  b. The time is half past one.
  The time is half pasØ one.

In these situations, other types of analysis can be employed as discussed below.

Marginal analysis

The most straightforward type of analysis is reporting the overall percentages of occurrence for each variant in relevant linguistic and social contexts as shown in table 14.13 for /aw/ fronting in southern Alberta.

Table 14.13 Percentage of variants of /aw/ by age group in Lethbridge, Alberta			
Age group	% front	% mid	% back
18–25	22	41	37
30–42	16	41	43

In fact, this is probably the best way to determine rates and occurrences of variants by context. However, since this variation may be subject to so many possibly interconnected factors, more sophisticated statistical methodology serves as a valuable tool for determining (1) if distinctions are significant and (2) if cross-cutting factors are falsely inflating or obscuring variation. Variable rule analysis is ideal for this purpose.

Variable rule analysis

Variable rule analysis is an important and frequently employed tool in the study of variation. Using statistical procedures specifically adapted for linguistic data, it indicates not only the probability that one variant or another will occur in any context but also whether there is a statistically significant difference between those contexts. More importantly, we can also find out which of a number of (possibly conflicting) explanations is most likely in accounting for any variation. Thus, a variety of social factors and linguistic factors can be simultaneously taken into account. As an example, a variable rule analysis of /aw/ fronting in southern Alberta showed that at least seven different factors, both linguistic and social, played a role in determining whether or not a speaker would front. These included the height of the onset vowel, relative stress, sex, age, and style.

Principal components analysis

Principal components analysis is markedly different from other methods of studying variation in that, instead of correlating particular variants of individual variables with predefined categories, a number of variables are examined simultaneously to see if any groups of speakers share linguistic features. A **principal component** is a set of variables that gives the best fit for the data with respect to how test items group together. In the Puerto-Rican Spanish speech community in New York City, principal components analysis was used to determine if factors like gender assignment, widespread usage or phonological and/or morphological integration were all relevant in loan word assimilation. Studies of speech communities in Sydney, Australia, and St. John's, Newfoundland, have studied the grouping of speakers with respect to their use of designated variables. Thus, which features are important and the social divisions which they mark fall out from the data rather than any specified social category. This has the advantage of revealing social distinctions that might not have been isolated if only correlations were examined.

In St. John's, six variables were found to make up one principal component. These are shown in table 14.14.

Table 14.14 Phonological variables in Newfoundland English PC1

Variable	Word	Phonetic realization
/e/	bay	a. standard [ej]
		b. non-standard [e:]
/o/	boat	a. standard [ow]
		b. non-standard [o:]
/θ/	three	a. standard [θ]
		b. non-standard [t]
/l/ (postvocalic)	mole	a. standard dark [ɫ]
		b. Irish-like clear [l]
		c. vocalic [ɤ] (a high, back, unrounded, lax vowel)
/or/	bore	a. standard [ɔr]
		b. non-standard [ar]
/ð/	them	a. standard [ð]
		b. non-standard [d] or flap

The speakers with the highest rate of non-standard variants for the variables in this component were found to be the older men in the community. No other social factors were discovered. A second principal component included the variables in table 14.15.

Table 14.15 Phonological variables in Newfoundland English PC2

Variable	Word	Phonetic realization
/ɪŋ/	fishing	a. standard [ɪŋ]
		b. non-standard/casual [ɪn]
/ð/	them	a. standard [ð]
		b. non-standard [d] or flap
/θ/	three	a. standard [θ]
		b. non-standard [t]

In the second component, it was speakers with high rates of standard features who formed a cluster and these were predominantly women and speakers from higher socioeconomic classes. The differing groups of speakers isolated for each component shows the conflict between standard and local non-standard language varieties and the importance of social identity in accounting for variation.

2.3   Social influence on variation

Although almost any social characteristic that plays a role in the formation and maintenance of group identities could hypothetically be a factor in variation, there are six main types of social influence which have been studied extensively. These are: geographical or regional location, socioeconomic class, social network, gender, age, and ethnicity.

Regional variation

Perhaps the most well-known factor affecting variation is geographical location. Most early work in sociolinguistics was in the field of **dialectology**, which allowed historical linguists to track sound changes across space although it quickly expanded to the study of differences in other levels of grammar, particularly the lexicon.

Dialectology studies usually involve **atlas surveys** of large numbers of speakers over wide areas designed to establish the geographical range and distribution of dialect difference. They are called atlas surveys because ultimately the variation is charted on a map. There are a number of methods by which data is collected for an atlas survey. The predominant method is a personal interview conducted by a fieldworker. Based on available information regarding social practice and likely areas of distinction between regions, the fieldworker follows an interview schedule constructed to elicit terms and pronunciations considered of interest. The interview includes both casual conversation on preselected topics or specific language questions like those in *24)*.

24)
a. Do you pronounce *news* like *cues* or *coos*?
b. 'There is a chicken in the yard'. Please repeat this sentence substituting the phrase 'three chickens' for 'a chicken'.

Since the main goal of a regional dialect study is to speak to people from as many areas as possible, a limited number of speakers are interviewed in each area. In early studies, only one male life-long resident of the area was chosen. Unfortunately, this resulted in problems related to **representativeness** since it ignored or disregarded many social influences in the community. For example, it provided little data on the speech of women. More recent studies include at least one woman and one man from each area and other possible social influences are noted. For example, *The Phonological Atlas of North America*, a study currently underway at the University of Pennsylvania, samples two speakers from cities with populations under 1 000 000 and four from larger centres. Prior to the widespread use of tape recorders, data was hand-transcribed by trained fieldworkers. Now, all interviews are tape-recorded.

Direct interviews are not the only way that researchers can gather data. *The Phonological Atlas of North America* uses **telephone survey** methods for some data collection. In cases where the interview schedule does not require access to recordings of the speakers, other methods can be used. For example, the *Survey of Canadian English* undertaken in 1972 and the more recent project on dialect topography of the Golden Horseshoe area around Lake Ontario involved written questionnaires. This kind of survey is called a **postal survey** and although the lack of direct contact with each speaker is a drawback, it has the advantage of more easily reaching a larger number of people than is possible with face-to-face interviews. Some questions from the dialect topography survey are shown in *25)*.

25)

a. What do you call the upholstered piece of furniture that two or three people sit on in the living room?

b. Does *leisure* rhyme with *measure*, or with *seizure*?

c. At meals, people are sometimes given a cloth to wipe their fingers on. What do you call it?

d. At meals, people are sometimes given a paper to wipe their fingers on. What do you call it?

e. Supply the past tense of *dive* in the following sentence: Yesterday he _____ into the quarry.

f. Which do you say? *The little devil sneaked into the theatre. The little devil snuck into the theatre.*

Surveys done over the Internet may also be valuable in the future, but since Internet access is still somewhat limited to more affluent, educated people, **Internet surveys** do not reach the entire population. Thus, they are not widely used although they were included in the study of Utah English.

Once the data has been collected, it is reported in a document called a dialect atlas. This document summarizes the responses to each item of interest from the interviews and plots them on a map such as that shown in figure 14.1.

Maps show either that different communities share features or that they are distinguished by different features. The map in figure 14.1 shows that there are similarities in

Figure 14.1 Words for 'fishhook' [Standard French *hameçon*] in French dialects of Atlantic Canada and western France (Péronnet and Arsenault, 1990)

vocabulary between francophone fishing villages in Atlantic Canada and a dialect in western France. Similarities between areas indicate some relationship between speakers, either because one community migrated from another area or because the areas are in close contact due to connecting trade routes or other lines of communication.

In many cases, it is possible to find distinct boundaries between areas which are shown on maps in the form of lines called **isoglosses**. A single isogloss indicates one point of distinction between areas. Where several isoglosses occur in roughly the same area on the map, it is referred to as an **isogloss bundle**. The larger the isogloss bundle, the more likely a true systematic difference among areas exists and, in that case, there are usually two distinct regional dialects. Isogloss bundles are also interesting for historical reasons because they often reveal a great deal about changing patterns of movement and communication among communities. For example, a study of isogloss bundles in Louisiana found that earlier patterns corresponded to the river systems, consistent with the fact that most transportation in that area of North America was along the water whereas modern patterns correspond to road systems.

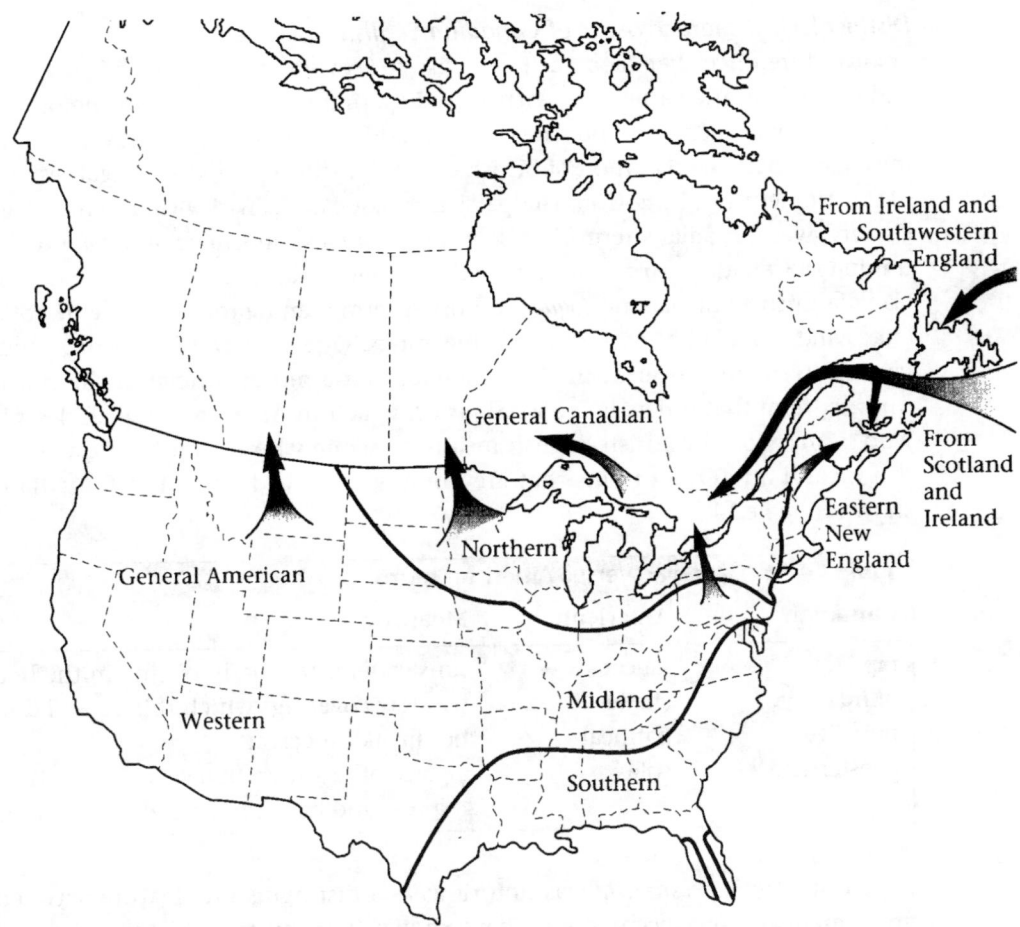

Figure 14.2 North American English: dialects and development

In fact, much of the existing dialect patterns in North America can be traced to routes of trade and immigration. Figure 14.2 shows the major dialect areas of North America and routes of immigration.

Canada's national languages

Canadian English

English Canada was founded by speakers of eighteenth-century North American English as a result of two great waves of migration from New England in the latter half of the 1700s. Many founding Canadians were North American in origin but retained an allegiance to Great Britain and this conflict in loyalties is still reflected in Canadian society and in the slightly British overtone of their language. Canadian English as a distinct dialect from general American English has been a much debated topic. Differences between Canadian and American English are subtle and have probably been exaggerated by those who wish to believe that Canadian English most resembles British English and therefore, is better. However, there are a few differences between Canadian and American English.

Distinct lexical characteristics of Canadian English

Lexical differences between varieties arise for several reasons. Words may become more widely used in one variety and either used sparingly or not at all in the other; new words may enter one variety and not the other; or both varieties may retain words but their meanings may differ. The retention of British cultural institutions like the legal system and system of government resulting from the persisting association with Britain and allegiance to the Crown gives Canadians terms like *solicitor, constable* and *Crown prosecutor*. Other terms are unique to Canada such as the term *riding* for electoral districts. Some terms originated in Canada, such as *canola* and *toque*. Still other terms can be found in use in both the United States and Canada but with different meanings. One such word is *sheriff*, which refers to a law enforcement officer in the United States but a minor official of the court in Canada. Another term that differs is the word *pissed*, which in American English describes someone who is angry but in British English means someone who is drunk. In Canadian English, it can mean both. Other terms that are notably more widespread in Canadian English are shown in table 14.16.

Table 14.16 Canadian versus American terms

Canadian	American	Meaning
tap	faucet	runs water into a basin or sink in the house
blinds	shades	window coverings which roll up and down
porridge	oatmeal	hot breakfast cereal
chesterfield	sofa	a piece of furniture that seats two or three people in a row and has upholstered arms and back

At one time, *chesterfield* was notorious as a distinguishing feature between Canadians and Americans, but recent studies have shown that this term is disappearing in Canadian English. Few young people use it anymore.

Other lexical differences between American and Canadian English are related to pronunciation. In the discussion of linguistic insecurity in section 2.1, a number of distinguishing pronunciations between Canada and the United States were presented. Interestingly, a postal survey studying the Americanization of Saskatchewan English found that while some lexical items (e.g., *lever, lieutenant*) showed an increased use by young rural Saskatchewanites of the variant associated with American usage, others (e.g., *either, route*) showed a reduction. In other words, in some cases, the American variant may have always been the local standard and both changes in use (either towards 'American' or 'Canadian' usage) are the result of movement toward a general Canadian norm.

Distinct phonological characteristics of Canadian English

Phonologically, Canadian and American English are remarkably the same. Only a few features distinguish American dialects from Canadian English. One major difference is the merger of the vowels in the words *caught* and *cot* discussed at the beginning of the chapter. However, since this merger has also been noted over vast areas of the western United States, it does not represent a clear isogloss between Canada and the United States.

Canadian English differs more sharply from American English for another phonological feature and this is the presence of a rule raising the diphthongs /aj/ and /aw/ before voiceless consonants, as shown in the minimal pairs in *26)*. This rule has long been considered a defining characteristic of Canadian English and is popularly known in linguistic circles as **Canadian Raising**.

26)

	Raised		Non-raised	
a.	bout	[bʌwt]	bowed	[bawd]
	lout	[lʌwt]	loud	[lawd]
b.	bite	[bʌjt]	bide	[bajd]
	light	[lʌjt]	lied	[lajd]

Interestingly, most Canadians do not realize that they are different in this respect and for the most part, are only aware of it because an American has commented on their pronunciation of *out* and *about*. Even then, Canadians often do not believe it because Americans hear and report the raised [ʌw] as [uː] and Canadians *do* know "we don't say *that!*" Raising of /aj/, on the other hand, goes unremarked for the most part, possibly because this phenomenom has also been observed in many parts of the United States and so it may not be as clearly a Canadian distinction. As for the raising of /aw/, although it also has been observed in some northerly parts of the United States, its rate of occurrence in Canada is generally far greater than any of these northern U.S. varieties.

Some studies have found that younger Canadian women seem to be using an increasing number of low variants before voiceless consonants, suggesting that Canadian English may be losing this distinctive feature under massive media and cultural influence from the United States. Studies in Victoria, Vancouver, Lethbridge, Toronto, Montreal, and Fredericton show that the fronting of /aw/ discussed earlier interacts with the Raising rule. Fronting is more likely in environments where Raising does not occur. However, despite the fact that fronting shows age distinctions clearly indicating a change in progress, evidence for the concomitant loss of the height distinction has been less conclusive. In most cases, men show no age distinction at all for Raising, and in southern Alberta, Canadian Raising is more prevalent among all younger speakers regardless of sex.

Distinct syntactic characteristics of Canadian English

Syntactically, Canadian English is virtually identical to standard American English. As with lexical items, the only real syntactic distinction is that some Canadian speakers use both the structures shown in *27)* whereas Americans would only use *27a)* and Britons would only use *27b)*.

27)
a. Do you have the time?
b. Have you the time?

The question of the presence and/or degree of American influence is frequently a consideration in studies of Canadian English. In particular, proximity to the Canada/U.S. border has been suggested as a factor determining the occurrence of particular lexical items in Canadian speech. American mass media such as television, films, and music may also have some influence on the way Canadians speak. Despite these claims, clear evidence that these exert any influence or even that Americanization of Canadian English is taking place has not been forthcoming.

Perhaps the most remarked-on characteristic of Canadian English is its uniformity from region to region. The study of /aw/ fronting shows that change is proceeding in almost exactly the same way in Toronto, Vancouver, and Victoria, a geographical range of over 3000 miles. However, there are dialect areas in Canada. For example, Maritime English has some differences from other areas, particularly in some lexical items, and phonologically, with a noted case being a fronted pronunciation of /a/ before [r]. The Ottawa Valley in Ontario is another noted dialect area as is the area around Lunenburg, Nova Scotia, with the former having many characteristics reminiscent of Hiberno-English (Irish English) and the latter reportedly affected by German English. However, these two areas may be losing their distinctive properties. Perhaps the most unique and robust dialect area is in Newfoundland.

Newfoundland English

The earliest English settlements in Canada were founded in Newfoundland by fishermen from the West Country of England who were later joined by Irish seamen. The fact that Newfoundland, unlike the rest of Canada, was not settled by speakers of North American English is reflected in their distinctive dialect. Relative isolation of both the Newfoundland area in general and isolated communities within Newfoundland makes for a unique dialect situation in North America. Newfoundlanders differ from other Canadians and from each other.

Phonological characteristics of Newfoundland English include all those noted in the section on principal components analysis. Other features include variable deletion of /h/ as in example *28a)* and /oj/ pronounced [ʌj] as in *28b)*.

28)
a. Put your 'at on the 'anger over 'ere.
b. Roy [rʌj] and Mary's two boys [bʌjz] left their toys [tʌjz] all over the place.

Lexically, Newfoundland English also differs from standard Canadian English. Table 14.17 shows both words unique to Newfoundland and words with unique meanings in Newfoundland.

Table 14.17	Lexical items specific to Newfoundland
drite	'dryness in the air'
dwall	'a short light sleep'
joog	'a drop (of liquid)'
package	'type of barrel for shipping dried fish'
hip	'to bump one's partner lightly with the hip (in a dance)'

Standard Canadian English and Newfoundland English also show syntactic and morphological differences as exemplified in *29)*.

29)

a. Use of *after* + gerund instead of *have* + past participle to express perfective aspect	*He's **after talking** to her twice already.*
b. 'me' as possession pronoun instead of 'my'	*I thought I put **me** tickets in **me** wallet.*
c. lack of plural marker on nouns following a plural number	*Six mile*
d. generalized use of 3rd person -*s*	*I thinks you better go home.*

Some of these such as the *after-* pattern can be traced to Irish English. Others are features of non-standard dialects of British English. Whatever the origin, studies of Newfoundland English show that these are all systematically employed in Newfoundland English and are not evidence of inferior language ability. The fact that they are considered non-standard is due to the social prestige of standard Canadian English in relation to Newfoundland English. Similar relationships between varieties can also be found in an examination of Canadian French.

Canadian French

Two early French settlements founded by Champlain in the early 1600s are the source of the two main varieties of Canadian French. Acadian French comes from what is now called Annapolis Royal, Nova Scotia, and Quebec French comes from Quebec City. These two communities were founded by people with very different origins. In Nova Scotia, the original settlers were largely agricultural workers from the Poitou, Aunis, and Saintonge area of western France. The Quebec settlers came from a wider variety of areas and backgrounds although most of the earliest arrivals came from Normandy and Île de France. These diverse backgrounds and origins are reflected in the differences between these two varieties.

Besides Acadian French, which influenced most of the French spoken in the Maritimes and Quebec French, there are several other varieties of French in Canada. There is a sizeable Franco-Ontarian population whose dialect is primarily based on that of Quebec, but that also may show influences from English since in Ontario there are very few communities where French is a majority language. In fact, the main property differentiating Franco-Ontarians from Franco-Quebecers is bilingualism. Further west, there are two main varieties of French. One variety was established by French fur traders at the beginning of the nineteenth century and is primarily spoken by Métis children of marriages between the traders and local indigenous women. The other variety is spoken by descendants of immigrants from both Quebec and France who established communities primarily in Manitoba and Saskatchewan, although there are also a few francophone areas in Alberta and British Columbia. For the most part, western French has not been extensively studied and most information on these varieties is anecdotal.

Quebec French

Quebec French differs from European French in much the same way as Canadian English differs from British English. While there are a few syntactic differences such as the construction shown in *30)*, which is not permitted in European French, most of the distinctions are either lexical or phonetic.

> 30)
> Avoir voulu, j'aurais pu finir plus vite.
> 'Had I wanted to, I could have finished faster.'

Phonetic distinctions

Table 14.18 shows some phonetic distinctions between Quebec French and European French.

Table 14.18 Characteristic features of Quebec French (QF) pronunciation as contrasted with those of European French (EF)

	EF	QF	Gloss
EF long vowels are often diphthongized in QF	[pɛːr]	[pɛjr]	'father'
EF nasalized vowels can be diphthongized in QF	[bãk]	[bãwk]	'bank'
EF short high vowels are lax in final closed syllables in QF	[vit]	[vɪt]	'quickly'
EF apical (dental) stops /t/ and /d/ are affricated before high front vowels or glides in QF	[ty]	[tˢy]	'you' (2 sg)
	[di]	[dᶻi]	'says'

Lexical distinctions

As in the case of Canadian English and British English, there are quite a few differences between the lexical inventories of Quebec French and European French. For example, Quebec French has retained some terms that are no longer used in France as shown in table 14.19.

Table 14.19 Comparison of Canadian French archaisms with European French

Canadian French	European French	Meaning
flambe	flamme	'flame'
acceptance	acceptation	'acceptance'
espérer	attendre	'wait for'
doutance	doute	'suspicion'

There are also several words which are found in both Canada and France but have come to have different meanings in each place. Some examples are shown in table 14.20.

Table 14.20 Comparison of Canadian French and European French meanings

Word	Canadian French	European French
traversier	ferry	crossing
poudrerie	blowing snow	powder
dépanneur	convenience store	repairman

As in English, Quebec French also has a number of neologisms resulting from contact with native languages such as *atoca/ataca* 'cranberry' and *ouaouaron* 'bullfrog'. Others appear to have arisen as **calques**, or translations, of words or phrases from other languages, particularly English. Some examples include *balle molle* 'softball', *papier de toilette* (QF) 'toilet paper' as opposed to *papier hygenique* (EF) and the colloquial use of *bienvenue* 'welcome' as a response to *merci* 'thank you' as well as the more standard European form *de rien*. There are also some English loan words that appear in Quebec French and not European French as shown in table 14.21.

Table 14.21 Canadian French borrowings from English

English loan word	European French form
bill	facture
gag (joke)	bon mot
beans	haricots
fan	ventilateur
gin	genièvre
pantry	armoire

Although the presence of English-origin calques and loan words may seem to indicate that Quebec French is more affected by contact with English than is European French, there are other cases where European French has an English loan word and Quebec French does not. For example, in Quebec the word for 'parking lot' is *stationnement*, while in France they use the English loan word *parking*. Furthermore, in both the Montreal and Ottawa-Hull French corpora, English loan words are a very small proportion of the total vocabulary (less than 1 percent). Therefore, while those who have concerns over the continued use of French in North America may worry about the loss of French *speakers* in Quebec, the language itself is still relatively 'uncorrupted' by English.

Acadian French

Acadian French also differs from Quebec French in a number of ways and like Maritime varieties of English, is considered non-standard in comparison to Quebec French. Some phonetic differences between Acadian French and Quebec French are shown in table 14.22.

There is also a lexically determined /h/ in Acadian French in words like *haut, homard* and *dehors* pronounced [ɥ] (a voiced glottal fricative), which does not appear in Quebec French.

As for grammatical distinctions, Acadian French differs from Quebec French in the retention of the third person plural suffix, which has disappeared from standard Quebec and

European French as shown in the examples in *31)*. In *31b)*, the suffix *-ent* is not pronounced while in *31c)*, the suffix *-ont* is pronounced as [ɔ̃].

	AF	QF	Gloss
Table 14.22 Characteristic features of Acadian French (AF) pronunciation as contrasted with those of Quebec French (QF)			
Long vowels are diphthongized only in open syllables	[pɛːr]	[pɛjr]	'father'
Apical (dental) stops /t/ and /d/ are not affricated before	[ty]	[tˢy]	'you' (2 sg)
high front vowels	[di]	[dᶻi]	'says'

31)
    a. Elle donne ([dʌn]) de l'argent à Robert. (Both Quebec and Acadian French)
       'She gives some money to Robert.'

    b. Ils donnent ([dʌn]) de l'argent à Robert. (Quebec French)

    c. Ils donnont ([dʌnɔ̃]) de l'argent à Robert. (Acadian French)
       'They give some money to Robert.'

With respect to lexical distinctions, as in English Canada, there are also a few regionalisms. In particular, Acadian French is often stigmatized by the claim that it contains more anglicisms than Quebec French. However, a study of borrowings in New Brunswick found roughly the same rate as had been found in studies of Quebec French. In general, the influence of English on French in Canada has been somewhat exaggerated.

This discussion shows that geographical area can be a factor in explaining patterns of variation. However, other factors within regional dialects can also play a role.

Social class

Patterning of variants according to socioeconomic class can give valuable clues to how language behaviour reflects social mobility. The theory rests on two basic findings; (1) the upper classes tend to use linguistic variants with higher **prestige**; and (2) speakers from the status group just below the highest class show the most linguistic insecurity. Studies of variation in New York City have shown that the second highest socioeconomic class often adopts even more variants with prestigious values than the highest class. This pattern is called **hyper-correction**.

However, just because a society can be grouped into classes on the basis of some objective socioeconomic criteria does not indicate that social class is necessarily the prime factor in determining the behaviour of individuals. Other societies may be organized according to different criteria even in Western culture. For example, Canadian voting patterns suggest that social class may have less significance for social behaviour in the general Canadian society than in the large metropolitan communities studied in the United States.

Another way to determine which are the standard variants in a community is with **linguistic market analysis**. Speakers can be ranked according to the degree to which they need the standard language for their work or hobbies and not necessarily according to their economic status. For example, two computer programmers could make the same salary but one might be required by her job to promote products at sales meetings whereas the other would not. The speakers' jobs may also not be the most important aspect of their linguistic life. Speakers may be very active in their community making public speeches before government committees or corporate sponsors. Studies of Montreal French have shown that linguistic market is not only a good predictor of linguistic behaviour, but also is closely tied to speakers' 'symbolic orientation' (i.e., individual preferences, social values, attitudes, etc.)— some of the very attributes that social class is purported to reflect. Speakers ranking higher for linguistic market are more likely to use standard variants particularly in more formal styles.

Of course, effects of social class may also be because people associate more with those in their own socioeconomic class. To examine possible effects of social association, a more direct approach uses social network analysis.

Social network

Individual social relationships can be examined as an explanation for patterns of variation by counting the ties between speakers according to relevant social network clusters such as family, neighbourhood, employment, religion, and friendships. This is called **social network analysis**.

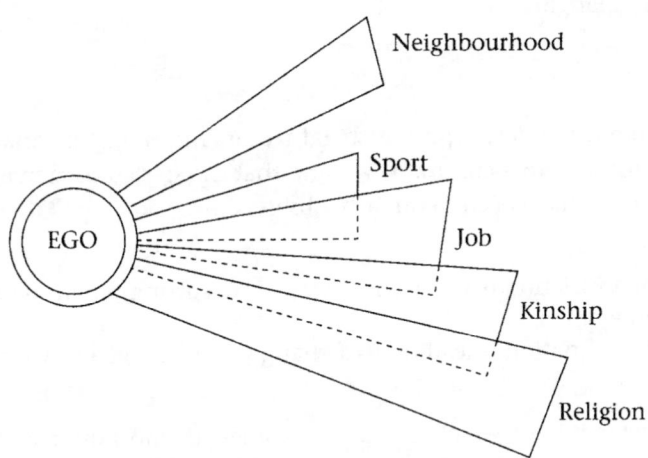

Figure 14.3 Social networks

The basic idea behind social network analysis is that people who talk to one another often are more likely to have the same speech patterns. Speakers are given individual network scores according to both the kinds of network ties they have and the **density** of the networks in which they are involved. Dense social networks are those where a large number of the speakers are interconnected. **Multiplex** networks are those where the relationships are formed on the basis of several clusters or kinds of relationships. In Northern Ireland, dense social networks act to enforce community norms so that speakers who are most closely integrated into the network show the highest rate of variants associated with it. Their relationships constrain their linguistic behaviour in much the same way as those in closely knit communities act to restrain other types of social behaviour such as moral values and work ethics. In a recent study of an Acadian-French community in New Brunswick, this was confirmed when it was found that speakers who held the weakest ties to the community were most closely associated with the introduction of external variants into the community.

The precise calculation of social network scores varies depending on the community since some types of network ties may be more important in one community than in another. For example, a study of a small Newfoundland fishing village found that ties related to traditional employment associations, such as fishing or shopkeeping were the most important for predicting language behaviour, whereas in Northern Ireland personal relationships and neighbourhood associations were the most important for maintaining local forms.

Age

Differences across age groups are another important social factor. When younger speakers use more new variants than older speakers, it may indicate the presence of natural changes in the language. However, age differences may have other explanations. In some cases, differences are merely the result of **age-grading**. Speakers may have different language behaviour depending on social situations associated with age. For example, as noted earlier, slang expressions are more closely associated with younger speakers. Furthermore, there may be differences associated with the aging process. Age also interacts with sex in cases where the language is changing.

Gender

One of the most widely reported social factors in linguistic variation is that of sex. Cross-linguistically and cross-culturally, we find that the speech of men and women tends to differ. Two tendencies have been frequently observed:

32)
  I. When variation is stable (no change is occurring), men use more non-standard forms than women.
  II. When variation is leading to a change in the language, women use more of the incoming forms than men.

In general, it has been observed that women are most often associated with greater use of variants that carry prestige, but agreement has not been reached as to the explanation for these tendencies. A number of theories have been suggested.

One possibility is that sex differences result from local network density. However, this is difficult to uphold since social groups always include members of both sexes. Even so, men and women will often form distinct social networks within social groups. As discussed earlier, linguistic differences related to sex may also be the result of power differentials in society associated with gender roles.

One extremely compelling explanation is associated with the observation that women tend to lead in situations where change is in progress. This is attributed to their role as child caregivers. Small children in the early stages of acquisition would be more likely to hear innovative forms produced by women than by men and thus the change is advanced *because it is transmitted to the younger generation*. Where men are in the lead, their limited contact with the next generation in their formative years limits the probability that their speech patterns will be passed on.

Ethnicity

In multicultural settings, ethnicity can be expressed linguistically either by the use of different languages or by means of phonological or other grammatical distinctions among varieties in the same language. The study of ethnicity is complicated because it is frequently entangled with a complex of social characteristics, any or all of which may influence variation. For example, proposing ethnicity as an explanation of African American Vernacular English (AAVE) as a distinct variety of American English has been confounded by the possible effects of geographical distribution and social class. A group's ancestral language or dialect may also have an effect on their variety. The speech of subordinate ethnic groups may feature speech markers due to direct influences from the substrate language or dialect. The study of ethnic variation in the English of Irish- and Italian-Americans in Boston, Cajuns in Louisiana, and Hispanic-Americans in other parts of the United States has confirmed this.

However, an appeal to linguistic origin has no account for why ethnic variation persists, or for that matter, why other potential transfer items do not. It has been suggested that the persistence of ethnic languages and dialects is related to their degree of **ethnolinguistic vitality**. Such factors as the number of speakers in a community, the degree to which the ethnic group and the language it speaks has institutional support from government, school, church, mass media, and culture, as well as pride in the community all may result in retention of ethnic varieties in a community.

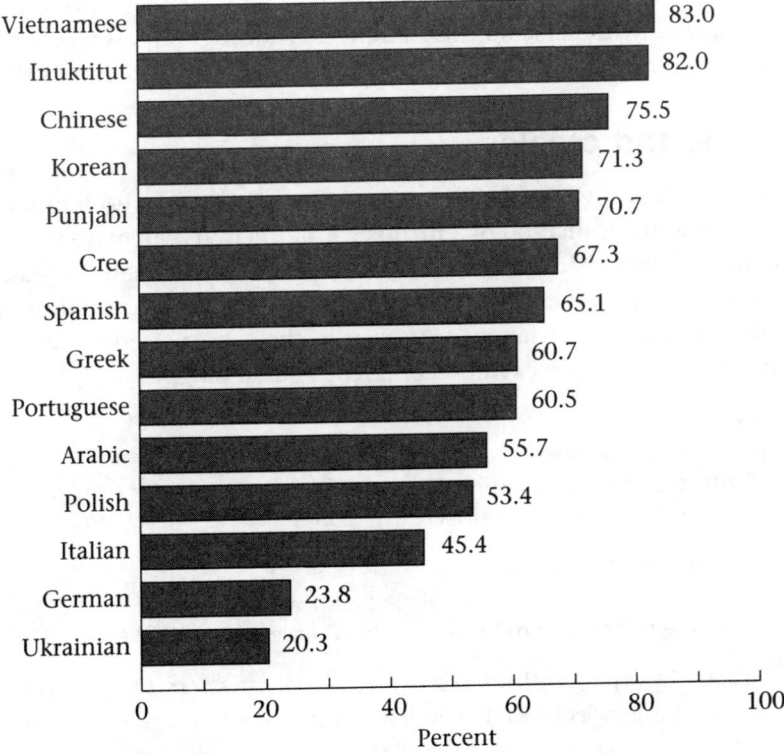

Figure 14.4 Language retention rates of some ethnic groups in Canada

In figure 14.4, we can compare groups that have only recently arrived in Canada like the Vietnamese to groups like the Germans, Italians, and Ukrainians who arrived in the early part of the 1900s. Naturally, the groups that are more established in the Canadian community are less likely to have retained their ethnic language. However, among the groups with a longer history of Canadian settlement, there are differences. Of particular note is that the Cree who undoubtedly predate all other ethnic groups in Canada are more likely to show native language retention than most other long-term European ethnic groups. Assuredly, assimilation of ethnic groups is not a foregone conclusion even when the group in question is strongly pressured to do so. Language retention brings up the question of variability, not only within varieties, but also variable use of different varieties.

2.4   Variable use of varieties

Lingua franca

Wherever there is social and commercial interaction between groups of people who speak different languages, we frequently find that speakers will maintain their own languages for interaction within the group and designate one semi-official language for the purpose of communicating between groups. A language used for this purpose is called a **lingua franca.** A lingua franca may be the native language of one of the interacting groups or it may be a 'neutral' language in that none of the groups speaks it natively. For example, in many colonized countries, where more than one language group exists, a European language, spread by traders and then adopted by local groups as a convention, may operate as the lingua franca. However, there are other ways for a lingua franca to arise.

Pidgins and creoles

Contact situations where speakers have restricted access to each other's language can sometimes lead to the formation of a **pidgin**, a rudimentary language with minimal grammatical rules and a small lexicon. By definition, a pidgin has no native speakers and many pidgins are predominantly used as a lingua franca. In fact, the term *lingua franca* comes from the name of a pidgin trade language spoken in the eastern Mediterranean in the Middle Ages. Example *33)* shows two examples of English-based pidgins.

> 33)
> a. *Neo-Melanesian*
>   mi stap lɔŋ bɪglajn, mi kətɪm kopra.
>   'I was in the work-group, cutting copra.'
>
> b. *Australian Pidgin English*
>   ðɪs púr nígər, ðé bín wə́rk əlɔ́ŋə kə́tɪm wʊ́d.
>   'These poor black men, they worked at cutting wood.'

Exactly how pidgins form is a controversial question. Pidgin languages are distinguished from other languages in that they have only a small number of grammatical categories and very little grammatical complexity. For example, pidgins generally do not have complement clauses, agreement marking, or tense marking. Temporal reference is frequently achieved by use of adverbs or aspect markers. Some have suggested that pidgins arise as a result of *foreigner talk* (discussed in chapter 11), which is also a simplified form of language. This suggestion, of course, assumes that native speakers of the **lexifier language**, or language from which the pidgin takes most of its words, who came into contact with speakers of other languages spoke to them using this reduced form of their language.

Pidgins tend to originate in two main social situations. One common situation where pidgins are found is in areas where there was a great deal of trade between groups of people who spoke different languages. Many known examples of pidgins were lexified by European or other internationally spoken languages as in the case of Australian Pidgin English, Russonorsk, Chinese Pidgin Portuguese, and Pidgin Arabic as a result of contact with traders. For example, Russonorsk arose in the early 1800s between Russian and Norwegian fishermen working on the Arctic coast of Norway. Apparently, both groups were under the impression that they were speaking the other's language partly due to the accidental fact that the word /pɔ/ 'in' had the same meaning in both base languages. As a result, Russonorsk had dual variants for many words, some lexified from Russian and some from Norwegian, as well as a few words of Dutch or English origin.

There are also several examples of pidgins formed from non-European languages as a result of trade as in Chinook Jargon, a trading language of North American natives in the Pacific northwest, and Sango, a pidgin form of Ngabandi, a language of west central Africa. Pidgins have also frequently been found in situations where people from a large number of language backgrounds come together as labourers, either as slaves or indentured workers, on large agricultural plantations.

Pidgins tend to be very short-lived for two reasons. They are generally held in great disdain by native speakers of the lexifier language, so it is socially advantageous for pidgin speakers to learn the standard form of the language when communicating with its speakers. Only in situations where the pidgin operates as a lingua franca between speech communities does it tend to endure for some time. In other cases, speakers of numerous languages have either come together in unified communities as a result of urbanization or they were forced into such communities as in the case of slave segregation. If their children then learn the pidgin as a first language and it is adopted as the native language of the new community, it becomes a **creole** and is no longer considered a pidgin.

When a pidgin becomes a creole, its inventory of lexical items and grammatical rules expands dramatically, usually in only one or two generations. Furthermore, creoles worldwide have remarkably similar grammatical characteristics. There are two basic theories for why this should occur. On the one hand, some people believe that creoles either (1) originated from a single, common proto-pidgin, with different lexical items taken from each individual lexifier language; or (2) are based on one or more of the native languages originally spoken by the founders of the community. The fact that creoles have many similarities simply reflects universal features of language and differences are accounted for by differences in the **substrate**, or base languages. This is called the **relexification hypothesis**.

Another prevailing theory is the **language bioprogram hypothesis** that claims that similarities among creoles reflect universal properties of an innate biological program found in the mental makeup of every human being that guides language acquisition. This theory has evolved and more recent versions of the bioprogram hypothesis are similar to the Universal Grammar (UG) hypothesis (see chapters 5 and 12). The bioprogram hypothesis is supported by studies of Tok Pisin, a recently formed creole in New Guinea, that have shown that there is a sharp difference in grammatical structure between the generation that speaks pidgin and the one that speaks the creole. According to the theory, since the first generation of children who acquired the creole must have done so on the basis of an impoverished input, any grammatical structure found in the newly formed creole must have come from their innate language program.

Both these theories have been criticized and the available evidence is not sufficient to decide unequivocally between the two. Critics of relexification note that there are too many differences across the possible substrate languages to account for the similarities in creoles. Furthermore, in slave populations, people who spoke a common language were often separated from each other to avoid rebellion, casting doubt on the possibility that one base language would have predominated. However, there have been studies of Pacific creoles that are consistent with the relexification hypothesis. The main problem in resolving the issue is that there are no current situations where both the resulting creole and the pidgin input can be observed, so even conclusions based on detailed quantitative comparative analysis are still subject to doubt. One difficulty is that creoles are not static in their development.

In most areas, creoles exist alongside a local version of the standard language which is termed the **acrolect**. As in most other non-standard language situations, the creole is highly variable and a number of stages or varieties of the creole can be identified. The variety that is least like the standard is called the **basilect**, while varieties intervening between the basilect and acrolect are termed **mesolects**. Therefore, grammatical features of some creoles may also have arisen from contact from the lexifier language.

In all the previous situations described, it is the speakers of each individual language who are in contact, so that while elements of two languages may combine in a resulting variety, there is no clear indication that any 'mixing' of languages is taking place. In the day-to-day use of bilinguals, two languages are used by a single speaker who may or may not combine languages in a number of ways.

Language mixture

In bilingual speech communities, speakers will often adopt a speech variety which involves alternation between languages in the same discourse. Where there is evidence that the grammatical systems of both languages are in operation during this alternation, this type of discourse, as shown in example *34)*, is referred to as **code-switching**.

34)
  a. *Acadian French-English*
     Pis, elle est toute seule, comme c'est (well, it is all alone as if it's) *in the middle of nowheres.*

  b. *Puerto Rican Spanish-English*
     Why make Carol *sentarse atras pa' que* (sit in the back so) everybody has to move *pa' que se salga* (for her to get out)?

c. Fongbe-French

mĕɖé	lé	nɔ́	ɖò	*gravement*	*blessés.*
someone	pl	hab	be	seriously	hurt

'Some are seriously hurt.'

Not all utterances that contain elements from two languages necessarily involve code-switching. In example *35)*, where a single word from one language is embedded in the syntax of another language, the speaker may merely be **borrowing** a word from one language (L1) into another (L2).

35)

a. J'ai ramassé une *bathtub,* pis j m'ai viré de bord avec la *bathtub.* (French-English)

b. Näitä kaks, kolme *bypassia* sillä on. (11a/399)

these-pl. two three   -pl. he-ad. is

'He has two, three bypasses.' (Finnish-English)

c. dartha f' l' *couloir* u yadi

put it (I) in the hallway and left (I) ...

'I put it in the hallway and I left' (2/2) (Arabic-French)

This is particularly true when the word in question shows phonological, morphological and syntactic properties of the L2 although borrowing does not always involve full integration on all these levels.

Another important question in the study of code-switching, besides that of distinguishing it from borrowing, is that of why speakers choose to do it. In some communities, the mere act of code-switching operates as a discourse mode and can signal solidarity between speakers in the same way as any other register of language. This is the case in the Puerto-Rican Spanish-English community in New York City and may also be true of French-English bilinguals in New Brunswick. Some researchers have suggested that code-switching may operate metaphorically to express solidarity with or distance from one community. When this occurs, it is called **metaphorical code-switching**.

When people switch from one code to another for clearly identifiable reasons, it is referred to as **situational code-switching**. For example, in some bilingual societies, one language may be more closely associated with government functions while the other is more closely associated with casual conversations. In this situation, a speaker may begin a conversation with an acquaintance at a government office in one language and when the conversation turns to more bureaucratic topics, the participants may switch to another language.

Studies of code-switching as a discourse mode have found that, contrary to popular belief, the ability to produce code-switching smoothly requires a great deal of language ability and counters any suggestion that code-switching is somehow degenerate and not *real* language, as derogatory terms like *Franglais* and *Spanglish* may imply.

Summing up

The study of **sociolinguistics** is concerned with language in its social context within the **speech community** involving both the **sociolinguistics of language** as well as the **sociolinguistics of society**. How language is used in discourse is affected by the **speech situation** and its components. Any given discourse can be analyzed and its overall structure identified. These structures can provide clues to the function of linguistic behaviour. Language is an important tool in the expression of **solidarity** and **power** between individuals. Sociolinguistic norms for language use can also give indications of how power is distributed in society in general.

The relationship between language and society is clearly shown by the existence of **standard** and **non-standard** language varieties. Whether or not a language or structure is considered standard is dependent on attitudes of speakers and not on any inherent notion of 'correctness'. In order to determine what features of each variety are affected by these attitudes, some form of variation analysis such as indexing, **variable** rule analysis, or **principal component analysis** can be used. Factors such as region, social class, social network, age, gender, and ethnicity may all have an effect on whether or not a form is considered non-standard. The designation of **official languages** and **language planning** are political ways for either reducing disadvantage for speakers of non-standard varieties or promoting varieties in the interest of increased power for speakers of standard varieties. Speakers can also vary between varieties for political reasons. A **lingua franca** can be used in societies where many languages are spoken to communicate between groups. Where communication is limited a **pidgin** or **creole** language may arise. In groups where speakers are multilingual, speakers may **code-switch** between languages for a number of reasons. At the very least, a language contact situation usually results in the **borrowing** of words between linguistic groups.

By confronting variation and studying its properties (both linguistic and social), over thirty years of research has confirmed that linguistic variation is not 'free' but rather shows complex, probabilistic patterns of social and linguistic conditioning that form a sociolinguistic structure reflecting the sociolinguistic competence and, in most cases, the social identity of speakers. Speakers will behave in a manner consistent with their own identity and according to the perceived identity of others.

Sources

The discussion of dialect and the terms *sociolinguistics of language* and *sociolinguistics of society* are adapted from R. Fasold, *The Sociolinguistics of Society* (Oxford: Blackwell, 1984) and R. Fasold, *Sociolinguistics of Language* (Oxford: Blackwell, 1990). The discussion of discourse analysis was informed by D. Schiffrin, *Approaches to Discourse* (Oxford: Blackwell, 1994). Examples of register were taken from R. Grable, J. Jernigan, C. Pogue, and D. Divis, "Metrics for Small Projects: Experiences at the SED" *Software* 16 (2): 21–29 (1999) and from Z. Segal, M. Gemar, and S. Williams, "Differential Cognitive Response to a Mood Challenge Following Successful Cognitive Therapy or Pharmacotherapy for Unipolar Depression," *Journal of Abnormal Psychology* 108 (1): 3–10 (1999).

The recipe for Dino-gettis on toast comes from *Time ... in the kitchen*, a cookbook compiled for the United Way by the 25th Anniversary Committee of Time Air; recipe contributed by Mike Exner, p. 117. Slang terms come from various Internet slang dictionaries.The study of slang in a Calgary high school is from J. P. Bowes, "Teenage Labelling: 'Are You a Jock or a Freak?'" *Calgary Working Papers in Linguistics* 9:7–16 (1983).

The discussion of solidarity and power is partly based on the discussion in J. Holmes, *An Introduction to Sociolinguistics* (New York: Longman, 1992) and in R. Brown and A. Gilman, "The Pronouns of Power and Solidarity," in *Style in Language*, edited by T. Sebeok (Cambridge, MA: MIT Press, 1960), pp. 253–76. Examples from Koasati come from M. Haas, "Men's and Women's Speech in Koasati" in *Language* 20:142–49 (1944). Examples from Bislama come from M. Meyerhoff, "Accommodating Your Data: The Use and Misuse of Accommodation Theory in Sociolinguistics" in *Language and Communication* 18:205–25 (1998). Examples from the Prijajis come from C. Geertz, "Linguistic Etiquette," in *Sociolinguistics,* edited by J.B. Pride and J. Holmes (New York: Penguin Books, 1972), pp. 167–79. Examples from Japanese are from S. Ide, "How and Why Do Women Speak More Politely in Japanese?" in *Aspects of Japanese Women's Language*, edited by S. Ide and N.H. McGloin (Tokyo: Kurosio Publishers, 1991), pp. 63–79. Discussion of gender and language, including some examples, comes from J. Coates, *Women, Men and Language* (New York: Longman, 1993).

The discussion of standard and non-standard language comes from I. Pringle, "The Complexity of the Concept of Standard," in *In Search of the Standard in Canadian English*, edited by W.C. Lougheed (Kingston, ON: Queen's University, 1985), pp. 20–38 and W. Labov, "The Logic of Non-Standard English," in *Georgetown Monographs on Languages and Linguistics*, edited by J. Alatis (Washington, DC: Georgetown University Press, 1970), pp. 1–43.

Canadian studies discussed in the section on attitudes are by T.W. Owens and P.M. Baker, "Linguistic Insecurity in Winnipeg, Canada: Validation of a Canadian Index of Linguistic Insecurity," *Language in Society* 13:337–50 (1984) and M. McKinnie and J. Dailey-O'Cain, *A Perceptual Dialectology of Anglophone Canada from the Perspective of Young Albertans and Ontarians* (Paper presented at NWAVE 27, University of Georgia, 1998). Results on /aw/ fronting in Toronto and Vancouver come from J.K. Chambers and M. Hardwick, "Comparative Sociolinguistics of a Sound Change in Canadian English" in *English World-Wide* 7:123–46 (1986).

The discussion of principal components analysis and reported figures are from S. Clarke, *Problems in the Analysis of Sociolinguistic Variability: From Social to Linguistic Groupings* (Paper presented at NWAVE 19, University of Pennsylvania, 1990). The map in figure 14.1 comes from L. Péronnet and P.-A. Arsenault, "Linguistic Atlas of French Maritime Terminology" *Journal of English Linguistics* 22(1): 25–29 (1990). The map in figure 14.2 comes from C. Von Baeyer, *The Ancestry of Canadian English* (Ottawa: Supply and Services, 1977). The study of water isoglosses in Louisiana is reported in C. Bodin, *Water-based Isoglosses in Louisiana Acadian French* (Paper presented at Methods IX, University of Wales, Bangor, 1996).

Canadian English sources include J. Edwards (ed.), *Language in Canada* (Cambridge: Cambridge University Press, 1998). Discussion of Newfoundland English takes material from S. Clarke, "The Role of Linguistic Feature Types in Dialect Stereotyping," in *Papers from the Eighth Annual Meeting of the Atlantic Province Linguistic Association*, edited by J. Barnstead et al. (Halifax: Dalhousie University Press, 1984), pp. 19–32 and from G.M. Story, W.J. Kirwin, and J.D.A. Widdowson, *Dictionary of Newfoundland English* (Toronto: University of Toronto,

1982). The discussion of Canadian French and examples are from P. Barbaud, "French in Quebec" in *Language in Canada*, edited by J. Edwards (Cambridge: Cambridge University Press, 1998), pp. 177–201; G. Dulong, *Dictionnaire correctif du français au Canada* (Québec: Les Presses de l'Université Laval, 1968); R. King, *Subject-Verb Agreement in Newfoundland French* (Paper presented at NWAVE 22, Ottawa, 1993); R.A. Papen, "French: Canadian Varieties" in *Language in Canada*, edited by J. Edwards (Cambridge: Cambridge University Press, 1998), pp. 160–76; D. Turpin, "'Le français c'est le last frontier': Le syntagme nominal dans le discours bilingue français/anglais," MA thesis, University of Ottawa, 1995; and D. Walker, *The Pronunciation of Canadian French* (Ottawa: University of Ottawa Press, 1984).

The social network discussion comes from L. Milroy, *Language and Social Networks* (Baltimore: University Park Press, 1980), with figures and examples from J. Boissevain, *Friends of Friends: Networks, Manipulators and Coalitions* (Oxford: Blackwell, 1974). Information on Canadian ethnic language retention comes from Statistics Canada publications: *Mother Tongue, The Nation* (1992) and *Home Language and Mother Tongue* (1992). The section on lingua franca and pidgins and creoles is based on a number of sources including R.A. Hall, Jr., *Pidgin and Creole Languages* (Ithaca, NY: Cornell University Press, 1966); D. Bickerton, "The Language Bioprogram Hypothesis" in *The Behavioral and Brain Sciences* 7(2): 173–221 (1984); and G. Sankoff and S. Laberge, "On the Acquisition of Native Speakers by a Language," in *Pidgins and Creoles: Current Trends and Prospects*, edited by D. DeCamp and I.F. Hancock (Washington: Georgetown University Press, 1974), pp. 73–84. The section on language mixture is informed by S. Poplack, "Sometimes I'll Start a Sentence in Spanish Y TERMINO EN ESPAÑOL: Toward a Typology of Code-Switching," *Linguistics* 18 (7/8): 581–618 (1980) as well as by J. Holmes, *An Introduction to Sociolinguistics* (New York: Longman, 1992). Additional examples come from D. Turpin, mentioned above; M. Meechan and S. Poplack, "Orphan Categories in Bilingual Discourse: Adjectivization Strategies in Wolof-French and Fongbe-French," *Language Variation and Change* 7:169–94 (1995); S. Poplack, S. Wheeler, and A. Westwood, "Distinguishing Language Contact Phenomena: Evidence from Finnish-English Bilingualism," in *The Nordic Languages and Modern Linguistics*, edited by P. Lilius and M. Saari (Helsinki: University of Helsinki Press, 1987), pp. 33–56; and M. Naït M'Barek and D. Sankoff, "Le discours mixte arabe/français: des emprunts ou des alternances de langue?" *Revue Canadienne de Linguistique* 33(2): 143–54 (1988).

Recommended reading

Chambers, J.K. 1995. *Sociolinguistic Theory*. Oxford: Blackwell.
Downes, W. 1998. *Language and Society*. Cambridge: Cambridge University Press.
Fasold, R. 1984. *The Sociolinguistics of Society*. Oxford: Blackwell.
Fasold, R. 1990. *Sociolinguistics of Language*. Oxford: Blackwell.
Holmes, J. 1992. *An Introduction to Sociolinguistics*. New York: Longman and Brown.
Schiffrin, D. 1994. *Approaches to Discourse*. Oxford: Blackwell.

Questions

1. Choose a speech situation and analyze it using the components discussed in the section on ethnography of communication.

2. Focusing on a particular adolescent or young adult social group in your community, make a list of slang terms that they use. Using this list, question an older member of the community and determine how terms differ and how they are the same.

3. Using the adjacency pair greeting-response, choose a specific situation and question four people from different cultural backgrounds to determine if there are any differences in kinds of utterances they would use.

4. Observe the way people around you close conversations. Make a list of some examples of closings. What made a closing particularly effective? Were any ineffective and why?

5. Examine the news articles in a newspaper or television news report and isolate any examples of euphemisms. Try to determine why the euphemism was employed. For example, was it used to avoid a taboo word or was the word it replaced avoided for some other reason?

6. Find some example of narrative discourse in either a contemporary play, television show, book or other source. Narrative involves the telling of the sequential events of a story. If it is not written down, transcribe it. Make a list of all the discourse markers and try to determine their function. For example, are they limited to bracketing any particular clause type?

7. Considering the discussion of language and gender, look for two examples where andro-centric bias might be found in three books on the prescriptive rules of English grammar. Try to choose books from three different timeframes, such as a book from the early 1900s as opposed to books that have been published more recently. Are all three books in agreement regarding the rules you have isolated? What might this indicate about the representation of gender in language?

8. Using the examples given in the section on language attitudes, ask ten people to give you their preferred pronunciation of the words given in table 14.8. Then, ask each person which is more 'correct'. Are there any discrepancies in their answers? What do the results say about the possible linguistic insecurity of the people you talked to?

9. Based on observation of people in your community, construct a questionnaire for elicit-ing terms, structures, and pronunciations that you have noticed are variable.

10. Words that have been borrowed into English may not always be completely integrated into English grammar. In that case, speakers may vary their pronunciation or use irregu-lar morphology such as deleted plurals or determiners. Make a list of borrowed words in your dialect that show signs of variable integration.

Fifteen

Michael Dobrovolsky
William O'Grady

Writing and language

Outside of a dog, a book is man's best friend;
inside of a dog, it's too dark to read.

GROUCHO

Speaking and writing are different in both origin and practice. Our ability to use language is as old as humankind, and reflects the biological and cognitive modification that has occurred during the evolution of our species. **Writing**, the symbolic representation of language by graphic signs or symbols, is a comparatively recent cultural development, having occurred within the past five thousand years and only in certain parts of the world.[1] The contrast between speech and writing comes into sharper focus when we consider that spoken language is acquired without specific formal instruction, whereas writing must be taught and learned through deliberate effort. There are entire groups of people in the world today, as well as individuals in every literate society, who are unable to write. While spoken language comes naturally to human beings, writing does not.

1 Types of writing

As different as they are, speech and writing share one major characteristic: just as spoken language shows an arbitrary link between sound and meaning, so written language exhibits an arbitrary link between symbol and sound.

All writing can be grouped into two basic types, called logographic and phonographic, depending on the technique that it uses to represent language.

1.1 Logographic writing

The term **logographic** (from Greek *logos* 'word') refers to a type of writing in which symbols represent morphemes or even entire words.

Logograms

Logographic writing is the oldest type of genuine writing. Ancient Mesopotamian cuneiform inscriptions, Egyptian hieroglyphics, and primordial Chinese characters were all highly logographic in their early stages. In fact, all writing systems maintain some logographic writing. Conventional abbreviations such as &, %, $, and the like are logographic, as are the symbols for numerals. To a certain extent, logographic writing can be read independently of its language of origin. For example, the Arabic numbers 1, 2, 7, 10, and so on can be read in any language.

1.2 Phonographic writing

No writing system is purely logographic, however. Nor can it be, since using a separate symbol to write each word in a language is simply too cumbersome. Throughout human history, writing systems have always evolved signs that represent some aspect of pronunciation. In **phonographic writing** (from Greek *phōnē* 'sound'), symbols represent syllables or segments. There are two principal types of phonographic writing systems—syllabic and alphabetic.

Syllabic writing

As the name suggests, **syllabic writing** employs signs to represent syllables (a set of syllabic signs is called a **syllabary**). Languages with relatively simple syllabic structures such as CV or CVC (Japanese and Cree, for example) are well suited to this type of writing, since they contain a relatively limited number of syllable types. In Japanese, for example, the word *kakimashita* '(s/he) wrote' can be written with the five syllabic signs か, き, ま, し, and た: かきました.

Alphabetic writing

Alphabetic writing represents consonant and vowel segments. Unlike the International Phonetic Alphabet, which is devised expressly to represent details of pronunciation, ordinary alphabets generally ignore non-phonemic phenomena. Thus, the spelling of the English words *pan* and *nap* represents the phonemes /p/, /n/, and /æ/, but ignores consonant aspiration, vowel nasalization, stress, and other subphonemic variation. As we will see in section 4 of this chapter, some spelling systems also capture certain morphophonemic alternations.

Writing systems emerged and spread around the earth over a long period of time. Though we can trace the spread of some systems over a wide area, writing may have emerged independently in several different places. The next sections trace the development of some writing systems from their pictorial origins.

2 The early history of writing

It is surprising that we cannot say with certainty how a comparatively recent cultural phenomenon like writing originated. We do know that writing developed in stages, the earliest of which involves direct representation of objects. This is sometimes called *pre-writing*.

2.1 Pre-writing

Figures and scenes depicted on cave walls and rock faces in the Americas, Africa, and Europe twelve thousand years ago, and perhaps even earlier, may have been forerunners of writing.

Some of these petroglyphs (scenes painted on stone) may represent a type of pre-literate stage that did not evolve into a full-fledged writing system.

These drawings depict a wide range of human and animal activity, and may even have been intended for purposes of linguistic communication. Some illustrations were doubtless a form of religious magic to guarantee a successful hunt or other benefits. Perhaps some were purely esthetic expression. Still others, such as those depicting the phases of the moon, may have been part of some form of record keeping. Figure 15.1a shows a pair of elk from a rock wall drawing in Sweden dating from the Old Stone Age (Paleolithic) period, perhaps as far back as 20 000 BC. Figure 15.1b shows an incised eagle bone from Le Placard, France, that dates back some 13 000 to 15 000 years. The incisions, which vary subtly, have been analyzed as a record of lunar phases. Pictorial records thus link the origins of writing with the history of representative art.

Figure 15.1 *a.* Paleolithic drawing, Sweden; *b.* Le Placard eagle bone

An even more direct connection links the origin of writing with record keeping. It has been suggested that the idea of writing had its origin in small clay tokens and counters that were used in record keeping and business transactions in the ancient Middle East. These small, fire-baked pieces of clay were apparently used for thousands of years before writing emerged (see figure 15.2). Counters representing cattle and other goods were stored on shelves or in baskets. Eventually, people began to make an impression of the tokens on soft clay tablets rather than storing and shipping the tokens themselves. This may have led to the idea that other objects and events in the world could be represented symbolically in graphic form.

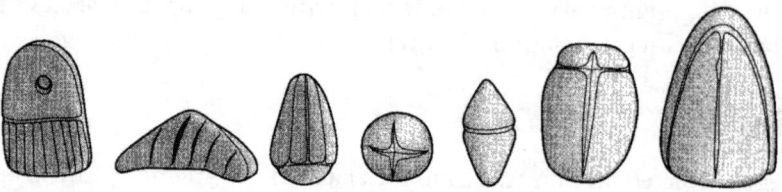

Figure 15.2 Ancient Mesopotamian tokens

2.2   Pictograms

Whatever their purpose, there is no doubt that pictures were among the precursors of the written word. Early writing systems all evolved from pictorial representations called **pictograms** or picture writing. Each pictogram was an image of the object or concept that it represented, and, as far as we know, offered no clues to pronunciation. Pictorial representations of this sort have been found among people throughout the ancient and modern world. Figure 15.3 is an example of Amerindian picture writing taken from a record kept by a Dakota named Lonedog; these pictures served as a kind of memory aid and not as a detailed record of events.

1800–01 Thirty Dakota were killed by Crow Indians.

1801–02 Many died of smallpox.

1802–03 A Dakota stole some horses with shoes (unusual amongst the Indians). (A horseshoe.)

1813–14 An epidemic of whooping-cough broke out.

1817–18 A Canadian built a log cabin out of dry wood. (Leafless tree.)

1824–25 A chieftain had all his horses killed.

1825–26 Many drowned in a flood. (The heads of the drowned floating in the water.)

1848–49 A Dakota called Humpback was killed by a spear.

1853–54 Spanish blankets were brought into the territory.

1869–70 An eclipse of the sun took place.

Figure 15.3 Amerindian pictography: a Dakota record of significant events

Like any other product of culture, pictography requires a knowledge of the conventions used by the author. Lonedog's record, for example, lists thirty Dakotas killed, but there are only twenty-four short vertical lines. To interpret the record correctly, it is necessary to know that the frame around the short lines consists of six additional joined lines.

Pictograms are still used today, often reflecting the function of this form of pre-writing as a memory aid. Signs indicating roadside services or information in parks are all pictographic in nature, as are the standardized set of symbols developed by the Canadian Olympic Association to indicate sporting events (see figure 15.4).

Figure 15.4 Contemporary pictograms: Canadian Olympic signs for sporting events

A contemporary and very sophisticated development of pictographic writing, **Blissymbolics** (originally called semantography), was developed by Charles K. Bliss. It makes use of a number of recombineable symbols that represent basic units of meaning, as the example in figure 15.5 illustrates.

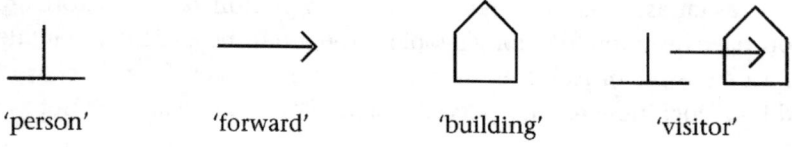

'person'   'forward'   'building'   'visitor'

Figure15.5   Blissymbolics

Though Blissymbolics was intended as a means of international, cross-linguistic communication by its inventor, its primary use today is as a means of communication for non-speaking individuals. The Blissymbolics Communication Institute of Toronto sets the standard for the training and application of Blissymbols for this specialized purpose.

As we consider developments that emerge from pictographic representation, it is important to remember that pictograms are not writing in any sense of the word. They do not represent linguistic elements such as segments, syllables, morphemes, or words. They are not written in a sequence that matches the language's word order. And they typically lend themselves to more than one interpretation, often providing only limited clues about their intended meaning.

3   The evolution of writing

The earliest known pictographic writing came from Sumeria, from where it spread to surrounding areas about five thousand years ago. Over time, inherently ambiguous pictograms came to be used to represent abstract notions as their use was extended to include related concepts. For example, in figure 15.6 the pictogram for 'fire' was also used for 'inflammation', the pictogram for 'hand' was employed to signify 'fist' as well as a particular unit of measurement, and the symbol for 'foot' came to stand for 'go', 'move' and 'go away'.

'to go, move, go
away'

'star, god'

'hand, fist, unit
of measurement'

'fire, inflammation'

Figure 15.6   Sumerian logograms

Sumerian writing also combined signs to express abstract meanings. For example, a head with fire coming out of the crown indicated 'anger'.

Figure 15.7 The Sumerian logogram for 'anger'

Although its evolution was gradual, we can state with some certainty that Sumerian writing was logographic because, from a fairly early stage, it was written in a consistent linear order that appears to reflect the order of words in speech. We cannot say with certainty at what date pictures began to be read as words, but once this practice took hold, the stage was set for the evolution to phonographic writing.

3.1 Rebuses and the emergence of writing

Phonographic writing made its appearance around 3000 BC with the first use of Sumerian symbols to represent sound rather than just meaning. This major development in the history of writing was made possible by the use of the **rebus principle**, which allows a sign to be used for any word that was pronounced like the word whose meaning it originally represented. In the inscription of an economic transaction in figure 15.8, for example, the symbol in the upper left-hand corner, was originally used to represent the word *GI* 'reed', here represents a homophonous word with the meaning 'reimburse'.

Figure 15.8 Sumerian rebus inscription (c. 3000 BC)

Thanks to the rebus principle, concepts that could not be directly depicted by a pictogram/logogram could be represented in writing. Thus, the sign for the word *ti* 'arrow', ➤— , was also used for the word *ti* 'life'.

3.2   Towards syllabic writing

Once the breakthrough towards phonographic writing had been made, it did not take long (in historical terms) before syllabic writing began to emerge. Within about 500 to 600 years, signs that clearly represent not just homophonous words, but parts of words—specifically, syllables—had become well established in Sumerian writing. For example, the word *kir* was represented by the syllabic signs for *ki* and *ir*, written in sequence. (By allowing the function of the symbols to overlap in this way, they avoided the need for a special sign for *r*.) Figure 15.9 illustrates this with the help of Sumerian cuneiform signs that are discussed in more detail in the following section.

ki   +   ir   =   kir

Figure 15.9 Overlapped Sumerian syllabic signs

Sumerian writing never developed into a pure syllabary. Logographic elements were interspersed with syllabic ones, and many syllabic signs were used to represent syllables with other pronunciations as well.

Cuneiform

Over the centuries, Sumerian writing was simplified and eventually came to be produced with the use of a wedge-shaped stylus that was pressed into soft clay tablets. This form of writing, initiated in the fourth millennium BC, has come to be known as **cuneiform** (from Latin *cuneus* 'wedge'). In time, a change in writing practices led the cuneiform signs to be rotated ninety degrees to the left. This resulted in their bearing even less resemblance to their pictographic origins than before. Figure 15.10 illustrates this development in two forms.

Figure 15.10 Changes in cuneiform writing

The cuneiform system was borrowed by the Elamites and Akkadians in the third millennium BC, a little later by the Persians, and in the second millennium BC by the Hittites far to the north in the ancient region of Anatolia (Modern Asian Turkey).

Cuneiform writing persisted until about the first few centuries of the Christian era in some areas, and then disappeared from use, not to be rediscovered until the nineteenth century. It was first deciphered from Old Persian texts, a breakthrough that led to the deciphering of Akkadian, Sumerian, and Hittite, among other languages that employed it. This script was used for thousands of years but then was generally replaced by systems of writing employed by the Semitic peoples of the Eastern Mediterranean.

3.3   Another Middle Eastern writing system: hieroglyphics

At about the time Sumerian pictography was flourishing, a similar system of pictorial communication was in use in Egypt. The Egyptian signs have become known as **hieroglyphics** (meaning 'sacred inscriptions' in Greek). The earliest texts display about five hundred such symbols. Like Sumerian pictograms, the hieroglyphic signs at first represented objects, but later they became logographic as they began to be associated with words.

Egyptian hieroglyphics developed into a mixed system of both word writing and phonographic writing. For example, the sign for a 'lute' was a picture of a lute: ; this represented the word itself: *nfr*. (Only the consonants of words represented by hieroglyphics are known with certainty. The Egyptians did not represent vowels—these can only be partially reconstructed from transcriptions in Greek and other languages that were made much later.) Eventually, the sign for 'lute' came to be disassociated from the word it represented, and was used to transcribe other words that consisted of or included the same sounds, such as the word for 'good', which also contained the consonants *nfr*.

Hieroglyphic symbols eventually came to be used to represent individual consonant phonemes by application of what is called the **acrophonic principle** (from Greek *acros* 'extreme'): sounds are represented by pictures of objects whose pronunciation begins with the sound to be represented. In this way, the first consonant of a word-sign came to be what the sign stood for. For example, the hieroglyph for 'horned viper':

is read logographically as *f(V)t*. Thanks to the acrophonic principle, this sign is also used to represent the phoneme /f/ in spellings such as *fen* 'pleasant'.

As we will see in section 3.4, the acrophonic principle was crucial to the development of true alphabets. In Egyptian writing, however, it was only part of a system that mixed logographic and phonographic elements.

Figure 15.11 provides some additional examples of hieroglyphics. (Throughout this chapter, a macron indicates a long vowel.) Hieroglyphics continued in decreasing use to Christian times. By the second century AD, Egyptian began to be written with Greek letters, and by the third century AD, hieroglyphics had been replaced by the Greek alphabet.

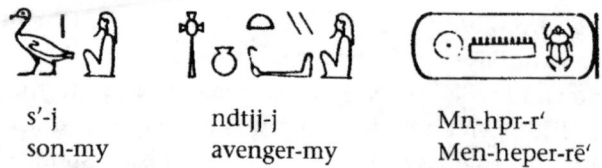

s'-j	ndtjj-j	Mn-hpr-r'
son-my	avenger-my	Men-heper-rē'

Figure 15.11 Egyptian hieroglyphics (c. 2000 BC)

3.4 The emergence of alphabets

Alphabetic writing emerged slowly from mixed writing systems over a long period in the Middle East. Building on this tradition, the Semitic peoples of ancient Phoenicia (modern Lebanon) devised a writing system of twenty-two consonantal signs as early as 1000 BC. This system was written horizontally, right to left, as had been common in earlier scripts. It ultimately led to the development of many alphabetic writing systems, including both the Greek and Latin alphabets.

The pictorial (and eventually logographic) origins of the Phoenician alphabet are evident in some of its symbols. Figure 15.12 illustrates the development of logograms for a stylized ox's head, a throwing stick, and a wavy flow of water into alphabetic symbols.

?āleph   gīmel   mēm

Figure 15.12 Pictorial and logographic origins of some signs in the Phoenician alphabet

These symbols eventually came to be used to represent the consonant phonemes of words by application of the acrophonic principle (see section 3.3). In this way, ?āleph was used to represent a glottal stop; *gīmel*, a /g/; and *mēm*, an /m/. Some of the symbols of the Phoenician alphabet had developed from Egyptian hieroglyphics, and, as in hieroglyphic writing, vowels were not represented (see figure 15.11).

The Phoenicians were a trading people, and their alphabetic writing spread to adjacent countries and beyond. Eventually, the Greeks acquired and adapted the Phoenician alphabet.

The Greek alphabet

The Greeks developed the Phoenician writing system into a full alphabet: each sign represented one phoneme and all phonemes were recorded by a sign. The Greeks were aware that some of the Phoenician symbols represented consonant sounds that were not found in Greek. Some of these symbols were adapted to represent Greek vowels, and other unneeded consonant signs were eventually dropped. Figure 15.13 illustrates the evolution of the Classical Greek and ultimately the Latin alphabet from the original Phoenician consonantal signs.

As we have seen, Phoenician *?āleph* represented a glottal stop. Since Greek had no such phoneme, the *?āleph* was employed to represent the vowel /a/ in Greek. Phoenician ⌂ (*h*)

	Symbols		Greek			Latin	
Phoenician	Hebrew Name	Phonetic value	Early	Classical	Name	Early	Monumental (Classical)
	'Aleph	ʔ			Alpha		A
	Beth	b			Beta		B
	Gimel	g			Gamma		C
	Daleth	d			Delta		D
	He	h			Epsilon		E
	Waw	w			Digamma		F
							G
	Zayin	z			Zeta		
	Ḥeth	ħ			Ēta		H
	Teth	ŧ			Theta		
	Yod	j			Iota		I (J)
	Kaph	k			Kappa		K
	Lamed	l			Lambda		L
	Mem	m			Mu		M
	Nun	n			Nu		N
	Samekh	s					
	'Ayin	ʕ			Ŏmicron		O
	Pe	p			Pi		P
	Tsade	s			San		
	Qoph	q			Qoppa		Q
	Reš	r			Rho		R
	Šin	ʃ-s			Sigma		S
	Taw	t			Tau		T
					Upsilon		V
					Chi		X
							Y
					Omega		Z

Figure 15.13 Evolution of the Greek and Latin alphabets

was used to represent the Greek vowel /e/, and other signs were added to the system by the Greeks, including Φ/f/, X/x/, Ψ/ps/, and Ω/ō/.

The Semitic names for the letters (*aleph, beth, gimel, daleth,* and so on) were maintained by the Greeks (as *alpha, beta, gamma, delta,* and so on), but the possible pictorial origins had been lost and the names carried no other meaning.[2] The writing system itself gained its name from the first two letters of the series: alphabet.

The Roman alphabet

When Greek colonists occupied southern Italy in the eighth and seventh centuries BC, they took their alphabet with them. It was in turn taken up and modified by the Etruscan inhabitants of central Italy, a non-Latin-speaking people who were a political and cultural power before the rise of Rome. It is believed that the Romans acquired their alphabet through the Etruscans. As the Romans grew in power and influence during the following centuries, first as masters of Italy and later of Europe, the Roman alphabet spread throughout their Empire.

Under the Romans, the Greek/Etruscan alphabet was again modified, this time with some symbols influenced by the Etruscans. The *G* in Greek writing developed into both *C* for the phoneme /k/ and *G* for /g/. The oldest inscriptions also retained *K* for /k/ in some words, but it was generally replaced by *C*. Similarly, *Q* was retained before /u/. Roman script also employed Greek *U* (= V), *X*, *Y*, and *Z* and moved *Z* to the end of the alphabet. The symbols Φ, Θ, Ψ, and Ω were among those discarded, and *H* was converted back to a consonant symbol.

Some subsequent changes were made in the alphabet as it was adapted by various peoples of the Roman Empire. In English, for example, *W* was created from two juxtaposed *V*s. Spanish employs a tilde (˜) over *n* (ñ) to signify a palatal nasal, as in *año* /aɲo/ 'year', and French uses a cedilla under c (ç) to indicate the dental fricative /s/, as in the spelling of *français*/frãsɛ/ 'French'.

3.5   Other developments, East and West

A large number of alphabetic systems other than those of Greek and Rome evolved and flourished in Europe and the Middle East. In this section, we briefly present some of these that are of historical significance or interest.

Runic writing

Germanic tribes occupying the north of Italy developed an early offshoot of the Greek/Etruscan tradition of writing into a script known as Runic writing. This system emerged shortly after the beginning of the Christian era, and its developments were eventually found as far north as Scandinavia. Runic writing persisted until the sixteenth century in some areas before giving way to the Roman alphabet.

Figure 15.14 illustrates some signs from one of the oldest known Runic inscriptions, which dates from about the third century AD. The angular style of the letters arose because the alphabet was carved in wood or stone, the former especially not readily lending itself to curved lines. The script is read from right to left.

= harigasti ['the warriors' guest'] (epithet for the god Odin)

Figure 15.14 Runic script

Cyrillic script

Another offshoot of the Greek script was created for the Slavic peoples in the ninth century AD. The Greek missionary brothers Constantine (Cyril) and Methodius introduced a writing system for the translation of the Bible that is now known as **Glagolitic script**. A later development, which combined adaptations of Glagolitic letters with Greek and Hebrew characters, has come to be known as the **Cyrillic alphabet**. The current Russian, Byelorussian, Ukrainian, Serbian, Macedonian, and Bulgarian alphabets, as well as those used to represent many non-Slavic languages spoken in the former Soviet Union, have evolved from this early Cyrillic script. Some examples of its development and adaptation are given in figure 15.15, followed by a short passage in contemporary Russian Cyrillic, which is transliterated for its letter values.

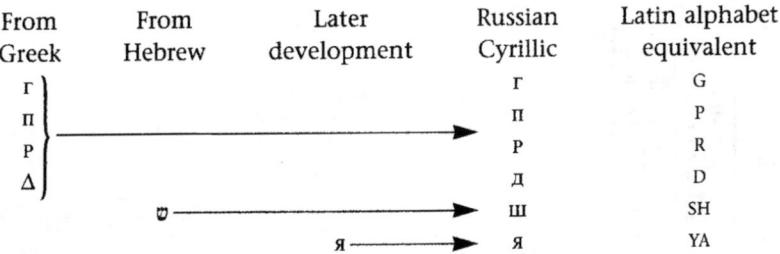

(Russian text below)

Мы все учились понемногу
Чему-нибудь и как-нибудь...

mɨ vse utʃilis' ponemnogu
tʃemu-nibud' i kak-nibud'...

'We all pick up our education
In bits and pieces as we can ...'
Pushkin, *Eugene Onegin*, I.5

Figure 15.15 Contemporary Russian Cyrillic transliterated

Two Semitic alphabets

Both Arabic and Hebrew are written with alphabets that descend from or are closely related to Phoenician script. Both are essentially consonant-writing systems (vowels are indicated with diacritic dots), and both are written from right to left.

The contemporary Arabic alphabet is the most widespread of all the descendants of Middle Eastern writing except the Roman alphabet. The earliest inscription dates back to the fourth century AD. In the latter half of the seventh century, this script was used to write the Koran, the sacred text of Islam, and its use spread rapidly along with the Islamic religion over the next centuries.

The Arabic alphabet contains twenty-eight consonants (vowels are indicated by diacritics above and below the consonants), and is written from right to left. An interesting feature of this alphabet is that twenty-two of its twenty-eight signs have different forms, depending on their position in (or outside of) a word. Figure 15.16 illustrates the forms of the letters *b* and *k* in initial, medial, and final position, as well as their forms when written in isolation.

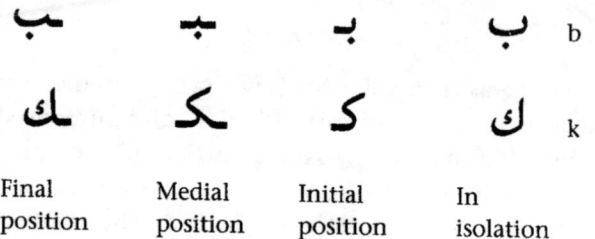

Final position	Medial position	Initial position	In isolation	
ـب	ـبـ	بـ	ب	b
ـك	ـكـ	كـ	ك	k

Figure 15.16 Variation in two Arabic letters according to position

The similarities among the symbols in figure 15.17 demonstrate the clear link between Phoenician script and the Hebrew and Arabic scripts.

Hebrew Letter name	Phonetic value	Phoenician	Modern Hebrew	Modern Arabic
'Alēph	ʔ		א	ا
Bêth	b		ב	ب
Gimel	g		ג	ج
Dāleth	d		ד	د
Hē	h		ה	ه
Wāw	w		ו	و
Zayin	z		ז	ز
Ḥēth	ħ		ח	ح
Ṭēth	ŧ		ט	ط
Yōdh	j		י	ي
Kaph	k		כ	ك
Lāmadh	l		ל	ل
Mêm	m		מ	م
Nūn	n		נ	ن
Sāmekh	s		ס	س
'Ayin	ʕ		ע	ع
Pê	p		פ	ف
Ṣādê	s		צ	ص
Qōph	q		ק	ق
Rêš	r		ר	ر
Šîn	ʃ		ש	ش
Tāw	t		ת	ت

Figure 15.17 The Phoenician, Hebrew, and Arabic alphabets

Other descendants of Middle Eastern Systems

Early Middle Eastern scripts gave rise to Aramaic, Old Hebrew, and South Arabic syllabaries, which, in turn, led to a host of further writing systems eventually stretching across the Near East and North Africa from India to Morocco. Figure 15.18 illustrates this widespread diffusion on a time scale.

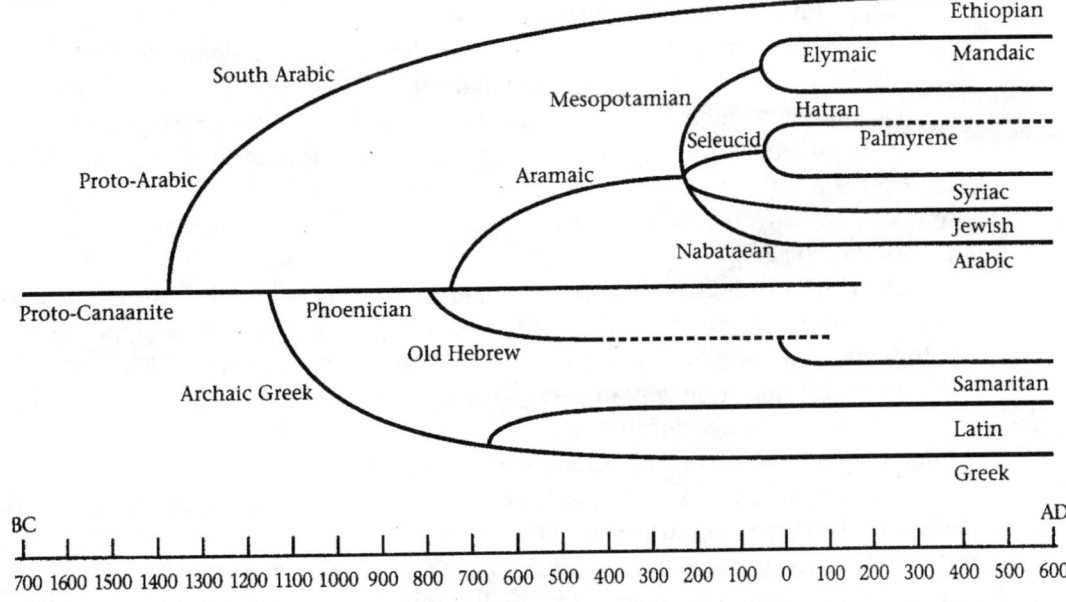

Figure 15.18 Development of writing systems (dotted lines indicate that the line of development is hypothetical)

4   Some non-European writing systems

This section focuses on the nature and development of writing systems that originated outside the Middle East. While some of these systems emerged in response to external influences, others seem to have been entirely independent innovations.

4.1   Chinese writing

The Chinese system of writing developed out of pictograms that eventually came to represent morphemes (most of which are also words). The oldest inscriptions are the oracle texts, written on animal bones and tortoise shells and dating back to about twelve hundred BC. These include many recognizable images, such as ☉ 'sun' and ☽ 'moon'.

A change toward more **symbolic signs** began at an early date as more abstract notions were symbolized, such as ‿ 'above' and ⌒ 'below'. Symbols were also combined to extend meanings metaphorically. For example, the sign for 'to tend' 牧 is composed of 牛 'cow' and 攴 'hand and whip'. 'To follow' 从 is two men in sequence, and so on. In time, the characters became more abstract. Figure 15.19 shows the historical development of the symbol for 'dog'.

Figure 15.19 Historical development of the Chinese symbol for 'dog'

Calligraphy is an ancient and respected art in China, and Chinese writing exists in a number of styles. The script is usually written from left to right along a horizontal axis, although newspapers and older texts begin in the right-hand margin and are read downwards.

The units of contemporary Chinese writing are called **characters**. Many monosyllabic words are presented in true logographic fashion by a character consisting of a single symbol. For example, the Mandarin words [ʃŏw] 'hand' and [mǎ] 'horse' are written 手 and 馬, respectively. However, the overwhelming majority of characters (one estimate is 99 percent) consist of two parts.

The main component of a multi-element character, called the **phonetic determinative**, provides information about the pronunciation of the corresponding morpheme. Although about 4000 different phonetic determinatives are used in Chinese writing, they represent pronunciation very imperfectly. Tone, which is contrastive in Chinese (see chapter 2), is not represented at all, and many phonetic determinatives indicate only part of the morpheme's pronunciation. For instance, the determinative 敖 is used for a wide variety of words ending in *ao* without regard for whether the initial consonant is *j, n, r,* or some other element. Furthermore, due to sound changes over the last centuries, about one-third of all phonetic determinatives provide little or no useful information about current pronunciation. Finally, because Chinese has many homophones, even the most informative phonetic determinatives can be used for many different words.

Chinese characters also include a semantic component, called the **radical** or key, which provides clues about the morpheme's meaning. There are about 200 different radicals in contemporary Chinese writing. Table 15.1 provides examples of some of the characters that can be formed by combining phonetic determinatives with radicals.

Table 15.1   Some Chinese characters

		Phonetic determinatives			
		A	B	C	D
	Semantic radical	敖 (*áo*)	參 (*cān*)	堯 (*yáo*)	甫 (*fŭ*)
1	亻 'person'	傲 (*ào*: 'proud')	傪 (*cān*: 'good')	僥 (*jiăo*: 'lucky')	俌 (*fŭ*: 'help')
2	扌 'hand'	撽 (*ào*: 'shake')	掺 (*shán*: 'seize')	撓 (*năo*: 'scratch')	捕 (*bŭ*: 'catch')
3	木 'wood'	橔 (*āo*: 'barge')	椮 (*shēn*: 'beam')	橈 (*náo*: 'oar')	楠 (*fŭ*: 'trellis')
4	氵 'water'	滶 (*ào*: 'stream')	渗 (*shèn*: 'leak')	澆 (*jiāo*: 'sprinkle')	浦 (*pŭ*: 'creek')

Notice that only the phonetic determinative in column A indicates the precise pronunciation (ignoring tone) of the four characters in which it appears. The other determinatives supply helpful, but incomplete, phonetic information. For instance, the determinative *yao* (column C) has a pronunciation that rhymes with that of the four morphemes it helps to represent.

The usefulness of the information supplied by the radicals also varies. The characters in row 1 represent morphemes whose meaning is at best indirectly associated with that of the radical ('person'), but the radicals in rows 2, 3, and 4 are much more informative. For example, the characters in row 2 all denote actions involving the hand while those in row 3 refer to things made of wood and those in row 4 all have something to do with liquids.

Although neither phonetic determinatives alone nor semantic radicals alone suffice to identify the morphemes that they are used to represent, they are more than adequate when used in conjunction with each other. Despite these complexities—one authority has described the system as "outsized, haphazard, inefficient, and only partially reliable"—Chinese writing provides its users with an effective way to represent the words and morphemes of the language. Moreover, the lack of efficiency is offset by the fact that the same literary script can be understood by speakers of different Chinese languages. Although a speaker of Mandarin and a speaker of Cantonese may pronounce the word for 'fire' differently—/xwǒ/ and /fɔ/, respectively—both can read it from the same character (火), since Chinese writing does not directly represent a word's phonemic segments.

In recent times, the government of the People's Republic of China has introduced simplified characters (some newly invented) in an attempt to promote literacy. At the same time, a system of writing Mandarin with a modified Latin alphabet, called **pinyin**, has also been introduced. Pinyin is used as a subsidiary system for writing such things as street signs, addresses, and brand names as well as for teaching children how to pronounce characters. It is also used for word processing and other computer-related activities, including electronic mail.

4.2 Japanese writing

The writing system of modern Japanese is arguably the most complicated in the entire world. Its use requires knowledge of three distinct scripts, including a pair of syllabaries—**hiragana** and **katakana**—which were created by modifying Chinese characters.

Although Japanese can be written exclusively with either syllabary, normal writing involves use of Chinese characters (called **kanji** in Japanese) in addition to hiragana and katakana. Kanji symbols are typically used to represent all or part of a word's root while affixes are represented by hiragana symbols. The phrase *the man's car*, for example, can be written as in figure 15.21, with the roots 'man' and 'car' represented by kanji, and the possessive morpheme *no* written in hiragana.

The katakana syllabary, whose symbols are less rounded than their hiragana counterparts, is used to write onomatopoeic words as well as words borrowed into Japanese from other languages. In addition, it is employed in advertising and in telegrams.

Finally, it should be noted that the Roman alphabet, which the Japanese call *romaji*, is also making inroads. It is not unusual to see all four writing systems used together, especially in advertising (see figure 15.22).

Katakana chart

COLUMN LINE	A	I	U	E	O
SINGLE VOWEL	ア A	イ I	ウ U	エ E	オ O
K	カ KA	キ KI	ク KU	ケ KE	コ KO
S	サ SA	シ SHI	ス SU	セ SE	ソ SO
T	タ TA	チ CHI	ツ TSU	テ TE	ト TO
N	ナ NA	ニ NI	ヌ NU	ネ NE	ノ NO
H	ハ HA	ヒ HI	フ FU	ヘ HE	ホ HO
M	マ MA	ミ MI	ム MU	メ ME	モ MO
Y	ヤ YA		ユ YU		ヨ YO
R	ラ RA	リ RI	ル RU	レ RE	ロ RO
W	ワ WA				ヲ O
N (in a coda)	ン N				

Hiragana chart

COLUMN LINE	A	I	U	E	O
SINGLE VOWEL	あ A	い I	う U	え E	お O
K	か KA	き KI	く KU	け KE	こ KO
S	さ SA	し SHI	す SU	せ SE	そ SO
T	た TA	ち CHI	つ TSU	て TE	と TO
N	な NA	に NI	ぬ NU	ね NE	の NO
H	は HA	ひ HI	ふ FU	へ HE	ほ HO
M	ま MA	み MI	む MU	め ME	も MO
Y	や YA		ゆ YU		よ YO
R	ら RA	り RI	る RU	れ RE	ろ RO
W	わ WA				を O
N (in a coda)	ん N				

Figure 15.20 Hiragana and katakana syllabaries and their phonetic values (The conventions for representing voicing, vowel length, and gemination are not indicated here.)

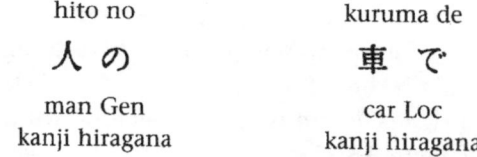

hito no	kuruma de
人 の	車 で
man Gen	car Loc
kanji hiragana	kanji hiragana

Figure 15.21 A phrase written in a mixture of kanji and hiragana

New Tomato

ほんのり 甘味　 さらっと　あと 味

(honnori　amami　saratto　ato　aji)

'Subtle sweetness and light after taste.'

トマト　の　新しい　ジュース　です

(tomato　no　atarashii　juusu　desu)

'It's a new tomato juice.'

——— --Hiragana
〰〰〰 --Katakana
═══ --Kanji

Figure 15.22 Kanji, hiragana, katakana, and romaji in a Japanese advertisement

Learning to read Japanese is a formidable task, in part because of the way the various scripts are intermingled and in part because of complexities in the use of kanji symbols, which can have more than one pronunciation depending on whether they are used to represent a word of Chinese or Japanese origin. (For example, Japanese has two morphemes with the meaning 'mountain'—/san/, which is of Chinese origin, and the native Japanese /yama/; both are written with the kanji character 山.)

4.3 Korean writing

Korean was once written with Chinese characters, which had been introduced in the first centuries AD. However, Korean suffixes could not be easily represented by Chinese writing. Various devices were used to alleviate this problem, but inadequacies persisted. Finally, King Sejong (1419–1452) commissioned an alphabetic script, called **hangul**. After some modifications over the centuries, it became the standard Korean writing system. An especially interesting feature of hangul is that symbols are grouped together into syllable-sized clusters (see figure 15.23).

Like Japanese, Korean also makes use of Chinese characters (called **hanja**), although in a more restricted way. Slightly more than half the vocabulary of contemporary Korean is of Chinese origin and many words of this type are written with the help of Chinese characters in newspapers and in scientific articles. However, this practice has been reduced somewhat in recent years in South Korea and it has been eliminated entirely in North Korea.

Hangul symbols

ㅂ   ㅜ   ㄹ   ㄱ   ㅗ   ㅣ

/p/   /u/   /l/   /k/   /o/   /i/

Grouped symbols

불   고기

'fire' /pul/   'meat' /koki/

Written form

불고기

'barbecued meat' *pulkoki*

Figure 15.23 Korean hangul

4.4 American scripts

A number of major civilizations developed on the American continents. In Mesoamerica alone more than eighteen writing systems have been discovered, including those of the Mayans of the Yucatan and the Aztecs of Mexico. In both systems, we can see the evolution of pictograms toward phonetic word signs, as with the Egyptian hieroglyphics illustrated in section 3.3.

Mayan symbols are called **glyphs** (see figure 15.24). Although some were read as word signs (logograms), they had other uses as well. The rebus principle was employed, although sometimes only partially, as in the use of the symbol for a smoking bundle of pine, 🗒 /taaʒ/, to represent the locative preposition /ta/ in a form of syllabic writing. Glyphs that mix syllabic writing with logographic representation are also found.

Figure 15.24 Six Mayan glyphs spelling 'Lord Pacal'

Cherokee

Some American writing systems are of more recent origin. After the colonization of North America by Europeans, a number of scripts were developed to provide Native peoples with a form of written communication. In one well-known case, the Cherokee leader Sikwayi (Sequoia) devised a syllabic script of more than eighty symbols, some based on the shapes of English letters and others newly invented (see figure 15.25).

Symbol	Value	Symbol	Value	Symbol	Value	Symbol	Value	Symbol	Value
Ꭰ	*a*	Ꭱ	*e*	Ꭲ	*i*	Ꭳ	*o*	Ꭴ	*u*
Ꭶ	*ga*	Ꭼ	*ge*	Ᏽ	*gi*	Ꭷ	*go*	Ꭻ	*gu*
Ꭽ	*ha*	Ꭾ	*he*	Ꭿ	*hi*	Ꮀ	*ho*	Ꮁ	*hu*
Ꮃ	*la*	Ꮄ	*le*	Ꮅ	*li*	Ꮆ	*lo*	Ꮇ	*lu*
Ꮉ	*ma*	Ꮊ	*me*	Ꮋ	*mi*	Ꮌ	*mo*	Ꮍ	*mu*

Figure 15.25 Some Cherokee syllabic symbols

Cree

Professional linguists have often played a role in the development of American scripts, as have missionaries. The syllabic script of the Cree Indians was the creation of a missionary, J. Evans, in the nineteenth century. It was employed for religious literature, and by 1861, the entire Bible appeared in the Cree syllabary. Today, in somewhat modified form, this script is used by Cree speakers across Canada.

Cree morphemes are made up of syllables that combine one of ten initial consonants with one of seven vowels; in some cases, there is also a postvocalic consonant. The Cree writing system provides a separate symbol for each V and CV syllable. As in syllabaries in general, the symbols representing the CV syllables bear no resemblance to those representing syllables consisting of a single vowel; there is no connection, for instance, between the symbols for the syllable /ki/ Ꮲ and the syllable /i/ ᐃ. However, the Cree system is not wholly syllabic since consonants that occur at the end of a syllable must be represented by a separate symbol.

A striking feature of the Cree syllabary is its phonetic symbolism. Vowels are indicated by the direction in which a syllabic symbol faces. Symbols that face 'south' (downward on the printed page) contain /e:/; those facing 'north' (upward) contain /i/ or /i:/; those pointing 'east' (rightward) have /o/ or /o:/, and those looking to the 'west' (leftward) contain /a/ or /a:/. Vowel length is indicated by a superposed dot, as in ᐢ = /si:/.

ᐃ *i, ī*	ᐁ *ē*	ᐅ *o, ō*	ᐊ *a*
ᐱ *pi, pī*	ᐯ *pē*	ᐳ *po, pō*	ᐸ *pa*
ᐱ *ti, tī*	ᐴ *tē*	ᐋ *to, tō*	ᐌ *ta*
ᕆ *ci, cī*	ᕃ *cē*	ᕊ *co, cō*	ᕍ *ca*
ᐱ *ki, kī*	ᑫ *kē*	ᑯ *ko, kō*	ᑲ *ka*
ᒥ *mi, mī*	ᒣ *mē*	ᒧ *mo, mō*	ᒪ *ma*
ᓂ *ni, nī*	ᓀ *nē*	ᓄ *no, nō*	ᓇ *na*
ᓯ *si, sī*	ᓭ *sē*	ᓱ *so, sō*	ᓴ *sa*
ᔨ *yi, yī*	ᔦ *yē*	ᔪ *yo, yō*	ᔭ *ya*

Finals

ᵖ *p* ᵗ *t* ᶜ *c* ᵏ *k* ᵐ *m* ˢ *s* ⁿ *n* ʸ *y* ᵂ *w* ʰ *h* ˣ *hk* ᶫ *l* ᵣ *r*

Figure 15.26 Western Cree syllabary

Plains Cree, a variety of Cree spoken in Western Canada, is written with the symbols in figure 15.26 (other dialects use slightly different ones).

The examples in figure 15.27 illustrate the use of the Cree syllabary.

ḋ ∧   σ ∧   ʔ ∧

nīpi   'leaf'   nipi   'water'   sīpi   'river'

Figure 15.27 Three words in Western Cree syllabary

Some other American scripts

The Cree syllabary, appropriately modified, is used by the Inuit of Baffin Island to represent their language, which is unrelated to Cree. A word-writing system developed by Alaskan Inuit toward the end of the nineteenth century eventually evolved into a partially syllabic system, although it did not become fully syllabic. A number of different systems are in use in regions of Alaska, and in some, tendencies toward alphabetization are discernible.

4.5   Some African scripts

In the past several centuries, societies in Central Africa have also produced syllabic scripts, which have either been invented as such or developed through stages from pictograms to refined syllabaries. Although the idea of writing appears to have been imported into these societies, the development of the various systems was indigenous.

The first sub-Saharan African writing seems to have been that of the Vai peoples in the region of Sierra Leone and Liberia. In the nineteenth century, a native of the area developed a syllabary from a system of picture communication. The new system, which grew to consist of 226 syllabic symbols plus a few logographic symbols, appears to have spawned a number of imitations throughout the area.

The writing of the Bamum people in the Cameroons was invented at the end of the nineteenth century by a native leader. The current seventy syllabic symbols show tendencies toward alphabetization.

The only sure example of alphabetic writing developed in modern times among African peoples is the Somali alphabet. The originator, acquainted with Arabic and Italian, devised an alphabet composed of nineteen consonants and ten vowels. The symbols themselves appear to have been invented, but their names are based on those used for the letters of the Arabic alphabet, and are listed and recited in the same order.

4.6   Some Indian scripts

A pictorial script appears to have had an independent origin in Northern India, where inscribed seals, pottery, and copper tablets dating back to the third millennium BC have been unearthed. The system seems to have consisted of about 250 symbols such as ꠟ, ▦, and ▲, but died away long before another writing system, seemingly derived from Semitic (see figure

15.28), was employed in the middle of the first millennium BC to record the ancient Sanskrit language.

The date of the first appearance of Indian Sanskrit symbols cannot be ascertained, but they resemble Aramaic and appeared as a full system of writing in the edicts of Ašoka (who ruled from 272 to 231 BC). They occurred in two types of writing—Kharosthi and Brahmi. The former continued in use until about the fifth century AD in Northern India. The Brahmi script gave rise to all later varieties of Indian writing.

One of these varieties, a cursive type called the Gupta script, was later employed to write Tocharian, Saka, and Turkish manuscripts discovered in eastern Turkestan. In India, it evolved into the Devanagari script, which became the most widespread type of writing in the subcontinent and which was used to record the voluminous literature of the Sanskrit language. Inscriptions in Devanagari are found throughout Southeast Asia, Indonesia, and as far afield as the southern Philippines.

Varieties of Indian writing were carried abroad by Buddhist missionaries and influenced writing systems in Tibet and Central and Southeast Asia. The Dravidian peoples of Southern India also developed a number of scripts under the influence of the Northern varieties. Another ancient Indian script, called Pali, gave rise to a number of Southeast Asian writing systems, including those used for Thai and Cambodian. Figure 15.28 illustrates Devanagari and some of the many other scripts found in India and Southeast Asia.

Figure 15.28 *a.* Devanagari; *b.* Gurmuki; *c.* Modern Malayalam; *d.* Modern Thai

The examples cited in this chapter only touch on the variety of writing systems past and present that scholars have investigated (the index of one standard work lists 470 scripts). Many of these systems are historically related, but the number nonetheless testifies to human ingenuity and creativity in devising writing systems.

5 English orthography

The set of conventions for representing language in written form is called an **orthography**. English employs an alphabetic orthography in which symbols are used to represent individual consonants and vowels rather than syllables or words. In this section, we will consider the nature and history of English orthography. Section 6 examines the relationship between writing and reading.

5.1 Irregularities

A frequently expressed complaint about English orthography is that it does not establish a one-to-one relationship between symbols and phonological segments. Table 15.2 lists some well-known examples of this.

Table 15.2 Some problems with English orthography	
Problem	**Examples**
Some letters do not represent any segments in a particular word.	throu_gh_, si_g_n, giv_e_, pa_l_m
A group of two or more letters can be used to represent a single segment.	_th_ink /θ/, _sh_ip /ʃ/, _ph_ilosophy /f/
A single letter can represent a group of two or more segments.	sa_x_ophone /ks/, e_x_ile /gz/
The same letter can represent different segments in different words.	_o_ in _o_n /ɑ/, b_o_ne /ow/, s_o_n /ʌ/, _o_ne /wʌ/
The same segment can be represented by different letters in different words.	/uw/ in r_u_de, l_oo_p, s_ou_p, n_ew_, s_ue_, t_o_, tw_o_

The following excerpt from a poem by Richard Krogh vividly illustrates the extent to which English orthography departs from the principle of one sound, one letter (one segment, one symbol).

> *Beware of heard, a dreadful word*
> *That looks like beard and sounds like bird.*
> *And dead; it's said like bed, not bead;*
> *For goodness sake, don't call it deed!*
> *Watch out for meat and great and threat*
> *(They rhyme with suite and straight and debt).*
> *A moth is not a moth in Mother,*
> *Nor both in bother, broth in brother.*

Historical factors

The relationship between symbol and segment in English orthography has not always been so indirect. In fact, the spelling system used throughout England during the Old English period provided a regular set of direct symbol-segment correspondences. The foundation for today's system, it lacked the symbols *j*, *v*, and *w*, but made use of four symbols that are not part of our current alphabet.

Table 15.3   Old English symbols not found in Modern English spelling

Symbol	Name	Segment(s) it represented
æ	ash	[æ]
ð	eth	[θ] and [ð]
þ	thorn	[θ] and [ð]
ƿ	wynn	[w]

The relationship between symbol and segment in English orthography was significantly disturbed in the Middle English period, as the phonological pattern of the language began to change. To see an example of this, we need only consider the Great Vowel Shift, which dramatically altered the pronunciation of long vowels—converting /iː/ into /aj/, /eː/ into /i/, /aː/ into /e/, and so on (see chapter 7). Because Old English orthography used the same symbol for long and short vowels, complications arose when the former vowels changed. Thus, the letter *i*, which had formerly been used only to represent the phonetically similar /iː/ and /i/, ended up representing the very dissimilar /aj/ (the descendent of /iː/) and /ɪ/ (the descendant of /i/). The end result can be seen in the spelling of *hide* and *hid, write* and *written, ride* and *ridden, wide* and *width,* and many other words.

Additional complications arose following the invasion of England by French-speaking Normans in the eleventh century. The use of English in official documents declined and regional orthographies developed in the absence of a national standard. To make matters worse, scribes who were trained primarily to write French and Latin, introduced a number of conventions from those languages into English spelling. Among those that have survived are the use of *ch* rather than *c* for /tʃ/ (*cheese, chin,* etc.), *th* rather than þ (thorn) and ð (eth) for /θ/ and /ð/ (*thin, this*), and *c* rather than *s* for /s/ (*grace, ice, mice*).

Toward the end of the fifteenth century, yet another trend developed—the practice of spelling words in a manner that reflected their etymological origin. Enduring examples of this influence are found in the spelling of the words *debt, doubt, receipt,* and *salmon* (formerly spelled *dette, doute, receite,* and *samon*), all of which were given a 'silent' consonant to make them look more like the Latin words from which they descended.

By the 1500s English orthography had become increasingly irregular and idiosyncratic, with many different spellings in use for the same word. The word *pity,* for example, could be spelled *pity, pyty, pitie, pytie, pittie,* and *pyttye.* As printing presses came into greater use and books became more widely available, the need to reform and regularize English orthography became apparent. In the late 1500s and early 1600s, a number of individuals (most notably Richard Mulcaster and Edmond Coote) formulated and published spelling rules, which were gradually adopted by printers and other literate speakers of English. While these rules retained many of the practices discussed above, they at least had the effect of stabilizing English spelling. By the 1700s, English orthography was more or less fixed.

The vast majority of the spelling conventions introduced during this period are still in use today. One of the most famous, proposed by Mulcaster in 1582, involves the use of 'silent' *e* at the end of words to indicate a preceding long (tense) vowel, as in *name, same,* and *mate.* Even here, though, there are complications and exceptions. In an earlier period, word-final *e* had represented [ə]. Following the loss of this sound in this position in the fourteenth century, final *e* was used quite haphazardly and was often added to words that would otherwise end in a single consonant. The *e* in the modern spelling of *have, done,* and *gone,* which contain lax vowels, reflects this practice and has survived even though it does not comply with Mulcaster's rule.

5.2   Obstacles to reform

Over the years, there have been numerous proposals for the reform of English orthography, including those put forward by Benjamin Franklin, George Bernard Shaw, and Noah Webster. However, far-reaching reforms are unlikely for a variety of reasons. For one thing, they would require a long and difficult period of transition. As the following letter to *The Economist* by M.J. Shields illustrates, reform would not be painless even if it took place over a period of many years.

> *For example, in Year 1 that useless letter 'c' would be dropped to be replased either by 'k' or 's', and likewise 'x' would no longer be part of the alphabet. The only kase in which 'c' would be retained would be the 'ch' formation, which will be dealt with later. Year 2 might reform 'w' spelling, so that 'which' and 'one' would take the same konsonant, wile Year 3 might well abolish 'y' replasing it with 'i' and Iear 4 might fiks the 'g-j' anomali wonse and for all.*
>
> *Jenerally, then, the improvement would kontinue iear bai iear with Iear 5 doing awai with useless double konsonants, and Iears 6 - 12 or so modifaiing vowlz and the rimeining voist and unvoist konsonants. Bai Iear 15 or sou, it wud fainali be posibl tu meik ius ov thi ridandant leterz 'c', 'y' and 'x' - bai now jast a memori in the maindz of ould doderers - tu replais 'ch', 'sh' and 'th' rispektivli.*
>
> *Fainali, xen, after sam 20 iers ov orxogrephkl riform, we wud hev a lojikl, kohirnt speling in ius xrewawt xe Ingliy spiking werld . . .*

People who knew only the reformed spelling system proposed in this letter would have difficulty reading books written in traditional orthography. Those who wished to read any of the millions of books or articles currently in print would therefore have to either learn the traditional spelling system or have the documents that interested them converted into the new orthography.

A second factor militating against serious orthographic reform has to do with the dialectal variation found within English. Because English is spoken in more parts of the world than any other language, it has many different dialects. Any attempt to establish an orthography based on a principle of one segment, one symbol would result in serious regional differences in spelling. For instance, speakers of Boston English would write *far* as *fa* since they do not pronounce syllable-final /r/. Speakers of some dialects of Newfoundland English would write both *tin* and *thin* as *tin* and *day* and *they* as *day* since they have no /t/-/θ/ or /d/-/ð/ distinction. Moreover, while most Canadians would have identical spellings for *cot* and *caught* (since these words are homophonous in their speech), speakers of English in many other parts of the world pronounce them differently and would therefore spell them differently as well.

Other considerations

Even if considerations relating to practicality and dialectal variation did not rule out major reforms to our orthography, there might still be reasons for retaining at least some of the current spelling conventions.

One advantage of the contemporary system is that it often indicates derivational relationships among words. For instance, if the words *music* and *musician* or *sign* and *signature* were spelled phonetically, it would be difficult to perceive the relationship between them since the root is pronounced differently in each case (see table 15.4).

1)

music	[mjuzɪk]	musician	[mjuzɪʃ-ən]
sign	[sajn]	signature	[sɪgn-ɪtʃər]

There are many other such cases where English orthography ignores differences in pronunciation so that a morpheme can have the same or nearly the same spelling in different words.

Table 15.4 Some cases in which English orthography provides a single spelling for roots with different pronunciations

electri<u>c</u> – electri<u>c</u>ity	[k] and [s] represented as *c*
inser<u>t</u> – inser<u>t</u>ion	[t] and [ʃ] as *t*
righ<u>t</u> – righ<u>t</u>eous	[t] and [tʃ] as *t*
bom<u>b</u> – bom<u>b</u>ard	Ø and [b] as *b*
dam<u>n</u> – dam<u>n</u>ation	Ø and [n] as *n*
impre<u>ss</u> – impre<u>ss</u>ion	[s] and [ʃ] as *ss*
all<u>e</u>g<u>e</u> – all<u>e</u>g<u>a</u>tion	[ɛ] and [ə] as *e*; [dʒ] and [g] as *g*
res<u>ig</u>n – res<u>ig</u>nation	[aj] and [ɪ] as *i*; Ø and [g] and *g*
ch<u>a</u>ste – ch<u>a</u>stity	[ej] and [æ] as *a*
prod<u>u</u>ce – prod<u>u</u>ctive	[u] and [ʌ] as *u*
pl<u>ea</u>se – pl<u>ea</u>sant	[i] and [ɛ] as *ea*

Examples such as these show that English orthography does not simply represent phonemic contrasts. Often, it provides a single representation for the variants of a morpheme, even if this means ignoring morphologically conditioned alternations among phonemes. (For this reason, some linguists have concluded that English orthography is a type of *morphophonemic* spelling system; see chapter 4, section 7 for a discussion of morphophonemic alternations.) Once this fact is taken into account, it is possible to see the usefulness of orthographic conventions that allow *c* to stand for either /k/ (*electric*) or /s/ (*electricity*) and *t* to represent /t/ (*react*) or /ʃ/ (*reaction*).

Morphological considerations are reflected in English orthography in other ways as well. Consider in this regard the spelling of the following words.

2)

mess	lapse
crass	dense
kiss	house
gloss	mouse

Although these words all end in the phoneme /s/, this segment cannot be represented as a simple *s*. Instead, the *s* is either doubled to *ss* (when preceded by a lax vowel, as in the first column) or followed by an *e* (all other cases, as exemplified in the second column). This reflects a general rule of English orthography, which reserves word-final *s* for inflectional suffixes (particularly, the plural and the third person singular). Thus, *s* is permitted in the word *laps* (the plural of *lap*) but not in *lapse*.

Another example of morphological influence is found in the rule that prohibits a final *ll* in polysyllabic words—*plentiful, excel, repel,* and so on. As the following examples show, this rule is systematically suspended in two morphological patterns: compounds (the first column) and derivations consisting of a prefix and its base (the second column).

3)

baseball	unwell
spoonbill	resell
landfill	recall

Yet another morphologically constrained rule of English orthography converts postconsonantal *y* to *i* in front of a suffix.

4)

carry	carri-ed
merry	merri-ly
marry	marri-age
candy	candi-es
beauty	beauti-ful

The existence of conventions and practices such as these demonstrates that English orthography is much more than a system for phonemic transcription. Its intricacies can be understood only through the careful study of the history and structure of the linguistic system that it is used to represent.

6 Writing and reading

The three types of writing described earlier in this chapter each represent different types of linguistic units—morphemes and words in the case of logographic systems, syllables in the case of syllabaries, and consonants and vowels in the case of alphabets. Because of these differences, each orthography places different demands on readers. We know that different parts of the brain are used for reading logographic writing systems and phonographic orthographies such as syllabaries and alphabets. Because phonological structure is largely irrelevant to logographic writing, people suffering from Broca's aphasia (see chapter 13) typically do not lose the ability to write and read logograms. However, the use of syllabaries and alphabets can be severely disrupted by this type of brain disorder. There are reports of Japanese patients suffering from Broca's aphasia who are unable to use hiragana or katakana (the Japanese syllabaries), but retain mastery of kanji (the logographic writing system).

Further information about the relationship between language and writing systems comes from the study of the congenitally deaf. Because they have never heard speech, congenitally deaf individuals have little or no understanding of the phonological units that alphabets represent. Significantly, they have a great deal of difficulty learning to read English.

The type of linguistic unit represented by an orthography also has an effect on how children with normal hearing learn to read. Each system has its own advantages and disadvantages. Children learning Chinese characters, for instance, have little difficulty understanding what each symbol represents, but it takes them many years to learn enough symbols to be able to write and read all the items in their vocabulary. (Knowledge of several thousand separate symbols is required just to read a newspaper.) Even educated people typically know only a few thousand characters and must use dictionaries for new or unfamiliar words.

This problem does not arise in syllabic and alphabetic orthographies. Because languages have far fewer syllables and phonemes than morphemes or words, the entire inventory of symbols can be learned in a year or two and then used productively to write and read new words. This is the major advantage of sound-based orthographies over word-based writing systems.

There is reason to think that children find syllabaries easier to master than alphabets. Children learning syllabaries (such as Japanese hiragana) are reported to have fewer reading problems than children learning alphabetic orthographies. Although at least some difficulties encountered by children learning to read English may be due to the complexity of English spelling conventions, Italian and German children learning to use their relatively regular alphabetic orthographies also have reading problems.

The advantage of syllabaries over alphabets for young readers apparently stems from the fact that children have less difficulty identifying syllables than phonemes. One study revealed that 46 percent of four year olds and 90 percent of six year olds can segment words into syllables. In contrast, virtually no four year olds and only about two-thirds of all six year olds can segment words into phoneme-sized units. Since learning to read involves an understanding of the type of unit represented by written symbols, it is not surprising that syllabaries are generally easier for young children to learn.

Of course, it must be remembered that syllabaries may have disadvantages of other sorts. While syllabic writing is feasible for languages such as Japanese that have a relatively small number of syllable types, it would be quite impractical in English where there are dozens of different syllable structures. Ultimately, an orthography must be judged in terms of its success in representing language for the purpose of reading and writing. There is no doubt that an alphabetic orthography is superior to a syllabary for representing the phonological structure of English.

Summing up

The development of writing has been one of humanity's greatest intellectual achievements. From **pictograms** and **logograms**, the graphic representation of language has developed through syllabic writing to the **alphabet**. This was achieved through the discovery of the relationship between graphic symbols and sounds.

Many of the large number of writing systems found throughout the modern world owe their origin directly or indirectly to the Semitic writing systems of the eastern Mediterranean. As the idea of writing spread, new forms of the signs were independently invented and sound-symbol correspondences were altered to accommodate individual languages. Some writing systems derived from the Graeco-Phoenician tradition are today scarcely recognizable as such, since so little remains of the original symbols. In cases where the entire system was invented, perhaps only the idea of writing is traceable to the early traditions.

In all cases, the historical line of development is clear. There seems to be no evidence of a culture that has developed an alphabet and then followed this with the development of, for example, a logographic script. But this cultural line of development does not imply that earlier forms of writing are inferior to alphabetic writing. In the case of languages such as Japanese or Cree, the syllabic writing system is as well suited to the phonological structure of the language as an alphabetic script would be.

Notes

[1] Scholars are still not in agreement on this question. Some claim a single common origin in the Middle East for all writing systems. Others state that certain systems, for example, Mayan writing (see section 4.4), must have emerged independently.

[2] Ancient Greek was represented by reversing the direction of writing at the end of each line. If the first line of a text was written right-to-left, the next line continued left-to-right, then right-to-left, and so on. This practice was typical of many old writing systems and is known as **boustrophedon** (Greek for 'as the ox turns'), since it was said to resemble the pattern made by plowing a field.

Sources

Comprehensive surveys of the development of writing and of the world's writing systems are found in Jensen, Gelb, and DeFrancis (all cited below). The possibility that pure syllabaries may not exist was called to the authors' attention by Prof. W. Poser of the University of British Columbia (personal communication). The idea that writing may have originated in record keeping with clay tokens is taken from Schmandt-Besserat (cited below). The following figures are adapted from Jensen: 15.1a, 15.3, 15.6, 15.11, 15.14, 15.25, 15.28; from Marshack, *The Roots of Civilization* (New York: McGraw-Hill, 1972): 15.1b; from Schmandt-Besserat: 15.2; from René Labat, *Manuel d'Epigraphie Akkadienne,* 5th ed., (Paris: P. Geuthner, 1976): 15.6; from DeFrancis (see Labat, further references to origins of these figures therein): 15.8, 15.9, 15.13, 15.17, 15.26 (adapted from *Visible Speech: The Diverse Oneness of Writing Systems* and reprinted by permission of the University of Hawaii Press); from Wayne M. Senner, "Theories and Myths on the Origins of Writing: A Historical Overview," in Senner (cited below: and reprinted by permission of the University of Nebraska Press): 15.10; from Samson (cited below): 15.12; from Frank Moore Cross, "The Invention and Development of the Alphabet," in Senner, p. 89 (cited below and reprinted by permission of the University of Nebraska Press): 15.18. The sport pictograms in figure 15.4 are courtesy of the Olympic Trust of Canada, ™Official Mark © Canadian Olympic Association, 1972. Figure 15.5 is courtesy of the Blissymbolics Communication Institute, exclusive licensee, 1982, and is derived from the symbols described in the work *Semantography*, original copyright C.K. Bliss 1949.

The discussion of Arabic writing is based on "The Arabic Alphabet" by James A. Bellamy in the book by Senner (cited below). John DeFrancis (University of Hawaii), Robert Fisher (York University), and Brian King (University of British Columbia) all provided insightful and helpful comments (especially regarding Chinese writing)—so many, in fact, that we were not able to make use of all of them here. Their views are not necessarily those reflected in the chapter, however. The discussion of Chinese writing is derived from DeFrancis (cited below), as is table 15.1; figure 15.9 was adapted from Jerry Norman, *Chinese* (Cambridge: Cambridge University Press, 1988); Chinese characters were kindly provided by Lin Zhiqiu. The presentation of Japanese writing is also indebted to DeFrancis, as well as to M. Shibatani, *The Languages of Japan* (Cambridge: Cambridge University Press, 1990). The hiragana and katakana charts (figure 15.20) are adapted from Len Walsh's *Read Japanese Today* (Tokyo: Charles E. Tuttle, 1971) and reprinted by permission of the publisher; Japanese examples were provided by Kazue Kanno. For a discussion of Cherokee writing, see "Native American Writing Systems" by W. Walker, in *Language in the USA*, edited by C. Ferguson et al. (New York: Cambridge University Press, 1981). Our presentation of the Cree syllabary is adapted from D. Pentland, *Nēhiyawasi-nahikēwin: A Standard Orthography for the Cree Language* (Saskatoon: Saskatchewan Indian Cultural College, 1977). David H. Kelley of the University of Calgary provided corrective and helpful advice on Mayan and other Mesoamerican writing. The examples of Northern Indian pictorial script are from John Marshall, *Mohenjo-Daro and the Indus Civilization* (London: A. Probsthain, 1931).

The discussion of the history of English spelling is based on *A History of English Spelling* by D.G. Scragg (New York: Barnes & Noble, 1974). The examples of spelling rules sensitive to morphological structure come from the book by D.W. Cummings cited below. Data on children's ability to segment words into syllables and phonemes comes from I. Y. Liberman, reported in the book by Gibson and Levin (cited below). John Sören Pettersson of Uppsala University commented extensively and helpfully on an earlier version of this chapter.

Recommended reading

Cummings, D.W. 1988. *American English Spelling.* Baltimore: The Johns Hopkins University Press.

DeFrancis, John. 1989. *Visible Speech: The Diverse Oneness of Writing Systems.* Honolulu: University of Hawaii Press.

Gelb, I. 1952. *A Study of Writing.* Chicago: University of Chicago Press.

Gibson, E., and H. Levin. 1975. *The Psychology of Reading.* Cambridge, MA: MIT Press.

Gleitman, L., and P. Rozin. 1977. "The Structure and Acquisition of Reading I: Relations Between Orthographies and the Structures of Language." In *Toward a Psychology of Reading.* Edited by A. Reber and D. Scarborough, 1–53. Hillsdale, NJ: Lawrence Erlbaum.

Jensen, H. 1970. *Sign, Symbol and Script.* G. Unwin, trans. London: George Allen and Unwin.

Sampson, G. 1985. *Writing Systems: A Linguistic Introduction.* Stanford, CA: Stanford University Press.

Schmandt-Besserat, Denise. 1989. "Two Precursors of Writing: Plain and Complex Tokens." In *The Origins of Writing.* Edited by W. M. Senner, 27-42. Lincoln, NE: University of Nebraska Press.

Senner, W.M., ed. 1989. *The Origins of Writing.* Lincoln, NE: University of Nebraska Press.

Wallace, Rex. 1989. "The Origins and Development of the Latin Alphabet." In *The Origins of Writing.* Edited by W. M. Senner, 121-136. Lincoln, NE: University of Nebraska Press.

Questions

1. Suppose you are the user of a pictographic writing system that can already represent concrete objects in a satisfactory way. Using the pictographic symbols of your system, propose ideographic extensions of these symbols to represent the following meanings.

   a) hunt   f) cook
   b) cold   g) tired
   c) fast   h) wet
   d) white   i) angry
   e) strength   j) weakness

2. Construct a syllabary for English that can be used to spell the following words. What problems do you encounter?

foe	law	shoe
slaw	slow	slowly
lee	day	daily
sue	pull	shop
ship	loop	food
lock	shock	unlock
locked	shocked	pulled
shops	locker	shod
float	splint	schlock

3. How does English orthography capture the morphophonemic alternations in the following words? Begin your analysis with a phonemic transcription of the forms.

   a) hymn   hymnal
   b) part   partial
   c) recite   recitation
   d) reduce   reduction
   e) design   designation
   f) critical   criticize   criticism
   g) analog   analogous   analogy

4. After discussing the forms in question 3, consider the following forms. Does the spelling system treat all cases of allomorphic variation the same way?

   a) invade   invasion
   b) concede   concession
   c) assume   assumption
   d) profound   profundity

5. Briefly outline the advantages and disadvantages of the three major types of writing that have evolved throughout history.

CHAPTER Sixteen
Michael Dobrovolsky

Animal communication

As I listened from a beach-chair in the shade
To all the noises that my garden made,
It seemed to me only proper that words
Should be withheld from vegetables and birds.

W.H. AUDEN

Communication—the passing on or exchange of information—distinguishes what is living from what is non-living in nature.[1] Communication is found even in the apparently passive world of plants; trees, for example, have been found to pass on information about advancing predators by means of chemical signals. Animals communicate among themselves and with humans so effectively that they are often said to use 'language'. But the words *communication* and *language* do not mean the same thing. Human language is a specific way of representing the world and passing on information. From the linguist's point of view, not just any communication qualifies as language as it is defined in this book.

A question that therefore interests many linguists is whether animals make use of any system of communication that genuinely resembles or approximates human language. Just as the use of communication sets what is living apart from what is non-living, the use of language is often said to set humans apart from all other animals. If animals communicate with a system that is structured like human language, then language as we know it is not the unique property of our species, and we will have to look for other ways of defining humanness. This chapter investigates the ways in which animal communication is like human language and the ways in which it is different.

1 Non-vocal communication

One of the most striking things about animal communication is the variety of means with which it is carried out. Animals communicate not only with sounds but with scent, light, ultrasound, visual signs, gestures, colour, and even electricity. From the slime mold to the giant blue whale, all living things appear to have some means of communication. Some non-vocal modes of communication are described here.

Scent Chemicals used by animals specifically for communicative purposes are called **pheremones**. Pheremones are used by species as different as molds, insects, and mammals. A female moth signals its reproductive readiness through the release of a pheremone into the air. Only a few of these molecules need to be sensed by a male moth for it to start flying zig-

571

zag upwind towards its potential mate. Dogs and other canines leave a urine-based phere-mone as an identification mark to stake out their territory, and many non-human primates have specialized scent glands for the same purpose.

Light   Probably the most well-known light user in North America is the firefly or lightning bug. This small flying beetle uses light flashes in varying patterns to signal its identity, sex, and location. Different species of these insects have different and distinguishing light patterns.

Electricity   Certain species of eels in the Amazon River basin communicate their presence and territoriality by means of electrical impulses at various frequencies. Each species signals at a specific frequency range, and the transmitting frequencies, like those of radio and television stations, do not overlap.

Colour   The colour (or colour pattern) of many animals plays an important role in their identification by members of their own species and other animals. The octopus changes colour frequently and this colouring is used for a range of messages that include territorial defence and mating readiness.

Posture   This is a common communicative device among animals. Dogs, for example, lower the front part of their bodies and extend their front legs when they are playful. They lower their whole bodies to the ground when they are submissive. Postural communication is found in both human and non-human primates as well.

Gesture   A gesture may be defined as active posturing. Humans wave their arms in recogni-

Figure 16.1 Some chimpanzee facial expressions: *a.* anger; *b.* fear-anger; *c.* affection; *d.* frustration-sadness; *e.* playfulness

tion or farewell, dogs wag their tails in excitement, and cats flick their tails when irritated. Many birds perform elaborate gestures of raising and lowering the head or racing back and forth across the water in their mating rituals. Some fish, such as the male stickleback, perform a series of distinct movements in the water as part of their mating ritual.

Facial expressions These are specific types of communicative gestures. When a male baboon yawns, bares its fangs, and retracts its eyebrows, it is indicating a willingness to fight. A wide and recognizable variety of facial expressions is found among chimpanzees, a number of which are shown in figure 16.1. Experiments have shown that humans can classify the meanings of these expressions quite accurately. For example, when humans draw back the corners of their mouths into a smile, they are generally indicating co-operation. A non-human primate's smile also indicates non-aggressiveness.

2 Communication structure: the study of signs

Certain common elements underlie the bewildering variety of communicative methods found in nature. An understanding of these is necessary for comparing the differences and similarities among systems of communication.

2.1 Signs

Communication relies on using something to stand for something else. Words are an obvious example of this: you do not have to have a car, a sandwich, or your cousin present in order to talk about them—the words *car, sandwich,* and *cousin* stand for them instead. This same phenomenon is found in animal communication as well. Instead of fighting over territory, for example, many animals produce sounds or make gestures that threaten and intimidate intruders—the message replaces the attack. Birds utter warning calls that represent the presence of a threat. A threatening animal or human need not be seen by other birds before they take flight—perception of the warning call replaces visual perception of the threat.

Each of these things that stand for other things is technically known as a **sign**. The sign is a unit of communication structure that consists of two parts: a **signifier**, be it a word, a scent, a gesture, or an electrical frequency, and something **signified** that exists in the real world, and which is mentally represented by the sign's conceptual content. The real world can be thought of as either external, mental, or emotional, and so what is signified by a sign can be as diverse as a tree, an abstract idea, a perception, or a feeling. Because their content is conceptual, all signs are associated with some **meaning**, such as 'danger', or 'item of furniture with legs and a flat top'. Individual instances of signs are called **tokens**. For example, in the sentence *The baby threw the rattle* there are five word tokens, but only four signs; *the* occurs twice as a token, but it is the same sign in both instances. Figure 16.2 illustrates these distinctions.

The study of signs is known as **semiotics**. Semiotics is a field of study that links many diverse disciplines, among them linguistics, anthropology, philosophy, zoology, genetics, literary study, and computer science. An understanding of signs is essential for understanding how messages are transmitted. So that we can understand signs better before proceeding to an analysis of animal communication, the next section examines their structure in more detail.

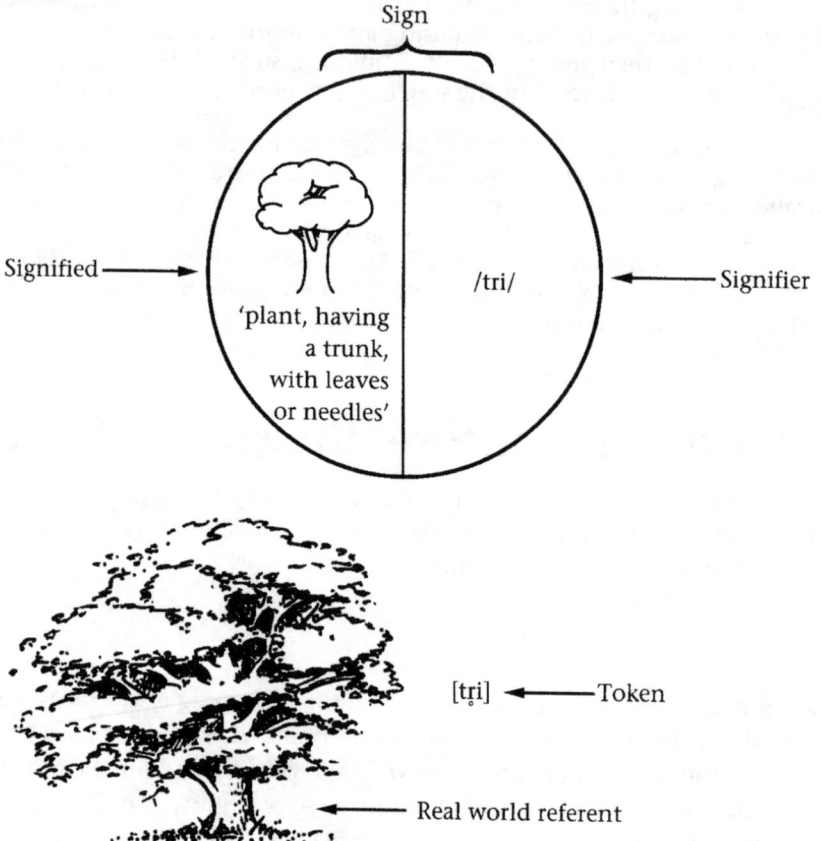

Figure 16.2 A sign

The signifier

A signifier is that part of a sign that stimulates at least one sense organ of the receiver of a message. The phonological component of the word *tree*, represented as /tri/ and pronounced [tri̥] is a typical linguistic signifier. A signifier can also be a picture, a photograph, a sign language gesture, or one of the many other words for *tree* in different languages.

The signified

The signified component of the sign refers to both the real world object it represents and its conceptual content.

The first of these is the real world content of the sign, its *extension* or *referent* (chapter 6, section 1.3) within a system of signs such as English, avian communication, or sign language. In our example, the referent is represented by a drawing since there is no room to include a real tree between the pages of this book. (Of course, the signifier /tri/ could also have a picture of a tree as its referent.) It is easiest to think of referents as concepts or persons or things but they may be ideas or feelings as well.

The signified component of a sign also evokes an *intension* (chapter 6, section 1.3) to users of the system in question. A word for 'tree' evokes concepts that probably include 'plant', 'having a trunk', and 'bearing leaves or needles' in the minds of speakers of any language who are familiar with trees. Some animals appear to conceptualize in terms of classes or categories as well. Certain monkeys, for example, distinguish among various types of predators on the basis of size, shape, and motion (see section 5.3).

2.2   Types of signs

Signs can be divided into three basic types, depending on (1) whether the signifier naturally resembles its referent, (2) whether the signifier is directly linked with the referent in a physical or mechanical sense, or (3) whether signifier and referent are arbitrarily associated.

Iconic signs

Iconic signs, or *icons,* always bear some resemblance to their referent. A photograph is an iconic sign; so too is a stylized silhouette of a female or a male on a restroom door. A baboon's open-mouth threat is iconic, resembling as it does the act of biting. Onomatopoeic words like *buzz, splat,* and *squish* in English and their counterparts in other human languages are also iconic in that they somewhat resemble what they signify. Because of this inherent resemblance to these referents—icons are considered non-arbitrary signs.

Figure 16.3 Some iconic tokens: *a.* open-mouth threat by a Japanese macaque (*Macaca fuscata*); *b.* park recreation signs; *c.* onomatopoeic words in English

Icons are widespread in the communication systems of all animals; many postures and gestures that are critical to animal communication are iconic, as are the postures and gestures used by humans. Human linguistic communication, however, does not make extensive use of iconic signs.

Indexical signs

An **indexical** sign, or *index,* fulfils its function by 'pointing out' its referent, typically by being a partial or representative sample of it. Indexes are not arbitrary, since their presence has in some sense been caused by their referent. For this reason it is sometimes said that there is a causal link between an indexical sign and its referent. The track of an animal, for example, points to the existence of the animal by representing a part of it. The presence of smoke is an index of fire.

Most important for our discussion here is a specific kind of indexical sign called a **symptomatic** sign, or *symptom*. Symptomatic signs spontaneously convey the internal state or emotions of the sender and thus represent the sender in an indexical manner. For example, the fact that our body temperature rises when we are ill is a spontaneous reflection of our internal state. When someone steps on our foot and we cry out, the cry is a spontaneous reflection of our internal state (surprise and pain) and thus constitutes a symptomatic sign.

Since symptomatic signs are spontaneous, we do not consider them to be deliberately selected by the sender for purposes of communication. We do not choose to cry out in pain in the same way as we might, for example, decide to call our dwelling place a *house, home, dwelling,* or *residence* in the appropriate circumstances. As forms of communication, symptomatic signs are therefore used primarily by the receiver of a message to assess the internal state of the sender. Since senders do not deliberately choose to transmit the sign, the message is assumed to be essentially beyond their control.[2]

Symbolic signs

Symbolic signs bear an arbitrary relationship to their referents and in this way are distinct from both icons and indexes. Human language is highly symbolic in that the vast majority of its signs bear no inherent resemblance or causal connection to their referents, as the following words show.

hana = ?
mazə = ?
talo = ?
kum = ?
berat = ?

Figure 16.4 Arbitrary sound-meaning correspondence in language

No phonological property of the words in figure 16.4 gives you any hint as to their possible meaning. (*Hana* means 'flower' or 'nose' in Japanese, *mazə* is 'forest' in Kabardian, *talo* is 'house' in Finnish, *kum* means 'sand' in Turkish, and *berat* means 'heavy' in Indonesian.)

We encounter many other symbolic signs in everyday life. The octagonal shape of a stop sign is symbolic; it bears no inherent connection with the message it helps to communicate. The colours used in traffic signals are symbolic as well; red has no more inherent connection with the act of stopping than yellow.

Mixed signs

Signs are not always exclusively of one type or another. Symptomatic signs, for example, may have iconic properties, as when a dog opens its mouth in a threat to bite. Symbolic signs such as traffic lights are symptomatic in that they reflect the internal state of the mechanism that causes them to change colour. Still, we classify a sign according to its major property: if it resembles its referent, it is iconic; if it is linked to its referent in some causal way or represents it partially in some non-arbitrary way, it is indexical (and symptomatic if it spontaneously expresses some internal state); and if its relationship to its referent is arbitrary, it is a symbol.

Signals

All signs can act as **signals** when they trigger a specific action on the part of the receiver, as do traffic lights, words in human language such as the race starter's "Go!", or the warning calls of birds. Typically, a signal releases more energy in the receiver than it takes for the transmitter to send it. For example, the simple release of a mating pheremone into the wind by a female moth (a symptomatic sign and also a signal) can cause the male to fly as much as six kilometres in search of her. Signals are very common in animal communication, but only a limited subset of human linguistic activity consists of signalling.

2.3   Sign structure

No matter what their type, signs show different kinds of structure. A basic distinction is made between **graded** and **discrete** sign structure.

Graded signs

Graded signs convey their meaning by changes in degree. A good example of a gradation in communication is voice volume. The more you want to be heard, the louder you speak along an increasing scale of loudness. There are no steps or jumps from one level to the next that can be associated with a specific change in meaning.

Gradation is common in many forms of communication. The hands of most clocks move (or appear to move) in a graded manner, as does the needle of an automobile speedometer. Many animal signs, such as the barking of dogs, are graded as well. A goose has essentially one type of honk, which may become louder and faster as it takes off in flight, but does not become another kind of honking. The gradually increasing fear in the facial expression of the monkey depicted in figure 16.5 is also a graded sign.

Figure 16.5 Some graded signs: the facial expressions *a, b,* and *c* of the macaque monkey represent just three points on a continuum expressing fear; *a.* is a neutral face; *b.* expresses slight fear; and *c.* expresses extreme fear. Each expression grades into the next. The hands of the clock in *d* express minutes and hours in a graded manner.

Discrete signs

Discrete signs are distinguished from each other by categorical (stepwise) differences. There is no gradual transition from one sign to the next. The words of human language are good examples of discrete signs. There is no intermediate stage between the words *stop* and *go* in English except that which can be expressed by other discrete words or combinations of words, such as *start to go*. The digital displays of watches are discrete as well, since they progress from one minute (or even second) to the next with no gradation. Traffic lights, too, are discrete signs; there is no gradual shifting from green to yellow to red.

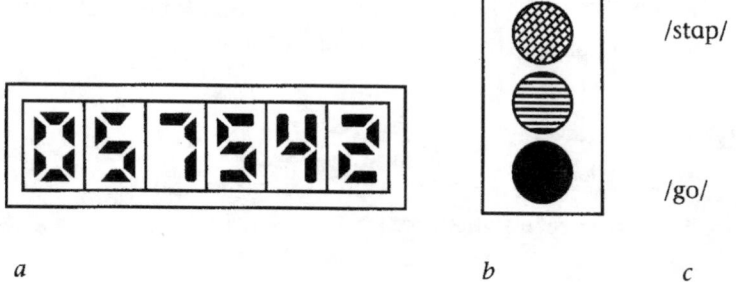

/stap/

/go/

a   *b*   *c*

Figure 16.6 Some discrete signs: *a.* digital time display; *b.* traffic lights; *c.* words of a human language

Sign types and structure

All three types of signs—*iconic, indexical/symptomatic,* and *symbolic*—can be graded or discrete. A photograph is iconic and discrete, but a threatening canine's gradual baring of its fangs is iconic and graded. Morse code is symbolic and discrete, but a slowly dimming light that signals the beginning of a theatrical performance is symbolic and graded. Symptomatic signs, too, may be discrete (the traffic light again) or graded (the crying of a child or the act of blushing).

It is possible for a discrete sign to be internally graded, and even to slip over into another type by degrees. Human crying, for example, is interpreted by experimental subjects as becoming gradually more like screaming as the audible intake of breath between sobs becomes shorter and shorter. Figure 16.7 illustrates this phenomenon.

At the extreme ends of the continuum, there is no difficulty interpreting the sound as one or the other, although it is difficult to say precisely when a 'sob' becomes a 'scream'. Thus we can say that 'sobbing' and 'screaming' are discrete symptomatic signs, but each of them is internally graded, and their gradations overlap. The same is true of many vocalizations in animal communication.

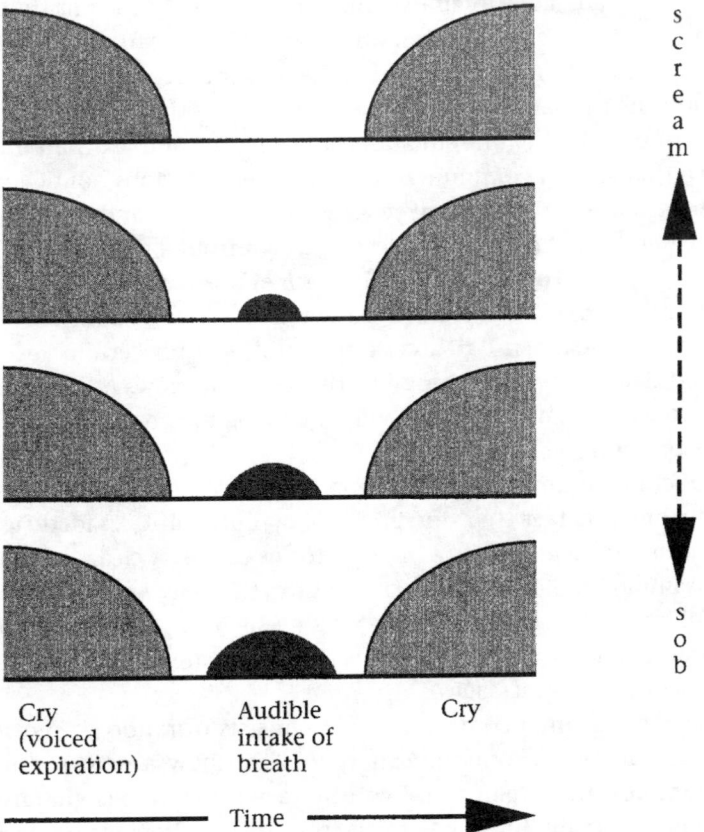

Figure 16.7 The graded continuum from sobbing to screaming (the height of the stippled and blackened areas represents the audibility of the vocalization and the width its duration): both sob and scream are discrete signs, even though each grades into the other

2.4   A view of animal communication

> *They're like Swiss watches . . . they just react. Their genes and hormones and experience tell them what to do. They don't think about it.*
>
> Zookeeper Ben Beck (on golden lion tamarin monkeys)

Most animal communication, it is claimed, shows little arbitrariness. It is said to be largely iconic and symptomatic and hence not deliberate or conscious in intent, nor symbolic in its sign repertory. For example, if a monkey gives a certain cry in the presence of danger, it is assumed that the monkey is spontaneously signalling its fear by vocalizing, but is not deliberately warning other group members of the danger. The symptomatic vocalization is interpreted and used by other members of a troop for their own benefit.

It follows from this view of animal communication that the acquisition of communicative systems by animals was in the past assumed to be largely devoid of learning and experience. Rather, it was claimed that the systems are rather strictly limited by genetic inheritance, and in this sense are radically unlike human language, the acquisition of which requires exposure to a mature system. This limitation certainly appears to be true in some cases. When raised in isolation, animals as diverse as the fox, the elephant seal, the cat, and certain monkeys develop the full range of vocalizations typical of their species. However, as we will see in section 4 of this chapter, the situation can be more complex than this.

It is further claimed that animal communication is neither conscious nor deliberate. It is not widely believed, for example, that a monkey assesses a situation and then deliberately chooses to warn group members of danger by selecting a sign from a repertoire of meaningful sound symbols at its disposal. For this reason, the term **stimulus-bound** is also used to describe animal communication, since it is often claimed that animal communication only occurs when it is triggered by exposure to a certain stimulus or for certain specific ends. Animals do not communicate about anything but the here and now. As the philosopher Bertrand Russell once noted, "No matter how eloquently a dog may bark, it cannot tell you that its parents were poor but honest."

With respect to structure, animal communication is said to show few traces of discrete structuring beyond the obvious fact that one group of symptomatic, graded signals may sound very different from another. Whining in dogs, for example, is clearly different from barking, but both are assumed to be symptomatic, and the two may grade into each other. Combining and recombining of discrete units of structure such as phonemes, morphemes, and words is not characteristic of the way animals communicate. Dogs do not combine whines and barks to produce novel messages.

This does not mean that animal communication consists of random emotional outbursts. Nor does it mean that animal communication does not show structure. Animal communication is both complex and organized. Evolutionary pressure has guaranteed that animal communication is optimally in tune with the survival requirements of each species. The electrical communication of Amazonian eels is an excellent means of communication in muddy waters. The danger whistle of a small, tree-dwelling primate like the galago is ideal for nocturnal communication in a dense forest. Small jungle frogs in South America communicate by sticking out their long and colourful legs, ideal for sending messages in the dim and noisy jungle. But jungle frogs do not try new combinations of leg movements in order to come up with an original message, any more than the electric eel recombines frequencies in order to signal something it has never conveyed before. Animal communication appears to be limited in the messages it can convey.

But is animal communication so very unlike human language in all respects? Recent work on animal communication has often focused on its relationship to human linguistic communication. The next sections examine the communication systems of several kinds of animals and compare them with human language.

3   The bees

> *I have no doubt that some will attempt to 'explain' the performances of the bees as the results of reflexes and instincts . . . for my part, I find it difficult to assume that such perfection and flexibility in behavior can be reached without some kind of mental processes going on in the small heads of the bees.*

August Krogh, *Scientific American*

3.1   The system

Forager bees display a remarkable system of communicating the location of a food source to other bees in their hive. When a food source has been discovered, the forager flies back to the hive and communicates information about it by performing special movements (which humans call *dancing*) before other members of the hive. The dancing conveys information about the location of the food source, its quality, and its distance from the hive.

Distance

Distance is conveyed by one of three different dances performed on the wall or floor of the hive (some species have only two different dances, and so may be said to have a different 'dialect'). In doing the round dance, the bee circles repeatedly. This indicates a food source within five metres or so of the hive. The *sickle dance* indicates a food source from five to twenty metres from the hive. It is performed by the bee dancing a curved figure eight shape. The *tail-wagging dance* indicates distances further than twenty metres. In this dance, the bee wags its abdomen as it moves forward, circles to the right back to its starting point, repeats the wagging forward motion, and circles left. The cycle then begins again.

Direction

The round dance does not communicate direction, presumably since the food source is so close to the hive. The direction of more distant food sources is indicated in the other two types of dance.

As the bee performs the sickle and tail-wagging dances, it is simultaneously indicating the direction of the food source. Bees orient themselves in flight relative to the angle of the sun. When danced on the floor of the hive, the angle of the open side of the sickle dance's figure eight or the angle of the wagging path during the tail-wagging dance indicates the direction of flight. When the dancing is performed on the vertical wall of the hive, it is apparently 'understood' that the top of the hive wall represents the current position of the sun in the sky. During the sickle dance, the angle of the open side of the figure eight relative to the hive's vertical alignment indicates the direction of flight toward the food source

Figure 16.8 Bee dancing

relative to the sun. When the bee performs the tail-wagging dance, the angle of its wagging path relative to the hive's vertical angle indicates the path of flight toward the food source relative to the sun. Figure 16.8 illustrates the dances and their manner of indicating the direction of the food source.

Quality

Quality of the food source is indicated by the intensity of the dancing and the number of repetitions of the circling movements. As the food source is depleted, the dance is performed with less vivacity.

Other factors

These messages are not communicated with perfect accuracy, nor are they the only ones involved in bee communication. Bees also leave a hive-specific pheremone trace at the site of the food source, thereby directing their fellow foragers to the precise location. The bees also carry back traces of the food source odours, which further aid other bees in the search. A complex of communicative modes operating on different channels—a constellation—is thus employed in bee communication. The use of different modalities to communicate the same information is called **redundancy**. Redundancy helps guarantee that communication will succeed in the event one or the other modalities fails or is imperfectly transmitted. All communication systems make use of redundancy, and human language is no exception. For example, the presence of allophonic features such as voicelessness and aspiration on syllable-initial voiceless stops, or both length and quality differences on vowels provides redundancy that assists in decoding the signals.

3.2   Bees and humans

How does bee communication compare with human language? The three patterns that the bees dance are not obviously connected with the messages they communicate and so are symbolic in nature (though it is possible to argue that relative distance is iconically represented in that a greater distance covered by the bee in each cycle of the dance corresponds to a greater distance of the nectar source from the hive). The communication of direction is indexical when carried out on the hive floor (in the sense that it points in the direction of flight), and in this sense may be comparable to a human gesture. Bees are, however, capable of transforming this information into a symbolic representation, since they transfer the horizontal flight path to a vertical representation on the hive wall. The expression of food source quality is, in all probability, symptomatic: the more stimulated a bee is by the quality of the food source, the faster it dances.

The total communicative constellation involves other, redundant sources of communication as well, such as pheremones and food source samples. The performance even involves audience participation. During its dancing, the returning bee is expected to provide samples from the food source. If it fails to do so, it may be stung to death.

Bee communication, then, like human language, shows symbolic, indexical, and symptomatic traits, and interaction between sender and receiver of the messages. But there is a major difference between the two systems of communication. The topic of bee language is severely constrained. Bees communicate only about food sources. Furthermore, their potential for communication is very limited. Only certain locations of food sources can be conveyed. Bees cannot communicate the notion of up or down. They can be easily tricked into communicating the wrong direction of the food source if a strong light source is placed in an incorrect position with relation to the food source. They can also be tricked into giving the wrong information about distance to the food source if they are forced to walk or stop several times during their trip. This indicates that they gauge distance by time. The bees show no means of assessing varying information and communicating this fact. Their system of communication appears to be close-ended and limited to a specific number of facts about a specific type of information.

It also appears that bee language is largely innate—that is, there is very little need for a new forager bee to be exposed to the system in the presence of other bees. Foragers on their first flight perform the appropriate dances, although they refine their performance to some extent with time and exposure to other dancing. Their flight orientation to the sun is imperfect at first, but it develops within a few hours.[3]

The innateness of bee dancing has been tested by cross-breeding Austrian bees, which do not perform the sickle dance to express intermediate distance of the food source from the hive, with Italian honeybees, which do. The results of such experiments further support a genetic interpretation of bee communication. In the cross-breeding experiment, the bees that bore a physical resemblance to their Italian parent performed the sickle dance to indicate intermediate distance 98 percent of the time. The bees that bore a physical resemblance to their Austrian parent performed the round dance to indicate intermediate distance 96 percent of the time; they did not perform the sickle dance at all. The dance pattern used in a specific situation appears to be inherited from a certain parent along with other more obvious genetic traits.

In 1948, when the Danish physiologist August Krogh made the statement quoted at the beginning of this section, he struck at the widely accepted notion that animal behaviour was either the result of some kind of conditioning, or, in some ill-defined way, instinctive. Much has been learned since then about the enormous quantity of information imparted by genetic transfer. It is now possible to state with a fair degree of certainty that the complex and sophisticated behaviour of bees and other equally remarkable insects is in all probability largely genetically predetermined and, unlike human language, it relies very little on exposure to the mature system in order to be acquired.

4   The birds

> *How intelligent is a creature that can amuse himself for 15 minutes by uttering, over and over, the following sounds: uhr, uhr, uhr, Uhr, URH, URH, Wah, Wah, wah, wah, wah.*

Jake Page (on his Amazon Parrot)

4.1   Bird vocalization

Birds, as Jake Page later found out, can do a lot more than utter sounds over and over. Even the parrot, which has been labelled for years as nothing but a stimulus-bound mimic, has been shown to have some capacity for meaningful labelling. The parroting of trained birds is generally accepted to be nothing more than non-intentional response to external stimuli arrived at through repetitive conditioning. But recently, it has been claimed that certain kinds of parroting have cognitive underpinning of a type shared with primates and perhaps even humans (although it took one test parrot four years to acquire a vocabulary of eighteen nouns). Research on natural communication among birds has already shed light on certain parallels in human linguistic communication.

Bird vocalization can be divided into two types, **call** and **song**. Calls are typically short bursts of sound or simple patterns of notes. Songs are lengthy, elaborate patterns of mostly pitched sounds.

Calls

Calls serve very specific functions in the bird community. They typically warn of predators, co-ordinate flocking and flight activity, express aggression, and accompany nesting or feeding behaviour. The cawing of crows is a typical call. It appears to convey a generalized mobilization to possible danger. When a crow hears cawing, it flies up to a tree if it is on the ground, or flies higher in a tree—or to another tree—if it is already in one. (If there are crows in your neighbourhood, you can test this yourself, as cawing is easy to imitate.)

In some birds, individual calls are associated with specific activities; a danger call is quite different from a call given when birds are grouped in flight. A flight call is generally short, crisp, and easy to locate by other group members. The honking of geese in flight is a typical example of this sort of call. Because it is loud and easy to locate, it is well suited to enable the bird flock to stay together. The call given by small birds when larger avian predators threaten them is very different. It is typically thin and high-pitched. This kind of sound is difficult to locate, and so can be given as a warning without revealing the position of the caller. Such functional utility is typical of bird calls, and in fact, calls that serve the same communicative purpose are often remarkably similar among different species of birds.

Song

Birdsong is different from calling. Although calls are produced year round, singing is largely limited to spring, summer, and autumn. Furthermore, it is generally only male birds that sing.

The main purposes of song are, as far as we know, to announce and delimit the territory of the male and to attract a mate. Birds establish territory for breeding purposes and defend it vigorously. Across Canada, as far north as Hudson Bay in the east, and well into the Northwest Territories and the Yukon in the west, it is a common sight in the spring to see a red-winged blackbird (*Agelaius phoeniceus*) and its mate team up to drive away a male of their species that has strayed into their territory. The use of song enables male birds to establish and maintain this territory without constant patrolling and fighting. Moreover, once a bird has established its territory, its song serves to attract and maintain contact with a mate. It follows that birdsong is unique from species to species, and even varies to some degree from bird to bird within the same species, since its purposes require species and individual recognition.[4]

In some species, songs are nothing more than a successive repetition of calls. In others, songs consist of complex patterns of pitches—sometimes called syllables—that form longer repeated units or themes. The sometimes elaborate complexity of song structure reflects individual variation among the singers, and, as pointed out previously, serves a specific purpose. Figure 16.9 shows a **spectrogram** (an acoustic recording that shows pitch and intensity of sound along a time axis) of the song of the European Robin (*Erithacus rubecula*). Note how the different subsections of the song are distinct and recognizable. There is also some evidence that sections of a song are combined in different orders by certain birds, but there is no evidence that recombination is associated with different meanings.

Figure 16.9 Spectrogram of a robin song; pitch is shown vertically along the L-R time axis, intensity by greater darkness

Avian dialects

There is evidence for both song and call dialects among bird species. Researchers even speak of avian *isoglosses* (lines drawn on a map to indicate shared characteristics among dialects; see chapter 14, section 2.3) that are based on variations in the melody of song 'syllables' or themes (see figure 16.10). The reason for the existence of dialects is still unclear; it may be no more than a reflection of individual avian variation in song and call learning. If it is, we are led to an intriguing issue in the relationship of bird vocalization to human language—the question of how bird vocalizations are acquired.

Figure 16.10 Avian isoglosses: call patterns of male Hill Mynas (black dots show myna groups; the shaded area shows forested hills and the unshaded, open plain; the heavier the black lines, the more song characteristics are shared by the group within its boundaries)

4.2   Birds and humans

The acquisition of call and song by birds shows interesting parallels with recent hypotheses about the acquisition of language by human children (see chapter 10). Though a great deal of bird vocalization—particularly calling—appears to be innate, there is much that appears to be acquired. Studies of avian dialects have shown that birds reared in the same nest acquire different song dialects when they live in different dialect areas. It also appears to be the case that singing ability is lateralized in the left brains of birds, as is linguistic ability in humans. Still more significant for linguistic study is the fact that some birds must acquire the species-specific characteristics of their song within a certain timespan or critical period. A number of bird species do not develop fully characteristic songs if they are deprived from hearing them during the early stages of their lives. The chaffinch (*Fringilla coelebs*) is one such bird. If chaffinches are reared in isolation, they sing, but replicate only in a general way the typical song of the species. If young chaffinches are reared away from fully developed singers, but with other young chaffinches, the entire experimental community develops an identical song. Finally, chaffinches that have been exposed to only some part of the fully developed song (those that are captured in the autumn of the first year of life) will, the following spring, develop a song that is partially typical but not completely well formed.

These experiments indicate that there are some songbirds that have both an innate and a learned component in their song. The innate component predisposes them to perform a general song that is extremely simplified. This has been called a **template** or a blueprint. Only exposure to the fully formed song of the species will enable them to produce the correct song. (Exposure to other song causes some species to imitate in this direction; other species simply do not acquire anything they are exposed to unless it is their own species-characteristic song.) Finally, it is clear that certain birds do not acquire their characteristic song in a brief span of time, but that several seasons of exposure are required. The evidence from songbird studies, while not transferable directly to humans, gives strong support to the idea that a combination of innate and acquired components is one way that the acquisition of complex behaviour takes place in nature.

5   Non-human primates

> *Some animals share qualities of both man and the four-footed beasts, for example, the ape, the monkey, and the baboon.*
>
> Aristotle, *On Animals*

Fascination with non-human primates goes far back in human history. Their social behaviour has long been seen as an amusing (and sometimes instructive) parody of human behaviour. Since the recent establishment of the fact that we are closely related genetically to these animals—some 99 percent of our genetic matter is shared with chimpanzees and gorillas—the resemblance of their behavioural, social, and communicative traits to ours has been seen as more than an amusing counterpart to human activity. Recently, the question of our shared cognitive, and especially linguistic ability, has become more important; it is thought that a better understanding of non-human primates may shed light on the evolution of human social and cognitive abilities.

Primates form a large class of mammals, which range from the tiny tarsier to the imposing mountain gorilla. Among the non-human primates, some are nocturnal, some diurnal in their activity cycle. Some are solitary, some form part of complex social groups. Many are tree-dwelling, and many are ground-dwelling. Some are quadrupeds, and some show periods of bipedal locomotion. The following figure 16.11 shows one widely accepted classification of the primates.

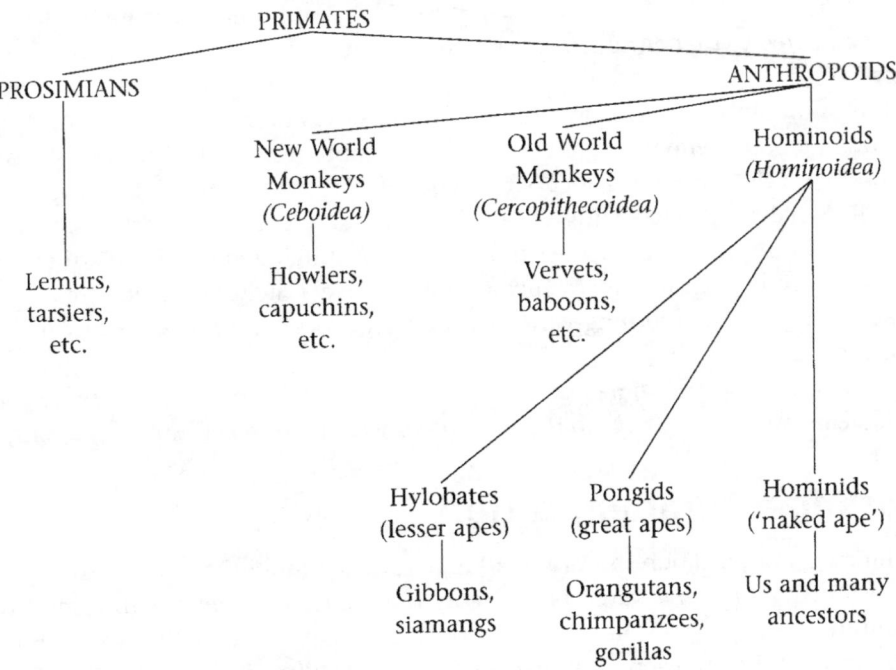

Figure 16.11 The primates

The prosimians are an evolutionarily early group found on the island of Malagasy, in sub-Saharan Africa, and in Southeast Asia. New World Monkeys range from Mexico through South America. Among them are the only primates with prehensile (grasping) tails. Old World Monkeys include the many tree- and ground-dwelling species of Africa and the Far East. The larger non-human primates—baboons, chimpanzees, and gorillas—are not native to North and South America. Baboons, large, mainly ground-dwelling primates, are found from central to northern Africa. They show a high degree of social organization, intelligence, and aggressiveness. The hominoids include the agile gibbons, solitary orangutans (both found only in Southeast Asia), the large but peaceful gorillas, the chimpanzees, and humans.

The validity of studies of communication among captive primates has been criticized because the animals' social existence is highly limited and compromised in zoos. Studies of non-human primate communication have largely left the zoo and laboratory and moved into the animals' natural habitat. While careful observation of non-human primate communication is still the basis of this work, the use of playback experiments, in which tape recordings of natural calls are played back over hidden loudspeakers, has led to a greater understanding of the communicative systems of these animals.

In the next section, we first turn our attention to non-human primate communication in the wild. It is there that we can gain an initial understanding of how forms of non-human primate communication resemble or differ from our own in terms of function and structure.

5.1 Some functions of non-human primate communication

Although the social life of even the most gregarious non-human primate is relatively simple when compared to that of humans, primates, like humans, communicate for many different reasons.

Typical non-human primate communication serves to mark and announce territory, to warn other group members of danger, to seek or maintain contact with a mate or other members of the species, and to interact with members of the troop or species in various ways we can call 'socializing'. Socializing vocalizations are particularly important in mother-child bonding and in primate groups with a complex and hierarchical social structure. In these groups, it is important to know which members have a higher or lower rank so that group members can behave accordingly in their presence. Vocalization is a key factor in maintaining this behaviour.

As we briefly survey some aspects of the structure of non-human primate communicative systems, we will also refer to the ways in which structure and function are linked.

5.2 Prosimian communication

Prosimian communication shows a small repertoire of sounds that are patterned into discrete groups. The lemur (*Lemur catta*) of Malagasy is a typical prosimian with respect to its vocal communication system. It has been described as making essentially two types of vocalization, noises and calls, each of which shows some grading. The vocalizations appear to be symptomatic. They are classified in table 16.1; quasi-phonetic descriptions like *spat* should be interpreted as onomatopoeic.

Table 16.1	Lemur vocalization		
Noises		**Calls**	
Sound	*Context*	*Sound*	*Context*
Single click	In response to strange objects	Light spat (yip)	When driving off threatening inferiors
Clicks, grunts	During locomotion, or for friendly greeting	Spat	When crowded or handled roughly
Purr	While grooming	Bark	When startled

Each graded set of sounds is used in a circumscribed range of situations. The calls, in particular, are limited to threat or fear encounters. They seem to form a graded series, ranging from the light spat to the bark in intensity. A small repertoire of distinct vocalizations is the norm among prosimians. The slow loris (*Nycticebus coucang*), an Asian prosimian, is reported to have no more than five calls.

5.3   Monkeys

The study of communication among the many varieties of New and Old World Monkeys is too vast for this chapter. An oversimplified picture reflects what most researchers agree is primarily a symptomatic system, but one that shows a larger number of signs, with more gradation among them, than does the communication of prosimians.

One study of the Bonnet Macaque (*Macaca radiata*), a South Asian monkey, presents a system of twenty-five different basic patterns that are used in various social interactions, including contact, agonistic encounters, foraging, greeting, sexual contact, and alarm giving. These vocalizations are determined by correlating observation with spectrographic analysis; descriptive labels are also given to the vocalizations, such as *whoo, rattle, growl, whistle,* and *bark*. These basic patterns are described as grading into each other. It is also claimed that they occur in combinations. There is no evidence, however, that these recombinations mean anything novel when they occur.

The communication systems of many monkeys appear to be genetically determined. This has been established by raising newborns in isolation. However, this statement cannot be made for all monkeys. For some monkeys, input from the adult system appears to be required. The study of one small monkey has suggested that not all monkey vocalizations are symptomatic, and that experience and learning can play a role in the acquisition of the communicative system.

The East African vervet monkey (*Cercopithecus aethiops*) is said to have three distinctive and arbitrary calls that announce the presence of either eagles, snakes, or large terrestial mammals posing a threat. These calls are associated with different responses by the monkeys. When they hear the eagle call, the monkeys look up or run into the bushes. The snake call causes them to look down at the ground near them. The mammal alarm sees them run up into the trees, or climb higher in a tree if they are already in one.

These findings, which appear to have been well established by playback experiments since they were first reported in 1967, suggest that not all non-human primates rely strictly on symptomatic signals to communicate or to trigger behaviour in others. It is claimed rather that the vervets assess the potential danger situation and then choose a specific call with a clearly defined referent to announce the danger. Furthermore, each call is a vocalization signifier that is arbitrarily linked with its referent. Other monkeys respond appropriately to the calls without necessarily observing the danger themselves. All this taken together suggests a cognitive ability for classification of objects in the world and an ability to link this classification system to arbitrary sounds for purposes of intentional communication (see figure 16.12).

The vervet may not be an isolated case. Goeldi's Monkey (*Callimico goeldii*), found in South America, is said to have five different alarm calls, three of which are used when terrestrial predators approach, and two of which have been heard in the presence of large birds. Such observations support the claim that certain monkeys have the cognitive capacity to associate perceptual categories with vocalizations.

The acquisition of these signals among vervets is interesting. Infant vervets appear to distinguish innately among broad classes of mammals, snakes, and birds, but they also give the 'eagle call' when other birds appear and the 'leopard call' when other terrestrial mammals appear. Adults distinguish between leopards and less dangerous mammals, and eagles and

Figure 16.12 Response of vervet monkeys to specific predators

less dangerous birds (as well as between snakes and sticks), and it is claimed that this ability must be perfected through experience. This once again suggests that a mixture of innate components and learning is typical of the way some communication systems are naturally acquired.

5.4 Gibbons, orangutans, and chimpanzees

Since the higher primates are close genetic relatives of humans, it is natural to expect their vocal communication to resemble that of humans. Perhaps surprisingly, communication among the higher primates does not show much indication of discrete vocal signs that could be interpreted as resembling human words. Rather, the communication systems of these animals are made up of groups of graded vocal signs.

Gibbons and orangutans

Gibbons display an interesting form of vocal interaction known as **duetting**. This is the interchange of calls in a patterned manner between two members of a species, and is found among certain birds, bats, and even antelopes. Duetting is, however, atypical of primate communication—among the hominoids, only gibbons perform it. Recent playback experiments show that duetting among gibbons serves to maintain spacing among territories much as does birdsong (see section 4.1). Playback of duetting within a gibbon's territory will cause it to approach the apparent source of the vocalizations, possibly with the intent of driving the intruders out. Playback of singing and duetting from outside a group's territory only infrequently evokes a response. Recognition of individuals does not appear to play a role in these vocalizations.

Unlike gibbons, which live in family groups, orangutans largely keep to themselves (except for mother-child pairs). Some sixteen distinct vocalizations have been identified, many of them straightforwardly symptomatic. Among the solitary forest males, loud calls up to three minutes long, serve a territorial and spacing function. These calls also identify the individuals who produce them. High-ranking males approach calls, presumably to confront the intruder, while low-ranking males stay away from areas where they hear the calls of high-ranking males. These calls are, in other words, indexes, which stand in for the individual animals themselves, and orangutans must identify and assess each of these calls before acting on them.

Chimpanzees

Chimpanzees vocalize with a number of graded calls. As many as thirty-four distinct calls have been reported for one species (*Pan troglodytes*). Some of these appear to show rather specific referents. Chimps typically hoot to signal location (a sound that carries well in dense forest). Hooting is also used in greeting or when chimps are excited about something. Another typical vocalization is known as rough grunting and is given in the presence of a favourite food source. 'Pant-grunting' appears to be used by lower-ranking animals in the presence of higher-ranking ones, signalling a reinforcing social hierarchy. A recent experiment has led to the claim that transmission of signs from one generation to the next plays a role in the acquisition of certain signs among chimpanzees. (For more on tradition, see section 7.1, number 10.)

'Language' in the wild?

Especially among highly socialized species, non-human primate vocalizations all show a great deal of variation. There is every indication that their vocalizations form part of a constellation of redundant communicative acts including gesture, posture, gaze (eye 'pointing'), and the expression of affect, all of which must be interpreted by other troop members. The obvious complexity of communication systems among these animals suggests that the level of mental activity devoted to communicative behaviour is sophisticated and well developed.

But despite the high degree of intelligence and social organization these animals demonstrate, there is very little evidence for arbitrary relationships between sound and meaning among apes. Even more significantly, there is no evidence of recombining various sections of a message to form new messages. Nothing that parallels the phonemic or morphological recombination of human language has been discovered in the natural communication systems of non-human primates.

It is possible that the lack of parallels with human linguistic communication in species closely related to our own may be because of the nature of their social organization. The small groups or family units typical of chimpanzees and gorillas living in a food-rich environment may not have required the development of any other mode of communication. What has evolved is suited to their needs. This does not mean, however, that our near-relatives do not possess any of the cognitive abilities necessary for using a system of communication akin to human language. There is some evidence, for example, of left hemisphere development of the type associated with human linguistic ability. A number of recent experiments with non-human primates have attempted to determine the extent—if any—of their linguistic abilities.

6 Testing non-human primates for linguistic ability

Much attention has been paid in recent years to non-human primates who communicate with humans through the use of sign language.

Controlled testing of the possible shared linguistic abilities of non-human primates and humans goes back to 1948, when two psychologists attempted to train Viki, a young chimpanzee, to say meaningful words in English. With great effort, Viki learned to approximate the pronunciations of a few words like *cup* and *papa* over a period of fourteen months. Unfortunately, the experiment was doomed to failure from the start, since the vocal fold structure and supralaryngeal anatomy of the chimpanzee is unsuited for producing human sounds.

Chimpanzee vocal folds are fatty and less muscular than those of humans, and the neurological pathways between the brain and vocal folds are less developed than in humans. The chimpanzee's epiglottis extends well up into the throat cavity, which lessens the range of sounds it can produce. Finally, the whole larynx-tongue linkage rests higher in the chimpanzee throat than in humans, which results in limitations on its human-like sound production as well. In short, chimpanzee anatomy is unsuited for human speech, and concentrating effort on teaching one to articulate words was distracting from the more provocative question: to what extent is the chimp mentally capable of linguistic behaviour?

6.1   Some experiments

An experiment conducted from 1965 to 1972 by Allen and Beatrice Gardner with a young female chimpanzee named Washoe created a new perspective on non-human primate linguistic abilities. The Gardners attempted to raise Washoe much as a human child would be raised, and to teach her American Sign Language (ASL), on the assumption that it was a genuinely linguistic form of communication (of which there is no doubt). Given the known manual dexterity of chimpanzees, it was felt that sign language might provide a window on chimpanzee linguistic abilities.

Washoe

The Gardners' reports claim that Washoe communicates intentionally with arbitrary signs in a creative manner, and thus shows the rudiments of human linguistic ability. Washoe learned to produce approximately 130 signs over a period of three years, and she recognized many more. Most significantly, it is claimed that Washoe spontaneously combined these signs to form novel utterances. She is reported to have signed WATER BIRD (in this chapter, signs are indicated by capital letters) on seeing ducks. Washoe also is said to have spontaneously produced BABY IN MY CUP when her toy doll was placed in her drinking cup and she was asked WHAT THAT?

Washoe was the first, but not the only chimpanzee to be taught sign language. The results have suggested to some linguists that chimpanzees show greater ability to associate arbitrary tokens with referents than was believed earlier, and that they demonstrate rudimentary syntactic behaviour. Other chimps, gorillas, and an orangutan that have been taught ASL since the pioneering Washoe experiment are reported to have performed even better.

Nim

Still other experiments in teaching chimpanzees sign language have produced contradictory results. The achievements of a chimpanzee named Nim have been interpreted by his teachers as consisting of frequent repetitions of a small number of all-purpose signs (NIM, ME, YOU, EAT, DRINK, MORE, and GIVE) that were largely appropriate to any context. These signs are said to have made up almost 50 percent of Nim's production. Furthermore, there are no reports of his engaging in creative combining of signs.

6.2   Non-signing experiments

Much of the criticism levelled at Washoe's performance centred on the relative informality of her training and claims at the time that ASL is a loose communicative system that does not require a strict adherence to syntactic rules (though we now know ASL to be a rule-governed natural language). Two very different experiments with chimpanzees attempted to forestall such criticism.

Lana

A chimpanzee called Lana was trained to fulfill her needs for food, fresh air, grooming, and entertainment (in the form of slide shows) by requesting these from a computer-controlled apparatus. Communication with the computer was carried out by means of a simple rule-governed language of nine arbitrary symbols. The symbols were on buttons that lit up and activated the computer when pressed. Any deviation from the syntactic role system invented for the experiment failed to get the desired responses from the computer. Human experimenters communicated directly with the chimpanzee through use of the same symbols. Lana learned to label and request food and other amenities through the computer. The experiment with Lana was criticized because she was said to have learned simple reflex associations among symbol, sequence, and reward. There was no evidence that she had acquired the roles underlying the sequences, and so could not be said to have displayed linguistic abilities.

Sarah

Another well-known experiment involved training a young female chimp named Sarah to manipulate arbitrary plastic symbols in a predetermined manner in order to obtain rewards. Sarah had to learn to use word order correctly, since only the following order would obtain a banana.

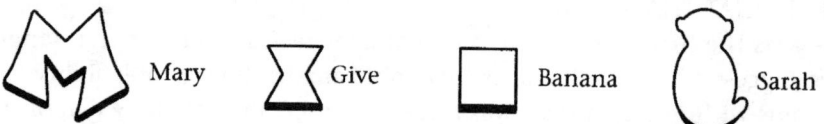

Mary   Give   Banana   Sarah

Figure 16.13 Arbitrary symbols used in experiments with the chimpanzee Sarah

She also seemed to show sensitivity to more abstract words like *if/then* in sentences like those shown in figure 16.14. But was Sarah learning aspects of human language or was she, too, trained? Humans who are taught similar skills perform them as well as Sarah but find it difficult to translate them into human language. They approach the exercise of moving plastic symbols around to obtain a reward as a puzzle that is not necessarily associated with language. It has been suggested that Sarah was performing the same kind of puzzle-solving and not demonstrating human-like linguistic capacities.

Interest in human-animal communications is not new. Language-using dogs, cats, pigs, and even turtles have been reported for thousands of years. The basis of much of the current criticism of these ancient reports and contemporary experiments rests on the performance of a horse in Germany at the turn of this century.

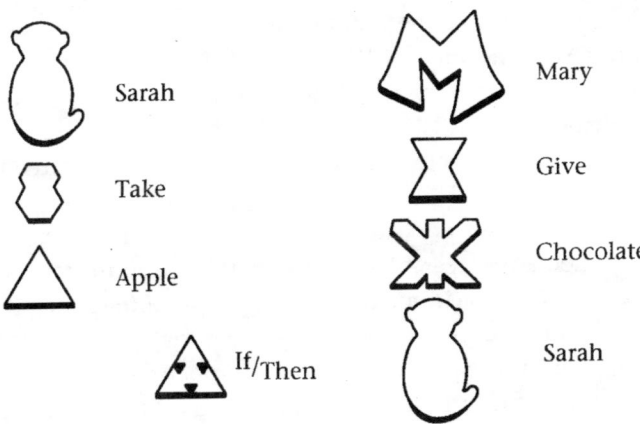

Figure 16.14 A 'sentence' understood by Sarah

6.3   The Clever Hans controversy

When I play with my cat, who is to say that my cat is not playing with me?

Michel de Montaigne, *Essays*

In 1904, a Berlin school teacher named Wilhelm von Osten claimed to possess a horse that showed evidence of a human-like capacity to think. His horse, Clever Hans (*der kluge Hans*), could supposedly calculate and convey messages by tapping out numbers or numbered letters of the alphabet with a front hoof or by nodding its head.

Experimentation by a skeptical scientist, Oskar Pfungst, eventually showed that Clever Hans was not so much a creative thinker as a careful observer: the horse perceived cues that indicated that he had performed correctly. For example, von Osten involuntarily moved his head very slightly when a correct answer had been reached. This movement (less than five millimetres) was outside the normal perceptual range of human observers, but the horse had learned to associate it with the correct answer. When observers did not know the answer to a question, or when Clever Hans was blindfolded, he failed to perform his miracles.

Clever Hans's performance resulted from **dressage**, a type of interaction between trainer and animal that depends on the animal's interpreting subtle cues given by the trainer. The Clever Hans phenomenon is an excellent example of dressage, which need not involve conscious communication on the part of humans. The highly developed perceptual ability displayed by Clever Hans is common to many animals. Many scientists believe that chimpanzees and gorillas that use sign language and perform other language-like tasks are demonstrating nothing more than the Clever Hans phenomenon.

The position is explained as follows. Human trainers want very much for their animal charges to succeed. This desire is translated into involuntary actions, which can be seized on by the animal because of its keen perceptual abilities; it is these cues that determine the animal's performance. A typical example of this is pointed out in Washoe's signing of BABY IN MY CUP which has been recorded on film (*First Signs of Washoe*). A careful examination of this interchange shows that the human repeatedly holds out the object to be signed and then points rapidly at the cup. Probably none of this cueing was intentional on the human's part.

Some so-called linguistic activity may be the result of factors other than the Clever Hans effect. Some reports of creative signing, such as Washoe's WATER BIRD, are dismissed as reflex signing that shows no intention of forming combinations on the part of the chimp. Reports of the gorilla Koko's displays of wit (she occasionally produces the opposite sign of the one requested, such as UP for DOWN) are also considered to be exaggerated or simply wishful thinking by researchers.

Some reports of linguistic behaviour are attributed to non-systematic or inaccurate observing. (For example, if Washoe answered WHAT THAT with any noun sign, the answer was considered correct.) Other reports are attributed to overoptimistic interpretation of signs. (Koko is reported to intentionally produce 'rhyming' signs—those that are very similar to the ones asked for or expected.) In short, those who do not view chimpanzee signing and symbol manipulation as linguistically relevant claim that this behaviour is more simply explained as arising from straightforward response-reward association and/or from dressage, and not a reflection of linguistic competence. As one researcher noted, training two pigeons to bat a ping-pong ball across a net does not mean that the birds know the rules of ping-pong.

6.4   The great ape debate

We believe that . . . there is no basis to conclude that signing apes acquired linguistic skills.

Mark S. Seldenberg and Laura Petitto

When these projects [Washoe, Lana, Sarah, and Nim] are taken together, it can be seen that chimpanzees are within the range of language behavior of humans and therefore have the capacity for language.

Roger Fouts

Researchers involved with the chimpanzees and gorillas who are being taught to sign attest to the emotional bonds they form with them, and also emphasize that in using human language, such bonds are a prerequisite to normal communication. They strongly insist that apes communicate spontaneously and creatively with humans. Roger Fouts, who has spent many years in close contact with Washoe and other chimpanzees, puts the case this way.

I reject the notion that there is some ultimate cut-and-dried criterion that distinguishes language from all other social and cognitive behaviors, or that distinguishes human communication and thought from that of all other species.

It is important to emphasize that most researchers sympathetic to the idea that apes show human linguistic abilities employ a broader definition of language than many of their critics. For these researchers, language use includes socialization and the use of communicative constellations.

For many linguists critical of these projects, a definition of language that rests on its social or functional aspects is unacceptable. In much current linguistic thinking, language is viewed as independent of the purposes it serves. This view, sometimes called the *linguistic autonomy hypothesis,* equates language with grammar—the "mental system that allows human beings to form and interpret the sounds, words, and sentences of their language," to quote from chapter 1 of this text. It follows from this definition that linguistic ability in non-human primates can only be claimed to exist if the animals produce, at the very least, spontaneous and intentional symbolic signs that are manipulated in a rule-governed manner.

Symbol use

All researchers who support the claim that non-human primates can employ intentional symbolic communication deny that cueing is a major factor in the apes' abilities, although most admit that it might be present on occasion. In order to refute charges of the Clever Hans effect, researchers employ a strict form of experimentation.

Primate sign language researchers try to avoid cueing by using the **double-blind test**. In this test, first a researcher shows the ape objects or pictures of objects that are invisible to a second human researcher. The ape's signing is then recorded by the second researcher and the record is interpreted by a third researcher who has not seen the signing. In this way, unintentional cueing is said to be avoided.

Critics of this research claim that even double-blind tests can be affected by human-animal interaction. First, the apes must be taught to perform the task. During this process they may be conditioned to provide certain responses. Secondly, it is difficult to avoid any human-animal interaction during these tests, and this could lead to subliminal cueing. As we have also seen, many claims for symbolic behaviour on any ape's part have been dismissed as stimulus-response conditioning—the mere apeing of behaviour in order to obtain a reward. We still have no way of knowing whether Washoe's use of a sign sequence like TIME-EAT indicates that she has a concept of time.

Ongoing work with two chimpanzees named Sherman and Austin has led to their exchanging signed information about classes of objects such as 'tool' and 'food'. These experiments are claimed to have circumvented any reliance on the Clever Hans effect and shown that signing apes can communicate about whole referential classes of items rather than be bound to simple stimulus-response association with individual items such as 'banana' and 'ice cream'.

Careful control of experiments has convinced some linguists that limited symbol use has been exhibited by some apes, perhaps even up to the level of a two-year-old human child. But some linguists who allow that a level of symbolic signing has been achieved have also denied this is a critical feature for defining language. Rather, rule-governed, creative symbol combinations and syntactic behaviour are said to be the critical features.

Creative signing?

A feature of language that sets it apart from most animal communication is its creativity—the fact that humans can use language to create novel messages. Sign researchers claim that such creativity is present in the many instances of novel combinations signed by the animals.

An early and famous instance of alleged creative signing was Washoe's WATER BIRD (referred to in section 6.3), which she signed on seeing a duck in the water for the first time. Such alleged compound signing behaviour has been noted in various signing apes. Some of the gorilla Koko's novel combinations are provided in table 16.2.

Table 16.2	Some sign combinations produced by Koko
Compound	**Referent**
Milk Candy	rich tapioca pudding
Fruit Lollipop	frozen banana
Pick Face	tweezers
Blanket White Cold	rabbit-fur cape
Nose Fake	mask
Potato Apple Fruit	pineapple

Critics say either that such combinations are accidental or that the ape produces the two signs independently of each other and thus does not display true compounding. There is no doubt that Washoe signed both WATER in the presence of water, and BIRD in the presence of the bird, but there is no consistent indication from her other output that she has a rule of compound formation.

It has been claimed that in more recent and carefully controlled experiments with a pygmy chimpanzee (*Pan pansicus*) named Kanzi, statistically significant differences in the spontaneous ordering of symbols has been observed. The conclusion that has been drawn from this is that Kanzi has exhibited a form of grammatical rule. For example, Kanzi frequently used combinations of signs that link two actions, such as CHASE HIDE, TICKLE SLAP, and GRAB SLAP. In fifty-four out of eighty-four cases, the first sign corresponded to the invitation to play and the second to the type of play requested.

Is there syntax?

Claims for syntactic behaviour among signing apes have also been made. Even though it has been claimed that the general (though flexible) syntax of ASL is copied by the apes, reports on the signing chimp Nim (section 6.1) showed that the animal had no consistent word order patterning. In fact, Nim's syntactic output was structurally incoherent. His longest sentence is reported as GIVE ORANGE ME GIVE EAT ORANGE ME EAT ORANGE GIVE ME EAT ORANGE GIVE ME YOU.

Koko is said to have developed her own word order in noun phrases—the adjective consistently follows the noun it modifies. It is difficult to prove claims for syntactic behaviour in animal signing, because (all) signing forms constellations with facial expression and gestures and so may be said to reduce the need for rigorous syntax. Koko, for example, can sign a meaning like 'I love Coca-Cola' by hugging herself (the sign for *love*) while signing *Coca-Cola* at the same time with her hands.

In spite of what is now widely considered to be the disappointment of the earlier studies (possibly because they expected too much), some controlled experimentation continues. Recently, the pygmy chimpanzee Kanzi is reported to have produced significant (though not wholly consistent) differences in the placement of animate agents in sign combinations. When another chimpanzee named Matata was grabbed, Kanzi produced GRAB MATATA, but when Matata performed an action such as biting, Kanzi produced MATATA BITE.

Lingering doubts

As we have seen, supporters of language use among apes have not yet proved to the satisfaction of all their critics that genuine symbolic behaviour is occurring, much less anything resembling rule-governed creativity in compounding or syntactic patterning.

Researchers who see the results of ape studies as positive evidence for linguistic ability in these animals claim that their opponents keep raising the stakes every time a chimp or a gorilla accomplishes something that could be interpreted as linguistic behaviour. Possible evidence of symbol use or creative signing to indicate linguistic ability is dismissed by these opponents as unsurprising or irrelevant.[5] Supporters of ape studies note that such critics are motivated by a long tradition of viewing animals as 'organic machines' that are locked into specific behavioural and communicative repertoires by their genetic inheritance, and that can therefore only respond automatically to a given situation with a narrow range of signs. Their own view, they claim, is at once more ancient and more modern in granting animals a certain as yet unknown degree of intentionality and cognitive ability in their behaviour.

In general, recent experiments have established more convincingly than earlier ape studies that symbol use and referential behaviour form part of the cognitive makeup of some non-human primates. Taken together with naturalistic studies, they help circumvent the claim that all evidence of symbol use among non-human primates is caused by the Clever Hans phenomenon.

Nonetheless, questions about creative sign combination and syntactic use still remain. Kanzi's alleged rules have been equated with those of a two-year-old child. But the major difference between a chimpanzee and a child at that point in their lives is that the elementary grammar of a two year old is the first hint of a full system that is rapidly developing and that will be in place in a matter of a few more years. While Kanzi's communicative behaviour constitutes interesting evidence for a chimpanzee's awareness of the world, it does not unequivocally imply a system of grammar. It has been noted, for example, that Kanzi's 'rules' are often bound up with a natural order of action or relationships (as when the sign GRAB precedes the sign SLAP).

To critics of these experiments, the apparent lack of rule-governed behaviour among signing apes (especially in the realm of syntax) remains the linguistic hurdle that the animals have not overcome. It is certain that apes do not show syntactic behaviour to any degree that humans do (for example, embedding is completely lacking) and many linguists claim that without such behaviour, the apes cannot be said to be using language. Syntax, in the strict linguistic sense, provides a system of rules capable of producing a sentence of potentially infinite length (even though in practice this is never required). There is no evidence that primates have shown this ability.

6.5   Implications

Critics of the ape studies have at this time carried the day. Many funding sources for ape-human research have dried up, and most of the subjects have lost their privileged relationships with humans and been returned to zoos. But the severe reaction to the apparent failure of ape-human linguistic communication research has had positive effects on the field as well. Recent trends—the number of experiments on animal cognition in the wild, and the more carefully controlled experiments with apes like Kanzi—are leading us slowly closer to new evidence that bears on this age-old issue.

The real significance of these experiments in ape-human linguistic communication goes far beyond popular enthusiasm about what an ape might say to us if it could talk. It has often been pointed out that an animal's view of the world must be totally unlike our own. It is perhaps not surprising that apes appear to communicate largely about their fundamental emotions and such basic needs as food and play.

In time, this research may help illuminate what is truly unique about human linguistic ability. As we have seen, many linguists claim that there is no connection between the communicative behaviour of non-human primates and the complex structures of human language. The opposing view claims that the capacity for true grammatical activity can be found in non-human primates. This implies that what we call language reflects a cognitive difference in *degree* and not in *kind* between humans and these animals. The optimistic view is that such research may ultimately shed light on the evolutionary origins of our species and its language use by demonstrating the degree of shared cognitive abilities between ourselves and our nearest genetic relatives.

7 Comparing communication systems: design features

Throughout this chapter, we have emphasized the distinction between communication and language. In this final section, we will compare human linguistic communication with what we have learned about systems of animal communication.

7.1 The features

Differences and similarities between human language and natural animal communication systems can be highlighted by comparing essential characteristics of the systems. These characteristics are called **design features**, and are set up (perhaps unfairly) with reference to human language. Since this book emphasizes the essentially mental nature of linguistic ability, the design features that follow do not include the traditional reference to vocal-auditory transmission. What is emphasized is the nature of the semantic and organizational structuring of each system. These design features represent an adaptation of those of Charles Hockett and W.H. Thorpe, as noted at the end of this chapter.

1. ***Interchangeability*** All members of the species can both send and receive messages.

   This is obviously true of human language. It is not the case with bee dancing (performed only by foragers) or birdsong (performed only by males). Non-human primate vocalizations appear to be largely interchangeable.

2. ***Feedback*** Users of the system are aware of what they are transmitting.

   Humans monitor their linguistic output and correct it. It is debatable whether bees do so when they dance, or whether birds monitor their calls. It is not known if birds monitor their song; it is likely that they do.

3. ***Specialization*** The communication system serves no other function but to communicate.

   Human language represents reality—both external (real world) and internal (states, beliefs)—symbolically in the mind. Manifested as speech, language serves uniquely as a communicative system. Bee dancing and birdsong also appear to be specialized communicative activity. Alarm calls of any species may be symptomatic but at the same time are specialized for different types of predators. Symptomatic tokens, on the other hand, are unspecialized. Crying is a symptomatic sign that may be interpreted by someone else and thus function communicatively, but its primary purpose is physiological (the clearing of foreign matter from the eye, the release of emotional tension). If animal communication is primarily symptomatic—a claim that is hotly disputed by specialists in animal communication—then it would not qualify as a specialized communicative system.

4. ***Semanticity*** The system conveys meaning through a set of fixed relationships among signifiers, referents, and meanings.

   Human language conveys meaning through arbitrary symbols. Bee dancing conveys meaning, but within a very limited range, as do bird calls and song. The range of meaning is broader and more subtle in non-human primate vocalizations. Although we cannot claim to know the minds of such near relations as chimpanzees and gorillas, it appears that the range of meanings suggested by their behaviour in the wild does not approach the vastness of human semanticity (see feature 8).

5. ***Arbitrariness*** There is no natural or inherent connection between a token and its referent.

   This is true of human language, with the possible exception of a few onomatopoeic terms. Bee dancing shows arbitrariness in that there may be no connection between the form of the dance and the distance from the hive. Expressions of food source quality and direction are not arbitrary, however. Many bird calls are highly suited for their purpose, such as danger calls which are difficult to locate, and in this sense are not arbitrary. Most non-human primate vocalization appears to be equally adaptive, though arbitrariness has been claimed for vervet monkey alarm calls.

6. ***Discreteness*** The communication system consists of isolatable, repeatable units.

   Human language shows distinctive features, phonemes, syllables, morphemes, words, and still larger combinations. There are two (three, in some dialects) discrete types of bee dances, but these dances are not combined in various ways to produce novel messages. There is some evidence for subunits in birdsong. They are also present in primate call systems.

7. ***Displacement*** Users of the system are able to refer to events remote in space and time.

   Bee dancing shows displacement. No evidence for displacement is found in bird calls or songs. Baboons occasionally produce threat and fight vocalizations long after an aggressive encounter, but there is no evidence that this is reflecting displacement; it probably reflects a slow winding down of the animal's emotional state. Among apes, it is not yet clear whether some degree of displacement is a feature of either their communication in the wild or the systems they have learned from humans. Non-human primates do not appear to communicate about imaginary pasts or futures, which humans are able to do with language.

8. ***Productivity***   New messages on any topic can be produced at any time. This is obviously true of human language. Bees show limited productivity. Bird calls show none. Birdsong shows evidence of recombination (the songs of laughing gulls are well documented in this respect), but it is doubtful whether these recombinations transmit novel messages. This is also true of recombination in the calls of certain monkeys, such as macaques.

9. ***Duality of patterning***   Meaningless units (phonemes) are combined to form arbitrary signs. These signs in turn can be recombined to form new, meaningful larger units.

In human language, phonemes can be combined in various ways to create different symbolic tokens: *spot*, *tops*, *opts*, and *pots*. These tokens in turn can be combined in meaningful ways: *Spot the tops of the pots*. There is no evidence of this type of patterning in any known animal communication system.

10. ***Tradition***   At least certain aspects of the system must be transmitted from an experienced user to a learner.

This is obviously a factor in the acquisition of human language. It is possibly present in a very limited way in bee communication, and it is definitely present in the acquisition of birdsong for some species. As noted in section 5.3, there is some recent evidence for a degree of tradition among chimpanzees.

11. ***Prevarication***   The system enables the users to talk nonsense or to lie.

Undoubtedly, this property is found in human language. There are specialized mimics among birds, fishes, and even insects. A few examples of animal deception have been noted among the arctic fox and among vervets, but it is not clear whether this is normal species-specific behaviour or the acts of a few isolated individuals. The question of intentionality is crucial here. Current work with birds suggests that some species learn as many songs as possible and use this repertoire to maintain territorial advantage by 'impersonating' other species. This may well be purely genetically determined behaviour, but, in any event, it is highly complex.

12. ***Learnability***   A user of the system can learn other variants.

Humans can learn a number of different languages. Bees are limited to their own genetically specified dialect. Bird calls are apparently limited in this same way. As noted previously, some birds learn the songs of other species, but this may well be simply mimicry. Non-human primates seem restricted to their own systems in the wild.

13. ***Reflexiveness***   The ability to use the communication system to discuss the system itself.

No evidence exists that any other species writes grammars or linguistics textbooks.

Tables 16.3 and 16.4 summarize this survey of design features.

Table 16.3 Summary of design features for bees and birds

Design feature	Bees	Birds
1. Interchangeability	no; foragers only	no; only males sing
2. Feedback	?	?
3. Specialization	yes	yes
4. Semanticity	yes, very limited	yes, limited
5. Arbitrariness	yes, for expressing distance	yes, though highly adaptive
6. Discreteness	in a limited way	yes, in song
7. Displacement	yes	no
8. Productivity	yes, very limited	possibly
9. Duality of patterning	no	no
10. Tradition	possibly, but highly limited	yes, limited
11. Prevarication	no	possibly
12. Learnability	no	possibly
13. Reflexiveness	no	no

Table 16.4 Summary of design features for non-human primates and humans

Design feature	Non-human primates	Humans
1. Interchangeability	yes	yes
2. Feedback	probably	yes
3. Specialization	in part	yes
4. Semanticity	yes	yes
5. Arbitrariness	limited confirmation; selectively adaptive	yes
6. Discreteness	in call systems	yes
7. Displacement	no	yes
8. Productivity	possibly	yes
9. Duality of patterning	no	yes
10. Tradition	possibly	yes
11. Prevarication	possibly	yes
12. Learnability	no	yes
13. Reflexiveness	no current evidence	yes

Summing up

This brief overview of animal communication systems emphasizes that human language is one communication system among the many that life forms on this planet employ.

Communication can be described with reference to the **sign**, which is composed of two components, a **signifier** and that which is **signified**. Tokens may be **iconic**, **symbolic**, or **indexical** (the latter including the **symptomatic** token), and structured as **graded** or **discrete** types. Most animal communication has traditionally been viewed as symptomatic, though studies of communication among birds and bees suggests symbolic signs are used. A significant innate component may interact with some exposure to the communication system, especially among birds. Non-human primate communication consists of graded series of vocalizations and appears to show little arbitrariness, though some has been reported for the alarm calls of several monkeys.

Experiments with non-human primates have created controversy over whether chimpanzees and gorillas have shown symbolic behaviour and a capacity for linguistic behaviour. Many researchers have dismissed the work as an example of **dressage** or the Clever Hans phenomenon.

Human language and systems of animal communication share certain **design features**. Humans, however, lack many communicative skills that animals possess. We are hopelessly inadequate at following scent trails, a feat that prosimians accomplish with ease; we cannot change colour for communicative purposes with the facility of an octopus; and we are not as gifted as horses and many other mammals at assessing and interpreting subtle body gestures. Humans do possess an ability to symbolize which far exceeds that of chimpanzees and gorillas (our nearest genetic relatives), even allowing for the most generous interpretation possible of recent experiments. Human language is also more flexible and productive in manipulating these symbols than any known animal communication system. Language is as suited for and as much a part of human life patterns as the communication systems of our fellow creatures are for their modes of existence.

Notes

1 Communication since the industrial revolution increasingly involves non-living things. Machines pass information to humans (for example, car speedometers, geiger counters, toasters), and among themselves (for example, computers, communication satellites). Still, non-living communicators have been designed by humans and use principles of communication based on living models.

2 Among humans, this fact about symptomatic signs can be turned on its head and symptoms such as tears or laughter can be feigned. The result is deception, trickery, or lying.

3 The bees are not perfect genetic machines, however. The fact that there are dancers that communicate more (or less) effectively than others shows the existence of varying ability among individuals.

4 You might wonder how song serves to establish and maintain territory. A recognized song is an indication to a bird that a certain amount of territory is occupied and that to stray onto that territory could provoke an attack. A recent hypothesis suggests that song also intimidates other males by disturbing their foraging patterns, since, again, hearing a song might lead a bird to think it was in another's territory and might have to flee or fight. Field studies support this hypothesis; they show that there is less singing among birds that co-exist in a forage-rich environment, where there is less competition for food resources (E.S. Morton, "Grading, Discreteness, Redundancy, and Motivation-Structure Rules" in *Acoustic Communication in Birds*, Vol. 1, edited by Kroodsma et al., pp. 183–212, cited in picture credits).

5 For example, the relevance of all non-syntactic communicative behaviour by non-human primates has been dismissed with these words: "virtually all of the nonsyntactic component of language predated the emergence of our species" in Derek Bickerton, review of

E. Sue Savage-Rumbaugh (1986), *Ape Language: From Conditioned Response to Symbol* in *International Journal of Primatology* 8 (3): 293–98 (1987).

Picture credits

Chimpanzee facial expressions in figure 16.1 and question 3, and monkey facial expressions in figure 16.5 are adapted from S. Chevalier-Skolnikoff's "Facial Expression and Emotion in Nonhuman Primates" in *Darwin and Facial Expression,* edited by E. Ekman (New York: Academic Press, 1973), pp. 11–90. The baboon open-mouth threat in figure 16.3 is adapted from a photograph in K.R.L. Hall and I. DeVore's "Baboon Social Behavior," in *Primate Behavior,* edited by I. DeVore (Toronto: Holt, Rinehart and Winston, 1965), pp. 53–110; park information signs in figure 16.3 are courtesy of Alberta Provincial Parks. Figure 16.7 is adapted from D. Todt's "Serial Calling as a Mediator of Interaction Processes: Crying" in *Primate Vocal Communication,* edited by D. Todt, D.E. Goedeking, and D. Symmes (Berlin: Springer-Verlag, 1988), pp. 88–107 and reprinted by permission of the publisher. Bee dancing (figure 16.8) is adapted from K. von Frisch's *The Dance Language and Orientation of Bees,* p. 57 (cited in sources). Copyright © 1967, 1993 by the President and Fellows of Harvard College. Reprinted by permission of Harvard University Press. The spectrogram of the robin song (figure 16.9) is from *Bird-Song* by W.H. Thorpe (cited in sources) copyrighted and reprinted with the permission of Cambridge University Press. Avian isoglosses in figure 16.10 are from Paul Mundinger's "Microgeographic and Macrogeographic Variation in Acquired Vocalizations of Birds," in *Acoustic Communication in Birds,* Vol. 2, edited by D.E. Kroodsma, E.H. Miller, and H. Ouellet (New York: Academic Press, 1982), pp. 147–208 and reprinted by permission. Figure 16.12 illustrating the response of vervet monkeys to predators is taken from *Animal Language* by Michael Bright (cited in sources). Tokens used in the Sarah experiments (figures 16.13 and 16.14) are taken from D. Premack and A.J. Premack as cited on p. 179 in E. Linden's *Apes, Men, and Language* (Baltimore, MD: Pelican Books, 1974).

Sources

The theory of semiotics outlined in this chapter is drawn from several recent works on semiotics, including T. Sebeok's *Contributions to the Doctrine of Signs, Studies in Semiotics* 5 (Bloomington, IN: Indiana University Press, 1976), *I Think I Am a Verb* (New York: Plenum Press, 1986), and U. Eco's *Semiotics and the Philosophy of Language* (Bloomington, IN: Indiana University Press, 1984). Bee communication is drawn from K. von Frisch's "Dialects in the Language of the Bees" in *Scientific American* 202 (2): 78–87 (1962) and his work *The Dance Language and Orientation of Bees,* translated by C.E. Chadwick (Cambridge, MA: Harvard University Press, 1967). Bird vocalization is based largely on W.H. Thorpe's *Bird-Song* (Cambridge, MA: Cambridge University Press, 1961). Jake Page's parrot is reported in *Science* (1982). Lemur vocalizations in table 16.1 are drawn from A. Jolly's *Lemur Behavior* (Chicago: University of Chicago Press, 1966). Vervet communication is drawn from R.M. Seyfarth and D.L. Cheney's "How Monkeys See the World," edited by Snowden et al. (cited below). Much information on primate communication in the wild was provided by Hugh Notman. Creative signing by Koko is reported in F. Patterson and E. Linden's work *The Education of Koko* (New York: Holt, Rinehart and Winston, 1981). The reference to cultural transmission of signs among chimpanzees is drawn from Michael Tomasello's "Cultural Transmission in the Tool Use and Communicatory Signaling of Chimpanzees?" in Parker and Gibson (cited below), pp. 274–311; some of the material on invented rules by the pygmy chimpanzee Kanzi is drawn from Patricia Marks Greenfield and E. Sue Savage-Rumbaugh's "Grammatical Combination in *Pan paniscus*,"also in Parker and Gibson, pp. 540–76; this volume contains a number of other articles relevant to the question of non-human primate cognitive and linguistic abilities. Some question material is drawn from various articles in *How Animals Communicate,* edited by Thomas A. Sebeok (Bloomington, IN: Indiana University Press, 1977).

Recommended reading

Bright, Michael. 1984. *Animal Language.* London: British Broadcasting Corporation.

Cheney, Dorothy L., and Robert M. Seyfarth. 1991. *How Monkeys See the World.* Chicago: University of Chicago Press.

de Luce, Judith, and Hugh T. Wilder, eds. 1983. *Language in Primates: Perspectives and Implications.* New York: Springer-Verlag.

Hauser, M. 1996. *The Evolution of Communication.* Cambridge, MA: MIT Press.

Hockett, Charles. 1960. "The Origin of Speech." *Scientific American* 203 (3): 88–96.

Lieberman, Philip. 1998. *Eve Spoke.* New York: W.W. Norton.

Parker, Sue Taylor, and Kathleen Rita Gibson. 1990. *"Language" and Intelligence in Monkeys and Apes: Comparative Developmental Perspectives.* Cambridge: Cambridge University Press.

Pinker, Steven. 1994. *The Language Instinct.* New York: Harper Perennial.

Sebeok, Thomas A., and Jean Umiker-Sebeok. 1980. *Speaking of Apes.* New York: Plenum Press.

Sebeok, Thomas A., and Robert Rosenthal, eds. 1981. *The Clever Hans Phenomenon: Communication with Horses, Whales, Apes, and People.* Annals of the New York Academy of Sciences, 364. New York: The New York Academy of Sciences.

Snowden, C.T., C.H. Brown, and M.R. Petersen, eds. 1982. *Primate Communication.* London: Cambridge University Press.

Thorpe, W.H. 1974. *Animal Nature and Human Nature.* Garden City, NY: Doubleday.

Questions

1. The following signs are all symptomatic.
   a) Dogs wag their tails when happy, cats flick their tails when irritated.
   b) An octopus, when showing aggressive behaviour, becomes bright red.
   c) The Canada goose shows aggressive intentions by opening its mouth, coiling its neck, and directing its head toward an opponent. When it is unlikely to attack, its mouth is closed, its head is horizontally extended, and its head is directed away from an opponent.
   d) Tree leaves change colour in the fall.
   e) The presence of stratocumulus clouds accompanies good weather.

   i) Why is this designation appropriate in each case?
   ii) State which of these signs are, in addition to being symptomatic, primarily *iconic,* which are primarily *symbolic,* and which are primarily *indexical.*

2. Find two examples each of *iconic, symbolic,* and *indexical* signs you encounter in the course of a day. Is it possible to classify unambiguously each sign as to type? If not, state why in each case.

3. What do the following chimpanzee facial expressions convey? Using a mirror, try to imitate the facial expressions; does this make it easier for you to label them? What characteristics of the signs lead you to your conclusion in each case?

4. Observe an animal in a zoo or at home for at least one-half hour. Try to discover at least three unambiguous signs the animal employs to communicate. Describe each one in terms of both *signifier* and *signified*. (A good way to do this is to note carefully the context in which the sign is given, to whom it is addressed, and what the receiver's response is to the communication.)

5. Add two columns to the list of design features presented in tables 16.3 and 16.4. For one column, take the perspective of a researcher who believes that apes show true linguistic ability in their signing, and fill in the column from this point of view. Fill in the other column from the perspective of a researcher who does not believe such ability has been shown. Be sure to comment on each design feature.

6. Now that you have been exposed to both sides of the ape language issue, summarize your own conclusions about it. Do you believe that human language is different in degree or in kind from the communicative behaviour of the great apes? Why?

Answer to question 3: *a*) submission; *b*) excitement, perhaps affection; *c*) desiring, perhaps mixed with frustration.

Glossary

Ablative The case form characteristically used to mark a noun indicating the point away from which there is movement.

Ablaut A vowel alternation that marks a grammatical contrast (e.g., *mouse/mice*).

Absolute universals Patterns or traits that occur in all languages.

Absolutive In some languages, the case associated with both the direct object of a transitive verb and the subject of an intransitive verb.

Abstract case Case that need not be expressed as inflection.

Abstract clause A type of narrative utterance that sometimes appears at the beginning of a narrative to provide a general summary of the story to be told.

Abstract representation A representation that is to a greater or lesser degree distinct from its phonetic realization.

Accent Phonetic qualities of a language variety which identifies it to speakers of other varieties as different from their own.

Accidental gaps Non-occurring but possible forms of a language (e.g., in English, *blork*).

Accommodation The modification of speech patterns to match those of other participants in a discourse.

Accuracy Second language speech in which the structures are nativelike.

Accusative The case form characteristically used to mark a direct object.

Acoustic phonetics An approach to phonetics that is concerned with measuring and analyzing the physical properties of sound waves produced when we speak.

Acquired agraphia *See* **Acquired dysgraphia**.

Acquired alexia *See* **Acquired dyslexia**.

Acquired dysgraphia The impairment of writing ability in patients who previously possessed normal writing ability (also called **acquired agraphia**).

Acquired dyslexia The impairment of reading ability in patients who previously possessed normal reading ability (also called acquired alexia).

Acrolect The variety most closely approximating the one that is considered standard in a creole speech community.

Acronym A word that is formed by taking the initial letters of (some or all) of the words in a phrase or title and pronouncing them as a word (e.g., *NATO* for *North Atlantic Treaty Organization*).

Acrophonic principle The representation of sounds by pictures of objects whose pronunciation begins with the sound to be represented (e.g., the sound [b] might be represented by a picture of a bird).

Active sentence A sentence in which the NP with the agent role is the subject (e.g., *Helen painted the room*).

Adjacency pair An ordered pair of utterances spoken by two different participants in a conversation.

Adjective (A) A lexical category that designates a property or attribute of an entity, can often take comparative and superlative endings in English, and functions as the head of an adjective phrase (e.g., *red, obese, hearty*).

Adstratum influence The mutual influence of two equally dominant languages on each other (e.g., the influence of English and French on each other in Montreal).

Adverb (Adv) A lexical category that typically denotes a property of the actions, sensations, and states designated by verbs (e.g., *quickly, fearfully*).

Affix A morpheme that does not belong to a lexical category and is always bound (e.g., *-ing, un-*).

Affixation The process that attaches an affix to a base.

Affricates Non-continuant consonants that

show a slow release of the closure (e.g., [tʃ, dʒ]).

Affrication A process in which palatalized stops become affricates.

Age-grading The correlation of a particular linguistic variant with social situations that are closely associated with a particular age group.

Agent The thematic role associated with the doer of an action (e.g., *Marilyn* in *Marilyn fed the dolphin*).

Agglutinating languages Languages in which words typically contain several morphemes, of which usually only one is a lexical category. The others are clearly identifiable affixes, each of which typically encodes a single grammatical contrast.

Agrammatism An aphasic disturbance characterized by the omission of function words and inflectional affixes and by syntactic comprehension deficits.

Agreement The result of one category being inflected to mark properties of another (e.g., the verb is marked for the person and/or the number of the subject).

Allomorphs Variants of a morpheme (e.g., [-s], [-z], and [-əz] are allomorphs of the English plural morpheme).

Allophones Variants of a phoneme, usually in complementary distribution and phonetically similar (e.g., voiced and voiceless *l* in English).

Alphabetic writing A type of writing in which symbols represent consonant and/or vowel segments.

Alveolar ridge The small ridge that protrudes from just behind the upper front teeth.

Alveopalatal (area) The area just behind the alveolar ridge where the roof of the mouth rises sharply (also called **palatoalveolar**).

Ambisyllabicity The simultaneous presence of a segment in two adjoining syllables.

Amelioration The process in which the meaning of a word becomes more favourable (e.g., *pretty* used to mean 'tricky, sly, cunning').

Amerind The group into which all the Amerindian languages (except for Na-Dené and Eskimo-Aleut stocks) have been placed, according to one controversial classification system.

Amerindian languages Languages spoken by the aboriginal peoples of North, South, and Central America.

Analogy A source of language change that involves the generalization of a regularity, on the basis of the inference that if elements are alike in some respects, they should be alike in others as well (e.g., *bring* becoming *brung* by analogy with *ring/rung*).

Analytic languages *See* **Isolating languages**.

Anaphoric reference Use of a pronominal form to refer to a preceding full noun phrase or verb phrase in discourse.

Angular gyrus An area of the brain that plays an important role in reading.

Animate A noun class category in some languages (e.g., both *duck* and *pipe* are animate nouns in Cree).

Antecedent The element that determines the interpretation of a pronoun (e.g., *Jeremy* in *Jeremy looked at himself in the mirror*).

Anterior A place feature that characterizes sounds articulated in front of the alveopalatal region.

Antonyms Words or phrases that are opposites with respect to some component of their meaning (e.g., *big* and *small*).

Aphasia A language deficit caused by damage to the brain.

Apocope The deletion of a word-final vowel (e.g., *name* used to be pronounced with a word-final schwa).

Areal classification An approach to language classification that identifies characteristics shared by languages that are in geographical contact.

Articulatory phonetics An approach to phonetics that studies the physiological mechanisms of speech production.

Articulatory simplification A process that facilitates acquisition (e.g., by deleting a consonant in a complex cluster or inserting a vowel to break up a cluster).

Arytenoids Two small cartilages in the larynx that are attached to the vocal folds, enabling the vocal folds to be drawn together or apart.

Aspiration The lag in the onset of vocalic voicing, accompanied by the release of air, that is heard after the release of certain stops in English (e.g., the first sound of *top* is aspirated).

Assimilation The influence of one segment on another, resulting in a sound becoming more like a nearby sound in terms of one or more of its phonetic characteristics (e.g., in English, vowels become nasal if followed by a nasal consonant).

Association line A line linking a symbol that represents a sound segment with a symbol that represents a tone or feature.

Atlas survey A linguistic survey that samples speakers according to regional speech communities.

Autopsy studies Studies based on a postmortem examination.

Autosegmental (notation) The type of notation that links segments with tones or features by association lines.

Autosegments Phonological features (e.g., tone) that have a certain autonomy from the segments.

Auxiliary verb (Aux) Verbs such as *will, can, may, be* and *have* that must always occur with another verb in complete sentences.

Back A dorsal feature that characterizes sounds articulated behind the palatal region in the oral cavity.

Back (of the tongue) The part of the tongue that is hindmost but still lies in the mouth.

Back vowel A vowel that is made with tongue positioned in the back of the oral cavity (e.g., the vowel sounds in *h**oo**t* and *b**oar**d*).

Backformation A word formation process that creates a new word by removing a real or supposed affix from another word in the language (e.g., *edit* came from *editor* through the removal of *-or*).

Banned language A language that is prohibited by authorities in a particular domain of use.

Base The form to which an affix is added (e.g., *book* is the base for the affix *-s* in *books, modernize* is the base for the affix *-ed* in *modernized*).

Basilect The variety that shows the greatest number of differences from the standard language in a creole speech community.

Bilingualism The state of possessing knowledge of two languages; the discipline devoted to the study of the simultaneous acquisition of two languages by children.

Blade (of the tongue) The area of the tongue just behind the tip.

Blend A word that is created from parts of two already existing items (e.g., *brunch* from *breakfast* and *lunch*).

Blissymbolics A contemporary development of pictographic writing that uses a number of recombineable symbols representing basic units of meaning; primarily used for non-speaking individuals.

Body (of the tongue) The main mass of the tongue.

Borrowing A source of language change that involves adopting aspects of one language into another.

Bottom-up processing A type of processing in which the activation of higher mental representations (e.g., words) occurs through the activation of simpler constituent representations (e.g., phonemes).

Bound morpheme A morpheme that must be attached to another element (e.g., the past tense marker *-ed*).

Boustrophedon The practice of reversing the direction of writing at the end of each line, which was typical of many old writing systems.

Broca's aphasia A non-fluent aphasia in which speech is very halting, there are numerous phonemic errors, and there is a lack of intonation.

Broca's area The area in the lower rear portion of the left frontal lobe that plays an important role in language production.

Canadian Raising The phonological phenomenon of using the allophones [ʌj] and [ʌw] in words such as *right* and *out*.

C-command A syntactic notion that is involved in pronoun interpretation and is formulated as: NP$_a$ c-commands NP$_b$, if the first category above NP$_a$ contains NP$_b$.

Call In avian communication, short bursts of sound or simple patterns of notes, typically used as warnings or other group-related signals.

Calque A borrowed word or expression that has been literally translated from the donor language into the recipient language.

Canonical Sentence Strategy A processing strategy that leads children to expect the first NP in a sentence to bear the agent role and the second NP to bear the theme role.

Caregiver speech The type of speech that is typically addressed to young language learners. (*See also* **Motherese**.)

Case A morphological category that encodes information about an element's grammatical role (subject, direct object, and so on) (e.g., the contrast between *he* and *him*).

Case Filter A constraint requiring that every NP in a grammatical sentence be assigned a case feature.

Cataphoric reference Use of a pronominal form to refer to a following full noun phrase or verb phrase in discourse.

Categorical A term used for a rule that always applies.

Central sulcus The sulcus that extends from the top of the cerebral cortex to the lateral fissure (also called the fissure of Rolando).

Cerebral cortex The grey wrinkled mass that sits like a cap over the rest of the brain and is the seat of cognitive functioning.

Cerebral hemispheres The left and right halves of the brain, separated by the longitudinal fissure.

Cerebrovascular accident *See* **Stroke**.

Characters The units of contemporary Chinese orthography, many of which consist of two parts, a phonetic **determinative** and a **radical**.

Class A group of sounds that shares certain phonetic properties (e.g., all voiced sounds).

Class 1 A group of affixes that (in English) often trigger changes in the consonant or vowel segments of the base and may affect the assignment of stress.

Class 2 A group of affixes that tend to be phonologically neutral in English, having no effect on the segmental makeup of the base or on stress assignment.

Class node A label that represents each feature grouping in the feature hierarchy (also called simply a **node**).

Clipping A word formation process that shortens a polysyllabic word by deleting one or more syllables (e.g., *prof* from *professor*).

Clitic A morpheme that is like a word in terms of its meaning and function, but is unable to stand alone as an independent form for phonological reasons.

Closed syllable A syllable with a coda (e.g., both syllables in *camping*).

Closing A discourse unit conventionally used to end a conversation.

Coda (Co) The elements that follow the nucleus in the same syllable (e.g., [rf] in *surfboard*).

Coda clause A type of narrative utterance sometimes found at the end of a narrative which shifts the time of the narrative into the present.

Code-switching The systematic alternation between language systems in discourse.

Cognates Words of different languages that have descended from a common source, as shown by systematic phonetic correspondences (e.g., English *father* and German *Vater*).

Cohesive device Any linguistic element that provides information about how participants and events in discourse relate to one another.

Cohort model A model of spoken word recognition that claims that word recognition proceeds by isolating a target word from a cohort of words that share initial segments.

Coinage *See* **Word manufacture**.

Communication strategies Strategies used by L2 learners when they are lacking the necessary linguistic knowledge to say what they want to say (e.g., paraphrasing).

Communicative competence A speaker's knowledge of the linguistic and social rules or principles for language production or perception.

Comparative method The reconstruction of properties of a parent language through comparison of its descendant languages.

Complement The element or elements for which a head is subcategorized and which provide information about entities and locations whose existence is implied by the meaning of the head (e.g., *the book* in *bought the book*).

Complement clause A sentence-like construction that is embedded within a larger structure (e.g., *that his car had been totalled* in *Jerry told Mary that his car had been totalled*).

Complementary distribution Variants of a phoneme that never occur in the same phonetic environment are in complementary distribution.

Complementizer (C) A functional category that takes an S complement, forming a CP (complementizer phrase) (e.g., *whether* in *I wonder whether Lorna has left*).

Complex word A word that contains two or more morphemes (e.g., *theorize, unemployment*).

Complicating action clause A type of narrative utterance that describes the events in a story.

Componential analysis The representation of a word's intension in terms of smaller semantic components called features.

Compound The formation of a word by combining two already existent words.

Compounding The combination of lexical categories (N, V, A, or P) to form a larger word (e.g., *fire + engine*).

Comprehensible input The linguistic input to which the L2 learner is exposed that is slightly beyond his or her competence in the target language (i+1).

Computerized Axial Tomography A technique for observing the living brain that uses a narrow beam of X-rays to create brain images that take the form of a series of brain slices (also called **CT scanning**).

Concatenative A term used for the morphological process that builds word structure by assembling morphemes in an additive, linear fashion.

Conflation pattern A class of meanings created by combining semantic elements such as manner and motion or direction and motion.

Conjugation The set of inflected forms associated with a verb (also called a **verbal paradigm**).

Conjunction (Con) A functional category that joins two or more categories of the same type, forming a coordinate structure (e.g., *and* in *a man and his dog*).

Connectionist model A psycholinguistic theory built around the claim that the mind can be best modelled by reference to complex associations of simple units that approximate neurons.

Connotation The set of associations that a word's use can evoke (e.g., in Canada *winter* evokes ice, snow, bare trees, etc.). (*See also* **Denotation**.)

Consonant deletion A phonetic process that deletes a consonant (e.g., the deletion of [θ] in *fifths*).

Consonant weakening A process that weakens a consonant, usually between vowels, according to the scale of consonantal strength.

Consonantal A major class feature that characterizes sounds produced with a major obstruction in the vocal tract.

Consonantal strength The relative placement of a consonant on a scale of consonantal strength.

Consonants Sounds that are produced with a narrow or complete closure in the vocal tract.

Constituent One or more words that make up a syntactic unit (e.g., *the apple* in *the apple fell onto the floor*). (*See also* **Coordination test**, **Substitution test**, and **Movement test**.)

Constricted Glottis ([CG]) A laryngeal feature that characterizes sounds made with the glottis closed (in English, only [ʔ]).

Constructional meaning The meaning associated with a structural pattern above and beyond the meaning of its component words.

Continuant A manner feature that characterizes sounds made with free or nearly free airflow through the oral cavity: vowels, fricatives, glides, and liquids.

Continuants Sounds that are produced with a continuous airflow through the mouth.

Contour tones Moving pitches on a single segment that signal meaning differences.

Contradiction A relationship between sentences wherein the truth of one sentence requires the falsity of another sentence (e.g., *Raymond is married* contradicts *Raymond is a bachelor*).

Contralateral The control of the right side of the body by the left side of the brain and vice versa.

Contrast Segments are said to contrast when their presence alone may distinguish forms with different meanings from each other (e.g., [s] and [z] in the words *sip* and *zip*).

Convergence The modification of language so that it becomes more similar to that of another speaker or group of speakers.

Conversation analysis *See* **Ethnomethodology**.

Conversational implicature Information that is conveyed through inference but is not actually said.

Conversion A word formation process that assigns an already existing word to a new syntactic category (also called **zero derivation**) (e.g., *nurse* (V) from *nurse* (N)).

Cooperative overlaps Overlapping of turns in a high involvement style conversation according to mutually held conventions of the participants.

Cooperative Principle, The The general overarching guideline thought to underlie conversational interactions: Make your contribution appropriate to the conversation.

Coordinate structure A pattern built around a conjunction such as *and, or,* or *but* (e.g., *Mary and the white horse*).

Coordination test A test used to determine if a group of words is a constituent by joining it to another group of words with a conjunction such as *and* or *or.*

CORONAL A place feature that characterizes sounds made with the tongue tip or blade raised (e.g., [t d s θ]).

Corpus callosum The bundle of nerve fibres that serves as the main connection between the cerebral hemispheres, allowing the two hemispheres to communicate with one another.

Creativity The characteristic of human language that allows novelty and innovation in response to new thoughts, experiences, and situations.

Creole A variety that arises as the native language of the children of members of a pidgin speech community.

Cricoid cartilage The ring-shaped cartilage in the larynx on which the thyroid cartilage rests.

Critical period A particular time frame during which children have to be exposed to language if the acquisition process is to be fully successful.

Cross-sectional Research that investigates and compares children (or groups of children) of distinct ages.

CT scanning *See* **Computerized Axial Tomography**.

Cuneiform Writing that was initiated in the fourth millenium BC and was produced by pressing a wedge-shaped stylus into soft clay tablets.

Cyrillic alphabet An alphabet that combined adaptations of Glagolitic letters with Greek and Hebrew characters, evolving into the alphabets that are currently used to represent some of the languages spoken in the former Soviet Union and in the Balkans.

D-structure *See* **Deep structure**.

Dative The case form characteristically used to mark a recipient.

Deaffrication A type of segmental simplification that turns affricates into fricatives by eliminating the stop portion of the affricate (e.g., [dʒ] becoming [ʒ]).

Declension *See* **Nominal paradigm**.

Deep dyslexia A type of acquired dyslexia in which the patient produces a word that is semantically related to the word he or she is asked to read (e.g., producing *father* when asked to read *mother*).

Deep structure The structure formed by the Merge operation in accordance with the X' schema and subcategorization properties of the heads.

Degemination The weakening of a geminate consonant to a non-geminate consonant (e.g., [tt] becoming [t]).

Degree word (Deg) A functional category that serves as the specifier of a preposition or an adjective (e.g., *quite* in *quite tired*, *very* in *very near the house*).

Deictics Forms whose use and interpretation depend on the location of the speaker and/or addressee within a particular setting (e.g., *this/that, here/there*).

Delayed release A manner feature that characterizes all and only affricate consonants.

Deletion A process that removes a segment from certain phonetic contexts (e.g., the pronunciation of *fifths* as [fifs]).

Denasalization A common substitution process in child language acquisition that involves the replacement of a nasal stop by a non-nasal counterpart (e.g., *come* is pronounced [kʌb]).

Denotation The set of entities to which a word or expression refers (also called its **referents** or **extension**).

Dentals Sounds made with the tongue placed against or near the teeth.

Dependent variable In an experiment, the behaviour or event that is measured in order to gauge the effect of an independent variable.

Derivation (morphology) An affixational process that forms a word with a meaning and/or category distinct from that of its base.

Derivation (syntax) The process whereby a syntactic structure is formed by syntactic operations such as Merge and Move.

Derived (phonology) Resulting from the application of phonological rules to underlying representations.

Descriptive A characteristic of linguistic research that seeks to describe human linguistic ability and knowledge, not to prescribe one system in preference to another. (*See also* **Prescriptive**.)

Design features Characteristics of human language that are used to compare animal communication systems with human language.

Determiner (Det) A functional category that serves as the specifier of a noun (e.g., *a, the, these*).

Developmental errors Errors that occur in language acquisition that result from the manner in which the language acquisition mechanisms operate (e.g., *goed* results from overgeneralization).

Devoicing Voicing assimilation in which a sound becomes voiceless because of a nearby voiceless sound (e.g., the *l* in *place* is devoiced because of the voiceless stop preceding it).

Diacritic A mark added to a phonetic symbol to alter its value in some way (e.g., a circle under a symbol to indicate voicelessness).

Dialect A language variety that is systematically different from another variety of the same language and spoken by a socially identifiable subgroup of some larger speech community.

Dialectology The study of the relationship between dialects and social groups.

Diaphragm The large sheet of muscle that separates the chest cavity from the abdomen and helps to maintain the air pressure necessary for speech production.

Diary study A type of naturalistic investigation in which a researcher (often a parent) keeps daily notes on a child's linguistic progress.

Dichotic listening A technique in which stimuli (either linguistic or non-linguistic) are presented through headphones to the left and right ears to determine the lateralization of various cognitive functions.

Diglossia The relationship between multiple varieties spoken by one speech community but with sharply distinct domains of use.

Diphthong A vowel that shows a noticeable change in quality during its production (e.g., the vowel sounds in *house* and *ride*).

Diphthongization A process in which a monophthong becomes a diphthong (e.g., [iː] became [aj] during the Great English Vowel Shift).

Direct negative evidence Language instruction involving correction or focus on form.

Direct object The NP complement of a verb (e.g., *a fish* in *Judy caught a fish*).

Discourse Any social interaction or expression involving language.

Discourse analysis The analysis of how utterances are structured in discourse.

Discourse markers Adverbial words or expressions that bracket utterances in discourse and organize the sequence and/or relationship between them.

Discrete sign A sign that is distinguished from other signs by stepwise differences (e.g., voiced and voiceless sounds, the numbers of a digital clock).

Dissimilation A process whereby one segment becomes less like another segment in its environment (e.g., *anma* 'soul' in Latin became *alma* in Spanish).

Distinctive feature A feature that is able to signal a difference in meaning by changing its plus or minus value (e.g., the feature [voice] in the words *peer* and *beer*).

Distribution The set of elements with which an item can co-occur.

Divergence The modification of language so that it becomes more different from that of another speaker or group of speakers.

Domains of use Speech situations where a particular variety is commonly used.

Dorsal features Features that represent placement of the body of the tongue.

Dorsum (of the tongue) The body and back of the tongue.

Double-blind test A type of test used in ape language studies in which the researcher is prevented from seeing the stimulus shown to the ape to avoid cueing certain behaviours.

Downdrift The maintenance of a distinction among the pitch registers of an utterance even as the overall pitch of the utterance falls.

Dressage A type of interaction between trainer and animal that depends on the animal's interpreting subtle cues given by the trainer.

Dual-route model A psycholinguistic theory built around the claim that a particular type of language processing can be accomplished in more than one manner.

Duetting The interchange of calls in a patterned manner between two members of a species.

Dysprosody The lack of sentence intonation, a common characteristic of the speech of Broca's aphasics.

Ebonics The cover term used to refer to a variety of English spoken by North Americans of African descent.

Economy constraint A grammatical constraint whose effect is to reduce the computational cost of derivations.

Enclitic A clitic that attaches to the end of a word.

Endocentric compound A compound whose rightmost component (in English) identifies the general class to which the meaning of the entire word belongs (e.g., *dumptruck* is a type of truck). (*See also* **Exocentric compound**.)

Entailment A relation between sentences in which the truth of one sentence necessarily implies the truth of another (e.g., *Gary is Bernice's husband* entails the truth of *Bernice is married*).

Environment The phonetic context in which a sound occurs.

Epenthesis A process that inserts a segment into a particular environment (e.g., the insertion of a schwa in the pronunciation of *athlete* as [æθəlit]).

Ergative The case associated with the subject of a transitive verb in some languages.

Ethnic dialect A dialect spoken by a particular ethnic group.

Ethnography of communication A type of discourse analysis that concentrates on how language is used to achieve communicative goals in particular social situations.

Ethnolinguistic vitality The strength of an ethnic group identity and the variety of language associated with it as measured by the number of people in the group relative to the majority, the degree of institutional support they receive and their relative pride in their identity.

Ethnomethodology A type of discourse analysis that focuses on the structural relationship between utterances in conversations.

Euphemisms Words or phrases used in place of taboo items.

Evaluation clause A type of narrative utterance that gives comments or evaluations regarding the events being narrated.

Event-related potentials (ERPs) A measurement of electrical activity in the brain that is correlated with the presentation of particular stimulus events.

Evidentiality A system of morphological contrasts indicating the type of evidence for the truth of a statement.

Exclusive A contrast in some languages that indicates that the addressee is to be excluded in the interpretation of the first person plural morpheme. (*See also* **Inclusive**.)

Exocentric compound A compound whose meaning does not follow from the meaning of its parts (e.g., *redneck,* since its referent is not a type of neck).

Experimental approach An approach to investigating language in which researchers make use of specially designed tasks to elicit linguistic activity relevant to a particular phenomenon.

Experimental paradigm A method of investigation that involves a particular way of presenting stimuli and a particular way of measuring responses.

Extension The set of entities to which a word or expression refers (also called its denotation or referents).

Feature (phonetic) The smallest unit of analysis of phonological structure, combina-

tions of which make up segments (e.g., [nasal], [continuant]).

Feature hierarchy A hierarchical representation of how features are related to each other.

Features (semantic) The semantic components that make up a word's intension.

Field dependent A cognitive style in which foreground and background information are integrated.

Field independent A cognitive style in which relevant information is perceived clearly against the information background.

Field technique A method of study that does not involve manipulation and control of factors in a laboratory, but rather involves observing phenomena as they occur.

Fissure A relatively deep sulcus of the cerebral cortex.

Fixed stress Stress whose position in a word is predictable.

Flap A sound commonly identified with *r* in some languages and produced when the tongue tip strikes the alveolar ridge as it passes across it (e.g., in North American English, the medial consonant in *bitter* and *bidder*).

Flapping An assimilation process in which a dental or alveolar stop ([-continuant]) changes to a flap ([+continuant]) in the environment of other continuants.

Fluency The ability to produce second language speech that is produced automatically and without noticeable hesitation.

Fluent aphasia The aphasia that occurs due to damage to parts of the left cortex behind the central sulcus, resulting in fluent speech but great difficulty in selecting, organizing, and monitoring language production (also called **sensory aphasia**).

Folk etymology Reanalysis of a word that is based on an incorrect historical analysis (e.g., *hamburger* being reanalyzed into two morphemes, *ham* and *burger*).

Foreigner talk The type of speech that is typically addressed to second language learners, characterized by such properties as simple word order and more common vocabulary items (also called **teacher talk**).

Fossilized A property of an interlanguage grammar that has reached a plateau, that has ceased to change.

Free form An element that does not have to occur in a fixed position with respect to neighbouring elements and may even be able to appear in isolation.

Free morpheme A morpheme that can be a word by itself (e.g., *fear*).

Free stress Stress whose position in a word is not predictable and must be learned on a case-by-case basis.

Free variation Sounds are in free variation when they do not contrast, can occur in identical phonetic environments, and are phonetically similar.

Frequency effect The common experimental finding that words that occur more commonly in a language are processed more quickly and more accurately.

Frication The weakening of a stop to a fricative (e.g., [d] becoming [ð]).

Fricatives Consonants produced with a continuous airflow through the mouth, accompanied by a continuous audible noise (e.g., [f], [ʃ]).

Front vowel A vowel that is made with the tongue positioned in the front of the oral cavity (e.g., the vowel sounds in *seal* and *bat).*

Frontal lobe The lobe of the brain that lies in front of the central sulcus and in which Broca's area is located.

Fronting A common substitution process in child language acquisition that involves the moving forward of a sound's place of articulation (e.g., *cheese* pronounced as [tsiz]).

Full reduplication A morphological process that duplicates the entire word (e.g., in Turkish, [tʃabuk] 'quickly'/tʃabuktʃabuk/ 'very quickly').

Function words Words such as determiners and conjunctions that are lacking in the speech of Broca's aphasics, resulting in telegraphic speech.

Functional analysis An approach to syntactic analysis that attempts to understand syntactic phenomena in terms of their communicative function.

Functional category A word-level syntactic category whose members are harder to define and paraphrase than those of lexical categories (e.g., auxiliary verbs, conjunctions, determiners, and degree words) (also called non-lexical category).

Functional magnetic resonance imaging (fMRI) A brain imaging technique that yields information on areas of high brain activity during the performance of cognitive tasks.

Fusion The process by which words develop into affixes over time.

Fusional languages Languages in which words typically consist of several morphemes and the morphemes that are affixes often mark several grammatical categories simultaneously (e.g., Russian).

Fuzzy concepts Concepts that do not have clear-cut boundaries that distinguish them from other concepts (e.g., the concept 'poor').

Garden path sentence A sentence that is difficult to process and interpret because its structure biases sentence parsing toward an incorrect analysis.

Gender roles Roles or occupations traditionally performed by only one sex.

Gender-exclusive The use of forms by one sex exclusively.

Gender-variable An increased tendency to use forms by one sex.

Generative grammar *See* **Transformational grammar**.

Genetic classification The categorization of languages according to the ancestor languages from which they developed.

Genetically related languages Languages that have descended from a common parent (e.g., German and Italian have both descended from Indo-European).

Genitive The case form characteristically used to mark a possessor.

Given information Knowledge that the speaker assumes is available to the addressee at the time of the utterance, either because it is shared by both or because it has already been introduced into the discourse (also called **old information**).

Glagolitic script A script that was introduced in Slavic-speaking areas in the ninth century AD for the translation of the Bible.

Glide strengthening The strengthening of a glide to an affricate (e.g., [j] becoming [dʒ]).

Glides Sounds that are produced with an articulation like that of a vowel, but move quickly to another articulation (e.g., [j], [w]).

Gliding A common substitution process in child language acquisition which involves the replacement of a liquid by a glide (e.g., *play* is pronounced [pwej]).

Global aphasia The most severe form of non-fluent aphasia, in which the patient is completely mute.

Glottals Sounds produced by using the vocal folds as the primary articulators (e.g., [h], [ʔ]).

Glottis The space between the vocal folds.

Glyphs The symbols used in Mayan writing.

Graded sign A sign that conveys its meaning by changes in degree (e.g., voice volume, a blush).

Grammar The mental system of rules and categories that allows humans to form and interpret the words and sentences of their language.

Grammatical The status of a sentence that speakers judge to be a possible sentence of their language.

Grammatical competence Competence in the structural aspects of language at or below the sentence level.

Grammaticalization The change of a lexical form into a grammatical form (e.g., an affix or member of a functional category).

Grammaticized concepts Concepts that are expressed as affixes or non-lexical categories (e.g., the concept of 'obligation' as expressed by the auxiliary verb *must*).

Grimm's Law A set of consonant shifts that took place between Proto-Indo-European and Proto-Germanic.

Gyrus An area where the cerebral cortex is folded out.

Hangul The alphabetic script used to represent Korean, the symbols of which are grouped to represent the syllables of individual morphemes.

Hanja The Korean word for the Chinese characters used in Korean writing.

Head (of a phrase) The word around which a phrasal category is built (e.g., V, N, A, P).

Head (of a word) The morpheme that determines the category of the entire word (e.g., *bird* in *blackbird*).

Hieroglyphics An Egyptian pictorial writing system, which later developed into a mixed writing system.

High A dorsal feature that characterizes sounds produced with the tongue body raised.

High involvement style A style of turn-taking in a conversation where speaker turns overlap.

Hiragana The Japanese syllabary that is used in conjunction with katakana and kanji to write Japanese.

Historical linguistics The linguistic discipline that is concerned with the description and the explanation of language change.

Holophrases Utterances produced by children in which one word expresses the type of meaning that would be associated with an entire sentence in adult speech (e.g., *up* used to mean 'Pick me up').

Homophony The situation in which a single form has two or more entirely distinct meanings (e.g., *club* 'a social organization', *club* 'a blunt weapon').

Host The element to which clitics are attached.

Hypercorrection The over- or under-use of a variant as a result of its prestige value.

Iconic sign A sign that bears some resemblance to its referent (e.g., a picture of a woman on a washroom door).

Illocutionary competence A speaker's knowledge of how a language functions.

Illocutionary force The intended meaning of an utterance.

Immersion A method of teaching a second language to children in which students are given most of their courses and school activities in the target language.

Implicational universal A universal of language which specifies that the presence of one trait implies the presence of another (but not vice versa).

Inanimate A noun class category in some languages. (*See also* **Animate**.)

Inclusive A contrast in some languages which indicates that the addressee is to be included in the interpretation of the first person plural morpheme. (*See also* **Exclusive**.)

Incorporation The combination of a word (usually a noun) with a verb to form a compound verb.

Indexical sign A sign that fulfills its function by pointing out its referent, typically by being a partial sample of it (e.g., the track of an animal).

Indirect negative evidence The assumption that non-occurring structures in the linguistic environment are ungrammatical.

Infix An affix that occurs within its base.

Inflection The modification of a word's form to indicate the grammatical subclass to which it belongs (e.g., the *-s* in *books* marks the plural subclass).

Inflectional language *See* **Fusional languages**.

Inherently variable The alternation between different forms to express the same linguistic function or meaning. It generally shows systematic influence from social and/or linguistic factors and cannot be expressed as a categorical rule.

Insertion rule An operation that adds an element to a tree structure.

Instrumental motivation The desire to achieve proficiency in a new language for utilitarian reasons, such as job promotion.

Integrative motivation The desire to achieve proficiency in a new language in order to participate in the social life of the language community.

Intension An expression's inherent sense; the concepts that it evokes.

Intercostals The muscles between the ribs that help to maintain the air pressure necessary for speech production.

Interdentals Sounds made with the tongue placed between the teeth (e.g., [θ], [ð]).

Interlanguage The dynamic grammatical system that an L2 learner is using at a particular period in his or her acquisition of a second language.

Internal change A process that substitutes one non-morphemic segment for another to mark a grammatical contrast.

Internal reconstruction The reconstruction of a proto-language that relies on the analysis of morphophonemic variation within a single language.

International Phonetic Alphabet (IPA) The universal system for transcribing the sounds of speech, which has been developing since 1888.

Internet survey A linguistic survey completed by subjects who happen to access a given Web site, Internet bulletin board, or special interest list on the Internet.

Intonation Pitch movement in spoken utterances that is not related to differences in word meaning.

Intransitive A verb that does not take a direct object (e.g., *sleep*).

Inversion A transformation that moves the element in the I position to the C position; formulated as: Move I to C.

Isogloss A line drawn on a dialect map to indicate that two regions differ for a particular linguistic feature.

Isogloss bundle Several isoglosses clustered along the same point on a map.

Isolating languages Languages whose words typically consist of only one morpheme (also called **analytic languages**) (e.g., Mandarin).

Jargon The vocabulary associated with a specific register.

Jargonaphasia A symptom of severe cases of Wernicke's aphasia in which speech contains very few real words of the language.

Kanji The Japanese word for the Chinese characters used to write Japanese.

Katakana The Japanese syllabary that is used in conjunction with hiragana and kanji to write Japanese.

Key *See* **Radical**.

LABIAL A place feature that characterizes sounds articulated with one or both lips.

Labials Sounds made with closure or near closure of the lips (e.g., the initial sounds of *bit* and *pot*).

Labiodentals Sounds involving the lower lip and upper teeth (e.g., the initial sounds of *freedom* and v*intage*).

Labiovelars Sounds made with the tongue raised near the velum and the lips rounded at the same time (e.g., the initial sound of *wound*).

Language bioprogram hypothesis The hypothesis that similarities among creoles reflect universal properties of an innate biological program for language acquisition found in the mental makeup of every human being.

Language contact A source of language change that involves the speakers of one language frequently interacting with the speakers of another language.

Language planning Official policy with the goal of increasing or limiting the domain of use of a particular language or languages.

Laryngeal features Features that represent voicing states.

Laryngeal node The node of the feature hierarchy from which branch out the features that capture voicing states.

Larynx The box-like structure located in the throat through which air passes during speech production, commonly known as the voicebox.

Late closure A proposed parsing principle that claims that, in sentence comprehension, humans tend to attach incoming material into the phrase or clause currently being parsed.

Lateral fissure The fissure that separates the temporal lobe from the frontal and parietal lobes.

Lateral fricative A lateral sound made with a narrow enough closure to be classified as a fricative.

Lateralization The unilateral control of cognitive functions by either the left or the right side of the brain (e.g., language is lateralized in the left hemisphere in most people).

Laterals Sounds made with the sides of the tongue lowered (e.g., varieties of *l*).

Lax vowel A vowel that is made with a placement of the tongue that results in relatively less vocal tract constriction (e.g., the vowel sounds in *hit* and *but*).

Learning strategies The ways in which language learners process language input and develop linguistic knowledge.

Length The auditory property of a sound that enables us to place it on a scale that ranges from short to long.

Lesion Severe damage to the brain.

Lexical ambiguity The result of homophony or polysemy in that a single form has two or more meanings, either related or not.

Lexical category The word-level syntactic categories noun (N), verb (V), adjective (A), and preposition (P).

Lexical decision An experimental paradigm in which a person sees or hears a stimulus and must judge as quickly as possible whether or not that stimulus is a word of his or her language.

Lexical diffusion Linguistic change that first manifests itself in a few words and then gradually spreads through the vocabulary of the language.

Lexical gaps Gaps in the lexicon that result from technological innovation or contact with another culture.

Lexicalization The process whereby concepts are encoded in the words of a language (e.g., the concepts of 'motion' and 'manner' are both encoded by the word *roll*).

Lexicon A speaker's mental dictionary, which contains information about the syntactic properties, meaning, and phonological representation of a language's words.

Lexifier language The language that provides

most of the lexical items to a contact variety.

Lingua franca A language used for the primary purpose of communicating across speech communities whose members speak different languages; usually the second lang age of all speakers involved.

Linguistic competence Speakers' knowledge of their language, which allows them to produce and understand an unlimited number of utterances, including many that are novel.

Linguistic insecurity The degree to which speakers believe that their own variety is not standard.

Linguistic market analysis The analysis of linguistic variation according to the degree to which speakers need the standard language in their everyday lives.

Linguistic typology An approach to language classification that classifies languages according to their structural characteristics without regard for genetic relationships.

Linguistic universals Structural characteristics that occur across the languages of the world.

Linguistics The discipline that studies the nature and use of language.

Lobes Substructures of the cerebral hemispheres that appear to have distinct responsibilities (e.g., frontal lobe, temporal lobe).

Logogram A written symbol representing a morpheme or word.

Logographic writing A type of writing in which symbols represent morphemes or even entire words.

Longitudinal fissure The fissure that extends from the front of the brain to the back and separates the left and right cerebral hemispheres.

Longitudinal studies Studies that examine language development over an extended period of time.

Loudness The auditory property of a sound that enables us to place it on a scale that ranges from soft to loud.

Low A dorsal feature that characterizes vowels made with the tongue body distinctly lowered from a central position in the oral cavity.

Macrofamilies *See* **Phyla**.

Major class features Features that represent the classes consonant, obstruent, nasal, liquid, glide, and vowel.

Majority rules strategy A secondary strategy used to reconstruct proto-forms which stipulates that the segment found in the majority of cognates should be assumed to be part of the proto-form. (*See also* **Phonetic plausibility strategy**.)

Manner features Features that represent manner of articulation.

Manners of articulation The various configurations produced by positioning the lips, tongue, velum, and glottis in different ways (e.g., nasal, fricative, liquid).

Marked traits Those characteristics of languages that are considered to be more complex and/or universally rarer in languages.

Markedness Differential Hypothesis The hypothesis that L2 elements that are different and more marked than the L1 elements will cause difficulty in learning.

Markedness theory A theory that classifies traits or patterns of languages as marked (those that are considered to be more complex and/or universally rarer) and unmarked (those that are considered to be less complex and/or universally more common).

Matched guise test A test of language attitudes used to measure linguistic insecurity and that asks subjects to evaluate recordings of the same person speaking different varieties as to their non-linguistic characteristics; e.g. honesty, intelligence, etc.

Matrix An array of features that represents a segment.

Matrix clause The larger S in which a complement clause occurs.

Maxim of Manner A principle that is thought to underlie the efficient use of language and is formulated as: Avoid ambiguity and obscurity; be brief and orderly.

Maxim of Quality A principle that is thought to underlie the efficient use of language and is formulated as: Try to make your contribution one that is true. (Do not say things that are false or for which you lack adequate evidence.)

Maxim of Quantity A principle that is thought to underlie the efficient use of language and is formulated as: Do not make your contribution more or less informative than required.

Maxim of Relation A principle that is thought to underlie the efficient use of language and is formulated as: Be relevant.

Maxims The specific principles that ensure that conversational interactions satisfy the Cooperative Principle.

Meaning The message or content that a sign conveys.

Mental lexicon *See* **Lexicon**.

Merge A syntactic operation that combines elements to create phrases and sentences.

Merger A change in a phonological system in which two or more phonemes collapse into one, thereby reducing the number of phonemes in that language.

Mesolect A variety with characteristics that place it at a mid point along the continuum between the acrolect and the basilect in a creole speech community.

Metaphor The understanding of one concept in terms of another (e.g., 'argument' understood in terms of 'war': *She annihilated him in the debate*).

Metaphorical code-switching The use of code-switching to express solidarity with or distance from the speech communities associated with the languages being switched.

Metathesis A process that reorders a sequence of segments (e.g., in child language, pronouncing *ask* as [æks]).

Mid vowel A vowel that is made with the tongue neither raised nor lowered (e.g., the vowel sounds in *set* and *Coke*).

Minimal attachment A proposed parsing principle that claims that, in sentence comprehension, humans tend to attach incoming material into phrase structure using the fewest nodes possible.

Minimal pair Two forms with distinct meanings that differ by only one segment found in the same position in each form.

Modifier An optional element that describes a property of a head (e.g., *blue* in *that blue car*).

Module A unit of processing that is relatively autonomous from other processing units.

Morpheme The smallest unit of language that carries information about meaning or function (e.g., *books* consists of the two morphemes *book* and *s*).

Morphology The system of categories and rules involved in word formation and interpretation.

Morphophonemics Rules that account for alternations among allomorphs.

Morphophonology *See* **Morphophonemics**.

Motherese The type of speech that is typically addressed to young children (also called **caregiver speech**).

Motor aphasia *See* **Non-fluent aphasia**.

Move A syntactic operation that transports an element to a new position within a particular sentence.

Movement test A test used to determine if a group of words is a constituent by moving it as a single unit to a different position within the sentence.

Multiplex The quality of a social network that indicates the degree to which social network connections are made on the basis of many different kinds of social relationships.

Murmur The glottal state that produces voiced sounds with the vocal folds relaxed enough to allow enough air to escape to produce a simultaneous whispery effect (also called **whispery voice**).

Mutual intelligibility The situation where speakers of two different varieties are able to understand one another's speech.

Narrative A type of discourse unit that tells a story.

Nasal A manner feature that characterizes any sound made with the velum lowered.

Nasal sounds Sounds produced by lowering the velum, allowing air to pass through the nasal passages.

Nasalization The nasalizing effect that a nasal

consonant can have on all adjacent vowels.

Native speaker One who has acquired a language as a child in a natural setting.

Nativism The view that certain grammatical knowledge is inborn.

Natural class A class of sounds that shares a feature or features (e.g., voiced stops).

Naturalistic approach An approach to investigating child language in which researchers observe and record children's spontaneous verbal behaviour.

Naturalness A criterion that guides language reconstruction by determining whether or not changes are natural.

Near-minimal pair Two forms with distinct meanings that contrast segments in nearly identical environments.

Negative evidence Information as to the ungrammatical nature of utterances.

Negative politeness The use of politeness conventions to express distance or lack of regard for other participants in discourse.

Network density The degree to which speakers in a network are interconnected with each other as determined by the number of connections.

Neurolinguistics The study of how language is represented and processed in the brain.

Neurons The basic information-processing units of the nervous system, also called nerve cells.

Neuroscience The scientific study of the brain.

New information Knowledge that is introduced into the discourse for the first time.

No-naming Avoiding the use of a person's name or title, usually due to uncertainty about their status with respect to power and/or solidarity in relation to the speaker.

Node *See* **Class node**.

Nominal paradigm The set of related forms associated with a noun (also called a **declension**).

Nominative The case form characteristically used to mark a subject.

Non-fluent aphasia Aphasia that results from damage to parts of the brain in front of the central sulcus and is characterized by slow, effortful speech production (also called

motor aphasia).

Non-lexical category *See* **Functional category**.

Non-standard variety A variety of language containing forms that are viewed pejoratively in the community; generally considered 'incorrect' by prescriptive grammarians.

Non-terminal (intonation) contour Rising or level intonation at the end of an utterance, often signalling that the utterance is incomplete.

Noun (N) A lexical category that typically names entities, can usually be inflected for number and possession (in English), and functions as the head of a noun phrase (e.g., *key, Bob, perception*).

NP movement A transformation that moves a noun phrase into the subject position.

Nucleus (N) A vocalic element that forms the core of a syllable (e.g., the vowel [æ] is the nucleus of the first syllable of *Patrick*).

Number The morphological category that expresses contrasts involving countable quantities (e.g., in English, the two-way distinction between singular and plural).

Object permanence A developmental milestone characterized by the ability to recognize that objects have an existence independent of one's interaction with them.

Oblique NP A noun phrase that combines with a preposition.

Obstruent Any non-sonorant consonant: fricatives, affricates, oral stops.

Obviative A verb form used in some languages to indicate that the referent of the subject is not the entity previously chosen as the focus of the conversation. (*See also* **Proximate**.)

Occipital lobe The area of the brain to the rear of the angular gyrus, in which the visual cortex is located.

Official language A language that has been designated by political or other official authorities as the working language of a region, nation, or other organization.

Old information *See* **Given information**.

Onomatopoeic words Words that sound like

the thing that they name (e.g., *plop, hiss*).

Onset (O) Within a syllable, the longest sequence of consonants to the left of each nucleus that does not violate the phonotactic constraints of the language in question (e.g., [st] forms the onset of the second syllable in *hamster*).

Ontogeny Model Predicts that during the course of SLA, transfer errors start out high in number and subsequently decrease, while developmental errors start out low in number, then increase, and finally decrease.

Open syllable A syllable that is not closed by a consonant.

Opening A discourse unit conventionally used to begin a conversation.

Oral sounds Sounds produced with the velum raised and the airflow through the nasal passage cut off.

Orderly heterogeneity Similar patterns of conditioning on variability across groups who show different overall rates of use.

Orientation clause A type of narrative utterance that gives background information to the story; e.g., the time and place where it occurred.

Orthography A set of conventions for representing language in written form.

Overextension A developmental phenomenon in which the meaning of the child's word is more general or inclusive than that of the corresponding adult form (e.g., *daddy* used to refer to any adult male).

Overgeneralization A developmental phenomenon that results from the overly broad application of a rule (e.g., *falled* instead of *fell*).

Overregularization *See* **Over–generalization**.

Palatalization The effect that front vowels and the palatal guide [j] typically have on velar, alveolar, and dental stops, making their place of articulation more palatal (e.g., the first sound of *keep* is palatalized).

Palatals Sounds produced with the tongue on or near the palate (e.g., [j]).

Palate The highest part of the roof of the mouth.

Palatoalveolar *See* **Alveopalatal (area)**.

Paragraphia A writing error associated with a linguistic deficit.

Parallel processing model A psycholinguistic theory built around the claim that phonological, lexical, and syntactic processes are carried out simultaneously.

Parameter The set of alternatives for a particular phenomenon made available by Universal Grammar to individual languages.

Parameter setting The determination of which option permitted by a particular parameter is appropriate for the language being learned.

Paraphrases Two sentences that have the same basic meaning (e.g., *A Canadian wrote that book* is a paraphrase of *That book was written by a Canadian*).

Parietal lobe The lobe of the brain that lies behind the central sulcus and above the temporal lobe.

Parsing The mechanism through which a listener or reader processes linguistic input by assigning categories to lexical elements and hierarchical structure to strings of lexical elements.

Partial reduplication A morphological process that duplicates part of the base to which it applies (e.g., in Tagalog, *takbuh* 'run' and *tatakbuh* 'will run').

Partial suppletion A morphological process that marks a grammatical contrast by replacing part of a morpheme (e.g., *think/thought*).

Passive sentence A sentence in which the NP bearing the theme role is encoded as subject (e.g., *The report was prepared by the committee members*).

Pejoration The process in which the meaning of a word becomes less favourable (e.g., *wench* used to mean simply 'girl').

Performance Actual language use in particular situations.

Person A morphological category that typically distinguishes among the first person (the speaker), the second person (the addressee), and the third person (anyone else) (e.g., in English, the difference between *I, you,* and *she/he/it*).

Pharyngeals Sounds made through the modification of airflow in the pharynx by retracting the tongue or constricting the pharynx.

Pharynx The area of the throat between the uvula and the larynx.

Pheremones Chemicals used by animals specifically for communicative purposes.

Phone Any sound used in human language (also called a **speech sound**).

Phoneme The phonological unit into which predictable variants of non-contrastive segments are grouped (e.g., in English, [t] and [tʰ] belong to the phoneme /t/).

Phonemic paraphasias Speech errors that result from phonemic substitutions and omissions (e.g., *spoon* may be pronounced as *poon*).

Phonemic representation The representation that consists of the phonemes to which allophones belong; predicable phonetic information is not represented.

Phonetic determinative The part of a Chinese character that provides information about the pronunciation of the corresponding morpheme.

Phonetic plausibility strategy The primary strategy used to reconstruct proto-forms that requires any sound changes posited to be phonetically plausible. (*See also* **Majority rules strategy**.)

Phonetic representation The representation that consists of predictable variants of allophones.

Phonetic sound change A sound change that results in a new allophone of an already existing phoneme.

Phonetically conditioned sound change Sound change that begins as subtle alterations in the sound pattern of a language in particular phonetic environments.

Phonetics The branch of linguistics that examines the inventory and structure of the sounds of language.

Phonographic writing A type of writing in which symbols represent syllables or segments.

Phonological change A sound change that results in the addition, elimination, or rearrangement of phonemes (e.g., splits, mergers).

Phonological dyslexia A type of acquired dyslexia in which the patient seems to have lost the ability to use spelling-to-sound rules and can only read words that they have seen before.

Phonological representation *See* **Phonemic representation**.

Phonological rules Rules that derive phonetic representations from underlying representations, accounting for alternations among allophones.

Phonology The component of a grammar made up of the elements and principles that determine how sounds pattern in a language.

Phonotactics The set of constraints on how sequences of segments pattern.

Phrase A unit of syntactic structure consisting of a head and an optional specifier and/or complements.

Phrase structure rule A rule of grammar that states the composition of a phrase (e.g., XP → (Specifier) X (Complement)).

Phrase structure schema The blueprint for the internal structure of phrases.

Phyla The groups into which purportedly related language stocks are placed (also called superstocks).

Pictograms Pictorial representations of objects or events.

Pidgin A variety that emerges when speakers of different languages are brought together in a stable situation requiring intergroup communication; it has no native speakers and generally is considered to have a reduced grammatical system relative to a non-pidgin.

Pinyin The system of writing Mandarin with a modified Latin alphabet, used for such things as street signs and brand names.

Pitch The auditory property of a sound that enables us to place it on a scale that ranges from low to high.

Place of articulation features Features that represent place of articulation.

Place node The node of the feature hierarchy from which branch out the major place features.

Places of articulation The points at which the airstream can be modified to produce different sounds.

Plural A contrast associated with the morphological category of number and associated with nouns that refer to more than one entity.

Points of articulation *See* **Places of articulation.**

Polysemy The situation in which a word has two or more related meanings (e.g., *bright* 'intelligent', *bright* 'shining').

Polysynthetic languages Languages in which single words can consist of long strings of lexical categories and affixes, often expressing the meaning of an entire sentence in English (e.g., Inuktitut).

Positive evidence Grammatical utterances in the learner's linguistic environment.

Positive politeness The use of politeness conventions to express regard and consideration for other participants in discourse.

Positron Emission Tomography (PET) A brain imaging technique that uses radioactive isotopes to measure changes in brain metabolism associated with particular cognitive and behavioural tasks.

Postal survey A linguistic survey given in the form of a written questionnaire and distributed by posting batches of questionnaires to selected intermediaries in the community who then pass them on to subjects.

Postposition A P that occurs after its complement. (*See also* **Preposition (P).**)

Power The degree of control that one group or individual may hold over another.

Pragmatics Speakers' and addressees' background attitudes and beliefs, their understanding of the context in which a sentence is uttered, and their knowledge of how language can be used for a variety of purposes.

Prefix An affix that is attached to the front of its base (e.g., *re-* in *replay*).

Preposition (P) A lexical category that functions as the head of a prepositional phrase and occurs before its complement (e.g., *into, with, for*).

Prescriptive A characteristic of certain non-linguistic approaches to grammar in that they seek to prescribe one system in preference to another. (*See also* **Descriptive**.)

Prestige The social value attached to a linguistic variant considered to be the one used by the group holding the highest esteem in the community; frequently also believed to be the grammatically 'correct' form.

Presupposition The assumption or belief implied by the use of a particular word or structure.

Primary stress The most prominent stress of a word.

Prime In a priming experiment, this is the stimulus that is expected to affect a subject's response accuracy and latency to a subsequent stimulus (called the target).

Priming A situation in which the presentation of a stimulus has a positive effect on the ease with which a subsequent related stimulus is processed.

Priming effect In a priming experiment, this is the extent to which a priming stimulus facilitates the processing of a target stimulus.

Principal component A set of variables that, when taken together, show patterns of variation that provide the best statistical fit for determining how test subjects should be grouped together.

Principle A The principle that constrains the interpretation of reflexive pronouns and is formulated as: A reflexive pronoun must have an antecedent that c-commands it in the same minimal S.

Principle B The principle that constrains the interpretation of pronominals and is formulated as: A pronominal must not have an antecedent that c-commands it in the same minimal S.

Principle of Compositionality, The A principle underlying sentence interpretation that is formulated as: The meaning of a sentence is determined by the meaning of its component parts and the manner in which they are arranged in syntactic structure.

Processes Articulatory adjustments that occur

during the production of speech (e.g., deletion, epenthesis, assimilation).

Proclitic A clitic that attaches to the beginning of a word.

Productivity The relative freedom with which affixes can combine with bases of the appropriate category.

Progressive assimilation Assimilation in which a sound influences a following segment (e.g., liquid-glide devoicing in English).

Pronominal A pronoun whose interpretation may be, but does not have to be, determined by an antecedent in the same sentence (e.g., *he, her*).

Pronoun A word whose interpretation can be determined by another element (an antecedent) (e.g., *him, she, themselves, herself*).

Prosodic properties *See* **Suprasegmental properties**.

Proto-forms Forms of a proto-language, written with a preceding asterisk to indicate their hypothetical character.

Proto-Indo-European (PIE) The proto-language from which evolved most of the languages of Europe, Persia (Iran), and the northern part of India.

Proto-language A language reconstructed through the methods of historical linguistics.

Prototypes The best exemplars of a concept (e.g., robins or magpies are prototypes of the concept 'bird').

Proximate A verb form used in some languages to indicate that the subject of the verb has been chosen as the focus of the conversation and any further use of which (without an overt subject) indicates a reference to that focused entity. (*See also* **Obviative**.)

Psycholinguistics The study of the mental processes and representations involved in language comprehension and production.

Radical The part of a Chinese character that provides clues about the morpheme's meaning (also called a **key**).

Reading The interpretation of a particular utterance.

Reanalysis A source of language change that involves an attempt to attribute an internal structure to a word that formerly was not broken down into component morphemes (e.g., *ham + burger*).

Rebus principle In writing, the use of a sign for any word that is pronounced like the word whose meaning the sign represented initially.

Recast A repetition of a child's utterance that includes adjustments to its form and/or content.

Reduced A dorsal feature that characterizes only schwa.

Reduced vowel *See* **Schwa**.

Redundancy The use of different modalities to convey the same information.

Reduplication A morphological process that duplicates all or part of the base to which it applies. (*See also* **Partial reduplication** and **Full reduplication**.)

Referents The set of entities to which a word or expression refers (also called its **denotation** or **extension**).

Reflexive pronoun A pronoun that must have a c-commanding antecedent usually in the same clause (e.g., *himself, herself*).

Regional dialect A dialect spoken in a specific geographical region.

Register A set of linguistic structures that is associated with a particular speech situation; it may carry an association with a particular style.

Register tones Level tones that signal meaning differences.

Regressive assimilation Assimilation in which a sound influences a preceding segment (e.g., nasalization in English).

Regressive saccades Eye movements in which the eyes dart backward to a section of text that has been previously read.

Related languages Languages that developed historically from the same ancestor language.

Relational analysis An approach to syntactic analysis in which syntactic phenomena are described in terms of grammatical relations such as subject and direct object.

Relexification hypothesis The hypothesis

that contact varieties of language are generated by using lexical items from one language and the grammatical system of another.

Representativeness The degree to which a subject sampling of a speech community accurately reflects the properties of the entire population under study.

Response accuracy The correctness of a subject's responses to particular stimuli provided in an experiment.

Response latency The amount of time taken by a subject in an experiment to respond to a stimulus.

Retroflex The *r* made by either curling the tongue tip back into the mouth or by bunching the tongue upward and back in the mouth.

Rhotacism A type of weakening that typically involves the change of [z] to [r].

Rhyme (R) The nucleus and the coda of a syllable (e.g., [uts] in the word *boots*).

Right ear advantage The phenomenon in which people with language in the left hemisphere hear speech louder and clearer with the right ear.

Root (of the tongue) The part of the tongue that is contained in the upper part of the throat.

Root (of a word) The morpheme in a word that carries the major component of the word's meaning and belongs to a lexical category (e.g., *collect* in the word *collections*).

Root node The highest node of the feature hierarchy.

Round A place feature that characterizes sounds made by protruding the lips (e.g., [ɔ], [w]).

Rounded (sounds) Sounds made with the lips protruding (e.g., [ow], [ɔ]).

S-structure *See* **Surface structure**.

Saccades The quick and uneven movement of the eyes during reading.

Schwa The lax vowel that is characterized by briefer duration than any of the other vowels (also called a **reduced vowel**) (e.g., the underlined vowels in *Ca*na*da, su*ppose).

Second language acquisition (SLA) The acquisition of proficiency in a language that is not one's first language.

Secondary stress The second most prominent stress in a word.

Segmental change Sound change that involves the simplification of a complex consonant (e.g., deaffrication).

Segments Individual speech sounds.

Self-praise avoidance The use of self-deprecating expressions in response to a compliment.

Semantic broadening The process in which the meaning of a word becomes more inclusive than its earlier form (e.g., *barn* used to mean 'a place to store barley').

Semantic decomposition *See* **Componential analysis**.

Semantic narrowing The process in which the meaning of a word becomes less inclusive than its earlier form (e.g., *meat* used to mean 'any type of food').

Semantic shift The process in which a word loses its former meaning, taking on a new, often related, meaning (e.g., *immoral* used to mean 'not customary').

Semantics The study of meaning in human language.

Semiotics The study of signs.

Sensory aphasia *See* **Fluent aphasia**.

Sequential change Sound change that involves sequences of segments (e.g., assimilation).

Serial processing model A psycholinguistic theory built around the claim that language processing proceeds in a step by step manner.

Shift A change in a phonological system in which a series of phonemes is systematically modified so that their organization with respect to each other is altered (e.g., the Great English Vowel Shift).

Shortest Move The requirement that moves should be as short as possible.

Sibilants *See* **Stridents**.

Sign A unit of communication structure that consists of two parts: a signifier and something signified.

Signal A sign that triggers a specific action on the part of the receiver (e.g., traffic lights).

Signified The real world object that a sign represents, as well as the sign's conceptual content.

Signifier That part of a sign that stimulates at least one sense organ of the receiver of a message.

Similarity Differential Rate Hypothesis The hypothesis that claims that the rates of acquisition for dissimilar phenomena in two languages are faster than for similar phenomena.

Simple vowels Vowels that do not show a noticeable change in quality during their production (also called **monophthongs**) (e.g., the vowel sounds of c*a*b and g*e*t).

Simple word A word that consists of a single morpheme (e.g., *horse*).

Single-route model A psycholinguistic theory built around the claim that a particular type of language processing is accomplished in one manner only.

Singular A contrast associated with the morphological category of number and associated with nouns that refer to a single entity.

Situational code-switching Switching between languages for clearly identifiable reasons such as reporting the speech of another or when the topic of conversation switches from personal to business affairs.

Slang Informal or faddish usages of language.

Social network analysis The analysis of linguistic variation according to the degree to which speakers participate in social networks.

Sociolect A dialect spoken by a particular social group.

Sociolinguistic norms Conventions for use of language structures in particular social situations.

Sociolinguistics The study of the relationship between language structures as they are used in discourse and the social roles and/or situations associated with them.

Sociolinguistics of language The study of how language structures are associated with particular social circumstances.

Sociolinguistics of society The study of how language structures are related to a speaker's social identity.

Solidarity The degree of intimacy or similarity that one group or individual may feel for another.

Song In avian communication, lengthy elaborate patterns of mostly pitched sounds.

Sonorant A major class feature that characterizes all and only the 'singables': vowels, glides, liquids, and nasals.

Sound shift The systematic modification of a series of phonemes (e.g., Grimm's Law).

Specifier A word that helps to make more precise the meaning of the head of the phrase and that occurs immediately beneath XP (e.g., *the* in *the book*).

Spectrogram An acoustic recording that graphically shows the frequency, intensity, and time of sounds.

Speech community Any group of people who share a set of conventions for language use.

Speech event An identifiable type of discourse associated with a particular speech situation.

Speech situation Any circumstance that may involve the use of speech.

Speech sound *See* **Phone**.

Spelling pronunciation A source of language change whereby a new pronunciation arises that reflects more closely the spelling of the word (e.g., *often* pronounced as [ɑftən] rather than [ɑfən]).

Split A situation in which allophones of the same phoneme come to contrast with each other due to the loss of the conditioning environment, resulting in one or more new phonemes.

Split brain experiments Studies that investigate the effects of surgically severing the corpus callosum.

Spoonerisms A type of speech error, named after Reverend William A. Spooner, in which words or sounds are re-arranged with often humorous results.

Spread Glottis ([SG]) A laryngeal feature that distinguishes unaspirated from aspirated sounds.

Standard variety The variety of language

spoken by the most powerful group in a community and generally held to be 'correct' by prescriptive grammarians.

Stem The base to which an inflectional affix is added (e.g., *modification* is the stem for *-s* in the word *modifications*).

Stimulus-bound communication Communication that only occurs when it is triggered by exposure to a certain stimulus or for certain specific ends (e.g., the warning call of a bird).

Stocks The groups into which purportedly related language families are placed.

Stopping A common substitution process in child language acquisition that involves the replacement of a fricative by a corresponding stop (e.g., *zebra* is pronounced [dibrə]).

Stops Sounds made with a complete and momentary closure of airflow through the vocal tract (e.g., the initial sounds of *pleasure* and *grab*).

Stressed vowels Vowels that are perceived as relatively more prominent due to the combined effects of pitch, loudness, and length.

Strident A place feature that characterizes the 'noisy' fricatives and affricates (in English, [s z ʃ ʒ tʃ dʒ]) (also called *sibilants*).

Stroke A hemorrhage in the brain or the blockage or rupture of an artery, causing brain damage (also called a **cerebrovascular accident**).

Structurally ambiguous A property of phrases or sentences whose component words can be combined in more than one way (e.g., *fast cars and motorcycles*).

Style The level of formality associated with a linguistic structure or set of structures classified along a continuum between most informal to most formal.

Subcategorization The classification of words in terms of their complement options (e.g., the verb *devour* is subcategorized for a complement NP).

Subject The NP occurring immediately under S (e.g., *Irene* in *Irene is a tailor*).

Subset Principle, The The initial or default setting of a parameter will correspond to the most restrictive option (i.e., the option that permits the fewest patterns).

Substitution A type of auditorily based change involving the replacement of one segment with another similar segment (e.g., in the history of English [f] replaced [x] in some words).

Substitution test A test used to determine if a group of words is a constituent by replacing them with a single word.

Substrate language A language hypothesized to have supplied the basic grammatical structure for a contact variety.

Substratum influence The influence of a politically or culturally non-dominant language on a dominant language in the area (e.g., the borrowing of words into English from Amerindian languages).

Suffix An affix that is attached to the end of its base (e.g., *-ly* in *quickly*).

Sulcus An area where the cerebral cortex is folded in.

Superstratum influence The influence of a politically or culturally dominant language on another language in the area (e.g., the effects of Norman French on English during the Middle English period).

Suppletion A morphological process that marks a grammatical contrast by replacing a morpheme with an entirely different morpheme (e.g., *be/was*).

Suprasegmental properties Those properties of sounds that form part of their makeup no matter what their place or manner of articulation: pitch, loudness, and length (also called **prosodic properties**).

Surface dyslexia A type of acquired dyslexia in which the patient seems unable to recognize words as wholes, but must process all words through a set of spelling-to-sound rules (e.g., *yacht* would be pronounced /jætʃt/).

Surface structure The structure that results from the application of whatever transformations are appropriate for the sentence in question.

Syllabary A set of syllabic signs used for representing a language.

Syllabic A major class feature that characterizes vowels.

Syllabic liquids Liquids that function as syllabic nuclei (e.g., the *l* in *bottle*).

Syllabic nasals Nasals that function as syllabic nuclei (e.g., the *n* in *button*).

Syllabic writing A type of writing in which each symbol represents a syllable.

Syllable A unit of linguistic structure that consists of a syllabic element and any segments that are associated with it. (*See also* **Onset**, **Nucleus**, **Coda**.)

Symbolic model A psycholinguistic theory built around the claim that models of linguistics knowledge make reference to rules and representations consisting of symbols, such as phonemes, words, syntactic category labels, and so forth.

Symbolic sign A sign that bears an arbitrary relationship to its referent (e.g., a stop sign, non-onomatopoeic words).

Symptomatic Spontaneously and involuntarily conveying an internal state or an emotion, as in a symptomatic sign such as crying.

Syncope The deletion of a word-internal vowel (e.g., the deletion of the schwa in *police*).

Synonyms Words or expressions that have the same meanings in some or all contexts (e.g., *buy* and *purchase*).

Syntactic category The category into which an element is placed depending on the type of meaning that it expresses, the type of affixes it takes, and the type of structure in which it occurs (includes both lexical and functional categories).

Syntactic parser The theoretical construct that accounts for the human ability to assign grammatical categories and hierarchical structure to elements in a stream of language input.

Syntax The system of rules and categories that underlies sentence formation in human language.

Systematic gaps Gaps in the occurring syllable structures of a language that result from the exclusion of certain sequences (e.g., *pfordv* in English).

Systematic phonetic correspondences Sound correspondences between two or more related languages that are consistent throughout the vocabularies of those languages.

Taboo Words or phrases that are considered to be impolite or that refer to topics that are conventionally avoided (e.g., death).

Target In a priming experiment, this is the stimulus to which a subject must respond and for which response accuracy and latency are measured.

Target language The language that an L2 learner is learning.

Teacher talk *See* **Foreigner talk**.

Telegraphic speech Speech lacking functional categories and bound morphemes.

Telegraphic stage The stage in child language acquisition in which children's utterances are generally longer than two words but lack bound morphemes and most functional categories.

Telephone survey A linguistic survey given over the telephone.

Template The innate blueprint of birdsong that predisposes birds to perform a general song that is extremely simplified.

Temporal lobe The lobe of the brain that lies beneath the lateral fissure and in which Wernicke's area is located.

Tense (feature) A dorsal feature that captures the tense-lax distinction among vowels.

Tense (verb) A morphological category that encodes the time of a situation with reference to the moment of speaking (e.g., in English, the two-way contrast between past and non-past).

Tense vowel A vowel that is made with a placement of the tongue that results in relatively greater vocal tract constriction (e.g., the vowel sounds in *heat* and *boat*).

Terminal (intonation) contour Falling intonation at the end of an utterance, signalling that the utterance is complete.

Text analysis A type of discourse analysis that studies how linguistic structures are used to perform particular discourse functions.

Thematic role A label (such as agent, theme,

goal, etc.) used to categorize the relation between the parts of a sentence and the event that it describes.

Thematic grid The part of a word's lexical entry that carries information about the thematic roles that it assigns.

Theme The thematic role of the entity directly affected by the action designated by the verb (e.g., *the ball* in *Tom caught the ball*).

Thyroid cartilage The cartilage that forms the main portion of the larynx, spreading outward like the head of a plow.

Tiers Levels on the feature hierarchy that reflect the relation of the nodes and features to each other.

Tip (of the tongue) The narrow area at the front of the tongue.

Token A single instantiation of a variable.

Tone Pitch movement in spoken utterances that is related to differences in word meaning.

Tone language A language in which differences in word meaning are signalled by differences in pitch.

Top-down processing A type of processing using a set of expectations to guide phonetic processing and word recognition.

Topic What a sentence or group of sentences is about.

Trace The empty element, marked by the symbol *t*, that is left in syntactic structure after an element has been moved.

Trachea The tube below the larynx through which air travels when it leaves the lungs, commonly known as the windpipe.

Transfer The process by which the first language (L1) influences the interlanguage grammar.

Transfer error An error made by a second language learner that can be traced to the first language.

Transformation A type of syntactic rule that can move an element from one position to another.

Transformational grammar A widely accepted approach to syntactic analysis in which syntactic phenomena are described with the help of transformations.

Transitive A verb that takes an NP complement (a direct object) (e.g., *hit*).

Tree structure A diagram depicting the internal organization of a linguistic unit such as a word, phrase, or sentence.

Trill An *r*-like sound that is made by passing air over the raised tongue tip, allowing it to vibrate.

Truth conditions The circumstances under which a sentence is true.

Turn-taking The change-over between speakers' turns in a conversation.

Typological plausibility A criterion that guides language reconstruction by referring to universals or existing properties of language.

Umlaut A phonological change in Germanic languages that results in the fronting of a vowel in the root under the influence of a front vowel in a suffix.

Underextension A developmental phenomenon in which a child uses a lexical item to denote only a subset of the items that it denotes in adult speech (e.g., *car* used to refer only to moving cars).

Underlying representations The unpredictable features of a phonemic segment are basic or underlying.

Universal Grammar (UG) The innate system of categories, operations and principles that are shared by all languages.

Universal tendencies Patterns or traits that occur in all or most languages.

Unmarked traits Those characteristics of language that are considered to be less complex and/or universally more common in languages.

Utterance The minimal unit of speech required to state a proposition.

Uvula The small fleshy flap of tissue that hangs down from the velum.

Uvulars Sounds made with the tongue near or touching the uvula.

Variable A set of forms, any of which may be used to express the same function or meaning and cannot be expressed by a categorical rule.

Variant One of a set of several possible forms that can be used to express the same function or meaning.

Variety A cover term used to refer to language used by a particular speech community; it merely implies that some set of sociolinguistic norms is present.

Velars Sounds made with the tongue touching or near the velum (e.g., [ŋ], [k]).

Velum The soft area towards the rear of the roof of the mouth.

Verb (V) A lexical category that typically designates actions, sensations, and states, can usually be inflected for tense, and functions as the head of a verb phrase (e.g., *see, feel, remain*).

Verbal hedges Expressions used to express lack of confidence in an assertion.

Verbal paradigm The set of inflected forms associated with a verb (also called a **conjugation**).

Vernacular The variety used by a speaker in the most formal style; generally hypothesized to be the one that they first acquired.

Verner's Law The explanation of apparent exceptions to Grimm's Law by taking into account the position of the original Proto-Indo-European accent.

Vocal cords *See* **Vocal folds**.

Vocal folds A set of muscles inside the larynx that may be positioned in various ways to produce different glottal states (also called **vocal cords**).

Vocal tract The oral cavity, nasal cavity, and pharynx.

Voice A laryngeal feature that distinguishes between voiced and voiceless sounds.

Voiced The glottal state in which the vocal folds are brought close together, but not tightly closed, causing air passing through them to vibrate (e.g., [æ], [z], [m] are voiced).

Voiceless The glottal state in which the vocal folds are pulled apart, allowing air to pass directly through the glottis (e.g., [t], [s], [f] are voiceless).

Voicing assimilation Assimilation in which one segment becomes more like a nearby segment in terms of voicing (e.g., liquid-glide devoicing in English).

Vowel reduction A process that reduces a full vowel, typically unstressed, to a schwa.

Vowels Sounds that are produced with little obstruction in the vocal tract and that are generally voiced.

Weakening (phonetic) A process that weakens a segment according to a particular scale of strength.

Weakening (semantic) The process in which the meaning of a word weakens (e.g., *soon* used to mean 'immediately' but now means 'in the near future').

Wernicke's aphasia The aphasia that results in fluent but nonsensical speech, sometimes characterized by **jargonaphasia**.

***Wh* movement** A transformation that moves a *wh* phrase to the beginning of the sentence, formulated as: Move a *wh* phrase to the specifier position under CP.

***Wh* question** A sentence that begins with a *wh*-word (e.g., *Who did you see?*).

Whisper The glottal state in which the vocal folds are adjusted so that the front portions are pulled close together, while the back portions are apart.

Whispery voice *See* **Murmur**.

Word level A level of representation above the syllable level.

Word manufacture The creation of a word from scratch, sometimes with the help of a computer (also called **coinage**) (e.g., *Kodak*).

Word-based morphology Morphology in which most complex words are formed from a base that can itself be a word.

Words The smallest free forms found in language.

Writing The representation of language by graphic signs or symbols.

Zero derivation *See* **Conversion**.

Language Index

635

Index

Ablative case, 149, 608
Ablaut, 128, 608
Absolute universals, 319, 608
Absolutive case, 150, 608
Abstract case, 206, 608
Abstract clause, 501, 608
Abstract representation, 157, 608
Accent, 608
   attitudes to, 511
   in L2 acquisition, 418–19
   of speech community, 494
Accidental gaps, 75, 608
Accommodation, 508–9, 608
Accuracy, 433, 608
Accusative case, 149, 150, 151,
   205, 608
Acoustic phonetics, 13, 608
Acquired agraphia, 486, 608
Acquired alexia, 486, 608
Acquired dysgraphia, 486, 608
Acquired dyslexia, 486–87, 608
Acquisition. *See* Language acqui-
   sition
Acrolect, 534, 608
Acronyms, 143, 287, 608
Acrophonic principle, 547, 608
Active structure, 208–12, 608
Adam's apple, 17
Address terms, 504–6
Adjacency pair, 499, 608
Adjective complements, 182, 185
Adjective phrase, 171–72, 203
Adjectives, 124, 170, 282–83,
   608
   as lexical category, 168, 169
Adstratum influence, 288, 289,
   608
Adverb phrase, 203
Adverbs, 608
   derived from adjectives,
      282–83
   as lexical category, 168, 169
   in word order, 330
Affixation, 126–27, 608
Affixes, 124, 126–27
   addition of, 279
   in agglutinating languages,
      325–26
   as bound morphemes, 124,
      608

in child language, 386
Class 1 and Class 2, 135–36
concepts associated with, 238
constraints, 460
derivational, 131–36, 145–47,
   327, 333–34
fusion of, 279, 326
inflectional, 144–47, 170,
   327, 333–34
languages lacking, 325
loss of, 280–81
to mark case, 149, 280–81
to mark topic, 252
omission with aphasia,
   489–90
order of, 146
productivity of, 146–47, 627
reanalysis, 282–83
selectional restrictions, 460
in tree structure, 125
See also Prefixes; Suffixes
Affricates, 25, 49–50
   contrasts among, 59
Affrication, 267, 609
Age factor
   in L1 acquisition, 403–4, 613
   in L2 acquisition, 430–31
   in linguistic variation, 530
Age-grading, 530, 609
Agent, 208, 243–46, 609
Agglutinating languages, 325–26,
   609
Agrammatism, 488–90, 609
Agraphia, acquired, 486, 608
Agreement, 609
   verb-object, 331–32
   verb-subject, 151, 331–32
Alexander the Great, 338
Alexia, acquired, 486, 608
Allomorphic variation, 123–24
Allomorphs, 123–24, 154–55,
   609
Allophones, 63–70, 609
Allophonic distribution, 69–70,
   100
Allophonic nasalization, 68–69
Allophonic variation, 63, 87–88
   feature representation, 98
   universality of, 68
Alpha notation, 103

Alphabetic writing, 541, 609
Alphabets, 548–50
Arabic, 551–52
   Cyrillic, 551
   Greek, 548–49
   Hebrew, 551–52
   Latin, 548–49
   Phoenician, 548, 552
   Roman, 550
Alveolar affricates, 50
Alveolar flap, 45
Alveolar fricatives, 24, 49
Alveolar lateral fricatives, 51
Alveolar laterals, 50, 51
Alveolar liquids, 28
Alveolar ridge, 20, 609
Alveolar stop, 22, 45, 48, 49
Alveolars, 20, 21, 29, 59, 91
Alveopalatal affricates, 25, 50
Alveopalatal area, 21, 609
Alveopalatal fricatives, 24, 49
Alveopalatals, 20, 29, 59, 91
Ambiguity
   lexical, 226
   structural, 241–42, 463–64,
      630
Ambisyllabicity, 109 n4, 609
Amelioration, 291, 609
American Sign Language (ASL),
   593
Analogy, 264–65, 281–82, 293,
   609
Analytic languages, 281, 325,
   609
Anaphoric reference, 502, 609
Angular gyrus, 475, 477, 478,
   486, 609
Animal communication,
   571–603
   acquisition of, 579–80
   critical period for learning,
      560, 586, 589
   design features, 600–603, 614
   dressage, 595–96
   innate vs. learned, 583, 586,
      588, 602
   limitations, 580, 582
   stimulus-bound, 580, 630
   studies of, 593–94, 596–600
   theories of, 579–80